MARKET SHARE REPORTER

ISSN 1052-9578

MARKET SHARE REPORTER

AN ANNUAL COMPILATION

OF REPORTED MARKET SHARE

DATA ON COMPANIES,

PRODUCTS, AND SERVICES

2 0 0 5

Volume 1

ROBERT S. LAZICH, Editor

THOMSON

★

GALE

Detroit • New York • San Francisco • San Diego • New Haven, Conn. • Waterville, Maine • London • Munich

Market Share Reporter 2005
Robert S. Lazich

Project Editor
Virgil L. Burton III

Editorial
Joyce Piwowarski, Susan Turner

Imaging and Multimedia
Michael Logusz

Manufacturing
Rita Wimberley

ISBN 0-7876-9414-2 (2 vol. set)
ISBN 0-7876-7444-3 (Vol. 1)
ISBN 0-7876-7368-4 (Vol. 2)
ISSN 0071-0210

Printed in the United States of America
10 9 8 7 6 5 4 3 2 1

TABLE OF CONTENTS

Table of Topics vii
Introduction. xvii

Volume I

General Interest and Broad Topics 1
SIC 01 - Agricultural Production - Crops 11
SIC 02 - Agricultural Production - Livestock 21
SIC 07 - Agricultural Services 26
SIC 08 - Forestry 27
SIC 09 - Fishing, Hunting, and Trapping 28
SIC 10 - Metal Mining 30
SIC 12 - Coal Mining 33
SIC 13 - Oil and Gas Extraction 36
SIC 14 - Nonmetallic Minerals, Except Fuels 41
SIC 15 - General Building Contractors 46
SIC 16 - Heavy Construction, Except Building 54
SIC 17 - Special Trade Contractors 56
SIC 20 - Food and Kindred Products 60
SIC 21 - Tobacco Products 185
SIC 22 - Textile Mill Products 190
SIC 23 - Apparel and Other Textile Products 194
SIC 24 - Lumber and Wood Products 209
SIC 25 - Furniture and Fixtures 214
SIC 26 - Paper and Allied Products 219
SIC 27 - Printing and Publishing 235
SIC 28 - Chemicals and Allied Products 257
SIC 29 - Petroleum and Coal Products 357
SIC 30 - Rubber and Misc. Plastics Products 360
SIC 31 - Leather and Leather Products 368
SIC 32 - Stone, Clay, and Glass Products 373
SIC 33 - Primary Metal Industries 381
SIC 34 - Fabricated Metal Products 389
SIC 35 - Industry Machinery and Equipment 398
SIC 36 - Electronic and Other Electric Equipment 436
SIC 37 - Transportation Equipment 495

Volume II

SIC 38 - Instruments and Related Products 533
SIC 39 - Miscellaneous Manufacturing Industries 561
SIC 40 - Railroad Transportation 586
SIC 41 - Local and Interurban Passenger Transit 588
SIC 42 - Trucking and Warehousing 589
SIC 43 - Postal Service 592
SIC 44 - Water Transportation 593
SIC 45 - Transportation by Air 598

SIC 46 - Pipelines, Except Natural Gas 614
SIC 47 - Transportation Services 615
SIC 48 - Communications 622
SIC 49 - Electric, Gas, and Sanitary Services 662
SIC 50 - Wholesale Trade - Durable Goods 668
SIC 51 - Wholesale Trade - Nondurable Goods 670
SIC 52 - Building Materials and Garden Supplies 672
SIC 53 - General Merchandise Stores 677
SIC 54 - Food Stores 681
SIC 55 - Automotive Dealers and Service Stations 699
SIC 56 - Apparel and Accessory Stores 703
SIC 57 - Furniture and Homefurnishings Stores 711
SIC 58 - Eating and Drinking Places 721
SIC 59 - Miscellaneous Retail 731
SIC 60 - Depository Institutions 757
SIC 61 - Nondepository Institutions 784
SIC 62 - Security and Commodity Brokers 796
SIC 63 - Insurance Carriers 806
SIC 64 - Insurance Agents, Brokers, and Service 828
SIC 65 - Real Estate 829
SIC 67 - Holding and Other Investment Offices 833
SIC 70 - Hotels and Other Lodging Places 836
SIC 72 - Personal Services 839
SIC 73 - Business Services 842
SIC 75 - Auto Repair, Services, and Parking 872
SIC 76 - Miscellaneous Repair Services 878
SIC 78 - Motion Pictures 879
SIC 79 - Amusement and Recreation Services 895
SIC 80 - Health Services 905
SIC 81 - Legal Services 910
SIC 82 - Educational Services 911
SIC 83 - Social Services 913
SIC 84 - Museums, Botanical, Zoological Gardens 916
SIC 86 - Membership Organizations 917
SIC 87 - Engineering and Management Services 919
SIC 92 - Justice, Public Order, and Safety 926
SIC 95 - Environmental Quality and Housing 927
SIC 96 - Administration of Economic Programs 928
SIC 97 - National Security and International Affairs 929

Indexes
Source Index 933
Place Names Index 961
Products, Services and Issues Index 971
Company Index 999
Brands Index 1061

Appendix I - Industrial Classifications. 1091
SIC Coverage 1091
NAICS Coverage 1099
ISIC Coverage 1107
Harmonized Code Coverage 1113
Appendix II - Annotated Source List 1115

TABLE OF TOPICS

The *Table of Topics* lists all topics used in *Market Share Reporter* in alphabetical order. One or more page references follow each topic; the page references identify the starting point where the topic is shown. The same topic name may be used under different SICs; therefore, in some cases, more than one page reference is provided. Roman numerals indicate volume number.

Abrasives, p. I-380
Accounting Services, pp. II-920-922
Adhesives, pp. I-352-353
Advanced Ceramics, p. I-376
Advertising, pp. II-842-850
Aerosol Cans, p. I-389
Aerospace, pp. I-530-531
Aerospace Contracting, p. II-928
Aftermarket Services, p. II-877
Agrichemicals, p. I-351
Agricultural Lending, pp. II-791-792
Air Cargo, pp. II-608-611
Air Force, p. II-929
Air Fresheners, p. I-356
Air Routes, pp. II-598-599
Aircraft, pp. I-520-521
Aircraft Engines, pp. I-522-523
Aircraft Services, p. I-523
Airlines, pp. II-599-608
Airport Security, p. II-864
Airports, pp. II-611-613
Alcoholic Beverages, pp. I-136-137
Alkalies and Chlorine, pp. I-259-260
Aluminum, pp. I-384-385
Aluminum Foil, p. I-386
Aluminum Rolling, p. I-386
Amusement Parks, pp. II-899-900
Analgesics, pp. I-273-283
Analytical Instruments, pp. II-537-538
Antennas, p. I-462
Apartments, p. II-830
Apparel, pp. I-194-202
Apple Sauce, p. I-92
Appliances, pp. I-437-438
Aquaculture Equipment, p. II-539
Architectural Services, pp. II-919-920
Army, p. II-929
Art, p. II-916
Artificial Turf, p. II-582
Athletic Footwear, pp. I-369-371

Atomic Power Plant Equipment, p. I-436
Auto Auctioning, p. I-495
Auto Insurance, pp. II-811-813
Auto Parts, pp. I-514-518
Auto Rental, pp. II-872-876
Auto Repair Services, p. II-877
Automated Beverage-Container Systems, p. I-433
Automated Teller Machines, pp. I-431-432
Automatic Ball Bonders, p. I-409
Automatic Meter Readers, p. II-537
Automotive Lighting, p. I-446
Automotive Mirrors, p. I-374
Automotive Trim, p. I-395
Autos, pp. I-495-509
Aviation Insurance, p. II-813
Avionics, p. II-533
Baby Care, pp. I-311-312
Baby Food, pp. I-88-90
Baby Products, p. II-582
Bacon, p. I-66
Baked Beans, p. I-92
Bakery Products, pp. I-112-114
Baking Mixes, p. I-108
Baking Needs, p. I-107
Bank Cards, p. II-782
Bank Holding Companies, p. II-833
Banking, pp. II-757-781
Banking Insurance, p. II-827
Bar Coding, p. II-538
Barley, p. I-13
Bars & Taverns, p. II-730
Bath Products, p. II-582
Batteries, pp. I-490-493
Bearings, p. I-414
Beer, pp. I-138-145
Beverages, pp. I-137-138
Bicycles, pp. I-526-527
Bill Payment, p. II-782
Biodiesel Fuels, p. I-357
Biological Substances, p. I-297

vii

Biometrics, pp. II-538-539
Biotechnology, p. I-299
Blood, p. I-299
Blood Testing, p. I-297
Boats, pp. I-524-525
Book Printing, p. I-251
Books, pp. I-244-249
Bottled Water, pp. I-160-163
Boxes, p. I-223
Bread, pp. I-114-117
Breath Fresheners, p. I-123
Bricks, pp. I-376-377
Broadcast Recording Services, p. II-657
Broadcasting Equipment, pp. I-462-464
Broilers, p. I-22
Brooms and Brushes, p. II-580
Building Construction, pp. I-52-53
Building Control Systems, p. II-536
Bus Companies, p. II-588
Buses, p. I-510
Business Loans, p. II-792
Butter, pp. I-73-74
Cable Broadcasting, pp. II-657-658
Cable Modems, p. I-460
Cakes, p. I-117
Call Centers, p. II-866
Camera Phones, p. I-464
Cameras, pp. II-554-555
Candles, p. II-582
Canned Food, pp. I-90-91
Canning Jars, p. I-374
Capacitors, p. I-487
Car Navigation Systems, p. II-533
Carbon Black, p. I-355
Card Shuffling Devices, p. II-583
Carpet Stores, p. II-712
Carpets and Rugs, pp. I-191-192
Carwashing Equipment, p. I-435
Castings, pp. I-383, 387-388
Catalogs, p. II-750
Catering, pp. II-721-722
Cellular Phones, pp. I-464-467
Cement, pp. I-374-375
Cereal, pp. I-107-108
Charities, pp. II-913-915
Check Processing, p. II-866
Cheese, pp. I-74-75
Cheese Spreads, p. I-76
Chemicals, pp. I-257-259
Chicken, pp. I-70-71
Child Care, p. II-913
Chilled Deserts, p. I-77
Chocolate, pp. I-131-134

Christmas Trees, p. I-27
Churches, p. II-918
Cigarette Making Machines, p. I-409
Cigarette Paper, p. I-234
Cigarettes, pp. I-185-189
Cigars, p. I-189
Circuit Boards, p. I-476
Clays, p. I-43
Cleaning Products, pp. I-307-310
Clinical Testing Industry, p. II-908
Coal, pp. I-33-35
Coated Paper, p. I-223
Coffee, pp. I-173-175
Coffee Drinks, p. I-175
Coffee Filters, p. I-234
Coffee Shops, p. II-722
Colleges, p. II-911
Comic Books, p. I-238
Compressors, p. I-412
Computer Data Storage, pp. I-424-425
Computer Peripherals, pp. I-426-427
Computer Printers, pp. I-427-431
Computer Services, p. II-864
Computers, pp. I-415-422
Concerts, p. II-895
Concrete, p. I-376
Condensed Milk, p. I-76
Condominiums, p. I-52
Condoms, p. I-364
Confectionery Products, pp. I-124-128
Connectors, p. I-487
Construction, pp. I-46-47
Construction Equipment, pp. I-402-403
Consulting Services, p. II-864
Consumer Electronics, pp. I-447-452
Consumer Spending, p. I-1
Contact Lenses, p. II-553
Contract Manufacturing, p. I-436
Contracting Work, p. I-54
Contracting Work - Air Conditioning, p. I-56
Contracting Work - Concrete, p. I-57
Contracting Work - Demolition Work, p. I-58
Contracting Work - Electrical, p. I-56
Contracting Work - Excavation, p. I-58
Contracting Work - Glazing/Curtain Wall, p. I-58
Contracting Work - Masonry, p. I-56
Contracting Work - Oil Pipelines, p. I-55
Contracting Work - Painting Work, p. I-56
Contracting Work - Railroads, p. I-55
Contracting Work - Roofing, p. I-57
Contracting Work - Sewers, p. I-55
Contracting Work - Steel, p. I-57
Contracting Work - Swimming Pools, p. I-58

Contracting Work - Transportation, p. I-54
Control Equipment, p. II-537
Convenience Stores, p. II-679
Conventions, p. II-866
Cookies, pp. I-118-120
Cooking Equipment, p. I-438
Cookware, p. I-395
Copper, pp. I-30-31
Copy Machines, pp. II-556-557
Corn, pp. I-12-13
Corrugated Boxes, p. I-222
Cosmaceuticals, p. I-313
Cosmetic Surgery, pp. II-905-906
Cosmetics, pp. I-313-316
Cosmetics Storage, p. I-366
Cottage Cheese, p. I-82
Cotton, pp. I-14-15
Cough Drops, pp. I-128-129
Countertops, p. I-1
Crackers, pp. I-120-121
Cranes, p. I-405
Cream, p. I-82
Credit Cards, pp. II-784-790
Credit Rating Agencies, p. II-850
Credit Unions, p. II-782
Crematories, p. II-839
Crops, p. I-11
Cruise Lines, pp. II-594-595
Crushed Stone, p. I-42
Crystal, p. I-374
Currency Equipment, p. I-432
Curtains and Draperies, p. I-204
Dairy Drinks, p. I-83
Dairy Products, pp. I-72-73
Danish, p. I-117
Debit Cards, pp. II-790-791
Decking, p. I-211
Deep-Sea Submersibles, p. I-523
Defense, pp. II-929-930
Defense Electronics, pp. II-533-534
Dental Equipment, pp. II-551-552
Denture Care, p. I-316
Deodorants, pp. I-316-318
Department Stores, pp. II-678-679
Depilatories, p. I-318
Design Services, pp. II-919-920
Detergents, pp. I-299-301
Diagnostics, p. I-298
Dialysis Centers, p. II-909
Diamond Grading, p. II-561
Diamonds, pp. I-44-45
Diapers, pp. I-225-227
Dies and Molds, p. I-408

Digital Video Recorders, p. I-453
Dimension Stone, p. I-41
Dips, pp. I-76, 97
Direct Marketing, p. II-851
Directories, pp. I-251-252
Dirtbikes, p. I-528
Discount Merchandising, pp. II-679-680
Dishwashers, pp. I-445-446
Dishwashing Detergents, p. I-302
Doctors, p. II-905
Dogs, p. I-24
Dolls, p. II-564
Donuts, p. I-117
Door Entry Devices, p. I-468
Doors, pp. I-1, 211
Dough, p. I-109
Drug Stores, pp. II-731-742
Drugs, pp. I-283-296
Dry Dinners, p. I-180
Dry Foods, p. I-95
Duct, p. I-394
DVDs and Videos, pp. II-879-884
Ear Care, p. I-319
Egg Substitutes, p. I-71
Eggs, p. I-23
Electromedical Equipment, pp. II-552-553
Electronic Commerce, pp. II-636-638
Elevators and Escalators, pp. I-404-405
Embroidery Shops, p. II-750
EMI/RFI Shielding, p. I-488
Energy, p. II-662
Energy Department, p. II-928
Energy Drinks, pp. I-163-164
Engineering Services, p. II-919
Engines, p. I-399
Entertainment, p. I-2
Environmental Services, p. II-927
Eye Care, p. I-319
Fabrics, pp. I-190-191
Fairs, p. II-901
Farm Equipment, pp. I-399-401
Farms, p. I-25
Fats and Oils, p. I-136
Fax Machines, p. I-460
Feminine Hygiene Products, pp. I-227-228
Ferries, p. II-595
Fiber Optics, p. I-387
Fibers, pp. I-270-271
Film Distribution, pp. II-889-891
Filters, p. I-435
Financial Information, p. II-804
Financial Services, p. II-783
Fire & Allied Insurance, p. II-816

Fire Pumps, p. I-412

Firearms, p. I-396

Firefighting Equipment, p. I-414

Firelogs, p. II-583

Firestarters, p. I-356

First Aid Products, pp. II-542-544

Fish Hatcheries, p. I-29

Fishing, pp. I-28-29

Flash Memory, p. I-477

Flashlights, p. II-583

Flat Panels, p. I-488

Flatware, p. II-562

Flooring, pp. I-2, 210-211, 581

Food, pp. I-60-63

Food and Trash Bags, p. I-224

Food Processing Equipment, p. I-409

Foodservice, pp. II-722-725

Foosball Tables, p. II-898

Foot Care, p. I-320

Footwear, pp. I-364, 368-369

Foreign Banks, p. II-782

Foundries, p. I-384

Fragrances, pp. I-321-323

Franchising, p. II-834

Freight Forwarding, p. II-620

Frequent Flier Programs, p. II-608

Frozen Bakery Products, pp. I-121-122

Frozen Desserts, pp. I-77-78

Frozen Foods, pp. I-101-106

Frozen Fruit, p. I-99

Frozen Vegetables, p. I-100

Fruit, pp. I-17-20

Fuel Testing Equipment, p. II-540

Full-Flight Simulators, p. I-523

Functional Foods, pp. I-63-64

Funeral Services, p. II-840

Furniture, pp. I-214-215

Furniture Stores, p. II-711

Gambling, pp. II-901-903

Gaming Systems, p. II-898

Garbage Trucks, p. I-509

Gas Cards, p. II-791

Gas Stations, pp. II-701-702

Gas Transmission, p. II-665

Gasoline, pp. I-357-358

Geotechnology, p. II-927

Gift Cards, p. I-2

Glass, p. I-373

Glassware, p. I-373

Global Positioning Satellites, p. I-467

Gold, pp. I-31-32

Golf Courses, p. II-898

Granite, p. I-43

Graphics Chips, p. I-478

Graphite, p. I-45

Green Goods, p. I-20

Greeting Cards, p. I-256

Grocery Stores, pp. II-681-695

Gum, p. I-134

Gyms, p. II-897

Gypsum, p. I-379

Hair Care, pp. I-323-328

Halloween Costumes, p. II-584

Hardware Stores, p. II-675

Hardwood, p. I-211

Hats, p. I-204

Hay, p. I-14

Health Clubs, p. II-897

Health Insurance, pp. II-813-814

Health Plans, pp. II-814-815

Hearing Aids, p. II-544

Heating and Cooling, p. I-434

Heavy Equipment Rental, p. II-851

Helicopter Transportation, p. II-594

Helicopters, p. I-522

Herbal Medicines, p. I-272

Herbicides, p. I-351

Holiday Decorations, p. II-584

Home Improvement Stores, pp. II-672-674

Home Owners Insurance, pp. II-816-818

Home Shopping, p. II-750

Home Warranties, p. II-823

Homefurnishings, pp. I-2-3, 204-207

Horizontal Directional Drilling, p. I-39

Horse Associations, p. II-917

Horse Racing, p. II-897

Horses, p. I-25

Hosiery, p. I-191

Hospital Beds, pp. I-217-218

Hospital Communications Services, p. II-658

Hospitals, pp. II-906-908

Hot Beverages, p. I-180

Hot Dogs, pp. I-66-67

Hot Sauce, p. I-97

Hotels, pp. II-836-838

Household Plastic Containers, p. I-366

Hubcaps, p. I-395

Ice Cream, pp. I-78-81

Incinerators, p. I-413

Industrial Gases, pp. I-260-262

Industrial Vehicles, p. I-405

Infant Formula, p. I-92

Information Technology, p. II-863

Ink, p. I-354

Inorganic Chemicals, pp. I-262-263

Inorganic Pigments, p. I-262

Insecticides, p. I-352

Insurance, pp. II-806-808

Interior Design, p. II-866

Interior Finishing, p. I-379

Internet, pp. II-638-643

Internet Phone Services, p. II-644

Internet Service Providers, pp. II-644-646

Investment Banking, pp. II-796-801

Iron Ore, p. I-30

Jewelry, pp. II-561-562

Jewelry Stores, p. II-748

Juices, pp. I-92-94

Ketchup, p. I-95

Kiosks, p. I-494

Labels, pp. I-255-256

Laboratory Instruments, p. II-536

Laminates, pp. I-354, 581

Landscaping Firms, p. I-26

Lasers, pp. I-478-480

Laundry Aids, pp. I-302-303

Laundry Equipment, pp. I-440-442

Lawn & Garden Equipment, p. I-402

Lawn & Garden Industry, pp. II-675-676

Lead, p. I-31

Lease Financing, p. II-792

Leasing, p. II-852

LED Equipment, p. I-488

Legal Services, p. II-910

Lettuce, p. I-181

Liability Insurance, pp. I-818, 823

Libraries, p. II-912

Licensed Merchandise, p. I-3

Life Insurance, pp. II-809-811

Lift Trucks, pp. I-405-406

Light Bulbs, p. I-446

Lighters, p. II-584

Limestone, p. I-42

Lingerie, p. I-203

Lip Care, p. I-328

Liquid Crystal Displays, pp. I-488-490

Liquor, pp. I-149-160

Livestock, p. I-26

Loan Arrangers, pp. II-792-793

Locks, p. I-392

Log Homes, p. I-212

Logistics, p. II-589

Luggage, pp. I-371-372

Luggage Boxes, p. I-392

Luggage Racks, p. I-392

Lumber, p. I-209

Lunch Kits, p. I-181

Lunch Meat, pp. I-67-68

Luxury Industry, p. I-4

Machine Tools, pp. I-406-408

Machine Vision, pp. II-535-536

Magazines, pp. I-239-243

Malt Beverages, p. I-145

Management Consulting Services, pp. II-924-925

Manufactured Homes, p. I-212

Marble and Limestone, p. I-42

Margarine, p. I-74

Marine Insurance, pp. II-818-820

Marine Voyage Recorders, p. II-534

Mass Transit, p. II-588

Massage Chairs, p. I-218

Mattresses, p. I-216

Mayonnaise, p. I-97

Meal Replacements, p. I-181

Meat, pp. I-65-66

Meat Snacks, pp. I-68-69

Media, pp. I-4-5

Medical Equipment, pp. II-540-542

Medical Laboratories, p. II-908

Medical Malpractice Insurance, pp. II-823-826

Medical Research, p. II-908

Medical Waste Disposal, p. II-909

Mergers & Acquisitions, pp. II-867-868

Metal Sashes and Doors, p. I-394

Microprocessors, pp. I-480-485

Milk, pp. I-83-86

Mining, p. I-30

Mints, p. I-129

Mobile Content, p. I-467

Mobile Gaming, p. II-622

Molding, p. I-212

Money Transfers, p. II-783

Mortgage Loans, pp. II-793-795

Motion Picture Libraries, p. II-888

Motion Pictures, pp. II-884-888

Motor Homes, p. I-519

Motor Oil, pp. I-358-359

Motorcycles, pp. I-528-530

Motors and Generators, p. I-437

Movie Rental Industry, p. II-894

Movie Theaters, pp. II-891-893

Moving Companies, p. II-589

Museums, p. II-916

Mushrooms, p. I-20

Music, pp. I-453-459

Musical Instruments, pp. II-562-564

Mutual Funds, p. II-802

Nail Care, pp. I-328-329

Nanotechnology, p. I-5

Nasal Care, p. I-330

Natural Gas, pp. I-36, 666

Natural Gas Liquids, p. I-39

Navy, p. II-931
Networking Equipment, pp. I-468-475
News Syndicates, p. II-865
Newspapers, pp. I-235-237
Nickel, p. I-385
Noise Barriers, p. I-5
Nonwoven Industry, p. I-192
Nuts, pp. I-18, 135
Nylons, p. I-272
Office Furniture, pp. I-216-217
Office Space, p. II-831
Office Supply Stores, p. II-670
Oil, pp. I-36-38
Oil & Gas Equipment, p. I-404
Oil Maintenance Dredging, p. I-40
Oil Wells, pp. I-39-40
Online Music Downloading, pp. I-459-460
Optical Good Stores, p. II-753
Optical Goods, p. II-554
Optoelectronics, p. I-476
Oral Care, pp. I-330-333
Organic Chemicals, pp. I-348-350
Organic Foods, pp. I-64-65
Orthopedic Appliances, pp. II-544-548
Outboard Motors, p. I-399
Package Delivery Services, pp. II-590-591
Packaging, pp. I-5-8
Packaging Machinery, p. I-413
Paint and Flooring Stores, p. II-675
Paints and Coatings, pp. I-344-347
Pallets, p. I-212
Paper, pp. I-219-220
Paper Tubes, p. I-222
Paperboard, pp. I-221-222
Pasta, pp. I-179-180
Patents, p. II-834
Pay Television, pp. II-659-661
Peanut Butter, p. I-95
Pencils, pp. II-579-580
Pens, p. II-579
Pensions, p. II-827
Personal Care Appliances, pp. I-442-444
Personal Care Products, pp. I-333-338
Personal Digital Assistants, pp. I-422-424
Personal Video Recorders, p. I-453
Pet Care, pp. II-584-585
Pet Food, pp. I-109-112
Pet Products, p. II-585
Petroleum Refining, p. I-358
Pets, p. I-8
Pharmacy Benefit Managers, p. II-743
Phosphate Rock, p. I-44
Photofinishing, p. II-866

Photographic Equipment, pp. II-557-558
Pipeline Trading, p. II-663
Pipelines, p. II-614
Plastic Bags, p. I-366
Plastic Cards, p. I-367
Plastic Film, p. I-364
Plastic Lumber, p. I-367
Plastic Pipe, p. I-365
Plastic Sheet, p. I-365
Plastics, pp. I-263-267
Plastics Machinery, p. I-410
Platemaking, p. I-256
Plumbing Fixtures, p. I-378
Police Cars, p. I-510
Political Action Committees, p. II-918
Polyester, p. I-272
Popcorn, p. I-181
Pork, pp. I-71-72
Portrait Studios, p. II-839
Ports, pp. II-595-596
POS Terminals, p. I-432
Postage Meters, p. I-433
Postal Bag Repair, p. II-878
Postal Service, p. II-592
Poultry, pp. I-21, 72
Powder Coatings, p. I-395
Powdered Milk, p. I-76
Powered Two Wheelers, p. I-530
Pre-Paid Industry, p. II-850
Pregnancy Test Kits, p. I-298
Prepared Meals, p. I-182
Prescription Drug Managers, p. II-670
Prescription Filling, pp. II-743-744
Primary Information Services, p. II-865
Printing, pp. I-253-255
Printing Equipment, p. I-409
Prison Health Care Services, p. II-905
Prison Uniforms, p. I-201
Prisons, p. II-926
Private Investigators, p. II-864
Projectors, p. II-558
Property Insurance, pp. II-820-821
Property Management, p. II-831
Psychiatric Hospitals, p. II-908
Public Relations Industry, p. II-925
Publishing, p. I-235
Pudding, pp. I-81-82
Pumps, p. I-412
Pumps and Mixing Equipment, p. I-434
Push Poles, p. I-395
Quick Printing, p. II-851
Radar and Search Equipment, p. II-534
Radiators, p. I-394

Radio Broadcasting, pp. II-649-653
Radio Frequency Identification Hardware, p. I-475
Railcar Leasing, p. II-852
Railroad Equipment, pp. I-525-526
Railroad Ties, p. I-209
Railroads, pp. II-586-587
Razor Blades, pp. I-389-391
Real Estate, pp. II-831-832
Real Estate Investment Trusts, pp. II-834-835
Recording Media, p. I-493
Recreational Vehicles, p. I-519
Recycling, p. II-666
Refractories, p. I-377
Refrigerated Storage, p. II-591
Refrigerators, pp. I-438-440
Registered Agents, p. II-922
Reinsurance, p. II-828
Rental Property Construction, p. I-52
Reposessions, p. II-869
Research, pp. II-922-923
Residential Construction, pp. I-47-52
Restaurants, pp. II-725-729
Retailing, pp. II-677-678
Retailing - Electronics, p. II-717
Retailing - Apparel, pp. II-703-709
Retailing - Appliances, pp. II-715-716
Retailing - Auto Supplies, pp. II-699-700
Retailing - Autos, p. II-699
Retailing - Beverages, p. II-696
Retailing - Books, pp. II-746-747
Retailing - Cameras, p. II-750
Retailing - Cards, p. II-747
Retailing - Coffee, p. II-729
Retailing - Computer Peripherals, p. II-717
Retailing - Consumer Electronics, p. II-717
Retailing - Flowers, p. II-752
Retailing - Food, pp. II-696-697
Retailing - Fruits & Vegetables, p. II-698
Retailing - Hobbies, p. II-748
Retailing - Homefurnishings, pp. II-712-715
Retailing - Ice Cream, p. II-698
Retailing - Magazines, p. II-752
Retailing - Meat, p. II-698
Retailing - Movies, pp. II-718-719
Retailing - Music, pp. II-719-720
Retailing - Music Products, p. II-720
Retailing - Personal Care Products, pp. II-753-755
Retailing - Pet Food, p. II-698
Retailing - Propane, p. II-752
Retailing - Religious Products, pp. II-755-756
Retailing - Sporting Goods, pp. II-745-746
Retailing - Supplements, p. II-756
Retailing - Swimming Pools, p. II-756

Retailing - Toys, pp. II-748-749
Retailing - Video Games, pp. I-718, 749
Retailing - Wedding Gowns, p. II-707
Retirement Homes, p. I-52
Rice, pp. I-12, 108
Robots, pp. I-414-415
Roofing, p. I-9
Rotocraft, p. I-522
Rubber, pp. I-268-269
Rubber Machinery, p. I-410
Salad Dressings, p. I-98
Salads, p. I-182
Salons, p. II-839
Sand & Gravel, p. I-43
Sanitary Paper Products, pp. I-229-233
Sanitaryware, p. I-378
Satellites, pp. I-467-468
Sauces, pp. I-98-99
Sausage, pp. I-69-70
Schools, p. II-911
Scooters, p. I-530
Screening Equipment, p. II-552
Seafood, pp. I-169-172
Seasonings, p. I-182
Seatbelts, pp. I-207-208
Securites Exchanges, p. II-802
Securities Exchanges, pp. II-803-804
Security Equipment, pp. I-475-476
Security Industry, p. II-865
Seeds, p. I-11
Self-Checkout Industry, p. I-433
Semiconductor Equipment, pp. I-410-412
Semiconductors, pp. I-485-487
Servers, pp. II-860-863
Shaving Cream, pp. I-338-339
Sheep and Goats, p. I-21
Ship Building, p. I-524
Shipping, pp. II-593-594
Shoe Stores, pp. II-709-710
Shopping Centers, pp. II-829-830
Side Dishes, p. I-183
Siding, p. I-9
Signs, p. II-580
Silver, p. I-32
Skin Care, pp. I-339-342
Slot Machines, pp. II-898-899
Small Appliances, p. I-444
Smartphones, p. I-460
Smoking Cessation Products, pp. I-296-297
Snack Bars, pp. I-130-131
Snack Cakes, p. I-118
Snacks, pp. I-176-178
Snuff, p. I-189

Soap, pp. I-303-307
Soft Drinks, pp. I-164-168
Software, pp. II-853-860
Softwood, p. I-210
Solar Equipment, pp. I-392-393
Sorghum, p. I-14
Soup, pp. I-96-97
Soybeans, p. I-13
Speakerphones, p. I-461
Spinach, p. I-183
Sporting Goods, pp. II-573-578
Sports, pp. II-903-904
Sports Drinks, p. I-169
Sports Teams, pp. II-896-897
Squeegees, p. II-585
Stadiums, p. II-901
Starches, p. I-310
Stationery, p. I-233
Steel, pp. I-381-382
Steel Beams, p. I-383
Steel Files, p. I-391
Steel Pipe, p. I-383
Steel Strapping, p. I-383
Stents, p. II-548
Stone, p. I-41
Sugar, p. I-122
Sugar Substitutes, p. I-122
Sugarbeets, p. I-16
Sun Blocking Films, p. I-365
Sun Care, p. I-343
Surety Insurance, p. II-826
Surfactants, p. I-260
Surgical Gloves, p. II-549
Surgical Supplies, pp. II-549-551
Sweeteners, p. I-169
Swimming Pool Heaters, p. I-393
Taco Kits, pp. I-183-184
Tanning Beds, p. II-585
Tape, pp. I-223-224
Tax Preparation, pp. II-840-841
Tea, p. I-184
Telecommunications, pp. II-623-624
Telephone Equipment, p. I-461
Telephone Recording Equipment, p. I-461
Telephone Services, pp. II-632-636
Teletypes, p. I-461
Television Broadcasting, pp. II-653-657
Temp Agencies, p. II-852
Terminal Operation, p. II-597
Testing Instruments, p. II-539
Testing Laboratories, p. II-923
Textbooks, pp. I-249-250
Textiles, p. I-190

Theater Screens, p. II-559
Theatrical Entertainment, p. II-895
Thermometers, p. II-540
Thermoses, p. I-365
Tiles, p. I-377
Tin, p. I-386
Tire Dealerships, p. II-701
Tire Retreading, p. II-876
Tires, pp. I-360-363
Title Insurance, p. II-826
Tobacco, p. I-15
Tobacco Retailing, p. II-752
Toll Collections, p. II-621
Toll Operators, p. II-621
Tour Operators, pp. II-619-620
Tourism, p. II-615
Toys and Games, pp. II-564-568
Trade Shows, pp. II-869-870
Trademarks, p. II-834
Trading Cards, p. I-252
Trailer Hitches, p. I-532
Training, pp. II-870-871
Translation Services, p. II-871
Travel, p. II-616
Travel Agencies, pp. II-616-617
Travel Arrangements, pp. II-617-619
Travel Trailers, p. I-532
Travelers Checks, p. II-783
Truck Trailers, p. I-519
Trucking, p. II-590
Trucks, pp. I-510-514
Trusts, p. II-833
Turbines, p. I-398
Turbochargers, p. I-518
Turbofans, p. I-399
Turkeys, pp. I-23-24
Tutoring, p. II-912
Unions, p. II-917
Utilities, pp. II-663-664
Utlities, p. II-664
Vacuum Cleaners, p. I-445
Valves, p. I-397
Vegetables, pp. I-16-17
Vehicle Stability Systems, p. I-493
Vending Machines, p. II-751
Veterinary Services, p. I-26
Video Game Consoles, pp. II-568-569
Video Game Manuals, p. I-251
Video Game Rental Industry, p. II-894
Video Games, pp. II-569-573
Video Tape, p. I-494
Vinegar, p. I-184
Vitamins, pp. I-272-273

Voting Machines, p. II-537
Wallboard, p. I-379
Waste Collection, pp. II-666-667
Watches, pp. II-559-560
Weather Measuring Equipment, p. II-536
Weight Control Products, p. I-297
Weight Loss Industry, p. I-9
Wheat, p. I-11
Whipped Toppings, p. I-86
Wholesale Trade, p. II-669
Wholesale Trade - Bicycles, p. II-669
Wholesale Trade - Comic Books, p. II-671
Wholesale Trade - Construction, p. II-668
Wholesale Trade - Convenience Stores, p. II-670
Wholesale Trade - Drugs, p. II-671
Wholesale Trade - Electronics, pp. II-668-669
Wholesale Trade - Pool Supplies, p. II-671
Wholesale Trade - Tires, p. II-668
Wholetrade Trade - Seafood, p. II-671
Wi-Fi, pp. II-647-648
Wind Power, p. II-664
Windows and Doors, pp. I-9-10
Wine, pp. I-145-149
Wine Cellars, p. I-440
Wine Chillers, p. I-440
Wipes, p. I-193
Wireless Services, pp. II-624-631
Wood Panels, p. I-210
Wool, p. I-21
Workers Compensation Insurance, pp. II-821-823
Writing Instruments, p. II-579
Yogurt, pp. I-86-88
Zinc, p. I-386
Zippers, p. II-580

INTRODUCTION

Market Share Reporter (MSR) is a compilation of market share reports from periodical literature. As shown by reviews of previous editions plus correspondence and telephone contact with many users, this is a unique resource for competitive analysis, diversification planning, marketing research, and other forms of economic and policy analysis.

This is the fifteenth edition of *Market Share Reporter*. In previous editions, *Market Share Reporter* presented market share data on the North American market. In 1997, *World Market Share Reporter* was first published, which provided international coverage -- market shares on global industries or markets in countries other than the United States, Canada and Mexico.

The editorial staff of *Market Share Reporter* decided that the needs of the users of *Market Share Reporter* would best be served by combining the two titles into one two-volume set. Previously, users would need to consult two separate books to gather research on market shares. The 2005 edition of *MSR* now provides market share information on domestic and international markets in one volume. A user seeking market share information on the autombile market, for example, will find entries covering the United States as well as foreign countries and the entire global industry. Having such data together in one chapter should be both entertaining and informative to readers.

However, little has changed from previous editions of *Market Share Reporter*. Frequent users will find that the book is still primarily arranged around the

Standard Industrial Classification (SIC) code. Features of the 2005 edition include—

- More than 3,600 entries, all new or updated.
- Entries arranged under both SIC and NAICS codes.
- Corporate, brand, product, service and commodity market shares.
- Coverage of private and public sector activities.
- Comprehensive indexes, including products, companies, brands, places, sources, NAICS, ISIC, Harmonized and SIC codes.
- Table of Topics showing topical subdivisions of chapters with page references.
- Graphics.
- Annotated source listing—provides publishers' information for journals cited in this edition of *MSR*.

MSR is a one-of-a-kind resource for ready reference, marketing research, economic analysis, planning, and a host of other disciplines.

Categories of Market Shares

Entries in *Market Share Reporter* fall into four broad categories. Items were included if they showed the relative strengths of participants in a market or provided subdivisions of economic activity in some manner that could assist the analyst.

- *Corporate market shares* show the names of companies that participate in an industry, produce a product, or provide a service. Each company's market share is shown as a percent of total industry or product sales for a defined period, usually a year. In some cases, the company's share represents the share of the sales of the companies shown (group total)—because shares of the total market were not cited in the source or were not relevant. In some corporate share tables, brand information appears behind company names in parentheses. In these cases, the tables can be located using either the company or the brand index.

- *Institutional shares* are like corporate shares but show the shares of other kinds of organizations. The most common institutional entries in *MSR* display the shares of states, provinces, or regions in an activity. The shares of not-for-profit organizations in some economic or service functions fall under this heading.

- *Brand market shares* are similar to corporate shares with the difference that brand names are shown. Brand names include equivalent categories such as the names of television programs, magazines, publishers' imprints, etc. In some cases, the names of corporations appear in parentheses behind the brand name; in these cases, tables can be located using either the brand or the company index.

- *Product, commodity, service, and facility* shares feature a broad category (e.g. household appliances) and show how the category is subdivided into components (e.g. refrigerators, ranges, washing machines, dryers, and dishwashers). Entries under this category cover products (autos, lawnmowers, polyethylene, etc.), commodities (cattle, grains, crops), services (telephone, child care), and facilities (port berths, hotel suites,

etc.). Subdivisions may be products, categories of services (long-distance telephone, residential phone service, 800-service), types of commodities (varieties of grain), size categories (e.g., horsepower ranges), modes (rail, air, barge), types of facilities (categories of hospitals, ports, and the like), or other subdivisions.

- *Other shares. MSR* includes a number of entries that show subdivisions, breakdowns, and shares that do not fit neatly into the above categorizations but properly belong in such a book because they shed light on public policy, foreign trade, and other subjects of general interest. These items include, for instance, subdivisions of governmental expenditures, environmental issues, and the like.

Coverage

MSR reports on *published* market shares rather than attempting exhaustive coverage of the market shares, say, of all major corporations and of all products and services. Despite this limitation, *MSR* holds share information on more than 6,100 companies, more than 3,000 brands, and more than 2,600 product, commodity, service, and facility categories. Several entries are usually available for each industry group in the SIC classification; omitted groups are those that do not play a conventional role in the market, e.g., Private Households (SIC 88).

As pointed out in previous editions, *MSR* tends to reflect the current concerns of the business press. In addition to being a source of market share data, it mirrors journalistic preoccupations, issues in the business community, and events abroad. Important and controversial industries and activities get most of the ink. Heavy coverage is provided in those areas that are—

- large, important, basic (autos, chemicals)
- on the leading edge of technological change (computers, electronics, software)
- very competitive (toiletries, beer, soft drinks)
- in the news because of product recalls, new product introductions, mergers and acquisitions, lawsuits, and for other reasons
- relate to popular issues (environment, crime), or have excellent coverage in their respective trade press.

Variation in coverage from previous editions is due in part to publication cycles of sources and a different mix of brokerage house reports for the period covered (due to shifting interests within the investment community).

How Entries Are Prepared

In many cases, several entries are provided on a subject each citing the same companies. No attempt was made to eliminate such seeming duplication if the publishing and/or original sources were different and the market shares were not identical. Those who work with such data know that market share reports are often little more than the "best guesses" of knowledgeable observers rather than precise measurements. To the planner or analyst, variant reports about an industry's market shares are useful for interpreting the data.

As a rule, material on market share data for 2004 were used by preference; in response to reader requests, we have included historical data when available. In some instances, information for earlier years was included if the category was unique or if the earlier year was necessary for context. In a number cases, projections for 2006 and later years were also included.

Because *Market Share Reporter* now holds entries on domestic and international markets, titles have become more descriptive than in previous editions. Each entry will indicate in the title if it is for a particular country, state, city or region. An entry may address a global market (Top Computer Makers Worldwide). In such entries, the title will feature "worldwide" or "global" so that the reader understands the market being discussed.

Many entries, such as the example on page xxii, do not feature any geographical reference in the title. In these instances, the entries are referring to the market in the United States. Market data on the United States make up well over half the entries in this book, so such an editorial decision seemed reasonable to the staff of *MSR*.

It is important to note that some sources do not explicitly state whether the market shares they are publishing are for the domestic or international market. Often, it is obvious by some measure in the article -- dollar sales or unit shipments, for example -- if the shares describe the United States or some global industry. However, in a handful of entries the staff of *MSR* has had to use their best judgment. As stated earlier, market share data is often best guesses of knowledgable observers. The staff of *MSR* feels that its own best guesses have been sufficient.

Time Period Covered in *MSR*

In previous editions of *Market Share Reporter*, entries were usually drawn from periodicals and government reports published during the previous 12 months. Entries for *World Market Share Reporter*, were taken from sources published during the previous two years.

In combining *Market Share Reporter* with *World Market Share Reporter*, the fifteenth edition of *MSR* will feature data from sources published after the previous edition of each of these titles. In short, entries that provide coverage on North America were drawn from sources published between January 2003 and July 2004. Those entries that provide international coverage were drawn from sources published after the final edition of *World Market Share Reporter*: December 2001 to July 2004.

This is, obviously, a very large time period. In preparing this edition of *Market Share Reporter*, preference is always given to the most current data. Many entries in this volume provide coverage of 2004 markets. The staff of *MSR* was also concerned with providing unique, interesting market share data across the SIC code range. Future editions of *MSR* will be drawn from a smaller time frame.

Some of the entries covering the global marketplace may be deemed "old" by the user. However, it is important to note that when analyzing the international marketplace the most recent data available may indeed be several years old. Such data are kept to a minimum and are used only if the share provides coverage of an unusual market or a popular, competitive one (diapers or toiletries, for example).

SIC and NAICS

The United States has used the *Standard Industrial Classification* code for roughly 60 years. It became clear, however, that the SIC code had its limitations. It was difficult to address the new technologies and ways of selling that had come to the global marketplace, such as warehouse clubs, office supply stores, and Internet businesses and technology. The *North American Industry Classification System (NAICS)* is intended to serve as a more comprehensive method to classify industries.

The transition between SIC and NAICS was implemented for the 1997 Economic Census. The new NAICS coding -- which is used in the United States, Canada and Mexico -- is a major revamping of the industrial classification system. *NAICS* coding includes new sectors and a more detailed study of the "services" category (industries that would fall under the 5300 and higher section of the SIC code).

Under *NAICS* coding, a 6-digit industry code replaces the old 4-digit SIC code. The first two digits indicate the sector, the third the subsector, the fourth designates the industry group, the fifth the NAICS industry and the sixth the national industry. There are 20 sectors in *NAICS* and 1,170 industries in *NAICS*.

Because the SIC code is still the more popular classification system, *Market Share Reporter* is organized around its coding. However, each entry now contains *NAICS* codes appropriate to the industry being discussed. Most entries will have only one *NAICS* code. However, some entries will have more than one code (three is the maximum). As stated, *NAICS* codes are more detailed than *SIC* classifications. Because of this, more than one *NAICS* code was sometimes necessary to provide the most accurate description of the industry being analyzed.

More information about *NAICS* is available through the U.S. Department of Commerce web site at http://www.ntis.gov/naics.

"Unusual" Market Shares

Some reviewers of the first edition questioned—sometimes tongue-in-cheek, sometimes seriously—the inclusion of tables on such topics as computer crime, the pet population, children's allowances, governmental budgets, and weapons system stockpiles. Indeed, some of these categories do not fit the sober meaning of "market share." A few tables on such subjects are present in every edition—because they provide market information, albeit indirectly, or because they are the "market share equivalents" in an industrial classification which is in the public sector or dominated by the public sector's purchasing power.

Organization of Chapters

Market Share Reporter is organized into chapters by 2-digit SIC categories (industry groups). The exception is the first chapter, entitled *General Interest and Broad Topics*; this chapter holds all entries that bridge two or more 2-digit SIC industry codes (e.g. retailing in general, beverage containers, building materials, etc.) and cannot, therefore, be classified using the SIC system without distortion. Please note, however, that a topic in this chapter will often have one or more additional entries later—where the table could be assigned to a detailed industry. Thus, in addition to tables on packaging in the first chapter, numerous tables appear later on glass containers, metal cans, etc.

Within each chapter, entries are shown by 4-digit SIC (industry level). Within blocks of 4-digit SIC entries, entries are sorted alphabetically by topic, then alphabetically by title.

SIC and Topic Assignments

MSR's SIC classifications are based on the coding as defined in the *Standard Industrial Classification Manual* for 1987, issued by the Bureau of the Census, Department of Commerce. This 1987 classification system introduced significant revisions to the 1972 classification (as slightly modified in 1977); the 1972 system is still in widespread use (even by the Federal government); care should be used in comparing data classified in the new and in the old way.

The closest appropriate 4-digit SIC was assigned to each table. In many cases, a 3-digit SIC had to be used because the substance of the table was broader than the nearest 4-digit SIC category. Such SICs always end with a zero. In yet other cases, the closest classification possible was at the 2-digit level; these SICs terminate with double-zero. If the content of the table did not fit the 2-digit level, it was assigned to the first chapter of *MSR* and classified by topic only.

Topic assignments are based on terminology for commodities, products, industries, and services in the SIC Manual; however, in many cases phrasing has been simplified, shortened, or updated; in general, journalistically succinct rather than bureaucratically exhaustive phraseology was used throughout.

Organization of Entries

Entries are organized in a uniform manner. A sample entry is provided below. Explanations for each part of an entry, shown in boxes, are provided below the sample.

1	*Entry Number.* A numeral between star symbols. Used for locating an entry from the index.
2	*Topic.* Second line, small type. Gives the broad or general product or service category of the entry. The topic for Top Pre-Laundry Treatment Brands, 2004 is Laundry Aids.

☆ 1142 ☆ 1

Laundry Aids   2

SIC: 2841; NAICS: 325611   3

Top Pre-Laundry Treatment Brands, 4
2003

5

Brands are ranked by supermarket, drug store and discount store (excluding Wal-Mart) sales for the year ended December 28, 2003.   6

	($ mil.)	Share 7
Shout	$ 64.9	17.54%
Spray & Wash	50.2	13.57
Oxi Clean	46.1	12.46 8
Woolite	43.3	11.70
Other	165.5	44.73

Source: *MMR*, May 31, 2004, p. 33, from Information Resources Inc.   9

3 *SIC and NAICS Code.* Second line, small type, follows the topic. General entries in the first chapter do not have an SIC code.

4 *Title.* Third line, large type. Describes the entry with a headline.

5 *Graphic.* When a graphic is present, it follows the title. Some entries will be illustrated with a pie or bar chart. The information used to create the graphic is always shown below the pie or bar chart.

6 *Note Block.* When present, follows the title and is in italic type. The note provides contextual information about the entry to make the data more understandable. Special notes about the data, information about time periods covered, market totals, and other comments are provided. Self-explanatory entries do not have a note block.

7 *Column headers.* Follow the note block. Some entries have more than one column or the single column requires a header. In these cases, column headers are used to describe information covered in the column. In most cases, column headers are years (2004) or indicators of type and magnitude ($ mil.). Column headers are shown only when necessary for clarity of presentation.

8 *Body.* Follows the note block or the column header and shows the actual data in two or more columns. In most cases, individual rows of data in the body are arranged in descending order, with the largest market share holder heading the list. Collective shares, usually labelled "Others" are placed last.

9 *Source.* Follows the body. All entries cite the source of the table, the date of publication, and the page number (if given). In many cases, the publisher obtained the information from another source (original source); in all such cases, the original source is also shown.

Continued entries. Entries that extend over two adjacent columns on the same page are not marked to indicate continuation but continue in the second column. Entries that extend over two pages are marked *Continued on the next page.* Entries carried over from the previous page repeat the entry number, topic (followed by the word *continued*), title, and column header (if any).

Use of Names

Company Names. The editors reproduced company names as they appeared in the source unless it was clearly evident from the name and the context that a name had been misspelled in the original. Large companies, of course, tend to appear in a large number of entries and in variant renditions. General Electric Corporation may appear as GE, General Electric, General Electric Corp., GE Corp., and other variants. No attempt was made to enforce a uniform rendition of names in the entries. In the Company Index, variant renditions were reduced to a single version or cross-referenced.

Use of Numbers

Throughout *MSR*, tables showing percentage breakdowns may add to less than 100 or fractionally more than 100 due to rounding. In those cases where only a few leading participants in a market are shown, the total of the shares may be substantially less than 100.

Numbers in the note block showing the total size of the market are provided with as many significant digits as possible in order to permit the user to calculate the sales of a particular company by multiplying the market total by the market share.

In a relatively small number of entries, actual unit or dollar information is provided rather than share information in percent. In such cases, the denomination of the unit (tons, gallons, $) and its magnitude (000 indicates multiply by 1,000; mil., multiply by

1,000,000) are mentioned in the note block or shown in the column header.

Data in some entries are based on different kinds of currencies and different weight and liquid measures. Where necessary, the unit is identified in the note block or in the column header. Examples are long tons, short tons, metric tons or Canadian dollars, etc.

Graphics

Pie and bar charts are used to illustrate some of the entries. The graphics show the names of companies, products, and services when they fit on the charts. When room is insufficient to accommodate the label, the first word of a full name is used followed by three periods (...) to indicate omission of the rest of the label.

In the case of bar charts, the largest share is always the width of the column, and smaller shares are drawn in proportion. Two bar charts, consequently, should not be compared to one another.

Sources

The majority of entries were extracted from newspapers and from general purpose, trade, and technical periodicals normally available in larger public, special, or university libraries. All told, 2,105 sources were used; of these, 1,039 were primary print sources. Many more sources were reviewed but lacked coverage of the subject. These primary sources, in turn, used 1,066 original sources.

In many cases, the primary source in which the entry was published cites another source for the data, the original source. Original sources include other publications, brokerage houses, consultancies and research organizations, associations, government agencies, special surveys, and the like.

Many sources have also been used from the World Wide Web. The citation includes the Web address, the date the article was retrieved, and, if possible, the title of the article or report. In many cases Web pages have no title or author name. As well, it is not uncommon for Web pages to be moved or temporarity out of operation.

Since many primary sources appear as original sources elsewhere, and vice-versa, primary and original sources are shown in a single Source Index under two headings. Primary sources included in *MSR* almost always used the market share data as illustrative material for narratives covering many aspects of the subject. We hope that this book will also serve as a guide to those articles.

Indexes

Market Share Reporter features five indexes and two appendices.

- **Source Index**. This index holds 2,105 references in two groupings. *Primary sources* (1,039) are publications where the data were found. *Original sources* (1,066) are sources cited in the primary sources. Each item in the index is followed by one or more entry numbers arranged sequentially, beginning with the first mention of the source.

- **Place Names Index**. This index provides references to cities, states, parks and regions in North America. 495 are included. References are to entry numbers.

- **Products, Services, Names and Issues Index**. This index holds 2,609 references to products, personal names and services in alphabetical order. The index also lists subject categories that do not fit the definition of a product or service but properly belong in the index. Examples include *aquariums, counties, crime, defense spending, economies, lotteries*, and the like. Some listings are abbreviations for chemical substances, computer software, etc. which may not be meaningful to those unfamiliar with the industries. Wherever possible, the full name is also provided for abbreviations commonly in use. Each listing is followed by one or more references to entry numbers.

- **Company Index**. This index shows references to more than 6,100 company names by entry number. Companies are arranged in alphabetical order. In some cases, the market share table from which the company name was derived showed the share for a combination of two or more companies; these combinations are reproduced in the index.

- **Brand Index**. The Brand Index shows references to 3,024 brands by entry number. The arrangement is alphabetical. Brands include names of publications, computer software, operating systems, etc., as well as the more conventional brand names (Coca Cola, Maxwell House, Budweiser, etc.)

Appendix I

- **SIC Coverage**. The first appendix shows SICs covered by *Market Share Reporter*. The listing shows major SIC groupings at the 2-digit level as bold-face headings followed by 4-digit SIC numbers, the names of the SIC, and a *page* reference (rather than a reference to an entry number, as in the indexes). The page shows the first occurrence of the SIC in the book. *MSR*'s SIC coverage is quite comprehensive, as shown in the appendix. However, many 4-digit SIC categories are further divided into major product groupings. Not all of these have corresponding entries in the book.

- **NAICS Coverage**. This section of the appendix contains a listing of the *North American Industry Classification System* codes that appear in *Market Share Reporter. NAICS* is a six digit classification system that covers 20 sectors and 1,170 industries. The page shows the first occurrence of the *NAICS* code in the book.

- **ISIC Coverage**. This section of the appendix provides a listing of the Industrial Standard Industrial Classification (ISIC) codes that appear in *Market Share Reporter*. ISIC codes, as with Harmonized Codes, are coding systems similar to NAICS. If features broader classfications and is less widely used. The ISIC listing shows the 4-digit level along with name of the industries. References to entries are not included.

- **HC Coverage**. This section provides a listing of the Harmonized Commodity classifications that appear in *MSR*. The listing shows industrial groups at the 2-digit, or chapter, level along with the names of the industries. Reference entries are not included. Both the Harmonized Code and the ISIC code sections are included in *MSR* because while they are older classification sytems they are still of interest to some readers.

Appendix II

- **Annotated Source List.** The second appendix provides publisher names, addresses, telephone

and fax numbers, and publication frequency of primary sources cited in *Market Share Reporter*, 15th Edition.

Available in Electronic Formats

Licensing. *Market Share Reporter* is available for licensing. The complete database is provided in a fielded format and is deliverable on such media as disk, CD-ROM or tape. For more information, contact Gale's Business Development Group at (800) 877-GALE or visit us on our web site at www.galegroup.com/bizdev.

Online. *Market Share Reporter* is accessible online as File MKTSHR through LEXIS-NEXIS and as part of the MarkIntel service offered by Thomson Financial Securities Data. For more information, contact LEXIS-NEXIS, P.O. Box 933, Dayton, OH 45401-0933, phone (937) 865-6800, toll-free (800) 227-4908,website: http://www.lexis- nexis.com; or Thomson Financial Securities Data, Two Gateway Center, Newark, NJ 07102, phone: (973) 622-3100, toll-free: (888)989-8373, website: www.tfsd.com.

Acknowledgements

Market Share Reporter is something of a collective enterprise which involves not only the editorial team but also many users who share comments, criticisms, and suggestions over the telephone. Their help and encouragement is very much appreciated. *MSR* could not have been produced without the help of many people in and outside of The Gale Group. The editors would like to express their special appreciation to Virgil Burton (Coordinating Editor, Gale Group) and to the staff of Editorial Code and Data, Inc.

Comments and Suggestions

Comments on *MSR* or suggestions for improvement of its usefulness, format, and coverage are always welcome. Although every effort is made to maintain accuracy, errors may occasionally occur; the editors will be grateful if these are called to their attention. Please contact:

> Editors
> *Market Share Reporter*
> The Gale Group
> 27500 Drake Road
> Farmington Hills, Michigan 48331-3535
> Phone:(248) 699-GALE
> or (800) 347-GALE
> Fax: (248) 699-8069

General Interest and Broad Topics

★ 1 ★

Consumer Spending

Back-to-School Spending

According to the survey, 43% of respondents did their back to school shopping 3 weeks to 1 month before school starting and 78% of respondents did their shopping at discount stores. Figures are in billions of dollars.

Clothing	$ 6.5
Electronics	2.7
Shoes	2.7
School supplies	2.3

Source: *Christian Science Monitor*, August 19, 2003, p. 18, from National Retail Foundation.

★ 2 ★

Countertops

Popular Types of Countertops

Total demand is projected to increase from 420 million square feet to 467 million square feet.

	2002	2007	Share
Laminates	259.1	277.0	59.31%
Solid surface	46.5	52.1	11.16
Natural stone	24.4	33.1	7.09
Engineered stone	15.9	25.0	5.35
Other	74.1	79.8	17.09

Source: *Professional Builder*, December 2003, p. 24, from Freedonia Group.

★ 3 ★

Doors

Entry Door Market, 2002

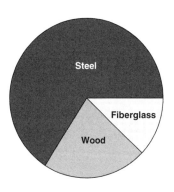

Data are shown based on shipments.

Steel	66.0%
Wood	22.0
Fiberglass	12.0

Source: *Wood & Wood Products*, May 2003, p. 67, from Window & Door Manufacturers Association.

★ 4 ★

Entertainment

Entertainment Spending

Spending is shown in billions of dollars.

DVD sales	$ 12.0
Music	11.9
Video gaming	10.3
Box office	9.3
DVD rentals	4.3

Source: *Investor's Business Daily*, May 19, 2004, p. A4, from Sony.

★ 5 ★

Flooring

Flooring Market in the U.K., 2001

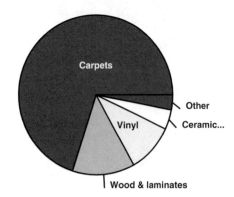

Market shares are shown in percent.

Carpets	70.0%
Wood & laminates	13.0
Vinyl	10.0
Ceramic tiles	4.0
Other	3.0

Source: *Contract Flooring Journal*, September 2002, p. 26, from AMA Research.

★ 6 ★

Gift Cards

Merchant Gift Cards

Visa estimates merchant gift cards to be a $300 billion market. About 18% of large merchants ($500 million or more in annual sales) have merchant loyalty and reward cards for their consumers, although the same percentage of firms are planning to launch them in the next year.

	($ bil.)	Share
Consumer gift cards	$ 174	58.39%
Other cards with commercial applications	124	41.61

Source: *Bank Technology News*, October 3, 2003, p. 1.

★ 7 ★

Homefurnishings

Houseware Sales

Department store sales are shown in millions of dollars.

	($ mil.)	Share
Cookware, accessories	$ 6,258	20.76%
Small electrics	5,642	18.71
Jewelry & watches	4,517	14.98
Soaps, cleaners	3,593	11.92
Tabletop	3,486	11.56
Plasticware storage	2,352	7.80
Paper goods	1,866	6.19
Vacuum cleaners, floor care	1,312	4.35
Picture frames, art	711	2.36
Giftware	412	1.37

Source: *Retail Merchandiser*, July 2003, p. 20, from *Retail Merchandiser*.

★ 8 ★

Homefurnishings

Kichenware Sales in Supermarkets and Drug Stores

Bradshaw International, through the brand Good Cook is top seller of cookware, bakeware, can openers, pizza wheels and similar items in supermarkets and drug stores. Its share is shown below.

Bradshaw International 43.0%
Other 57.0

Source: *Inland Valley Daily Bulletin*, February 18, 2004, p. NA.

★ 9 ★

Licensed Merchandise

College Merchandise Market

The company has agreements with about 200 schools, which gives it about 90% of the market.

Collegiate Licensing Co. 90.0%
Other 10.0

Source: *Town Talk*, November 28, 2003, p. NA.

★ 10 ★

Licensed Merchandise

Licensed Merchandise Sales in North America

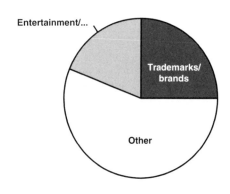

Retail sales in the U.S. and Canada declined slightly to $13.6 billion. The 4% drop has been attributed to a lack of a merchandising blockbuster such as the Spider-Man movie. Figures show share of total North American licensed product retail sales.

Trademarks/brands 25.0%
Entertainment/character 19.0
Other 56.0

Source: *Entertainment Marketing Letter*, January 15, 2004, p. 5, from *Licensing Letter*.

★ 11 ★

Licensed Merchandise

Licensing Revenues, 2003

Makers of licensed goods such as toys and clothing spent $5.8 billion in 2003. The largest increase over 2002 was the collegiate category, with revenues up 11.5%. Fashion was down 4.9% largely because of the weak economy. Analysts are hopeful about the entertainment category with new films starring Shrek, Spider-Man, and Batman.

	($ mil.)	Share
Entertainment characters	$ 2,502	43.10%
Trademarks/brands	1,060	18.26
Fashion	848	14.61
Sports	807	13.90
Collegiate	203	3.50
Art	167	2.88

Continued on next page.

★ 11 ★

[Continued]
Licensed Merchandise

Licensing Revenues, 2003

Makers of licensed goods such as toys and clothing spent $5.8 billion in 2003. The largest increase over 2002 was the collegiate category, with revenues up 11.5%. Fashion was down 4.9% largely because of the weak economy. Analysts are hopeful about the entertainment category with new films starring Shrek, Spider-Man, and Batman.

	($ mil.)	Share
Music	$ 113	1.95%
Publishing	43	0.74
Non-profit	40	0.69
Other	22	0.38

Source: *USA TODAY*, June 8, 2004, p. B1, from Licensing Industry Manufacturers Association.

★ 12 ★

Luxury Industry

Leading Luxury Product Makers in Europe, 2002

Companies are ranked by sales in millions of dollars. Chanel's figure is estimated.

Louis Vuitton	$ 3,260.0
Chanel	2,000.0
Giorgio Armani	1,830.0
Gucci	1,670.0
Prada	1,400.0
Hermes	1,350.0
Max Mara	1,190.0
Burberry	973.5
Escada	840.6
Salvatore Ferragamo	636.2
Dolce & Gabbana	589.0
Christian Dior	534.9

Source: *WWD*, December 8, 2003, p. 45S.

★ 13 ★

Luxury Industry

Luxury Good Sales in Europe

Sales are in billions of euros.

	1999	2001	Share
France	4.78	5.02	22.81%
Germany	3.85	4.05	18.40
U.K.	3.57	3.77	17.13
Italy	2.79	2.96	13.45
Spain	1.14	1.24	5.63
Netherlands	0.58	0.62	2.82
Sweden	0.50	0.53	2.41

Source: *Horizont*, September 12, 2002, p. NA, from Datamonitor.

★ 14 ★

Media

Largest Media Firms in Canada

Firms are ranked by revenues from media holdings as of September 30, 2003.

Bell Globemedia	$ 2,734.0
CanWest Global	1,897.0
Quebecor Media	1,216.5
Torstar	893.7
Rogers	844.6
Corus Entertainment	532.9
CHUM Limited	528.8
Transcontinental	504.2
Astral Media	475.7
Standard Radio	241.0

Source: *Strategy*, November 17, 2003, p. 4.

★ 15 ★
Media
Largest Media Groups

Companies are ranked by revenues in billions of dollars.

AOL Time Warner . . . . $ 41.0
Walt Disney 25.3
Viacom 24.6
Comcast 21.1
Sony 20.0
Vivendi Universal 19.7
News Corp. 15.2
Cox Enterprises 9.9
Hughes Electronics 8.9
Clear Channel 8.4

Source: *Broadcasting & Cable*, May 12, 2003, p. 12.

★ 16 ★
Nanotechnology
Global Nanoparticle Market, 2005

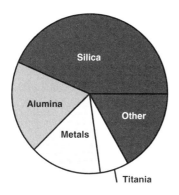

Nanotechnology refers to miniature structures measuring between .000000001 and .0000001, or 1 to 100 nanometers. Nanotechnology includes high-tech equipment, antimicrobial agents, MRI contrast media, sunscreens and orthopedic materials. The total market was worth $492.5 million in 2000 and is projected to hit $900.1 million in 2005.

Silica 43.9%
Alumina 18.5
Metals 14.9
Titania 6.2
Other 16.6

Source: *American Ceramic Society Bulletin*, March 2002, p. 36, from Business Communications Co.

★ 17 ★
Nanotechnology
Nanotechnology Demand, 2007

Nanotechnology refers to miniature structures measuring between .000000001 and .0000001, or 1 to 100 nanometers. Total demand is expected to reach $1.1 billion.

Minerals 61.0%
Polymers and chemicals 14.0
Metals 14.0
New materials 9.0

Source: *Chemical Week*, October 8, 2003, p. 21, from Freedonia Group.

★ 18 ★
Noise Barriers
Outdoor Noise Barrier Market, 2002 and 2007

Total demand for outdoor noise barriers is expected to grow to $116 million in 2007. The transportation sector is the leading segment but the industry will also see sales around industrial equipment (chillers, substations) in highly populated areas. Demand is shown in millions of dollars.

	2002	2007	Share
Highway	$ 84.6	$ 101.5	87.50%
Aviation	7.3	7.9	6.81
Other nonbuilding	3.9	4.8	4.14
Other transportation	1.6	1.8	1.55

Source: *Research Studies - Freedonia Group*, September 23, 2003, p. NA, from Freedonia Group.

★ 19 ★
Packaging
Beverage Container Market, 2007

Total demand is expected to increase from 205 billion units in 1992 to 223.5 billion in 2007. Soft drinks take up the bulk of the metal container segment (66.1 billion out of 102.6 billion). In the glass container field, beer took 21.7 billion out of 28.6 billion units.

	(bil.)	Share
Metal	102.6	45.91%
Plastic	68.5	30.65
Glass	28.7	12.84
Paper	23.7	10.60

Source: *Beverage Industry*, April 2004, p. 36, from Freedonia Group.

★ 20 ★
Packaging

Digital Package Printing Market, 2002 and 2007

Sales of digitally printed labels and folding cartons are expected to increase 20% over the next four years. Figures are shown in millions of dollars.

	2002	2007	Share
Digital labels	$ 70	$ 178	78.41%
Carton printing	17	42	18.50
Flexible packaging	4	7	3.08

Source: *Converting*, September 2003, p. 2, from Packaging Strategies.

★ 21 ★
Packaging

European Market for Modified-Atmosphere Packaging, 2001

The 2001 market is shown by country. Modified atmosphere packaging involves the packaging of food for optimum safety and reduced chances of food deterioration.

United Kingdom	35.0%
France	23.0
Germany	15.0
Spain	14.0
Italy	5.0
Other	8.0

Source: *Converting*, August 2002, p. 2, from Pira International, Ltd.

★ 22 ★
Packaging

Flexible Packaging Demand Worldwide, 2000 and 2005

Market data shown as millions of metric tons. The total market size is estimated to reach $53 billion in 2005.

	2000	2005	Share
Asia/Pacific	3.65	5.16	36.06%
North America	3.50	3.95	27.60
Western Europe	2.74	3.10	21.66
Other	1.52	2.10	14.68

Source: *Converting*, March 2002, p. 8, from The Freedonia Group, Inc.

★ 23 ★
Packaging

Flexible Packaging Market, 2003

Polyethylene
Polypropylene
Paper
Aluminum foil
Other

The U.S. market for converted flexible packaging is expected to grow to 6.8 billion pounds of material in 2008.

Polyethylene	47.0%
Polypropylene	20.0
Paper	17.0
Aluminum foil	4.0
Other	11.0

Source: *Packaging Digest*, April 2004, p. 4, from Freedonia Group.

★ 24 ★
Packaging

Flexible Packaging Market Worldwide

North America (mostly U.S.) is the largest market for the industry. The flexible packaging market stood at $20 billion in 2002 and represented the second largest segment of the packaging industry.

North America	29.0%
Western Europe	27.0
Japan	15.0
Asia Pacific	13.0
Rest of world	7.0
Latin America	6.0
Eastern Europe	3.0

Source: *Flexible Packaging*, June 2003, p. 14, from *World Packaging Companies 2002* and C.S. First Boston.

★ 25 ★
Packaging

Flexible Packaging Market Worldwide, 2001

Market shares are shown in percent. The entire market was estimated to total $30 billion in 2001.

North America	36.0%
Western Europe	23.0
Southeast Asia	13.0
Japan	10.0
Other	18.0

Source: *Plastic News*, December 2, 2002, p. 3, from PCI Films Consulting Ltd.

★ 26 ★
Packaging

Food Packaging Market, 2007

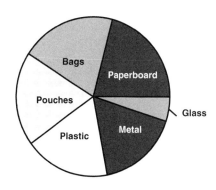

Demand in the United States is forecasted to reach $18.7 billion in 2007.

Paperboard	21.0%
Bags	20.0
Pouches	19.0
Plastic	18.0
Metal	17.0
Glass	5.0

Source: *Converting*, April 2004, p. 2, from Freedonia Group.

★ 27 ★
Packaging

Lawn & Garden Packaging

The popularity of gardening has translated into a growing market for lawn & garden packaging. Demand is expected to grow 2.8% annually through 2006 to reach sales of $545 million. Demand is shown in millions of dollars.

	2001	2006
Bags & sacks	$ 475	$ 545
Plastic bottles	155	185
Bulk packaging	130	160
Pouches	35	80
Other	90	95

Source: *Canadian Packaging*, May 2003, p. 6, from Freedonia Group.

★ 28 ★
Packaging

Personal Care Packaging Demand, 2007

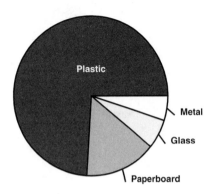

Figures are for cosmetics and toiletries. In 2007, the market is forecasted to be 23.1 billion pounds.

Plastic	74.0%
Paperboard	15.0
Glass	6.0
Metal	5.0

Source: *Plastics News*, December 15, 2003, p. 3, from Freedonia Group.

★ 29 ★
Packaging

Storage Drum Market in North America

Data show share of production.

Wood fiber	50.0%
Steel	40.0
Plastic	10.0

Source: *Plastics News*, August 25, 2003, p. 1, from Plastics Custom Research Services.

★ 30 ★
Packaging

Top Packaging Firms in Australia

The value of the packaging industry (excluding machinery) is about $4.7 billion. Paperboard packaging has about 36% of the market, plastic 30% and metal 20%.

Amcor	27.3%
Visy Industries	23.2
ACI Packaging	13.0
Other	36.5

Source: "Packaging." [online] from http://www.usatrade.gov [accessed January 5, 2004], from U.S. Commercial Service, Research Analyst, and BIS Shrapnel Lty. Ltd.

★ 31 ★
Pets

Pet Population, 2003

The category "fish" includes 185 million freshwater fish and 7 million saltwater fish, according to the report. Americans spent $31 billion on the care and feeding of pets.

Fish	192
Cats	78
Dogs	65
Birds	17
Small mammals	17
Reptiles	9

Source: *National Geographic Explorer*, November-December 2003, p. 3, from American Pet Product Manufacturers Association National Pet Owners Survey.

★ 32 ★
Roofing

Residential Roofing Market

The market was placed at 129.4 million squares in 1997 and 148 million squares in 2002.

	1997	2002	Share
Asphalt shingles	112.7	128.0	84.77%
Roofing tile	6.2	7.6	5.03
Wood shingles and shakes . .	3.3	3.5	2.32
Built-up roofing	1.6	1.5	0.99
Elastomeric roofing	1.4	1.9	1.26
Modified bitumen roofing . .	1.2	1.5	0.99
Metal roofing	1.0	1.7	1.13

Source: *Research Alert*, March 21, 2003, p. 3, from Freedonia Group.

★ 33 ★
Siding

Residential Siding Market

The market was placed at 74.4 million squares in 1997 and 81.5 million squares in 2002. 56% of the industry was devoted to new construction with the balance held by repairs and improvement.

	1997	2002	Share
Vinyl	35.0	36.2	44.47%
Wood	20.2	15.2	18.67
Brick	8.2	8.9	10.93
Stucco and related	7.4	10.0	12.29
Fiber cement	1.8	9.4	11.55
Other	1.8	1.7	2.09

Source: *Research Alert*, March 21, 2003, p. 3, from Freedonia Group.

★ 34 ★
Weight Loss Industry

Weight Loss Market

According to the report, weight loss products saw roughly 4% annual growth in household penetration in the last four years. In 2002, nearly one-third of the population purchased a weight control product. In the nearly $50 billion market anti-obesity drugs saw 40% growth between 2002 and 2003. Figures are in billions of dollars.

	2002	2003	Share
Diet soft drinks	$ 14.86	$ 16.76	33.65%
Health clubs	13.52	17.85	35.84

	2002	2003	Share
Meal replacements & appetite suppress . . .	.$ 2.38	$ 3.52	7.07%
Medical supervision diet programs	2.12	2.44	4.90
Low calorie/diet entrees . .	2.07	2.66	5.34
Artificial sweeteners	1.79	2.05	4.12
Commercial weight loss centers	1.44	1.83	3.67
Diet books, tapes, videos . .	1.38	1.76	3.53
Anti-obesity drugs	0.75	0.93	1.87

Source: *Nutraceuticals World*, October 2003, p. 32, from *2003 Health & Wellness Trends Report*.

★ 35 ★
Windows and Doors

New Window Market in Spain, 2003

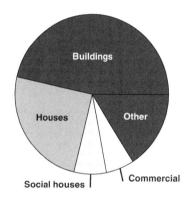

New construction has 79% of the window market (renovation has about 19% and ampliation the rest). New construction will lose share until about 2005, however, while renovation will increase to 20%. 51.5% of windows were PVC, 22.1% were wood, 20.6% metal and 5.8% wood aluminum combinations.

Buildings	.46.7%
Houses	.24.8
Social houses	.6.7
Commercial	.6.1
Other	.15.6

Source: *M2 Presswire*, January 19, 2004, p. NA, from *Windows in Spain, 2003*.

★ 36 ★
Windows and Doors
Window and Door Demand

Demand is shown in millions of dollars.

	2002	2007	Share
Wood	$ 10,370	$ 11,900	38.33%
Metal	9,780	12,950	41.71
Plastic	4,350	6,200	19.97

Source: *Wood & Wood Products*, May 2003, p. 68, from Freedonia Group.

★ 37 ★
Windows and Doors
Window Market in Europe

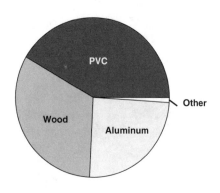

Market shares are shown in percent.

	2002	2003
PVC	42.2%	41.5%
Wood	32.5	32.7
Aluminum	24.3	24.8
Other	1.0	1.0

Source: *Wood & Wood Products*, May 2003, p. 67, from Eurowindow.

★ 38 ★
Windows and Doors
Window Market in France, 2002

Total sales of windows were estimated at $2.2 billion, representing 8 million units. Other market sizes: 24 million units in Germany, 12 million in the U.K. and 10 million in Spain.

Framed PVC	54.0%
Wooden	24.0
Aluminum	20.0
Mixed	2.0

Source: "Building Products." [online] from http://www.usatrade.gov [accessed January 5, 2004], from U.S. Commercial Service.

★ 39 ★
Windows and Doors
Windows Market in Austria

Shares are projected for 2005.

	2002	2005
Plastic	60.4%	61.5%
Wood	24.6	22.3
Wood-aluminum	10.3	11.3

Source: *M2 Presswire*, January 19, 2004, p. NA, from *Windows in Austria, 2003*.

SIC 01 - Agricultural Production - Crops

★ 40 ★
Crops
SIC: 0110; NAICS: 11114, 11115

Leading Bio-Tech Crop Producers Worldwide, 2002

Debate continues over bio-tech crops. The EU had a moratorium on testing new biotech crops for more than four years (although some think this ban may be lifted). Figures are in millions of acres.

U.S.	96.3
Argentina	33.3
Canada	8.6
South Africa	0.7
China	0.2

Source: *Wall Street Journal*, January 31, 2003, p. A8, from International Service for the Acquisition of Agri-Biotech Applications.

★ 41 ★
Seeds
SIC: 0111; NAICS: 11114

Seed Demand

Figures are in millions of dollars. Data for 2007 are projected.

	2002	2007	Share
Field crops	$ 5,020	$ 5,940	67.89%
Grass & forage	825	1,045	11.94
Vegetables	750	860	9.83
Flowers	640	800	9.14
Fruit, trees & novelties	85	105	1.20

Source: *Landscape Managment*, November 2003, p. 21, from Freedonia Group.

★ 42 ★
Wheat
SIC: 0111; NAICS: 11114

Wheat Plantings in the United Kingdom

Shares are shown based on acreage for quality wheats. Tanekr and Napier lead the feed wheat category with 4% shares each. In the category of second wheats (white wheats) Consort controls 31% of sowings.

Malacca	13.0%
Hereward	8.0
Option	7.0
Other	72.0

Source: *Arable Farming*, December 17, 2002, p. 3, from Kynetec.

★ 43 ★
Wheat
SIC: 0111; NAICS: 11114

Wheat Production by State, 2003

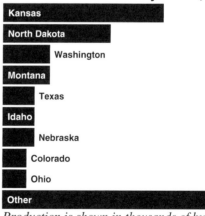

Production is shown in thousands of bushels.

	(000)	Share
Kansas	480,000	20.54%
North Dakota	317,090	13.57

Continued on next page.

★ 43 ★

[Continued]
Wheat
SIC: 0111; NAICS: 11114

Wheat Production by State, 2003

Production is shown in thousands of bushels.

	(000)	Share
Washington	139,345	5.96%
Montana	137,530	5.89
Texas	96,600	4.13
Idaho	87,300	3.74
Nebraska	83,720	3.58
Colorado	78,160	3.35
Ohio	68,000	2.91
Other	848,781	36.33

Source: *Crop Production*, January 2004, p. 11, from National Agricultural Statistics Services, U.S. Department of Agriculture.

★ 44 ★

Rice
SIC: 0112; NAICS: 11116

Rice Production by State, 2003

Production is shown in thousands of acres.

	(000)	Share
Arizona	1,455	48.55%
California	507	16.92
Louisiana	450	15.02
Mississippi	234	7.81
Texas	180	6.01
Missouri	171	5.71

Source: *Crop Production*, January 2004, p. 11, from National Agricultural Statistics Services, U.S. Department of Agriculture.

★ 45 ★

Corn
SIC: 0115; NAICS: 11115

Corn Production by State, 2003

Production of corn grain is shown in thousand of bushels.

	(000)	Share
Iowa	1,884.00	18.63%
Illinois	1,812.20	17.92
Nebraska	1,124.20	11.12
Minnesota	970.90	9.60
Indiana	786.90	7.78
Ohio	478.90	4.74
South Dakota	427.30	4.22
Wisconsin	367.50	3.63
Missouri	302.40	2.99
Kansas	300.00	2.97
Other	1,659.58	16.41

Source: *Crop Production*, January 2004, p. 5, from National Agricultural Statistics Services, U.S. Department of Agriculture.

★ 46 ★

Corn
SIC: 0115; NAICS: 11115

Leading Corn Producing Nations, 2001-2002

Data are in millions of bushels.

	(mil.)	Share
United States	9,507	40.43%
China	4,492	19.11
European Union	1,528	6.50
Brazil	1,398	5.95
Mexico	803	3.42
Argentina	567	2.41
India	532	2.26
South Africa	358	1.52
Canada	323	1.37
Hungary	299	1.27
Romania	276	1.17
Other	3,429	14.58

Source: *Corn and Soybean Digest*, April 2003, p. 1, from U.S. Department of Agriculture.

★ 47 ★

Soybeans
SIC: 0116; NAICS: 11111

Largest Soybean Exporters Worldwide, 1999-2001

Market shares are shown in percent.

United States	34.0%
Brazil	27.0
Argentina	23.0
Other	16.0

Source: *Chicago Tribune*, June 13, 2004, p. 1, from United States of Department of Agriculture, Food and Agricultural Policy Research Institute, ESRI, and GlobeExplorer.

★ 48 ★

Soybeans
SIC: 0116; NAICS: 11111

Soybean Production by State, 2003

Illinois
Iowa
Minnesota
Indiana
Nebraska
Ohio
Missouri
South Dakota
Other

Production is shown in thousands of bushels.

	(000)	Share
Illinois	374,125	15.48%
Iowa	337,600	13.96
Minnesota	229,400	9.49
Indiana	203,300	8.41
Nebraska	179,600	7.43
Ohio	162,640	6.73
Missouri	143,260	5.93
South Dakota	113,130	4.68
Other	674,510	27.90

Source: *Crop Production*, January 2004, p. 11, from National Agricultural Statistics Services, U.S. Department of Agriculture.

★ 49 ★

Barley
SIC: 0119; NAICS: 111199

Barley Production by State, 2003

Production is shown in thousand of bushels.

	(000)	Share
North Dakota	118,800	43.03%
Idaho	47,520	17.21
Montana	31,590	11.44
Washington	14,570	5.28
Michigan	12,750	4.62
Colorado	8,938	3.24
Wyoming	7,125	2.58
Pennsylvania	3,965	1.44

Continued on next page.

★ 49 ★
[Continued]
Barley
SIC: 0119; NAICS: 111199

Barley Production by State, 2003

Production is shown in thousand of bushels.

	(000)	Share
Oregon	3,840	1.39%
Other	26,989	9.78

Source: *Crop Production*, January 2004, p. 11, from National Agricultural Statistics Services, U.S. Department of Agriculture.

★ 50 ★
Hay
SIC: 0119; NAICS: 111199

Hay Production by State, 2003

Production is shown in thousands of tons.

	(000)	Share
Texas	12,388	7.55%
California	9,310	5.67
Missouri	8,168	4.98
Nebraska	7,600	4.63
South Dakota	7,210	4.39
Kansas	7,000	4.27
Kentucky	6,375	3.88
Iowa	5,515	3.36
Tennessee	4,726	2.88
Other	95,831	58.39

Source: *Crop Production*, January 2004, p. 11, from National Agricultural Statistics Services, U.S. Department of Agriculture.

★ 51 ★
Sorghum
SIC: 0119; NAICS: 111199

Sorghum Production by State, 2003

Production is shown in thousand of bushels.

	(000)	Share
Texas	153,900	37.42%
Kansas	130,500	31.73
Nebraska	31,000	7.54

	(000)	Share
Arizona	17,220	4.19%
Missouri	16,170	3.93
Louisiana	14,025	3.41
Oklahoma	9,250	2.25
South Dakota	6,750	1.64
Colorado	4,320	1.05
Other	28,102	6.83

Source: *Crop Production*, January 2004, p. 5, from National Agricultural Statistics Services, U.S. Department of Agriculture.

★ 52 ★
Cotton
SIC: 0131; NAICS: 11192

Cotton Production by State, 2003

Production is shown in thousands of bales.

	(000)	Share
Texas	4,292	23.55%
Georgia	2,100	11.52
Mississippi	2,100	11.52
California	1,870	10.26
Arizona	1,800	9.88
North Carolina	1,100	6.04
Tennessee	875	4.80
Alabama	820	4.50
Missouri	710	3.90
Other	2,557	14.03

Source: *Crop Production*, January 2004, p. 39, from National Agricultural Statistics Services, U.S. Department of Agriculture.

★ 53 ★
Cotton
SIC: 0131; NAICS: 11192

Leading Cotton Exporters Worldwide, 2003-2004

United States
Uzbekistan
Australia
Brazil
Mali
Greece
Burkina
Others

A total of 33.34 million 480-pound bales were exported from 2003-2004. Compared to 2002-2003 figures, Brazil's shipments increased 186.3%, the United States increased 16% and Australia fell 27.5%.

	Bales	Share
United States	13,800,000	41.4%
Uzbekistan	3,075,000	9.3
Australia	1,925,000	5.8
Brazil	1,400,000	4.2
Mali	1,125,000	3.4
Greece	1,100,000	3.3
Burkina	950,000	2.9
Others	9,969,000	29.9

Source: *USATODAY*, April 28, 2004, p. 3B, from U.S. Department of Agriculture, Foreign Agricultural Service.

★ 54 ★
Tobacco
SIC: 0132; NAICS: 11191

Largest Tobacco Producing Nations, 2003

Data are in metric tons dry weight for the calendar year.

	Tons	Share
China	2,224,481	38.45%
India	595,000	10.29
Brazil	515,720	8.91
United States	363,168	6.28
Indonesia	144,700	2.50
Turkey	142,190	2.46
Other	1,799,741	31.11

Source: "World's Leading Unmanufactured Tobacco Producing, Trading and Consuming Countries." [online] from http://www.fas.usda.gov, from Foreign Agricultural Service, U.S. Department of Agriculture.

★ 55 ★
Tobacco
SIC: 0132; NAICS: 11191

Tobacco Production by State, 2003

Production is shown in thousands of pounds.

	(000)	Share
North Carolina	310,695	37.38%
Kentucky	229,840	27.65
Tennessee	72,870	8.77
South Carolina	63,000	7.58
Georgia	60,480	7.28
Virginia	42,679	5.13
Florida	11,000	1.32
Ohio	9,010	1.08
Indiana	8,400	1.01
Other	23,230	2.79

Source: *Crop Production*, January 2004, p. 41, from National Agricultural Statistics Services, U.S. Department of Agriculture.

★ 56 ★
Sugarbeets
SIC: 0133; NAICS: 111991

Sugarbeet Production by State, 2003

Production is shown in thousands of tons.

	(000)	Share
Minnesota	10,032	32.78%
Idaho	6,065	19.82
North Dakota	5,202	17.00
Michigan	3,400	11.11
California	1,832	5.99
Montana	1,308	4.27
Other	2,766	9.04

Source: *Crop Production*, January 2004, p. 41, from National Agricultural Statistics Services, U.S. Department of Agriculture.

★ 57 ★
Vegetables
SIC: 0161; NAICS: 111219

Global Asparagus Market

Data are in thousands of hectares for selected countries. Asparagus production has risen noticeably in recent years to about one million tons. Much of the rise comes from expansion in China. Production in the United States has fallen by about a third during the last six years.

China	75.00
United States	21.90
Germany	18.22
Peru	18.00
Spain	13.80
Mexico	10.60
France	7.40
Italy	6.60
Japan	6.50
Greece	4.50

Source: *Agra Europe*, April 6, 2004, p. M6, from B.L. Benson, ZMP, and national statistics.

★ 58 ★
Vegetables
SIC: 0161; NAICS: 111219

Largest Vegetable Growers in the North

Companies are ranked by acreage devoted to vegetable operations.

R.D. Offutt Co.	65,000
Hartung Brothers Inc.	23,956
Bird's Eye Foods	18,900
Heartland Farms Inc.	11,066
Black Gold Farms	10,850
Wysocki Produce Farm Inc.	10,039
Paramount Farms Inc.	9,500
Walther Farms	8,222
Torrey Farms Inc.	7,486
Charles H. West Farms Inc.	7,307

Source: *AVG*, October 2003, p. 12.

★ 59 ★
Vegetables
SIC: 0161; NAICS: 111219

Largest Vegetable Growers in the Southeast

Companies are ranked by acreage devoted to vegetable operations.

A. Duda & Sons Inc.	20,000
Pacific Tomato Growers/Triple E Produce Corp.	16,098
Thomas Produce Co.	14,930
Hundley Farms Inc.	14,732
Six L's Packing Co.	12,500
Gargiulo Inc.	9,500
Suwannee Farms/Eagle Island Farms . . .	7,589
Pero Family Farms Inc.	7,428
Nash Produce Company	5,910
Barnes Farming Corp.	5,550

Source: *AVG*, October 2003, p. 12.

★ 60 ★
Vegetables
SIC: 0161; NAICS: 111219
Largest Vegetable Growers in the Southwest

Companies are ranked by acreage devoted to vegetable operations.

Martori Farms	10,850
Navajo Agricultural Products Industry	7,585
Amigo Farms Inc.	7,398
Pasquinelli Produce Co.	6,748
Greer Farms	5,800
Wyatt Hidalgo Farms	5,426
Del Monte Fresh Produce	4,834
Nakasawa Farms	4,541
Barkley Co.	4,500
Rousseau Farming Co.	4,309

Source: *AVG*, October 2003, p. 12.

★ 61 ★
Vegetables
SIC: 0161; NAICS: 111219
Largest Vegetable Growers in the West

Companies are ranked by acreage devoted to vegetable operations.

Grimmway Farms	47,500
Tanimura & Antle	47,398
D'Arrigo Bros. Co. of California Inc.	27,469
J.G. Boswell Co.	22,832
Mission Ranches	22,266
Larsen Farms	21,743
Ocean Mist Farms/Boutonnet Farms	19,753
Nunes Vegetables Inc.	15,379
Rio Farms	14,910
Betteravia Farms	13,758

Source: *AVG*, October 2003, p. 12.

★ 62 ★
Fruit
SIC: 0171; NAICS: 111339
Cranberry Market Worldwide

The company is the largest producer of cranberry products in the world.

Ocean Spray	70.0%
Other	30.0

Source: *Australasian Business Intelligence*, May 3, 2004, p. NA.

★ 63 ★
Fruit
SIC: 0171; NAICS: 111334
Leading Cranberry Producers, 2002

Production is shown in millions of pounds.

Wisconsin	321.0
Massachusetts	145.0
Oregon	43.2
New Jersey	42.7
Washington	16.0

Source: *USA TODAY*, November 28, 2003, p. 1, from Cranberry Marketing Committee.

★ 64 ★
Fruit
SIC: 0172; NAICS: 111332
Largest Grape Growers

Companies are ranked by total acreage.

E&J Gallo Winery	12,851
Beringer Wine Estates	10,400
Giumarra Vineyards Corp.	10,210
Michael Hat Faming	10,000
Vino Farms	7,353

Continued on next page.

17

★ 64 ★

[Continued]
Fruit
SIC: 0172; NAICS: 111332

Largest Grape Growers

Companies are ranked by total acreage.

Monterey Pacific	6,974
Godlen State Vintners	6,830
Delicato Vineyards	6,700
Gerawan Farming	6,227
Trinchero Family Estates	5,454

Source: *American Fruit Grower*, June 2003, p. 18.

★ 65 ★

Nuts
SIC: 0173; NAICS: 111335

Global Almond Production, 2002

Figures are for fiscal years and based on thousand metric tons.

United States	45.0%
Spain	12.0
Syria	8.0
Iran	6.0
Italy	5.0
Other	24.0

Source: "World Almond Situation & Outlook." [online] from http://www.fas.usda.gov [accessed June 10, 2004], from National Agriculture Statistics Services, U.S. Department of Agriculture.

★ 66 ★

Nuts
SIC: 0173; NAICS: 111335

Peanut Production by State, 2003

Production is shown in thousands of pounds.

	(000)	Share
Georgia	1,863,000	44.95%
Texas	810,000	19.55
Alabama	508,750	12.28
Florida	345,000	8.32
North Carolina	320,000	7.72
Oklahoma	98,000	2.36
Virginia	95,700	2.31
New Mexico	45,900	1.11
Other	57,800	1.39

Source: *Crop Production*, January 2004, p. 11, from National Agricultural Statistics Services, U.S. Department of Agriculture.

★ 67 ★

Fruit
SIC: 0175; NAICS: 111331

Apple Production by State, 2003

Red delicious has about 41% of the entire crop, down from 56% in 2000. Figures are in thousands of 42 pound units.

	(000)	Share
Washington	116,667	52.88%
New York	24,286	11.01
Michigan	23,095	10.47
California	12,143	5.50
Pennsylvania	10,476	4.75
Virginia	7,143	3.24
North Carolina	3,333	1.51
Oregon	2,857	1.29
Other	20,633	9.35

Source: *American/Western Fruit Grower*, September/October 2003, p. 16, from U.S. Department of Agriculture.

★ 68 ★
Fruit
SIC: 0175; NAICS: 111339
Cherry Production by State, 2003

Production is shown in million of pounds.

	(mil.)	Share
Michigan	150.0	68.81%
Utah	24.0	11.01
Washington	20.0	9.17
Wisconsin	11.0	5.05
New York	7.0	3.21
Oregon	3.6	1.65
New York	1.9	0.87
Colorado	0.5	0.23

Source: *Crop Production*, April 2004, p. 41, from National Agricultural Statistics Services, U.S. Department of Agriculture.

★ 69 ★
Fruit
SIC: 0175; NAICS: 111339
Fresh Pineapple Market

Market shares are shown in percent.

Fresh Del Monte	70.0%
Other	30.0

Source: *Wall Street Journal*, October 7, 2003, p. 1.

★ 70 ★
Fruit
SIC: 0175; NAICS: 111339
Popular Apricot Varieties

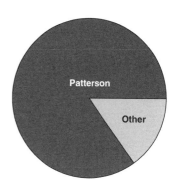

Sales are shown by variety.

Patterson	85.0%
Other	15.0

Source: *Knight Ridder/Tribune News Service*, August 11, 2003, p. NA.

★ 71 ★
Fruit
SIC: 0179; NAICS: 111336, 111339
Leading Stone Fruit Producers

Companies are ranked by total acreage devoted to stone fruit production.

Gerawan Farming	5,858
Fowler Packing	4,095
Ito Packing	3,586
Taylor Orchards	3,500
Southern Orchard/Lane Packaging	3,100
California Prune Packing	3,097
Thiara Brothers Orchards	2,650
Wilbur Ranch	2,645
Titan Peach Farms	2,400
Sun Valley Packing	2,185

Source: *American/Western Fruit Grower*, September/October 2003, p. 12.

★ 72 ★
Fruit
SIC: 0179; NAICS: 111339

Pomegranate Industry

The pomegranate season runs from October through December. A total of 1.3 (28 pound) million boxes were shipped in 2003, up significantly from 950,000 boxes in 2002 and 660,000 boxes in 2000. The pomegranate received attention largely because of its antioxidant properties.

Wonderful 80.0%
Other 20.0

Source: *Rocky Mountain News*, October 29, 2003, p. 3D.

★ 73 ★
Fruit
SIC: 0179; NAICS: 111339

Pomegranate Market, 2003

Paramount Farms sold $20 million in cartons of pomegranates in 2003, four times what it sold in 2001.

Paramount Farms 60.0%
Other 40.0

Source: *Forbes*, February 2, 2004, p. 50.

★ 74 ★
Green Goods
SIC: 0181; NAICS: 111421, 111422

Green Goods Sales, 2003

Total sales were $14.5 billion.

Evergreens 35.9%
Bedding plants 19.0
Flowering plants 11.5
Shrubs 11.0
Foliage 10.2
Decidous trees 4.3
Flowering trees 3.0
Fruit & nut plants 2.2
Blubs 1.5
Roses 1.4

Source: *Nursery Retailer*, January/February 2004, p. 83.

★ 75 ★
Mushrooms
SIC: 0182; NAICS: 111411

Specialty Mushroom Sales, 2002-2003 Season

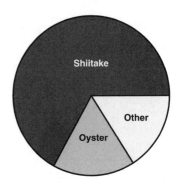

Mushroom sales for the 2002-2003 season (July 1, 2002 through June 30, 2003) were 844 million pounds, essentially unchanged from 2001-2002.

	($ mil.)	Share
Shiitake	25,249	67.02%
Oyster	6,353	16.86
Other	6,074	16.12

Source: "Mushrooms." [online] from http://ffas.usda.gov [accessed June 10, 2004], from National Agricultural Service, U.S. Department of Agriculture.

SIC 02 - Agricultural Production - Livestock

★ 76 ★
Sheep and Goats
SIC: 0214; NAICS: 11241

Sheep and Goats by State, 2004

There were 6.09 million heads as of January 1, 2004. Figures are in thousand head of sheep and goats.

	(000)	Share
California	680	11.17%
Wyoming	430	7.06
South Dakota	370	6.08
Colorado	360	5.91
Montana	300	4.93
Utah	265	4.35
Idaho	260	4.27
Iowa	250	4.11
Oregon	215	3.53
Texas	100	1.64
Other	2,860	46.96

Source: "Sheep and Goats." [online] from http://usda.manlibb.cornell.edu/reports/nass/livetock/pgs [accessed June 10, 2004], from National Agricultural Statistics Service, U.S. Department of Agriculture.

★ 77 ★
Wool
SIC: 0214; NAICS: 11241

Wool Production by State, 2003

Total production of wool was 38.11 million pounds in 2003.

	(000)	Share
Texas	5,600	14.69%
Wyoming	3,650	9.58
California	3,500	9.18
Montana	2,597	6.81
Colorado	2,580	6.77

	(000)	Share
Utah	2,230	5.85%
Iowa	1,360	3.57
New Mexico	1,240	3.25
Other	15,357	40.29

Source: "Sheep and Goats." [online] from http://usda.manlibb.cornell.edu/reports/nass/livetock/pgs [accessed June 10, 2004], from National Agricultural Statistics Service, U.S. Department of Agriculture.

★ 78 ★
Poultry
SIC: 0250; NAICS: 11231, 11232

Poultry Production by Segment, 2003

Production is shown in thousands of dollars.

	2001	2002	2003
Broilers	$ 16,696	$ 13,437	$ 15,214
Eggs	4,446	4,281	5,315
Turkeys	2,796	2,732	2,720
Chickens	47	49	47

Source: *Poultry - Production and Value*, April 2004, p. 41, from National Agricultural Statistics Services, U.S. Department of Agriculture.

★ 79 ★

Broilers

SIC: 0251; NAICS: 11232

Broiler Production by State, 2003

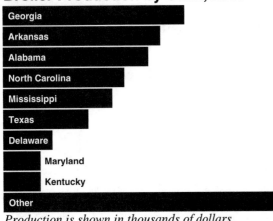

Production is shown in thousands of dollars.

	($ 000)	Share
Georgia	$ 1,935,750	14.80%
Arkansas	1,743,870	13.33
Alabama	1,608,480	12.29
North Carolina	1,367,472	10.45
Mississippi	1,223,520	9.35
Texas	893,327	6.83
Delaware	494,208	3.78
Maryland	440,512	3.37
Kentucky	421,050	3.22
Other	2,955,623	22.59

Source: *Poultry - Production and Value*, April 2004, p. 41, from National Agricultural Statistics Services, U.S. Department of Agriculture.

★ 80 ★

Broilers

SIC: 0251; NAICS: 11232

Largest Chicken Breeders Worldwide

The top three companies in the industry control 90% of the market. Aviagen is the largest provider of chicken genetics with its Arbor Acres, Ross and Lohmann lines, giving it a 45% share of that market.

Aviagen/Merial/Tyson	90.0%
Other	10.0

Source: *Feedstuffs*, December 1, 2003, p. 9.

★ 81 ★

Broilers

SIC: 0251; NAICS: 11232

Leading Broiler Firms Worldwide

The shares of world production are estimated. Aviagen has 35-45%, Cobb 30-40%, Hubbard 10-20%, Hybro 5-10%.

Aviagen	45.0%
Cobb	40.0
Hubbard	20.0
Hybro	10.0
Other	20.0

Source: *WATTPoultryUSA*, March 2002, p. 12.

★ 82 ★

Broilers

SIC: 0251; NAICS: 11232

Top Broiler Firms

Companies are ranked by ready-to-cook production in millions of pounds. The top 40 companies produced 666.2 million pounds. Pilgrim's Pride recently acquired ConAgra Poultry, the largest poultry industry acquisition in history.

	(mil.)	Share
Tyson Foods	149.20	22.60%
Pilgrim's Pride Corporation	106.19	16.08
Gold Kist Inc.	62.44	9.46
Perdue Farms Inc.	42.83	6.49
Wayne Farms	28.90	4.38
Sanderson Farms Inc.	27.63	4.19
Mountaire Farms Inc.	21.50	3.26
Foster Farms	15.90	2.41
Cagle's Inc.	15.65	2.37
House of Raeford Farms Inc.	15.09	2.29
O.K. Foods Inc.	14.10	2.14
George's Inc.	13.38	2.03
Other	147.39	22.33

Source: *WATTPoultryUSA*, January 2004, p. 18C.

★ 83 ★
Eggs
SIC: 0252; NAICS: 11231

Egg Production by State, 2003

Production is shown in thousands of dollars.

	($ 000)	Share
Iowa	$ 460,495	8.66%
Georgia	395,769	7.45
Ohio	374,458	7.04
Pennsylvania	370,907	6.98
Arkansas	344,040	6.47
Texas	310,007	5.83
Alabama	295,650	5.56
California	282,375	5.31
North Carolina	241,788	4.55
Mississippi	169,228	3.18
Other	2,070,594	38.96

Source: *Poultry - Production and Value*, April 2004, p. 41, from National Agricultural Statistics Services, U.S. Department of Agriculture.

★ 84 ★
Eggs
SIC: 0252; NAICS: 11231

Egg Production Worldwide, 2001

Egg production is measured in million eggs raised in 2001 by country or region.

	(mil.)	Share
China	389,000	48.9%
United States	85,020	10.7
European Union	73,835	9.3
Japan	42,000	5.3
Russian Federation	34,200	4.3
Mexico	33,640	4.3
Brazil	16,435	2.1
Canada	6,400	0.8
Others	115,181	14.5

Source: *World Poultry*, February 2004, p. 19, from U.S. Department of Agriculture and Foreign Agricultural Service.

★ 85 ★
Eggs
SIC: 0252; NAICS: 11231

Top Fresh Egg Brands, 2003

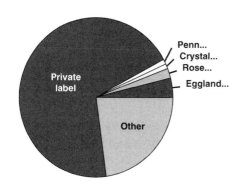

Brands are ranked by sales in millions of dollars for the 12 weeks ended August 10, 2003.

	($ mil.)	Share
Eggland Best	$ 24.01	4.21%
Rose Acre	11.21	1.97
Crystal Farms	6.58	1.15
Penn Dutch Farms	3.68	0.65
Private label	396.21	69.50
Other	128.42	22.53

Source: *Frozen Food Age*, October 2003, p. 44, from Information Resources Inc.

★ 86 ★
Turkeys
SIC: 0253; NAICS: 11233

Largest Turkey Exporters Worldwide, 2003

Exports have been on the decline for the last two years after experiencing strong growth in the 1990s. The poultry export market experienced further setbacks with the avian influenza, which prompted countries to tighten their rules regarding poultry trade. Market shares are shown in percent.

European Union	38.8%
United States	34.6
Brazil	15.9
Hungary	5.4
Canada	2.4
Poland	2.2
Mexico	0.8

Source: *WATT PoultryUSA*, May 2004, p. 23.

★ 87 ★
Turkeys
SIC: 0253; NAICS: 11233
Leading Turkey Processors, 2002

Companies are ranked by millions of live pounds processed.

Jennie-O Turkey Store	1,200.0
Cargill Turkey Products	1,023.0
ConAgra Foods (Butterball)	830.0
Carolina Turkeys	705.0
Pilgrim's Pride	499.0
Bil Mar Foods (Sara Lee)	300.0
Kraft Foods (Louis Rich)	300.0
House of Raeford	245.0
Foster Farms	243.8
Perdue Farms	239.0

Source: *WATT PoultryUSA*, January 2004, p. 60.

★ 88 ★
Turkeys
SIC: 0253; NAICS: 11233
Leading Turkey Producers in Europe, 2000

France's poultry production dipped slightly in 1999 but then rebounded in 2000. Turkey now represents 36% of the weight of poultry slaughtered in France.

France	40.7%
Italy	19.9
Portugal	17.0
Germany	17.0
U.K.	16.6
Netherlands	2.2
Ireland	1.7
Other	2.5

Source: *World Poultry*, No. 2, 2002, p. 27.

★ 89 ★
Turkeys
SIC: 0253; NAICS: 11233
Turkey Production by State, 2003

Production is shown in thousands of dollars.

	($ 000)	Share
North Carolina	$ 429,293	15.71%
Minnesota	413,424	15.13
Missouri	281,826	10.31
Arkansas	198,417	7.26
Virginia	165,020	6.04
California	158,026	5.78
Indiana	145,080	5.31
South Carolina	136,630	5.00
Iowa	94,046	3.44
Other	710,719	26.01

Source: *Poultry - Production and Value*, April 2004, p. 41, from National Agricultural Statistics Services, U.S. Department of Agriculture.

★ 90 ★
Dogs
SIC: 0279; NAICS: 11299
Leading Dog Registrations, 2003

Figures show the top registrations by breed. Some of the breeds with striking growth between 2002 and 2003 are: Havanese (+42%), Brussels griffon (+20%), French bulldog (+20%), and the Cavalier King Charles spaniel (+32%).

Labrador retrievers	144,934
Golden retrievers	52,530
Beagles	45,033
German shepherds	43,950
Dachshunds	39,473
Yorkshire terriers	38,256
Boxers	34,136

Continued on next page.

★ 90 ★

[Continued]
Dogs
SIC: 0279; NAICS: 11299

Leading Dog Registrations, 2003

Figures show the top registrations by breed. Some of the breeds with striking growth between 2002 and 2003 are: Havanese (+42%), Brussels griffon (+20%), French bulldog (+20%), and the Cavalier King Charles spaniel (+32%).

Poodles 32,176
Shih Tzu 26,935

Source: *USA TODAY*, June 9, 2004, p. 8D, from American Kennel Club.

★ 91 ★

Horses
SIC: 0279; NAICS: 11292

Horse Registrations

According to various associations, the number of registrations has been relatively consistent in recent years. Only the Morgan Paint Horse and Standardbred expect registrations to decline. Figures for 2003 are forecasted.

	2001	2003
Quarter horse	150,956	160,000
Paint horse	56,862	55,000
Thoroughbred	31,000	37,000
Tennessee walking horse	14,974	15,500
Standardbred	11,261	11,500
Appaloosa	9,322	9,100
Arabian	9,266	9,400
Morgan Horse	3,475	3,700
Saddlebred	3,055	3,000

Source: *Equus*, November 2003, p. 48.

★ 92 ★

Farms
SIC: 0291; NAICS: 11299

Farm Locations by Region, 2003

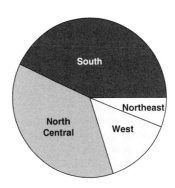

Distribution is shown in percent.

South 43.0%
North Central 37.0
West 14.0
Northeast 6.0

Source: *Poultry - Production and Value*, April 2004, p. 41, from National Agricultural Statistics Services, U.S. Department of Agriculture.

SIC 07 - Agricultural Services

★ 93 ★
Veterinary Services
SIC: 0740; NAICS: 54194
Popular Fields for Vets

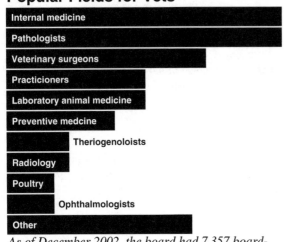

As of December 2002, the board had 7,357 board-certified diplomates. Spending on pet care increased from $11.1 billion in 1996 to $19 billion in 2001. Recent estimates show there were 61.6 million dogs and 68.9 million cats in American households.

	No.	Share
Internal medicine	1,338	18.19%
Pathologists	1,326	18.02
Veterinary surgeons	926	12.59
Practicioners	691	9.39
Laboratory animal medicine	669	9.09
Preventive medcine	491	6.67
Theriogenoloists (reproduction) . . .	293	3.98
Radiology	261	3.55
Poultry	240	3.26
Ophthalmologists	232	3.15
Other	890	12.10

Source: *USA TODAY*, September 22, 2003, p. 6D, from American Veterinary Medical Association.

★ 94 ★
Livestock
SIC: 0751; NAICS: 11521
Livestock Sales in the Northeast

The company controls more than 50% of all livestock sales in the Northeast. It operates nine markets in the region.

Empire Livestock	50.0%
Other	50.0

Source: *Rural Cooperatives*, September - October 2003, p. 14.

★ 95 ★
Landscaping Firms
SIC: 0782; NAICS: 56173
Largest Landscaping Firms

Companies are ranked by revenues in millions of dollars. Weedman's figure is in Canadian dollars.

The TruGreen Cos.	$ 1,500,000.0
ValleyCrest Companies	620.0
The Davey Tree Expert Co.	325.0
The Brickman Group Ltd.	323.0
Scotts Lawn Service	125.0
Weed Man	85.0
Gothic Landscape Inc.	80.0
OneSource Landscape & Golf Svcs. . . .	80.0
Lawn Doctor Inc.	73.0
American Civil Constructors Inc.	57.8

Source: *Landscape Managment*, July 2003, p. 24, from company reports.

★ 96 ★

Christmas Trees

SIC: 0811; NAICS: 111421

Leading Christmas Tree Producers

Oregon	
North Carolina	
Michigan	
Wisconsin	
Washington	

Production is shown in millions of trees. Of trees in the Northwest, 46% go to California and 13% go to the Northwest.

Oregon	8.3
North Carolina	4.5
Michigan	3.5
Wisconsin	3.0
Washington	3.0

Source: *Statesman Journal*, November 26, 2003, p. B8.

SIC 09 - Fishing, Hunting, and Trapping

★ 97 ★

Fishing

SIC: 0910; NAICS: 114111, 114112

Global Aquaculture and Commercial Catches, 2001

Data are in thousands of live weight metric tons.

	Tons	Share
Herrings, sardines, anchovies . .	20,460.64	16.04%
Carps, barbels, cyprinids	16,975.24	13.31
Cods, hakes, haddocks	9,224.57	7.23
Tunas, bonitos, billfishes	5,835.25	4.58
Oysters	4,406.83	3.46
Clams, cockies, arkshells . . .	3,917.96	3.07
Squids, cuttlefishes, octopus . .	3,346.84	2.62
Salmons, trouts, smelts	2,673.04	2.10
Tilapias	2,068.17	1.62
Flatfish	1,068.17	0.84
Other	57,557.64	45.13

Source: ''World Fisheries.'' [online] from http://st.nmfs.gov [accessed June 1, 2004], from National Marine Fisheries Service.

★ 98 ★

Fishing

SIC: 0910; NAICS: 114111, 114112

Largest Fishing Ports, 2002

| Dutch Harbor-Unalaska, AK |
| Empire-Venice, LA |
| Reedville, VA |
| Intracoastal City, LA |
| Cameron, LA |
| Kodiak, AK |
| Pascagoula-Moss Point, MS |
| Los Angeles, CA |
| New Bedford, MA |

Ports are ranked by value of landings in millions of pounds.

Dutch Harbor-Unalaska, AK	908.1
Empire-Venice, LA	398.9
Reedville, VA	367.4
Intracoastal City, LA	358.5
Cameron, LA	349.9
Kodiak, AK	250.4
Pascagoula-Moss Point, MS	198.5
Los Angeles, CA	170.1
New Bedford, MA	108.9

Source: *National Fisherman*, December 2003, p. 13.

★ 99 ★
Fishing
SIC: 0910; NAICS: 114111, 114112

Leading Fishing Nations, 2001

Data are in millions of live weight metric tons.

	Tons	Share
China	42.57	32.70%
Peru	7.99	6.14
India	5.96	4.58
Japan	5.52	4.24
United States	5.40	4.15
Indonesia	5.06	3.89
Chile	4.36	3.35
Russian Federation	3.71	2.85
Thailand	3.60	2.76
Norway	3.19	2.45
Other	42.84	32.90

Source: ''World Fisheries.'' [online] from http://
st.nmfs.gov [accessed June 1, 2004], from National Marine
Fisheries Service.

★ 100 ★
Fishing
SIC: 0910; NAICS: 114111, 114112

Seafood Industry

*The United States primarily raises catfish, trout,
crawfish, salmon, oysters and tilapia. Alaska is the
largest producer and processor of seafood and
aquaculture. Figures are in billions of dollars.*

Processing	$ 8.3
Commercial	3.1
Aquaculture	1.0

Source: *AgExporter*, January 2003, p. NA.

★ 101 ★
Fish Hatcheries
SIC: 0921; NAICS: 112511

Trout Sold by Point of Sale, 2003

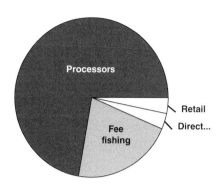

*Figures refer to trout 12 inches or longer. Sales of
such fish totaled 45.9 million fish, down 8% from
2002. For trout 6 -12 inches fee fishing took 54.2%
of point of first sales.*

Processors	68.4%
Fee fishing	19.5
Direct to consumers	3.2
Retail	2.8

Source: ''Trout Production.'' [online] from http://
ffas.usda.gov [accessed June 10, 2004], from National Agricultural Statistics Service, U.S. Department of Agriculture.

SIC 10 - Metal Mining

★ 102 ★

Mining

SIC: 1000; NAICS: 21221, 212234

Worldwide Investments in Mining Projects, 2002

Data are based on 1,350 reported projects world-wide with capital investment totaling $97 billion. Latin America had the largest share (30%) of active mine investment. PGM stands for platinum group metals.

	($ bil.)	Share
Copper	$ 24	31.58%
Gold	16	21.05
Nickel	12	15.79
Magnesium	6	7.89
Lead/Zinc	5	6.58
PGMs	3	3.95
Iron Ore	3	3.95
Other	7	9.21

Source: *E&MJ*, January 2003, p. 28, from Raw Materials Data.

★ 103 ★

Iron Ore

SIC: 1011; NAICS: 21221

World Iron Ore Production, 2003

China has become the major source of growth in iron ore demand. Production is in million metric tons of useable ore.

	(mil.)	Share
China	240	21.5%
Brazil	215	19.2
Australia	190	17.0
Russia	92	8.3
India	80	7.2
Ukraine	63	5.7
United States	50	4.5
South Africa	38	3.4
Canada	32	2.9
Sweden	21	1.9

	(mil.)	Share
Kazakhstan	18	1.6%
Venezuela	17	1.6
Iran	11	1.0
Mauritania	10	0.9
Other countries	40	3.6

Source: *Mineral Commodity Summaries — Iron Ore*, January 2004, p. 85, from U.S. Geological Survey.

★ 104 ★

Copper

SIC: 1021; NAICS: 212234

Global Copper Production, 2002

Shares are by country and based on copper production for the year 2002, measured in thousand metric tons.

	(000)	Share
Chile	4,450	33.2%
United States	1,130	8.7
Indonesia	1,100	8.2
Peru	850	6.4
Australia	850	6.4
Russia	680	5.1
Canada	625	4.7
China	580	4.4
Poland	500	3.8
Kazakhstan	450	3.5
Mexico	330	2.5
Zambia	320	2.4
Other countries	1,500	11.2

Source: *Mineral Commodity Summaries — Copper*, January 2003, p. 57, from U.S. Geological Survey.

★ 105 ★

Copper

SIC: 1021; NAICS: 212234

Leading Copper Producers in Arizona, 2002

Production is shown in millions of pounds. Companies are shown in parentheses.

Morenci (Phelps Doge and Sumitomo)	825.4
Ray (Asarco)	382.1
Bagdad (Phelps Dodge)	168.0
Sierrita (Phelps Dodge)	152.4
Mission (Asarco)	80.7
Silver Bell (Asarco and Mitsui)	45.0
Pinto Valley (BHP)	25.1
Miami (Cyprus)	21.0
San Manuel (BHP)	4.0
Mineral Park (Equitorial Mining)	3.1

Source: *Mining Engineering*, May 2003, p. 21.

★ 106 ★

Lead

SIC: 1031; NAICS: 212231

Lead Production Worldwide, 2002-2003

Figures are in thousands of tons of lead content.

	2002	2003	Share
America	1,022	1,030	33.02%
Asia	772	1,096	35.14
Oceania	714	658	21.10
Europe	247	217	6.96
Africa	130	118	3.78

Source: "Lead Statistics." [online] from http://www.ilzsg.org/statistics.asp?pglead [accessed June 10, 2004], from International Lead and Zinc Study Group.

★ 107 ★

Gold

SIC: 1041; NAICS: 212221

Gold Production by State, 2002

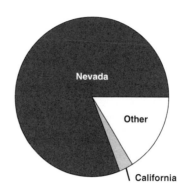

Companies are ranked by production in thousands of kilograms.

	Kilograms	Share
Nevada	240,000	80.62%
California	9,180	3.08
Other	48,500	16.29

Source: "Gold Statistics." [online] available from http://www.nma.org [accessed March 1, 2004], from National Mining Association.

★ 108 ★

Gold

SIC: 1041; NAICS: 212221

Top Gold Producers, 2002

Companies are ranked by production in thousands of ounces.

	(000)	Share
Barrick Gold	6,082	54.87%
Newmont Mining	2,775	25.03
Placer Dome Inc.	988	8.91
Anglo Gold	461	4.16
Echo Bay Mines	441	3.98
Glamis Gold Inc.	122	1.10
Couer d'Alene Mines	72	0.65
Canyon Resources	57	0.51
Kinross Gold Corporation	41	0.37
Hecla Mining	31	0.28
Meridian Gold	9	0.08

Continued on next page.

★ 108 ★

[Continued]
Gold

SIC: 1041; NAICS: 212221

Top Gold Producers, 2002

Companies are ranked by production in thousands of ounces.

	(000)	Share
Vista Gold	3	0.03%
MK Gold	3	0.03

Source: "Gold Statistics." [online] available from http://www.nma.org [accessed March 1, 2004], from National Mining Association.

★ 109 ★

Gold

SIC: 1041; NAICS: 212221

Top Gold Producing Nations, 2002

A total of 2,590 metric tons of gold were produced from above ground stocks in 2002.

South Africa	15.0%
United States	12.0
Australia	10.0
China	8.0
Russia	7.0
Canada	6.0
Indonesia	6.0
Peru	6.0
Other	30.0

Source: "Mine Production" [online] http://www.gold.org/value/market/supply-demand/mine_production.html [accessed March 16, 2004], p. NA, from World Gold Council.

★ 110 ★

Silver

SIC: 1044; NAICS: 212222

Largest Silver Mines in Nevada

Nevada is the top gold and silver producing state. Its silver production for the year was 13.5 million ounces. Figures are shown in millions of ounces.

	mil.	Share
Rochester Mines (Coeur d'Alene Mines)	6.42	51.36%
Midas Mine (Newmont)	2.87	22.96
McCoy/Cove Mine (Echo Bay)	1.90	15.20
Other	1.31	10.48

Source: *Mining Engineering*, May 2003, p. 21.

★ 111 ★

Silver

SIC: 1044; NAICS: 212222

Top Silver Producers Worldwide, 2002

Shares are shown based on millions of ounces of silver produced during 2002.

	(mil.)	Share
Industries Penoles	52.7	8.99%
BHP Minerals	44.5	7.60
KGHM Polska Miedz	38.3	6.54
Grupo Mexico	19.6	3.35
Barrick Gold	17.8	3.04
Rio Tinto plc	17.2	2.94
Coeur d'Alene Mines Corp.	14.8	2.53
MIM Holdings Ltd.	13.2	2.25
Cia. De Minas Buenaventura	11.7	2.00
Noranda Inc.	11.3	1.93
Volcan Cia. Minera SA	10.9	1.86
Pasminco Ltd.	9.5	1.62
Hecla Mining Company	8.7	1.48
Boliden AB	8.5	1.45
Codelco	8.2	1.40
Pan American Silver	7.8	1.33
Comsur	7.6	1.30
Societe Metallurgique d'lmiter	7.1	1.21
Luismin SA de CV	5.9	1.01
Soc. Minera Corona	5.6	0.96
Others	265.0	45.23

Source: "Top World Silver Producers" [online] http://www.nma.org [accessed March 22, 2004], from Silver Institute.

SIC 12 - Coal Mining

★ 112 ★
Coal
SIC: 1220; NAICS: 212111, 212112
Coal Consumption by Sector, 2002

Data are in millions of short tons. Western United States produced 550.8 million of the 1.09 billion short tons produced in 2002. CHP stands for combined heat and power.

	(mil.)	Share
Electric power	981.9	86.51%
Non-CHP	36.6	3.22
Combined heat and power	26.5	2.33
Coke plants	22.5	1.98
Residential/commercial	4.4	0.39
Other industrial plants	63.1	5.56

Source: *Electric Light & Power*, June 2003, p. 20, from Energy Information Administration.

★ 113 ★
Coal
SIC: 1220; NAICS: 212111, 212112
Largest Coal Reserves Worldwide

According to the source, total recoverable reserves of coal worldwide are about 1,083 billion tons, enough to last another 210 years at current rates of consumption. The top three countries have 60% of holdings with Australia, India, Germany and South Africa taking almost 30% of the total.

United States	25.0%
Former Soviet Union	23.0
China	12.0
Other	40.0

Source: "Coal." [online] from http://www.eia.doe.gov/oiaf/ieo/coal.html [accessed June 10, 2004], from International Energy Outlook.

★ 114 ★
Coal
SIC: 1220; NAICS: 212111, 212112

Leading Coal Producing Counties in Kentucky, 2001

Kentucky ranks third in the nation in coal production. Figures are in millions of metric tons.

Pike	34.27
Perry	14.07
Knott	13.30
Harlan	12.22
Webster	10.88

Source: *Mining Engineering*, May 2003, p. 21, from Kentucky's Department of Mines and Minerals.

★ 115 ★
Coal
SIC: 1220; NAICS: 212111, 212112

Top Coal Producers, 2002

Market shares are shown based on production.

Peabody Corporation	18.1%
Arch Coal Inc.	10.7
Kennecott Energy Corporation	10.6
RAG American Coal Holding	6.5
CONSOL Energy Inc.	6.1
Massey Energy Company	4.0
Triton Coal Company	3.9
Horizon Natural Resources Company	3.4
The North American Coal Corporation	3.1
Westmoreland Coal Company	2.3
Other	31.3

Source: "Major U.S. Coal Producers." [online] from http://www.nma.org [accessed April 1, 2004], from National Mining Association.

★ 116 ★
Coal
SIC: 1220; NAICS: 212111, 212112

Top Coal Producers in China, 2001

Market shares are shown based on output.

Shenhua Group	4.98%
Yankuang Group	3.31
Datong Co.	3.21
Kailuan Co.	2.05
Pingdingshan Group	1.98
Huaibei Group	1.83
Xishan Group	1.75
Other	80.89

Source: *AsiaPulse News*, December 11, 2003, p. NA, from State Coalmine Safety Supervision Administration.

★ 117 ★
Coal
SIC: 1220; NAICS: 212111, 212112

Top Coal Producing States, 2002

Production is shown in millions of short tons.

	mil.	Share
Wyoming	373.5	34.15%
West Virginia	150.6	13.77
Kentucky, eastern	98.9	9.04
Pennsylvania	68.7	6.28
Tennessee	67.4	6.16
Texas	45.2	4.13
Montana	37.4	3.42
Indiana	35.5	3.25
Colorado	35.1	3.21
Illinois	33.3	3.04
Other	148.2	13.55

Source: *Mining Engineering*, May 2003, p. 21.

★ 118 ★
Coal
SIC: 1220; NAICS: 212111, 212112

Top Coal Producing States, 2004

Data are in thousands of short tons from January 1 - June 5, 2004. Colorado has seen its output rise by 16% so far this year.

Wyoming	164,257
West Virginia	59,319
Kentucky	47,585
Pennsylvania	28,805
Texas	20,130
Colorado	16,869
Montana	15,820
Indiana	15,744
North Dakota	13,609
Virginia	13,285

Source: *New York Times*, June 16, 2004, p. A14, from Energy Information Administration, U.S. Department of Energy.

SIC 13 - Oil and Gas Extraction

Natural Gas

SIC: 1311; NAICS: 211111

Leading Natural Gas Producers, 2002

Companies are ranked by natural gas production in millions of cubic feet per day. The top 10 firms have 40% of the U.S. production. The top 50 firms (41.3 billion cubic feet per day) have 74% of the total production.

BP	5,512
ExxonMobil	3,130
ChevronTexaco Inc.	2,846
ConocoPhillips Co.	2,445
Shell Oil Co.	2,377
Devon Energy Corp.	2,020
El Paso Energy	1,894
Burlington Resources Oil & Gas Co.	1,875
Anadarko Petroleum Corp.	1,776
Unocal Corp.	1,261

Source: ''Top 100 Oil and Gas Field Fields for 2002.'' [online] from http://eia.doc.gov [accessed June 9, 2004], from Energy Information Administration.

Natural Gas

SIC: 1311; NAICS: 211111

Natural Gas Wells by State, 2003

Total wells increased from 371,862 in 2002 to 391,336 in 2003.

	Wells	Share
Texas	66,315	16.94%
Pennsylvania	46,397	11.86
West Virginia	40,186	10.27
New Mexico	36,437	9.31
Oklahoma	34,283	8.76
Ohio	33,780	8.63
Wyoming	23,217	5.93
Kansas	18,639	4.76%
Louisiana	15,694	4.01
Kentucky	12,551	3.21
Other	63,867	16.32

Source: *World Oil*, February 2004, p. 54, from state agencies and *World Oil* estimates.

Oil

SIC: 1311; NAICS: 211111

Largest Oil Exporters Worldwide, 2002

Countries are ranked by millions of barrels per day.

Saudi Arabia	7.0
Russia	5.0
Norway	3.1
Venezuela	2.5
Iran	2.3
United Arab Emirates	2.1

Continued on next page.

36

★ 121 ★

[Continued]
Oil
SIC: 1311; NAICS: 211111

Largest Oil Exporters Worldwide, 2002

Countries are ranked by millions of barrels per day.

Nigeria	1.9
Kuwait	1.7
Mexico	1.7
Iraq	1.6

Source: *USA TODAY*, May 11, 2004, p. 4B, from Energy Information Administration.

★ 122 ★

Oil
SIC: 1311; NAICS: 211111

Largest Oil Reserves Worldwide, 2002

Countries are ranked by millions of barrels per day.

Saudi Arabia	261.7
Iraq	115.0
Iran	99.1
Kuwait	98.9
United Arab Emirates	62.8
Russia	53.9
Nigeria	30.0
Libya	30.0
China	29.5

Source: *USA TODAY*, May 11, 2004, p. 4B, from Energy Information Administration and International Energy Outlook.

★ 123 ★

Oil
SIC: 1311; NAICS: 211111

Leading Oil Firms in Denmark, 2002

Over the last five years Danish oil production has grown 61%. Average daily production is just under 59,000 cubic meters in 2002. Market shares are estimated in percent.

Shell	37.8%
A.P. Moeller	32.0
Texaco	12.3

Amerada Hess	6.2%
DONG	6.1
Paladin	1.9
Denerco	1.8
Statoil	1.7
Danoil	0.2

Source: ''Danish Oil and Gas Market.'' [online] from http://www.usatrade.gov [accessed January 5, 2004], from U.S. Commercial Service and Danish Energy Authority.

★ 124 ★

Oil
SIC: 1311; NAICS: 211111

Top Oil Producers, 2002

Companies are ranked by crude oil production in thousands of barrels per day. The top 10 firms have 60% of the total production. The top 50 firms (4.42 million barrels per day) have 78% of the U.S. production.

BP	868
ChevronTexaco Inc.	620
Shell Oil Co.	462
ConocoPhillips	350
ExxonMobil Corp.	297
Occidental Petroleum Corp.	261
Aera Energy	232
Amerada Hess Corp.	106
Anadarko Petroleum Corp.	103
Marathon Oil Co.	97

Source: ''Top 100 Oil and Gas Field Fields for 2002.'' [online] from http://eia.doc.gov [accessed June 9, 2004], from Energy Information Administration.

★ 125 ★

Oil

SIC: 1311; NAICS: 211111

Top Oil Producing Companies Worldwide

Companies are ranked by production in millions of barrels per day.

Saudi Aramco	8.3
National Iranian Oil Co.	3.8
Pemex	3.6
PDV	3.2
Exxon Mobil	2.5
Iraq National Oil Co.	2.4
Royal Dutch/Shell	2.2
PetroChina	2.1
ChevronTexaco	2.0
BP	1.8

Source: *Wall Street Journal*, April 30, 2003, p. A1, from Energy Intelligence Group.

★ 126 ★

Oil

SIC: 1311; NAICS: 211111

U.S. Oil Imports, 2002

The U.S. produces 7.191 million barrels of oil annually. The gap between oil production and consumption of oil products has been increasing since the 1970s.

Saudi Arabia	17.0%
Canada	16.0
Mexico	16.0
Venezuela	13.0
Nigeria	6.0
Iraq	5.0
Other	27.0

Source: *National Geographic*, June 2004, p. 90.

★ 127 ★

Oil

SIC: 1311; NAICS: 211111

World Crude Oil Reserves, 2003

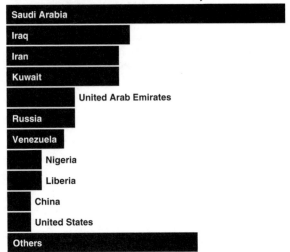

Countries are ranked by oil reserves in billions of barrels as of January 1, 2003.

	(bil.)	Share
Saudi Arabia	261.8	25.30%
Iraq	115.0	11.11
Iran	100.1	9.67
Kuwait	98.9	9.56
United Arab Emirates	63.0	6.09
Russia	58.8	5.68
Venezuela	53.1	5.13
Nigeria	32.0	3.09
Liberia	30.0	2.90
China	23.7	2.29
United States	22.7	2.19
Others	175.6	16.97

Source: *Financial Times*, April 30, 2004, p. 8, from Energy Information Administration.

★ 128 ★
Natural Gas Liquids
SIC: 1321; NAICS: 211112

Largest Natural Gas Liquid Reserves, 2002

Fields are ranked by reported production volume. Figures are in million barrels of 42 U.S. gallons. The top 10 firms have 21.3% of the U.S. production. The top 50 (803.3 million barrels) represent 38.6% of total production.

Prudhoe Bay	151.6
Kuparuk River	58.6
Mississippi Canyon Blk 807	52.1
Midway-Sunset	50.4
Belridge South	39.9
Kern River	38.6
Alpine	35.0
Mississippi Canyon Blk 810	31.8
Wasson	25.5

Source: "Top 100 Oil and Gas Field Fields for 2002." [online] from http://eia.doc.gov [accessed June 9, 2004], from Energy Information Administration.

★ 129 ★
Natural Gas Liquids
SIC: 1321; NAICS: 211112

Natural Gas Liquid Production Worldwide, 2002

Data show 10 month average production in thousands of barrels per day.

	(000)	Share
United States	1,892	31.10%
Canada	688	11.31
Saudi Arabia	644	10.59
Mexico	411	6.76
Russia	244	4.01
United Arab Emirates	220	3.62
United Kingdom	202	3.32
Algeria	190	3.12
Venzuela	180	2.96
China	180	2.96
Other	1,232	20.25

Source: *Oil and Gas Journal*, February 3, 2003, p. 79.

★ 130 ★
Horizontal Directional Drilling
SIC: 1381; NAICS: 213111

Horizontal Directional Drilling, 2003

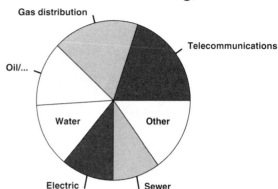

At the beginning of 2003, approximately 18,335 units had entered the market since 1992. Shares are based on industrial sector into which horizontal directional drilling equipment was sold. In 2000 the telecom sector accounted for 47% of the market. Shares are estimates based on a survey of contractors in 2000.

Telecommunications	20.0%
Gas distribution	17.6
Oil/gas pipeline	13.1
Water	13.1
Electric	10.6
Sewer	10.2
Other	15.4

Source: *Underground Construction*, June 2003, p. 25, from Underground Contruction's *5th Annual HDD Survey*.

★ 131 ★
Oil Wells
SIC: 1381; NAICS: 213111

Floating Drilling Rigs

Oceaneering's market share is shown based on its plans to acquire 116 remotely operated vehicles from Subsea 7, Halliburton and DSNS. Its share currently stands at 30%.

Oceaneering International	51.0%
Sonsub	14.0
Thales	9.0
Stolt Offshore fleet	8.0
Subsea 7 fleet	6.0
Other	12.0

Source: *Petroleum Finance Week*, December 8, 2003, p. NA.

★ 132 ★
Oil Wells
SIC: 1381; NAICS: 213111

Jack-up Rigs in the Gulf of Mexico

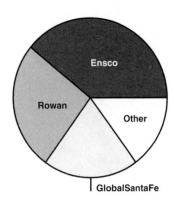

Ensco forecasts a surge in demand for jack-up rigs that can drill past 15,000 feet.

Ensco	39.0%
Rowan	26.0
GlobalSantaFe	20.0
Other	15.0

Source: *Natural Gas Week*, September 22, 2003, p. 6.

★ 133 ★
Oil Wells
SIC: 1381; NAICS: 213111

Oil & Gas Well Drilling Worldwide, 2003

There are 72,540 wells forecasted to be drilled worldwide in 2003, an increase of 3.6% over the number drilled in 2002.

	Wells	Share
United States	29,519	40.74%
Canada	18,018	24.87
China	10,183	14.06
Former Soviet Union	4,700	6.49
Argentina	1,358	1.87
Indonesia	905	1.25
Venezuela	699	0.96
Oman	425	0.59
Saudi Arabia	290	0.40%
Egypt	231	0.32
South Pacific	223	0.31
Other	5,899	8.14

Source: *World Oil*, August 2003, p. 23, from *World Oil*, oil companies, and government agencies and industry associations.

★ 134 ★
Oil Wells
SIC: 1381; NAICS: 213111

Oil Well Drilling by State, 2003

Second half of the year drilling will be 16,653 wells, 30% more than the first six months. The number of wells is up 2% overall from 2002.

	No.	Share
Texas	8,375	28.37%
Wyoming	2,492	8.44
California	2,235	7.57
Pennsylvania	2,196	7.44
Oklahoma	2,143	7.26
Kansas	1,672	5.66
New Mexico	1,204	4.08
Louisiana	1,149	3.89
West Virginia	1,042	3.53
Gulf of Mexico	942	3.19
Other	6,069	20.56

Source: *World Oil*, August 2003, p. 28.

★ 135 ★
Oil Maintenance Dredging
SIC: 1389; NAICS: 213112

Oil Dredging Industry in India

Market shares are shown in percent.

DCI	90.0%
Other	10.0

Source: *Asia Africa Intelligence Wire*, November 19, 2003, p. NA, from *Economic Times*.

SIC 14 - Nonmetallic Minerals, Except Fuels

★ 136 ★

Dimension Stone

SIC: 1411; NAICS: 212311

Dimension Stone Market, 2003

Dimension stone valued at $236 million was produced by roughly 132 companies. Total production was about 1.35 million tons. Indiana and Wisconsin were the top producers. Figures are based on tonnage.

Granite	34.0%
Limestone	28.0
Sandstone	16.0
Marble	5.0
Slate	1.0
Other	16.0

Source: ''Dimension Stone.'' [online] from http://www.ers.usgs.gov [accessed March 22, 2004], from U.S. Geological Survey.

★ 137 ★

Stone

SIC: 1411; NAICS: 212311

Leading Stone Markets, 2002

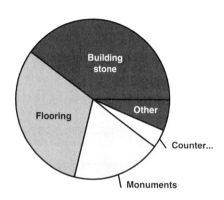

$3.3 billion in stone was consumed in the United States during 2002.

Building stone	31.8%
Flooring	25.1
Monuments	14.8
Counter tops	3.3
Other	5.0

Source: *Stone World*, January 2004, p. 32, from Catalina Research.

★ 138 ★
Crushed Stone
SIC: 1420; NAICS: 212312

Crushed Stone Market, 2003

Crushed stone valued at $8.6 billion was manufactured by roughly 1,600 companies. Florida and Texas were the top producers. Demand is shown by use.

Limestone and dolomite 71.0%
Granite 15.0
Traprock 7.0
Other 7.0

Source: ''Crushed Stone.'' [online] from http://www.ers.usgs.gov [accessed March 22, 2004], from U.S. Geological Survey.

★ 139 ★
Limestone
SIC: 1422; NAICS: 212312

Largest Limestone Producers in Ohio, 2002

National Lime & Stone
Hanson Aggregates Midwest
Shelly Materials
Martin Marietta Aggregates
Stoneco

Total production of limestone and dolomite was 69.9 million metric tons, valued at $390 million.

National Lime & Stone 11.33
Hanson Aggregates Midwest 10.88
Shelly Materials 6.40
Martin Marietta Aggregates 5.27
Stoneco 4.56

Source: *Mining Engineering*, May 2003, p. 21.

★ 140 ★
Limestone
SIC: 1422; NAICS: 212312

World Limestone Production, 2003

Shares are by country and based on lime production for the year 2003, measured in thousand metric tons.

	(000)	Share
China	23,500	20.0%
United States	18,200	15.6
Russia	8,000	6.9
Japan	7,400	6.4
Germany	6,800	5.9
Brazil	6,500	5.6
Mexico	6,500	5.6
Italy	3,000	2.6
France	2,500	2.2
Canada	2,250	2.0
Australia	2,000	1.7
Iran	2,000	1.7
Poland	2,000	1.7
United Kingdom	2,000	1.7
South Africa	1,600	1.4
Other countries	23,000	19.7

Source: *Mineral Commodity Summaries — Lime*, January 2004, p. 97, from U.S. Geological Survey.

★ 141 ★
Marble and Limestone
SIC: 1422; NAICS: 212312

Top Marble/Limestone/Travertine Exporters to the United States, 2002

Total imports to the U.S. increased from $230.2 million in 1992 to $638.7 million in 2002. The top exporters to the U.S. in 2002 were Italy, Spain, and Greece.

	($ mil.)	Share
Italy	$199.35	31.21%
Spain	120.58	18.88
Greece	90.05	14.10
France	72.79	11.40
Taiwan	28.56	4.47
Mexico	18.92	2.96
Turkey	18.20	2.85
Portugal	10.96	1.72
China	9.16	1.43
Other	70.13	10.98

Source: *Stone World*, March 2004, p. 168, from Catalina Research Inc. and Ceramic Tile and Stone Consultants.

★ 142 ★

Granite

SIC: 1423; NAICS: 212313

Top Granite Exporters to the United States, 2002

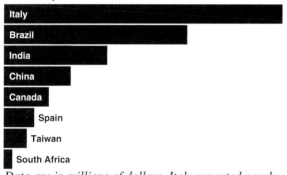

Data are in millions of dollars. Italy exported nearly $195 million worth of granite to the U.S. in 2002, almost four times its $53.1 million figure in 1992. Total granite imported to the U.S. in 2002 was $523.7 million, up from $115.4 million in 1992.

	($ mil.)	Share
Italy	$ 194.88	38.44%
Brazil	127.70	25.19
India	70.33	13.87
China	43.29	8.54
Canada	30.15	5.95
Spain	21.94	4.33
Taiwan	14.23	2.81
South Africa	4.51	0.89

Source: *Stone World*, March 2004, p. 168, from Catalina Research Inc. and Ceramic Tile and Stone Consultants.

★ 143 ★

Sand & Gravel

SIC: 1442; NAICS: 212321

Construction Sand and Gravel Market

Construction sand and gravel valued at $5.8 billion was manufactured by roughly 4,000 companies. California and Texas were the top producers. Demand is shown by use.

Unspecified	54.0%
Concrete aggregates	42.0
Road base, coverings, road stabilization	23.0
Construction fill	15.0
Asphaltic concrete aggregates	12.0
Concrete blocks, pipes, etc.	3.0
Plaster and gunite sands	1.0

Source: "Sand and Gravel." [online] from http://www.ers.usgs.gov [accessed March 22, 2004], from U.S. Geological Survey.

★ 144 ★

Sand & Gravel

SIC: 1442; NAICS: 212321

Largest Sand & Gravel Producers in Ohio, 2002

Ohio ranked fourth in the nation in sand & gravel production. Total production fell 6% over the previous year to 48.3 million metric tons.

	mil.	Share
Martin Marietta Aggregates	8.65	17.91%
Shelly Materials	3.57	7.39
Olen	2.99	6.19
Watson Gravel	2.01	4.16
Barrett Paving Materials	1.28	2.65
Other	29.80	61.70

Source: *Mining Engineering*, May 2003, p. 21.

★ 145 ★

Clays

SIC: 1450; NAICS: 212324, 212325

Clay Production

Production is shown in thousands of metric tons.

	2000	2002
Common clay	23,700	24,200
Kaolin	8,800	7,450
Bentonite	3,760	4,110
Fuller's earth	2,910	3,400
Ball clay	1,140	1,070
Fire clay	476	355

Source: *American Ceramic Society Bulletin*, August 2003, p. 32, from U.S. Geological Survey.

★ 146 ★
Phosphate Rock
SIC: 1475; NAICS: 212392

World Phosphate Rock Production, 2003

Production is shown in thousands of metric tons. More than 95% of phosphate ore rock mined in the United States was used in the production of wet-process phosphoric acid and superphosphoric acid, which are used in the production of fertilizers and fedd supplements.

	(000)	Share
United States	33,300	24.2%
China	24,000	17.4
Morocco and Western Sahara	24,000	17.4
Russia	11,000	8.0
Tunisia	7,700	5.6
Jordan	7,200	5.3
Other countries	7,000	5.1
Brazil	4,960	3.6
Israel	4,000	2.9
South Africa	2,500	1.9
Syria	2,400	1.8
Togo	2,100	1.6
Australia	2,200	1.5
Egypt	1,500	1.1
Senegal	1,500	1.1
Canada	1,200	0.9
India	1,250	0.9

Source: *Mineral Commodity Summaries — Phosphate Rock*, January 2004, p. 123, from U.S. Geological Survey.

★ 147 ★
Diamonds
SIC: 1499; NAICS: 212399

Diamond Imports by the United States, 2002 and 2003

The value of rough diamonds imported in previous years: $733.5 million in 1999, $741.2 million in 2000, $550.4 million in 2001 and $567.2 million in 2002. Shares are shown based on imports fot the first six months of 2003, which were $300.13 million.

	2002	2003
South Africa	$ 352.63	$ 199.36
United Kingdom	68.60	31.59
Congo	24.23	7.98
Guinea	19.38	4.63
Botswana	18.19	2.45
Israel	14.90	7.66
Brazil	$ 14.21	$ 12.37
Belgium	11.57	2.10
Guyana	6.24	6.63
Canada	2.04	2.78

Source: *Diamond Intelligence Briefs*, September 12, 2003, p. 279.

★ 148 ★
Diamonds
SIC: 1499; NAICS: 212399

Leading Diamond Producing Nations, 2002

Countries are ranked by production of uncut (or rough) diamonds, (industrial and gems). Figures are in millions of carats.

	(mil.)	Share
Australia	33.6	25.51%
Botswana	28.4	21.56
Russia	23.0	17.46
Congo	18.2	13.82
South Africa	10.9	8.28
Angola	6.0	4.56
Canada	5.0	3.80
Other	6.6	5.01

Source: *Wall Street Journal*, February 24, 2003, p. A1, from U.S. Geological Survey.

★ 149 ★
Diamonds
SIC: 1499; NAICS: 212399
Rough Diamond Production Worldwide

The company has over 60% of the rough diamond market worldwide. The company also has just less than half of the wholesale polished diamond market in the United States.

	2001	2002	2003
DeBeers	56.0%	66.0%	62.0%
Other	44.0	34.0	38.0

Source: *New York Times*, July 10, 2004, p. B1, from Rapaport Research.

★ 150 ★
Diamonds
SIC: 1499; NAICS: 212399
World Industrial Diamond Mining, 2003

Diamond production is shown measured in million carats. The United States is the leading market for industrial diamonds. The construction sector will be a major contributor to the increased domestic demand (industrial diamonds coat the edge of saws used to cut concrete).

	(mil.)	Share
Australia	19.0	29.0%
Congo	15.0	22.9
Russia	11.8	18.1
Botswana	9.0	13.8
South Africa	6.7	10.3
Other countries	3.0	4.6
China	1.0	1.6

Source: *Mineral Commodity Summaries — Diamonds*, January 2004, p. 57, from U.S. Geological Survey.

★ 151 ★
Graphite
SIC: 1499; NAICS: 212399
World Graphite Production, 2003

Graphite production is shown in thousands of metric tons. Leading uses include refractory applications, brake linings, and lubricants.

	(000)	Share
China	450	57.2%
India	110	14.1
Brazil	65	8.4
Canada	25	3.2
North Korea	25	3.2
Mexico	20	2.6
Czech Republic	15	2.0
Madagascar	10	1.3
Other countries	62	8.0

Source: *Mineral Commodity Summaries — Natural Graphite*, January 2004, p. 75, from U.S. Geological Survey.

SIC 15 - General Building Contractors

★ 152 ★

Construction

SIC: 1500; NAICS: 23321, 23331, 23332

Construction Industry, 1999 and 2003

The construction industry saw spending increase in 2003. Residential construction takes just over half of all construction spending. It remains strong. Non-residential sectors were less successful. Figures show percent of total industry by volume.

	1999	2003
Single-family homes	29.2%	32.2%
Residential improvements	13.0	15.5
Highways and streets	6.1	4.0
Private office and professional (new) .	5.1	4.2
Utilities	4.5	4.7
Education (new)	4.3	4.7
Multifamily homes	3.6	8.0
Stores and other mercantile (new) . .	3.3	3.0
Education and improvements	2.0	2.2
Other	28.9	21.5

Source: *Contractor's Business Management Report*, March 2004, p. 1, from *2003-2004 U.S. Market's Construction Update.*

★ 153 ★

Construction

SIC: 1500; NAICS: 23321, 23331, 23332

Construction Industry in Europe, 2003

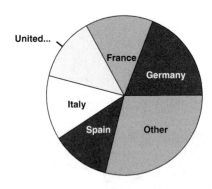

The top 5 countries have not changed in recent years but some of their shares have. In 1998, Germans took 27% of activity and Spain had 7% the other countries were essentially flat.

Germany	19.0%
France	14.0
United Kingdom	13.0
Italy	13.0
Spain	12.0
Other	29.0

Source: *International Construction*, March 20, 2004, p. 17.

★ 154 ★

Construction

SIC: 1500; NAICS: 23321, 23331, 23332

Leading Construction Firms, 2002

Firms are ranked by construction revenues in millions of dollars.

Bechtel	$ 9,688.0
Fluor Corp.	7,796.3

Continued on next page.

★ 154 ★

[Continued]

Construction

SIC: 1500; NAICS: 23321, 23331, 23332

Leading Construction Firms, 2002

Firms are ranked by construction revenues in millions of dollars.

Centex	$ 7,111.7
The Turner Corp.	6,245.7
Skanska	5,874.7
Kellogg Brown & Root	5,741.1
Peter Kiewit Sons Inc.	3,745.0
Bovis Lend Lease	3,230.4
Washington Group International	3,054.9
The Shaw Group Inc.	3,017.5

Source: *ENR*, May 19, 2003, p. 85.

★ 155 ★

Construction

SIC: 1500; NAICS: 23331, 23321, 23332

Leading General Construction Firms, 2002

Firms are ranked by construction revenues in billions of dollars.

Centex	$ 6.7
The Turner Corp.	5.2
Skanska (USA) Inc.	3.5
Bovis Lend Lease	2.7
The Clark Construction Group Inc.	2.2
Gilbane Building Co.	2.2
The Whiting-Turner Contracting Co.	1.5
J.E. Dunn Group	1.5
Hensel Phelps Construction Co.	1.5
Hunt Construction Group	1.4

Source: *ENR*, May 19, 2003, p. 85.

★ 156 ★

Residential Construction

SIC: 1521; NAICS: 23321

Top Builders in Atlanta, GA, 2002

Market shares are shown based on number of closings.

Pulte Homes	3.4%
D.R. Horton/Torrey Dobson Homes	2.3
Colony Homes	2.1
Ryland Homes	1.8
Bowen Builders Group	1.8
M.D.C. Holdings/Richmond American Homes	1.7
John Wieland Homes & Neighborhoods	1.5
Brayson Homes	1.4
Other	84.0

Source: *Builder*, May 2003, p. 196.

★ 157 ★

Residential Construction

SIC: 1521; NAICS: 23321

Top Builders in Chicago, IL, 2002

Market shares are shown based on number of closings.

Pulte Homes	4.7%
Neumann Homes	4.2
Lennar Corp./Concord Homes/Summit Homes	4.2
Lakewood Homes	4.2
D.R. Horton/Cambridge Homes	4.1
Ryland Homes	3.8
Town & Country Homes	2.6
Pasquinelli Construction Co.	1.6
Kirk Homes	1.6

Continued on next page.

★ 157 ★

[Continued]
Residential Construction
SIC: 1521; NAICS: 23321

Top Builders in Chicago, IL, 2002

Market shares are shown based on number of closings.

Centex Homes	1.6%
Other	67.4

Source: *Builder*, May 2003, p. 196.

★ 158 ★

Residential Construction
SIC: 1521; NAICS: 23321

Top Builders in Columbus, OH, 2002

Market shares are shown based on number of closings.

Dominion Homes	22.1%
M/I Homes	20.1
Rockford Homes	4.0
Beazer Homes USA/Deluxe Homes	3.7
Centex Homes	2.8
Diyanni Homes	2.3
Joshua Homes	1.3
Virginia Homes	0.9
Duffy Homes	0.9
Bob Webb Builders	0.9
Other	41.0

Source: *Builder*, May 2003, p. 196.

★ 159 ★

Residential Construction
SIC: 1521; NAICS: 23321

Top Builders in Denver, CO, 2002

Market shares are shown based on number of closings.

D.R. Horton/Continental Homes/Trimark Homes/Melody Homes	19.8%
Lennar Corp./U.S. Home Corp.	11.8
M.D.C. Holdings/Richmond American Homes	11.7

KB Home	10.2%
Pulte Homes	5.0
Ryland Homes	4.6
American West Homes/Oakwood Homes	4.5
Shea Homes	4.4
Village Homes of Colorado	3.6
Other	24.4

Source: *Builder*, May 2003, p. 196.

★ 160 ★

Residential Construction
SIC: 1521; NAICS: 23321

Top Builders in Detroit, MI, 2002

Market shares are shown based on number of closings.

Pulte Homes	8.5%
Crosswinds Communities	6.5
MJC Cos.	2.3
Toll Brothers	2.2
Centex Homes	2.0
S.R. Jacobson Development Corp.	1.8
Ivanhoe-Huntley	1.5
Delcor Homes	1.3
Other	73.9

Source: *Builder*, May 2003, p. 196.

★ 161 ★

Residential Construction
SIC: 1521; NAICS: 23321

Top Builders in Fort Worth/Arlington, TX, 2002

Market shares are shown based on number of closings.

Choice Homes	10.5%
Centex Homes	7.1
Pulte Homes	5.9
Lennar Corp.	5.9
D.R. Horton/Continental Homes	5.9
KB Home	5.5
Meritage Corp./Legacy Homes	3.9
Highland Homes	3.7

Continued on next page.

★ 161 ★

[Continued]
Residential Construction
SIC: 1521; NAICS: 23321

Top Builders in Fort Worth/Arlington, TX, 2002

Market shares are shown based on number of closings.

David Weekley Homes	2.7%
Other	48.9

Source: *Builder*, May 2003, p. 196.

★ 162 ★

Residential Construction
SIC: 1521; NAICS: 23321

Top Builders in Indianapolis, IN, 2002

Market shares are shown based on number of closings.

C.P. Morgan	16.4%
Beazer Homes USA/Crossman Communities .	15.8
Davis Homes	8.6
Ryland Homes	5.7
American West Homes/Arbor Homes	5.5
Trinity Homes	4.5
Dura Builders	3.6
The Estridge Cos.	3.5
Centex Homes	3.2
Other	33.2

Source: *Builder*, May 2003, p. 196.

★ 163 ★

Residential Construction
SIC: 1521; NAICS: 23321

Top Builders in Kansas City, MO/KS, 2002

Market shares are shown based on number of closings.

Pulte Homes	1.4%
Prieb Homes	1.1
Duggan Homes	0.8
J.S. Robinson Construction	0.8
Don Bell Homes	0.7
Don Julian Builders	0.7
Lambie-Geer Homes	0.7
Thomas French Builders	0.7
Three J's Construction	0.7
Other	92.4

Source: *Builder*, May 2003, p. 196.

★ 164 ★

Residential Construction
SIC: 1521; NAICS: 23321

Top Builders in Las Vegas, NV, 2002

Market shares are shown based on number of closings.

KB Home	11.8%
Pulte Homes	8.5
D.R. Horton	5.4
M.D.C. Holdings/Richmond American Homes	4.9
Weyerhaeuser Real Estate Co./Pardee Homes .	4.9
American West Homes	3.7
Beazer Homes USA	3.5
Lennar Corp./Greystone Homes/U.S. Home Corp.	3.5
Woodside Homes of Nevada	3.2
Other	50.6

Source: *Builder*, May 2003, p. 196.

★ 165 ★
Residential Construction
SIC: 1521; NAICS: 23321

Top Builders in Los Angeles/Long Beach CA, 2002

Market shares are shown based on number of closings.

Beazer Homes	10.1%
D.R. Horton/Western Pacific Housing	9.3
KB Home	8.4
Lennar Corp./Greystone Homes	4.6
Shea Homes	4.4
Hovnanian Enterprises/Forecast Homes	4.0
John Laing Homes	3.4
Shapell Industries	3.3
M.D.C. Holdings/Richmond American Homes	3.2
Other	49.3

Source: *Builder*, May 2003, p. 196.

★ 166 ★
Residential Construction
SIC: 1521; NAICS: 23321

Top Builders in Minneapolis/St. Paul, MN, 2002

Market shares are shown based on number of closings.

Rottlund Homes	5.8%
Pulte Homes	4.9
Centex Homes	4.6
Lennar Corp./Lundgren Bros./Orrin Thompson Homes	3.8
D.R. Horton	3.3%
M.W. Johnson Construction	3.3
Ryland Homes	2.6
Key-Land Homes	2.1
Wensmann Homes	2.0
Other	67.6

Source: *Builder*, May 2003, p. 196.

★ 167 ★
Residential Construction
SIC: 1521; NAICS: 23321

Top Builders in Nashville, TN, 2002

Market shares are shown based on number of closings.

Beazer Homes USA/Phillips Builders	5.9%
Ole South Properties	5.9
Pulte Homes	2.4
Continental Development	1.7
Butler J Construction	1.6
Centex Homes	1.5
Newmark Homes	1.4
Jones Custom Homes	1.3
Greenvale Construction	1.1
Hovnanian Enterprises	1.1
The Drees Co.	1.1
Other	75.0

Source: *Builder*, May 2003, p. 196.

★ 168 ★
Residential Construction
SIC: 1521; NAICS: 23321

Top Builders in Tampa Bay, FL, 2002

Market shares are shown based on number of closings.

Lennar Corp./U.S. Home Corp.	10.8%
Ryland Homes	5.7
Pulte Homes	5.4
Maronda Homes	4.1
Windward Homes	3.8
Inland Homes	3.0
M/I Homes	2.8

Continued on next page.

★ 168 ★

[Continued]
Residential Construction
SIC: 1521; NAICS: 23321

Top Builders in Tampa Bay, FL, 2002

Market shares are shown based on number of closings.

Rottlund Homes	2.5%
Suarez Housing Corp.	2.4
Other	59.5

Source: *Builder*, May 2003, p. 196.

★ 169 ★

Residential Construction
SIC: 1521; NAICS: 23321

Top Home Builders, 2004

Market shares are estimated.

DR Horton	2.7%
Pulte Homes	2.5
Lennar	2.3
Centex	2.2
Other	90.3

Source: *Forbes*, June 21, 2004, p. 196, from company reports, Greenhouse Associates, and Reuters Fundamentals via FactSet Research Systems.

★ 170 ★

Residential Construction
SIC: 1521; NAICS: 23321

Top Home Builders in Japan, 2002

Market shares are shown based on domestic housing starts.

Sekisui House	4.0%
Misawa Homes	3.4
Daiwa House Industry	2.7
Sekisui Chemical	2.5
Asaki Kasei	2.3
Other	85.1

Source: "Market Share Survey Report 2002." [online] from http://www.nni.nikkei.co.jp [accessed January 20, 2004], from Nikkei estimates.

★ 171 ★

Residential Construction
SIC: 1521; NAICS: 23321

Top Housing Markets

Markets are ranked by 12 months of single-family permits.

Atlanta, GA	53,956
Phoenix, AZ	46,731
Riverside, CA	35,832
Houston, TX	34,121
Chicago, IL	31,281
Washington D.C.	30,804
Las Vegas	30,289
Dallas, TX	26,881
Orlando, FL	22,398
Minneapolis, MN	20,480

Source: *Professional Builder*, April 2004, p. S10, from U.S. Bureau of Census and John Burns Real Estate Consulting.

★ 172 ★

Residential Construction
SIC: 1521; NAICS: 23321

Top Markets for Luxury Homes

According to the source, more than one out of every three new U.S. homes is valued at a million dollars or more. States are ranked by number of such properties.

	Homes	Share
California	128,619	41.0%
New York	22,327	7.1
Florida	18,094	5.8
Connecticut	13,906	4.4
Illinois	12,386	3.9
New Jersey	11,869	3.8
Texas	10,137	3.2
Massachusetts	10,090	3.2

Source: *Builder*, September 15, 2003, p. 10, from National Association of Home Builders and U.S. Bureau of the Census.

★ 173 ★
Residential Construction
SIC: 1521; NAICS: 23321

Top Residential Home Builders, 2002

Companies are ranked by gross revenues in millions of dollars.

Centex Corp.	$ 8,824
Pulte Homes	7,512
D.R. Horton	7,324
Lennar Corp.	7,320
KB Home	5,031
NVR	3,136
The Ryland Group	2,877
Beazer Homes	2,852
Hovnanian Enterprises	2,551
Toll Brothers	2,329
M.D.C. Holdings	2,319
Standard Pacific Corp.	2,051

Source: *Builder*, May 2003, p. 174.

★ 174 ★
Retirement Homes
SIC: 1521; NAICS: 23321

Retirement Home Market in the U.K.

The group's core business is selling one and two bedroom flats to people over 60 years of age. Market shares are shown in percent.

McCarthy & Stone	75.0%
Other	25.0

Source: *Contract Journal*, November 13, 2002, p. 9.

★ 175 ★
Rental Property Construction
SIC: 1522; NAICS: 23322

Top Multifamily Rental Home Builders, 2002

Companies are ranked by number of rental starts.

A.G. Spanos	5,832
Bostic Brothers Construction	4,413
Clark Realty Builders	4,153
Simpson Housing Limited Partnership	4,125
JPI Investment Co.	3,570
Colson & Colson Construction	3,495
Lincoln Property Co.	3,431
Trammel Crow Residential	3,374
Picerne Real Estate Group	3,055
The Cornerstone Group	2,897

Source: *Builder*, May 2003, p. 174.

★ 176 ★
Condominiums
SIC: 1531; NAICS: 23322

Top Condominium Builders in Japan, 2002

Market shares are shown based on total sales of 169,790 new units.

Daikyo	4.2%
Sumitomo Realty	2.7
Anabuki Construction	2.6
Mitsui Fudosan	2.6
Towa Real Estate	2.4
Other	85.5

Source: "Market Share Survey Report 2002." [online] from http://www.nni.nikkei.co.jp [accessed January 20, 2004], from Real Estate Economic Institute Co.

★ 177 ★
Building Construction
SIC: 1540; NAICS: 23331, 23332

Nonresidential Construction Spending, 2004

Figures are in billions of dollars and are shown by category.

	($ bil.)	Share
Education	$ 73.6	26.08%
Commercial	67.7	23.99
Office	42.2	14.95
Health care	32.7	11.59
Amusement & recreation	20.4	7.23

Continued on next page.

★ 177 ★

[Continued]
Building Construction
SIC: 1540; NAICS: 23331, 23332

Nonresidential Construction Spending, 2004

Figures are in billions of dollars and are shown by category.

	($ bil.)	Share
Manufacturing	$ 15.6	5.53%
Lodging	11.7	4.15
Public safety	9.4	3.33
Religious	8.9	3.15

Source: *Construction Equipment*, January 2004, p. S6, from U.S. Commerce Department.

★ 178 ★

Building Construction
SIC: 1541; NAICS: 23331, 23332

South Korea's Building Construction Industry, 2002

In 2002, there were 6,079 construction companies registered as general builidng contractors in South Korea. The major contracted segments are ranked by share of 95 billion Korean Won in contracts.

Apartments	34.9%
Industrial Plants	8.3
Office-residential hybrids	8.0
Commerical (retail) buildings	7.2
Schools	6.9
Residential-commercial hybrids	6.7
Office Buildings	5.2
Hotels, lodging facilities	2.8
Houses	2.5
Government Buildings	2.5
Hospitals	1.4

Source: "Korea's Faucet and Sanitary Ware Market" [online] http://www.export.gov/comm_svc/index.html [accessed March 30, 2004], March 10, 2020, p. NA.

SIC 16 - Heavy Construction, Except Building

★ 179 ★
Contracting Work
SIC: 1600; NAICS: 23321, 23332, 23331

Largest Contractors Worldwide, 2002

Companies are ranked by sales in millions of dollars. Shares are shown based on sales of $428 billion by the top 100 firms.

	($ mil.)	Share
Vinci	.$ 18,285	4.27%
Skanska Group	16,557	3.87
Kajima	15,755	3.68
Taisei	15,263	3.57
Bouygues Construction Divisions	14,760	3.45
Shimizu	14,386	3.36
Hochtief	13,315	3.11
Bechtel	11,600	2.71
Obayashi	11,269	2.63
Fluor	9,959	2.33
Other	.286,851	67.02

Source: *International Construction*, July/August 2003, p. 15, from *International Construction's Top 100 League Table.*

★ 180 ★
Contracting Work
SIC: 1600; NAICS: 23412, 23411

Leading Heavy Construction Firms, 2002

Firms are ranked by heavy construction revenues in millions of dollars.

Bechtel	$ 3,550.0
Peter Kiewit Sons Inc.	2,255.7
APAC Inc.	2,087.0
Skanska (USA) Inc.	1,465.0
Granite Construction Inc.	1,256.2
Washington Group International Inc.	1,174.9
The Walsh Group	964.4

Modern Continental Construction	$ 866.9
Fluor Corp.	850.5
The Shaw Group Inc.	621.1

Source: *ENR*, May 19, 2003, p. 85.

★ 181 ★
Contracting Work - Transportation
SIC: 1611; NAICS: 23411, 23412

Transportation Construction Spending, 2003

Highway
Bridge & tunnels
Airports
Railroads
Docks, piers & wharfs

Value of contracts are shown in millions of dollars. There were 29,431 contracts awarded in 2003, down from 32,544 in 2002 and 31, 353 in 2001.

	($ mil.)	Share
Highway	$ 30,897.297	66.32%
Bridge & tunnels	11,675.354	25.06
Airports	1,601.737	3.44
Railroads	1,507.590	3.24
Docks, piers & wharfs	907.410	1.95

Source: *U.S. Transportation Construction Market Report*, January 2004, p. 1, from American Road & Transportation Builders Association.

★ 182 ★

Contracting Work - Sewers

SIC: 1623; NAICS: 23491, 23492

Underground Construction Spending

Figures show annual spending in millions of dollars on selected underground construction projects.

Sewer pipe	$ 8,900
Tranchless renovation	5,000
Sewer renovation	2,600
Water pipe	2,600
Water renovation	1,100
Manhole renovation	100

Source: *Underground Construction*, April 2003, p. R9.

★ 183 ★

Contracting Work - Oil Pipelines

SIC: 1629; NAICS: 23493, 23499

Shallow-Water Pipe-Laying Market

The company takes 40% of the shallow-water pipe laying market. The article states how the subsea company has invested considerable resources in the move to deep water construction.

Torch Offshore	40.0%
Other	60.0

Source: *New Orleans CityBusiness*, April 26, 2004, p. NA.

★ 184 ★

Contracting Work - Railroads

SIC: 1629; NAICS: 23499

Expenditures on Railway Tracks Worldwide, 2003

Shares are shown for annual expenditures on main line and metropolitain line rail tracks by region. Expenditures are measured in millions of euros. CIS stands for Commonwealth of Independent States.

	(mil.)	Share
Western Europe	10,054	40.0%
Asia	5,390	21.5
Canada and the United States	4,664	18.6
CIS	2,017	8.1
Eastern Europe	1,503	6.0
Latin America	681	2.8
Africa and the Middle East	420	1.7
Austrial and New Zealand	400	1.6

Source: *Railway Age*, January 2004, p. NA, from SCI Verkehr for Vossloh.

SIC 17 - Special Trade Contractors

★ 185 ★
Contracting Work - Air Conditioning
SIC: 1711; NAICS: 23511

Air Conditioning Contracting in Greater Phoenix

Market shares are shown in percent.

Mention Chas Roberts Air Conditioning Co.	75.0%
Other	25.0

Source: *Air Conditioning, Heating & Refrigeration News*, September 8, 2003, p. 24.

★ 186 ★
Contracting Work - Painting Work
SIC: 1721; NAICS: 23521

Largest Painting Contractors, 2002

Firms are ranked by revenues in millions of dollars.

Protherm Services Group LLC	$ 44.0
Techno Coatings Inc.	35.6
Robison-Prezioso Inc.	35.5
Avalotis Corp.	30.3
Certified Coatings of California	25.2
Ascher Brothers Co. Inc.	24.4
Fine Painting Co.	22.8
F.D. Thomas Inc.	20.4
Aulson Co.	19.8

Source: *ENR*, October 20, 2003, p. 52, from *ENR's Top 600 Report*.

★ 187 ★
Contracting Work - Electrical
SIC: 1731; NAICS: 23531

Largest Electrical Contractors, 2002

Firms are ranked by revenues in millions of dollars.

EMCOR Group	$ 1,547.5
Integrated Electrical Services	1,449.0
Infrasource Inc.	1,449.0
Myr Group Inc.	494.4
Mass. Electric Construction Co.	378.7
Cupertino Electric Inc.	260.1
Xcelecom Inc.	243.9
Rosendin Electric Inc.	235.0
FischBach & Moore Electric Inc.	235.0

Source: *ENR*, October 20, 2003, p. 52, from *ENR's Top 600 Report*.

★ 188 ★
Contracting Work - Masonry
SIC: 1741; NAICS: 23541

Leading Masonry Contractors

Firms are ranked by revenues in millions of dollars.

McGee Brothers Co. Inc.	$ 83.0
J.D. Long Masonry Inc.	49.3
The Western Group	41.5
Sun Valley Masonry Inc.	40.9
Dee Brown Inc.	40.8
Leonard Masonry Inc.	39.8
Caretti Inc.	39.4
Seedorf Masonry Inc.	37.4
Masonry Arts Inc.	35.2
D'Agostino Associates	35.0

Source: *Masonry Construction*, October 2003, p. 29.

★ 189 ★
Contracting Work - Roofing
SIC: 1761; NAICS: 23561

Largest Roofing Contractors, 2002

Firms are ranked by revenues in millions of dollars.

GeneralRoofing	$ 263.2
Centimark Corp.	240.0
Tecta American Corp.	181.0
The Hartford Roofing Co.	56.2
Birdair Inc.	51.0
Latite Roofing & Sheet Metal Co. Inc. . . .	49.9
Baker Roofing Co.	42.2
The Holland Roofing Group	36.0
Best Roofing & Waterproofing Inc.	35.0
W.R. Kelso Co. Inc.	29.7

Source: *ENR*, October 20, 2003, p. 52, from *ENR's Top 600 Report*.

★ 190 ★
Contracting Work - Roofing
SIC: 1761; NAICS: 23561

Roofing Market Shares

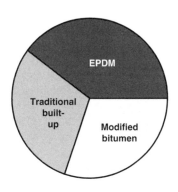

Data are based on a 2001 survey. EPDM stands for ethlene propylene diene monomer. Traditonal built-up roofing's share is between 20-25% of the market. Polyvinyl chloride and thermoplastic polyolefin single-ply are the two fastest-growing roofing sectors.

EPDM	33.0%
Traditional built-up	25.0
Modified bitumen	25.0

Source: *Building Design & Construction*, September 2003, p. 66, from National Roofing Contractors Association.

★ 191 ★
Contracting Work - Concrete
SIC: 1771; NAICS: 23571

Leading Concrete Contractors

Firms are ranked by concrete revenues in millions of dollars.

Baker Concrete Construction	$ 384.0
Clayco Construction	291.4
Walsh Group	270.8
Miller & Long	264.7
S&F Concrete Construction	175.0
Interstate Highway Construction	159.6
Webcor Concrete	151.0
Structural Group	134.0
CECO Concrete Construction	130.2
Campbell Concrete of Nevada	127.0

Source: *Concrete Construction*, July 2003, p. 35.

★ 192 ★
Contracting Work - Steel
SIC: 1791; NAICS: 23591

Largest Steel Contractors, 2002

Firms are ranked by revenues in millions of dollars.

Schuff International Inc.	$ 96.6
The Williams Group	80.0
Area Erectors Inc.	62.8
Pacific Coast Steel Inc.	60.0
Interstate Iron Works Corp.	54.0
Ben Hur Construction Co.	41.9
Danny's Construction Co. Inc.	40.3
Derr Construction Co.	36.7
Midwest Steel Inc.	35.0
Sowles Co.	33.1
National Riggers & Erectors Inc.	31.8

Source: *ENR*, October 20, 2003, p. 52, from *ENR's Top 600 Report*.

★ 193 ★
Contracting Work - Glazing/Curtain Wall
SIC: 1793; NAICS: 23592

Largest Glazing/Curtain Wall Contractors, 2002

Firms are ranked by revenues in millions of dollars.

Enclos Corp.	$ 152.0
Harmon Inc.	146.2
Walters & Wolf Glass	85.4
W&W Glass Systems Inc.	57.4
Architectural Glass & Aluminum Co. Inc.	52.8
Trainor Glass Co.	50.0
Architectural Wall Solutions Inc. (Awalls)	42.5
APG - America Inc.	33.9
Karas & Karas Glass Co. Inc.	32.6
Masonry Arts	28.8

Source: *ENR*, October 20, 2003, p. 52, from *ENR's Top 600 Report.*

★ 194 ★
Contracting Work - Excavation
SIC: 1794; NAICS: 23593

Largest Excavation/Foundation Contractors, 2002

Firms are ranked by revenues in millions of dollars.

Hayward Baker Inc. (A Keller Co.)	$ 157.5
Ryan Inc. Central	95.2
Berkel & Co. Contractors Inc.	92.0
Malcolm Drilling Co. Inc.	91.2
Independence Excavation Inc.	83.8
Case Foundation Co.	81.7
Urban Foundation/Engineering Co.	70.1
Beaver Excavating Co.	68.6
Nicholson Construction Co.	63.8
American Asphalt & Grading Co.	62.8

Source: *ENR*, October 20, 2003, p. 52, from *ENR's Top 600 Report.*

★ 195 ★
Contracting Work - Demolition Work
SIC: 1795; NAICS: 23594

Largest Demolition Contractors, 2002

Firms are ranked by revenues in millions of dollars.

Penhall Co.	$ 129.5
Brandenburg Industrial Service Co.	80.2
Cleveland Wrecking Co.	54.4
North American Site Dev. Inc. (NASDI)	50.0
D.H. Griffing Wrecking Co.	48.0
Mazzocchi Wrecking Inc.	40.1
Bierlein Demolition Contractors	34.3
Testa Corp.	34.2
CST Environmental Inc.	32.4
Railworks Corp.	26.0

Source: *ENR*, October 20, 2003, p. 52, from *ENR's Top 600 Report.*

★ 196 ★
Contracting Work - Swimming Pools
SIC: 1799; NAICS: 23599

Largest Swimming Pool Builders, 2002

Data show number of pools constructed.

Blue Haven Pools & Spas	5,880
Anthony & Sylvan	3,700
Shasta Industries	2,157
Paddock Pool Construction Co.	1,936
Pacific Pools	980
Premier Pools	872
Riverbend Sandler Pools	675

Continued on next page.

★ 196 ★

[Continued]
Contracting Work - Swimming Pools
SIC: 1799; NAICS: 23599

Largest Swimming Pool Builders, 2002

Data show number of pools constructed.

Mission Pools	607
Patio Pools & Spas	483
White Water Pools & Spas	480

Source: *Pool & Spa News*, September 5, 2003, p. 56.

SIC 20 - Food and Kindred Products

★ 197 ★
Food

SIC: 2000; NAICS: 311513, 311612

Deli Sales by Product

Supermarket deli sales climbed from $10.5 billion in 1996 to $13.6 billion in 2001.

	1996	2001
Sliced meats	34.2%	28.5%
Cheese	13.0	13.8
Salads, prepared	12.4	12.5
Hot entrees	10.2	11.0
Chicken	7.3	10.5
Sandwiches	7.0	6.9
Refrigerated entrees	3.5	3.8

Source: *Refrigerated & Frozen Foods*, June 2003, p. 32, from International Dairy-Deli-Bakery Association and *Progressive Grocer*.

★ 198 ★
Food

SIC: 2000; NAICS: 11231, 311821

High and Low Carb Foods, 2003

The table looks at sales of selected high and low carbohydrate foods in millions of dollars. Such foods have benefited from the popularity of the Atkins diet and similar diets. Potato sales fell 10% over 2002. Eggs saw an 18.5% increase over 2002, meat snacks were up 16%, bacon was up 10% and nuts 11%.

Cookies	$ 4,000.0
Eggs	2,600.0
White bread	2,200.0
Bacon	2,000.0
Nuts	1,800.0
Potatoes	1,500.0
Meat snacks	296.0
Instant rice	168.7

Source: *USA TODAY*, February 25, 2004, p. D1, from ACNielsen.

★ 199 ★
Food

SIC: 2000; NAICS: 31213, 311612, 311513

Largest Fine-Dining Foods Markets in Europe, 2008

Shares are shown based on sales in billion pounds sterling.

France	7.00
U.K.	5.50
Italy	4.40
Germany	3.90
Spain	2.30
Netherlands	0.95

Source: *Caterer & Hotelkeeper*, February 19, 2004, p. 20, from Datamonitor.

★ 200 ★
Food

SIC: 2000; NAICS: 31123, 311615, 31211

Largest Food and Beverage Categories at Wal-Mart

Sales are shown in thousands of dollars for the year ended March 22, 2003. Sales exclude Sam's Club. The fastest growing categories during this period (sales compared to previous time period a year ago) were scotch (1366.3%), dessert wine (241.9%) and breakfast bars (150%).

Fresh milk	$ 1,091,850.34
Produce, fresh	1,057,769.13
Cereal, ready-to-eat	1,009,249.68
Dog food, dry	1,006,368.31
Cookies	696,236.37
Bread, fresh	650,748.01
Chocolate candy	576,918.97
Cola, regular	564,268.53
Infant formula	520,778.96

Source: *Retail Merchandiser*, May 2003, p. 26, from ACNielsen Wal-Mart Channel Service.

★ 201 ★
Food
SIC: 2000; NAICS: 311611, 311615, 312111

Largest Food and Drink Firms Worldwide

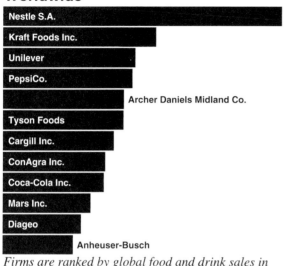

Nestle S.A.
Kraft Foods Inc.
Unilever
PepsiCo.
Archer Daniels Midland Co.
Tyson Foods
Cargill Inc.
ConAgra Inc.
Coca-Cola Inc.
Mars Inc.
Diageo
Anheuser-Busch

Firms are ranked by global food and drink sales in millions of dollars.

Nestle S.A.	$ 54,254
Kraft Foods Inc.	29,723
Unilever	25,670
PepsiCo.	25,112
Archer Daniels Midland Co.	23,454
Tyson Foods	23,367
Cargill Inc.	21,500
ConAgra Inc.	19,839
Coca-Cola Inc.	19,564
Mars Inc.	17,000
Diageo	15,137
Anheuser-Busch	13,566

Source: *Food Engineering*, November 2003, p. 30.

★ 202 ★
Food
SIC: 2000; NAICS: 31192, 31133, 325411

Largest Natural Food Categories, 2003

Categories are ranked in millions of dollars for the year ended January 25, 2003.

Vitamins and minerals	$ 1,507.9
Meal replacements and supplement powders	878.9
Produce, packaged fresh	842.0
Energy bars and gels	602.0
Bottled water	593.4
Carbonated beverages and single-serve drinks	560.6
Non-dairy beverages	367.3
Diet formulas	358.4
Teas	350.3

Source: *Supermarket News*, December 29, 2003, p. 19, from ACNielsen Scantrack and Spins Naturaltrack.

★ 203 ★
Food
SIC: 2000; NAICS: 311812, 31152, 311511

Largest Private Label Food Categories

Studies show that 15-20% of shoppers primarily purchase private label products for their grocery needs. In 2002, private label had the lead volume share in 25% of categories, up from 21% in 1997. Sales are shown in millions of dollars.

Milk	$ 6,500.0
Bread and rolls, fresh	2,300.0
Natural cheese	2,000.0
Eggs, fresh	1,700.0
Ice cream/sherbert	1,100.0
Beverages, carbonated	848.5
Vegetables	746.6
Vegetables, frozen and plain	702.0
Juices/drinks, refrigerated	633.3
Sugar	628.0
Juices, bottled shelf-stable	624.9

Source: *Grocery Headquarters*, November 2003, p. 14, from *Private Label Manufacturers Association 2003 Private Label Yearbook.*

★ 204 ★

Food

SIC: 2000; NAICS: 311421

Leading Fruits and Vegetable Processors, 2002

Companies are ranked by fruit and beverage sales in millions of dollars.

ConAgra Specialty Foods	$ 1,500.0
Simplot Food Group	1,300.0
McCain Foods	900.0
Dole Foods	732.0
Fresh Express (div. of Performance Group)	716.0
Agrilink Foods	687.0
H.J. Heinz Co.	650.0
General Mills Inc.	640.0
Ready Pac Foods	400.0
Seneca Foods Corp.	303.2

Source: *Refrigerated and Frozen Foods*, February 2003, p. 12.

★ 205 ★

Food

SIC: 2000; NAICS: 311999

Leading Meal/Entree Producers

Companies are ranked by meals and entree sales in millions of dollars.

Nestle USA	$ 3,200.0
ConAgra Foods Inc.	2,800.0
Kraft Foods Inc.	1,900.0
The Schwan Food Co.	1,100.0
H.J. Heinz	539.0
Kellogg Co.	448.5
General Mills Inc.	426.0
Pinnacle Food Corp.	415.0
Luigino's Inc.	400.0
Tyson Foods	250.0

Source: *Refrigerated and Frozen Foods*, February 2003, p. 12.

★ 206 ★

Food

SIC: 2000; NAICS: 311412

Leading Snack/Appetizer/Side Dish Producers, 2002

Companies are ranked by snack, appetizer and side dish sales in millions of dollars.

McCain Snack Foods	$ 600.0
H.J. Heinz Co.	495.0
Kraft Foods Inc.	395.0
Reser's Fine Foods	365.0
Chef Solutions Inc.	360.0
ConAgra Foods Inc.	280.0
J&J Snack Foods	250.0
General Mills Inc.	214.2
Specialty Brands	145.0
Rich-SeaPak Corp.	140.0

Source: *Refrigerated and Frozen Foods*, February 2003, p. 12.

★ 207 ★

Food

SIC: 2000; NAICS: 311513, 311812, 311421

Luncheon Foods Sales in the United Kingdom, 2002

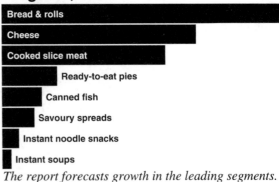

The report forecasts growth in the leading segments. Bread and roll sales will increase from 2,410 in 2003 to 2,555 in 2007 (in pounds sterling). Cheese will increase from 1,671 to 1,844. Cooked sliced meats from 1,392 to 1,696.

Bread & rolls	36.0%
Cheese	25.0
Cooked slice meat	21.0
Ready-to-eat pies	7.0

Continued on next page.

★ 207 ★

[Continued]
Food
SIC: 2000; NAICS: 311513, 311812, 311421

Luncheon Foods Sales in the United Kingdom, 2002

The report forecasts growth in the leading segments. Bread and roll sales will increase from 2,410 in 2003 to 2,555 in 2007 (in pounds sterling). Cheese will increase from 1,671 to 1,844. Cooked sliced meats from 1,392 to 1,696.

Canned fish	5.0%
Savoury spreads	4.0
Instant noodle snacks	2.0
Instant soups	1.0

Source: *Brand Strategy*, April 2004, p. 20, from Mintel.

★ 208 ★

Food
SIC: 2000; NAICS: 311511, 311513, 311612

Refrigerated Food Sales at Wal-Mart Supercenters

Sales are shown for the 52 weeks ended December 28, 2002.

Milk, fresh	$ 1,064.57
Produce, fresh	1,012.47
Lunch meat, sliced	484.54
Beer	469.00
Sausage	301.68
Orange juice	258.62
Yogurt	255.73
Natural cheese	240.79
Cheese, sliced processed	236.24
Cheese, shredded, grated	232.76

Source: *Frozen Food Age*, May 2003, p. 1, from ACNielsen's Homescan Panel.

★ 209 ★

Food
SIC: 2000; NAICS: 311422, 311999

Thanksgiving Food Sales

Figures show sales of Thanksgiving items for the week ended November 30, 2002. Sales of electric knifes and peelers hit $261,163 and oven bag sales were $5,803,146. In a typical supermarket week, fresh cranberry sales were $541,361, canned sweet potatoes and yams were $1.2 million and eggnog was $1.9 million.

Stuffing products	$ 38,135,794
Canned cranberries	18,449,321
Fresh & canned eggnog	13,965,423
Canned onions	12,106,780
Canned pumpkin	10,378,532
Canned sweet potatoes and yams . . .	10,295,464
Fresh (UPC-coded) cranberries	8,276,021
Canned mincemeat	907,151

Source: *Business Wire*, November 18, 2003, p. NA, from ACNielsen.

★ 210 ★

Functional Foods
SIC: 2000; NAICS: 312111, 31123, 311421

European Functional Foods Market, 2003 and 2007

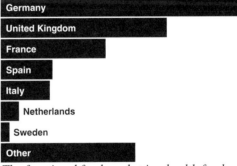

The functional food market is a health food sector. In Europe this sector measured 2 billion United Kingdom pounds sterling in 2003.

	2003 (mil.)	2007 (mil.)	Share
Germany	£ 298	£ 412	33.66%
United Kingdom	179	256	20.92
France	112	163	13.32
Spain	54	80	6.54

Continued on next page.

★ 210 ★
[Continued]
Functional Foods
SIC: 2000; NAICS: 312111, 31123, 311421

European Functional Foods Market, 2003 and 2007

The functional food market is a health food sector. In Europe this sector measured 2 billion United Kingdom pounds sterling in 2003.

	2003 (mil.)	2007 (mil.)	Share
Italy	£ 51	£ 71	5.80%
Netherlands	18	27	2.21
Sweden	8	11	0.90
Other	144	204	16.67

Source: *Nutraceuticals International*, January 2004, p. NA, from Datamonitor.

★ 211 ★
Functional Foods
SIC: 2000; NAICS: 312111, 31123, 311421

Functional Food Market

Analysts often give vague definitions about what constitutes functional foods. The source describes the industry as any food which claims to have health benefits (this claim may or may not be proven to be accurate). Because of the broad definition the size of the market can be difficult. Estimates are shown in millions of dollars below.

	($ mil.)	Share
Breakfast cereals	$ 5,000	23.17%
Orange juice	3,900	18.07
Other juices and waters	3,000	13.90
Soy foods	2,500	11.58
Meal replacements	2,300	10.66
Sports drinks	2,100	9.73
Nutrition bars	1,700	7.88
Energy drinks	800	3.71
Yogurts and dairy	200	0.93
Cholesterol-lowering spreads	80	0.37

Source: *just-food.com (Management Briefing)*, September 2003, p. 18, from *New Nutrition Business* estimate.

★ 212 ★
Organic Foods
SIC: 2000; NAICS: 311421, 111219, 311612

Organic Food Industry in Germany

According to one source, organic food refers to "produce that has been certified to have been grown free of chemicals." The market was valued at $2.1 billion in 1998, $2.5 billion in 2000 and $3.5 billion in 2002.

Fruit & vegetables	29.70%
Dairy food	27.60
Bakery & cereals	26.30
Juices	21.00
Meat	11.20
Ready meals	0.03
Other	2.90

Source: *Datamonitor Industry Market Research*, October 1, 2003, p. NA, from Datamonitor.

★ 213 ★
Organic Foods
SIC: 2000; NAICS: 311421, 111219, 311612

Organic Food Industry in the Netherlands

The Netherlands represented 4.4% of the European organic food market in terms of value. Organic farms represent about 1.4% of all the farms in the country.

Dairy food	33.90%
Fruit & vegetables	29.40
Bakery & cereals	26.30
Meat	4.90
Juices	2.30
Ready meals	0.02
Other	2.90

Source: *Datamonitor Industry Market Research*, October 1, 2003, p. NA, from Datamonitor.

★ 214 ★
Organic Foods
SIC: 2000; NAICS: 311421, 111219, 311612

Popular Organic Products

According to the survey, 54% of Americans said they had tried organic foods and 29% claimed to consume more organic foods and beverages than a year ago. Data are based on a survey of 1,084 adults.

Produce	72.0%
Bread or bakery	30.0
Non-dairy beverages	29.0
Packaged goods	24.0
Dairy	23.0
Meat	19.0
Frozen foods	17.0
Prepared foods and ready-to-go meals	12.0
Baby food	7.0

Source: *Supermarket News*, November 10, 2003, p. 22, from *2003 Whole Foods Market Organic Foods Trend Tracker* and Synovate.

★ 215 ★
Meat
SIC: 2011; NAICS: 311611

Beef Production by State

Production is shown in billions of dollars.

Texas	$ 5.9
Nebraska	5.0
Kansas	4.8
Colorado	2.8
Oklahoma	1.9
Iowa	1.8
South Dakota	1.5
California	1.2
Idaho	1.0
Minnesota	0.9

Source: *USA TODAY*, December 26, 2003, p. B1, from United States Department of Agriculture.

★ 216 ★
Meat
SIC: 2011; NAICS: 311611, 311615

Meat and Poultry Production Worldwide, 2002

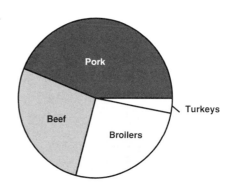

Global production stood at 187 million tons. Figures exclude sheep meat totaling 11 million tons.

Pork	44.0%
Beef	27.0
Broilers	26.0
Turkeys	3.0

Source: *Watt PoultryUSA*, November 2003, p. 26.

★ 217 ★
Meat
SIC: 2011; NAICS: 311611

Top Beef Producers

Companies are ranked by share of commercial slaughter.

Tyson Foods	27.7%
Excel Corp.	20.1
Swift & Co.	15.3
Farmland National	7.9
Smithfield Foods	5.5
Other	23.5

Source: *Feedstuffs*, June 16, 2003, p. 1, from *Cattle Buyers Weekly*.

★ 218 ★
Meat
SIC: 2011; NAICS: 311611

Top Meat Packers, 2002

The top five companies slaughter and package over three quarters of all beef consumed in the United States.

IBP/Tyson	27.1%
Excel/Cargill	20.6
Swift	16.1
Farmland National Beef	7.8
Smithfield	6.6
Other	21.8

Source: "Big Beef." [online] from http://www.oligopolywatch.com/2003/10/04.html [accessed November 19, 2003], from Illinois Farm Bureau figures.

★ 219 ★
Meat
SIC: 2011; NAICS: 311611

U.S. Beef Imports, 2002

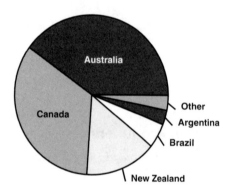

Imports represent 20% of all beef sales in the country.

Australia	40.0%
Canada	34.0
New Zealand	15.0
Brazil	5.0
Argentina	3.0
Other	3.0

Source: *Christian Science Monitor*, April 14, 2003, p. 20, from U.S. Department of Agriculture.

★ 220 ★
Bacon
SIC: 2013; NAICS: 311612

Top Refrigerated Bacon Brands, 2004

Market shares are shown based on sales at supermarkets, drugstores and mass merchandisers (but not Wal-Mart) for the year ended January 25, 2004.

Oscar Mayer	18.92%
Hormel Black Label	6.65
Bar-S	3.42
Farmland	3.41
Gwaltney	3.24
Smithfield	3.11
Wright	2.95
Louis Rich	2.45
Other	55.85

Source: *Grocery Headquarters*, April 2004, p. 16, from Information Resources Inc.

★ 221 ★
Bacon
SIC: 2013; NAICS: 311612

Top Refrigerated Bacon Makers, 2004

Market shares are shown based on sales at supermarkets, drugstores and mass merchandisers (but not Wal-Mart) for the year ended January 25, 2004.

Kraft/Oscar Mayer	18.94%
Hormel Foods	10.23
Gwaltney of Smithfield	4.02
Farmland Foods	3.76
Private label	18.46
Other	44.59

Source: *Grocery Headquarters*, April 2004, p. 16, from Information Resources Inc.

★ 222 ★
Hot Dogs
SIC: 2013; NAICS: 311612

Top Hot Dog Brands, 2003

Market shares are shown based on sales at supermarkets, drugstores and mass merchandisers (but not Wal-Mart) for the year ended May 18, 2003.

Oscar Mayer Rfg. Frankfurters	19.6%
Ball Park Rfg. Frankfurters	16.4
Bar-S Rfg. Frankfurters	6.1

Continued on next page.

★ **222** ★

[Continued]
Hot Dogs
SIC: 2013; NAICS: 311612

Top Hot Dog Brands, 2003

Market shares are shown based on sales at super-markets, drugstores and mass merchandisers (but not Wal-Mart) for the year ended May 18, 2003.

Hebrew National	4.5%
Nathan	3.3
Bryan	3.1
Armour	2.8
Eckrich	2.3
Kahns	2.0
Private label	6.0
Other	33.9

Source: *National Provisioner*, July 2003, p. 32, from Information Resources Inc.

★ **223** ★

Hot Dogs
SIC: 2013; NAICS: 311612

Top Hot Dog Makers, 2004

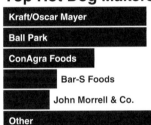

Market shares are shown based on sales at super-markets, drugstores and mass merchandisers (but not Wal-Mart) for the year ended January 25, 2004.

Kraft/Oscar Mayer	18.90%
Ball Park	18.55
ConAgra Foods	11.78
Bar-S Foods	7.13
John Morrell & Co.	6.38
Other	37.26

Source: *Grocery Headquarters*, April 2004, p. 16, from Information Resources Inc.

★ **224** ★

Lunch Meat
SIC: 2013; NAICS: 311612

Lunch Meat Sales by Year

Figures show sales of packaged, refrigerated and sliced lunch meat in millions of dollars. The 2002 figure is estimated.

2002	$ 3,186
2001	3,128
2000	3,050
1999	2,945

Source: *Prepared Foods*, May 2003, p. 21, from Mintel International Group.

★ **225** ★

Lunch Meat
SIC: 2013; NAICS: 311612

Top Deli Brands

Brands are ranked by sales at supermarket delis in millions of dollars.

Oscar Mayer sliced lunchmeat	$ 819.00
Oscar Mayer Lunchables	601.43
Private label sliced lunchmeat	472.25
Hillshire Farm dinner sausage	388.16
Private label bacon	361.17
Oscar Mayer bacon	349.86
Oscar Mayer frankfurters	325.48
Ball Park frankfurters	282.38
Jimmy Dean breakfast sausage	222.33
Private label uncooked meats	213.38

Source: *Frozen Food Age*, May 2003, p. 1, from ACNielsen.

★ **226** ★

Lunch Meat
SIC: 2013; NAICS: 311612

Top Lunch Meat (Refrigerated) Brands, 2003

Market shares are shown based on sales at super-markets, drug stores and mass merchandisers (but not Wal-Mart) for the year ended September 7, 2003. Total sales of sliced, refrigerated lunch meat were $3.08 billion.

Oscar Mayer	25.7%
Butterball	5.1
Hillshire Farm Deli Selects	4.8

Continued on next page.

★ 226 ★

[Continued]
Lunch Meat
SIC: 2013; NAICS: 311612

Top Lunch Meat (Refrigerated) Brands, 2003

Market shares are shown based on sales at super-markets, drug stores and mass merchandisers (but not Wal-Mart) for the year ended September 7, 2003. Total sales of sliced, refrigerated lunch meat were $3.08 billion.

Buddig	3.9%
Louis Rich	2.9
Land O Frost Premium	2.4
Bar S	2.3
Hormel	2.0
Bryan	1.9
Private label	15.5
Other	33.5

Source: *National Provisioner*, November 2003, p. 10, from Information Resources Inc.

★ 227 ★

Lunch Meat
SIC: 2013; NAICS: 311612

Top Lunch Meat (Refrigerated Non-Sliced) Brands

Market shares are shown based on sales for super-markets, drug stores and mass merchandisers (but not Wal-Mart) for the year ended May 18, 2003.

Hickory Farms	8.5%
Oscar Mayer	4.9
Hebrew National	4.4
Hillshire Farm	4.3
John Morrell	4.1
Farmland	3.7
Old Wisconsin	3.5
Kahns	3.5
Johnsonville	3.4
Private label	4.3
Other	55.4

Source: *National Provisioner*, August 2003, p. 52, from Information Resources Inc.

★ 228 ★

Lunch Meat
SIC: 2013; NAICS: 311612

Top Lunch Meat (Sliced, Refrigerated) Makers, 2004

Market shares are shown based on sales at super-markets, drugstores and mass merchandisers (but not Wal-Mart) for the year ended January 25, 2004.

Kraft/Oscar Mayer	25.69%
ConAgra Foods	11.40
Hillshire Farm & Kahns	5.57
Carl Buddig & Co.	4.35
Private label	15.18
Other	37.81

Source: *Grocery Headquarters*, April 2004, p. 16, from Information Resources Inc.

★ 229 ★

Meat Snacks
SIC: 2013; NAICS: 311612

Meat Snack Sales, 2002

Sales reached $2.22 billion in 2002, up from $1.74 billion in 2000. Sales are projected to climb $3 billion. The snacks have enjoyed being a part of the low-carb diet craze.

	($ mil.)	Share
Regular	$910	40.97%
Hot & spicy	533	24.00
Smoked	433	19.50
Teriyaki	178	8.01
Other	167	7.52

Source: *Prepared Foods*, October 2003, p. 25, from Mintel.

★ 230 ★
Meat Snacks
SIC: 2013; NAICS: 311612

Top Dried-Snack Meat Brands, 2003

Market shares are shown for supermarkets, drug stores and mass merchandisers (excluding Wal-Mart) for the year ended September 7, 2003.

Oberto	21.7%
Slim Jim	15.8
Jack Links	15.7
Pemmican	11.0
Bridgford	7.9
Other	27.9

Source: *National Provisioner*, October 2003, p. 48, from Information Resources Inc.

★ 231 ★
Sausage
SIC: 2013; NAICS: 311612

Leading Ham/Sausage Makers in Japan, 2002

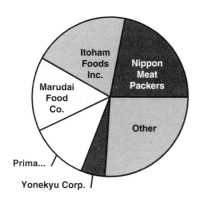

Market shares are shown based on domestic sales of 530,250 tons.

Nippon Meat Packers	21.6%
Itoham Foods Inc.	20.4
Marudai Food Co.	14.9
Prima Meat Packers	11.8
Yonekyu Corp.	5.0
Other	26.3

Source: "Market Share Survey Report 2002." [online] from http://www.nni.nikkei.co.jp [accessed January 20, 2004], from Nikkei estimate and Agriculture Ministry, Japan.

★ 232 ★
Sausage
SIC: 2013; NAICS: 311612

Top Frozen Sausage Brands, 2003

Brands are ranked by sales for the year ended June 15, 2003.

	($ mil.)	Share
Swift Premium Brown & Serve	$ 93.53	44.03%
Johnsonville	40.87	19.24
Jones	13.28	6.25
Jones Golden Brown	11.51	5.42
Swift Premium Brown n Serve Lite	8.07	3.80
Butterball	3.98	1.87
Jimmy Dean Smokehouse	3.87	1.82
Hormel Jennie-O	1.87	0.88
Private label	23.89	11.25
Other	11.53	5.43

Source: *Frozen Food Age*, August 2003, p. 32, from Information Resources Inc.

★ 233 ★
Sausage
SIC: 2013; NAICS: 311612

Top Refrigerated Dinner Sausage Brands, 2003

Brand shares are shown for the 52 weeks ended May 18, 2003. Sales include supermarkets, drug and mass merchandisers but not Wal-Mart.

Hillshire Farm	25.0%
Johnsonville	10.2
Eckrich	7.6
Bryan	2.7
Bar-S	1.6
John Morrell	1.4
Premio	1.2
Hillshire Farm Liti Beef Smokies	1.2
Butterball	1.2
Private label	7.8
Other	40.1

Source: *National Provisioner*, July 2003, p. 36, from Information Resources Inc.

★ 234 ★
Sausage
SIC: 2013; NAICS: 311612

Top Refrigerated Sausage Brands, 2003

Brands are ranked by sales for the year ended June 15, 2003.

	($ mil.)	Share
Jimmy Dean	$ 217.46	24.01%
Bob Evans	118.71	13.11
Tennessee Pride	51.24	5.66
Jimmy Dean Fresh Taste Fast	41.72	4.61
Johnsonville	41.10	4.54
Farmer John	34.39	3.80
Owens	26.34	2.91
Hormel Little Sizzler	25.15	2.78
Purnell Old Folks	22.41	2.47
Private label	59.26	6.54
Other	267.84	29.58

Source: *Frozen Food Age*, August 2003, p. 32, from Information Resources Inc.

★ 235 ★
Chicken
SIC: 2015; NAICS: 311615

Chicken Purchases

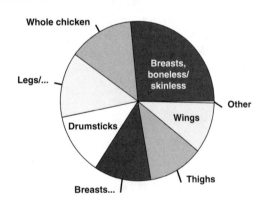

Data show how chicken is purchased in supermarkets. Figures are based on a survey.

Breasts, boneless/skinless	65.6%
Whole chicken	33.6
Legs/leg quarters	32.8
Drumsticks	31.1
Breasts, bone-in/skin-on	29.7

Thighs	29.4%
Wings	26.0
Other	1.0

Source: *Supermarket News*, October 13, 2003, p. 41, from National Chicken Council.

★ 236 ★
Chicken
SIC: 2015; NAICS: 311615

Largest Chicken Firms

Market shares are shown based on average weekly production.

	(mil.)	Share
Tyson Foods	145	22.7%
Pilgrim's Pride	106	16.6
Gold Kist	60	9.4
Perdue Farms	47	7.4
Wayne Poultry	28	4.4
Sanderson Farms	24	3.8
Fosters Farms	20	3.1
Mountaire Farms	18	2.8
Peco Foods	12	1.9
O.K. Foods	12	1.9
House of Raeford	12	1.9
George's	12	1.9
Fieldale Farms	12	1.9

Source: *Feedstuffs*, December 1, 2003, p. 1, from *Feedstuffs Reference Issue*.

★ 237 ★
Chicken
SIC: 2015; NAICS: 311615

Top Frozen Chicken/Chicken Substitute Brands, 2003

Brands are ranked by sales in millions of dollars for the 12 weeks ended June 15, 2003.

	($ mil.)	Share
Tyson	$ 95.60	21.42%
Banquet	39.64	8.88
Gold Kist Farms	15.19	3.40
Barber	12.78	2.86
Private label	125.62	28.15
Other	157.41	35.27

Source: *Frozen Food Age*, September 2003, p. 12, from Information Resources Inc.

★ 238 ★
Egg Substitutes
SIC: 2015; NAICS: 311615

Top Egg Substitute Brands, 2003

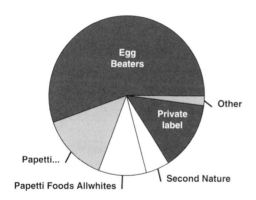

Brands are ranked by sales in millions of dollars for the 12 weeks ended May 18, 2003.

	($ mil.)	Share
Egg Beaters	$ 19.36	55.78%
Papetti Foods Better N Eggs	4.79	13.80
Papetti Foods Allwhites	3.40	9.80
Second Nature	1.74	5.01
Private label	4.69	13.51
Other	0.73	2.10

Source: *Frozen Food Age*, July 2003, p. 12, from Information Resources Inc.

★ 239 ★
Pork
SIC: 2015; NAICS: 311615

Largest Pork Processors

Companies are ranked by number of sows.

Smithfield Foods	756,226
Premium Standard Farms	225,000
Seaboard Farms	213,600
Prestage Farms	129,000
Cargill	118,000
The Pipestone System	100,000
Iowa Select Farms	100,000
Christensen Farms	94,000
Goldsboro Hog Farm	74,000
The Hanor Company	73,500
Tyson Foods	65,000
Land O'Lakes	62,900

Source: *Successful Farming*, October 2003, p. 38.

★ 240 ★
Pork
SIC: 2015; NAICS: 311615

Largest Pork Processors in Canada

Companies are ranked by number of sows.

Maple Leaf Foods	122,000
Premium Pork	47,000
Hytek	40,000
Isoporc	33,000
F. Menard	32,000
Big Sky Farms	26,000
The Puratone Corporation	25,000
Heartland Pork	18,000

Source: *Successful Farming*, October 2003, p. 38.

★ 241 ★
Pork
SIC: 2015; NAICS: 311615

Largest Pork Producers

Companies are ranked by share of industrywide kill capacity.

	Capacity	Share
Smithfield Foods	79,600	21.1%
Tyson Foods	67,600	18.0
Swift	39,500	10.5
Hormel Foods	31,700	8.4
Excel	29,500	7.8
Farmland Foods	22,000	5.8
Premium Standard Farms	19,000	5.0
Seaboard Farms	16,000	4.2
Indian Packers	13,000	3.5
Sara Lee	8,200	2.2

Source: *Feedstuffs*, July 21, 2003, p. 1, from Sterling Marketing Inc.

★ 242 ★
Poultry
SIC: 2015; NAICS: 311615

Poultry Sales, 2002

Per capita consumption is about 80.5 pounds per year for chicken, 67.6 pounds for beef and 51.5 pounds for pork.

Deboning for processing	43.0%
Foodservice	29.0
Retail	25.0

Source: *Meat Retailer*, December 2003, p. 26, from U.S. Department of Agriculture.

★ 243 ★
Dairy Products
SIC: 2020; NAICS: 311511, 311513, 311514

Dairy Industry Worldwide

Figures show percent of market value.

	1998	1999	2000
Western Europe	32.1%	31.2%	30.1%
Latin America	21.2	20.2	21.4
North America	19.9	20.9	20.3
Asia Pacific	11.9	13.5	13.9
Eastern Europe	8.8	8.1	8.1
Africa & Middle East	4.6	4.6	4.7
Australasia	1.5	1.6	1.6

Source: *Dairy Foods*, January 2002, p. 10, from Dairy Management Inc. and Euromonitor.

★ 244 ★
Dairy Products
SIC: 2020; NAICS: 311511, 311513, 311514

Dairy Products Market in Denmark, 2003

The company Arla Foods was created in 1999 when the two milk products cooperatives merged, MD Foods of Denmark and Arla of Sweden. Arla Foods produces nearly 2 billion gallons of milk annually.

Arla Foods	92.0%
Other	8.0

Source: *America's Intelligence Wire*, March 31, 2004, p. NA.

★ 245 ★
Dairy Products
SIC: 2020; NAICS: 311511, 311513, 311514
Private Label Dairy Products, 2003

Categories are ranked by dollar share for the year ending November 2, 2003.

Eggs, fresh	70.7%
Milk	62.1
Butter	46.3
Natural cheese	39.4
Cottage cheese	37.9
Baked goods	37.6
Cheesecakes	33.9
Sour cream	30.5
Cream cheese/cream cheese spreads	29.8

Source: *Progressive Grocer*, January 1, 2004, p. 55, from Information Resources Inc.

★ 246 ★
Dairy Products
SIC: 2020; NAICS: 311511, 311513, 311514
Top Dairy Brands in Inner Mongolia

Market shares are shown as of September 2003.

Yili	17.7%
Mengniu	15.0
Bright Dairy	14.0
Other	53.3

Source: *Business Daily Update*, December 16, 2003, p. NA, from ACNielsen.

★ 247 ★
Dairy Products
SIC: 2020; NAICS: 311511, 311513, 311514
Top Dairy Brands in Supermarkets, 2002

Brands are ranked by sales at supermaret dairy departments in millions of dollars. Figures are for the year ended December 29, 2002.

Private label skim/lowfat milk	$ 4,185.89
Private label whole milk	2,099.51
Private label eggs	1,661.19
Private label natual cheese	999.94

Private label natural shredded cheese	$ 821.70
Fresh Express fresh-cut salad	688.98
Dole fresh-cut salad	612.05
Minute Maid Premium orange juice	598.14
Private label butter	569.83
Private label orange juice	555.98

Source: *Frozen Food Age*, May 2003, p. 1, from ACNielsen.

★ 248 ★
Butter
SIC: 2021; NAICS: 311512
Top Butter Brands, 2004

Market shares are shown based on sales at supermarkets, drugstores and mass merchandisers (but not Wal-Mart) for the year ended January 25, 2004.

Land O'Lakes	30.24%
Challenge	4.91
Breakstone	2.33
Tillamook	2.11
Kellers	1.74
Crystal Farms	1.65
Hotel Bar	1.59
Cabot	1.15
Other	34.28

Source: *Grocery Headquarters*, April 2004, p. 16, from Information Resources Inc.

★ 249 ★

Butter

SIC: 2021; NAICS: 311512

Top Butter Makers, 2004

Market shares are shown based on sales at super-markets, drugstores and mass merchandisers (but not Wal-Mart) for the year ended January 25, 2004.

Land O'Lakes	30.27%
Kellers Creamery	5.94
Challenge Dairy Products	5.33
Tillamook Country Creamery	2.11
Private label	45.35
Other	11.00

Source: *Grocery Headquarters*, April 2004, p. 16, from Information Resources Inc.

★ 250 ★

Margarine

SIC: 2021; NAICS: 311512

Top Margarine/Spread/Butter Blend Brands, 2004

Market shares are shown based on sales at super-markets, drugstores and mass merchandisers (but not Wal-Mart) for the year ended January 25, 2004.

I Can't Believe It's Not Butter	15.93%
Shedds Country Crock	15.02
Parkay	8.49
Blue Bonnet	6.84
Land O'Lakes	5.80
Imperial	5.05
I Can't Believe It's Not Butter	4.81
Fleischmanns	4.51
Brummel & Brown	3.24
Private label	8.97
Other	21.34

Source: *Grocery Headquarters*, April 2004, p. 16, from Information Resources Inc.

★ 251 ★

Margarine

SIC: 2021; NAICS: 311512

Top Margarine/Spread/Butter Blend Makers, 2004

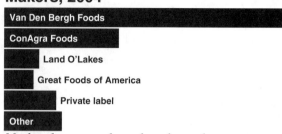

Market shares are shown based on sales at super-markets, drugstores and mass merchandisers (but not Wal-Mart) for the year ended January 25, 2004.

Van Den Bergh Foods	48.93%
ConAgra Foods	20.42
Land O'Lakes	6.12
Great Foods of America	5.12
Private label	8.97
Other	10.44

Source: *Grocery Headquarters*, April 2004, p. 16, from Information Resources Inc.

★ 252 ★

Cheese

SIC: 2022; NAICS: 311513

Top American Cheese Brands, 2003

Brands are ranked by supermarket sales in millions of dollars for the year ended August 10, 2003.

	($ mil.)	Share
Kraft Singles	$ 538.00	29.89%
Kraft Velvetta	296.42	16.47
Borden	124.79	6.93
Kraft Deli Deluxe	110.94	6.16
Private label	450.14	25.01
Other	279.88	15.55

Source: *Frozen Food Age*, October 2003, p. 48, from Information Resources Inc.

★ 253 ★

Cheese

SIC: 2022; NAICS: 311513

Top American Cheese Makers, 2004

Market shares are shown based on sales at super-markets, drugstores and mass merchandisers (but not Wal-Mart) for the year ended January 25, 2004.

Kraft Foods	60.32%
American Dairy Brands	7.42
Land O'Lakes Inc.	2.10
Crystal Farms Inc.	1.31
Private label	24.47
Other	4.38

Source: *Grocery Headquarters*, April 2004, p. 16, from Information Resources Inc.

★ 254 ★

Cheese

SIC: 2022; NAICS: 311513

Top Cheese Brands in the U.K., 2003

Brands are ranked by sales in thousands of pounds sterling for the year ended October 4, 2003.

	(000)	Share
Cathedral City Cheddar	£ 52,445	9.68%
Philadelphia	34,717	6.41
McLelland Cheddar	32,793	6.06
Pilgrims Choice Cheddar	18,701	3.45
Anchor Cheddar	7,319	1.35
Boursin	7,243	1.34
Cheese Co. Cheddar	4,084	0.75
Port Salut	3,592	0.66
Other	380,671	70.29

Source: *Grocer*, December 13, 2003, p. 66, from Information Resources Inc.

★ 255 ★

Cheese

SIC: 2022; NAICS: 311513

Top Cheese Vendors, 2003

Market shares are shown based on supermarket sales for the year ended August 10, 2003.

Kraft Foods	19.9%
Tillamook Country Creamery	6.0
Sorrento Cheese Co.	3.8
Sargento Food Co.	3.5
Private label	36.5
Other	30.3

Source: *Refrigerated & Frozen Foods*, October 2003, p. 60, from Information Resources Inc. InfoScan.

★ 256 ★

Cheese

SIC: 2022; NAICS: 311513

Top Natural Cheese Brands, 2003

Brands are ranked by sales at supermarkets, drug stores and mass merchandisers (but not Wal-Mart) for the year ended September 7, 2003.

	($ mil.)	Share
Private label (Not Shredded) . . .	$ 1,102	20.39%
Private label (Shredded)	869	16.08
Kraft Shredded	483	8.94
Kraft Natural (Not Shredded) . . .	283	5.24
Tillamook (Not Shredded)	182	3.37
Kraft SS Grated	145	2.68
Kraft Cracker Barrel (Not Shredded)	103	1.91
Sargento (Not Shredded)	93	1.72
Sargento Shredded	89	1.65

Continued on next page.

★ 256 ★
[Continued]
Cheese
SIC: 2022; NAICS: 311513

Top Natural Cheese Brands, 2003

Brands are ranked by sales at supermarkets, drug stores and mass merchandisers (but not Wal-Mart) for the year ended September 7, 2003.

	($ mil.)	Share
Sargento Fancy Shredded	$ 71	1.31%
Other	1,984	36.71

Source: *Dairy Foods*, November 2003, p. 34, from Information Resources Inc.

★ 257 ★
Cheese Spreads
SIC: 2022; NAICS: 311513

Top Cheese Spead/Ball Brands, 2003

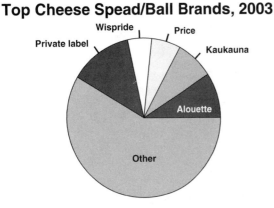

Brands are ranked by sales in millions of dollars for the 12 weeks ended May 18, 2003.

	($ mil.)	Share
Alouette	$ 5.19	9.27%
Kaukauna	4.65	8.31
Price	3.60	6.43
Wispride	2.78	4.97
Private label	7.35	13.13
Other	32.40	57.89

Source: *Frozen Food Age*, July 2003, p. 12, from Information Resources Inc.

★ 258 ★
Dips
SIC: 2022; NAICS: 311513

Prepared Dip Market in New Zealand

Market shares are shown for the $20 million category.

Country Goodness	60.0%
Other	40.0

Source: *Grocer's Review*, November 2003, p. NA, from ACNielsen.

★ 259 ★
Condensed Milk
SIC: 2023; NAICS: 311514

Top Condensed Milk Makers in Brazil, 2003

Brazil is the main consumer of condensed milk in the world. Market shares are shown for August 2003.

Itambe	15.0%
Mococa	11.0
Gloria	9.0
Parmalat	8.0
Elege	7.0
Other	50.0

Source: *America's Intelligence Wire*, October 3, 2003, p. NA.

★ 260 ★
Powdered Milk
SIC: 2023; NAICS: 311514

Leading Powdered Milk Makers in Thailand

The industry is valued at 1 billion baht annually.

Nestle	30.0%
Mead Johnson	20.0
Dumex	20.0
Other	30.0

Source: *Bangkok Post*, March 12, 2003, p. NA.

★ 261 ★
Chilled Deserts
SIC: 2024; NAICS: 31152

Chilled Desert Market in Western Europe

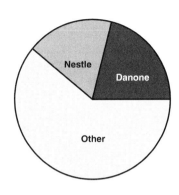

Market shares are shown in percent.

Danone 21.2%
Nestle 18.2
Other 60.6

Source: *Eurofood*, May 23, 2002, p. 6.

★ 262 ★
Frozen Desserts
SIC: 2024; NAICS: 31152

Frozen Dessert Industry

Sales are shown by segment.

Ice cream 92.0%
Frozen yogurt 5.0
Sherbets and ice milk 3.0

Source: *The Tampa Tribune*, November 3, 2003, p. 12, from Information Resources Inc.

★ 263 ★
Frozen Desserts
SIC: 2024; NAICS: 31152

Frozen Dessert Sales, 2003

Total sales were $1.16 billion.

	($ mil.)	Share
Whipped topping	$ 365	31.33%
Pie	362	31.07
Cake & pastry	342	29.36
Cheesecake	92	7.90
Mousse and pudding	4	0.34

Source: *Prepared Foods*, April 2004, p. 15, from Information Resources inc. InfoScan.

★ 264 ★
Frozen Desserts
SIC: 2024; NAICS: 311512

Leading Frozen Dessert Makers, 2003

Companies are ranked by sales in millions of dollars. Sales are down about 5% form 2001 as the industry faces more competition and consumers turn away from carbohydrate and sugar rich products.

	($ mil.)	Share
Schwan Foods Co.	$ 264	11.31%
Kraft	262	11.22
Mrs. Smiths	197	8.44
Sara Lee	180	7.71
Campbell Soup Co.	75	3.21
Edwards	68	2.91
Private label	124	5.31
Other	1,165	49.89

Source: *Prepared Foods*, April 2004, p. 15, from Information Resources Inc. InfoScan.

★ 265 ★
Frozen Desserts
SIC: 2024; NAICS: 31152

Top Frozen Dessert Brands, 2004

Market shares are shown based on sales at super-markets, drugstores and mass merchandisers (but not Wal-Mart) for the year ended January 25, 2004.

Klondike 6.95%
Silhouette 5.03
Nestle Drumstick 4.66

Continued on next page.

★ 265 ★

[Continued]
Frozen Desserts
SIC: 2024; NAICS: 31152

Top Frozen Dessert Brands, 2004

*Market shares are shown based on sales at super-
markets, drugstores and mass merchandisers (but not
Wal-Mart) for the year ended January 25, 2004.*

Popsicle	4.28%
Weight Watchers Smart Ones	4.23
Carvel	3.01
Haagen Dazs	1.98
Private label	14.47
Other	55.39

Source: *Grocery Headquarters*, April 2004, p. 16, from Information Resources Inc.

★ 266 ★

Frozen Desserts
SIC: 2024; NAICS: 311512

Top Frozen Novelty Makers, 2004

*Market shares are shown based on sales at super-
markets, drugstores and mass merchandisers (but not
Wal-Mart) for the year ended January 25, 2004.*

Good Humor/Breyers	21.91%
Ice Cream Partners USA	9.49
Silhouette Brands Inc.	5.16
Masterfoods USA	4.62
Private label	14.47
Other	44.35

Source: *Grocery Headquarters*, April 2004, p. 16, from Information Resources Inc.

★ 267 ★

Ice Cream
SIC: 2024; NAICS: 31152

Ice Cream Sales by Type

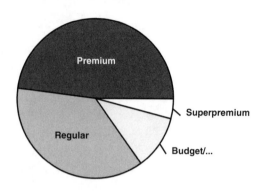

*The superpremium category has been growing in re-
cent years but still has only 4% of the market.*

Premium	48.0%
Regular	37.0
Budget/economy	11.0
Superpremium	4.0

Source: *Dairy Foods*, July 2003, p. 10, from International
Dairy Foods Association.

★ 268 ★

Ice Cream
SIC: 2024; NAICS: 31152

Top Ice Cream Brands, 2003

*Market shares are shown in percent based on
supermarket sales for the year ended August 10,
2003.*

Breyers	14.8%
Dreyers Edy's Grand	10.3
Blue Bell	5.1
Haagen Dazs	4.6
Ben & Jerrys	4.4
Turkey Hill	2.5
Wells Blue Bunny	2.5
Healthy Choice	2.3
Dreyers Edy's Grand Light	2.2

Continued on next page.

★ 268 ★

[Continued]
Ice Cream
SIC: 2024; NAICS: 31152

Top Ice Cream Brands, 2003

Market shares are shown in percent based on supermarket sales for the year ended August 10, 2003.

Friendly	2.0%
Dreyers Edy's	1.9
Private label	22.5
Other	24.9

Source: *Supermarket News*, September 15, 2003, p. 16, from Information Resources Inc.

★ 269 ★

Ice Cream
SIC: 2024; NAICS: 31152

Top Ice Cream Brands in the U.K., 2003

Brands are ranked by sales in thousands of pounds sterling for the year ended October 4, 2003.

	(000)	Share
Wall's Magnum	£ 86,763	9.73%
Wall's Cornetto	46,455	5.21
Haagen-Dazs	43,059	4.83
Care d'Or	42,529	4.77
Ben & Jerry's	35,921	4.03
Mars	28,726	3.22
Solero	26,558	2.98
Wall's Blue Ribbon	22,746	2.55
Wall's Caippo	21,068	2.36
Other	538,136	60.33

Source: *Grocer*, December 13, 2003, p. 66, from Information Resources Inc.

★ 270 ★

Ice Cream
SIC: 2024; NAICS: 31152

Top Ice Cream Flavors, 2003

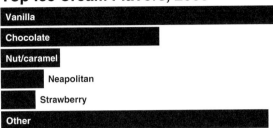

Data show percentage of flavors eaten during the year ended February 2003. Figures are based on 2,000 households.

Vanilla	33.0%
Chocolate	19.0
Nut/caramel	7.0
Neapolitan	5.0
Strawberry	4.0
Other	32.0

Source: *USA TODAY*, May 25, 2004, p. A1, from NPD Group's National Eating Trends Services.

★ 271 ★

Ice Cream
SIC: 2024; NAICS: 31152

Top Ice Cream Makers, 2004

Market shares are shown based on sales at supermarkets, drugstores and mass merchandisers (but not Wal-Mart) for the year ended January 25, 2004.

Dreyer's Grand	17.49%
Good Humor/Breyers	15.64
Blue Bell Creameries	5.23
Ice Cream Partners	4.45
Private label	20.35
Other	36.84

Source: *Grocery Headquarters*, April 2004, p. 16, from Information Resources Inc.

★ 272 ★
Ice Cream
SIC: 2024; NAICS: 31152
Top Ice Cream Makers in Israel, 2003

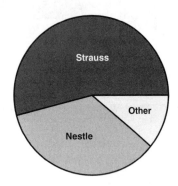

Shares are for the retail ice cream market and do not include institutions, kiosks, restaurants, and entertainment sites.

Strauss	54.0%
Nestle	34.9
Other	11.1

Source: *Haaretz*, March 21, 2004, p. NA, from ACNielsen.

★ 273 ★
Ice Cream
SIC: 2024; NAICS: 31152
Top Ice Cream Makers in Japan

Market shares are shown in percent.

Ezaki Glico	13.00%
Morinaga Milk Industry	12.32
Meiji Dairies	12.28
Other	62.40

Source: *Nikkei Weekly*, July 21, 2003, p. 1, from Nihon Keizai Shimbun.

★ 274 ★
Ice Cream
SIC: 2024; NAICS: 31152
Top Ice Cream Makers in Shanghai, China

The top five firms are Nestle, Mengniu Dairy Co. Ltd., Unilever's Wall, Bright Dairy & Food Co. Ltd. Yili Industrial Co.

Top 5 firms	85.0%
Other	15.0

Source: *Ice Cream Reporter*, April 20, 2004, p. 8.

★ 275 ★
Ice Cream
SIC: 2024; NAICS: 31152
Top Ice Cream Makers in South Africa, 2003

Shares are for ice cream sales in tubs during the period December 2002 through November 2003.

Nestle	49.0%
Ola	22.7
Other	28.3

Source: *Business Report*, March 31, 2004, p. PN, from ACNielsen.

★ 276 ★
Ice Cream
SIC: 2024; NAICS: 31152
Top Ice Cream (Pint) Makers

Market shares are shown in percent.

Ben & Jerry's	40.0%
Haagen-Dazs	40.0
Other	20.0

Source: *Daily Record*, April 23, 2004, p. NA.

★ 277 ★

Ice Cream

SIC: 2024; NAICS: 31152

Top Ice Cream Producing Nations, 2000

The introduction of premium brands in the 1980s brought significant change to the ice cream and frozen dessert market. Branding became important. Sales of frozen desserts and ice cream is a $20 billion industry in the United States alone. Production is shown in millions of hectoliters.

U.S.	61.3
China	23.6
Canada	5.4
Italy	4.6
Australia	3.3
France	3.2
Germany	3.1
Sweden	1.3
Switzerland	1.0
New Zealand	1.0

Source: *Dairy Industries International*, October 2002, p. 27, from U.S. Department of Agriculture, Foreign Agricultural Service.

★ 278 ★

Ice Cream

SIC: 2024; NAICS: 31152

Top Ice Cream/Sherbert Brands, 2003

Brands are ranked by sales in millions of dollars for the year ended December 28, 2003.

	($ mil.)	Share
Breyers	$ 659	13.36%
Dreyer's Edy's Grand	474	9.61
Blue Bell	242	4.91
Haagen Dazs	215	4.36
Ben & Jerry's	200	4.06
Wells' Blue Bunny	108	2.19
Turkey Hill	107	2.17
Dreyer's Edy's Grand Light	100	2.03
Healthy Choice	94	1.91
Private label	1,002	20.32
Other	1,730	35.08

Source: *Dairy Foods*, March 2004, p. 44, from Information Resources Inc.

★ 279 ★

Ice Cream

SIC: 2024; NAICS: 31152

Top Sherbert/Sorbet/Ice Brands, 2003

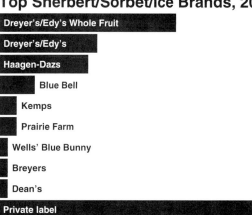

Brands are ranked by sales in millions of dollars for the year ended November 30, 2003.

	($ mil.)	Share
Dreyer's/Edy's Whole Fruit	$ 42.47	19.85%
Dreyer's/Edy's	23.79	11.12
Haagen-Dazs	21.26	9.94
Blue Bell	9.25	4.32
Kemps	4.98	2.33
Prairie Farm	3.45	1.61
Wells' Blue Bunny	3.14	1.47
Breyers	2.82	1.32
Dean's	2.58	1.21
Private label	66.48	31.07
Other	33.75	15.77

Source: *Frozen Food Age*, January 2004, p. 22, from Information Resources Inc.

★ 280 ★

Pudding

SIC: 2024; NAICS: 31152

Top Pudding/Gelatin Brands

Market shares are shown based on sales at supermarkets, drug stores and mass merchandisers for the 52 weeks ended May 18, 2003. Figures exclude Wal-Mart.

Hunt's Snack Packs	31.8%
Kraft Handi Snacks	22.2
Dole Fruit and Gel Bowls	14.5
Del Monte	4.6
Hunt's Snack Pack Dessert Favorites	3.9

Continued on next page.

★ 280 ★
[Continued]
Pudding
SIC: 2024; NAICS: 31152

Top Pudding/Gelatin Brands

*Market shares are shown based on sales at super-
markets, drug stores and mass merchandisers for the
52 weeks ended May 18, 2003. Figures exclude Wal-
Mart.*

Hunt's Snack Pack Juicy Gels	3.4%
Kraft Handi Snacks Gels	3.2
Hunt's Snack Pack Squeez 'n Go	2.5
Private label	6.7
Other	7.2

Source: *Dairy Field*, July 2003, p. 22, from Information
Resources Inc.

★ 281 ★
Pudding
SIC: 2024; NAICS: 31152

Top Pudding/Mousse/Gelatin/Parfait Brands

*Market shares are shown based on sales at super-
markets for the 52 weeks ended May 18, 2003.
Figures exclude Wal-Mart.*

Jell-O	23.5%
Kozy Shack	13.6
Jell-O Gelatin Snacks	12.3
Jell-O Free	11.0
Swiss Miss	8.0
Jell-O Extreme	5.0
Jell-O Creme Savers	4.7
Jolly Rancher	2.9
Hershey's	2.0
Private label	6.2
Other	10.8

Source: *Dairy Field*, July 2003, p. 22, from Information
Resources Inc.

★ 282 ★
Cottage Cheese
SIC: 2026; NAICS: 311514

Top Cottage Cheese Brands, 2004

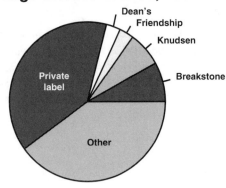

*Brands are ranked by unit sales for the 22 weeks
ended February 22, 2004.*

	(mil.)	Share
Breakstone	7.11	7.86%
Knudsen	6.14	6.79
Friendship	3.01	3.33
Dean's	2.61	2.89
Private label	35.06	38.76
Other	36.52	40.38

Source: *Frozen Food Age*, May 2004, p. 44, from Information Resources Inc.

★ 283 ★
Cream
SIC: 2026; NAICS: 311511

Fresh Cream Market in France

Market shares are shown in percent.

Lactalis	17.6%
Elle et Vire	12.9
Yoplait	12.4
Private label	36.1
Other	21.0

Source: *LSA*, April 11, 2002, p. NA, from ACNielsen.

★ 284 ★
Dairy Drinks
SIC: 2026; NAICS: 311511

Fermented Dairy Drinks Market in Africa and the Middle East, 2002

The fermented dairy drinks (for example, yogurt drinks) market grew at a rate of 9.3 percent worldwide in 2003. The table shows market shares for leaders in this market in Africa and the Middle East during 2002.

Danone Group	47.9%
Parmalat Finanziaria SpA	29.1
Societe Chergui	8.6
Others	14.4

Source: *Dairy Industries International*, March 2004, p. 20, from Euromonitor.

★ 285 ★
Dairy Drinks
SIC: 2026; NAICS: 311511

Fermented Dairy Drinks Market in Latin America, 2002

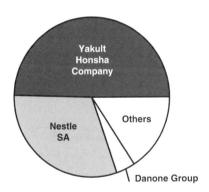

The fermented dairy drinks (for example, yogurt drinks) market grew at a rate of 9.3 percent worldwide in 2003. The table shows market shares for leaders in this market in Latin America during 2002.

Yakult Honsha Company Ltd	49.9%
Nestle SA	31.3
Danone Group	3.8
Others	15.5

Source: *Dairy Industries International*, March 2004, p. 20, from Euromonitor.

★ 286 ★
Dairy Drinks
SIC: 2026; NAICS: 311511

Top Dairy-Based Drink Brands, 2003

Market shares are shown based on $198.9 million in sales at drug stores, mass merchandisers and supermarkets (but not Wal-Mart) for the year ended September 7, 2003.

Yoo-hoo	22.4%
Rice Dream	12.6
Parmalat	8.4
Soy Dream	7.3
West Soy	6.3
Edensoy Extra	4.2
West Soy Plus	4.2
Hersheys	3.4
Edensoy	3.2
Private label	3.5
Other	24.5

Source: *Beverage Industry*, November 2003, p. 24, from Information Resources Inc.

★ 287 ★
Milk
SIC: 2026; NAICS: 311511

Fluid Milk Market

Shares are shown based on volume. For the last two decades the industry has stood at about 6.3 - 6.4 billion gallons.

White	93.0%
Flavored	7.0

Source: *Beverage Aisle*, May 15, 2003, p. 40, from Beverage Marketing Corp.

★ 288 ★
Milk
SIC: 2026; NAICS: 311511

Largest Milk Markets, 2004

Markets are ranked by sales in millions of gallons for the year ended February 29, 2004.

Los Angeles, CA	$ 171.81
New York City, NY	141.43
Baltimore/Washington D.C.	85.75
Chicago, IL	75.84
San Antonio/Corpus Christi, TX	67.02

Continued on next page.

★ 288 ★
[Continued]
Milk
SIC: 2026; NAICS: 311511

Largest Milk Markets, 2004

Markets are ranked by sales in millions of gallons for the year ended February 29, 2004.

Dallas/Fort Worth, TX . . . .$ 65.29
San Francisco/Oakland, CA 63.53
Philadelphia, PA 56.56
Miami/Fort Lauderdale, FL 55.92
Boston, MA 54.42

Source: *Supermarket News*, March 29, 2004, p. 46, from *Dairy Management* and Information Resources Inc.

★ 289 ★
Milk
SIC: 2026; NAICS: 311511

Largest Milk Processors in Germany

Companies are ranked by turnover in millions of euros.

Humana 2.53
Nordmilch 2.31
Muller-Gruppe 1.33
Campina Deutschland 1.19
Hochwald-Gruppe 0.64

Source: *Der Spiegel*, September 22, 2003, p. 131.

★ 290 ★
Milk
SIC: 2026; NAICS: 311511

Largest Milk Producers in Europe, 2002

A total of 114.53 million tons of milk was collected in 2002, up from 113.73 million tons in 1995.

Germany 24.0%
France 20.0
United Kingdom 12.5
Other 43.5

Source: *Europe Agri*, December 5, 2003, p. 309.

★ 291 ★
Milk
SIC: 2026; NAICS: 311511

Leading Milk Producers in Scotland

Arla has less than 10% of the market.

Wiseman 70.0%
Arla 10.0
Other 20.0

Source: *The Herald (Glasgow, Scotland)*, May 26, 2004, p. 21.

★ 292 ★
Milk
SIC: 2026; NAICS: 311511

Leading Milk Producers in the U.K.

Market shares are shown in percent.

Arla 45.0%
Wiseman 20.0
Other 35.0

Source: *The Herald (Glasgow, Scotland)*, May 26, 2004, p. 21.

★ 293 ★
Milk
SIC: 2026; NAICS: 311511

Milk Sales in the U.K.

Distribution is shown by type.

	1994	2004
Whole milk	45.7%	27.1%
Semi-skimmed milk	40.9	56.9
Skimmed milk	12.3	14.5
Other	1.1	1.5

Source: *Dairy Farmer*, April 1, 2004, p. 51.

★ 294 ★

Milk

SIC: 2026; NAICS: 311511

Refrigerated Soy Milk Sales

Market share is for sales at natural food stores.

Silk 85.0%
Other 15.0

Source: *New York Times*, December 5, 2003, p. C5, from Spence Information Systems.

★ 295 ★

Milk

SIC: 2026; NAICS: 311511

Soy Milk Market

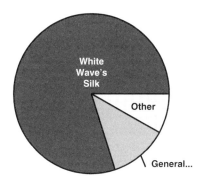

Market shares are shown for sales at grocery stores. The category "other" includes Eden Soy and Imagine Food's Soy Dream.

White Wave's Silk 80.0%
General Mills 8th Continent 12.0
Other 8.0

Source: *Business 2.0*, April 2004, p. 74, from company reports and Information Resources Inc.

★ 296 ★

Milk

SIC: 2026; NAICS: 311511

Top Flavored Milk Brands, 2004

Brands are ranked by sales in millions of dollars for the year ended January 25, 2004. Figures are for supermarkets, drug and mass merchandiser sales and exclude Wal-Mart.

	($ mil.)	Share
Nestle Nesquik	$ 115.00	15.25%
Deans	33.00	4.38
Kemps	19.00	2.52
Borden Milk Products	13.90	1.84
Hershey's	13.87	1.84
Mayfield	12.30	1.63
Garelick Farms	11.40	1.51
Hershey's Morningstar	11.00	1.46
Prairie Farms	10.60	1.41
Private label	216.00	28.65
Other	297.93	39.51

Source: *Dairy Foods*, April 2004, p. 34, from Information Resources Inc.

★ 297 ★

Milk

SIC: 2026; NAICS: 311511

Top Flavored Milk/Eggnog/Buttermilk Brands

Market shares are shown in percent based on sales at supermarkets, drug stores and mass merchandisers (but not Wal-Mart) for the year ended December 1, 2002.

Nestle Nesquik 14.6%
Deans 4.9
Kemps 2.8
Borden 2.7
Hiland 1.9
Mayfield 1.7
Prairie Farms 1.6
Barbers 1.5
Hershey's 1.2
Private label 24.9
Other 42.2

Source: *Dairy Field*, March 2003, p. 45, from Information Resources Inc.

★ 298 ★

Milk

SIC: 2026; NAICS: 311511

Top Low Fat/Skim Milk Brands, 2003

Lactaid 100

Kemps

Deans

Horizon Organic

Garelick Farms

Mayfield

Prairie Farms

Farmland

Hood

Private label

Other

Brands are ranked by sales in millions of dollars for the year ended April 20, 2003.

	($ mil.)	Share
Lactaid 100	$ 175	2.69%
Kemps	89	1.37
Deans	85	1.31
Horizon Organic	71	1.09
Garelick Farms	66	1.01
Mayfield	65	1.00
Prairie Farms	62	0.95
Farmland	45	0.69
Hood	44	0.68
Private label	4,170	64.05
Other	1,639	25.17

Source: *Dairy Foods*, June 2003, p. 34, from Information Resources Inc.

★ 299 ★

Milk

SIC: 2026; NAICS: 311511

Top Refrigerated Milk Brands, 2003

Brands are ranked by sales in millions of dollars for the year ended November 30, 2003. Figures are for supermarkets, drug and mass merchandiser sales and exclude Wal-Mart.

	($ mil.)	Share
Breakstone	$ 106	15.68%
Daisy	100	14.79
Knudsen Hampshire	55	8.14
Friendship	14	2.07

	($ mil.)	Share
Knudson Nice N Light	$ 11	1.63%
Dean's	11	1.63
Land O Lakes	10	1.48
Tillamook	9	1.33
Gandy's	8	1.18
Private label	204	30.18
Other	148	21.89

Source: *Dairy Foods*, November 2003, p. 34, from Information Resources Inc.

★ 300 ★

Whipped Toppings

SIC: 2026; NAICS: 311511

Top Whipped Topping Brands, 2003

Brands are ranked by sales for the 12 weeks ended June 15, 2003.

	($ mil.)	Share
Cool Whip	$ 35.15	39.52%
Cool Whip Lite	13.41	15.08
Cool Whip Free	12.59	14.15
Real Whip	0.16	0.18
Private label	27.54	30.96
Other	0.10	0.11

Source: *Frozen Food Age*, August 2003, p. 10, from Information Resources Inc.

★ 301 ★

Yogurt

SIC: 2026; NAICS: 311511

Top Children's Yogurt Makers in the U.K., 2003

Shares are shown for the leading manufacturers of children's yogurt and chilled desserts sold in the United Kingdom.

Yoplait	40.0%
Nestle	25.0
Muller	16.5
Other	18.5

Source: *Marketing*, February 26, 2004, p. 7.

★ 302 ★
Yogurt
SIC: 2026; NAICS: 311511

Top Yogurt Brands in Israel, 2001

About 170,000 tons of yogurt is consumed annually in the country.

Danona	47.0%
Ami	19.0
PriLi	14.0
Ski	5.4
Vitmina	5.0
Tara	4.0
Tnuva Cream	2.0
Other	2.0

Source: *Jerusalem Post*, December 17, 2001, p. NA.

★ 303 ★
Yogurt
SIC: 2026; NAICS: 311511

Top Yogurt Brands in the U.K., 2003

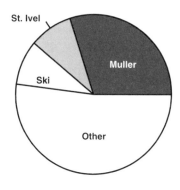

Sales hit 923 million British pounds for the year.

Muller	30.2%
St. Ivel	9.3
Ski	8.7
Other	51.8

Source: *Marketing Week*, January 15, 2004, p. 27, from Euromonitor.

★ 304 ★
Yogurt
SIC: 2026; NAICS: 311511

Top Yogurt/Yogurt Drink Brands, 2003

Brands are ranked by sales in millions of dollars for the year ended September 7, 2003. Figures are for supermarkets, drug and mass merchandiser sales and exclude Wal-Mart.

	($ mil.)	Share
Yoplait	$ 329	12.00%
Dannon	196	7.15
Dannon Light N Fit	185	6.75
Yoplait Light	145	5.29
Yoplait Go Gurt	126	4.60
Yoplait Trix	95	3.47
Yoplait Custard Style	88	3.21
Dannon Danimals	87	3.17
Dannon La Creme	86	3.14
Private label	358	13.06
Other	1,046	38.16

Source: *Dairy Foods*, November 2003, p. 34, from Information Resources Inc.

★ 305 ★
Yogurt
SIC: 2026; NAICS: 311511

Top Yogurt/Yogurt Drink Makers, 2003

Market shares are shown based on supermarket, drug and mass merchandiser (but not Wal-Mart) unit sales for the year ended December 28, 2003.

Yoplait USA	34.0%
Dannon Co.	22.9
Kraft Foods	6.1
Colombo	2.7
Stonyfield Farm	2.6
Yofarm Corp.	2.2
Johanna Foods	2.2
Crowley Foods	1.8
Private label	18.6
Other	6.9

Source: *Food Processing*, June 2004, p. 38, from Information Resources Inc.

★ 306 ★

Yogurt

SIC: 2026; NAICS: 31152

Top Yogurts and Dairy Dessert Brands in the U.K., 2003

Brands are ranked by sales in thousands of pounds sterling for the year ended October 4, 2003.

	(000)	Share
Muller	£ 301,116	26.19%
Ski	53,419	4.65
Onken	46,048	4.01
Petits Filous	43,572	3.79
Shape	36,214	3.15
Cadbury	35,983	3.13
Yeo Valley	35,607	3.10
Weight Watchers	35,371	3.08
Munch Brunch	28,660	2.49
Wild Life	27,449	2.39
Other	506,224	44.03

Source: *Grocer*, December 13, 2003, p. 66, from Information Resources Inc.

★ 307 ★

Baby Food

SIC: 2032; NAICS: 311422

Baby Food Market, 2003

Sales are shown in thousands of dollars for the 52 weeks ended April 19, 2003. Figures include food, drug and mass merchandisers but exclude Wal-Mart.

	($ mil.)	Share
Infant formulas	$ 2,498,426.1	73.18%
Strained baby food	422,124.1	12.36
Junior baby food	197,651.9	5.79
Baby cereal & biscuits	185,002.2	5.42
Juice	110,865.1	3.25

Source: *Grocery Headquarters*, July 2003, p. 37, from ACNielsen.

★ 308 ★

Baby Food

SIC: 2032; NAICS: 311422

Leading Baby Electrolyte Products, 2003

Brands are ranked by sales at supermarkets, drug stores and discount stores (but not Wal-Mart) for the year ended September 7, 2003.

	($ mil.)	Share
Pedialyte	$ 70.7	68.64%
Gerber	6.8	6.60
Nutra Max	0.9	0.87
Revital	0.6	0.58
Revital Ice	0.5	0.49
Revital Jel	0.4	0.39
Naturalyte	0.3	0.29
Kaolectrolyte	0.2	0.19
Private label	21.9	21.26
Other	0.7	0.68

Source: *MMR*, December 8, 2003, p. 32, from Information Resources Inc.

★ 309 ★

Baby Food

SIC: 2032; NAICS: 311422

Leading Baby Food Brands, 2003

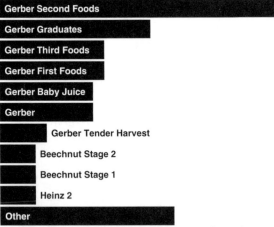

Brands are ranked by sales at supermarkets, drug stores and discount stores (but not Wal-Mart) for the year ended September 7, 2003.

	($ mil.)	Share
Gerber Second Foods	$ 211.8	23.84%
Gerber Graduates	112.4	12.65
Gerber Third Foods	81.4	9.16
Gerber First Foods	80.8	9.10

Continued on next page.

★ 309 ★
[Continued]
Baby Food
SIC: 2032; NAICS: 311422
Leading Baby Food Brands, 2003

Brands are ranked by sales at supermarkets, drug stores and discount stores (but not Wal-Mart) for the year ended September 7, 2003.

	($ mil.)	Share
Gerber Baby Juice	$ 75.0	8.44%
Gerber	73.4	8.26
Gerber Tender Harvest	37.5	4.22
Beechnut Stage 2	28.1	3.16
Beechnut Stage 1	26.8	3.02
Heinz 2	24.3	2.74
Other	136.9	15.41

Source: *MMR*, December 8, 2003, p. 32, from Information Resources Inc.

★ 310 ★
Baby Food
SIC: 2032; NAICS: 311422
Organic Baby Food Market, 2004

Market share is for the 24 weeks ended January 24, 2004.

Earth's Best	65.6%
Other	34.4

Source: *Brandweek*, April 12, 2004, p. 38, from SpinsScan.

★ 311 ★
Baby Food
SIC: 2032; NAICS: 311422
Top Baby Food Makers in China, 2002

Market shares are shown in percent.

Nestle	21.0%
Heinz	11.0
Other	68.0

Source: *just-food.com (Management Briefing)*, July 2003, p. 11, from just-food.

★ 312 ★
Baby Food
SIC: 2032; NAICS: 311422
Top Baby Food Makers in Indonesia

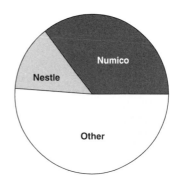

Market shares are shown in percent.

Numico	32.0%
Nestle	12.0
Other	46.0

Source: *Forbes*, January 12, 2004, p. 132.

★ 313 ★
Baby Food
SIC: 2032; NAICS: 311422
Top Baby Food Makers in the Netherlands, 2002

Market shares are shown in percent.

Royal Numico	60.0%
Friesland Coberco	32.0
Other	8.0

Source: *just-food.com (Management Briefing)*, July 2003, p. 11, from just-food.

★ 314 ★
Baby Food
SIC: 2032; NAICS: 311422

Top Baby Food Makers in the U.K., 2002

Market shares are shown in percent.

Royal Numico	30.0%
Heinz	30.0
SMA Nutrition	20.0
Hipp	10.0
Other	10.0

Source: *just-food.com (Management Briefing)*, July 2003, p. 11, from just-food.

★ 315 ★
Baby Food
SIC: 2032; NAICS: 311422

Top Baby Food Makers Worldwide, 2002

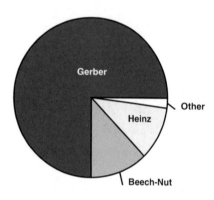

Market shares are shown in percent.

Gerber	75.0%
Beech-Nut	12.0
Heinz	11.0
Other	2.0

Source: *just-food.com (Management Briefing)*, July 2003, p. 11, from just-food.

★ 316 ★
Canned Food
SIC: 2032; NAICS: 311422

Canned Food Sales in New Zealand

Sales are shown in millions of dollars. Heinz-Wattie is the leader in the baked beans and spaghetti segments with more than 87% of the market. It also has 55% of the canned vegetable category but 27% of the cooking sauces category.

Fruit	$ 66.40
Fish & seafood	64.50
Corned meats	10.70
Puddings	8.00
Meals	3.40
Beans and salads	3.30
Mushrooms	1.90
Meats	1.40
Other vegetables	0.83

Source: *Grocer's Review*, November 2003, p. NA.

★ 317 ★
Canned Food
SIC: 2032; NAICS: 311422

Canned Food Sales in the U.K., 2003

Sales of brands are shown in thousands of pounds sterling for the year ended October 4, 2003.

	(000)	Share
Heinz baked beans	£ 90,290	8.75%
John West tuna	56,935	5.52
Princes tuna	36,830	3.57
John West salmon	22,666	2.20
Princes salmon	21,397	2.07
Green Giant giblets sweetcorn	17,748	1.72
Princes corned beef	17,281	1.67
John West (other canned fish)	16,242	1.57
Fray Bentos pies	15,074	1.46
Napolina tomatoes	14,752	1.43
Other	722,640	70.03

Source: *Grocer*, December 13, 2003, p. 49, from Information Resources Inc.

★ 318 ★

Canned Food

SIC: 2032; NAICS: 311421

Canned Fruit Sales, 2002

Data show supermarket sales in millions of dollars.
Total supermarket sales were $1.94 billion.

	($ mil.)	Share
Pineapple	$ 236.78	12.38%
Peaches, cling	232.52	12.16
Applesauce	192.24	10.05
Pears	106.34	5.56
Pie & pastry filling, canned	105.70	5.53
Fruit cocktail	105.48	5.51
Cranberries, shelf-stable	101.68	5.32
Oranges	90.94	4.75
Cherries, maraschino	44.47	2.32
Apricots	23.99	1.25
Other	672.60	35.16

Source: *Progressive Grocer*, September 15, 2003, p. 19,
from *Progressive Grocer's 56th Consumer Expenditures Study.*

★ 319 ★

Canned Food

SIC: 2032; NAICS: 311422

Canned Pork Market in Hawaii

Market shares are shown in percent.

Spam	95.0%
Other	5.0

Source: *Honolulu Star Bulletin*, March 9, 2004, p. NA.

★ 320 ★

Canned Food

SIC: 2032; NAICS: 311421

Canned Vegetable Sales, 2002

Data show supermarket sales in millions of dollars.
Total supermarket sales were $4.23 billion.

	($ mil.)	Share
Green beans	$ 381.44	9.00%
Corn, whole kernel	339.03	8.00
Tomato sauce	243.81	5.75
Peas	167.27	3.95
Mushrooms	157.53	3.72
Beans, kidney or red	115.98	2.74
Tomatoes, whole	98.05	2.31
Tomato paste	94.94	2.24
Tomatoes, stewed	81.68	1.93
Mixed vegetables	74.00	1.75
Other	2,485.86	58.63

Source: *Progressive Grocer*, September 15, 2003, p. 19,
from *Progressive Grocer's 56th Consumer Expenditures Study.*

★ 321 ★
Infant Formula
SIC: 2032; NAICS: 311422

Leading Infant Formula Makers in Brazil

Market shares are shown in percent.

Nestle 65.0%
Support Produtos Nutricionais (Royal
   Numico) 11.5
Nutrimental 9.5

Source: *America's Intelligence Wire*, March 11, 2004, p. NA.

★ 322 ★
Apple Sauce
SIC: 2033; NAICS: 311421

Apple Sauce Market

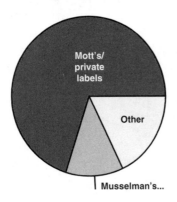

The industry saw sales of $380 million for the year ended August 10, 2003.

Mott's/private labels 70.0%
Musselman's and Lucky Leaf 12.0
Other 18.0

Source: *Adweek*, September 15, 2003, p. 14, from Information Resources Inc.

★ 323 ★
Baked Beans
SIC: 2033; NAICS: 311421

Baked Beans Market

Market shares are shown in percent.

Bush Brothers 80.0%
Other 20.0

Source: *Knoxville News-Sentinel*, March 14, 2004, p. NA.

★ 324 ★
Juices
SIC: 2033; NAICS: 311421

Fruit Juice Market in Germany

Market shares are shown for 2002.

Migros 41.6%
Coop 20.7
Henneiz 14.5
Rivella 4.3
Granador 2.0
Coca-Cola 1.9
Other 15.0

Source: *HandelsZeitung*, April 23, 2003, p. NA.

★ 325 ★
Juices
SIC: 2033; NAICS: 311421

Fruit Juice Market in Poland, 2002

Shares are for the leading manufacturers of fruit and vegetable juices in Poland in 2002.

Maspex and Sonda 32.1%
Agros-Fortuna 21.6
Hortex 10.1
Other 36.2

Source: *European Intelligence Wire*, July 1, 2003, p. NA.

★ 326 ★

Juices

SIC: 2033; NAICS: 311421

Global Fruit Juice Consumption, 2002

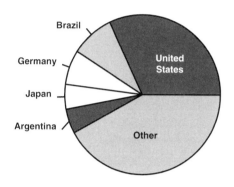

The industry has enjoyed modest growth in recent years, with consumption growing from 434 million hectoliters in 1993 to 490 million hectoliters in 2002.

United States	32.4%
Brazil	8.8
Germany	6.8
Japan	5.1
Argentina	4.8
Other	42.1

Source: *Beverage World*, June 15, 2004, p. 1.

★ 327 ★

Juices

SIC: 2033; NAICS: 311421

Leading Bottled Juice (Shelf-Stable) Brands, 2003

Brands are ranked by sales at supermarkets, drug stores and discount stores (but not Wal-Mart) for the year ended September 7, 2003.

	($ mil.)	Share
Ocean Spray	$ 383.6	10.28%
Libby's Juicy	176.6	4.73
Welch's	167.8	4.50
Hawaiian Punch	120.4	3.23
V8	108.0	2.90
Tropicana Twister	104.3	2.80
Motts	81.0	2.17
Tree Top	70.4	1.89

	($ mil.)	Share
Private label	$ 387.6	10.39%
Other	2,130.3	57.11

Source: *MMR*, December 8, 2003, p. 32, from Information Resources Inc.

★ 328 ★

Juices

SIC: 2033; NAICS: 311421

Leading Juice Producers, 2002

Companies are ranked by juice sales in millions of dollars.

Tropicana (div. of PepsiCo.)	$ 2,000
Minute Maid Co. (div. of Coca-Cola)	1,600
Pasco Beverage Group	800
Florida's Natural Growers	620
Welch Foods	158

Source: *Refrigerated and Frozen Foods*, February 2003, p. 12.

★ 329 ★

Juices

SIC: 2033; NAICS: 311421

Orange Juice Sales by Type

Not from concentrate has grown to take nearly half of the market from its 8% share in 1987. Tropicana has about 70% of this market. FCOJ - frozen concentrated orange juice.

	1987	2002
Not from concentrate	8.0%	47.0%
Chilled reconstituted orange juice	44.0	41.0
FCOJ	47.0	12.0

Source: *The Ledger*, June 29, 2003, p. NA, from ACNielsen.

★ 330 ★
Juices

SIC: 2033; NAICS: 311421

Orange Juice Sales in Hackensack, NJ

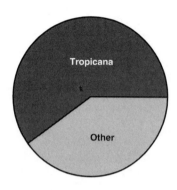

Market shares are shown in percent.

Tropicana	60.0%
Other	40.0

Source: *The Record*, August 27, 2003, p. NA.

★ 331 ★
Juices

SIC: 2033; NAICS: 311421

Tomato Juice Market

The bottled tomato juice market had sales of $272 million. Campbell makes V8 and V8 Splash.

Campbell Soup	83.0%
Other	17.0

Source: *Philadelphia Inquirer*, October 16, 2003, p. NA, from Information Resources Inc.

★ 332 ★
Juices

SIC: 2033; NAICS: 311421

Top Orange Juice Makers, 2004

Market shares are shown based on sales at super-markets, drugstores and mass merchandisers (but not Wal-Mart) for the year ended January 25, 2004.

Tropicana Dole Beverages	46.36%
Minute Maid Co.	21.35
Citrus World	9.83
Dean Foods Co.	0.61
Odwalla Inc.	0.35
Johanna Foods	0.33
Freshco Ltd.	0.29
Private label	16.53
Other	8.35

Source: *Grocery Headquarters*, April 2004, p. 16, from Information Resources Inc.

★ 333 ★
Juices

SIC: 2033; NAICS: 311421

Top Orange Juices, 2003

Companies are ranked by supermarket, drugstore and mass merchandiser sales (but not Wal-Mart) for the 12 months ended April 20, 2003.

	($ mil.)	Share
Tropicana Pure Premium . . .	$ 1,407.0	44.2%
Minute Maid Premium	594.3	18.7
Florida Natural	293.2	9.2
Simply Orange	65.9	2.1
Private label	557.7	17.5

Source: *Sarasota Herald Tribune*, May 17, 2003, p. D3, from Information Resources Inc.

★ 334 ★
Ketchup
SIC: 2033; NAICS: 311421

Ketchup Market in Russia

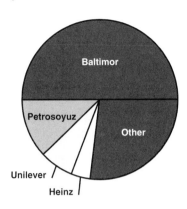

Market shares are shown in percent.

Baltimor	50.0%
Petrosoyuz	12.0
Unilever	7.0
Heinz	4.0
Other	27.0

Source: *Kommersant*, August 22, 2003, p. 7.

★ 335 ★
Ketchup
SIC: 2033; NAICS: 311421

Ketchup Market in the U.K.

The company also has 60% of the U.S. market.

Heinz	72.0%
Other	28.0

Source: *Philadelphia Inquirer*, February 20, 2003, p. NA.

★ 336 ★
Peanut Butter
SIC: 2033; NAICS: 311421

Peanut Butter Market

Total sales were placed at $856.3 million in 2002.

Jif	32.0%
Skippy	23.0
Peter Pan	12.0
Private label	20.0

Source: *Washington Post*, March 3, 2003, p. NA, from Information Resources Inc.

★ 337 ★
Dry Foods
SIC: 2034; NAICS: 311423, 311999

Dry Food Sales, 2002

Data show supermarket sales in millions of dollars.

	($ mil.)	Share
Dry dinners, pasta	$ 1,323.72	29.37%
Mexican tortillas	822.81	18.26
Rice mixes	526.97	11.69
Potatoes, mashed and dry	200.25	4.44
Mexican shells	170.41	3.78
Potatoes, specialty dry	129.06	2.86
Mexican dinners, dry/kit	116.06	2.58
Dry dinners, rice	53.15	1.18
Mixes, ethnic specialty	41.14	0.91
Pizza pie & crust mixes	32.03	0.71
Other	1,091.47	24.22

Source: *Progressive Grocer*, September 15, 2003, p. 19, from *Progressive Grocer's 56th Consumer Expenditures Study*.

★ 338 ★
Soup
SIC: 2034; NAICS: 311422
Soup Market in North America

The market is estimated at $3.1 billion annually. For the year ended January 3, 1999, Campbell had 74.5% and Progresso had a 9.2% share.

Campbell	67.0%
Progresso	14.5
Other	18.5

Source: *Baseline*, December 15, 2003, p. NA, from Information Resources Inc.

★ 339 ★
Soup
SIC: 2034; NAICS: 311422
Soup Market Leaders, 2002

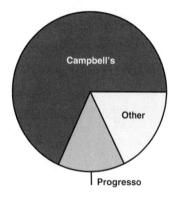

Total soup sales were $3.1 billion. Sales of condensed soups are on the decline, falling from $1.55 billion in 1998 to $1.33 billion in 2002.

	1998	2002
Campbell's	74.5%	68.6%
Progresso	9.2	13.5
Other	16.3	17.9

Source: *Wall Street Journal*, July 31, 2003, p. A2, from Information Resources Inc.

★ 340 ★
Soup
SIC: 2034; NAICS: 311422
Top Condensed Soup Brands, 2004

Market shares are shown based on sales at supermarkets, drugstores and mass merchandisers (but not Wal-Mart) for the year ended January 25, 2004.

Campbell's Chunky	26.51%
Progresso	24.64
Campbell's Select	11.48
Campbell's Soup at Hand	4.17
Healthy Choice	3.45
College Inn	2.77
Wolfgang Puck	2.55
Campbell	1.94
Private label	5.40
Other	17.09

Source: *Grocery Headquarters*, April 2004, p. 16, from Information Resources Inc.

★ 341 ★
Soup
SIC: 2034; NAICS: 311422
Top Frozen Soup Brands, 2003

Brands are ranked by sales for the 12 weeks ended November 30, 2003.

	Sales	Share
Tabatchnick	$ 1,790,348	28.12%
Phillips	869,637	13.66
Culinary Delights	521,437	8.19
Boston Chowda	377,844	5.94
Private label	826,043	12.98
Other	1,980,453	31.11

Source: *Frozen Food Age*, January 2004, p. 12, from Information Resources Inc.

★ 342 ★
Soup
SIC: 2034; NAICS: 311422

Top Soup Brands in the U.K.

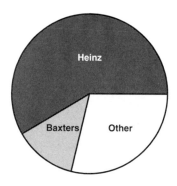

Market shares are shwon in percent.

Heinz	. 58.5%
Baxters	. 13.0
Other	. 28.5

Source: *Marketing*, August 14, 2003, p. 2.

★ 343 ★
Dips
SIC: 2035; NAICS: 311941

Top Refrigerated Dip Brands, 2003

The top brands are ranked by supermarket sales for the year ended December 28, 2003.

	($ mil.)	Share
T. Marzetti	$ 73.74	18.49%
Dean's	47.67	11.95
Kraft	39.81	9.98
Heluva Good	28.39	7.12
Classic Guacamole	17.17	4.31
Marie's	10.86	2.72
Calavo	5.72	1.43
Bison	5.69	1.43
Yoder's	3.75	0.94
Other	166.00	41.62

Source: *Frozen Food Age*, May 2004, p. 41, from Information Resources Inc.

★ 344 ★
Hot Sauce
SIC: 2035; NAICS: 311941

Top Hot Sauce Brands, 2003

Brands are ranked by unit sales for the year ended July 13, 2003.

McIlhenny Tabasco	. 16.19
Bruce's Louisiana	. 13.22
Crystal	. 10.20
Frank's Original	. 9.99
Texas Pete	. 7.88
Tapatio	. 5.22
Valentina	. 3.24
Chilula	. 1.85
Hooters	. 0.63
Private label	. 10.09

Source: *Progressive Grocer*, October 15, 2003, p. 33, from Information Resources Inc.

★ 345 ★
Mayonnaise
SIC: 2035; NAICS: 311941

Mayonnaise Market

Market shares are shown in percent.

Kraft	. 43.0%
Hellman's	. 40.0
Other	. 17.0

Source: *Christian Science Monitor*, July 28, 2003, p. 13.

★ 346 ★
Salad Dressings
SIC: 2035; NAICS: 311941

Top Salad Dressing Brands, 2003

Brands are ranked by sales in millions of dollars for the year ended February 2003.

	($ mil.)	Share
Kraft	$ 452.0	31.2%
Wishbone	274.3	18.9
Hidden Valley	190.0	13.1
Ken's Steak House	109.0	7.5
Newman's Own	54.7	3.8
Annie's Natural	7.2	0.5
Private label	116.1	8.0

Source: *Food Processing*, May 2003, p. 32, from Information Resources Inc.

★ 347 ★
Salad Dressings
SIC: 2035; NAICS: 311941

Top Salad Dressing Makers, 2004

Market shares are shown based on sales at supermarkets, drugstores and mass merchandisers (but not Wal-Mart) for the year ended January 25, 2004.

Kraft Foods Inc.	31.54%
Lipton	17.70
Clorox Co.	13.72
Ken's Foods Inc.	8.51
Newman's Own Inc.	4.48
T Marzetti Co.	1.76
Girard's Fine Foods Inc.	1.50
Agrilink Foods Inc.	1.41
Other	19.38

Source: *Grocery Headquarters*, April 2004, p. 16, from Information Resources Inc.

★ 348 ★
Salad Dressings
SIC: 2035; NAICS: 311941

Top Spoonable Dressing Brands, 2003

Sales are shown for the 12 weeks ended December 28, 2003.

	Sales	Share
Marie's	$ 15,973,683	37.32%
Litehouse	9,477,867	22.14
T. Marzetti	6,549,798	15.30
Naturally Fresh	3,566,163	8.33
Walden Farms	1,453,097	3.39
Other	5,781,352	13.51

Source: *Frozen Food Age*, February 2004, p. 10, from Information Resources Inc.

★ 349 ★
Sauces
SIC: 2035; NAICS: 311421, 311941

Condiment and Sauce Sales, 2002

Data show supermarket sales in millions of dollars.

	($ mil.)	Share
Spaghetti/marinara sauce	$ 1,379.84	19.65%
Mexican sauces	887.41	12.64
Catsup	458.16	6.53
Barbecue sauces	338.96	4.83
Mustard	298.15	4.25
Vinegar	221.46	3.15
Gravy, canned	193.27	2.75
Oriental sauces	168.49	2.40
Gravy mixes, packaged	166.43	2.37
Cooking sauces	142.24	2.03
Other	2,766.69	39.41

Source: *Progressive Grocer*, September 15, 2003, p. 19, from *Progressive Grocer's 56th Consumer Expenditures Study*.

★ 350 ★
Sauces
SIC: 2035; NAICS: 311941
Top Cooking Sauce Brands in the U.K., 2003

Brands are ranked by sales in thousands of pounds sterling for the year ended October 4, 2003.

	(000)	Share
Dolmio	£ 81,115	14.60%
Homepride	38,721	6.97
Chicken Tonight	38,401	6.91
Colman's	29,702	5.35
Uncle Ben's	26,669	4.80
Ragu	25,098	4.52
Schwartz	21,475	3.87
Lloyd Grossman	20,353	3.66
Other	274,013	49.32

Source: *Grocer*, December 13, 2003, p. 66, from Information Resources Inc.

★ 351 ★
Sauces
SIC: 2035; NAICS: 311941
Top Pasta Sauce Brands, 2004

Market shares are shown based on sales at supermarkets, drugstores and mass merchandisers (but not Wal-Mart) for the year ended January 25, 2004.

Prego	16.49%
Classico	10.97
Ragu	9.19
Ragu Old World Style	6.63
Hunts	6.57
Ragu Chunky Gardenstyle	6.25
Five Brothers Bertolli Lucca	5.40
Barilla	4.37
Ragu Hearty	3.44
Private label	4.94
Other	25.75

Source: *Grocery Headquarters*, April 2004, p. 16, from Information Resources Inc.

★ 352 ★
Sauces
SIC: 2035; NAICS: 311941
Top Pasta Sauce Makers, 2004

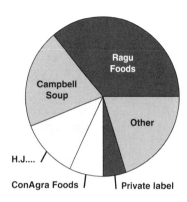

Market shares are shown based on sales at supermarkets, drugstores and mass merchandisers (but not Wal-Mart) for the year ended January 25, 2004.

Ragu Foods	36.32%
Campbell Soup	19.94
H.J. Heinz Co.	11.80
ConAgra Foods	7.15
Private label	4.94
Other	19.85

Source: *Grocery Headquarters*, April 2004, p. 16, from Information Resources Inc.

★ 353 ★
Frozen Fruit
SIC: 2037; NAICS: 311411
Top Fruit Brands, 2003

Brands are ranked by sales for the 12 weeks ended June 15, 2003.

	($ mil.)	Share
Big Valley	$ 5.30	9.22%
Birdseye	2.77	4.82
VIP	2.05	3.57
Cascadian Farm	1.60	2.78
Private label	45.07	78.40
Other	0.70	1.22

Source: *Frozen Food Age*, August 2003, p. 10, from Information Resources Inc.

★ 354 ★

Frozen Vegetables

SIC: 2037; NAICS: 311411

Frozen Vegetable Sales, 2003

Sales are for the first six months of the year. The sales of frozen carrots was up 40% over the same period in 2002.

	($ mil.)	Share
Potatoes/fries/hashbrowns	$ 449.4	31.22%
Mixed vegetables	239.1	16.61
Beans	108.9	7.57
Corn	103.7	7.20
Peas	103.4	7.18
Broccoli	96.8	6.73
Prepared vegetables	92.8	6.45
Corn on the cob	64.4	4.47
Spinach	59.3	4.12
Carrots	21.3	1.48
Onion rings	15.3	1.06
Onions	5.8	0.40
Other	79.2	5.50

Source: *Food Institute Report*, October 6, 2003, p. 17, from Information Resources Inc. InfoScan.

★ 355 ★

Frozen Vegetables

SIC: 2037; NAICS: 311411

Top Bean Brands, 2003

Brands are ranked by sales for the 12 weeks ended June 15, 2003.

	($ mil.)	Share
Pictsweet	$ 4.31	8.87%
Birdseye	3.60	7.41
Hanover	3.36	6.92
California and Washington	2.95	6.07
Private label	23.00	47.33
Other	11.37	23.40

Source: *Frozen Food Age*, August 2003, p. 10, from Information Resources Inc.

★ 356 ★

Frozen Vegetables

SIC: 2037; NAICS: 311411

Top Broccoli Brands, 2003

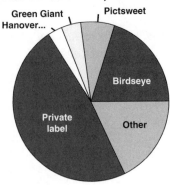

Brands are ranked by sales for the 12 weeks ended June 15, 2003.

	($ mil.)	Share
Birdseye	$ 8.47	19.74%
Pictsweet	3.16	7.37
Green Giant	1.68	3.92
Hanover Premium	1.44	3.36
Private label	20.60	48.02
Other	7.55	17.60

Source: *Frozen Food Age*, August 2003, p. 10, from Information Resources Inc.

★ 357 ★

Frozen Vegetables

SIC: 2037; NAICS: 311411

Top Carrot Brands, 2003

Brands are ranked by sales for the 12 weeks ended June 15, 2003.

	Sales	Share
Green Giant	$ 1,224,775	12.95%
Hanover Country Fresh		
Classics	320,833	3.39
Birdseye	313,444	3.31
Pictsweet	108,379	1.15
Private label	7,076,273	74.81
Other	415,622	4.39

Source: *Frozen Food Age*, August 2003, p. 10, from Information Resources Inc.

★ 358 ★
Frozen Foods
SIC: 2038; NAICS: 311412

Dipping-at-Breakfast Food Industry

Food makers are preparing a variety of handheld foods — french toast sticks, apple slices and mini pancakes — to be packaged with disposable cups with sauces for dipping. Sales of dippable foods are up 35% and the industry is valued at $100 million.

General Mills	50.0%
Other	50.0

Source: *USA TODAY*, April 8, 2004, p. 4B.

★ 359 ★
Frozen Foods
SIC: 2038; NAICS: 311412

Frozen Food Sectors

Data show retail and institutional sales.

	($ mil.)	Share
Prepared foods	$ 25,058	35.25%
Fish & seafood	20,312	28.57
Vegetables	12,235	17.21
Juices and drinks	4,441	6.25
Meat	3,750	5.28
Poultry	3,272	4.60
Fruit	2,021	2.84

Source: *Quick Frozen Foods International*, October 2003, p. 121.

★ 360 ★
Frozen Foods
SIC: 2038; NAICS: 311412

Frozen Potato Market, 2003

Market shares are shown based on supermarket sales for the year ended August 10, 2003.

H.J. Heinz	50.5%
ConAgra Foods	5.7
McCain Foods	3.5
Simplot Food Group	1.2
Private label	33.8
Other	5.3

Source: *Refrigerated & Frozen Foods*, October 2003, p. 60, from Information Resources Inc. InfoScan.

★ 361 ★
Frozen Foods
SIC: 2038; NAICS: 311412

Frozen Potato Market in Germany

Market shares are shown in percent.

McCain's	28.0%
Agrafrost	15.0
Aviko	2.0
Private label	26.0
Other	29.0

Source: *Quick Frozen Foods International*, April 2002, p. 58.

★ 362 ★
Frozen Foods
SIC: 2038; NAICS: 311412

Frozen Potato Products

According to the institute, french fry consumption has been on the increase since 2000.

Foodservice	90.0%
Retail	10.0

Source: *Idaho Business Review*, June 2, 2003, p. NA, from Frozen Potato Processing Institute.

★ 363 ★
Frozen Foods
SIC: 2038; NAICS: 311412

Frozen Potato Suppliers in Netherlands, 2001

Market shares are shown in percent.

Aviko 33.3%
McCain Foods 8.8
Private label 44.3
Other 13.5

Source: *Quick Frozen Foods International*, January 2002, p. 58, from Information Resources Inc.

★ 364 ★
Frozen Foods
SIC: 2038; NAICS: 311412

Largest Frozen Food Sectors in Europe, 2002

Frozen food consumption exceeded 12 million metric tons. The United Kingdom was the largest market. Eastern Europe is seeing noticeable growth in consumption as these economies grow. Poland was the largest market in this region.

	Tons	Share
Prepared foods	3,663,600	30.68%
Potato products	2,396,600	20.07
Vegetables	2,311,200	19.35
Fish/mollusc/shellfish	1,355,700	11.35
Poultry	1,155,100	9.67
Meat	953,100	7.98
Fruits/juices	105,500	0.88
Other	2,300	0.02

Source: *Quick Frozen Foods International*, October 2003, p. 108, from FAFPAS.

★ 365 ★
Frozen Foods
SIC: 2038; NAICS: 311412

Private Label Frozen Food Sales

Selected sales are shown in millions of dollars. Seafood sales were driven by a glut of shrimp.

	($ mil.)	Share
Seafood	$ 624.5	39.2%
Chicken	524.2	27.4
Fried potatoes	292.1	33.7
Pizza	176.4	6.5
Meat	129.4	20.5
Entrees	102.9	2.7
Appetizers/snacks	38.9	4.9

Source: *Quick Frozen Foods International*, October 2003, p. 80, from Information Resources Inc.

★ 366 ★
Frozen Foods
SIC: 2038; NAICS: 311412

Top Frozen Appetizer Brands, 2003

Bagel Bites
T.G.I. Fridays
Delimex
Poppers
El Monterey
Jose Ole Mexi Minis
Red Baron
Pagoda Cafe
Other

Brands are ranked by supermarket sales for the year ended September 7, 2003.

	($ mil.)	Share
Bagel Bites	$ 88.05	11.35%
T.G.I. Fridays	67.11	8.65
Delimex	47.08	6.07
Poppers	33.24	4.29
El Monterey	33.13	4.27
Jose Ole Mexi Minis	25.75	3.32
Red Baron	23.03	2.97
Pagoda Cafe	21.24	2.74
Other	436.86	56.33

Source: *Frozen Food Age*, December 2003, p. 20, from Information Resources Inc.

★ 367 ★
Frozen Foods
SIC: 2038; NAICS: 311412
Top Frozen Dinner/Entrees, 2004

Market shares are shown based on sales for the year ended February 22, 2004.

Stouffer's Entrees	5.8%
Stouffer's Lean Cuisine Cafe Classics	5.3
Banquet Select Menu	4.9
Hot Pockets Handheld Entrees (non-breakfast)	4.4
Stouffers Lean Cuisine Everyday Favorites . .	4.3
Weight Watchers Smart Ones	4.1
Banquet Value Menu	4.0
Lean Pockets Handheld Entrees (non breakfast)	2.8
Healthy Choice	2.5
Kid Cuisine	2.1
Other	59.8

Source: *Food Processing*, April 2004, p. 43, from Information Resources Inc. InfoScan.

★ 368 ★
Frozen Foods
SIC: 2038; NAICS: 311412
Top Frozen Dinner Makers, 2004

Market shares are shown based on sales at super-markets, drugstores and mass merchandisers (but not Wal-Mart) for the year ended January 25, 2004.

ConAgra Foods	46.71%
Pinnacle Food Products	20.54
Nestle USA	15.14
Marie Callender's	11.79
Freezer Queen Foods	1.42
Other	4.40

Source: *Grocery Headquarters*, April 2004, p. 16, from Information Resources Inc.

★ 369 ★
Frozen Foods
SIC: 2038; NAICS: 311412
Top Frozen Entree Brands, 2003

Market shares are shown based on supermarket sales for the 52 weeks ended August 10, 2003. Figures exclude Wal-Mart and refer to supermarkets with sales of $2 million or more.

	($ mil.)	Share
Healthy Choice	$ 204.5	5.46%
Swanson Hungry Man	160.7	4.29
Marie Callender's	144.0	3.85
Banquet Select	131.5	3.51
Banquet Value	109.7	2.93
Other	2,993.8	79.96

Source: *Refrigerated & Frozen Foods*, October 2003, p. 61, from Information Resources Inc. InfoScan.

★ 370 ★
Frozen Foods
SIC: 2038; NAICS: 311412
Top Frozen Entree Makers, 2003

Market shares are shown based on supermarket sales for the 52 weeks ended August 10, 2003. Figures exclude Wal-Mart and refer to supermarkets with sales of $2 million or more.

Nestle Prepared Foods	44.7%
ConAgra Foods	13.1
H.J. Heinz	9.4
Luigino's	7.6
Masterfoods USA	3.9
Other	21.3

Source: *Refrigerated & Frozen Foods*, October 2003, p. 61, from Information Resources Inc. InfoScan.

★ 371 ★
Frozen Foods
SIC: 2038; NAICS: 311412
Top Frozen Food Makers, 2004

Market shares are shown based on sales at super-markets, drugstores and mass merchandisers (but not Wal-Mart) for the year ended January 25, 2004.

Kraft/Tombstone	31.74%
Tony's Pizza	28.62
General Mills	8.33
Kraft/Jack's	6.09
Nestle USA	5.32

Continued on next page.

★ 371 ★

[Continued]
Frozen Foods
SIC: 2038; NAICS: 311412

Top Frozen Food Makers, 2004

Market shares are shown based on sales at supermarkets, drugstores and mass merchandisers (but not Wal-Mart) for the year ended January 25, 2004.

Aurora Foods	2.92%
McCain Ellio's	1.38
Weight Watchers	1.32
Private label	6.88
Other	7.40

Source: *Grocery Headquarters*, April 2004, p. 16, from Information Resources Inc.

★ 372 ★

Frozen Foods
SIC: 2038; NAICS: 311412

Top Frozen Meal Makers, 2003

Market shares are shown based on supermarket sales for the 52 weeks ended August 10, 2003. Figures exclude Wal-Mart and refer to supermarkets with sales of $2 million or more.

ConAgra Foods	57.1%
Pinnacle Foods	21.8
Nestle Prepared Foods	15.7
Other	5.4

Source: *Refrigerated & Frozen Foods*, October 2003, p. 61, from Information Resources Inc. InfoScan.

★ 373 ★

Frozen Foods
SIC: 2038; NAICS: 311412

Top Frozen Pizza Brands, 2003

Brands are ranked by supermarket sales for the year ended September 7, 2003.

	($ mil.)	Share
DiGiorno	$481.21	17.91%
Tombstone	335.30	12.48
Red Baron	256.73	9.56

	($ mil.)	Share
Freschetta	$186.63	6.95%
Totino's Party Pizza	178.04	6.63
Tony's	162.89	6.06
Stouffer's	103.07	3.84
Jack's Original	95.07	3.54
Celeste	80.64	3.00
Other	807.19	30.04

Source: *Frozen Food Age*, November 2003, p. 18, from Information Resources Inc.

★ 374 ★

Frozen Foods
SIC: 2038; NAICS: 311412

Top Frozen Pizza Brands in the U.K., 2003

Brands are ranked by sales in thousands of pounds sterling for the year ended October 4, 2003.

	(000)	Share
Goodfella's 9 in standard	£41,113	14.75%
Chicago Town Individual Pizza Pie	34,584	12.41
Dr. Oetker Ristorante 9 in standard	16,711	5.99
Freschetta 9 ins rising	12,551	4.50
McCain Micro Pizza	8,596	3.08
Goodfella's Stone Baked	8,057	2.89
McCain Pizza fingers	7,367	2.64
Other	149,802	53.73

Source: *Grocer*, December 13, 2003, p. 66, from Information Resources Inc.

★ 375 ★

Frozen Foods
SIC: 2038; NAICS: 311412

Top Frozen Pizza Makers, 2003

Companies are ranked by sales at food stores for the 52 weeks ended June 15, 2003.

	($ mil.)	Share
Kraft Foods Inc./Tombstone Pizza Corp.	$909.82	33.70%
Schwan's Consumer Brands	759.11	28.12
General Mills	227.39	8.42

Continued on next page.

★ 375 ★

[Continued]
Frozen Foods
SIC: 2038; NAICS: 311412

Top Frozen Pizza Makers, 2003

Companies are ranked by sales at food stores for the 52 weeks ended June 15, 2003.

	($ mil.)	Share
Kraft Foods/Jack's	$ 167.45	6.20%
Nestle USA	123.00	4.56
Aurora Foods Inc.	83.52	3.09
McCain Ellio's Food Inc.	36.74	1.36
Weight Watchers	36.03	1.33
ConAgra Inc.	29.82	1.10
Private label	173.74	6.43
Other	153.38	5.68

Source: *Baking & Snack*, August 1, 2003, p. NA, from Information Resources Inc.

★ 376 ★

Frozen Foods
SIC: 2038; NAICS: 311412

Top Frozen Pretzel Brands, 2003

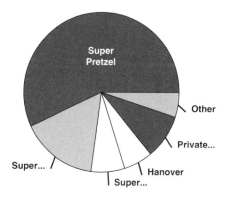

Sales are shown for the 12 weeks ended December 28, 2003.

	Sales	Share
Super Pretzel	$ 4,222,074	56.98%
Super Pretzel Softstix	1,159,324	15.65
Super Pretzel Pretzelfils	520,892	7.03
Hanover	408,197	5.51
Private label	698,216	9.42
Other	401,260	5.42

Source: *Frozen Food Age*, February 2004, p. 10, from Information Resources Inc.

★ 377 ★

Frozen Foods
SIC: 2038; NAICS: 311412

Top Frozen Ravioli Brands, 2003

Brands are ranked by supermarket sales for the year ended November 30, 2003.

	($ mil.)	Share
Rosetto	$ 28.65	25.89%
Celentano	11.54	10.43
Mama Rosies	9.38	8.48
Louisa	3.70	3.34
Pede Brothers	3.04	2.75
Andrea	2.85	2.58
Lucca	2.13	1.92
Seviroli	2.01	1.82
Private label	15.46	13.97
Other	31.89	28.82

Source: *Frozen Food Age*, January 2004, p. 30, from Information Resources Inc.

★ 378 ★

Frozen Foods
SIC: 2038; NAICS: 311412

Top Frozen Waffles Brands, 2003

Brands are ranked by sales in millions of dollars for the 12 weeks ended June 15, 2003.

	($ mil.)	Share
Eggo	$ 60.10	52.66%
Pillsbury Hungry Jack	12.95	11.35
Aunt Jemima	8.51	7.46
Nutri Grain Eggo	5.90	5.17
Private label	14.93	13.08
Other	11.73	10.28

Source: *Frozen Food Age*, September 2003, p. 12, from Information Resources Inc.

★ 379 ★
Frozen Foods
SIC: 2038; NAICS: 311412

Top Hand-Held Entree Makers, 2003

Market shares are shown based on supermarket sales for the 52 weeks ended August 10, 2003. Figures exclude Wal-Mart and refer to supermarkets with sales of $2 million or more.

Nestle Prepared Foods	48.2%
Sara Lee Foods	5.8
Camino Real Foods	5.5
Ruiz Foods	5.3
Foster Farms	4.2
Other	31.0

Source: *Refrigerated & Frozen Foods*, October 2003, p. 61, from Information Resources Inc. InfoScan.

★ 380 ★
Frozen Foods
SIC: 2038; NAICS: 311412

Top Hand-Held Entrees, 2003

Market shares are shown based on supermarket sales for the 52 weeks ended August 10, 2003. Figures exclude Wal-Mart and refer to supermarkets with sales of $2 million or more.

	($ mil.)	Share
Hot Pockets	$ 262.2	24.91%
Lean Pockets	154.3	14.66
Croissant Pockets	89.9	8.54
State Fair	60.6	5.76
El Monterey	53.9	5.12
Other	431.8	41.02

Source: *Refrigerated & Frozen Foods*, October 2003, p. 61, from Information Resources Inc. InfoScan.

★ 381 ★
Frozen Foods
SIC: 2038; NAICS: 311412

Top Pierogi Brands, 2003

Brands are ranked by supermarket sales in millions of dollars for the year ended August 10, 2003.

	($ mil.)	Share
Mrs. T's	$ 37.08	70.63%
Mrs. T's Rogie's	3.64	6.93
Poppy's Pierogies	2.35	4.48
Naleway Baker's Dozens	1.54	2.93

	($ mil.)	Share
Kasias	$ 1.51	2.88%
Delicious Fresh Pierogi	1.27	2.42
Golden Gourmet	0.60	1.14
Dudek	0.43	0.82
Other	4.08	7.77

Source: *Frozen Food Age*, October 2003, p. 48, from Information Resources Inc.

★ 382 ★
Frozen Foods
SIC: 2038; NAICS: 311412

Top Turkey/Turkey Substitutes, 2003

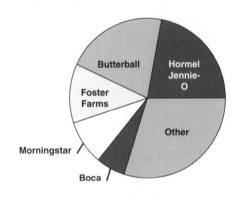

Sales are shown for the 12 weeks ended December 28, 2003.

	Sales	Share
Hormel Jennie-O	$ 8,058,768	22.23%
Butterball	7,477,922	20.63
Foster Farms	4,247,926	11.72
Morningstar	3,367,515	9.29
Boca	2,288,004	6.31
Other	10,807,957	29.82

Source: *Frozen Food Age*, February 2004, p. 10, from Information Resources Inc.

★ 383 ★
Baking Needs
SIC: 2040; NAICS: 311822, 311812, 31132
Baking Supply Sales, 2002

Data show supermarket sales in millions of dollars. Total supermarket sales were $2.33 billion.

	($ mil.)	Share
Frosting ready-to-spread	$ 248.65	10.63%
Stuffing products	242.85	10.38
Breading products	228.16	9.76
Chocolate chips & morsels . . .	194.73	8.33
Croutons	135.60	5.80
Cake decorations & icing . . .	116.85	5.00
Pie & pastry shells, prepared . .	71.25	3.05
Yeast, dry	61.23	2.62
Baking chips, nonchocolate . .	61.19	2.62
Baking chocolate	45.15	1.93
Other	932.91	39.89

Source: *Progressive Grocer*, September 15, 2003, p. 19, from *Progressive Grocer's 56th Consumer Expenditures Study*.

★ 384 ★
Cereal
SIC: 2043; NAICS: 31123
Cereal Sales by Type

Sales are shown in millions of dollars for the year ended July 15, 2003. Figures are for food, drug and mass merchandisers but exclude Wal-Mart.

	($ mil.)	Share
Ready-to-eat	$ 6,409.76	69.50%
Hot cereal	849.87	9.21
Granola & yogurt bars	793.67	8.61
Health bars & sticks	474.26	5.14
Breakfast bars	450.40	4.88
Granola & natural	145.72	1.58
Hominy grits	84.91	0.92
Wheat germ	14.58	0.16

Source: *Grocery Headquarters*, October 2003, p. 41, from ACNielsen.

★ 385 ★
Cereal
SIC: 2043; NAICS: 31123
Top Cereal Makers

The $6.7 billion category remains flat.

Kellogg	33.2%
General Mills	31.6
Other	35.2

Source: *Brandweek*, January 5, 2004, p. 4, from Information Resources Inc.

★ 386 ★
Cereal
SIC: 2043; NAICS: 31123
Top Cereal Makers in Israel

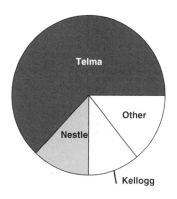

The cereal market is worth NIS 300 million.

Telma	63.0%
Nestle	12.0
Kellogg	11.0
Other	14.0

Source: *Globes Online*, December 23, 2003, p. NA.

★ 387 ★
Cereal
SIC: 2043; NAICS: 31123

Top Cereal Makers in the U.K.

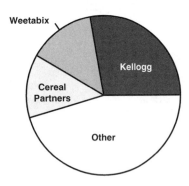

Market shares are shown in percent.

Kellogg	28.2%
Weetabix	13.6
Cereal Partners	12.7
Other	45.5

Source: *Marketing Week*, November 27, 2003, p. 22.

★ 388 ★
Cereal
SIC: 2043; NAICS: 31123

Top Cold Cereal Brands, 2003

Market shares are shown based on sales at food, drug and mass retailers for the 52 weeks ended October 5, 2003. Figures exclude Wal-Mart.

Cheerios	4.9%
Frosted Flakes	4.1
Honey Nut Cheerios	3.8
Honey Bunches of Oats	3.3
Cinnamon Toast Crunch	2.9
Frosted Mini Wheats	2.4
Raisin Bran	2.3
Lucky Charms	2.3
Life	2.1
Private label	8.1
Other	36.2

Source: *Grocery Headquarters*, December 2003, p. 23, from Information Resources Inc.

★ 389 ★
Rice
SIC: 2044; NAICS: 311212

Top Rice Brands in France, 2002

Rice sales in grocery stores stood at $261.1 million for the year ended September 2002.

Uncle Ben's	21.0%
Taureau Aile	19.5
Lustucru	18.0
Other	41.5

Source: *LSA*, November 28, 2002, p. 66, from ACNielsen.

★ 390 ★
Baking Mixes
SIC: 2045; NAICS: 311822

Baking Mix Sales, 2002

Data show supermarket sales in millions of dollars.

	($ mil.)	Share
Cake, layer over 10 oz.	$ 310.49	17.77%
Brownies	200.18	11.46
Muffin	182.18	10.43
Pancake	175.03	10.02
Rolls & biscuits	120.37	6.89
Bread	92.20	5.28
Cookie	69.29	3.97
Dessert, misc.	60.29	3.45
Cake, specialty over 10 oz.	51.31	2.94
Other	485.44	27.79

Source: *Progressive Grocer*, September 15, 2003, p. 19, from *Progressive Grocer's 56th Consumer Expenditures Study*.

★ 391 ★
Dough
SIC: 2045; NAICS: 311822

Refrigerated Dough Market

Market shares are shown in percent.

General Mills 71.0%
Other 29.0

Source: *Food & Drug Packaging*, October 2003, p. 24, from ACNielsen.

★ 392 ★
Dough
SIC: 2045; NAICS: 311822

Top Cookie/Brownie Dough Brands, 2004

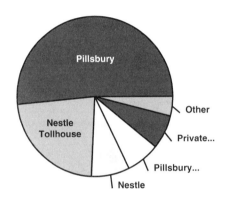

Brands are ranked by sales for the 22 weeks ended February 22, 2004.

	(mil.)	Share
Pillsbury	26.57	51.88%
Nestle Tollhouse	11.67	22.79
Nestle	4.04	7.89
Pillsbury Ready to Bake Big		
Deluxe Classics	3.78	7.38
Private label	3.34	6.52
Other	1.81	3.53

Source: *Frozen Food Age*, May 2004, p. 44, from Information Resources Inc.

★ 393 ★
Dough
SIC: 2045; NAICS: 311822

Top Refrigerated Biscuit Doughs, 2003

Brands are ranked by supermarket sales for the year ended November 30, 2003.

	($ mil.)	Share
Pillsbury Grinds	$ 190.52	56.16%
Pillsbury Hungry Jack	47.91	14.12
Pillsbury	33.24	9.80
Pillsbury Hungry Jack Butter		
Tasting	11.77	3.47
Pillsbury Tender Layer	6.36	1.87
Pillsbury Golden Homestyle . . .	5.93	1.75
Merico	4.52	1.33
Other	38.99	11.49

Source: *Frozen Food Age*, January 2004, p. 30, from Information Resources Inc.

★ 394 ★
Pet Food
SIC: 2047; NAICS: 311111

Dog Food Market in Japan

There are roughly 9.8 million dogs and 7.5 million cats in Japan. Roughly $2 billion is spent on pet food each year, with cat and dog food sales representing 90% of the market. Over half of all pet food sales (57%) take place at home centers, followed by general merchandise stores (26%).

Dry 47.0%
Wet 24.0
Semi-moist 17.0
Other 12.0

Source: *AgExporter*, August 2003, p. 12.

★ 395 ★
Pet Food
SIC: 2047; NAICS: 311111

Pet Food Industry in New Zealand

Sales are shown in millions of dollars. Masterfoods is the leading making of pet food with a 33.4% share. Its brands include Whiskas for cats, Top Kitecat, Pedigree, Optimum, Lucky and Schmakos.

	($ mil.)	Share
Canned cat food	$ 80.3	37.07%
Wet dog food	44.2	20.41
Dry cat food	41.2	19.02
Dry dog food	26.5	12.23
Canned dog food	12.5	5.77
Wet cat food	11.7	5.40
Other	0.2	0.09

Source: *Grocer's Review*, August 2003, p. NA.

★ 396 ★
Pet Food
SIC: 2047; NAICS: 311111

Pet Food Market in Italy

Market sectors are shown in millions of euros.

	(mil.)	Share
Cats	506	44.86%
Dogs	420	37.23
Fish	81	7.18
Birds	79	7.00
Rodents	17	1.51
Reptiles	4	0.35
Other	21	1.86

Source: "Pet Products Market in Italy." [online] from http://www.usatrade.gov [accessed January 5, 2004], from U.S. Commercial Service.

★ 397 ★
Pet Food
SIC: 2047; NAICS: 311111

Premium Pet Food Imports in Hong Kong, 2003

Procter & Gamble makes IAMS. Eukanuba and Hill makes Science Diet. The Hong Kong market was valued at $32 million, all of which was imported. The U.S. took 40% of that market.

IAMS	80.0%
Science Diet	20.0

Source: "Pet Foods and Pet Supplies" [online] http://www.export.gov/comm_svc/index.html [accessed March 30, 2004], p. NA.

★ 398 ★
Pet Food
SIC: 2047; NAICS: 311111

Top Dry Cat Food Brands, 2003

Market shares are shown based on food store sales for the 52 weeks ended April 20, 2003.

Iams	13.3%
Meow Mix	10.2
Purina Cat Chow	9.0
Friskies	7.8
Friskies Chefs Blend	5.6
Purina One	5.6
Kal Kan Whiskas Savory Nuggets	5.4
Purina Kit N Kaboodle	4.8
Purina Deli Cat	3.2
Private label	8.5
Other	73.4

Source: *Supermarket News*, May 26, 2003, p. 37, from Information Resources Inc.

★ 399 ★
Pet Food
SIC: 2047; NAICS: 311111
Top Dry Cat Food Makers in Australia

Market shares are shown in percent for 2000. In the wet cat food segment, Uncle Ben's leads with a 64.7% value share and a 67.5% volume share.

	Value	Volume
Friskies	48.4%	47.9%
Uncle Ben's	43.0	41.7
Generics	4.9	7.2
Ralston Purina	1.4	0.6
Green's	0.7	0.7
Private label	1.6	1.8

Source: "Australia Product Brief Pet Food 2003." [online] from http://www.fas.usda.gov [accessed January 1, 2004], from *Grocery Industry Marketing Guide 1999-2001.*

★ 400 ★
Pet Food
SIC: 2047; NAICS: 311111
Top Dry Dog Food Brands

Market shares are shown in percent.

Iams	14.8%
Pedigree	12.3
Purina One	10.2
Other	62.3

Source: *St. Louis Post-Dispatch*, June 6, 2003, p. C1, from Information Resources Inc.

★ 401 ★
Pet Food
SIC: 2047; NAICS: 311111
Top Dry Dog Food Brands, 2003

Market shares are shown on food store sales for the 52 weeks ended April 20, 2003.

Iams	13.7%
Pedigree Mealtime	11.0
Purina One	10.3
Purina Dog Chow	7.3
Beneful	4.4
Purina Puppy Chow	3.4
Ken L Ration Kibbles	3.3
Purina Dig Chow Little Bites	2.9
Friskies Come & Get It	2.8
Private label	9.5
Other	68.6

Source: *Supermarket News*, May 26, 2003, p. 37, from Information Resources Inc.

★ 402 ★
Pet Food
SIC: 2047; NAICS: 311111
Top Dry Dog Food Makers, 2004

Market shares are shown based on sales at supermarkets, drugstores and mass merchandisers (but not Wal-Mart) for the year ended January 25, 2004.

Nestle Purina Products	45.00%
The Iams Co.	16.05
Masterfoods USA	15.24
Heinz Pet Products	9.30
Dad's Products	2.01
Sunshine Mills	1.51

Continued on next page.

★ 402 ★
[Continued]
Pet Food

SIC: 2047; NAICS: 311111

Top Dry Dog Food Makers, 2004

Market shares are shown based on sales at super-markets, drugstores and mass merchandisers (but not Wal-Mart) for the year ended January 25, 2004.

Nunn Milling	0.65%
American Nutrition	0.59
Windy Hill Pet Food	0.48
Private label	8.41
Other	0.76

Source: *Grocery Headquarters*, April 2004, p. 16, from Information Resources Inc.

★ 403 ★
Pet Food

SIC: 2047; NAICS: 311111

Top Dry Dog Food Makers in Australia

Market shares are shown in percent for 2000. In the wet dog food segment, Uncle Ben's leads with a 65.3% value share and a 68.4% volume share.

	Value	Volume
Uncle Ben's	53.6%	51.6%
Friskie's	24.8	25.1
Generics	10.3	12.6
Green's	7.7	6.5
Ralston Purina	0.8	0.3
Private label	1.5	1.7
Other	1.4	2.2

Source: "Australia Product Brief Pet Food 2003." [online] from http://www.fas.usda.gov [accessed January 1, 2004], from *Grocery Industry Marketing Guide 1999-2001*.

★ 404 ★
Pet Food

SIC: 2047; NAICS: 311111

Top Pet Food Brands in the U.K., 2003

Brands are ranked by sales in thousands of pounds sterling for the year ended October 4, 2003.

	(000)	Share
Whiskas (pouch)	103,907	9.37%
Whiskas (canned)	85,161	7.68
Pedigree (canned)	78,392	7.07%
Felix (canned)	73,363	6.62
Bakers (complete)	37,179	3.35
Friskies Go Cat (complete)	36,963	3.33
Iams Cat (complete)	35,473	3.20
Butchers (canned)	35,079	3.16
Other	623,286	56.21

Source: *Grocer*, December 13, 2003, p. 66, from Information Resources Inc.

★ 405 ★
Pet Food

SIC: 2047; NAICS: 311111

Top Pet Food Makers Worldwide, 2000

Market shares are shown in percent.

Mars	20.9%
Nestle	13.5
Ralston Purina	8.7
Colgate-Palmolive	5.2
Procter & Gamble	4.9
Heinz	4.5
Royal Canin	1.7
Other	40.6

Source: *Eurofood*, December 20, 2001, p. 8, from Euromonitor.

★ 406 ★
Bakery Products

SIC: 2050; NAICS: 311812, 311821

Baked Goods Market in Thailand

The market is estimated to be worth 3.3 billion baht.

Crackers	40.0%
Cookies	35.0
Wafers	25.0

Source: *Bangkok Post*, April 23, 2004, p. NA, from ACNielsen.

★ 407 ★

Bakery Products

SIC: 2050; NAICS: 311812, 311821

Foodservice Bakery Sales

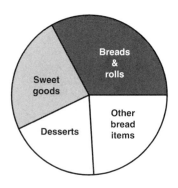

Total manufacturer sales reached $13 billion.

Breads & rolls	33.0%
Sweet goods	24.0
Desserts	19.0
Other bread items	24.0

Source: *Snack Food & Wholesale Bakery*, August 2003, p. 22, from Strategic Growth Partners Inc.

★ 408 ★

Bakery Products

SIC: 2050; NAICS: 311812, 311821

Leading Bakery Product Producers, 2002

Companies are ranked by bakery product sales in millions of dollars.

General Mills	$ 1,500
Sara Lee	1,100
Rich Productts Corp.	570
Mrs. Smith's	570
Otis Spunkmeyer	280
The Schwan Food Co.	250
Chef Solutions	200
The Bama Cos.	180
Pepperidge Farms (div. of Campbell's Soup) .	170
Country Home Bakers	170

Source: *Refrigerated and Frozen Foods*, February 2003, p. 12.

★ 409 ★

Bakery Products

SIC: 2050; NAICS: 311812, 311821

Top Sweet Goods Brands, 2003

Brands are ranked by sales at food stores (no supercenters) for the 52 weeks ended October 12, 2003.

	($ mil.)	Share
Entenmann's	$ 459.29	15.60%
Hostess (Interstate Brands Corp.) .	334.66	11.37
Little Debbie (McKee Foods) . . .	329.19	11.18
Krispy Kreme	223.32	7.59
Tatykake (Tasty Baking Co.) . . .	96.03	3.26
Dolly Madison (I.B.C.)	67.53	2.29
Drake (I.B.C.)	62.14	2.11
Svenhards	43.04	1.46
Otis Spunkmeyer	30.81	1.05
Private label	833.15	28.30
Other	464.89	15.79

Source: *Baking & Snack*, December 2003, p. 56, from Information Resources Inc.

★ 410 ★

Bakery Products

SIC: 2050; NAICS: 311812, 311821

Top Sweet Goods Vendors, 2003

Brands are ranked by sales at food stores (no supercenters) for the 52 weeks ended October 12, 2003.

	($ mil.)	Share
Interstate Brands Corp.	$ 489.79	16.64%
Enternmann's	459.79	15.62
McKee Baking Co.	334.20	11.35
Krispy Kreme	223.32	7.59
Tasty Baking Co.	96.04	3.26
Flowers Foods	53.89	1.83
Svenhards Swedish Bakery	43.14	1.47
Sara Lee Bakery Group	34.56	1.17
Bimbo Bakeries	33.45	1.14
Private label	833.36	28.31
Other	342.51	11.63

Source: *Baking & Snack*, December 2003, p. 56, from Information Resources Inc.

★ 411 ★
Bakery Products
SIC: 2051; NAICS: 311812, 311821
Bakery Product Sales, 2002

Market shares are shown based on supermarket,
drug store and mass merchandiser sales.

	($ mil.)	Share
Bread aisle	$ 12,355.8	36.53%
Cookies & crackers	11,128.1	32.90
Baked sweet goods	4,643.4	13.73
Refrigerated & frozen baked goods	3,312.2	9.79
Snack bars	2,383.1	7.05

Source: *Snack Food & Wholesale Bakery*, June 2003,
pp. SI-61, from Information Resources Inc.

★ 412 ★
Bread
SIC: 2051; NAICS: 311812
Bread Market in Germany

Market shares are shown in percent.

Mixed flour	47.0%
Rye flour	20.0
Multi grain	11.0
Soft white (toastbrot)	10.0
Wheat flour	9.0
Other	3.0

Source: *Frankfurter Allgemeine*, October 23, 2003, p. 14,
from GfK.

★ 413 ★
Bread
SIC: 2051; NAICS: 311812
Bread Market Shares, 2002

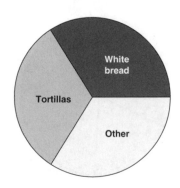

Tortilla sales have grown by just under 10% a year.
It has helped to greatly expand the bread market.

White bread	34.0%
Tortillas	32.0
Other	34.0

Source: *San Jose Mercury News*, December 2, 2003,
p. NA, from Tortilla Industry Association.

★ 414 ★
Bread
SIC: 2051; NAICS: 311812
Leading Bread/Roll Markets in Europe, 2002 and 2006

Data show the value of the top markets in billions of
dollars. Sweet biscuits have the largest share of the
bakery/cereal market.

	2002	2006
Germany	$ 9.28	$ 10.06
France	8.59	10.31
Italy	6.38	7.50
United Kingdom	5.39	5.80
Spain	2.66	3.01

Source: *Food Engineering & Ingredients*, April 2003, p. 4,
from Datamonitor.

★ 415 ★

Bread

SIC: 2051; NAICS: 311812

Top Bagel Brands, 2003

Market shares are shown based on supermarket sales for the 52 weeks ended January 5, 2003. Figures exclude Wal-Mart.

	($ mil.)	Share
Thomas'	$ 162.1	36.2%
Sara Lee	86.1	19.3
Lenders Bagel Shop	32.1	7.2
Earth Grains	26.3	5.9
Private label	64.2	14.0

Source: *Snack Food & Wholesale Bakery*, June 2003, p. SI-37, from Information Resources Inc.

★ 416 ★

Bread

SIC: 2051; NAICS: 311812

Top Bread Brands, 2003

Brands are ranked by sales at food stores for the year ended March 30, 2003.

	($ mil.)	Share
Wonder	$ 330.37	5.64%
Pepperidge Farm	280.04	4.78
Oroweat	256.60	4.38
Nature's Own	203.64	3.48
Home Pride	174.70	2.98
Sun Beam	170.10	2.90

	($ mil.)	Share
Arnold	$ 165.54	2.83%
Merita	94.52	1.61
Brownberry	89.70	1.53
Other	4,094.49	69.88

Source: *Baking & Snack*, June 1, 2003, p. NA, from Information Resources Inc.

★ 417 ★

Bread

SIC: 2051; NAICS: 311812

Top Bread Brands in the U.K., 2003

Sales of pre-packaged brands are shown in thousands of pounds sterling for the year ended October 5, 2003.

	(000)	Share
Hovis	£ 230,113	26.37%
Kingsmill	180,699	20.70
Warburtons	178,969	20.51
Weight Watchers	17,929	2.05
Nimble	16,158	1.85
Other	248,890	28.52

Source: *Grocer*, December 13, 2003, p. 49, from Information Resources Inc.

★ 418 ★

Bread

SIC: 2051; NAICS: 311812

Top Bread/Roll/Pastry Dough Makers, 2003

Market shares are shown based on supermarket sales for the year ended August 10, 2003.

	($ mil.)	Share
Rhodes International	$ 44.5	32.04%
General Mills	23.5	16.92
Hom'ade Foods	21.2	15.26
Bridgford Foods	9.6	6.91
Private label	15.3	11.02
Other	24.8	17.85

Source: *Refrigerated & Frozen Foods*, October 2003, p. 60, from Information Resources Inc. InfoScan.

★ 419 ★
Bread
SIC: 2051; NAICS: 311812
Top Dinner Roll/Biscuit Brands, 2003

Market shares are shown based on supermarket sales for the 52 weeks ended January 5, 2003. Figures exclude Wal-Mart.

King's Hawaiian	11.9%
Francisco International	7.2
Private label	24.2
Other	56.7

Source: *Snack Food & Wholesale Bakery*, June 2003, p. SI-37, from Information Resources Inc.

★ 420 ★
Bread
SIC: 2051; NAICS: 311812
Top English Muffin Brands, 2003

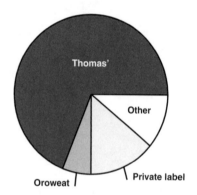

Market shares are shown based on supermarket sales for the 52 weeks ended January 5, 2003. Figures exclude Wal-Mart.

Thomas'	69.3%
Oroweat	5.7
Private label	14.3
Other	10.7

Source: *Snack Food & Wholesale Bakery*, June 2003, p. SI-37, from Information Resources Inc.

★ 421 ★
Bread
SIC: 2051; NAICS: 311812
Top Fresh Bread Makers, 2004

Market shares are shown based on sales at supermarkets, drugstores and mass merchandisers (but not Wal-Mart) for the year ended January 25, 2004.

Interstate Brands Corp.	14.1%
George Weston Inc.	14.1
Sara Lee Bakery Group	10.0
Flowers Bakeries	7.1
Private label	27.9
Other	30.6

Source: *Grocery Headquarters*, April 2004, p. 16, from Information Resources Inc.

★ 422 ★
Bread
SIC: 2051; NAICS: 311812
Top Frozen Bread/Roll/Biscuit Brands, 2003

Market shares are shown based on supermarket, drugstore and mass merchandiser sales for the 52 weeks ended March 23, 2003. Figures exclude Wal-Mart.

Pillsbury Home Baked Classics	21.4%
Pepperidge Farm	19.0
New York	18.8
Cole's	12.1
Private label	9.8
Other	18.9

Source: *Snack Food & Wholesale Bakery*, June 2003, p. SI-37, from Information Resources Inc.

★ 423 ★
Bread
SIC: 2051; NAICS: 311812

Top Hamburger/Hot Dog Bun Brands, 2003

Market shares are shown based on supermarket sales for the 52 weeks ended January 5, 2003. Figures exclude Wal-Mart.

	($ mil.)	Share
Wonder	$ 56.7	5.9%
Rainbo	31.2	3.3
Sunbeam	30.8	3.2
Oroweat	22.3	2.3
Private label	455.7	47.8

Source: *Snack Food & Wholesale Bakery*, June 2003, p. SI-37, from Information Resources Inc.

★ 424 ★
Cakes
SIC: 2051; NAICS: 311812

Top Cake Brands in the U.K., 2003

Brands are ranked by sales in thousands of pounds sterling for the year ended October 4, 2003.

	(000)	Share
Cadbury MiniRolls	£ 27,753	5.31%
Mr. Kipling Pies	22,732	4.35
Soreen Malt Loaf	8,330	1.59
Mr. Kipling Cherry Bakewells	7,998	1.53
McVitie's Jaff Cake Bars	6,543	1.25
Mr. Kipling Country Slices	6,051	1.16
Mr. Kipling Lemon Slices	5,921	1.13
Mr. Kipling Viennese Whirls	5,919	1.13
Mr. Kipling Angel Slices	4,959	0.95
Other	426,723	81.60

Source: *Grocer*, December 13, 2003, p. 66, from Information Resources Inc.

★ 425 ★
Danish
SIC: 2051; NAICS: 311812

Top Danish Brands, 2003

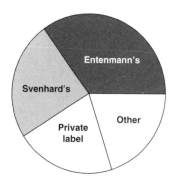

Market shares are shown based on supermarket sales for the 52 weeks ended February 2, 2003. Figures exclude Wal-Mart.

Entenmann's	35.4%
Svenhard's	23.7
Private label	21.1
Other	19.8

Source: *Snack Food & Wholesale Bakery*, June 2003, p. SI-37, from Information Resources Inc.

★ 426 ★
Donuts
SIC: 2051; NAICS: 311812

Top Donut Brands, 2003

Market shares are shown based on supermarket sales for the 52 weeks ended February 2, 2003.

Krispy Kreme	24.6%
Entenmann's	22.1
Hostess	13.7
Dolly Madison	5.8
Private label	14.4
Other	19.4

Source: *Snack Food & Wholesale Bakery*, June 2003, p. SI-37, from Information Resources Inc.

★ 427 ★

Snack Cakes

SIC: 2051; NAICS: 311812

Top Snack Cake Brands, 2003

Brands are ranked by food store sales (not supercenters) in millions of dollars for the 52 weeks ended May 25, 2003.

	($ mil.)	Share
Little Debbie	$ 219.70	31.8%
Hostess	209.47	30.3
Tastykake	69.52	10.1
Drake	42.00	6.1
Dolly Madison	13.26	1.9
Entenmann's	12.93	1.9
Freeds Bakery	9.93	1.4
Marinela	5.62	0.8
BlueBird	5.16	0.7
Private label	75.62	10.9

Source: *Baking & Snack*, July 1, 2003, p. NA, from Information Resources Inc.

★ 428 ★

Snack Cakes

SIC: 2051; NAICS: 311812

Top Snack Cake Vendors, 2003

Market shares are shown based on supermarket sales for the 52 weeks ended August 17, 2003. Figures exclude Wal-Mart.

Entenmann's	15.7%
Hostess	11.5
Little Debbie	11.3
Krispy Kreme	7.2
Tastykake	3.3
Dolly Madison	2.3
Drake	2.2
Svenhards	1.5
Private label	28.5
Other	16.5

Source: *Snack Food & Wholesale Bakery*, September 2003, p. SI-37, from Information Resources Inc.

★ 429 ★

Snack Cakes

SIC: 2051; NAICS: 311812

Top Snack Pie Brands, 2003

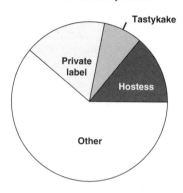

Market shares are shown based on supermarket sales for the 52 weeks ended February 2, 2003. Figures exclude Wal-Mart.

Hostess	14.0%
Tastykake	8.3
Private label	17.1
Other	60.6

Source: *Snack Food & Wholesale Bakery*, June 2003, p. SI-37, from Information Resources Inc.

★ 430 ★

Cookies

SIC: 2052; NAICS: 311821

Chocolate Wafer Cookie Market, 2002

Total sales were $200 million.

Kit Kat	32.0%
Twix	29.0
Reese's Sticks	28.0
Other	11.0

Source: *Food Processing*, January 2004, p. 18.

★ 431 ★
Cookies
SIC: 2052; NAICS: 311821

Cookie Market in Argentina, 2003

The biscuits market in Argentina is worth 900 million peso per year.

Kraft	26.0%
Danone	22.0
Arcor	21.5
Other	30.5

Source: *South American Business Information*, April 1, 2004, p. NA, from COMTEX.

★ 432 ★
Cookies
SIC: 2052; NAICS: 311821

Top Biscuits (Savory and Sweet)/ Cookie Brands Worldwide, 2001

Market shares are shown in percent.

Nabisco	3.0%
Oreo	2.5
Keebler	2.5
Ritz	2.1
Pepperidge Farm	1.8
Mulino Bianco	1.4
Chips Ahoy!	1.4
Sunshine	1.0
Arnotts	0.9
Other	83.4

Source: *just-food.com (Management Briefing)*, October 2003, p. NA, from Euromonitor.

★ 433 ★
Cookies
SIC: 2052; NAICS: 311821

Top Cookie Brands, 2003

Sales at food stores are shown for the 52 weeks ended August 10, 2003. Figures exclude supercenters.

	($ mil.)	Share
Nabisco Oreo	$ 549.30	13.62%
Nabisco Chips Ahoy	355.87	8.82
Keebler Chips Deluxe	142.13	3.52
Nabisco Newtons	133.41	3.31
Pepperidge Farm Distinctive . . .	123.42	3.06
Keebler Fudge Shoppe	105.45	2.61
Nabisco Teddy Grahams	94.13	2.33
Nabisco Snackwells	91.03	2.26
Nabisco Nilla	87.18	2.16
Pepperidge Farm Classics	82.80	2.05
Other	2,268.78	56.25

Source: *Baking & Snack*, October 1, 2003, p. NA, from Information Resources Inc.

★ 434 ★
Cookies
SIC: 2052; NAICS: 311821

Top Cookie Brands in the U.K., 2003

Brands are ranked by sales in thousands of pounds sterling for the year ended October 4, 2003.

	(000)	Share
Nestle Kit Kat	£ 76,812	4.32%
McVitie's Homewheat	67,933	3.82
Quaker Snack-a-Jacks	47,735	2.68
Kellogg's Nutri-grain	42,838	2.41

Continued on next page.

★ 434 ★

[Continued]

Cookies

SIC: 2052; NAICS: 311821

Top Cookie Brands in the U.K., 2003

Brands are ranked by sales in thousands of pounds sterling for the year ended October 4, 2003.

	(000)	Share
McVitie's Jaffa cakes	£ 42,067	2.37%
Mcvitie's Penguin	39,387	2.21
Twix	35,206	1.98
McVitie's Digestive	32,850	1.85
Cadbury Fingers	31,244	1.76
Other	1,362,469	76.61

Source: *Grocer*, December 13, 2003, p. 66, from Information Resources Inc.

★ 435 ★

Cookies

SIC: 2052; NAICS: 311821

Top Cookie Brands (Unit Sales)

Nabisco Oreo
Nabisco Chips Ahoy!
Keebler Chips Deluxe
Keebler Fudge Shoppe
Nabisco Newtons
Pepperidge Farm Distinctive
Nabisco Teddy Grahams
Nabisco Snackwell's
Pepperidge Farm Classics
Nabisco 'Nilla Wafers

Brands are ranked by unit sales at food stores, drug stores and mass merchandisers for the year ended February 23, 2003. Figures exclude Wal-Mart.

Nabisco Oreo	202.7
Nabisco Chips Ahoy!	136.4
Keebler Chips Deluxe	62.3
Keebler Fudge Shoppe	51.6
Nabisco Newtons	47.9
Pepperidge Farm Distinctive	47.5

Nabisco Teddy Grahams	43.3
Nabisco Snackwell's	40.7
Pepperidge Farm Classics	33.1
Nabisco 'Nilla Wafers	28.1

Source: *Progressive Grocer*, May 1, 2003, p. 75, from Information Resources Inc.

★ 436 ★

Cookies

SIC: 2052; NAICS: 311821

Top Cookie Makers, 2003

Sales at food stores are shown for the 52 weeks ended August 10, 2003. Figures exclude supercenters.

	($ mil.)	Share
Nabisco	$ 1,538.91	38.15%
Keebler (Kellogg's)	517.50	12.83
Parmalat	291.39	7.22
Pepperidge Farm Inc.	274.39	6.80
Little Debbie (McKee Foods)	197.51	4.90
Murray Biscuit Co.	188.11	4.66
Voortman	57.17	1.42
Masterfoods USA/Mars	55.40	1.37
Stella D'Oro (Kraft)	39.88	0.99
Other	873.24	21.65

Source: *Baking & Snack*, October 1, 2003, p. NA, from Information Resources Inc.

★ 437 ★

Crackers

SIC: 2052; NAICS: 311821

Top Cracker Brands, 2003

Sales at food stores are shown for the 52 weeks ended August 10, 2003. Figures exclude supercenters.

	($ mil.)	Share
Nabisco Ritz Everyday	$ 325.51	9.55%
Sunshine Cheez-it	313.46	9.20
Nabisco Wheat Thins	278.56	8.18
Pepperidge Farm Goldfish	259.23	7.61
Nabisco Premium	230.03	6.75
Nabisco Triscuit	204.29	6.00
Nabisco Graham	167.42	4.91
Keebler Club	114.27	3.35
Nabisco Ritz Bits Bite Size	112.02	3.29

Continued on next page.

★ 437 ★

[Continued]

Crackers

SIC: 2052; NAICS: 311821

Top Cracker Brands, 2003

Sales at food stores are shown for the 52 weeks ended August 10, 2003. Figures exclude supercenters.

	($ mil.)	Share
Nabisco Cheese Nips	$ 102.47	3.01%
Other	1,299.69	38.15

Source: *Baking & Snack*, October 1, 2003, p. NA, from Information Resources Inc.

★ 438 ★

Crackers

SIC: 2052; NAICS: 311821

Top Cracker Vendors, 2003

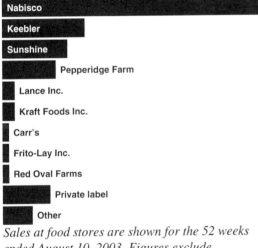

Nabisco
Keebler
Sunshine
Pepperidge Farm
Lance Inc.
Kraft Foods Inc.
Carr's
Frito-Lay Inc.
Red Oval Farms
Private label
Other

Sales at food stores are shown for the 52 weeks ended August 10, 2003. Figures exclude supercenters.

	($ mil.)	Share
Nabisco (Kraft)	$ 1,597.82	46.90%
Keebler (Kellogg's)	488.06	14.33
Sunshine (Kellogg's)	358.88	10.53
Pepperidge Farm	294.03	8.63
Lance Inc.	72.89	2.14
Kraft Foods Inc.	57.75	1.70
Carr's	49.47	1.45
Frito-Lay Inc.	27.06	0.79
Red Oval Farms (Kraft)	25.65	0.75
Private label	258.65	7.59
Other	176.69	5.19

Source: *Baking & Snack*, October 1, 2003, p. NA, from Information Resources Inc.

★ 439 ★

Frozen Bakery Products

SIC: 2053; NAICS: 311813

Cheesecake Market

Shares of the $85 million market are shown for the year ended June 15, 2003.

Sara Lee	60.6%
Other	39.4

Source: *St. Louis Business Journal*, July 28, 2003, p. NA, from Information Resources Inc.

★ 440 ★

Frozen Bakery Products

SIC: 2053; NAICS: 311813

Leading Sweet Good Brands

Data are for the 12 weeks ended August 10, 2003 and exclude cheesecakes.

	($ mil.)	Share
Pillsbury Toaster Streudl	$ 22.86	32.69%
Sara Lee	11.73	16.78
Pepperidge Farm Three Layer Cake	9.23	13.20
Mrs. Smith's	6.93	9.91
Pepperidge Farm	3.40	4.86
Other	15.77	22.55

Source: *Frozen Food Age*, October 2003, p. 14, from Information Resources Inc.

★ 441 ★

Frozen Bakery Products

SIC: 2053; NAICS: 311813

Top Frozen Pie Brands, 2003

Market shares are shown based on supermarket, drug store and mass merchandiser sales for the 52 weeks ended July 13, 2003. Figures exclude Wal-Mart.

Mrs. Smith's	24.2%
Edwards	11.4
Sara Lee	11.1
Marie Callenders	9.5
Pet Ritz	8.7
Pepperidge Farm	3.7
Mrs. Smith's Special Recipe	3.4
Sara Lee Oven Fresh	2.7

Continued on next page.

★ 441 ★

[Continued]
Frozen Bakery Products
SIC: 2053; NAICS: 311813

Top Frozen Pie Brands, 2003

Market shares are shown based on supermarket, drug store and mass merchandiser sales for the 52 weeks ended July 13, 2003. Figures exclude Wal-Mart.

Sara Lee Signature Collections	1.7%
Private label	7.6
Other	16.0

Source: *Snack Food & Wholesale Bakery*, August 2003, p. SI-37, from Information Resources Inc.

★ 442 ★

Frozen Bakery Products
SIC: 2053; NAICS: 311813

Top Frozen Pie Makers, 2003

Market shares are shown based on supermarket sales for the 52 weeks ended August 10, 2003. Figures exclude Wal-Mart and refer to supermarkets with sales of $2 million or more.

Schwan Food Co.	56.2%
Sara Lee Bakery	15.6
American Pie	9.6
General Mills	8.7
Other	19.9

Source: *Refrigerated & Frozen Foods*, October 2003, p. 53, from Information Resources Inc. InfoScan.

★ 443 ★

Sugar
SIC: 2060; NAICS: 311311, 311312

U.S. Sugar Imports

Imports account for 15% of sugar use.

Dominican Republic	17.9%
Brazil	14.7
Philippines	13.7
Australia	8.2
Guatemala	4.8
Other	40.7

Source: *USA TODAY*, February 11, 2004, p. 3B, from United States Department of Agriculture Economic Research Service.

★ 444 ★

Sugar Substitutes
SIC: 2061; NAICS: 311311

Top Sugar Substitutes, 2003

Market shares are shown for the 52 weeks ended June 15, 2003. Figures exclude Wal-Mart.

Splenda	28.6%
Equal	26.8
Sweet & Low	19.7
Natrataste	6.1
Private label	6.9
Other	11.9

Source: *St. Louis Post-Dispatch*, August 1, 2003, p. C1, from Information Resources Inc.

★ 445 ★
Breath Fresheners
SIC: 2064; NAICS: 31134

Mouth Freshening Industry Worldwide, 2002

The breath strip category — also known as the breath freshening category — was created by Pfizer's Warner Lambert division in August 2000 with Listerine Pocketpak strips. The global market was worth $502.9 million.

	($ bil.)	Share
United States	$ 348.7	69.34%
Japan	10.8	2.15
United Kingdom	6.7	1.33
Spain	4.9	0.97
France	2.5	0.50
Italy	1.6	0.32
Other	127.7	25.39

Source: *Soap & Cosmetics*, August-September 2003, p. 10, from Euromonitor.

★ 446 ★
Breath Fresheners
SIC: 2064; NAICS: 31132

Top Breath Freshener Firms, 2003

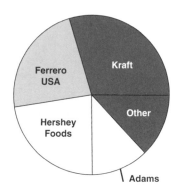

Shares are shown based on sales at food, drug and mass merchandisers for the 52 weeks ended February 23, 2003. Figures exclude Wal-Mart.

Kraft	29.8%
Ferrero USA	23.1
Hershey Foods	22.7
Adams	11.6
Other	12.8

Source: *Candy Industry*, April 2003, p. 39, from Information Resources Inc.

★ 447 ★
Breath Fresheners
SIC: 2064; NAICS: 31134

Top Breath Fresheners (Sprays/Drops), 2004

Brands are ranked by sales at supermarkets, drugstores and discount stores (but not Wal-Mart) for the year ended January 25, 2004.

	($ mil.)	Share
Binaca	$ 5.2	32.30%
Sweet Breath	2.9	18.01
Mint Asure	1.9	11.80
Dentek Breath Remedy	1.6	9.94
Breath Asure	1.3	8.07
Crystal	0.5	3.11
Binaca Blasters	0.5	3.11
Therabreath	0.4	2.48
Puretek Breath Relief	0.4	2.48
Rembrandt Dazzling	0.3	1.86
Private label	0.7	4.35
Other	0.4	2.48

Source: *MMR*, April 19, 2004, p. 59, from Information Resources Inc.

★ 448 ★
Breath Fresheners
SIC: 2064; NAICS: 31134

Top Mini Mint Brands in New Zealand

Smint
Tic Tac
Other

Market shares are shown in percent.

Smint	46.0%
Tic Tac	37.2
Other	16.8

Source: *Grocer's Review*, August 2003, p. NA.

★ 449 ★
Confectionery Products
SIC: 2064; NAICS: 31133, 31134

Best-Selling Candy Occasions, 2002

Figures are in billions of dollars. Chocolate confectionery sales stood at about $14.4 billion in 2003. Only about 5% come from gourmet and specialty shops.

Halloween/Back-to-school	$ 2.0
Easter	1.8
Winter holidays	1.5
Valentine's Day	1.0

Source: *Gourmet Retailer*, February 2004, p. 22, from National Confectionery Association and Mintel.

★ 450 ★
Confectionery Products
SIC: 2064; NAICS: 31133, 31134

Confectionery Market in Australia, 2002

Total sales reached $1.24 billion from July 2001 - June 2002 (Australia's fiscal year). Cadbury, Nestle and Mars/Kenman are the confectionery leaders with 75% of the market. Wrigley has 98% of the gum market.

	($ mil.)	Share
Chocolate	$ 708	55.66%
Sugar	485	38.13
Chewing gum	79	6.21

Source: *AgExporter*, July 2003, p. 10.

★ 451 ★
Confectionery Products
SIC: 2064; NAICS: 31133, 31134

Functional Confectionery Market Worldwide

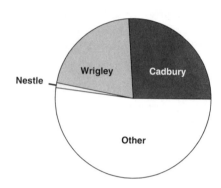

The industry refers to gums and candy with oral care properties, such as teeth whitening. The market was valued at $10 billion by Cadbury and is growing at 5.2% a year.

Cadbury	26.0%
Wrigley	21.0
Nestle	0.6
Other	52.4

Source: *Wall Street Journal*, June 18, 2003, p. D3, from Cadbury.

★ 452 ★
Confectionery Products
SIC: 2064; NAICS: 31133, 31134

Hard Candy Market in Indonesia

Market shares are shown in percent.

Relaxa	16.0%
Kopiko	13.5
Hexos	2.5
Fox	2.4
Other	67.1

Source: *Indonesian Commercial Newsletter*, June 25, 2002, p. 16.

★ 453 ★

Confectionery Products

SIC: 2064; NAICS: 31133, 31134

Largest Confectionery Markets Worldwide, 2002 and 2007

The market is forecasted to grow from $112.4 billion in 2002 to $122.5 billion in 2008. Chocolate confectionery will take $64.3 billion, followed by sugar with $42.1 billion and gum with $16.3 billion. Sales are shown for 2002 and projected for 2007 in billions of dollars.

	2002	2007
United States	$ 25.2	$ 27.2
United Kingdom	7.9	8.2
Germany	7.8	8.4
Japan	7.4	8.1
Russia	5.0	6.1
China	4.0	5.9
France	3.8	4.1
Brazil	3.2	4.0
Italy	3.2	3.4
Mexico	2.8	3.0

Source: *Candy Industry*, August 2003, p. 30, from Euromonitor, *The World Market for Confectionery 2003.*

★ 454 ★

Confectionery Products

SIC: 2064; NAICS: 31133, 31134

Non-Chocolate Candy Industry, 2003

Sales are shown at food stores, drug stores and mass merchandiser sales for the year ended December 28, 2003. Figures exclude Wal-Mart.

	($ mil.)	Share
Chewy	$ 659.43	27.24%
Hard packaged & rolled	318.54	13.16
Novelty	270.82	11.19
Breath fresheners	237.14	9.80
Diet candy	154.99	6.40
Licorice box/bags > 3.5 oz	153.43	6.34
Plain mints	123.94	5.17
Easter	113.20	4.68
Christmas	100.52	4.15
Valentine's Day	79.52	3.29
Specialty nut/coconut candy	76.59	3.16

Source: *Candy Business*, January - February 2004, p. 8, from Information Resources Inc.

★ 455 ★

Confectionery Products

SIC: 2064; NAICS: 31133, 31134

Retail Confectionery Sales in Canada

Sales are shown for the year ended February 22, 2003.

	($ mil.)	Share
Chocolate bars	$ 758	43.61%
Gum	345	19.85
Boxed chocolates/packaged confections	210	12.08
Non-chocolate confections	167	9.61
Cough drops incl. alpine & fisherman friends	97	5.58
Portable breath fresheners	44	2.53
Energy and nutritional bars	40	2.30
Hard rolled candy, single and multi	39	2.24
Mini mints	38	2.19

Source: *Food in Canada*, May 2003, p. 52, from ACNielsen MarketTrack.

★ 456 ★

Confectionery Products

SIC: 2064; NAICS: 31133, 31134

Top Christmas Candy Makers, 2003

The top brands of non-chocolate Christmas candies are shown for the year ended January 26, 2003. Sales are shown for food, drug and mass merchandiser sales (except Wal-Mart) and seasonally wrapped products only.

	($ mil.)	Share
Bobs Candies Inc.	$ 12.12	11.66%
Spangler Candy Co.	11.13	10.71
Kraft/Nabisco	9.47	9.11

Continued on next page.

★ 456 ★
[Continued]
Confectionery Products
SIC: 2064; NAICS: 31133, 31134

Top Christmas Candy Makers, 2003

The top brands of non-chocolate Christmas candies are shown for the year ended January 26, 2003. Sales are shown for food, drug and mass merchandiser sales (except Wal-Mart) and seasonally wrapped products only.

	($ mil.)	Share
Brach's Confections	$ 9.16	8.81%
Jaret International Inc.	7.78	7.49
Asher Candy Co.	5.00	4.81
Galerie Au Chocolat Inc.	4.81	4.63
Nestle USA Inc.	3.62	3.48
Hershey Foods Corp.	3.47	3.34
Masterfoods USA	3.14	3.02
Other	34.22	32.93

Source: *Professional Candy Buyer*, May-June 2003, p. 106, from Information Resources Inc.

★ 457 ★
Confectionery Products
SIC: 2064; NAICS: 31133, 31134

Top Confectionery Makers Worldwide, 2002

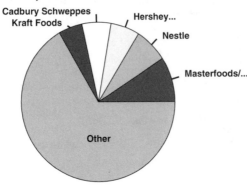

Market shares are shown in percent.

Masterfoods/Mars	9.4%
Nestle	7.4
Hershey Food Group	6.3
Cadbury Schweppes	6.0
Kraft Foods	5.0
Other	65.9

Source: *Duty-Free News International*, August 1, 2003, p. 9, from Euromonitor.

★ 458 ★
Confectionery Products
SIC: 2064; NAICS: 31133, 31134

Top Confectionery Producers in Brazil, 2003

Market shares are shown in percent. Nestle acquired Garoto in February 2002. The Brazilian Administrative Council for Economic Defense (CADE) has yet to rule on this merger however.

Kraft	33.0%
Nestle	29.0
Garoto	21.0
Other	17.0

Source: *South American Business Information*, January 22, 2004, p. NA.

★ 459 ★
Confectionery Products
SIC: 2064; NAICS: 31133, 31134

Top Confectionery Producers in Russia

The industry is valued at 2 million tons per year. Market shares are shown based on value.

Nestle	18.9%
Babaevskij	10.1
Stollwerck	9.8
Mars	8.2
Krasnyj Oktyabr	7.2
SladKo	5.7
Cadbury	4.2
Rot-Front	4.1
Other	31.8

Source: *Kommersant*, April 17, 2002, p. 17.

★ 460 ★
Confectionery Products
SIC: 2064; NAICS: 31133, 31134

Top Diet Candy Makers, 2003

Companies are ranked by sales for the year ended November 2, 2003. Figures exclude Wal-Mart.

	($ mil.)	Share
Russell Stover	$ 45.6	32.50%
Hershey Foods	10.0	7.13

Continued on next page.

★ 460 ★

[Continued]
Confectionery Products
SIC: 2064; NAICS: 31133, 31134

Top Diet Candy Makers, 2003

Companies are ranked by sales for the year ended November 2, 2003. Figures exclude Wal-Mart.

	($ mil.)	Share
Sweet N Low	$ 8.3	5.92%
Whitman's	6.5	4.63
Creme Savers	6.4	4.56
Reeses	5.7	4.06
Velamints	4.8	3.42
Estee	4.6	3.28
Carbolite	4.3	3.06
Private label	6.3	4.49
Other	37.8	26.94

Source: *Grocey Headquarters*, February 2004, p. 29, from Information Resources Inc.

★ 461 ★

Confectionery Products
SIC: 2064; NAICS: 31133, 31134

Top Licorice Brands > 3.5 oz, 2002

Market shares are shown based on sales at food, drug stores and mass merchandisers (but not Wal-Mart) for the year ended December 29, 2002.

Twizzlers	61.3%
American Licorice	21.1
Good & Plenty	7.4
Kenny's	3.5
Bassett's	2.1
Panda	0.7
Nibs	0.6
Twizzler Twist n Fill	0.4
Private label	0.8
Other	2.1

Source: *Professional Candy Buyer*, May - June 2003, p. 86, from Information Resources Inc.

★ 462 ★

Confectionery Products
SIC: 2064; NAICS: 31133, 31134

Top Non-Chocolate Chewy Brands, 2002

Market shares are shown based on sales at food, drug stores and mass merchandisers (but not Wal-Mart) for the year ended December 29, 2002.

Starburst	11.3%
Skittles	8.0
Tootsie Roll	4.2
Lifesavers Gummisavers	3.7
Jelly Belly	3.7
Mentos	3.0
Farley's	2.7
Air Heads	2.6
Brach's	2.4
Other	58.4

Source: *Professional Candy Buyer*, May - June 2003, p. 86, from Information Resources Inc.

★ 463 ★

Confectionery Products
SIC: 2064; NAICS: 31133, 31134

Top Packaged/Rolled Hard Candy Brands, 2002

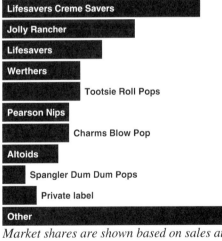

Lifesavers Creme Savers
Jolly Rancher
Lifesavers
Werthers
Tootsie Roll Pops
Pearson Nips
Charms Blow Pop
Altoids
Spangler Dum Dum Pops
Private label
Other

Market shares are shown based on sales at food, drug stores and mass merchandisers (but not Wal-Mart) for the year ended December 29, 2002.

Lifesavers Creme Savers	18.1%
Jolly Rancher	12.2
Lifesavers	8.9
Werthers	7.4
Tootsie Roll Pops	6.7

Continued on next page.

★ 463 ★

[Continued]
Confectionery Products
SIC: 2064; NAICS: 31133, 31134

Top Packaged/Rolled Hard Candy Brands, 2002

Market shares are shown based on sales at food, drug stores and mass merchandisers (but not Wal-Mart) for the year ended December 29, 2002.

Pearson Nips	5.9%
Charms Blow Pop	5.5
Altoids	4.9
Spangler Dum Dum Pops	2.3
Private label	3.3
Other	24.8

Source: *Professional Candy Buyer*, May - June 2003, p. 86, from Information Resources Inc.

★ 464 ★

Confectionery Products
SIC: 2064; NAICS: 31133, 31134

Top Specialty Nut/Coconut Candy Brands, 2002

Market shares are shown based on sales at food, drug stores and mass merchandisers (but not Wal-Mart) for the year ended December 29, 2002.

Payday	30.5%
Brach's Maple Nut Goodies	8.1
Pearson's	5.3
Sophie Mae	4.0
Planters	3.2
Brach's	3.1
Annabelle Big Hunk	2.4
Russell Stover	1.8
FP Boston Baked Beans	1.8
Other	39.8

Source: *Professional Candy Buyer*, May - June 2003, p. 86, from Information Resources Inc.

★ 465 ★

Confectionery Products
SIC: 2064; NAICS: 31133, 31134

Top Sugar Candy Makers, 2003

Market shares are shown based on food, drug and mass merchandiser sales (but not Wal-Mart) for the year ended December 28, 2003.

Hershey	13.0%
Kraft Foods	12.1
Mars	9.2
Tootsie Roll	7.2
Nestle	6.4
Other	52.1

Source: *Candy Industry*, March 2004, p. 37, from Information Resources Inc.

★ 466 ★

Cough Drops
SIC: 2064; NAICS: 325412

Top Cough Drop Brands, 2004

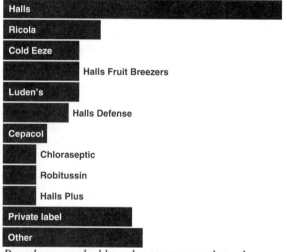

Brands are ranked by sales at supermarkets, drug stores and discount stores (but not Wal-Mart) for the year ended January 25, 2004.

	($ mil.)	Share
Halls	$ 99.8	26.41%
Ricola	35.7	9.45
Cold Eeze	27.1	7.17
Halls Fruit Breezers	26.0	6.88
Luden's	24.6	6.51
Halls Defense	22.7	6.01
Cepacol	13.6	3.60
Chloraseptic	12.6	3.33
Robitussin	11.6	3.07

Continued on next page.

★ 466 ★

[Continued]
Cough Drops
SIC: 2064; NAICS: 325412

Top Cough Drop Brands, 2004

Brands are ranked by sales at supermarkets, drug stores and discount stores (but not Wal-Mart) for the year ended January 25, 2004.

	($ mil.)	Share
Halls Plus	$ 10.7	2.83%
Private label	44.4	11.75
Other	49.1	12.99

Source: *MMR*, April 19, 2004, p. 59, from Information Resources Inc.

★ 467 ★

Cough Drops
SIC: 2064; NAICS: 325412

Top Cough/Sore Throat Drops

Market shares are shown based on sales at drug stores.

Halls	22.4%
Ricola	10.5
Cold Eeze	7.9
Luden's	6.8
Hall's Fruit Breezers	5.9
Halls Defense	5.7
Cepacol	3.6
Halls Plus	3.1
Sucrets	2.8
Chloraseptic	2.8
Other	28.5

Source: *Chain Drug Review*, January 5, 2004, p. 52.

★ 468 ★

Mints
SIC: 2064; NAICS: 31134

Top Mint Brands, 2002

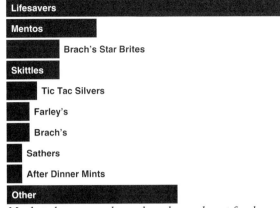

Lifesavers
Mentos
Brach's Star Brites
Skittles
Tic Tac Silvers
Farley's
Brach's
Sathers
After Dinner Mints
Other

Market shares are shown based on sales at food, drug stores and mass merchandisers (but not Wal-Mart) for the year ended December 29, 2002.

Lifesavers	37.4%
Mentos	11.8
Brach's Star Brites	7.2
Skittles	6.9
Tic Tac Silvers	3.5
Farley's	3.3
Brach's	3.1
Sathers	2.4
After Dinner Mints	1.9
Other	22.5

Source: *Professional Candy Buyer*, May - June 2003, p. 86, from Information Resources Inc.

★ 469 ★

Mints
SIC: 2064; NAICS: 31134

Top Mint Makers, 2003

Market shares are shown based on food, drug and mass merchandiser sales for the year ended December 28, 2003. Figures exclude Wal-Mart.

Kraft Foods	31.0%
Ferrero	17.0
Hershey	14.5
Cadbury Schweppes	6.0

Continued on next page.

[Continued]
Mints
SIC: 2064; NAICS: 31134

Top Mint Makers, 2003

Market shares are shown based on food, drug and mass merchandiser sales for the year ended December 28, 2003. Figures exclude Wal-Mart.

Perfetti Van Melle	5.8%
Barry Callebaut	3.2
Masterfoods	2.2
Other	20.3

Source: *Candy Industry*, March 2004, p. 37, from Information Resources Inc.

★ 470 ★
Snack Bars
SIC: 2064; NAICS: 31134

Leading Snack Bar Brands, 2003

Brands are ranked by sales at supermarkets, drug stores and discount stores (but not Wal-Mart) for the year ended September 7, 2003.

	($ mil.)	Share
Kellogg's Nutri Grain	$ 113.0	20.48%
General Mills Milk 'N Cereal Bars	73.0	13.23
Quaker Fruit & Oatmeal	45.8	8.30
Kellogg's Special K	41.6	7.54
Slim Fast Snack Options	40.4	7.32
Quaker Fruit & Oatmeal Bites	30.4	5.51
Kellogg's Nutri Grain Yogurt Bars	26.2	4.75
Kellogg's Nutri Grain Minis	22.3	4.04
Kellogg's Cereal & Milk Bars	22.2	4.02
Private label	30.7	5.56
Other	106.1	19.23

Source: *MMR*, December 8, 2003, p. 32, from Information Resources Inc.

★ 471 ★
Snack Bars
SIC: 2064; NAICS: 31134

Top Energy/Nutrition Bars, 2003

Market shares are shown based on supermarket, drug store and mass merchandiser (but not Wal-Mart) based on the year ended October 5, 2003.

Slim Fast Meal on the Go Bar	10.4%
Atkins Diet Advantage Bar	9.2
Clif Luna Bar	6.9
Zone Perfect Nutritional Bar	6.8
Carb Solutions Bar	6.2
Power Bar	5.4
Balance Gold Bar	5.1
EAS Carb Control Bar	3.6
Clif Bar	3.6
Power Bar Protein Plus	3.4
Other	39.4

Source: *Candy Industry*, November 2003, p. 36, from Information Resources Inc.

★ 472 ★
Snack Bars
SIC: 2064; NAICS: 31134

Top Nutritional/Intrinsic Health Bars, 2003

Market shares are shown for the year ended November 30, 2003. Atkins Nutritional is the top company with a 16% market share.

Slim Fast Meal-on-the-Go	9.5%
Atkins Diet Advantage	9.4
Zone Perfect	6.8
Clif Luna	6.4
Carb Solutions	6.3

Continued on next page.

★ 472 ★
[Continued]
Snack Bars
SIC: 2064; NAICS: 31134

Top Nutritional/Intrinsic Health Bars, 2003

Market shares are shown for the year ended November 30, 2003. Atkins Nutritional is the top company with a 16% market share.

Balance Gold	5.3%
PowerBar	5.1
Atkins Endulge	4.4
Other	46.8

Source: *Snack Food & Wholesale Bakery*, January 2004, p. 14, from Information Resources Inc.

★ 473 ★
Snack Bars
SIC: 2064; NAICS: 31134

Top Snack/Granola Bar Makers, 2004

Market shares are shown based on sales at supermarkets, drugstores and mass merchandisers (but not Wal-Mart) for the year ended January 25, 2004.

Kellogg Co.	13.33%
Quaker Oats	10.58
General Mills	9.39
Atkins Nutritional	6.23
Quaker Oats	5.42
Power Bar Inc.	4.90
Slim Fast Foods Inc.	4.67
Kellogg Co.	4.12
General Mills	3.62
Other	37.74

Source: *Grocery Headquarters*, April 2004, p. 16, from Information Resources Inc.

★ 474 ★
Chocolate
SIC: 2066; NAICS: 31132, 31133

Chocolate Candy Industry, 2003

Sales are shown at food stores, drug stores and mass merchandiser sales for the year ended December 28, 2003. Figures exclude Wal-Mart.

	($ mil.)	Share
Boxes/bags/bars > 3.5 oz.	$ 1,386.21	32.21%
Candy bars < 3.5 oz.	835.55	19.41

	($ mil.)	Share
Snack size	$ 649.84	15.10%
Easter	459.55	10.68
Christmas	325.69	7.57
Valentine's Day	289.11	6.72
Gift box chocolates	242.29	5.63
Halloween	80.72	1.88
Novelty	12.13	0.28
Other seasonal	22.74	0.53

Source: *Candy Business*, January-February 2004, p. 8, from Information Resources Inc.

★ 475 ★
Chocolate
SIC: 2066; NAICS: 31132, 31133

Largest Chocolate Markets Worldwide, 2000 and 2003

Eastern European countries are seeing the fastest growth rates. Figures are in millions of kilograms.

	2000	2003	Share
U.K.	649.0	684.6	24.51%
Germany	407.2	391.0	14.00
France	382.5	395.9	14.17
Russia	304.4	351.0	12.57
Poland	124.1	137.5	4.92
Italy	94.4	96.0	3.44
Austria	85.7	96.1	3.44
Belgium	84.2	87.8	3.14
Netherlands	79.0	84.3	3.02
Switzerland	73.9	79.0	2.83

Source: *International Food Ingredients*, June-July 2003, p. 20, from Datamonitor.

★ 476 ★
Chocolate
SIC: 2066; NAICS: 31132, 31133

Top Chocolate Candy Boxes/Bags/ Bar Brands > 3.5oz, 2002

Market shares are shown based on sales at food, drug stores and mass merchandisers (but not Wal-Mart) for the year ended December 29, 2002.

M&M's	14.5%
Hershey's	12.4

Continued on next page.

★ 476 ★
[Continued]
Chocolate
SIC: 2066; NAICS: 31132, 31133

Top Chocolate Candy Boxes/Bags/ Bar Brands > 3.5oz, 2002

Market shares are shown based on sales at food, drug stores and mass merchandisers (but not Wal-Mart) for the year ended December 29, 2002.

Hershey's Kisses	7.1%
Hershey's Nuggets	4.8
Snickers	4.1
Reese's	3.8
York Peppermint Patty	2.7
Nestle Treasures	2.5
Ferrero Rocher	2.3
Other	45.8

Source: *Professional Candy Buyer*, May-June 2003, p. 86, from Information Resources Inc.

★ 477 ★
Chocolate
SIC: 2066; NAICS: 31132, 31133

Top Chocolate Candy Brands, 2003

Shares are for chocolate candy brands less than 3.5 ounces. Market shares are shown based on food, drug and mass merchandiser sales for the year ended December 28, 2003. Figures exclude Wal-Mart.

	($ mil)	Share
M&Ms	$ 103.9	12.43%
Hershey's	88.7	10.62
Snickers	76.6	9.17
Reese's Peanut Butter Cups	69.9	8.37
Kit Kat	38.0	4.55
Nestle Crunch	34.2	4.09
Butterfinger	26.2	3.14
Twix	25.3	3.03
Three Musketeers	23.3	2.79
York Peppermint Patty	22.5	2.69
Other	327.0	39.13

Source: *Candy Industry*, March 2004, p. 37, from Information Resources Inc.

★ 478 ★
Chocolate
SIC: 2066; NAICS: 31132, 31133

Top Chocolate Candy Makers, 2003

Companies are ranked by sales for the year ended November 2, 2003. Figures exclude Wal-Mart.

	($ mil.)	Share
Hershey Foods	$ 1,836	42.73%
Masterfoods USA	1,160	27.00
Nestle USA	377	8.77
Russell Stover	209	4.86
P.M. Palmer Co.	69	1.61
Ferrero US Inc.	54	1.26
Whitman's	54	1.26
Kraft Foods	43	1.00
Storck USA	23	0.54
Private label	40	0.93
Other	432	10.05

Source: *Grocey Headquarters*, February 2004, p. 29, from Information Resources Inc.

★ 479 ★
Chocolate
SIC: 2066; NAICS: 31132, 31133

Top Chocolate Candy Makers in Australia

Market shares are shown in percent.

Cadbury Schweppes	36.1%
Nestle	18.2
MasterFoods	13.9
Wrigley	6.8
Private label	6.3
Other	18.7

Source: *Australasian Business Intelligence*, October 22, 2003, p. NA, from ACNielsen.

★ 480 ★
Chocolate
SIC: 2066; NAICS: 31132, 31133

Top Chocolate Candy Makers Worldwide

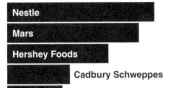

Market shares are shown in percent.

Nestle 19.0%
Mars 17.0
Hershey Foods 13.0
Cadbury Schweppes 8.0
Kraft Foods 7.0
Other 36.0

Source: *just-food.com (Management Briefing)*, October 2003, p. NA, from Leatherhead Food International.

★ 481 ★
Chocolate
SIC: 2066; NAICS: 31132, 31133

Top Chocolate Halloween Candy Brands, 2003

Brands are ranked by supermarkets, drug stores and mass merchandiser sales for the year ended November 3, 2003.

	($ mil.)	Share
M&M's Halloween Candy	$ 15.80	20.12%
Reeses	11.20	14.26
Hershey's Kisses	10.33	13.16
Hershey's	9.92	12.63
Nestle Seasonal Chocolate	7.03	8.95
York Peppermint Patty	2.99	3.81
Russell Stover	2.03	2.59
Nestle Ultimate Scream Collection	1.93	2.46
M&M's 9.5 ounce bag	1.85	2.36
R.M. Palmer	1.53	1.95
Other	13.91	17.72

Source: *Professional Candy Buyer*, March-April 2004, p. 30, from Information Resources Inc.

★ 482 ★
Chocolate
SIC: 2066; NAICS: 31132, 31133

Top Chocolate Producers in Poland

The country's confectionery industry has been fueled by exports. Market shares are shown in percent.

Kraft Foods 32.5%
Cadbury Wedel 31.2
Nestle/Goplana 10.2
Ferrero 3.8
Terravita 3.8
Wawel 3.0
Milano 2.5
Other 6.8

Source: *Europe Intelligence Wire*, September 19, 2003, p. NA, from *Polish News Bulletin* and MAMRB.

★ 483 ★
Chocolate
SIC: 2066; NAICS: 31132, 31133

Top Easter Candy Brands, 2003

The top brands of chocolate Easter candies are shown for the year ended May 18, 2003. Sales are shown for food, drug and mass merchandiser sales (except Wal-Mart) and seasonally wrapped products only.

	($ mil.)	Share
M&M's	$ 52.58	11.53%
Reese's	49.30	10.81
Hershey's	32.96	7.23
Russell Stover	31.61	6.93
Hershey's Kisses	26.69	5.85
Cadbury Creme Eggs	19.55	4.29
Leaf Robin Eggs	17.22	3.78
Cadbury Mini Eggs	17.05	3.74
Dove	15.26	3.35
Cadbury	13.03	2.86
Other	180.90	39.66

Source: *Professional Candy Buyer*, September-October 2003, p. 106, from Information Resources Inc.

★ 484 ★

Chocolate

SIC: 2066; NAICS: 31132, 31133

Top Gift Chocolate Brands, 2002

Market shares are shown based on sales at food, drug stores and mass merchandisers (but not Wal-Mart) for the year ended December 29, 2002.

Russell Stover	44.6%
Whitman's Sampler	18.5
Hershey's Pot of Gold	15.7
Queen Anne	5.3
Fannie May	3.5
Whitman's	3.0
Esther Price	1.5
Maxfield's	1.0
Mrs. Fields	1.0
Other	5.9

Source: *Professional Candy Buyer*, May-June 2003, p. 86, from Information Resources Inc.

★ 485 ★

Gum

SIC: 2067; NAICS: 31134

Chewing Gum Market in Norway

Market shares are shown in percent.

Wrigley	90.0%
Other	10.0

Source: *Aftenposten*, June 17, 2002, p. NA.

★ 486 ★

Gum

SIC: 2067; NAICS: 31134

Top Gum Makers Worldwide

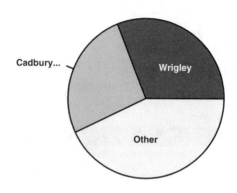

Market shares are shown in percent. Cadbury is acquiring Pfizer Inc's gum business, which includes Trident. The share reflects this merger.

Wrigley	31.0%
Cadbury Schweppes	26.0
Other	43.0

Source: *Crain's Chicago Business*, March 24, 2003, p. 39.

★ 487 ★

Gum

SIC: 2067; NAICS: 31134

Top Gum Makers, 2003

Market shares are shown based on food, drug and mass merchandiser sales for the year ended December 28, 2003. Figures exclude Wal-Mart.

	($ mil.)	Share
Wrigley	$535.2	60.3%
Cadbury Schweppes	200.3	22.6
Hershey	118.8	13.4
Topps	7.2	0.8
Concord Confections	4.1	0.5
Private label	6.4	0.7

Source: *Candy Industry*, March 2004, p. 37, from Information Resources Inc.

★ 488 ★
Nuts
SIC: 2068; NAICS: 311911
Nut Sales, 2002

Data show supermarket sales in millions of dollars.

	($ mil.)	Share
Nuts, bags	$ 569.04	19.19%
Nuts, cans	452.31	15.26
Nuts, jars	167.96	5.67
Unshelled	104.49	3.52
Other	1,670.91	56.36

Source: *Progressive Grocer*, September 15, 2003, p. 19, from *Progressive Grocer's 56th Consumer Expenditures Study*.

★ 489 ★
Nuts
SIC: 2068; NAICS: 311911
Top Snack Nut Brands, 2003

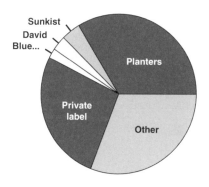

Market shares are shown based on sales at supermarkets, drug stores and mass merchandisers (but not Wal-Mart) for the 52 weeks ended March 23, 2003.

Planters	33.9%
Sunkist	3.6
David	2.9
Blue Diamond	1.7
Private label	26.6
Other	31.3

Source: *Snack Food & Wholesale Bakery*, June 2003, p. SI-59, from Information Resources Inc.

★ 490 ★
Nuts
SIC: 2068; NAICS: 311911
Top Snack Nut Makers in the U.K.

Supermarkets had 49% of sales for the year. Pubs and bars took the bulk of small package sizes. Shares are for 2000.

KP Snacks	24.0%
Private label	60.0
Other	16.0

Source: "The U.K. Peanut Market." [online] from http://www.fas.usda.gov [accessed January 1, 2004], from Mintel's *Nuts and Dried Fruit, 2001*.

★ 491 ★
Nuts
SIC: 2068; NAICS: 311911
Top Snack Nut Producers in Australia

Market shares are shown in percent.

	2000	2001
Smith's Snackfood Co.	25.1%	26.2%
Olympic	3.0	2.7
Snack Brands Australia	2.9	3.5
Private label	52.6	50.8
Other	16.4	16.8

Source: "Australia Product Brief Snack Food 2003." [online] from http://www.fas.usda.gov [accessed January 1, 2004], from *Retail World Grocery Guides 1999-2001*.

★ 492 ★
Fats and Oils
SIC: 2079; NAICS: 311225

Salad and Cooking Oil Sales, 2002

Data show supermarket sales in millions of dollars.

	($ mil.)	Share
Salad and cooking oil	$ 783.44	35.09%
Olive oil	405.06	18.14
Cooking sprays	219.24	9.82
Shortening	131.47	5.89
Lard	23.30	1.04
Other	670.28	30.02

Source: *Progressive Grocer*, September 15, 2003, p. 19, from *Progressive Grocer's 56th Consumer Expenditures Study*.

★ 493 ★
Fats and Oils
SIC: 2079; NAICS: 311225

Yellow Fats Market Worldwide

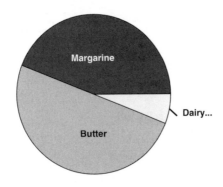

The market is valued at 13.8 billion euros. Market shares are estimated in percent.

	Volume	Value
Margarine	58.0%	44.0%
Butter	35.0	50.0
Dairy spreads	7.0	6.0

Source: *Dairy Industries International*, July 2003, p. 27.

★ 494 ★
Alcoholic Beverages
SIC: 2080; NAICS: 31212, 31213, 31214

Alcohol Consumption Worldwide, 2007

Figures are projected.

Beer (incl. cider)	42.0%
Spirits	37.5
Wine	18.8
Flavored alcoholic beverages	1.8

Source: *Beverage Aisle*, December 15, 2003, p. 6, from Euromonitor.

★ 495 ★
Alcoholic Beverages
SIC: 2080; NAICS: 31212, 31213, 31214

Alcoholic Beverage Market

Vodka is the best-selling type of spirit with sales projected to reach $2.97 billion.

	2002	2003
Beer	54.4%	53.3%
Spirits	29.7	30.4
Wine	15.9	16.3

Source: *Food & Drink Weekly*, December 15, 2003, p. 2, from Distilled Spirits Council.

★ 496 ★
Alcoholic Beverages
SIC: 2080; NAICS: 31212, 31213, 31214

Alcoholic Beverage Market in Australia, 2003

The industry is shown in percent. Per capita beer consumption fell from 1999 to 2003. Wine and spirits levels remained mostly unchanged.

Beer	42.0%
Wine	29.0
Spirits	18.0
RTDs	11.0

Source: *Hospitality*, November 6, 2003, p. NA.

★ **497** ★
Alcoholic Beverages
SIC: 2080; NAICS: 31212, 31213, 31214

Alcoholic Beverage Market in Russia, 2002

The spirits market in Russia was estimated at $20.3 billion. It represents a quarter of the alcoholic beverage market. In some regions vodka makes up nearly 100% of the market.

Vodka	79.3%
Brandy and cognac	14.2
Other	6.5

Source: *Izvestia*, July 31, 2003, p. 2, from Russian Federation.

★ **498** ★
Beverages
SIC: 2080; NAICS: 312111, 312112

Beverage Consumption

Data are in millions of gallons.

	2001	2003	Share
Soft drinks	15,023	15,310	31.67%
Coffee	7,710	7,790	16.12
Milk	6,910	7,000	14.48
Beer	6,241	6,316	13.07
Bottled water	4,800	5,800	12.00
Tea	1,910	1,950	4.03
Juices	1,790	1,860	3.85
Powdered drinks . . .	1,340	1,310	2.71
Wine	556	612	1.27
Distilled spirits	357	378	0.78
Cider	12	10	0.02

Source: *Wine Handbook*, Annual 2004, p. 138, from Adams Research Database.

★ **499** ★
Beverages
SIC: 2080; NAICS: 312111, 312112

Beverage Production in China, 2002

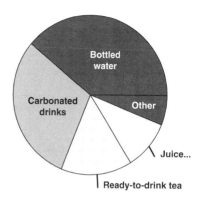

Production is shown in percent.

Bottled water	39.0%
Carbonated drinks	30.0
Ready-to-drink tea	15.0
Juice, juice drink	10.0
Other	6.0

Source: *Wall Street Journal*, October 15, 2003, p. B1, from China Soft Drinks Association and Rabobank International.

★ **500** ★
Beverages
SIC: 2080; NAICS: 312111, 312112

Largest Drink Firms, 2002

Companies are ranked by sales in billions of dollars.

The Coca-Cola Company	$ 19.56
Nestle SA	17.75
Coca-Cola Enterprises	16.88
Diageo	14.31
Anheuser-Busch	13.56
Heineken	11.78
PepsiCo	9.23
Dean Foods	8.99
SABMiller	8.90
Interbrew	7.99
Dairy Farmers of America	6.44

Source: *Beverage World*, October 2003, p. 33.

★ 501 ★
Beverages
SIC: 2080; NAICS: 312111, 312112

Leading Beverage Brands in Drug Stores, 2002

Brands are ranked by drug store sales in millions of dollars for the 52 weeks ended December 29, 2002. Total beverage sales in drug stores were $3.61 billion.

	($ mil.)	Share
Coca-Cola	$ 193.9	5.36%
Bud Light	152.7	4.22
Pepsi	145.2	4.01
Budweiser	135.8	3.75
Diet Coke	129.8	3.59
Miller Lite	80.3	2.22
Diet Pepsi	72.7	2.01
Sprite	61.7	1.71
Coors Light	56.0	1.55
Mountain Dew	54.0	1.49
Dr. Pepper	52.1	1.44
Other	2,482.5	68.64

Source: *Drug Store News*, May 19, 2003, p. 60, from Information Resources Inc.

★ 502 ★
Beverages
SIC: 2080; NAICS: 312111, 312112

Nutrition Enhanced Beverages

Sales are in millions of dollars.

	2000	2002	Share
Fruit drinks	$ 192.8	$ 183.6	33.51%
Teas	61.2	86.0	15.70
Dairy	37.5	43.3	7.90
Waters	20.0	230.6	42.09
Other	3.7	4.4	0.80

Source: *Beverage World*, November 15, 2003, p. 18, from Beverage Marketing Corp.

★ 503 ★
Beverages
SIC: 2080; NAICS: 311411, 312112

Store-Brand Beverage Sales, 2003

Milk is still the top store-branded beverage. 64% of milk sales are private label. Figures are shown in millions of dollars.

	2001	2003	Share
Milk	$ 6,812	$ 6,435	63.73%
Juice/juice drinks	1,794	1,612	15.97
Carbonated beverages . . .	1,104	1,097	10.86
Bottled water	546	632	6.26
Tea/coffee	323	321	3.18

Source: *Supermarket News*, October 27, 2003, p. 52, from Mintel.

★ 504 ★
Beer
SIC: 2082; NAICS: 31212

Beer Consumption by State, 2003

Consumption is shown in thousands of 31 gallon barrels.

	(000)	Share
California	20,976	11.15%
Texas	18,145	9.64
Florida	12,992	6.90
New York	10,597	5.63
Pennsylvania	9,726	5.17
Illinois	9,145	4.86
Ohio	8,819	4.69

Continued on next page.

★ 504 ★

[Continued]
Beer
SIC: 2082; NAICS: 31212

Beer Consumption by State, 2003

Consumption is shown in thousands of 31 gallon barrels.

	(000)	Share
Michigan	6,801	3.61%
North Carolina	6,002	3.19
Virginia	4,972	2.64
New Jersey	4,645	2.47
Arizona	4,471	2.38
Other	70,873	37.67

Source: *Wine Handbook*, Annual 2004, p. 128.

★ 505 ★

Beer
SIC: 2082; NAICS: 31212

Beer Market in Australia

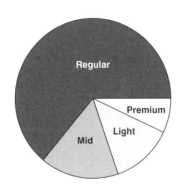

Market shares are shown in percent.

Regular	55.0%
Mid	14.0
Light	11.0
Premium	6.0

Source: *Sydney Morning Herald*, February 4, 2004, p. 1, from ACNielsen.

★ 506 ★

Beer
SIC: 2082; NAICS: 31212

Beer Market in Sarasota-Manatee County, FL

Market shares are shown in percent.

Gold Coast Eagle	69.6%
Other	30.4

Source: *Sarasota Herald Tribune*, October 13, 2003, p. 12.

★ 507 ★

Beer
SIC: 2082; NAICS: 31212

Beer Market in Southeast Michigan

The area is the company's central distributor area, which includes most of Wayne County (but not Detroit) and the Novi Northville area of Oakland County.

Anheuser-Busch	57.5%
Other	42.5

Source: *Detroit News*, July 1, 2003, p. 2.

★ 508 ★

Beer
SIC: 2082; NAICS: 31212

Beer Market in Wisconsin, 2002

Market shares are shown in percent.

Miller	45.2%
Anheuser-Busch	32.3
Other	22.5

Source: *Modern Brewery Age*, June 30, 2003, p. 1.

★ 509 ★

Beer

SIC: 2082; NAICS: 31212

Beer Market Shares, 2001 and 2006

Market shares are shown in percent.

	2001	2006
Light	43.0%	49.6%
Premium	22.7	17.8
Popular	13.2	8.8
Imports	11.0	14.8
Superpremium	4.3	4.1
Malt liquor	2.8	2.0
Other	2.9	2.9

Source: *Beverage Aisle*, July 15, 2003, p. 16, from Beverage Marketing Corp.

★ 510 ★

Beer

SIC: 2082; NAICS: 31212

Beer Sales in Convenience Stores

Market shares are shown in percent.

Anheuser-Busch	58.4%
SAB Miller	17.0
Other	24.6

Source: *St. Louis Business Journal*, January 23, 2004, p. NA, from Information Resources Inc.

★ 511 ★

Beer

SIC: 2082; NAICS: 31212

Top Beer Brands, 2003

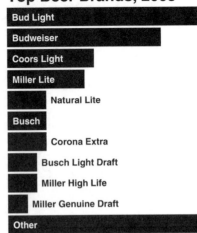

Market shares are shown based on 197.5 million cases.

Bud Light	19.5%
Budweiser	15.6
Coors Light	8.5
Miller Lite	8.1
Natural Lite	4.2
Busch	3.8
Corona Extra	3.5
Busch Light Draft	2.7
Miller High Life	2.6
Miller Genuine Draft	2.3
Other	29.2

Source: *Beverage World*, April 15, 2004, p. 35, from Beverage Marketing Corp.

★ 512 ★

Beer

SIC: 2082; NAICS: 31212

Top Beer Brands in the U.K., 2003

Beer brands are ranked by sales in the United Kingdom in 2003 in thousand British pounds.

Stella Artois	£ 619,288
Carling	293,194
Foster's	260,246
Budweiser	156,507
Grolsch	119,775
Kronenbourg	111,446

Continued on next page.

★ 512 ★

[Continued]
Beer
SIC: 2082; NAICS: 31212

Top Beer Brands in the U.K., 2003

Beer brands are ranked by sales in the United Kingdom in 2003 in thousand British pounds.

Carlsberg	£ 93,472
Carlsberg Export	79,746
Beck's	71,232
Tennent's	62,792

Source: *European Intelligence Wire*, March 5, 2004, p. NA, from *Off Licence News*.

★ 513 ★

Beer
SIC: 2082; NAICS: 31212

Top Beer Brands Worldwide, 2002

Brands are ranked by shipments in billions of gallons. As of March 2004, Interbrew was planning to merge with AmBev, which manufactures Skol and Brahma Chopp.

Budweiser	1.19
Bud Light	1.17
Skol	0.78
Corona	0.71
Heineken	0.61
Asahi Super Dry	0.54
Coors Lite	0.53
Miller Lite	0.49
Brahma Chopp	0.48
Polar	0.38

Source: *New York Times*, March 2, 2004, p. C7, from Impact's *2003 Global Drink Study*.

★ 514 ★

Beer
SIC: 2082; NAICS: 31212

Top Beer Firms in Russia

Market shares are shown in percent.

BBH	33.0%
Sun Interbrew	15.0
Other	52.0

Source: *Sunday Times*, May 16, 2004, p. 1.

★ 515 ★

Beer
SIC: 2082; NAICS: 31212

Top Beer Makers, 2003

Shares are shown based on a 197.5 million barrel market.

Bud Light	19.5%
Budweiser	15.6
Coors Light	8.5
Miller Lite	8.1
Natural Lite	4.2
Busch	3.8
Corona Extra	3.5
Busch Light	2.7
Miller High Life	2.6
Miller	2.3
Other	29.2

Source: *Beverage World*, April 15, 2004, p. NA, from Beverage Marketing Corp.

★ 516 ★
Beer
SIC: 2082; NAICS: 31212
Top Beer Makers in Canada

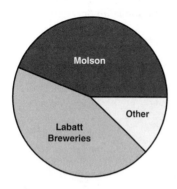

Market shares are shown in percent.

Molson 44.0%
Labatt Breweries 44.0
Other 12.0

Source: *Financial Post*, August 9, 2003, p. NA.

★ 517 ★
Beer
SIC: 2082; NAICS: 31212
Top Beer Makers in Central/Eastern Europe, 2002

Market shares are shown in percent.

SABMiller 25.0%
BBAG 16.0
Heineken 15.0
Interbrew 11.0
Carlsberg 5.0
Other 27.0

Source: *Financial Times*, May 3, 2003, p. 8, from Cazenove.

★ 518 ★
Beer
SIC: 2082; NAICS: 31212
Top Beer Makers in China

China's beer market is worth $6 billion. It is the world's largest beer market by volume (25.9 billion liters annually, just ahead of the U.S. with 23.8 billion liters).

Tsingtai Brewery 12.9%
China Resources Breweries 10.0
Beijing Yanjing Beer Group 9.4
Harbin Brewery Group 4.3
Zhujian Brewery Group 3.4
Other 60.0

Source: *Time Canada*, May 17, 2004, p. 40, from Euromonitor.

★ 519 ★
Beer
SIC: 2082; NAICS: 31212
Top Beer Makers in the U.K.

Market shares are shown in percent.

Scottish Courage Ltd. 26.4%
Interbrew UK 21.3
Coors Brewers 20.1
Carlsberg Tetley Brewing 12.0
Other 20.2

Source: *just-drinks.com (Management Briefing)*, January 2004, p. NA, from P.A.S.H. Beverage Research/Trade.

★ 520 ★
Beer
SIC: 2082; NAICS: 31212
Top Beer Makers in the Ukraine, 2003

Production increased to 190.78 million liters. Market shares are shown for the first eight months of the year.

Sun Interbrew 31.7%
Obolon 25.8
BBH 17.7
Other 24.8

Source: *Food & Agriculture Report*, October 1, 2003, p. NA.

★ 521 ★
Beer
SIC: 2082; NAICS: 31212

Top Beer Makers Worldwide, 2002

Market shares are shown in percent.

Anheuser-Busch	9.0%
SAB/SABMiller	8.5
Heineken	6.2
Interbrew	6.0
Carlsberg	5.0
AmBev	4.4
Asahi Breweries	3.0
Modelo	2.8
Coors	2.8
Scottish & Newcastle	2.7
Other	49.6

Source: *Beverage World*, February 15, 2003, p. 24, from Beverage Marketing Corp.

★ 522 ★
Beer
SIC: 2082; NAICS: 31212

Top Beer Makers Worldwide, 2002

China recently surpassed the United States as the world's largest beer market. The top 10 brewers now have over half the market, an industry first.

China	16.8%
United States	15.2
Gernamy	7.6
Brazil	6.0
Japan	4.9
Russia	4.9
Mexico	4.5%
United Kingdom	4.0
Spain	2.0
Poland	1.8
Other	32.3

Source: *Beverage World*, February 15, 2004, p. 39, from Beverage Marketing Corp.

★ 523 ★
Beer
SIC: 2082; NAICS: 31212

Top Beer Wholesalers

Companies are ranked by sales in millions of cases.

The Reyes Family	39.0
Ben E. Keith Beers	32.7
Manhattan Beer Distributors	27.6
Silver Eagle Distributors	25.3
JJ Taylor Companies Inc.	23.0
Topa Equities Ltd.	22.8
The Sheehan Family	22.5
Hensley	22.4
Gold Coast Beverage Trust	20.7
Liquid Investments Inc.	18.2
The Banko Family	16.4
Standard Sales Company	13.5

Source: *Beverage World*, August 2003, p. 32.

★ 524 ★
Beer
SIC: 2082; NAICS: 31212

Top Craft Brewers, 2002

Market shares are shown in percent.

Boston Beer Co.	24.9%
Sierra Nevada Brewing Co.	11.1
Jacob Leinenkugel Brewing Co.	6.7
Spoetzl Brewing Co.	5.0
New Belgium Brewing	5.0
Other	47.3

Source: *Adams Wine Handbook*, 2003, p. 101, from *Adams Handbook Advance 2003*.

★ 525 ★
Beer
SIC: 2082; NAICS: 31212

Top Ice Brands, 2002

Ice beers are conventional brews that have been frozen at some stage in the fermentation process. Since 2000, consumption has been on the decline, from 106.2 million to 96.87 million 2.25-gallon cases.

Natural Ice	33.6%
Icehouse	26.5
Bud Ice	15.6
Milwaukee's Best Ice	15.2
Keystone Ice	3.3
Other	5.9

Source: *Adams Wine Handbook*, 2003, p. 101, from *Adams Handbook Advance 2003*.

★ 526 ★
Beer
SIC: 2082; NAICS: 31212

Top Imported Beer Makers, 2003

Market shares are shown in percent.

Barton/Gambrinus	36.1%
Heineken USA	22.2
Labatt USA	16.5
Diageo	4.6
Molson	3.6
Other	17.0

Source: *Wine Handbook*, Annual 2004, p. 132.

★ 527 ★
Beer
SIC: 2082; NAICS: 31212

Top Light Beers, 2002

Market shares are shown in percent.

Bud Light	19.1%
Budweiser	16.3
Coors Light	8.5
Miller Lite	7.9
Natural Lite	4.1
Busch	3.9

Corona Extra	3.4%
Miller High Life	2.7
Busch Light Draft	2.7
Miller Genuine Draft	2.5
Other	28.9

Source: *Beverage Aisle*, May 15, 2003, p. 36, from Beverage Marketing Corp.

★ 528 ★
Beer
SIC: 2082; NAICS: 31212

Top Non-Alcoholic Beer Makers, 2003

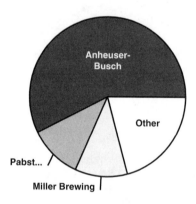

Market shares are shown in percent.

Anheuser-Busch	58.0%
Pabst Brewing	10.6
Miller Brewing	10.5
Other	20.9

Source: *Wine Handbook*, Annual 2004, p. 133.

★ 529 ★
Beer
SIC: 2082; NAICS: 31212

Top Premium Beer Markets, 2002

Premium beer has lost market share to light beers over the last 25 years. Market shares are shown based on thousands of 2.25-liter cases.

	(000)	Share
California	51,000	9.58%
Florida	37,160	6.98

Continued on next page.

★ 529 ★

[Continued]
Beer
SIC: 2082; NAICS: 31212

Top Premium Beer Markets, 2002

Premium beer has lost market share to light beers over the last 25 years. Market shares are shown based on thousands of 2.25-liter cases.

	(000)	Share
Texas	33,700	6.33%
Ohio	25,055	4.71
New York	24,450	4.59
Illinois	21,100	3.96
Pennsylvania	20,885	3.92
Michigan	18,610	3.50
North Carolina	17,432	3.27
Georgia	17,280	3.25
Other	265,608	49.90

Source: *Adams Wine Handbook*, 2003, p. 101, from *Adams Handbook Advance 2003*.

★ 530 ★

Beer
SIC: 2082; NAICS: 31212

Top Premium/Micro/Spec/FMB Brands, 2002

The segment stood at 214.3 million 2.25 gallon cases in 2002, up from 158.59 million in 1997. FMB stands for flavored malt beverage. Figures are shown in thousands of 2.25 gallon cases.

	(000)	Share
Michelob	18,000	8.40%
Yuengling Traditional Lager	16,336	7.62
Samuel Adams Boston Lager	9,900	4.62
George Killian's Irish Red	8,700	4.06
Sierra Nevada Pale Ale	7,106	3.31
Michelob Amber Bock	5,570	2.60
Henry Weinhard	3,800	1.77
Shiner Bock	3,195	1.49
Fat Tire Amber Ale	3,030	1.41
Other	138,733	64.72

Source: *Adams Wine Handbook*, 2003, p. 101, from *Adams Handbook Advance 2003*.

★ 531 ★

Malt Beverages
SIC: 2082; NAICS: 31212

Top Malt Liquor Brands, 2002

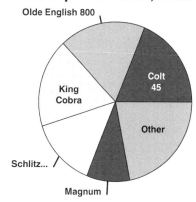

Advertisers have shifted their dollars into the light and import segments.

Colt 45	19.3%
Olde English 800	18.0
King Cobra	18.0
Schlitz Malt Liquor	13.6
Magnum	8.7
Other	22.3

Source: *Adams Wine Handbook*, 2003, p. 101, from *Adams Handbook Advance 2003*.

★ 532 ★

Wine
SIC: 2084; NAICS: 31213

Largest Wineries

Wineries are ranked by production in millions of gallons.

E&J Gallo Winery	443.00
Canandaigua Wine Co.	133.95
The Wine Group	87.00
Bronco Wine Co./JFJ Bronco Inc.	72.50
Korbel & Bros.	60.29
Vie-Del Co.	59.20
Golden State Vntnrs.	54.70
Robert Mondavi	50.10
Trinchero Family Estates	46.00
Delicato Vyds.	45.80

Source: *Wines & Vines*, July 2003, p. 31.

★ 533 ★
Wine
SIC: 2084; NAICS: 31213

Leading Wine Importers, 2002

Total wine sales reached $21.1 billion.

Italy	37.1%
Australia	20.9
France	18.5
Chile	10.4
Spain	3.4
Germany	2.9
Argentina	2.2
Portugal	1.1
New Zealand	1.0
South Africa	0.8
Other	1.7

Source: *USA TODAY*, August 1, 2003, p. B1, from Gomberg-Fredrikson Report.

★ 534 ★
Wine
SIC: 2084; NAICS: 31213

Leading Wine Producing Countries, 2006

The source discusses a rivalry between well known European producers and those described as New World producers. Between 2001 and 2006 wine production is forecasted to jump 24% in Chile, 20.9% in Germany, 20.3% in Australia, and 17.9% in Argentina.

Italy	18.8%
France	18.5
Spain	13.4
United States	7.8
Argentina	4.9
Australia	4.8
Germany	4.2
Portugal	2.6
Chile	2.3
Romania	2.1
South Africa	2.0
Other	18.8

Source: *Financial Times*, August 19, 2003, p. 15, from Vinexpo.

★ 535 ★
Wine
SIC: 2084; NAICS: 31213

Top Dessert Wine Makers, 2002

Richardson's Wild Irish is the leading brand of domestic dessert and fortified wine. The market was valued at 9.3 million 9-liter cases.

Canandaigua Wine	41.4%
E&J Gallo Winery	25.2
The Wine Group	18.2
Other	15.2

Source: *Adams Wine Handbook*, 2003, p. 101, from Adams Media.

★ 536 ★
Wine
SIC: 2084; NAICS: 31213

Top Domestic Sparkling Wine Brands, 2003

Brands are ranked in thousands of 9-liter cases. Figures are estimated.

Andre/Wycliff	1,930
Cook's	1,390
Korbel	1,116
Ballatore	600
J. Roget	590
Domaine Chandon	335
Domaine Ste. Michelle	280
Tott's	170
Mumm Cuvee Napa	121
Gloria Ferrer	95

Source: *Wine Handbook*, Annual 2004, p. 112.

Wine
SIC: 2084; NAICS: 31213

Top Imported Sparkling Wine Brands, 2003

Brands are ranked in thousands of 9-liter cases.
Figures are estimated.

Martini & Rossi Asti	750
Freixenet	625
Moet & Chandon	585
Verdi Spumante	499
Tosti Asti	355
Veuve Clicquot/La Grande Dame	270
Taittinger	90
Perrier-Jouet	75
Dom Perignon	69

Source: *Wine Handbook*, Annual 2004, p. 112.

★ 538 ★
Wine
SIC: 2084; NAICS: 31213

Top Imported Sparkling Wine Makers, 2002

Market shares are shown in percent.

Bacardi USA	18.0%
Freixenet USA	16.6
Schueffelin & Somerset	14.6
Carriage House Imports	12.3
Shaw-Ross Importers	8.4
Clicquot	6.1

Kobrand	3.4%
Other	20.6

Source: *Adams Wine Handbook*, 2003, p. 101, from Adams Media.

★ 539 ★
Wine
SIC: 2084; NAICS: 31213

Top Sparkling Wine Makers, 2002

Andre/Wycliffe is the top brand of the 7.78 million 9-liter case market.

E&J Gallo Winery	38.0%
Canandaigua Wine	29.1
Brown-Forman Beverages	14.3
Schieffelin & Somerset	4.1
Weibel Vineyards	3.5
Stimson Lane Vineyards	3.4
Other	7.6

Source: *Adams Wine Handbook*, 2003, p. 101, from Adams Media.

★ 540 ★
Wine
SIC: 2084; NAICS: 31213

Top Table Wine Makers, 2003

Market shares are shown in percent.

Banfi Vintners	11.1%
W J Deutsch	9.8
Southcorp Wines USA	8.5
Palm Bay Imports	7.2
E & J Gallo Winery	5.6
Constellation Brands	4.0
Shaw-Ross International	3.8
Other	50.0

Source: *Wine Handbook*, Annual 2004, p. 112.

★ 541 ★

Wine

SIC: 2084; NAICS: 31213

Top Table Wine Varieties

Market shares are shown based on sales of 52 weeks ended April 20, 2003. Data exclude Wal-Mart.

	2001	2002
Chardonnay	26.6%	26.4%
Merlot	14.6	14.9
Cabernet Sauvignon	12.5	12.3
Superpremium	11.0	11.0
White zinfandel	8.8	8.1

Source: *Beverage Industry*, June 2003, p. 16, from Information Resources Inc.

★ 542 ★

Wine

SIC: 2084; NAICS: 31213

Top Wine Makers in Japan, 2003

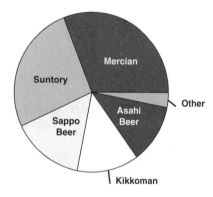

Wine sales reached 124 billion yen in fiscal year 2002. Liquor stores (mainly individually operated) took 74% of sales, mass merchandisers took 18% and convenience stores 8%. Market shares are forecasted for 2003.

	2001	2003
Mercian	33.2%	30.9%
Suntory	25.5	25.8
Sappo Beer	14.6	15.3
Kikkoman	12.5	13.3
Asahi Beer	5.5	11.7
Other	3.5	3.0

Source: ''Japan Wine Manual Annual Report.'' [online] from http://www.fas.usda.gov [accessed January 1, 2004], from Fuji Keizai.

★ 543 ★

Wine

SIC: 2084; NAICS: 31213

Top Wine Suppliers, 2002

Market shares are shown based on total sales of 246.26 million 9-liter cases.

E&J Gallo Winery	26.2%
Canandaigua Wine	14.9
The Wine Group	12.7
Beringer Blass Wine Estates	4.2
Robert Mondavi Winery	3.6
Trinchero Family Estates	3.2
Banfi Vintners	2.4
Brown-Forman Beverage	2.3
Kendall-Jackson Wine Estates	1.9
Southcorp Wines USA	1.7
Classic Wines of California (Bronco)	1.5
Other	25.4

Source: *Adams Wine Handbook*, 2003, p. 101, from Adams Media.

★ 544 ★

Wine

SIC: 2084; NAICS: 31213

Wine Consumption by Segment, 2003

Consumption is shown in thousands of 9-liter cases. Total domestic wine consumption was 196.4 million cases and imported was 61 million cases.

	(000)	Share
Table wine	232,350	93.50%
Champagne & sparkling	12,210	4.91
Vermouth/aperitif	1,920	0.77
Dessert & fortified	1,080	0.43
Wine coolers	940	0.38

Source: *Wine & Spirit Industry Marketing*, April 2004, p. 11.

★ 545 ★
Wine
SIC: 2084; NAICS: 31213

Wine Sales by Price

Bottles that cost over $7 make up 30% of the market but 62% of industry revenue.

Cost less than $3	35.0%
$3 - $7	35.0
More than $7	30.0

Source: *Orange County Register*, March 16, 2004, p. NA, from Wine Institute.

★ 546 ★
Wine
SIC: 2084; NAICS: 31213

Wine Sales by Segment, 2003

Wine sales grew 2.3% to reach $14.3 billion in 2003. Much of the increase came from restaurant sales.

California	67.0%
Foreign wines	26.0
Other states	7.0

Source: *Modesto Bee*, April 2, 2004, p. NA, from Wine Institute.

★ 547 ★
Liquor
SIC: 2085; NAICS: 31214

Largest Distilled Spirit Markets, 2003

Data are in 9-liter cases.

	(000)	Share
California	18,925	11.90%
Florida	12,250	7.70
New York	9,960	6.26
Texas	8,704	5.47
Illinois	7,063	4.44
Michigan	6,039	3.80
New Jersey	5,658	3.56
Pennsylvania	5,367	3.37
Georgia	4,565	2.87
Ohio	4,541	2.85
Other	76,000	47.78

Source: *Wine Handbook*, Annual 2004, p. 41.

★ 548 ★
Liquor
SIC: 2085; NAICS: 31214

Liquor Industry Worldwide

Market values are shown in millions of dollars. The industry is forecasted to be worth $231.9 billion in 2007.

	2002	2007	Share
Whisky	$ 62,169	$ 60,311	26.01%
White spirits	. 45,245	49,216	21.23
Liquers	. 19,263	20,692	8.92
Brandy and cognac . .	. 18,150	20,023	8.64
Rum	. 15,144	19,372	8.36
Tequila and mezcal . .	. 6,102	8,575	3.70
Other	. 51,050	53,664	23.15

Source: *Travel Retailer International*, October - November 2003, p. 104, from Datamonitor.

★ 549 ★
Liquor
SIC: 2085; NAICS: 31214

Popular Spirits Sales

Categories are ranked by sales in millions of dollars for the year ended August 10, 2003. Data are for food stores, drug stores and mass merchandiser sales, excluding Wal-Mart.

	($ mil.)	Share
Vodka	. $ 662.9	25.24%
North American whiskey	. 548.5	20.88
Rum	. 321.2	12.23
Cordials	. 294.5	11.21
Tequila	. 174.8	6.65
Scotch whiskey	. 165.9	6.32
Brandy/cognac	. 158.3	6.03
Prepared cocktails	. 136.7	5.20
Gin	. 136.6	5.20
Flavored brandy	. 16.5	0.63
Irish whiskey	. 9.0	0.34
Grain	. 1.7	0.06

Source: *Beverage Industry*, October 2003, p. 20, from Information Resources Inc.

★ 550 ★
Liquor
SIC: 2085; NAICS: 31214

Top Blended Whiskey Brands, 2003

Brands are ranked in thousands of 9-liter cases. Figures are estimated.

	(000)	Share
7 Crown	. 2,452	45.22%
Kessler	. 785	14.48
McCormick Blend	211	3.89
Kentucky Deluxe	200	3.69
Calvert Extra	160	2.95
Old Thompson	159	2.93
Fleischmann's Preferred	158	2.91
Beam's 8 Star	155	2.86
Heaven Hill Blended Whiskey . . .	150	2.77
Philadelphia	115	2.12
Other	877	16.17

Source: *Wine Handbook*, Annual 2004, p. 45.

★ 551 ★
Liquor
SIC: 2085; NAICS: 31214

Top Brandy/Cognac Brands, 2003

Brands are ranked in thousands of 9-liter cases. Figures are estimated.

	(000)	Share
E & J	. 2,440	24.49%
Hennessy	. 1,880	18.87
Paul Masson Brandy	. 1,230	12.35
Christian Brothers	. 1,150	11.54

Continued on next page.

★ 551 ★

[Continued]
Liquor
SIC: 2085; NAICS: 31214

Top Brandy/Cognac Brands, 2003

*Brands are ranked in thousands of 9-liter cases.
Figures are estimated.*

	(000)	Share
Remy Martin	620	6.22%
Courvoisier	535	5.37
Korbel	380	3.81
Raynal	250	2.51
Presidente	205	2.06
Other	1,273	12.78

Source: *Wine Handbook*, Annual 2004, p. 45.

★ 552 ★

Liquor
SIC: 2085; NAICS: 31214

Top Canadian Whiskey Brands Worldwide, 1998 and 2002

Crown Royal
Canadian Club
Canadian Mist
Black Velvet
Seagram's

*The top brands are ranked by sales of millions of
nine-liter cases.*

	1998	2002
Crown Royal	2.75	3.80
Canadian Club	2.68	2.34
Canadian Mist	2.68	2.34
Black Velvet	2.20	2.00
Seagram's	1.80	1.50

Source: *just-drinks.com (Management Briefing)*, April
2004, p. NA, from P.A.S.H. Beverage Research/Trade.

★ 553 ★

Liquor
SIC: 2085; NAICS: 31214

Top Champagne Brands Worldwide, 2002

*The top brands are ranked by sales of millions of
bottles.*

	(mil.)	Share
Moet Hennessy Group	52.91	18.39%
Marne & Champagne Diffusion	19.61	6.80
Vranken Pommery Monopole	14.19	4.90
Remy Cointreau	9.81	3.40
Laurent-Perrier	9.44	3.28
Allied Domecq	7.30	3.33

Source: *just-drinks.com (Management Briefing)*, May
2004, p. NA, from Banque de France, BNP Paribas, Impact
International, and companies.

★ 554 ★

Liquor
SIC: 2085; NAICS: 31213, 31214

Top Champagne/Sparkling Wine Markets, 2002

Total consumption was 11.58 million cases.

Chicago	8.0%
Los Angeles-Long Beach	7.2
New York	4.8
Detroit	2.2
Orange County	2.2
Boston-Lawrence-Lowell-Brockton	2.1
Riverside-San Bernadino	2.0
San Diego	2.0
Nassau-Suffolk	1.9
Washington D.C.	1.9
Other	65.7

Source: *Adams Wine Handbook*, 2003, p. 101, from Adams
Media.

★ 555 ★
Liquor
SIC: 2085; NAICS: 31214
Top Cider Brands, 2003

Brands are ranked in thousands of 9-liter cases. Figures are estimated.

Hornsby's	1,250
Woodchuck	900
Cider Jack	700
HardCore	390
Magner's Original Vintage Cider	300
Woodpecker	260
Wyder's	200
K Cider	140

Source: *Wine Handbook*, Annual 2004, p. 112.

★ 556 ★
Liquor
SIC: 2085; NAICS: 31214
Top Cider Makers, 2003

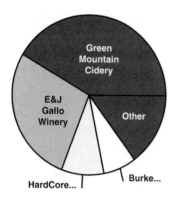

Market shares are shown in percent.

Green Mountain Cidery	41.7%
E&J Gallo Winery	27.8
HardCore Cider/Boston Beer	8.6
Burke Distributing/Manhattan Beer	6.6
Other	15.3

Source: *Wine Handbook*, Annual 2004, p. 112, from Adams Research Database.

★ 557 ★
Liquor
SIC: 2085; NAICS: 31214
Top Cognac Brands, 2002

Brands are ranked by sales of nine-liter cases. Cognac sales increased 6% over the previous year. Much of the growth comes from the young African American population.

	(000)	Share
Hennessey	1,710	52.70%
Remy Martin	590	18.18
Courvoisier	535	16.49
Martell	215	6.63
Salignac	75	2.31
Other	120	3.70

Source: *Research Alert*, October 3, 2003, p. 10, from Impact Databank.

★ 558 ★
Liquor
SIC: 2085; NAICS: 31214
Top Cooler/Malternative Brands, 2003

Figures are for the four week period ending August 10, 2003.

Smirnoff Ice	261,137
Mike's Hard Lemonade	192,122
Smirnoff Triple Black Ice	129,887
Mike's Hard Cranberry	129,581
Bacardi Silver o3	86,714
Zima	56,855
Skyy Blue	54,372
Bacardi Silver	47,980
Tequiza	40,577

Source: *St. Louis Post-Dispatch*, August 26, 2003, p. C1, from Information Resources Inc.

★ 559 ★
Liquor
SIC: 2085; NAICS: 31214

Top Cordials/Liquer Brands, 2003

Brands are ranked in thousands of 9-liter cases.
Figures are estimated.

	(000)	Share
DeKuyper	2,735	13.99%
Southern Comfort	1,322	6.76
Jagermeister	1,300	6.65
Kahlua	1,300	6.65
Baileys	1,275	6.52
Hiram Walker Cordials	1,050	5.37
Other	10,564	54.05

Source: *Wine Handbook*, Annual 2004, p. 55.

★ 560 ★
Liquor
SIC: 2085; NAICS: 31214

Top Distilled Spirit Brands, 2003

Bacardi
Smirnoff
Absolut
Captain Morgan
Jack Daniel's
Jose Cuervo
Crown Royal
Jim Beam
Seagram's Gin
DeKuyper
7 Crown

Brands are ranked in thousands of 9-liter cases.
Figures are estimated.

Bacardi	8,130
Smirnoff	7,185
Absolut	4,488
Captain Morgan	4,210
Jack Daniel's	3,935
Jose Cuervo	3,240
Crown Royal	3,195
Jim Beam	3,100
Seagram's Gin	2,800

DeKuyper	2,735
7 Crown	2,452

Source: *Wine Handbook*, Annual 2004, p. 43.

★ 561 ★
Liquor
SIC: 2085; NAICS: 31214

Top Gin Brands, 2003

Brands are ranked in thousands of 9-liter cases.
Figures are estimated.

	(000)	Share
Seagram's Gin	2,800	25.39%
Tanqueray	1,440	13.06
Gordon's Gin	900	8.16
Bombay Sapphire	650	5.90
Beefeater	615	5.58
Gilbey's Gin	605	5.49
Burnett's White Satin Gin	380	3.45
Barton Gin	359	3.26
Fleischmann's Gin	345	3.13
McCormick Gin	213	1.93
Other	2,719	24.66

Source: *Wine Handbook*, Annual 2004, p. 57.

★ 562 ★
Liquor
SIC: 2085; NAICS: 31214

Top Irish Whiskey Brands, 2003

Brands are ranked in thousands of 9-liter cases.
Figures are estimated.

	(000)	Share
Jameson (includes 1780)	262	53.04%
Bushmills	130	26.32
Tullamore Dew	35	7.09
John Power	20	4.05
Kilbeggan Irish Whiskey	11	2.23
Black Bush	11	2.23
Other	25	5.06

Source: *Wine Handbook*, Annual 2004, p. 55.

★ 563 ★
Liquor
SIC: 2085; NAICS: 31214

Top Liquer Brands in Canada, 2002

Market shares are shown in percent.

Bailey's Original Irish Cream	13.7%
Kahlua	9.2
Southern Comfort	4.1
Grand Marnier	4.0
McGuinness	4.0
Other	65.0

Source: *just-drinks.com (Management Briefing)*, July 2003, p. 16.

★ 564 ★
Liquor
SIC: 2085; NAICS: 31214

Top Liquer Brands in Germany, 2002

Market shares are shown in percent.

Bailey's Original Irish Cream	5.0%
Verpoorten Advocaat	4.5
Batida de Coco	3.0
Other	87.5

Source: *just-drinks.com (Management Briefing)*, July 2003, p. 16.

★ 565 ★
Liquor
SIC: 2085; NAICS: 31214

Top Liquer Brands in Greece, 2002

Market shares are shown in percent.

Bailey's Original Irish Cream	20.0%
Southern Comfort	15.0
Kahlua	10.0
Drambuie	10.0
Other	35.0

Source: *just-drinks.com (Management Briefing)*, July 2003, p. 16.

★ 566 ★
Liquor
SIC: 2085; NAICS: 31214

Top Liquer Brands Worldwide, 2002

Market shares are shown in percent.

De Kuyper	14.4%
Kahlua	7.5
Southern Comfort	7.3
Bailey's Original Irish	6.0
Hiram Walker range	5.7
Alize	3.3
E&J Cask Cream	3.0
Jacquin range	2.7
Bols range	2.7
Other	47.4

Source: *just-drinks.com (Management Briefing)*, July 2003, p. 16.

★ 567 ★
Liquor
SIC: 2085; NAICS: 31214

Top Liquer Brands Worldwide by Cases Sold, 2002

Brands are ranked by sales in millions of 9-liter cases.

Bailey's Original Irish Cream	6.00
De Kuyper	4.70
Kahlua	3.10
Malibu	2.20
Southern Comfort	2.13
Disaronno	1.70
Grand Marnier	1.40
Cointreau	1.24
Bois	1.20
Hiram Walker	1.10
Marie Brizard	1.10

Source: *just-drinks.com (Management Briefing)*, July 2003, p. NA.

★ 568 ★
Liquor
SIC: 2085; NAICS: 31214

Top Liquer (Traditional) Brands in the U.K.

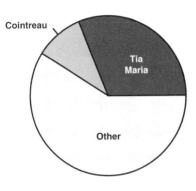

Market shares are shown in percent.

Tia Maria	31.0%
Cointreau	10.0
Other	59.0

Source: *Marketing*, April 15, 2004, p. 3, from ACNielsen.

★ 569 ★
Liquor
SIC: 2085; NAICS: 31214

Top Prepared Cocktail Brands, 2003

Brands are ranked in thousands of 9-liter cases. Figures are estimated.

	(000)	Share
TGI Friday's	1,100	20.54%
Jack Daniel's Country Cocktails . .	1,081	20.19
Jose Cuervo Authentic Margarita's .	1,050	19.61
Bacardi Party	425	7.94
Chi-Chi's	394	7.36
Club Cocktails	345	6.44
Beam Cocktails--cooler	150	2.80
Seagram's Gin & Juice	135	2.52
Other	675	12.61

Source: *Wine Handbook*, Annual 2004, p. 55.

★ 570 ★
Liquor
SIC: 2085; NAICS: 31214

Top Ready-to-Drink Liquor Brands in the U.K., 2003

The ready-to-drink market in the United Kingdom was valued at 12 billion British pounds during 2003.

	(000)	Share
Bacardi Breezer	£ 696,849	5.8%
Smirnoff Ice	693,463	5.8
WKD	492,658	4.1
Reef	280,985	2.4
Red Square	272,771	2.3
Archers Aqua	272,717	2.3
VHF	97,695	0.9

Source: *Europe Intelligence Wire*, March 5, 2004, p. NA, from *Off Licence News*.

★ 571 ★
Liquor
SIC: 2085; NAICS: 31214

Top Regional Whiskey Brands Worldwide

The top brands are ranked by sales of millions of nine-liter cases.

Bagpiper	5.78
McDowell's	4.02
Officer's Choice	3.52
Director's Special	2.98
Royal Stag	2.27
Hayward's	2.25
Suntory Kakubin	2.21
Gilbey's Green Label	1.97
Kerala Malt	1.80

Source: *just-drinks.com (Management Briefing)*, April 2004, p. NA, from P.A.S.H. Beverage Research/Trade.

★ 572 ★
Liquor
SIC: 2085; NAICS: 31214

Top Rum Brands, 2003

Brands are ranked in thousands of 9-liter cases.
Figures are estimated.

	(000)	Share
Bacardi	8,130	41.67%
Captain Morgan	4,210	21.58
Castillo	1,195	6.13
Malibu	1,040	5.33
Ronrico	560	2.87
Cruzan Rum	380	1.95
Myers'	294	1.51
Mount Gay	183	0.94
Monarch Rum	175	0.90
Other	3,342	17.13

Source: *Wine Handbook*, Annual 2004, p. 45.

★ 573 ★
Liquor
SIC: 2085; NAICS: 31214

Top Scotch Whiskey Brands, 2002

Brands are ranked by sales of nine-liter cases. Sales
have been on the decline in recent years. Whiskey
sales fell below 8 millionc ases in 2002 (down from
24 million in 1995).

	(000)	Share
Dewar's	1,395	17.58%
Johnnie Walker Red	655	8.25
Johnnie Walker Black	645	8.13
Clan MacGregor	610	7.69
Chivas Regal	470	5.92
Other	4,160	52.43

Source: *Research Alert*, October 3, 2003, p. 10, from Impact Databank.

★ 574 ★
Liquor
SIC: 2085; NAICS: 31214

Top Scotch Whiskey Brands Worldwide, 1998 and 2002

The top brands are ranked by sales of millions of
nine-liter cases.

	1998	2002
Johnnie Walker Red Label	7.40	6.80
J&B Rare	6.20	6.00
Ballantine's Finest	4.60	4.80
William Grant's	3.80	4.20
Johnnie Walker Black Label	3.00	4.00
Dewar's	3.10	3.50
Chivas Regal	3.15	2.76
The Famous Grouse	2.22	2.54
Bell's	2.70	2.00
Cutty Sark	1.80	1.88

Source: *just-drinks.com (Management Briefing)*, April 2004, p. NA, from P.A.S.H. Beverage Research/Trade.

★ 575 ★
Liquor
SIC: 2085; NAICS: 31214

Top Single-Malt Scotch Brands Worldwide

Global sales of single malts grew by 37% from 1992
to 2002. Scotch whiskey as a whole shrunk by 1%.
Market shares are shown in percent.

	1992	2002
Glenfiddich	20.9%	26.5%
Glen Grant	10.8	20.4
The Glenlivet	9.8	9.8
Cardhu	7.9	3.3

Continued on next page.

★ 575 ★

[Continued]

Liquor

SIC: 2085; NAICS: 31214

Top Single-Malt Scotch Brands Worldwide

Global sales of single malts grew by 37% from 1992 to 2002. Scotch whiskey as a whole shrunk by 1%. Market shares are shown in percent.

	1992	2002
The Macalian	7.1%	4.8%
Glenmorangie	7.0	4.8
Aberlour	5.2	3.1
Other	31.3	27.3

Source: *Wall Street Journal*, December 30, 2003, p. B1, from Impact Databank.

★ 576 ★

Liquor

SIC: 2085; NAICS: 31213

Top Sparking Wine Brands in the U.K., 2003

Leading brands of champagne and sparkling wine sold in the United Kingodm in 2003 are listed by value of sales in thousand pounds sterling.

Moet Hennessy	£ 44,754
Negro Freixenet	21,374
Veuve Clicquot	20,657
MCD	20,556
Bacardi Martini	18,476
Pernod Ricard	13,589
Allied Domecq	11,679
Mentzendorff	11,675
Laurent-Perrier	11,589
Vranken Monopole	10,152

Source: *Europe Intelligence Wire*, April 9, 2004, p. NA, from ACNielsen.

★ 577 ★

Liquor

SIC: 2085; NAICS: 31213, 31214

Top Spirits Producers, 2002

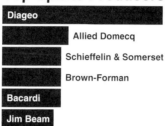

Market shares are shown in percent.

Diageo	22.0%
Allied Domecq	9.0
Schieffelin & Somerset	8.0
Brown-Forman	8.0
Bacardi	8.0
Jim Beam	7.0
Other	38.0

Source: *Wall Street Journal*, August 29, 2003, p. C1, from Goldman Sachs and companies.

★ 578 ★

Liquor

SIC: 2085; NAICS: 31214

Top Straight Whiskey Brands, 2003

Brands are ranked in thousands of 9-liter cases. Figures are estimated.

	(000)	Share
Jack Daniel's	3,935	29.50%
Jim Beam	3,100	23.24
Evan Williams	925	6.93
Early Times	817	6.12
Wild Turkey	511	3.83
Ten High	502	3.76
Old Crow	500	3.75
Maker's Mark	490	3.67
Heaven Hill Bourbon	250	1.87
Other	2,311	17.32

Source: *Wine Handbook*, Annual 2004, p. 43.

★ 579 ★
Liquor
SIC: 2085; NAICS: 31214
Top Tequila Brands, 2003

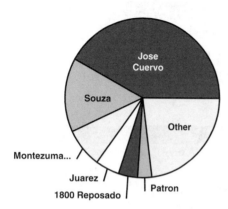

Brands are ranked in thousands of 9-liter cases.
Figures are estimated.

	(000)	Share
Jose Cuervo	3,240	42.36%
Souza	1,110	14.51
Montezuma Tequila	594	7.77
Juarez	400	5.23
1800 Reposado	307	4.01
Patron	205	2.68
Other	1,793	23.44

Source: *Wine Handbook*, Annual 2004, p. 59.

★ 580 ★
Liquor
SIC: 2085; NAICS: 31214
Top Vermouth/Aperitifs Makers, 2003

Market shares are shown in percent.

Bacardi USA	32.0%
E & J Gallo Winery	20.8
The Wine Group	12.8
Distillerie Stock USA	10.2
Other	24.2

Source: *Wine Handbook*, Annual 2004, p. 118.

★ 581 ★
Liquor
SIC: 2085; NAICS: 31214
Top Vermouth Brands, 2003

Brands are ranked in thousands of 9-liter cases.
Figures are estimated.

Martini & Rossi Vermouth	565
Gallo Vermouth	400
Tribuno	245
Stock Vermouth	196
Dubonnet	80
Noilly Prat	50
Cinzano	47
Lillet	21

Source: *Wine Handbook*, Annual 2004, p. 112.

★ 582 ★
Liquor
SIC: 2085; NAICS: 31214
Top Vodka Brands, 2003

Brands are ranked in thousands of 9-liter cases.
Figures are estimated.

	(000)	Share
Smirnoff	7,185	17.30%
Absolut	4,488	10.80
Stolichnoya	1,850	4.45
McCormick Vodka	1,800	4.33
Popov Vodka	1,775	4.27
Skyy	1,690	4.07
Barton Vodka	1,496	3.60
Gordon's Vodka	1,470	3.54
Grey Goose	1,400	3.37
Skol Vodka	1,206	2.90
Other	17,178	41.35

Source: *Wine Handbook*, Annual 2004, p. 55.

★ 583 ★
Liquor
SIC: 2085; NAICS: 31214
Top Vodka Brands in Austria, 2002

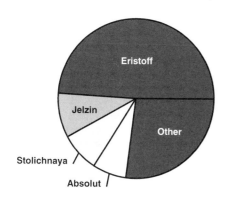

Market shares are shown in percent.

Eristoff	49.0%
Jelzin	9.0
Stolichnaya	8.0
Absolut	7.0
Other	27.0

Source: *just-drinks.com (Management Briefing)*, May 2003, p. 16.

★ 584 ★
Liquor
SIC: 2085; NAICS: 31214
Top Vodka Brands in Canada, 2002

Market shares are shown in percent.

Smirnoff	34.0%
Absolut	9.0
Alberta	8.0
Russian Prince	6.0
Polar Ice	5.0
Other	38.0

Source: *just-drinks.com (Management Briefing)*, May 2003, p. 16.

★ 585 ★
Liquor
SIC: 2085; NAICS: 31214
Top Vodka Brands in Denmark, 2002

Market shares are shown in percent.

Smirnoff	38.0%
Absolut	13.0
Danzka	10.0
Other	39.0

Source: *just-drinks.com (Management Briefing)*, May 2003, p. 16.

★ 586 ★
Liquor
SIC: 2085; NAICS: 31214
Top Vodka Brands in France, 2002

Market shares are shown in percent.

Eristoff	39.0%
Smirnoff	25.0
Absolut	11.0
Other	25.0

Source: *just-drinks.com (Management Briefing)*, May 2003, p. 16.

★ 587 ★
Liquor
SIC: 2085; NAICS: 31214
Top Vodka Brands in Ireland, 2002

Market shares are shown in percent.

Smirnoff	56.0%
Huzzar	22.0
Other	22.0

Source: *just-drinks.com (Management Briefing)*, May 2003, p. 16.

★ 588 ★
Liquor
SIC: 2085; NAICS: 31214
Top Vodka Brands in Norway, 2002

Market shares are shown in percent.

Absolut 17.0%
Smirnoff 16.0
Koskenkorva 16.0
Vikingfjord 10.0
Kalinka 10.0
Other 31.0

Source: *just-drinks.com (Management Briefing)*, May
2003, p. 16.

★ 589 ★
Liquor
SIC: 2085; NAICS: 31214
Top Vodka Brands in Sweden, 2002

Market shares are shown in percent.

Explorer 19.0%
Renat 17.0
Absolut 17.0
Kron 7.0
Other 40.0

Source: *just-drinks.com (Management Briefing)*, May
2003, p. 16.

★ 590 ★
Liquor
SIC: 2085; NAICS: 31214
Top Vodka Brands Worldwide, 2002

*The top brands are ranked by sales of millions of
nine-liter cases.*

Stolichnaya 55.00
Moskovskaya 32.00
Smirnoff 17.50
Absolut 7.50
Nemiroff 3.53
Finlandia 1.68
Gorbatschow 1.32
Wyborowa 1.09
Kristoff 1.00

Source: *just-drinks.com (Management Briefing)*, April
2004, p. NA, from P.A.S.H. Beverage Research/Trade.

★ 591 ★
Bottled Water
SIC: 2086; NAICS: 312112
Bottled Water Industry

Data show type of distribution.

Grocery/off premise 57.3%
Home 13.8
Commercial 12.8
Restaurants 5.7

Source: *Beverage World*, September 15, 2003, p. 20, from
Beverage Marketing Corp.

★ 592 ★
Bottled Water
SIC: 2086; NAICS: 312112

Global Bottled Water Market, 2002

Europe's lead over North America has been shrinking in the last five years. Data are in thousands of hectolitres.

	(000)	Share
Europe	505,624.4	35.11%
North America	417,780.1	29.01
Asia	331,034.7	22.98
South America	126,768.9	8.80
Africa/Mideast/Oceania	44,994.5	3.12
Other	14,074.4	0.98

Source: *Beverage World*, May 15, 2004, p. 16, from Beverage Marketing Corp.

★ 593 ★
Bottled Water
SIC: 2086; NAICS: 312112

Top Bottled Water Brands, 2003

Shares are shown based on the $8.3 billion wholesale market.

Aquafina	11.3%
Dasani	10.0
Poland Spring	7.8
Arrowhead	6.6
Deer Park	4.3
Crystal Geyser	4.0
Okarka	2.8
Zephyrhills	2.6
Ice Mountain	2.5

Evian	1.7%
Other	46.4

Source: *Business Wire*, April 8, 2004, p. NA, from Beverage Marketing Corp.

★ 594 ★
Bottled Water
SIC: 2086; NAICS: 312112

Top Bottled Water Brands in Convenience Stores

Market shares are shown in percent.

Aquafina	12.1%
Dasani	11.8
Dannon	8.1
Pure American	7.1
Evian	6.6
Poland Spring	6.0
Veryfine Fruit 20	5.3
Propel	2.0
Other	41.0

Source: *Chain Drug Review*, February 2, 2004, p. 39, from Information Resources Inc.

★ 595 ★
Bottled Water
SIC: 2086; NAICS: 312112

Top Bottled Water Brands in India

The industry is estimated at Rs 1,000 crore. Roughly 250-300 companies operate in this market.

Bisleri	37.0%
Kinley	30.8
Aquafina	11.6
Bailey	5.0
Yes	1.0
Purelife	1.0
Other	13.6

Source: *Business India*, June 23, 2002, p. 15.

★ 596 ★
Bottled Water
SIC: 2086; NAICS: 312112
Top Bottled Water Brands in New Zealand

Market shares are shown based on supermarket sales.

Kiwi Blue	12.5%
Pump	11.1
Other	76.4

Source: *Grocer's Review*, October 2003, p. NA, from CCANZ.

★ 597 ★
Bottled Water
SIC: 2086; NAICS: 312112
Top Bottled Water Firms, 2003

Shares are shown based on the $8.3 billion wholesale market.

Nestle Waters	32.4%
Coca-Cola	15.1
PepsiCo.	11.3
Suntory Water Group	5.9
Crystal Geyser	4.5
Danone Waters	3.5
DPSU Bottling	2.1
Culligan International	1.4
Vermont Pure	0.9
Glacier Water	0.8
Other	22.1

Source: *Beverage Aisle*, May 15, 2004, p. 24, from Beverage Marketing Corp.

★ 598 ★
Bottled Water
SIC: 2086; NAICS: 312112
Top Bottled Water Firms Worldwide, 2003

Bottled water includes spring water (obtained from underground formations) and purified water (water produced by distillation or deonization or a similar method).

All others	71.2%
Groupe Danone	11.6
Nestle	11.4
Coca-Cola	3.8
Pepsico	2.0

Source: *The Atlanta Journal-Constitution*, March 25, 2004, p. D1, from Beverage Marketing Corp. and International Bottled Water Association.

★ 599 ★
Bottled Water
SIC: 2086; NAICS: 312112
Top Sources for Water, 2002

Roughly 55 million gallons of bottled water were imported from France, down from 65 million gallons the previous year.

France	44.5%
Canada	22.0
Italy	15.8
Fiji	6.2
Germany	3.4
Mexico	2.8
Poland	1.5
Portugal	1.0
Norway	0.3
New Zealand	0.3

Source: *Beverage World*, September 15, 2003, p. 20, from Beverage Marketing Corp.

★ 600 ★
Bottled Water
SIC: 2086; NAICS: 312112

Top Sparkling/Mineral Water Brands, 2003

Shares are shown based on sales at food, drug and mass merchandisers for the 52 weeks ended August 10, 2003. Figures exclude Wal-Mart.

Perrier	13.7%
San Pellegrino	7.8
La Croix	6.4
Poland Spring	5.5
Calistoga	3.7
Canada Dry	3.4
Clearly Canadian	3.1
Arrowhead	2.6
Mendota Springs	2.3
Private label	30.2
Other	21.3

Source: *Beverage Industry*, September 2003, p. 22, from Information Resources Inc.

★ 601 ★
Energy Drinks
SIC: 2086; NAICS: 312111

Best-Selling Energy Drinks

Unit shares are shown based on April 2002 - April 2003 sales.

Red Bull	49.5%
SoBe Adrenaline Rush	10.2
Amp (Mountain Dew)	9.9
Rockstar	7.2
KMX	5.6
Other	17.6

Source: *New York Times*, April 4, 2004, p. 4, from Beverage Digest/Maxwell.

★ 602 ★
Energy Drinks
SIC: 2086; NAICS: 312111

Energy Drink Market in Thailand

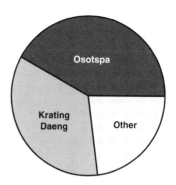

Market shares are shown in percent.

Osotspa	42.0%
Krating Daeng	35.0
Other	23.0

Source: *Bangkok Post*, May 27, 2004, p. NA.

★ 603 ★
Energy Drinks
SIC: 2086; NAICS: 312111

Energy Drink Market in Western Europe

Red Bull has about two thirds of the Western European market by volume. The rest of the top 20 brands took a combined share of 17% for the year.

U.K.	26.0%
Germany	20.0
Spain	13.0
Austria	11.0
Other	30.0

Source: *Nutraceuticals World*, March 2004, p. 32, from Zenith.

★ 604 ★
Energy Drinks
SIC: 2086; NAICS: 312111

Top Energy Drink Brands

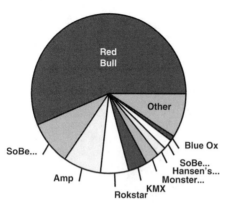

Market shares are shown based on sales of $748.3 million at food, drug and mass merchandisers for the year ended November 2, 2003. Figures exclude Wal-Mart.

Red Bull	56.7%
SoBe Adrenaline Rush	8.7
Amp	8.1
Rokstar	5.9
KMX	3.8
Monster Energy	2.9
Hansen's Energy	2.4
SoBe No Fear	1.7
Blue Ox	1.2
Other	8.6

Source: *Beverage Industry*, December 2003, p. 20, from Information Resources Inc.

★ 605 ★
Energy Drinks
SIC: 2086; NAICS: 312111

Top Energy Drinks in Western Europe, 2001

Market shares are shown based on retail value.

Red Bull	53.1%
Black Booster	3.8
Battery	3.8
Flying Horse	2.6
Purdey's	1.7
V	1.0
Red Devil	1.0

Dark Dog	0.7%
Indigo	0.6
Solstis	0.5
Private label	12.2
Other	19.0

Source: *Beverage Industry*, February 2003, p. 12, from Euromonitor.

★ 606 ★
Soft Drinks
SIC: 2086; NAICS: 312111

Fountain Drink Market

Market shares are shown in percent.

Coca-Cola	66.0%
Other	34.0

Source: *Wall Street Journal*, August 26, 2003, p. A6.

★ 607 ★
Soft Drinks
SIC: 2086; NAICS: 312111

Global Soft Drink Market, 2002

North America's market share was 43.9% in 1998 and has been on the decline since. Europe's share increased slightly from 22.1% in 1998 to 23.1% in 2002.

North America	42.1%
Europe	23.1
Asia	13.6
South America	13.1
Africa	3.4
Middle East	3.1
Oceania	1.5

Source: *Beverage World*, May 15, 2004, p. 16, from Beverage Marketing Corp.

★ 608 ★
Soft Drinks
SIC: 2086; NAICS: 312111
Health Drink Industry

The natural health beverage industry is growing by about 20% a year. Market shares are shown in percent.

Odwalla	67.0%
Other	33.0

Source: *The Fresno Bee*, August 8, 2003, p. C1, from company representatives.

★ 609 ★
Soft Drinks
SIC: 2086; NAICS: 312111
Leading New Beverage Firms, 2002

PepsiCo.
Coca-Cola
Nestle Waters North America
Cadbury-Schweppes
Danone Waters of North America
Ferolito, Vultaggio & Sons
Red Bull
Crystal Geyser
Other

The category includes sparkling waters, premium sodas, fruit beverages and ready-to-drink teas. Total gallons increased from 2.8 billion in 1998 to 4.6 billion in 2002.

PepsiCo.	35.0%
Coca-Cola	16.1
Nestle Waters North America	10.6
Cadbury-Schweppes	9.2
Danone Waters of North America	3.1
Ferolito, Vultaggio & Sons	2.6
Red Bull	2.2
Crystal Geyser	2.0
Other	19.3

Source: *Beverage World*, February 15, 2004, p. 20.

★ 610 ★
Soft Drinks
SIC: 2086; NAICS: 312111
Soft Drink Market in Belgium, 2002

Shares are shown based on 2.61 million litres.

Bottled water	38.5%
Carbonates	31.0
Fruit/vegetable juice	8.0
RTD + tea	2.5
Functional drinks	0.8
Concentrates	0.5
Other	18.7

Source: *just-drinks.com (Management Briefing)*, August 2003, p. 16, from Euromonitor and just-drinks.

★ 611 ★
Soft Drinks
SIC: 2086; NAICS: 312111
Soft Drink Market in France, 2002

Shares are shown based on 12.75 million litres.

Bottled water	66.0%
Carbonates	12.0
Fruit/vegetable juice	9.9
RTS + tea	1.5
Concentrates	1.0
Other	9.6

Source: *just-drinks.com (Management Briefing)*, August 2003, p. 14, from Euromonitor and just-drinks.

★ 612 ★
Soft Drinks
SIC: 2086; NAICS: 312111
Top Diet Soft Drink Brands, 2003

Market shares are shown in percent.

Diet Coke	9.4%
Diet Pepsi	5.5
Caffeine Free Diet Coke	1.7
Diet Dr. Pepper	1.2
Diet Mountain Dew	1.1

Continued on next page.

★ 612 ★

[Continued]
Soft Drinks

SIC: 2086; NAICS: 312111

Top Diet Soft Drink Brands, 2003

Market shares are shown in percent.

Caffeine Free Diet Pepsi	0.9%
Diet Sprite	0.6
Diet 7Up	0.5
Diet Sierra Mist	0.3
Diet Rite	0.3
Other	78.5

Source: *Beverage World*, March 15, 2020, p. 50, from Beverage Marketing Corp.

★ 613 ★

Soft Drinks

SIC: 2086; NAICS: 312111

Top RTD Tea and Coffee Brands

Market shares are shown based on sales of $748.3 million at food, drug and mass merchandisers for the year ended November 2, 2003. Figures exclude Wal-Mart.

	($ mil.)	Share
Frappuccino Cappuccino	$ 115.6	15.45%
Lipton Brisk	109.7	14.66
Arizona	100.8	13.47
Snapple	97.4	13.02
Diet Snapple	75.8	10.13
Neste Cool	57.2	7.64
Nestea	38.5	5.14
Lipton Iced Tea	24.9	3.33
Lipton	20.2	2.70
SoBe	19.4	2.59
Private label	17.9	2.39
Other	70.9	9.47

Source: *Beverage Industry*, December 2003, p. 20, from Information Resources Inc.

★ 614 ★

Soft Drinks

SIC: 2086; NAICS: 312111

Top Soft Drink Brands, 2003

Market shares are shown in percent.

Coke Classic	18.6%
Pepsi-Cola	11.9
Diet Coke	9.4
Mountain Dew	6.3
Sprite	5.9
Diet Pepsi	5.8
Dr. Pepper	5.7
Caffeine-Free Diet Coke	1.7
Sierra Mist	1.4
7Up	1.2
Other	32.1

Source: *Atlanta Journal-Constitution*, March 5, 2004, p. NA, from Beverage Digest/Maxwell.

★ 615 ★

Soft Drinks

SIC: 2086; NAICS: 312111

Top Soft Drink Brands in Dallas, TX

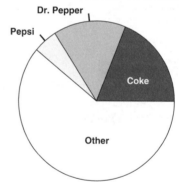

Market shares are shown in percent.

Coke	19.3%
Dr. Pepper	14.7
Pepsi	5.4
Other	60.6

Source: *Dallas Morning News*, May 25, 2004, p. NA, from *Beverage Digest*.

★ 616 ★
Soft Drinks
SIC: 2086; NAICS: 312111

Top Soft Drink Brands in the U.K., 2003

Shares are provided by brand for the leading soft drink and bottled water brands sold in the United Kingdom during 2003.

Coca-Cola	£ 899,281
Robinsons	269,042
Pepsi-Cola	219,501
Lucozade	207,684
Fanta	184,713
Ribena	163,328
Tropicana Pure Premium	129,586
Volvic	97,992
Red Bull	92,805
Schweppes	88,756

Source: *Europe Intelligence Wire*, March 5, 2004, p. NA, from *Off Licence News*.

★ 617 ★
Soft Drinks
SIC: 2086; NAICS: 312111

Top Soft Drink Firms in Ecuador

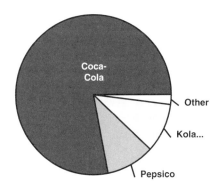

Market shares are shown in percent.

Coca-Cola	78.0%
Pepsico	10.0
Kola Real	10.0
Other	2.0

Source: *The Houston Chronicle*, October 28, 2003, p. 11.

★ 618 ★
Soft Drinks
SIC: 2086; NAICS: 312111

Top Soft Drink Firms in Guatemala, 2003

Market shares are shown in percent.

Cabcorp	41.0%
Femsa	34.0
Other	25.0

Source: *Beverage World*, February 2004, p. 12.

★ 619 ★
Soft Drinks
SIC: 2086; NAICS: 312111

Top Soft Drink Firms in Japan, 2002

Market shares are shown based on domestic sales of 1.61 billion cases.

Coca-Cola Group	31.6%
Suntory Ltd.	17.5
Kirin Beverage Corp.	9.7
Ito En Ltd.	6.2
Otsuka Pharmaceutical Co.	5.9
Other	29.1

Source: "Market Share Survey Report 2002." [online] from http://www.nni.nikkei.co.jp [accessed January 20, 2004], from Nikkei estimate.

★ 620 ★
Soft Drinks
SIC: 2086; NAICS: 312111

Top Soft Drink Firms in Mexico, 2002

Market shares are shown in percent.

Coca-Cola	71.9%
Pepsi	15.1
Kola Real	4.0
Cadbury Schweppes	2.0

Source: *just-drinks.com*, May 17, 2004, p. NA, from Euromonitor and just-drinks.

★ 621 ★
Soft Drinks
SIC: 2086; NAICS: 312111
Top Soft Drink Makers, 2003

Shares are shown based on 10.14 billion cases. Carolina Beverage actually has less than 0.1% of the market. Other includes private label.

Coca-Cola Co. 44.0%
Pepsi-Cola Co. 31.8
Cadbury Schweppes 14.3
Cott Corp. 4.7
National Beverage 2.4
Big Red 0.4
Red Bull 0.2
Monarch Co. 0.1
Hansen Natural 0.1
Carolina Beverage 0.1
Other 2.0

Source: "Beverage Digest/Maxwell Ranks U.S. Soft Drink Industry for 2003." [online] from http://www.bevnet.com [Press release March 4, 2003], from Beverage Digest/ Maxwell.

★ 622 ★
Soft Drinks
SIC: 2086; NAICS: 312111
Top Soft Drink Makers in Jordan, 2002

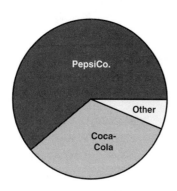

Market shares are shown in percent.

PepsiCo. 61.0%
Coca-Cola 33.0
Other 6.0

Source: *Wall Street Journal*, January 7, 2004, p. B4, from *Beverage Digest*.

★ 623 ★
Soft Drinks
SIC: 2086; NAICS: 312111
Top Soft Drink Makers in Kuwait, 2002

Market shares are shown in percent.

PepsiCo. 74.0%
Coca-Cola 25.0
Other 1.0

Source: *Wall Street Journal*, January 7, 2004, p. B4, from *Beverage Digest*.

★ 624 ★
Soft Drinks
SIC: 2086; NAICS: 312111
Top Soft Drink Makers in Lebanon, 2002

Market shares are shown in percent.

PepsiCo. 83.0%
Coca-Cola 15.0
Other 2.0

Source: *Wall Street Journal*, January 7, 2004, p. B4, from *Beverage Digest*.

★ 625 ★
Soft Drinks
SIC: 2086; NAICS: 312111
Top Soft Drink Makers in Peru

Market shares are shown based on volume.

Coca-Cola 35.0%
Kola Real 19.0
PepsiCo. 11.0
Other 35.0

Source: *Wall Street Journal*, October 27, 2003, p. A1, from *Beverage Digest* and Kola Real.

★ 626 ★
Sports Drinks
SIC: 2086; NAICS: 312111
Leading Sports Drink Brands, 2003

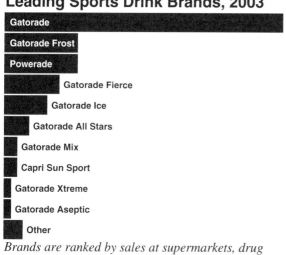

Brands are ranked by sales at supermarkets, drug stores and discount stores (but not Wal-Mart) for the year ended September 7, 2003.

	($ mil.)	Share
Gatorade	$ 520.4	46.46%
Gatorade Frost	139.5	12.46
Powerade	136.1	12.15
Gatorade Fierce	101.7	9.08
Gatorade Ice	75.4	6.73
Gatorade All Stars	40.1	3.58
Gatorade Mix	25.0	2.23
Capri Sun Sport	22.1	1.97
Gatorade Xtreme	15.6	1.39
Gatorade Aseptic	12.8	1.14
Other	31.3	2.79

Source: *MMR*, December 8, 2003, p. 32, from Information Resources Inc.

★ 627 ★
Sports Drinks
SIC: 2086; NAICS: 312111
Sports Drink Market

Market shares are shown in percent.

Gatorade	85.0%
Other	15.0

Source: *Indianapolis Business Journal*, June 16, 2003, p. 3.

★ 628 ★
Sports Drinks
SIC: 2086; NAICS: 312111
Top Sports Drinks in Denmark, 2003

Market shares are shown in percent.

Cult Energy Activator	83.0%
Other	17.0

Source: *just-drinks (Management Briefing)*, March 1, 2004, p. NA.

★ 629 ★
Sweeteners
SIC: 2087; NAICS: 31193, 311999
Sweetener Production, 2002 and 2007

Over 120 million tons of sugar are produced each year. Consumption is on the increase, although the increase is largely from processed food and beverage consumption and not table sugar use.

	2002	2007	Share
Sweeteners	$ 4,925	$ 5,496	52.71%
Sugars	3,870	4,330	41.53
HIS	520	601	5.76

Source: *Food Processing*, April 2003, p. 52, from BCC Inc.

★ 630 ★
Seafood
SIC: 2091; NAICS: 311711
Canned Sardine Market in Canada

The company also holds 53% of the U.S. market.

Connors Bros.	78.0%
Other	22.0

Source: *San Diego Union-Tribune*, February 12, 2004, p. NA.

★ 631 ★
Seafood
SIC: 2091; NAICS: 311711
Seafood Industry in Canada

Canada's domestic harvest is growing at 3% annually. The 2002 catch was valued at $2 billion (1.25 million tons). The Atlantic has about 80% of the catch.

	Tons	Share
Ocean fish, fresh and frozen	75,422	32.53%
Ocean fish, processed	51,760	22.32
Shellfish	45,003	19.41
Fish, fresh water	816	0.35
Other	58,888	25.39

Source: *AgExporter*, January 2003, p. 15.

★ 632 ★
Seafood
SIC: 2091; NAICS: 311711
Top Canned Seafood Brands in the Caribbean, 2004

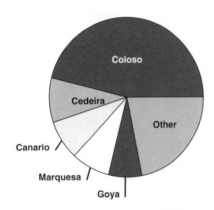

Shares are for the first quarter of 2004.

Coloso	46.0%
Cedeira	9.0
Canario	8.0
Marquesa	8.0
Goya	7.0
Other	22.0

Source: *Caribbean Business*, June 3, 2004, p. 27.

★ 633 ★
Seafood
SIC: 2091; NAICS: 311711
Top Fish/Herring/Seafood Brands, 2004

Brands are ranked by sales for the 22 weeks ended February 22, 2004.

	(mil.)	Share
Louis Kemp Crab Delight	2.69	14.39%
Vita	1.98	10.59
Lascoo	0.64	3.42
Acme	0.53	2.84
Private label	2.13	11.40
Other	10.72	57.36

Source: *Frozen Food Age*, May 2004, p. 44, from Information Resources Inc.

★ 634 ★
Seafood
SIC: 2091; NAICS: 311711
Top Seafood Suppliers in North America

Companies are ranked by sales in millions of dollars.

ConAgra Foods Sales	$ 1,200
Red Chamber Co.	680
Trident Seafoods Corp.	650
StarKist Seafood Co.	630
Pacific Seafood Group	595
Nippon Suisan USA (Nissui)	575
Ocean Beauty Seafoods	500
Tri-Marine International	475
Fishery Products International	472
Chicken of the Sea International	445

Source: *Seafood Business*, May 2003, p. 1.

★ 635 ★
Seafood
SIC: 2091; NAICS: 311711
Top Tuna Brands

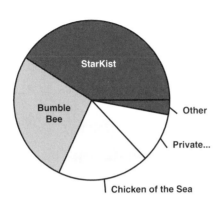

Market shares are shown in percent.

StarKist	41.4%
Bumble Bee	27.2
Chicken of the Sea	19.1
Private label	9.6
Other	2.7

Source: *Seafood Business*, August 2003, p. 1.

★ 636 ★
Seafood
SIC: 2092; NAICS: 311712
Fresh Fish Consumption in France

Data are in tons.

	2000	2001
Coley	9,216	8,958
Cod	7,885	7,425
Whiting	5,997	6,334
Sole	2,800	2,181
Hake	2,030	1,983
Monkfish	1,981	2,107
Perch	1,501	3,591
Bream	1,416	1,635
Bass	1,230	1,280
Tutbot	136	84

Source: *LSA Libre Services Actualities*, June 6, 2002, p. 67, from Secodip.

★ 637 ★
Seafood
SIC: 2092; NAICS: 311712
How Salmon is Processed

Figures are averages for 1998-2002. Pink salmon accounts for just under half (48%) of processed salmon. Sockeye is second with 24%.

Frozen	46.0%
Canned	42.0
Fresh	8.0
Other	4.0

Source: *Seafood Business*, October 2003, from McDowell Group.

★ 638 ★
Seafood
SIC: 2092; NAICS: 311712
Top Frozen Fish Brands in the U.K., 2003

Brands are ranked by sales in thousands of pounds sterling for the year ended October 4, 2003.

	(000)	Share
Captain Birds Eye Premium Fish Fingers	£ 39,760	17.64%
Young's Chip Shop Battered Fillets	29,375	13.03
Young's Prawns	27,012	11.98
Young's Scampi	11,580	5.14
Other	117,727	52.22

Source: *Grocer*, December 13, 2003, p. 66, from Information Resources Inc.

★ 639 ★
Seafood
SIC: 2092; NAICS: 311712

Top Frozen Seafood Brands, 2003

Brands are ranked by supermarket sales for the year ended September 7, 2003.

	($ mil.)	Share
Gorton's	$ 173.33	10.76%
Van de Kamps	94.32	5.86
SeaPak	55.30	3.43
Mrs. Paul's	49.73	3.09
Aqua Star	47.05	2.92
Singleton	44.62	2.77
Other	1,146.08	71.17

Source: *Frozen Food Age*, December 2003, p. 20, from Information Resources Inc.

★ 640 ★
Seafood
SIC: 2092; NAICS: 311712

Top Frozen Seafood Makers, 2004

Market shares are shown based on sales at supermarkets, drugstores and mass merchandisers (but not Wal-Mart) for the year ended January 25, 2004.

Gorton's Corp.	12.10%
Aurora Foods Inc.	5.98
Mrs. Paul's Kitchens	4.38
Rich-Seapak Corp.	3.35
Private label	39.59
Other	34.60

Source: *Grocery Headquarters*, April 2004, p. 16, from Information Resources Inc.

★ 641 ★
Seafood
SIC: 2092; NAICS: 311712

Top Refrigerated Seafood Brands, 2003

Brands are ranked by supermarket sales for the year ended September 7, 2003.

	($ mil.)	Share
Louis Kamp Crab Delights	$ 35.77	11.82%
Vita	21.75	7.19
Acme	12.58	4.16
Lasoco	11.45	3.78
Louis kemp Lobster Delights	9.37	3.10
Philips	8.63	2.85
Other	203.01	67.10

Source: *Frozen Food Age*, December 2003, p. 20, from Information Resources Inc.

★ 642 ★
Seafood
SIC: 2092; NAICS: 311712

Top Shrimp Suppliers

In 2001 for the first time shrimp was the number one seafood product consumed in the United States. Per capita intake was 3.4 lbs (tuna was 2.9 lbs).

Thailand	28.8%
China	11.5
Vietnam	10.4
India	10.3
Ecuador	6.9
Mexico	5.6
Indonesia	4.0
Venezuela	2.4
Bangladesh	1.9
Other	18.2

Source: *Quick Frozen Foods International*, April 2003, p. 28.

★ 643 ★
Coffee
SIC: 2095; NAICS: 31192

Coffee Beverage Service Sales

Figures show results of a survey of coffee cafes, coffee & tea retail stores, specialty food stores and similar retailers. Regular bagged/ground coffee was the sales leader. Coffee & tea retailers had the highest average gross sales in 2002, with sales totaling $199,133.

Drip coffee	40.1%
Espresso-based beverages	34.2
Cold/iced coffee	11.6
Brewed	8.1
Chai	5.9

Source: *Gourmet Retailer*, May 2003, p. 88, from *Gourmet Retailer/SCAA Specialty Coffee Market Research Report*.

★ 644 ★
Coffee
SIC: 2095; NAICS: 31192

Coffee Market in Southern Louisiana

Community is the leader in the regional coffee market. Its share is estimated. Mello Joy, a once popular brand in the area, has been out of the market for some time but is now returning.

Community	70.0%
Other	30.0

Source: *Greater Baton Rouge Business Report*, October 14, 2003, p. 13.

★ 645 ★
Coffee
SIC: 2095; NAICS: 31192

RTD Coffee Market Sales, 2002

Each region recorded double digit growth in 2002. RTD stands for ready-to-drink.

	($ mil.)	Share
West	$ 115.5	40.84%
Northeast	70.5	24.93
South	52.0	18.39
Midwest	44.8	15.84

Source: *Beverage World*, March 2003, p. 30, from Beverage Marketing Corp.

★ 646 ★
Coffee
SIC: 2095; NAICS: 31192

Top Coffee Brands, 2003

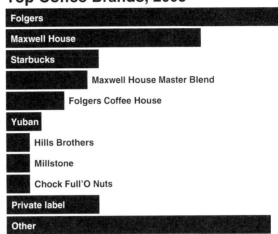

Folgers
Maxwell House
Starbucks
Maxwell House Master Blend
Folgers Coffee House
Yuban
Hills Brothers
Millstone
Chock Full'O Nuts
Private label
Other

Market shares are shown based on sales at food stores, drug stores and mass merchandisers (but not Wal-Mart) for the year ended June 15, 2003.

Folgers	24.0%
Maxwell House	17.0
Starbucks	8.0
Maxwell House Master Blend	7.0
Folgers Coffee House	4.5
Yuban	2.6
Hills Brothers	2.2
Millstone	2.2
Chock Full'O Nuts	2.0
Private label	8.0
Other	22.5

Source: *Beverage Industry*, July 2003, p. 32, from Information Resources Inc.

★ 647 ★
Coffee
SIC: 2095; NAICS: 31192

Top Coffee Brands in Spain, 2000

Market shares are shown in percent.

Saimaza	4.77%
Brasilia	2.16
La Estreka	1.38
Soley	1.35
Marcilla	1.03
Bonka	0.85
Other	88.46

Source: *Expansion*, May 2, 2002, p. 4, from ACNielsen.

★ 648 ★
Coffee
SIC: 2095; NAICS: 31192

Top Coffee Brands (Whole Bean), 2002

Market shares are shown based on sales at food stores, drug stores and mass merchandisers for the year ended November 3, 2002. Figures exclude Wal-Mart.

Eight O'Clock	31.9%
Starbucks	21.7
Folgers Select	8.1
Millstone	7.8
Seattle's Best	2.3
Don Francisco	2.2
Brothers	1.8
Green Mountain	1.7
The Roasterie	1.3
Private label	9.8
Other	11.4

Source: *Beverage Industry*, January 2003, p. 11, from Information Resources Inc.

★ 649 ★
Coffee
SIC: 2095; NAICS: 31192

Top Ground Coffee Brands, 2003

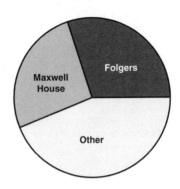

Shares are as of December 2003.

Folgers	30.0%
Maxwell House	26.0
Other	44.0

Source: *The Daily Oklahoman*, December 28, 2003, p. NA, from Information Resources Inc.

★ 650 ★
Coffee
SIC: 2095; NAICS: 31192

Top Ground Coffee Makers, 2004

Market shares are shown based on sales at super-markets, drug stores and mass merchandisers (but not Wal-Mart) for the year ended January 25, 2004.

Kraft Foods Co.	36.37%
Procter & Gamble	32.32
Sara Lee Corp.	3.44
Hillstone Coffee Inc.	2.46
Chock Full O'Nuts	2.33
Community Coffee Co.	1.86
F. Gavina & Sons	1.85
Private label	7.98
Other	11.39

Source: *Grocery Headquarters*, April 2004, p. 16, from Information Resources Inc.

★ 651 ★
Coffee
SIC: 2095; NAICS: 31192

Top Instant Coffee Brands, 2002

Market shares are shown based on sales at food stores, drug stores and mass merchandisers for the year ended November 3, 2002. Figures exclude Wal-Mart.

General Foods International	19.2%
Folgers	19.1
Tasters Choice	12.8
Maxwell House	12.0
Folgers Cafe Latte	4.8
Tasters Choice Original Blend	4.2
Nescafe Clasico	2.8
Maxwell House Cafe Cappuccino	2.7
Nescafe Mountain Blend	2.4
Other	20.0

Source: *Beverage Industry*, January 2003, p. 11, from Information Resources Inc.

★ 652 ★
Coffee
SIC: 2095; NAICS: 31192

Top Instant Coffee Makers in the U.K., 2001

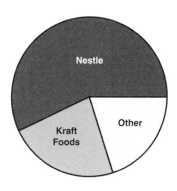

The industry had sales of 700 million British pounds.

Nestle	57.0%
Kraft Foods	23.0
Other	20.0

Source: *Brand Strategy*, December 3, 2002, p. 18.

★ 653 ★
Coffee
SIC: 2095; NAICS: 31192

Top Selling Coffee Brands, 2003

The top brands are ranked by retail sales in millions of dollars for the year ended November 2, 2003.

	($ mil.)	Share
Folgers ground coffee	$ 399.04	14.25%
Maxwell House Ground Coffee	282.99	10.11
Starbucks Ground Coffee	133.82	4.78
Maxwell House Master Blend Ground Coffee	106.98	3.82
Folgers Instant Coffee	93.07	3.32
Eight O Clock Whole Coffee Beans	91.33	3.26
General Foods International Coffee Instant Coffee	90.59	3.24
Folgers Coffee House Ground Coffee	78.00	2.79
Starbucks Whole Coffee Beans	70.13	2.50
Other	1,454.05	51.93

Source: *Food Processing*, January 2004, p. 32, from Information Resources Inc.

★ 654 ★
Coffee Drinks
SIC: 2095; NAICS: 31192

Chilled Coffee Drink Market

Frappuccino

■ **DoubleShot**

■ **Other**

Market shares are shown in percent.

Frappuccino	86.4%
DoubleShot	4.5
Other	9.1

Source: *Wall Street Journal*, May 12, 2004, p. B4, from *Beverage Digest*.

★ 655 ★
Snacks
SIC: 2096; NAICS: 311919
Salty Snack Market in Australia, 2003

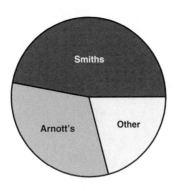

The market was valued at $A484.5 million (Australian dollars) in 2003.

Smiths	47.4%
Arnott's	31.6
Other	21.0

Source: *Australasian Business Intelligence*, May 26, 2004, p. NA.

★ 656 ★
Snacks
SIC: 2096; NAICS: 311919
Salty Snack Market in Canada, 2002

The salty snack market was worth about $1.1 billion in 2002, up from $875 million in 1998. Food stores represent about 60% of the market with convenience stores take about 16%, pharmacies take 7.5% and other channels 16%.

Potato chips & sticks	42.5%
Corn chips & similar	31.7
Popcorn	11.3
Cheese snacks	8.7
Pretzels	5.9

Source: ''Snack Food Market in Canada.'' [online] from http://www.usda.gov [accessed November 1, 2003].

★ 657 ★
Snacks
SIC: 2096; NAICS: 311919
Salty Snack Sales, 2002

Figures exclude Wal-Mart sales. Sales of salty snacks in 2002 were $15 billion (up 33% from 1997). Frito-Lay commands 41% of the category. RTE stands for Ready-to-eat.

	2000	2002	Share
Potato chips	$ 2,614	$ 2,770	32.47%
Tortilla chips	1,805	1,930	22.63
Snack nuts & seeds	1,132	1,165	13.66
Pretzels	530	555	6.51
Corn snacks	478	467	5.47
Cheese snacks	460	495	5.80
RTE popcorn	217	208	2.44
Other	830	940	11.02

Source: *Prepared Foods*, August 2003, p. 12, from Mintel and Information Resources Inc.

★ 658 ★
Snacks
SIC: 2096; NAICS: 311919
Snack Food Market Shares, 2002

Snack revenues have been increasing steadily from $18.2 billion in 1998 to $22.5 billion in 2002.

Potato chips	26.5%
Tortilla chips	19.9
Meat snacks	9.4
Nuts	8.4
Microwave popcorn	5.9
Pretzels	5.7
Cheese snacks	4.7
Other	19.5

Source: *USA TODAY*, January 23, 2004, p. 4B, from Snack Food Association.

★ 659 ★
Snacks
SIC: 2096; NAICS: 311919
Snack Food Sales at Wal-Mart

Sales are shown in millions of dollars for the year ended June 14, 2003.

Tortilla chips	$ 318.5
Popcorn, unpopped	199.2
Puffed cheese	113.1
Pretzels	82.8
Corn chips	62.5
Dips, shelf stable	60.7
Caramel corn/popped popcorn	43.6
Potato chips	42.8

Source: *Retail Merchandiser*, September 2003, p. 26, from ACNielsen Wal-Mart Channel Service.

★ 660 ★
Snacks
SIC: 2096; NAICS: 311919
Top Potato Chip Brands, 2004

Market shares are shown based on sales at supermarkets, drug stores and mass merchandisers (but not Wal-Mart) for the year ended January 25, 2004.

Lays	30.72%
Ruffles	12.22
Wavy Lays	11.08
Pringles	8.40
Utz	4.86
Wise	2.09
Private label	4.86
Other	25.77

Source: *Grocery Headquarters*, April 2004, p. 16, from Information Resources Inc.

★ 661 ★
Snacks
SIC: 2096; NAICS: 311919
Top Potato Chip Makers, 2004

Market shares are shown based on sales at supermarkets, drug stores and mass merchandisers (but not Wal-Mart) for the year ended January 25, 2004.

Frito Lay	59.46%
Procter & Gamble	11.45
Utz Quality Foods	3.39
Wise Foods	3.26
Private label	4.86
Other	17.58

Source: *Grocery Headquarters*, April 2004, p. 16, from Information Resources Inc.

★ 662 ★
Snacks
SIC: 2096; NAICS: 311919
Top Potato Chip Makers in Chicago, IL

Shares are shown based on supermarket sales for the 52 weeks ended July 13, 2003.

Frito-Lay	59.0%
Jay's	28.0
Other	13.0

Source: *Crain's Chicago Business*, August 11, 2003, p. 1, from Information Resources Inc.

★ 663 ★
Snacks
SIC: 2096; NAICS: 311919
Top Potato Chip Makers in Dayton/ Cincinnati Market, 2004

Frito-Lay has more than 40% of the local market and 60% of the $6 billion U.S. market overall. Shares are from March 2003 - March 2004.

Frito-Lay	41.8%
Mike-sell's Potato Chip Co.	23.1
Shearer's Foods	2.2
Other	32.9

Source: *Dayton Business Journal*, May 21, 2004, p. NA.

★ 664 ★

Snacks

SIC: 2096; NAICS: 311919

Top Pretzel Brands, 2003

Market shares are shown based on supermarket, drug store and mass merchandiser sales for the 52 weeks ended September 7, 2003.

	($ mil.)	Share
Rold Gold	$ 176.98	30.56%
Snyders of Hanover	153.21	26.46
Utz	28.16	4.86
Combos	20.28	3.50
Bachman	15.62	2.70
Herrs	13.22	2.28
Pepperidge Farm	10.31	1.78
Jays	8.80	1.52
Anderson	7.54	1.30
Other	144.98	25.04

Source: *Professional Candy Buyer*, November - December 2003, p. 58, from Information Resources Inc.

★ 665 ★

Snacks

SIC: 2096; NAICS: 311919

Top Tortilla Chip/Tostado Makers, 2004

Market shares are shown based on sales at super-markets, drug stores and mass merchandisers (but not Wal-Mart) for the year ended January 25, 2004.

Frito-Lay	79.37%
Mission Foods	2.35
Hain Celestial Group	1.78
Old Dutch Foods	0.83
Private label	4.71
Other	10.96

Source: *Grocery Headquarters*, April 2004, p. 16, from Information Resources Inc.

★ 666 ★

Snacks

SIC: 2096; NAICS: 311919

Top Tortilla/Tostada Chips, 2003

Market shares are shown based on supermarket, drug store and mass merchandiser sales for the year ended February 23, 2003. Figures exclude Wal-Mart.

Doritos	36.3%
Tostitos	26.4
Tostitos Scoops	5.8
Santitas	3.0
Mission	2.5
Doritos Extremes	1.8
Baked Tostitos	1.4
Torengos	1.3
Baked Doritos	1.3
Tostitos Wow!	1.2
Private label	4.6
Other	14.4

Source: *Snack Food & Wholesale Bakery*, April 2003, p. 14, from Information Resources Inc.

★ 667 ★

Pasta

SIC: 2098; NAICS: 311823

Leading Spaghetti Makers in the European Union, 2002

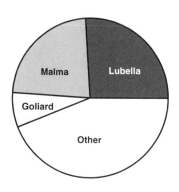

Market shares are shown in percent.

Lubella 26.0%
Malma 23.0
Goliard 7.0
Other 44.0

Source: Europe Intelligence Wire, July 23, 2003, p. NA, from *Polish News Bulletin.*

★ 668 ★

Pasta

SIC: 2098; NAICS: 311823

Pasta Sales, 2002

Data show supermarket sales in millions of dollars. Total supermarket sales were $1.54 billion.

	($ mil.)	Share
Macaroni	$ 567.81	36.69%
Spaghetti	425.66	27.51
Noodles & dumplings	207.82	13.43
Oriental noodles	36.26	2.34
Other	309.98	20.03

Source: Progressive Grocer, September 15, 2003, p. 19, from *Progressive Grocer's 56th Consumer Expenditures Study.*

★ 669 ★

Pasta

SIC: 2098; NAICS: 311823

Pasta Sales in the U.K., 2003

Shares are shown based on sales 95.5 million pounds sterling for the 52 weeks ended August 17, 2003. The market is growing about 4% annually. About 75% of the population buy into the market consuming about 100g a week per household.

Spaghetti 19.0%
Twists 17.1
Quills 8.2
Shells 8.1
Lasagna 7.1
Tagliatelle 5.5
Fusilli 4.5
Macaroni 4.3
Bows 3.5
Penne Rigate 3.2
Other 19.5

Source: Grocer, November 8, 2003, p. 43, from TNS Superpanel.

★ 670 ★

Pasta

SIC: 2098; NAICS: 311823

Top Noodle Makers in Japan

Market shares ae shown in percent.

Tingyi (Cayman Islands) Holding Corp. 40.0%
Hebei Hualong 20.0
Other 40.0

Source: Knight Ridder/Tribune Business News, April 13, 2004, p. NA.

★ 671 ★
Pasta
SIC: 2098; NAICS: 311823

Top Pasta Brands, 2003

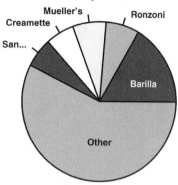

Dry pasta sales reach roughly $1.1 billion each year. Current share is based on supermarket sales from the end of September 2002 through the end of September 2003.

	2000	2003
Barilla	8.2%	16.9%
Ronzoni	7.1	6.9
Mueller's	6.9	6.6
Creamette	6.0	6.2
San Giorgio	5.6	5.7
Other	66.2	57.7

Source: *USA TODAY*, November 10, 2003, p. B1, from ACNielsen and Food Institute Report.

★ 672 ★
Pasta
SIC: 2098; NAICS: 311823

Top Pasta Firms in Japan, 2002

Market shares are shown based on domestic shipments.

Nissin Foods Co.	30.0%
Nippon Flour Mills Co.	23.3
Showa Sangyo Co.	7.8
Hagoromo Foods Corp.	7.1
Okumoto Flour Milling Co.	3.3
Other	28.5

Source: "Market Share Survey Report 2002." [online] from http://www.nni.nikkei.co.jp [accessed January 20, 2004], from Nikkei estimate and Japan Pasta Association.

★ 673 ★
Dry Dinners
SIC: 2099; NAICS: 311423

Leading Dry Dinner Brands, 2003

Brands are ranked by sales at supermarkets, drug stores and discount stores (but not Wal-Mart) for the year ended September 7, 2003.

	($ mil.)	Share
Betty Crocker Hamburger Helper	$ 237.0	14.36%
Kraft	186.6	11.31
Kraft Velveeta	131.1	7.95
Kraft Deluxe	92.4	5.60
Banquet Homestyle Bakes	89.9	5.45
Rice A Roni Pasta Roni	87.3	5.29
Lipton Noodles & Sauce	83.6	5.07
Kraft Easy Mac	71.3	4.32
Betty Crocker Tuna Helper	46.6	2.82
Private label	112.4	6.81
Other	511.8	31.02

Source: *MMR*, December 8, 2003, p. 32, from Information Resources Inc.

★ 674 ★
Hot Beverages
SIC: 2099; NAICS: 31192

Top Hot Beverage Brands in the U.K., 2003

Brands are ranked by sales in thousands of pounds sterling for the year ended October 4, 2003.

	(000)	Share
Nescafe Original	126,936	12.94%
Tetley Tea Bags	80,748	8.23
PG Tips Pyramid tea bags	80,748	8.23
Nescafe Gold Blend	58,497	5.96
Kenco instant coffee	49,783	5.07
Typhoo tea bags	22,511	2.29
Yorkshire Tea Bags	20,894	2.13
Twinings Specialty Tea Bags	17,854	1.82
Kenco Rappor	16,915	1.72
Other	506,343	51.60

Source: *Grocer*, December 13, 2003, p. 66, from Information Resources Inc.

★ 675 ★
Lettuce
SIC: 2099; NAICS: 311991

Leading Fresh Lettuce Brands, 2003

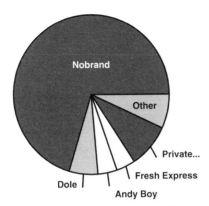

Sales of uniform weight fresh lettuce are shown by brand for the 12 weeks ended November 30, 2003.

	Sales	Share
Nobrand	$ 95,679,520	71.43%
Dole	7,805,308	5.83
Andy Boy	5,150,314	3.84
Fresh Express	4,845,386	3.62
Private label	11,397,822	8.51
Other	9,070,754	6.77

Source: *Frozen Food Age*, January 2004, p. 30, from Information Resources Inc.

★ 676 ★
Lunch Kits
SIC: 2099; NAICS: 311999

Lunch Kit Market, 2003

Market shares are shown based on sales for the year ended September 7, 2003.

	($ mil.)	Share
Oscar Mayer Lunchables	$ 590	82.17%
Other	128	17.83

Source: *Brandweek*, October 13, 2003, p. 13, from Information Resources Inc.

★ 677 ★
Meal Replacements
SIC: 2099; NAICS: 311999

Global Meal Replacement Sales, 2003

Data compare sales at mainstream and natural food stores. Figures are for the year ended December 21, 2003

Ready-to-drink replacements (mainstream) .	$ 713.6
Powdered meal replacements & supplements (mainstream)	112.9
Powdered meal replacements & supplements (natural)	60.1
Ready-to-drink meal replacements (natural) .	5.8

Source: *Prepared Foods*, March 2004, p. NS3, from ACNielsen ScanTrack, SPINS NaturalTrack, and SPINSscan.

★ 678 ★
Popcorn
SIC: 2099; NAICS: 311919

Top RTE Popcorn Brands

Market shares are shown based on sales at supermarkets, drug stores and mass merchandisers for the 52 weeks ended December 24, 2002. Figures exclude Wal-Mart.

Smart Food	13.5%
Poppycock	10.0
Cracker Jack	9.8
Crunch 'n Munch	9.5
Houston Harvet	7.9
Other	49.3

Source: *Snack Food & Wholesale Bakery*, June 2003, p. SI-59, from Information Resources Inc.

★ 679 ★
Prepared Meals
SIC: 2099; NAICS: 311999

Chilled and Prepared Food Market in Europe, 2002

The market for chilled prepared foods was worth an estimated 13.5 billion euros in 2002.

U.K.	38.0%
France	24.0
Germany	18.0
Netherlands	4.0
Spain	3.0
Other	13.0

Source: *Frozen & Chilled Foods*, November-December 2003, p. 16, from Leatherhead Food International.

★ 680 ★
Prepared Meals
SIC: 2099; NAICS: 311999

Prepared Meals Industry in Europe

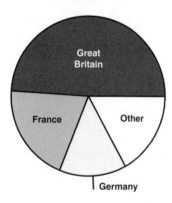

The U.K. is thought to take 51% of the market for prepared meals by 2007. It will be worth about 7.1 billion euros, a 25% increase from 2002.

Great Britain	49.0%
France	20.0
Germany	14.0
Other	17.0

Source: *Frozen & Chilled Foods*, November-December 2003, p. 6, from Datamonitor.

★ 681 ★
Salads
SIC: 2099; NAICS: 311991

Top Fresh-Cut Salad Makers, 2003

Market shares are shown based on supermarket sales for the year ended August 10, 2003.

Dole Packaged Foods	37.8%
Fresh Express	35.9
Ready Pac	6.9
Earthbound Farm	4.0
Private label	10.6
Other	4.8

Source: *Refrigerated & Frozen Foods*, October 2003, p. 60, from Information Resources Inc. InfoScan.

★ 682 ★
Seasonings
SIC: 2099; NAICS: 311942

Best-Selling Spices, 2003

Brands are ranked by sales in millions of dollars for the year ended September 7, 2003.

McCormick	$ 314.16
Spice Islands	38.54
A&A Spice World	32.20
Mrs. Dash	26.55
Durkee	23.67
Sazon Goya	20.26
Mojave	19.17
McCormick Grill Mate	16.44
Accent	16.37
Private label	133.80

Source: *Supermarket News*, October 20, 2003, p. 48, from Information Resources Inc.

★ 683 ★
Seasonings
SIC: 2099; NAICS: 311942

Spice and Seasoning Sales, 2002

Data show supermarket sales in millions of dollars.

Spices & herbs, dry	$ 808.10
Pepper	205.67

Continued on next page.

★ 683 ★
[Continued]
Seasonings
SIC: 2099; NAICS: 311942

Spice and Seasoning Sales, 2002

Data show supermarket sales in millions of dollars.

Marinades & tenderizers	$ 187.16
Salt, cooking and seasoned	142.85
Salt, table	89.93
Seasonings, liquid & remaining	72.47
Salt substitutes	29.47
Vegetables, onions and instant	23.30

Source: *Progressive Grocer*, September 15, 2003, p. 19, from *Progressive Grocer's 56th Consumer Expenditures Study*.

★ 684 ★
Side Dishes
SIC: 2099; NAICS: 311991

Top Refrigerated Side Dish Brands, 2003

Brands are ranked by supermarket sales for the year ended September 7, 2003.

	($ mil.)	Share
AFC	$ 59.27	31.09%
Simply Potatoes	45.84	24.04
Bob Evans	12.69	6.66
Express Bake Potaotes	8.91	4.67
Diner's Choice	8.02	4.21
Yoder's	7.01	3.68
Reser's	4.70	2.47
Reser's Potato Express	2.77	1.45
Purely Idaho	2.72	1.43
Private label	28.21	14.80
Other	10.51	5.51

Source: *Frozen Food Age*, December 2003, p. 20, from Information Resources Inc.

★ 685 ★
Spinach
SIC: 2099; NAICS: 111998

Top Fresh Spinach Brands (Uniform Weight), 2003

Brands are ranked by sales in millions of dollars for the 12 weeks ended August 10, 2003.

	($ mil.)	Share
Fresh Express	$ 16.38	32.67%
Dole	5.31	10.59
Nobrand	3.62	7.22
River Ranch Popeye	2.80	5.58
Private label	9.00	17.95
Other	13.03	25.99

Source: *Frozen Food Age*, October 2003, p. 44, from Information Resources Inc.

★ 686 ★
Taco Kits
SIC: 2099; NAICS: 311999

Top Taco Kit Brands, 2003

Brands are ranked by sales at food stores for the 52 weeks ended July 13, 2003.

	($ mil.)	Share
Guerrero	$ 140.56	16.60%
Mission	140.29	16.57
Old El Paso	132.31	15.63
Tia Rosa	38.30	4.52
Ortega	29.11	3.44
Taco Bell Home Originals	27.77	3.28
Diane's	25.67	3.03
Taco Bell	18.04	2.13
Mission Estilo	17.97	2.12
Other	276.55	32.67

Source: *Baking & Snack*, September 1, 2003, p. NA, from Information Resources Inc.

★ 687 ★
Taco Kits
SIC: 2099; NAICS: 311999

Top Taco Kit Makers, 2003

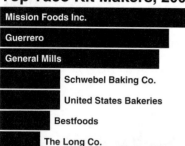

Mission Foods Inc.
Guerrero
General Mills
Schwebel Baking Co.
United States Bakeries
Bestfoods
The Long Co.
Other

Companies are ranked by sales at food stores for the 52 weeks ended July 13, 2003.

	($ mil.)	Share
Mission Foods Inc.	$ 159.23	18.81%
Guerrero	140.56	16.60
General Mills	132.30	15.63
Schwebel Baking Co.	49.62	5.86
United States Bakeries	48.51	5.73
Bestfoods	46.38	5.48
The Long Co.	34.79	4.11
Other	235.18	27.78

Source: Baking & Snack, September 1, 2003, p. NA, from Information Resources Inc.

★ 688 ★
Tea
SIC: 2099; NAICS: 31192

Tea Sales by Segment

Retail tea sales increased nearly $1 billion over 2002 to $5.5 billion in sales in 2003.

Ready-to-drink	75.0%
Loose and bagged	25.0

Source: Beverage Aisle, March 15, 2004, p. 6, from U.S. Market for Tea and Ready-to-Drink Tea by Packaged Facts.

★ 689 ★
Tea
SIC: 2099; NAICS: 31192

Top Tea (Loose/Leaf) Brands, 2003

Market shares are shown based on sales at food stores, drug stores and mass merchandisers (but not Wal-Mart) for the year ended June 15, 2003.

Lipton	26.7%
Celestial Seasonings	14.9
Bigelow	13.5
Luzianne	5.6
Twinnings	5.4
Tetley	4.5
Lipton Cold Brew	3.0
Salada	2.7
Stash	2.6
Private label	7.3
Other	13.8

Source: Beverage Industry, July 2003, p. 32, from Information Resources Inc.

★ 690 ★
Vinegar
SIC: 2099; NAICS: 311999

Vinegar Market Shares, 2002

Unit shares are shown in percent.

White	46.0%
Cider	22.0
Red wine	12.0
Balsamic	10.0
Rice	5.0
Other	5.0

Source: "Vinegar Statistics." [online] available from http://www.versatilevinegar.org/vinegarstats.html [accessed November 24, 2003], from ACNielsen.

SIC 21 - Tobacco Products

★ 691 ★
Cigarettes
SIC: 2111; NAICS: 312221
Top Cigarette Brands

Market shares are shown in percent.

Marlboro	39.0%
Newport	7.8
Camel	6.4
Doral	5.9
Basic	5.0
Winston	4.7
GPC	3.2
Kool	2.8
Salem	2.4
Virginia Slims	2.3
Other	20.5

Source: *Tobacco Retailer*, December 2003, p. 28.

★ 692 ★
Cigarettes
SIC: 2111; NAICS: 312221
Top Cigarette Brands in Finland, 2003

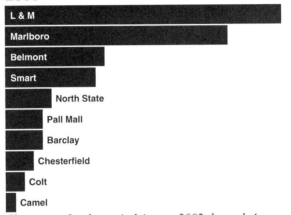

Shares are for the period August 2002 through August 2003 based on sales of 4,751 million pieces.

L & M	31.0%
Marlboro	25.1
Belmont	10.7
Smart	9.6
North State	5.1
Pall Mall	4.0
Barclay	4.0
Chesterfield	2.8
Colt	2.0
Camel	1.2

Source: *World Tobacco*, January 2004, p. 34, from Amer Tobacco.

★ 693 ★
Cigarettes
SIC: 2111; NAICS: 312221

Top Cigarette Brands in France, 2002

Market shares are shown based on sales in April 2002. Philip Morris (39.1% share) and Altadis (29.1% share) were the top two firms.

Marlboro	30.3%
Gauloises brunes	9.7
Gauloises blondes	7.0
Winfield	5.3
Camel	5.3
Gitanes brunes	4.5
Philip Morris	4.1
Winston	3.8
Chesterfield	3.6
Peter Stuyvesant	3.4
Other	23.0

Source: *Tobacco Europe*, July-August 2002, p. 10, from Revue des Tabacs.

★ 694 ★
Cigarettes
SIC: 2111; NAICS: 312221

Top Cigarette Brands in Germany, 2001

Market shares are shown in percent. Philip Morris was market leader with a 37% share, followed by BAT with a 22.9% share and Reetsma with a 22.2% share.

Marlboro	30.1%
West	10.4
HB	5.1
Lucky Strike	4.7
F6	4.4
Gauloises Blonde	4.1
Camel	2.7
Peter Stuyvesant	2.6
Lord	2.2
R1	2.1
Other	31.6

Source: *Tobacco Europe*, March-April 2002, p. 13.

★ 695 ★
Cigarettes
SIC: 2111; NAICS: 312221

Top Cigarette Brands in Spain, 2003

Shares are based on volume sales of blond tobacco cigarettes during the first half of 2003. Blond tobacco cigarettes are a segment of the total cigarette market in Spain where dark tobacco cigarettes are also popular.

Fortuna	21.89%
Marlboro	19.92
Chesterfield	14.26
L & M	7.90
Camel	7.60
Noble	5.85
Lucky Strike	4.97
Winston	2.99
Gold Coast	1.84
Lambert & Butler	1.73
Others	11.02

Source: *World Tobacco*, November 2003, p. 4, from La Boutique del Fumador.

★ 696 ★
Cigarettes
SIC: 2111; NAICS: 312221

Top Cigarette Brands in the U.K., 2003

Brands are ranked by sales in millions of sticks for the year ended September 2003.

	(mil.)	Share
Lambert & Butler KS	6,394.6	12.32%
Benson & Hedges Gold KS	4,474.1	8.62
Mayfair KS	3,031.0	5.84
Marlboro Gold KS	2,757.0	5.31

Continued on next page.

★ 696 ★

[Continued]
Cigarettes
SIC: 2111; NAICS: 312221

Top Cigarette Brands in the U.K., 2003

Brands are ranked by sales in millions of sticks for the year ended September 2003.

	(mil.)	Share
Richmond SK	2,345.9	4.52%
Superkings	2,134.6	4.11
Silk Cut KS	1,934.8	3.73
Richmond KS	1,851.5	3.57
Royals KS	1,788.6	3.45
Regal KS	1,756.3	3.38
Other	23,432.5	45.15

Source: *Grocer*, December 13, 2003, p. 95, from ACNielsen.

★ 697 ★

Cigarettes
SIC: 2111; NAICS: 312221

Top Cigarette Makers, 2003

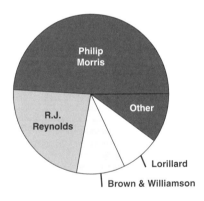

Market shares are shown as of September 2003.

Philip Morris	49.2%
R.J. Reynolds	22.7
Brown & Williamson	9.6
Lorillard	8.1
Other	10.4

Source: *New York Times*, October 28, 2003, p. C2, from Information Resources Inc., Capstone Research Inc., and R.J. Reynolds Tobacco.

★ 698 ★

Cigarettes
SIC: 2111; NAICS: 312221

Top Cigarette Makers in Belgium/ Luxembourg, 2001

Market shares are shown in percent.

Philip Morris Belgium	35.7%
BAT	26.3
Cinta	18.1
JTI (Japan Tobacco)	4.6
HVL (Handewyck)	3.6
Other	11.5

Source: *Tobacco Europe*, July-August 2002, p. 13.

★ 699 ★

Cigarettes
SIC: 2111; NAICS: 312221

Top Cigarette Makers in France, 2002

Market shares are shown in percent.

Philip Morris	38.9%
Altadis	29.3
BAT	16.3
JTI	9.0
Imperial	3.4
Gallaher	2.9
Other	0.2

Source: "Tobacco and Products Annual 2004." [online] from http://ffas.usda.gov [accessed June 1, 2004], from Foreign Agricultural Service, U.S. Department of Agriculture and Business Analytica.

★ 700 ★

Cigarettes
SIC: 2111; NAICS: 312221

Top Cigarette Makers in India

Market shares are shown in percent.

ITC Ltd.	75.0%
Other	25.0

Source: *Asia Africa Intelligence Wire*, May 2, 2004, p. NA, from India Business Insight.

★ 701 ★
Cigarettes
SIC: 2111; NAICS: 312221

Top Cigarette Makers in Indonesia, 2002

Market shares are shown in percent. Roughly 60% of adult males in Indonesia smoke. Indeed, the market grew 43% between 1990 and 1999, making it the fastest growing cigarette market in the world, according to the World Health Organization.

Gudang Garam	29.3%
PT HM Sampoerna	19.1
PT Djarum	16.6
Philip Morris	5.9
BAT	3.8
Lestari Putra	2.2
Noyorono	1.3
Gelora Djaya	1.2
Filasta	1.0
Other	19.6

Source: *World Tobacco*, September 2003, p. 21, from Gappri.

★ 702 ★
Cigarettes
SIC: 2111; NAICS: 312221

Top Cigarette Makers in Ireland

Market shares are shown in percent.

Gallaher	47.8%
John Players (Imperial)	29.0
PJ Carroll's & Co. (BAT)	24.0

Source: *Tobacco Europe*, January-February 2002, p. 13, from World Tobacco File.

★ 703 ★
Cigarettes
SIC: 2111; NAICS: 312221

Top Cigarette Makers in Pakistan

Abour 24 tobacco companies are though to operate in Pakistan. 20 of these companies do not register production with the Tobacco Board, making official figures estimates. Total consumption is thought to be 65 million pieces.

Lakson Tobacco	40.0%
Pakistan Tobacco Company	38.0
Other	22.0

Source: "Tobacco and Products Annual 2004." [online] from http://ffas.usda.gov [accessed June 1, 2004], from Foreign Agricultural Service, U.S. Department of Agriculture.

★ 704 ★
Cigarettes
SIC: 2111; NAICS: 312221

Top Cigarette Makers in Peru, 2002

Market shares are shown as a percent of the legal market for cigarettes. The illegal trade in cigarettes is estimated to represent between 30 and 35 percent of the domestic market totalling about 200 million boxes.

National Tobacco Company	75.0%
British American Tobacco	15.0
Distribuidora Dinamica	8.5
Other	1.5

Source: *South American Business Information*, January 22, 2020, p. NA.

★ 705 ★
Cigarettes
SIC: 2111; NAICS: 312221

Top Cigarette Makers in Russia, 2003

Russia is expected to have its second year of declining output.

Philip Morris	24.0%
JTI	15.0
BAT	14.3
Gallaher	14.2

Continued on next page.

★ 705 ★

[Continued]
Cigarettes
SIC: 2111; NAICS: 312221

Top Cigarette Makers in Russia, 2003

Russia is expected to have its second year of declining output.

Balkanskaya Zvezda	7.6%
Donskoy Tabak	7.4
Imperial Tobacco	4.9
Other	12.6

Source: "Tobacco and Products Annual 2004." [online] from http://ffas.usda.gov [accessed June 1, 2004], from Foreign Agricultural Service, U.S. Department of Agriculture and Business Analytica.

★ 706 ★

Cigarettes
SIC: 2111; NAICS: 312221

Top Cigarette Makers in the Dominican Republic

E. Leon Jiminez is a private company associated with Philip Morris.

E. Leon Jiminez	85.0%
Other	15.0

Source: "Tobacco and Products Annual 2004." [online] from http://ffas.usda.gov [accessed June 1, 2004], from Foreign Agricultural Service, U.S. Department of Agriculture.

★ 707 ★

Cigars
SIC: 2121; NAICS: 312229

Cigar Market

Market shares are shown in percent.

Altadis	50.0%
Other	50.0

Source: "Industry Center - Tobacco." [online] from http://biz.yahoo.com/ic/profile/tobacco_1203.html [June 1, 2004].

★ 708 ★

Snuff
SIC: 2131; NAICS: 312229

Snuff Market in Germany

Market shares are shown in percent. Poschl has 50% of the global market.

Poschl	90.0%
Other	10.0

Source: "NeGeCo Implements." [online] from http://www.suse.de [accessed May 5, 2004].

SIC 22 - Textile Mill Products

★ 709 ★

Fabrics

SIC: 2200; NAICS: 31321

Largest Fabric/Fiber Mills in Italy

The largest mills are ranked by sales in millions of euros.

Legnano	224.95
Carvico	211.30
Legler	202.79
Zegan Baruffa	201.00
Mantero	183.66
Frangi	175.80
Limonta	170.09
Lineapi	166.10
Alcantara	149.96

Source: *Daily News Record*, August 26, 2002, p. 120, from Pambianco Consultancy.

★ 710 ★

Textiles

SIC: 2200; NAICS: 31321

U.S. Textile and Apparel Imports, 2002

CBTPA stands for Caribbean Basin Trade Partnership Act.

China	15.0%
CBTPA countries	12.0
Mexico	12.0
Canada	5.0
Hong Kong	5.0
India	4.0
Korea	4.0
Other	43.0

Source: *American Shipper*, March 2004, p. 30, from Government Accounting Office and U.S. Bureau of the Census.

★ 711 ★

Fabrics

SIC: 2211; NAICS: 31321

Coated Fabric Demand in China

Demand is shown in millions of square meters.

	2002	2007	Share
Nylon coated fabrics	929.7	1,289.1	47.70%
Polyester coated fabrics	187.9	288.4	10.67
Cotton coated fabrics	183.4	265.0	9.81
Polyester and cotton coated fabrics	172.7	264.6	9.79
Other coated fabrics	401.0	595.6	22.04

Source: *Chinese Markets for Coated Fabrics*, December 2003, p. NA.

★ 712 ★

Fabrics

SIC: 2221; NAICS: 31321

Chemical-Protection Suit Liners

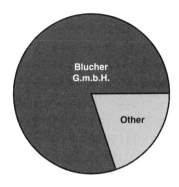

The company has 80% of the global market for fabric that goes into chemical-protection suits.

Blucher G.m.b.H.	80.0%
Other	20.0

Source: *New York Times*, April 8, 2003, p. W1.

★ 713 ★

Hosiery

SIC: 2251; NAICS: 315111

Leading Hosiery Brands

Brands are ranked by sales in millions of dolalrs for the year ended August 10, 2003.

	(mil.)	Share
L'Eggs Sheer Energy	$ 65.15	15.29%
No Nonsense	53.33	12.52
L'Eggs Silken Mist	34.54	8.11
Everday by L'Eggs	21.10	4.95
Just My Size	17.80	4.18
No Nonsense Sheer Endurance	17.69	4.15
No Nonsense Great Shapes Figure Enhancement	16.66	3.91
L'Eggs Sheer Comfort	13.53	3.18
No Nonsense Almost Bare	12.80	3.00
Private label	61.10	14.34
Other	112.31	26.36

Source: *Grocery Headquarters*, October 2003, p. 84, from Information Resources Inc.

★ 714 ★

Hosiery

SIC: 2251; NAICS: 315111

Top Women's Hosiery Makers, 2003

Market shares are shown based on sales at super-markets, drug stores and mass merchandisers (but not Wal-Mart) for the year ended May 18, 2003.

Legg's Products Inc.	54.0%
Kayser-Roth Corp.	25.1
Smith Hosiery Inc.	2.4
Americal Corp.	1.4
Private label	14.4
Other	2.7

Source: *Grocery Headquarters*, August 2003, p. S6, from Information Resources Inc.

★ 715 ★

Hosiery

SIC: 2252; NAICS: 315119

Men's Hosiery Market

Market shares are shown in percent. The company has 54% of the department store market.

Gold Toe	64.0%
Other	36.0

Source: *Daily News Record*, August 25, 2003, p. 16, from NPD Fashion Group.

★ 716 ★

Carpets and Rugs

SIC: 2273; NAICS: 31411

Leading Bath Rug Makers

Firms are ranked by sales in millions of dollars.

Mohawk Home	$ 172
Springs Industries	160
Maples Rugs	80
Shaw Living	30
Lacey Mills	24

Source: *Home Textiles Today*, January 12, 2004, p. 1.

★ 717 ★

Carpets and Rugs
SIC: 2273; NAICS: 31411

Leading Carpet/Rug Makers in Egypt

Market shares are shown in percent.

Oriental Weavers	80.0%
Other	20.0

Source: *Business Today*, October 3, 2003, p. NA.

★ 718 ★

Nonwoven Industry
SIC: 2297; NAICS: 31323

Largest Nonwoven Goods Producers

Firms are ranked by sales in millions of dollars.

Freudenberg & Co.	$ 1,400
DuPont Nonwovens	1,200
Kimberly-Clark Corp.	900
BBA Fiberweb	850
PGI Nonwovens	750
Ahlstrom FiberComposites	651
Johns Manville	525
Buckeye Technologies	225
Colbond BV	223
Japan Vilene	168

Source: *Nonwovens Industry*, September 2003, p. 36.

★ 719 ★

Nonwoven Industry
SIC: 2297; NAICS: 31323

Nonwoven Fabric Demand

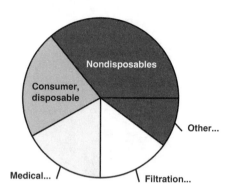

Advances in the industry will be driven by incontinence products, filters and protective apparel. Total demand is forecasted to reach nearly $5 billion in 2007.

	2002	2007	Share
Nondisposables	$ 1,470	$ 1,770	35.98%
Consumer, disposable . . .	935	1,085	22.05
Medical, disposable	670	820	16.67
Filtration, disposable	580	740	15.04
Other disposable	400	505	10.26

Source: *Research Studies - Freedonia Group*, October 22, 2003, p. NA, from Freedonia Group.

★ 720 ★
Wipes
SIC: 2297; NAICS: 31323

Household Wipes Market in North America

The household segment breaks down like this: glass $47 million, auto care $40 million, electrostatic $154, furniture polish $72 million, floor cleaners $102, hard surface $190 and the rest of the market includes such things as mop heads and dry wipes. Wal-Mart and mass merchants take about $200 - $230 million of the market.

	($ mil.)	Share
Baby	$ 882	41.00%
Household	715	33.24
Personal	554	25.76

Source: *Nonwovens Industry*, February 2004, p. 34, from Euromonitor.

★ 721 ★
Wipes
SIC: 2297; NAICS: 31323

Household Wipes Market Segments

The global market was valued at $5.2 billion in 2003.

	($ mil.)	Share
Personal wipes	$ 3,225.1	16.96%
Baby wipes	2,152.5	11.32
Household cleaning wipes	1,989.8	10.46
Cleanser impregnated wet wipes	1,040.6	5.47
Cosmetic wipes	691.4	3.64
Wipes and refills	683.9	3.60
Facial cleansing wipes	612.2	3.22

	($ mil.)	Share
Wet floor wipes	$ 378.2	1.99%
All purpose cleaning wipes	358.0	1.88
Starter kits/sweepers/sticks	265.3	1.40
Other	7,619.0	40.07

Source: *Global Cosmetic Industry*, April 2004, p. 40, from Euromonitor.

★ 722 ★
Wipes
SIC: 2297; NAICS: 31323

Leading Wipes Makers Worldwide, 2003

Western Europe led the $5.2 billion market with sales of $2.3 billion.

Procter & Gamble	23.9%
Kimberly-Clark	9.6
Kao Corp.	5.8
Johnson & Johnson Inc.	5.6
SC Johnson & Son Inc.	5.2
Reckitt Benckiser	3.6
Unilever	3.6
Beiersdorf	2.1
Other	40.6

Source: *Global Cosmetic Industry*, April 2004, p. 40, from Euromonitor.

SIC 23 - Apparel and Other Textile Products

★ 723 ★

Apparel

SIC: 2300; NAICS: 315211, 315212

Apparel Sales by Type

Figures are for the 12 months ended April 2003. Since 1998 private and proprietary apparel brands have increased 5% while total apparel sales fell 1.2%.

Private/proprietary	36.0%
National	34.0
Designer	7.0
Other	23.0

Source: *WWD*, July 23, 2003, p. 21, from NPD Group.

★ 724 ★

Apparel

SIC: 2300; NAICS: 315211, 315212

Apparel Spending by Teenagers and Tweens

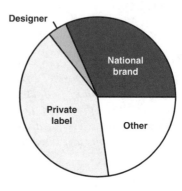

Spending is shown by type of apparel. Private label brands have begun to take share from national brands in recent years.

	2001	2003
National brand	32.0%	32.0%
Designer	5.5	3.5
Private label	39.0	42.0
Other	23.5	22.5

Source: *WWD*, October 29, 2003, p. 14.

★ 725 ★
Apparel
SIC: 2300; NAICS: 315211, 315212

Children's Apparel Brand Leaders

Figures show the most popular brands of survey respondents when asked " if you were shopping in a discount department store, what brand would you want?"

Hanes	16.0%
Levi's	10.0
Nike	9.0
Fruit of the Loom	5.0
Carter's	5.0

Source: *DSN Retailing Today*, October 13, 2003, p. F18, from Leo J. Shapiro & Associates Inc.

★ 726 ★
Apparel
SIC: 2300; NAICS: 315211, 315212

Children's Apparel Sales

Boy's apparel sales grew steadily from $7.3 billion in 2001 to $8.8 billion in 2003. Girl's apparel sales grew from $7.5 billion to $10 billion during the same period.

Tops	26.9%
Bottoms	25.3
Knit shirts	15.7
Pants/sacs	8.1
Jeans	8.1
Children's/infantsets	7.0
Tailored clothing	6.6
Fleecewear	5.4
Sleepwear	5.2
Special infantswear	4.9

Source: *Children's Business*, May 2004, p. 7, from NPD Data.

★ 727 ★
Apparel
SIC: 2300; NAICS: 315228, 315239

Clothing Industry in South Korea, 2004

The clothing industry is expected to surpass $16.7 billion in 2004.

Casual wear	52.6%
Female suits	12.8
Accessories	12.2
Infantwear	8.3
Male suits	7.3
Underwear	6.9

Source: *Yonhap News Agency Korea*, January 6, 2004, p. NA, from MPI.

★ 728 ★
Apparel
SIC: 2300; NAICS: 315239, 315228

Compression Apparel Market, 2003

Compression apparel refers to fabric that is specially designed to absorb moisture. The fabric is popular with athletes. Under Armour is one of the fastest growing companies with annual sales of $120 million.

Under Armour	69.0%
Nike	3.5
Reebok	1.2
Other	26.3

Source: *New York Times*, November 27, 2003, p. C4, from SportScanINFO.

★ 729 ★
Apparel
SIC: 2300; NAICS: 315211, 315239

Jeans Market in the U.K.

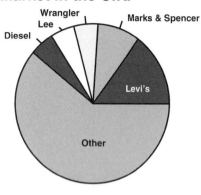

The number of pairs of jeans grew nearly 40% between 1998 and 2002. The women's jeans sector is expected to decline in the coming years, however.

Levi's	15.0%
Marks & Spencer	9.0
Wrangler	5.0
Lee	5.0
Diesel	5.0
Other	61.0

Source: *Marketing*, September 4, 2003, p. 20, from Mintel.

★ 730 ★
Apparel
SIC: 2300; NAICS: 315211, 315239

Jeans Sales by Type

Sales are shown in billions of dollars.

	April 2002	April 2003	Share
National brand	$ 5.25	$ 5.64	48.54%
Designer	1.03	0.93	8.00
Private label	3.87	3.65	31.41
Other/unclassified	1.52	1.40	12.05

Source: *Advertising Age*, June 30, 2003, p. 4, from NPD Group/NPD Fashionworld and consumer data estimates.

★ 731 ★
Apparel
SIC: 2300; NAICS: 315223

Leading T-Shirt Makers

Market shares are estimated in percent.

Gildan	29.0%
Haynes	19.0
Delta	10.0
Other	42.0

Source: *Fayetteville Observer*, February 21, 2004, p. NA.

★ 732 ★
Apparel
SIC: 2300; NAICS: 315228, 315239

Performance/Sport Swimwear Market

Market shares are shown in percent.

Speedo	70.0%
Other	30.0

Source: *Brandweek*, March 8, 2004, p. 9.

★ 733 ★
Apparel
SIC: 2300; NAICS: 315228, 315239

Sports Apparel Market (Loose Fitting)

Under Armour has taken control of the compression apparel market for the sports clothing market. The tables compares its rising share in the loose fitting sports apparel market.

	Dec. 2003	Feb. 2004
Nike	50.7%	44.7%
Under Armour	14.2	17.0
Other	35.1	38.3

Source: *Daily Record*, February 20, 2004, p. NA.

★ 734 ★

Apparel

SIC: 2300; NAICS: 315228, 315239

Sports Apparel Purchases, 2002

Figures show the activities for which Americans purchased sports apparel.

Walking for exercise	10.9%
Basketball	6.6
Golf	6.5
Running/jogging	5.8
Baseball/softball	3.6
Hiking/camping/climbing	2.9
Soccer/rugby	2.7
Football	2.5
Aerobics/dance	2.3
Skiing	1.7
Other	54.5

Source: *just-style.com (Management Briefing)*, April 2004, p. 3, from NPD Fashionworld.

★ 735 ★

Apparel

SIC: 2300; NAICS: 315228, 315239

Sports Apparel Sales, 2002

Figures are in billions of dollars. Sports apparel represented 21.3% of the total apparel market in 2002, up from 20% in 2001. Overall, consumers spent 11.7% less for each item than in 2001.

	($ bil.)	Share
T-shirts	$ 13.12	35.27%
Polo/golf/rugby shirts	4.44	11.94
Tanks/sleaveless tops	3.26	8.76
Swimwear	3.24	8.71
Fleece sweatshirts	1.98	5.32

	($ bil.)	Share
Outerwear/jackets	$ 1.73	4.65%
Shorts	1.31	3.52
Socks	1.29	3.47
Fleece sweatpants/shorts	1.26	3.39
Underwear/intimates	0.76	2.04
Pants/slacks	0.74	1.99
Other	4.07	10.94

Source: *Research Alert*, December 19, 2003, p. 1, from NPD Fashionworld and Sporting Goods Manufacturers Association International.

★ 736 ★

Apparel

SIC: 2300; NAICS: 315228, 315239

Swimwear Market in Australia

Speedo has 70% of the active swimwear market. Nike and Sydney-based Seafolly company (which has 30% of the fashion swimwear market) recently announced plans to partner and enter the active swimwear market.

Speedo	70.0%
Other	30.0

Source: *The Business Journal - Portland*, March 17, 2003, p. NA.

★ 737 ★

Apparel

SIC: 2300; NAICS: 315228, 315239

Top Apparel Exporters, 2003

The top exporters to the U.S. are ranked by market share for the year ending July 2003.

Mexico	11.60%
China	10.86
Honduras	6.81
Hong Kong	5.23
Bangladesh	4.99
El Salvador	4.35
Other	56.16

Source: *Apparel*, November 2003, p. 36.

★ 738 ★
Apparel
SIC: 2300; NAICS: 315228, 315239

Top Apparel Firms (Private-Label), 2002

Market shares are shown in percent.

Wal-Mart	8.6%
Old Navy	7.0
The Gap	6.6
J.C. Penney	6.4
Kmart	5.1
Target	3.6
Express	3.4
Kohl's	2.8
American Eagle	2.8
Abercrombie & Fitch	2.7
Other	51.0

Source: *Research Alert*, December 19, 2003, p. 1, from STS Market Research.

★ 739 ★
Apparel
SIC: 2300; NAICS: 315228, 315239

Top Apparel Makers

Firms are ranked by sales in millions of dollars.

Sara Lee	$ 6,455.0
VF Corporation	5,519.0
Levi Strauss & Co.	4,258.7
Jones Apparel Group	4,048.3
Liz Clairborne	3,448.5
Polo Ralph Lauren	2,363.7
Kellwood Company	2,281.8
Tommy Hilfiger	1,876.7
Benetton Group	1,869.6
Wacoal Corp.	1,227.0

Source: *World Trade*, March 2003, p. 22.

★ 740 ★
Apparel
SIC: 2311; NAICS: 315228, 315239

Outerwear Market Sales

Sales are shown by model for the 12 months ended September 2003. By shell, synthetics and synthetic blends lead the market with 46% of sales followed by leather with 23%, and with the blance held by cottons and wools.

Bombers - 27 inches	37.0%
Barn and barcoats - 32-36 inches	35.0
Lightweight zipper jackets - 29 inches	24.0
Three quarter toppers - 38 inches +	4.0

Source: *Daily News Record*, November 17, 2003, p. 22, from NPD Fashionworld.

★ 741 ★
Apparel
SIC: 2320; NAICS: 315211, 315221

Leading Men's Sportswear Firms

In 2002, just under half of all men (48%) 13 and older made a sportswear purchase at a discount store.

Wrangler	11.6%
Hanes	6.4
Fruit of the Loom	6.1
Cherokee	5.5
Route 66	5.4
Faded Glory	4.5
Puritan	3.8
Rustler	2.8
Basic Editions	2.8
Other	51.1

Source: *Daily News Record*, March 10, 2003, p. 24, from STS Market Research.

★ 742 ★

Apparel

SIC: 2320; NAICS: 315211, 315223, 315221

Men's and Boy's Wear Sales

Men's and boy's apparel sales in department stores was $20.2 billion.

	($ mil.)	Share
Tops, men's	$ 4,919	24.33%
Bottoms, men's	3,875	19.17
Furnishings, men's	2,586	12.79
Tops, boy's	1,874	9.27
Activewear, men's	1,398	6.91
Bottoms, boy's	1,127	5.57
Outerwear, men's	991	4.90
Suits, sportcoats, men's	922	4.56
Furnishings, boy's	780	3.86
Activewear, boy's	722	3.57
Other	1,024	5.06

Source: *Retail Merchandiser*, July 2003, p. 20, from *Retail Merchandiser*.

★ 743 ★

Apparel

SIC: 2320; NAICS: 315211

Popular Men's Apparel Brands

Figures show the most popular brands of survey respondents when asked '' if you were shopping in a discount department store, what brand would you want?''

Hanes	30.0%
Levi's	15.0
Fruit of the Loom	11.0
Wrangler	10.0
Dockers	7.0

Source: *DSN Retailing Today*, October 13, 2003, p. F18, from Leo J. Shapiro & Associates Inc.

★ 744 ★

Apparel

SIC: 2320; NAICS: 315228

Top Markets for Men's Dress Clothing

Areas are ranked by share of total dress pants and shirt spending for the year ended July 2003.

Houston, TX	30.7%
New York City, NY	26.8
Boston-Worcester, MA	24.6
Los Angeles-Long Beach, CA	23.8
Phoenix-Mesa, AZ	22.2
Denver, CO	21.5
Atlanta, GA	21.5
Miami, FL	20.8
Tampa-St. Petersburg, FL	20.2

Source: *Daily News Record*, September 29, 2003, p. 24, from STS Market Research.

★ 745 ★
Apparel
SIC: 2320; NAICS: 315228

Top Men's Apparel Firms in Japan, 2002

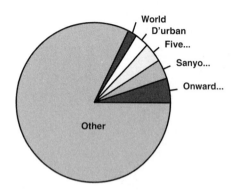

Market shares are shown based on domestic sales of 1.09 trillion yen.

Onward Kashiyama	5.0%
Sanyo Shokai	3.8
Five Foxes	3.6
D'urban	2.6
World	2.4
Other	82.6

Source: "Market Share Survey Report 2002." [online] from http://www.nni.nikkei.co.jp [accessed January 20, 2004], from Nikkei estimate.

★ 746 ★
Apparel
SIC: 2320; NAICS: 315228

Top Men's Sportswear Brands Among Hispanics, 2003

Data show the top brands for Hispanic males 13-24 years of age. Figures are for the 12 months ended May 2003. Tommy Hilfiger had a 2.3% share for non-Hispanic men.

Tommy Hilfiger	8.2%
Polo Ralph Lauren	5.3
Gap	4.4
Nike	4.4
Old Navy	4.4
Levi's	4.1
Nautica	3.4
Anchor Blue	2.8
Abercrombie & Fitch	2.4

Dockers	2.3%
Other	58.3

Source: *Daily News Record*, August 4, 2003, p. 20, from STS Market Research.

★ 747 ★
Apparel
SIC: 2321; NAICS: 315223

Top Dress Shirt Brands, 2003

Market shares are for the 12 months ended September 2003.

Van Heusen	7.7%
Polo/Ralph Lauren	7.6
Arrow	5.4
Stafford	4.1
Geoffrey Beene	2.6
Tommy Hilfiger	2.4
Brooks Brothers	2.3
Nautica	2.2
Land's End	2.2
Express	2.0
Other	61.5

Source: *Daily News Record*, December 1, 2003, p. 10, from 2002-2003 STS Market Research.

★ 748 ★
Apparel
SIC: 2322; NAICS: 315221

Men's Underwear Market

Jockey holds more than half the market.

Jockey	50.0%
Other	50.0

Source: *Daily News Record*, November 10, 2003, p. 14.

★ 749 ★

Prison Uniforms

SIC: 2326; NAICS: 315211

Prison Uniform Market

The company makes 70-80% of the country jail uniforms in the United States. Solids have about 70% of the market, although stripes are coming back. Stripes cost about $1 more per top or pant to make than solids.

Robinson Textiles	80.0%
Other	20.0

Source: *Denver Post*, August 31, 2003, p. B2.

★ 750 ★

Apparel

SIC: 2330; NAICS: 315212

Popular Women's Apparel Brands

Figures show the most popular brands of survey respondents when asked "if you were shopping in a discount department store, what brand would you want?"

Hanes	19.0%
Levi's	7.0
Faded Glory	5.0
Cherokee	4.0
Polo	2.0

Source: *DSN Retailing Today*, October 13, 2003, p. F18, from Leo J. Shapiro & Associates Inc.

★ 751 ★

Apparel

SIC: 2330; NAICS: 315239

Top Women's Apparel Firms in Japan, 2002

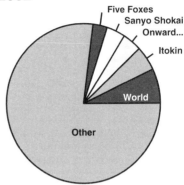

Market shares are shown based on domestic sales of 2.36 trillion yen.

World	6.8%
Itokin	4.9
Onward Kashiyama	4.4
Sanyo Shokai	3.8
Five Foxes	3.4
Other	76.7

Source: "Market Share Survey Report 2002." [online] from http://www.nni.nikkei.co.jp [accessed January 20, 2004], from Nikkei estimate.

★ 752 ★

Apparel

SIC: 2330; NAICS: 315212, 315232, 315221

Women's and Girl's Wear Sales, 2002

Women's and girl's apparel sales in department stores were $27 billion.

	($ mil.)	Share
Tops, women's	$ 8,430	31.12%
Dresses, skirts, suits (women)	4,845	17.89
Bottoms, women's	4,548	16.79
Intimate apparel (women)	4,027	14.87
Activewear, women's	1,599	5.90
Tops, girl's	1,008	3.72

Continued on next page.

★ 752 ★
[Continued]
Apparel
SIC: 2330; NAICS: 315212, 315232, 315221

Women's and Girl's Wear Sales, 2002

Women's and girl's apparel sales in department stores were $27 billion.

	($ mil.)	Share
Bottoms, girl's	$ 799	2.95%
Intimate apparel, girl's	651	2.40
Outerwear, girl's	600	2.22
Dresses, skirts (girl's)	581	2.14

Source: *Retail Merchandiser*, July 2003, p. 20, from *Retail Merchandiser*.

★ 753 ★
Apparel
SIC: 2330; NAICS: 315212

Women's Apparel by Size

More than one-third of American women are size 14 or larger.

size 0-6	12.5%
size 14	10.9
size 12	10.8
size 16	9.2
Other	56.6

Source: *WWD*, September 24, 2003, p. 14, from NPD.

★ 754 ★
Apparel
SIC: 2330; NAICS: 315212, 315231

Women's Apparel Sales in France, 2002

The womenswear market represented 53% of the total French apparel market. The 473 companies generate $6.4 billion in annual sales. Sales are shown in thousands of pieces.

	(000)	Share
T-shirts	80,027	23.14%
Pull overs	57,589	16.65
Town pants	43,578	12.60
Skirts	28,724	8.30
Blouses	26,214	7.58
Jeans	21,887	6.33

	(000)	Share
Leisure pants	19,251	5.57%
Dresses	14,277	4.13
Suits and ensembles	13,693	3.96
Other	40,638	11.75

Source: "Womenswear." [online] from http://www.usatrade.gov [accessed February 1, 2004], from Women's Wear Trade Association in France.

★ 755 ★
Apparel
SIC: 2330; NAICS: 315228, 315239

Women's Sportswear Market

Figures are for October 2002 - September 2003. Data are drawn from AccuPanelSM, a representative consumer panel comprised of over 10,000 men and women ages 13 and older, who report each month on their casual sportswear purchases.

	($ mil.)	Share
Casual wear	$ 22,723	58.27%
Business	8,900	22.82
Special event	3,583	9.19
School	2,015	5.17
Active sport	1,577	4.04
Other	200	0.51

Source: *WWD*, December 3, 2003, p. 8, from STS Market Research and AccuPanelSM.

★ 756 ★
Lingerie
SIC: 2341; NAICS: 315231
Intimate Apparel Sales, 2003

Sales are shown for the year ended October 2003.

	($ mil.)	Share
Bras	$ 4,360	35.66%
Sleepwear	3,750	30.67
Panties	2,630	21.51
Daywear	686	5.61
Shapewear	564	4.61
Thermals	237	1.94

Source: *WWD*, December 1, 2003, p. 16, from NPD
Fashionworld.

★ 757 ★
Lingerie
SIC: 2341; NAICS: 315231
Popular Intimate Apparel Brands

*Figures show the most popular brands of survey
respondents when asked " if you were shopping in a
discount department store, what brand would you
want?"*

Hanes	39.0%
Playtex	16.0
Victoria's Secret	6.0
Vanity Fair	5.0
L'eggs	5.0

Source: *DSN Retailing Today*, October 13, 2003, p. F18,
from Leo J. Shapiro & Associates Inc.

★ 758 ★
Lingerie
SIC: 2341; NAICS: 315231
Top Women's Underwear Firms in Japan, 2002

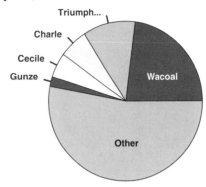

*Market shares are shown based on domestic sales of
418 billion yen.*

Wacoal	23.1%
Triumph International	10.6
Charle	5.9
Cecile	5.1
Gunze	2.4
Other	52.9

Source: "Market Share Survey Report 2002." [online]
from http://www.nni.nikkei.co.jp [accessed January 20,
2004], from Nikkei estimate.

★ 759 ★
Lingerie
SIC: 2341; NAICS: 315231
Women's Lingerie Market in India

*Branded products have a small share of the Rs 2,000
crore market. The market is developing enough, however, that a few national brands are becoming popular: Ashok Reddy has 40-45% of the premium bra
market. BodyCare has about 25% of the market in
the North.*

Below Rs 80	55.0%
Rs 80 to Rs 150	30.0
Rs 150 and above	15.0

Source: *Business World*, February 9, 2004, p. NA, from
KSA Technopak estimates.

★ 760 ★
Hats
SIC: 2353; NAICS: 315991
Global Hat Market

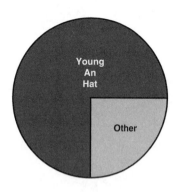

Market shares are shown in percent.

Young An Hat Co. 75.0%
Other 25.0

Source: *Knight Ridder/Tribune Business News*, January 29, 2003, p. NA.

★ 761 ★
Curtains and Draperies
SIC: 2391; NAICS: 314121
Leading Curtain/Drapery Makers, 2003

Firms are ranked by sales in millions of dollars.

CHF Industries . . . . $ 140
S. Lichtenberg 135
Springs Industries 104
Croscill Home 84
Miller Curtain 70

Source: *Home Textiles Today*, January 12, 2004, p. 1, from *Home Textiles Today* market research.

★ 762 ★
Curtains and Draperies
SIC: 2391; NAICS: 314121
Soft Windowcovering Sales, 2002

Mid-price chains took 39% of soft window covering sales. By construction, synthetics took 75% of sales. By pattern, sheers to 36% of sales, solids took 28% of sales.

Panels only 29.0%
Top treatments only 20.0
Toppers with side panels 17.0
Tabletops 8.0
Kitchen/novelty tiers 8.0
Pinch-pleat draperies 7.0
Pole tops 6.0
Blousson/valences 5.0

Source: *Home Textiles Today*, January 30, 2004, p. 42, from *The Facts: Soft Window Coverings*.

★ 763 ★
Homefurnishings
SIC: 2392; NAICS: 31321, 31411
Bath Product Market, 2002

Sales grew to $3.5 billion in 2003.

Bath towels 53.0%
Bath/scatter rugs 24.0
Bath accessorites 12.0
Shower curtains 10.0
Tank sets 1.0

Source: *Home Textiles Today*, January 30, 2004, p. 40, from *The Facts: Bath Products*.

★ 764 ★
Homefurnishings
SIC: 2392; NAICS: 314129
Bedding Industry, 2003

The $6.8 billion market is shown by segment. Discount department stores lead the market with a 36% share.

Sheets & pillowcases 36.0%
Comforters 20.0
Sleep pillows 10.0
Blankets 6.0
Bed-in-a-bag 6.0

Continued on next page.

★ 764 ★

[Continued]
Homefurnishings
SIC: 2392; NAICS: 314129

Bedding Industry, 2003

The $6.8 billion market is shown by segment. Discount department stores lead the market with a 36% share.

Mattress pads	5.0%
Duvet covers	4.0
Decorative pillows	4.0
Bedspreads	4.0
Other	5.0

Source: *Home Textiles Today*, May 3, 2004, p. 8.

★ 765 ★

Homefurnishings
SIC: 2392; NAICS: 314129

Consumer Bed Market in the U.K., 2003

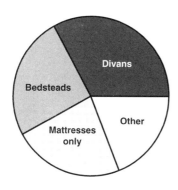

Divans held 50% of the market a decade ago (although sales are up 14% year on year from March 2002 to March 2003). The volume of mattress only sales increased 16% for the same period.

Divans	33.0%
Bedsteads	25.0
Mattresses only	23.0
Other	19.0

Source: *Furniture Manufacturer*, July-August 2003, p. 28, from GfK.

★ 766 ★

Homefurnishings
SIC: 2392; NAICS: 314129

Leading Blanket Makers, 2002

Firms are ranked by sales in millions of dollars.

WestPoint Stevens	$ 130
Sunbeam	115
Charles D. Owen (div. of Springs)	100
Biddeford Textile	18
Pendleton Woolen Mills	16

Source: *Home Textiles Today*, January 12, 2004, p. 1, from *Home Textiles Today* market research.

★ 767 ★

Homefurnishings
SIC: 2392; NAICS: 314129

Leading Comforter Makers, 2002

Firms are ranked by sales in millions of dollars.

Springs Industries	$ 445
WestPoint Stevens	260
Dan River	153
American Pacific	135
Croscill Home	124

Source: *Home Textiles Today*, January 12, 2004, p. 1, from *Home Textiles Today* market research.

★ 768 ★

Homefurnishings
SIC: 2392; NAICS: 314129

Leading Decorative Pillow Makers, 2003

Firms are ranked by sales in millions of dollars.

Brentwood Originals	$ 121
Arlee	74
Mohawk Home	31
Newport	25
Fashion Industries	22

Source: *Home Textiles Today*, January 12, 2004, p. 1, from *Home Textiles Today* market research.

★ 769 ★
Homefurnishings
SIC: 2392; NAICS: 314129
Leading Foam Pillows/Toppers Makers, 2003

Firms are ranked by sales in millions of dollars.

Sleep Innovations	$ 130
Carpenter Co.	50
Leggett & Platt	23
Louisville Bedding	22
Hudson Industries	18

Source: *Home Textiles Today*, January 12, 2004, p. 1, from *Home Textiles Today* market research.

★ 770 ★
Homefurnishings
SIC: 2392; NAICS: 314129
Leading Kitchen Textile Makers, 2003

Firms are ranked by sales in millions of dollars.

Barth & Dreyfuss	$ 60
Franco Mfg.	56
Cecil Saydah Co.	48
John Ritzenthaler Co.	34
Charles Craft	18

Source: *Home Textiles Today*, January 12, 2004, p. 1, from *Home Textiles Today* market research.

★ 771 ★
Homefurnishings
SIC: 2392; NAICS: 314129
Leading Quilt Makers, 2003

Firms are ranked by sales in millions of dollars.

Keeco	$ 90
Sunham Home Fashions	70
PHI	57
Britannica Home Fashions	50
American Pacific	48

Source: *Home Textiles Today*, January 12, 2004, p. 1, from *Home Textiles Today* market research.

★ 772 ★
Homefurnishings
SIC: 2392; NAICS: 314129
Leading Sheet/Pillowcase Makers, 2003

Firms are ranked by sales in millions of dollars.

Springs Industries	$ 740
WestPoint Stevens	500
Dan River	179
Franco Manufacturing	95
Divatex Home Products	85

Source: *Home Textiles Today*, January 12, 2004, p. 1, from *Home Textiles Today* market research.

★ 773 ★
Homefurnishings
SIC: 2392; NAICS: 314129

Leading Sleep Pillow Makers, 2003

| Pacific Coast Feather |
| Hollander Home Fashions |
| Springs Industries |
| WestPoint Stevens |
| Louisville Bedding |

Firms are ranked by sales in millions of dollars.

Pacific Coast Feather	$ 130
Hollander Home Fashions	128
Springs Industries	105
WestPoint Stevens	80
Louisville Bedding	42

Source: *Home Textiles Today*, January 12, 2004, p. 1, from *Home Textiles Today* market research.

★ 774 ★
Homefurnishings
SIC: 2392; NAICS: 314129, 31321

Leading Towel Makers, 2002

Firms are ranked by sales in millions of dollars.

WestPoint Stevens	$ 560
Springs Industries	310
J.R. United	65
Santens	53
1888 Mills	32

Source: *Home Textiles Today*, January 12, 2004, p. 1, from *Home Textiles Today* market research.

★ 775 ★
Homefurnishings
SIC: 2392; NAICS: 314129

Slip Cover Market

Market shares are shown in percent.

Sure Fit	85.0%
Other	15.0

Source: *The Morning Call*, March 10, 2004, p. NA.

★ 776 ★
Homefurnishings
SIC: 2392; NAICS: 314129, 313241

Table Linen Market by Category, 2002

Sales grew to $603 million in 2003. By fiber, cotton took 38% of the market and cotton-blend took 25%.

Place mats	39.0%
Tablecloths	37.0
Napkins	18.0
Runners	4.0
Napkin rings	2.0

Source: *Home Textiles Today*, January 30, 2004, p. 40, from *The Facts: Table Linens*.

★ 777 ★
Seatbelts
SIC: 2399; NAICS: 33636

Global Seatbelt Market, 2000

Market shares are shown in percent.

Autoliv (inc. NSK)	30.0%
TRW	29.0
Takata (inc. Petri)	17.0
Breed	14.0
Other	10.0

Source: ''Market Consolidation Occupies Airbag Manufacturers.'' [online] from http://www.just-auto.com [accessed January 6, 2003], from just-auto.com and industry estimates.

★ 778 ★
Seatbelts
SIC: 2399; NAICS: 33636

Seatbelt Market in Western Europe, 2000

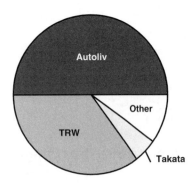

Market shares are shown in percent.

Autoliv 50.0%
TRW 35.0
Takata (inc. Petri) 5.0
Other 10.0

Source: ''Market Consolidation Occupies Airbag Manufacturers.'' [online] from http://www.just-auto.com [accessed
January 6, 2003], from just-auto.com and industry estimates.

SIC 24 - Lumber and Wood Products

★ 779 ★
Lumber
SIC: 2411; NAICS: 321113, 321912
How Wood is Used in Mexico

Lumber	73.0%
Cellulose and paper	15.0
Fuel and charcoal	5.0
Plywood	4.0
Poles, piles and posts	3.0

Source: ''Wooden Building Products for the Construction Industry.'' [online] from http://www.usatrade.gov [accessed January 7, 2004], from U.S. Commercial Service.

★ 780 ★
Lumber
SIC: 2421; NAICS: 321113, 321912
Alder Lumber Market

The company has 65-75% of the market.

Weyerhaeuser	75.0%
Other	25.0

Source: *The Oregonian*, September 10, 2003, p. NA.

★ 781 ★
Lumber
SIC: 2421; NAICS: 321113, 321912
How Lumber is Used in Australia

New Zealand is the top supplier of lumber to Australia. Its share increased from 21% in 1989 to 57% in 2002.

House framing	68.0%
Fencing for landscaping	7.0
Joinery/furniture	7.0

Source: *New Zealand Forest Industries Magazine*, February 2004, p. 16, from 2001 New South Wales Survey.

★ 782 ★
Railroad Ties
SIC: 2421; NAICS: 321999
Railroad Tie Market in North America

Wood makes up 90% of the North American market.

Wood	90.0%
Other	10.0

Source: *Railway Age*, August 2003, p. 19.

★ 783 ★
Softwood
SIC: 2421; NAICS: 321113, 321912

Largest Softwood Lumber Producers, 2001

The industry saw further consolidations in 2001. Companies are ranked by production in millions of board feet (MMbf).

	MMbf	Share
Weyerhaeuser	6,281	4.49%
International Paper	3,638	2.60
Stora Enso	2,415	1.73
Canfor	2,265	1.62
West Fraser	2,007	1.43
Georgia-Pacific	1,882	1.34
Finnforest	1,801	1.29
Abitibi-Consolidated	1,704	1.22
Louisiana-Pacific	1,420	1.01
Slocan	1,384	0.99
Other	115,203	82.29

Source: *Wood Markets Monthly*, May 2002, p. 2, from company reports and WOOD Markets.

★ 784 ★
Wood Panels
SIC: 2421; NAICS: 321113, 321912

Wood Panel Market in Europe, 2002

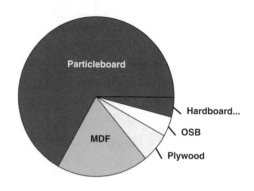

The wood panel market is shown by share of the total market. MDF stands for medium density fiberboard. OSB stands for oriented strandboard.

Particleboard	67.0%
MDF	19.0
Plywood	6.0
OSB	4.0
Hardboard and softboard	4.0

Source: *Wood Based Panels International*, August-September 2003, p. 10, from European Panel Federation.

★ 785 ★
Flooring
SIC: 2426; NAICS: 321113, 321918

Leading Wood Floor Makers in Poland

Market shares are shown in percent.

Barlinek	70.0%
Other	30.0

Source: *Poland Business News*, June 3, 2004, p. NA.

★ 786 ★
Flooring
SIC: 2426; NAICS: 321113, 321918
Wood Flooring Market in the U.K.

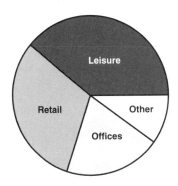

The market is forecasted to be worth 44 million British pounds by 2006. In 2002, the total floorcovering market (wood included) stood at 2.1 billion pounds. Market growth to 2006 will be about 4-5% per year, according to AMA Research.

Leisure	39.0%
Retail	31.0
Offices	20.0
Other	10.0

Source: *Contract Flooring Journal*, October 2003, p. 23, from AMA Research.

★ 787 ★
Hardwood
SIC: 2426; NAICS: 321113, 321912, 321918
Temperate Hardwood Production in Mexico

Production is shown by state.

Michoacan	30.0%
Durango	20.0
Chihuahua	16.0
Jalisco	5.0
Other	20.0

Source: ''Wooden Building Products for the Construction Industry.'' [online] from http://www.usatrade.gov [accessed January 7, 2004], from U.S. Commercial Service.

★ 788 ★
Decking
SIC: 2430; NAICS: 321911
Composite Decking Market

Trex has more than half of the wood/plastic composite decking market. Composites are used in 6% of the nation's decking.

Trex	50.0%
Other	50.0

Source: *Investor's Business Daily*, May 22, 2003, p. A10.

★ 789 ★
Decking
SIC: 2430; NAICS: 321911
Decking Market Shares

The market is valued at $3 billion.

Wood	85.0%
Composite	10.0
Other plastics (vinyl)	5.0

Source: *Building Products*, May - June 2003, p. 109.

★ 790 ★
Doors
SIC: 2431; NAICS: 321911
Wood Door Market

Figures show wood door manufacturing by volume. MDF stands for medium density fiberboard.

Edge-glued panels	59.0%
MDF	15.0
Particleboard	11.0
Hardboard	7.0
OSB	4.0
Plywood	3.0
Other	1.0

Source: *Forest Products Journal*, July-August 2003, p. 19.

★ 791 ★

Molding

SIC: 2431; NAICS: 321918

Leading Molding Importers, 2003

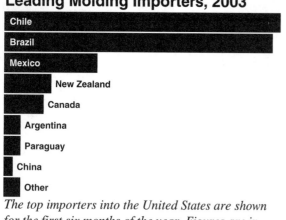

The top importers into the United States are shown for the first six months of the year. Figures are in thousands of meters.

	Meters	Share
Chile	164.86	35.78%
Brazil	161.14	34.97
Mexico	53.24	11.56
New Zealand	28.29	6.14
Canada	21.56	4.68
Argentina	9.12	1.98
Paraguay	7.24	1.57
China	5.04	1.09
Other	10.25	2.22

Source: *New Zealand Forest Industries Magazine*, September 2003, p. 10.

★ 792 ★

Pallets

SIC: 2448; NAICS: 32192

Pallet Market in Central Mississippi

The company is closing in on controlling 50% of the market. Its recycling efforts have saved nearly 250,000 trees and significantly reduced wood waste in landfills.

A-1 Pallet	50.0%
Other	50.0

Source: *Mississippi Business Journal*, October 27, 2003, p. S6.

★ 793 ★

Pallets

SIC: 2448; NAICS: 32192

Pallets Market

Pallets have 90% of the $10 billion pallet market.

Wood	90.0%
Other	10.0

Source: *Business Wire*, October 7, 2003, p. NA.

★ 794 ★

Manufactured Homes

SIC: 2451; NAICS: 321991

Top Manufactured Home Builders, 2002

Companies are ranked by number of homes shipped.

Champion Enterprises	29,217
Oakwood Homes	27,549
Fleetwood Enterprises	24,212
Clayton Homes	19,056
Cavalier Homes	13,555
Palm Harbor Homes	9,938
Skyline Corp.	9,849
Genesis Homes	9,640
Patriot Homes	4,838
Southern Energy Homes	4,411

Source: *Builder*, May 2003, p. 174.

★ 795 ★

Log Homes

SIC: 2452; NAICS: 321992

Top Log Home Builders

Companies are ranked by number of units.

Honka Log Homes	4,000
Jim Barna Log Systems	505
Town & Country Cedar Homes	150
Gastineau Log Homes	125
Wholesale Log Homes	100

Continued on next page.

★ 795 ★

[Continued]
Log Homes
SIC: 2452; NAICS: 321992

Top Log Home Builders

Companies are ranked by number of units.

Log Homes of America	100
B.K. Cypress Log Homes	80
Mountaineer Log & Siding	42
Garland Homes	35
Fall Creek Housing	22

Source: *Builder*, May 2003, p. 174.

SIC 25 - Furniture and Fixtures

★ 796 ★
Furniture
SIC: 2500; NAICS: 337122, 337211, 337124

Top Furniture Firms, 2002

Companies are ranked by furniture shipments in millions of dollars.

Furniture Brands International	$ 2,301.8
La-Z-Boy	2,059.5
Ashley Furniture Inds..	1,267.2
Klaussner	860.4
Ethan Allen	757.2
Sauder Woodworking	621.2
Berkline BenchCraft	456.0
Dorel	455.1
Lacquer Craft	400.0
Natuzzi	365.2
Brown Jordan International	337.0
Bassett Furniture	312.4

Source: *Furniture Today*, Winter 2003, p. 37, from *Furniture Today* market research.

★ 797 ★
Furniture
SIC: 2500; NAICS: 337122, 337211, 337124

Top Furniture Firms in Canada

Companies are ranked by furniture and bedding shipments in millions of Canadian dollars.

Dorel Inds.	$ 712.9
Palliser Furniture	518.8
Shermag Inc..	188.0
Canadel Furniture	155.0
Sealy Canada	139.7
Simmons Canada Inc.	130.9
Ka-Z-Boy Canada Ltd.	117.9
Magnussen Home Furnishings	106.8
Gusdorf Canada	105.0
South Shore Inds.	100.0
Durham Furniture	91.2
El Ran Furniture	90.2

Source: *Furniture Today*, Winter 2003, p. 37, from *Furniture Today* market research.

★ 798 ★
Furniture
SIC: 2511; NAICS: 337122, 337125

College Dormitory Room/Apartment Furniture

Market shares are shown in percent.

University Loft	33.0%
Other	67.0

Source: *Indianapolis Business Journal*, June 16, 2003, p. 15.

★ 799 ★

Furniture

SIC: 2511; NAICS: 337122, 337125

Furniture Market in Germany, 2001

During the first nine months of 2001 the industry had turnover in $16.6 billion. Germany is the largest furniture market in Europe with sales of over $19.6 billion in 2001. Schieder Group and Steinhoff Holding International are the top furniture makers.

Living/dining/bedroom furniture	34.0%
Kitchen furniture	17.0
Office and shop fitting furniture	13.0
Mattresses	3.0
Other	23.0

Source: "Furniture." [online] from http://www.usatrade.gov [accessed February 1, 2004].

★ 800 ★

Furniture

SIC: 2511; NAICS: 337122, 337125

High-End Furniture Market in Europe

On average, 20% of European furniture sales are devoted to high-end furniture. Independents dominate the 16.6 billion pound (at retail prices) industry. The market share for such furniture is shown for each country.

Switzerland	38.0%
Germany	38.0
Holland	24.0
Italy	19.9
U.K.	17.7
Belgium	17.7
Austria	17.7
France	16.0
Denmark	14.3

Source: *Cabinet Maker*, March 28, 2003, p. 2, from CSIL's *The European Market for Upper End Furniture*.

★ 801 ★

Furniture

SIC: 2512; NAICS: 337121

Leading Upholstered Furniture Makers in the U.K.

Companies are ranked by turnover in millions of British pounds. Figures are for 2000-2001.

DFS Furniture	£ 401.9
Slb Holdings	63.7
Cambria Mobel	49.0

Lebus Furniture	£ 38.9
Collins & Hayes	20.2
G Plan Upholstery	18.2
Ultra Furniture	16.5
Lifestyle Upholstery	16.3
Wyvern Furniture	15.7
Alstons (upholstery)	15.4

Source: *Cabinet Maker*, October 18, 2002, p. 9, from *U.K. Domestic Furniture Manufacturers Report*.

★ 802 ★

Furniture

SIC: 2514; NAICS: 337125, 337122, 337124

Outdoor Furniture Sales, 2003

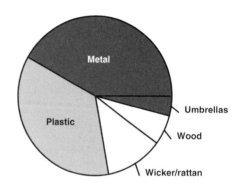

Retail sales of outdoor and casual furniture and accessories reached $5.97 billion in 2003.

Metal	42.0%
Plastic	36.0
Wicker/rattan	12.0
Wood	6.0
Umbrellas	4.0

Source: *Research Alert*, November 21, 2003, p. 9, from Packaged Facts.

★ 803 ★
Mattresses
SIC: 2515; NAICS: 33791

Top Bedding Producers, 2002

Companies are ranked by bedding sales in millions of dollars.

Sealy	23.1%
Serta	15.3
Simmons	14.8
Spring Air	7.4
King Koil	2.5
Therapedic	2.3
England/Englander	2.3
Kingsdown	2.1
Restonic	1.9
Lady Americana	1.5
Other	26.8

Source: *Furniture Today*, Winter 2003, p. 49, from *Furniture Today* market research.

★ 804 ★
Mattresses
SIC: 2515; NAICS: 33791

Viscoeleastic Foam Mattress/Pillow Sales, 2002

Market shares are estimated in percent.

Tempur-Pedic	70.0%
Other	30.0

Source: *Lexington Herald-Leader*, December 9, 2003, p. NA.

★ 805 ★
Office Furniture
SIC: 2520; NAICS: 337214

High-Performance Desk Chairs

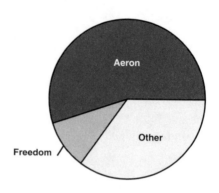

The industry is valued at $280 million annually. High-performance office furniture includes ergonomic products and similar design improvements.

Aeron	55.0%
Freedom	10.0
Other	35.0

Source: *Forbes*, March 29, 2004, p. 86.

★ 806 ★
Office Furniture
SIC: 2520; NAICS: 337214

Home Office Furniture Demand in China, 2007

The industry is one of the fastest growing in China because at the booming construction industry. Total sales are forecasted to reach 11.96 billion rembini in 2007.

Desks	29.0%
Home office chairs	25.0
Tables	18.0
Bookcases and bookshelves	15.0
File cabinets	13.0

Source: *Chinese Markets for Home Office Furniture*, December 2003, from Asian Market Information & Development Company.

★ 807 ★
Office Furniture
SIC: 2520; NAICS: 337214

Leading Office Furniture Vendors to the Federal Government, 2002

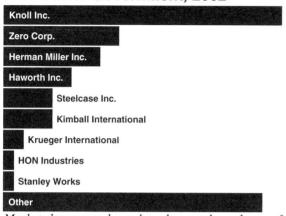

Market shares are shown based on total purchases of $707 million.

Knoll Inc.	28.98%
Zero Corp.	12.34
Herman Miller Inc.	10.40
Haworth Inc.	6.52
Steelcase Inc.	5.21
Kimball International	4.84
Krueger International	2.34
HON Industries	1.07
Stanley Works	1.02
Other	27.28

Source: *Government Executive*, September 4, 2003, p. NA.

★ 808 ★
Office Furniture
SIC: 2520; NAICS: 337214

Office Furniture Market, 2002

Production of office furniture was valued at $8.9 billion.

Systems	30.9%
Seating	25.7
Files	14.3
Desks	11.9
Tables	6.8
Storage	6.3
Other	4.1

Source: *Wood & Wood Products*, December 2003, p. 58, from Business and Institutional Furniture Manufacturers Association.

★ 809 ★
Office Furniture
SIC: 2520; NAICS: 337214

Office Furniture Market in Canada

The market is evenly divided between seats, other metal office furniture and other non-metal furniture. Sales are shown in millions of dollars.

	($ mil.)	Share
Ontario	$ 1,490	42.23%
Quebec	793	22.48
British Columbia	448	12.70
Alberta	357	10.12
Other	440	12.47

Source: *M2 Presswire*, September 22, 2003, p. NA, from Researchandmarkets.com.

★ 810 ★
Hospital Beds
SIC: 2599; NAICS: 337127

Hospital Bed Market in Japan

The company also has 60% of the homecare market.

Paramount	70.0%
Other	30.0

Source: *Asia Africa Intelligence Wire*, January 12, 2004, p. NA.

★ 811 ★
Hospital Beds
SIC: 2599; NAICS: 337127

Hospital Bed Sales in India, 2003

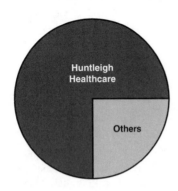

The hospital bed market is expected to grow 10-12% annually. The company has 95% of the market in the United Kingdom.

Huntleigh Healthcare 75.0%
Others 25.0

Source: *The Financial Express*, April 2, 2004, p. NA.

★ 812 ★
Massage Chairs
SIC: 2599; NAICS: 337127

Massage Chair Market in Malaysia, 2004

This market share forecast is based on the launch in 2004 of a new message chair called the Osim iSymphonic.

Osim (M) Sdn Bhd 95.0%
Other 5.0

Source: *Asia Africa Intelligence Wire*, March 30, 2004, p. NA.

SIC 26 - Paper and Allied Products

★ 813 ★
Paper
SIC: 2621; NAICS: 322121

Leading Supercalendered Makers in North America, 2003

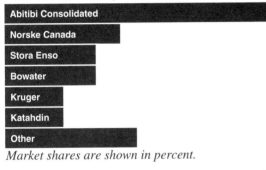

Market shares are shown in percent.

Abitibi Consolidated	34.0%
Norske Canada	14.0
Stora Enso	11.0
Bowater	11.0
Kruger	7.0
Katahdin	7.0
Other	16.0

Source: *Graphic Arts Monthly*, January 2004, p. 27.

★ 814 ★
Paper
SIC: 2621; NAICS: 322121

Release Liner Market in North America

The market is expected to see a 3-5% growth rate annually, with self-adhesive applications taking 90% of the market.

Polyethylene	53.0%
Polyester	30.0
Polypropylene	15.0
Other	2.0

Source: *Paper, Film & Foil Converter*, October 1, 2003, p. NA, from AWA Alexander Watson Associates.

★ 815 ★
Paper
SIC: 2621; NAICS: 322121

Top Kraft Paper Makers in North America, 2003

Market shares are shown based on total North American capacity of 2.5 billion tons.

International Paper	18.0%
Smurfit-Stone	12.0
Georgia-Pacific	10.1
Longview Fibre	8.6
Tolko Industries	6.4
Delta Natural Kraft	5.8
Port Townsend	5.0
Canfor	4.8
West Fraser	4.8
Grupo Durango	4.6
Other	20.0

Source: *Pulp & Paper*, November 2003, p. 7, from Canadian Paper Analyst and company profiles and data.

★ 816 ★
Paper
SIC: 2621; NAICS: 322122

Top Newsprint Makers in North America, 2003

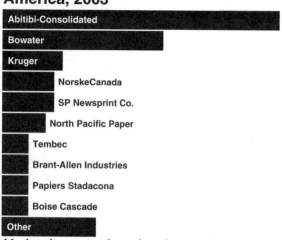

Abitibi-Consolidated
Bowater
Kruger
NorskeCanada
SP Newsprint Co.
North Pacific Paper
Tembec
Brant-Allen Industries
Papiers Stadacona
Boise Cascade
Other

Market shares are shown based on total North American capacity of 15,280 tons.

Abitibi-Consolidated	33.3%
Bowater	18.8
Kruger	7.4
NorskeCanada	6.4
SP Newsprint Co.	6.2
North Pacific Paper	4.9
Tembec	3.3
Brant-Allen Industries	3.2
Papiers Stadacona	2.8
Boise Cascade	2.6
Other	11.1

Source: *Pulp & Paper*, December 2003, p. 7, from company reports.

★ 817 ★
Paper
SIC: 2621; NAICS: 322121

Top Paper Firms in Poland, 2002

There were 156 companies operating in the total sector. Sales grew across nearly all sectors with the total reaching 11.9 billion zlotys. Firms are ranked by sales in millions of zlotys.

	(mil.)	Share
International Paper SA	1,757.7	14.77%
Frantschach Swiecie	1,184.2	9.95
Arctic Paper Kostrzyn	575.7	4.84
Intercell SA	570.8	4.80

	(mil.)	Share
Antalis Poland	308.7	2.59%
Cezex	232.4	1.95
Kimberly-Clark	222.1	1.87
ICT Poland	221.9	1.86
DS Smith Polska	214.7	1.80
TPF sp. Z.o.o.	161.0	1.35
Other	6,450.8	54.21

Source: *Europe Intelligence Wire*, October 28, 2003, p. NA, from *Polish News Bulletin* and Rzeczpospolita.

★ 818 ★
Paper
SIC: 2621; NAICS: 322121

Top Tissue Paper Makers in North America, 2003

Market shares are shown based on total North American capacity of 8.8 billion tons.

Georgia-Pacific	34.7%
Kimberly-Clark	18.0
Procter & Gamble	14.4
Cascades	5.2
SCA Tissue	5.1
Kruger	3.9
J.D. Irving	2.5
Cellu Tissue	2.4
Potlatch	2.0
Marcal	1.8
Other	10.1

Source: *Pulp & Paper*, February 2004, p. 7, from company reports.

★ 819 ★
Paper
SIC: 2621; NAICS: 322121

Top Uncoated Groundwood Makers in North America, 2003

Market shares are shown based on total North American capacity of 5.79 million tons.

Abitibi-Consolidated	34.3%
NorskeCanada	14.3
Bowater	11.4
Stora Enso	10.8

Continued on next page.

★ 819 ★

[Continued]
Paper
SIC: 2621; NAICS: 322121

Top Uncoated Groundwood Makers in North America, 2003

Market shares are shown based on total North American capacity of 5.79 million tons.

Katahdin Paper Co.	7.4%
Kruger	6.7
St. Marys	3.9
Irving	3.7
Madison	3.7
Papiers Stadacona	2.5
Other	1.3

Source: *Pulp & Paper*, September 2003, p. 7, from Canadian Paper Analyst and company profiles and data.

★ 820 ★

Paperboard
SIC: 2631; NAICS: 32213

Containerboard Industry Worldwide, 2001

Production is shown by region.

North America	36.0%
Asia	32.0
Europe	25.0
Central and South America	4.0
Africa and Oceania	3.0

Source: *Paperboard Packaging*, July 2002, p. 17, from International Corrugated Case Association.

★ 821 ★

Paperboard
SIC: 2631; NAICS: 32213

Leading White Top Makers in North America

Market shares are shown based on capacity of 2.2 million metric tons.

SSCC	28.0%
SS Canada	17.0
Green Bay	12.0
Simpson	11.0
IP	11.0
Weyerhaeuser	7.0
Other	14.0

Source: *Paperboard Packaging*, February 2004, p. 23, from Jacobs-Sirrine.

★ 822 ★

Paperboard
SIC: 2631; NAICS: 32213

Top 10 Containerboard Producers in China

Companies are ranked by production in thousands of tons.

	(000)	Share
Nine Dragons	1,000	25.74%
Lee Man	585	15.06
Guangdong Yinzhou	400	10.30
Zhongshan Rengo	350	9.01
Zhejiang Jinxin	320	8.24
Hebei Jiteng	300	7.72
Anhui Shayin	300	7.72
Wuxin Longda	250	6.44
Shandong Huazhong	200	5.15
Guangdong Wangda	180	4.63

Source: *Paperboard Packaging*, September 2003, p. 21, from Paccess.

★ 823 ★

Paperboard

SIC: 2631; NAICS: 32213

Top Bleached Paperboard Makers, 2003

Market shares are shown based on total North American capacity of 7.3 million tons.

International Paper	33.9%
MeadWestvaco	22.2
Potlatch	8.5
Georgia-Pacific	7.7
Smurfit-Stone	4.3
Blue Ridge Paper	3.7
Gulf States Paper	3.6
Weyerhaeuser	3.0
Tembec	2.7
Durango-Georgia	2.7
Other	7.6

Source: *Pulp & Paper*, September 2003, p. 7, from Canadian Paper Analyst and company profiles and data.

★ 824 ★

Paperboard

SIC: 2631; NAICS: 32213

Top Kraft Linerboard Makers, 2003

Market shares are shown based on total North American capacity of 27.76 million tons.

Smurfit-Stone	17.3%
Weyerhaeuser	15.5
International Paper	13.9
Inland Paper	10.6
Georgia-Pacific	9.9
Packaging Corp. of America	5.2
Norampac	2.5
Green Bay Packaging	2.3
Longview Fibre	2.1
Boise Cascade	1.9
Other	18.5

Source: *Pulp & Paper*, January 2004, p. 7, from company reports.

★ 825 ★

Corrugated Boxes

SIC: 2653; NAICS: 322211

Leading Corrugated Packaging Makers

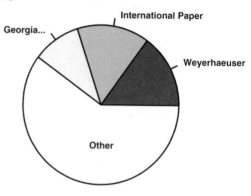

Market shares are shown in percent.

Weyerhaeuser	15.0%
International Paper	15.0
Georgia Pacific	10.0
Other	60.0

Source: *The Ledger*, May 14, 2004, p. NA, from Pratt Industries.

★ 826 ★

Paper Tubes

SIC: 2655; NAICS: 322214

Paper Cores and Tube Sales, 2002

Shars are shown based on sales volume.

Paper mill cores	25.7%
Film cores	21.9
Cloth & floor covering sores	13.0
Yarn carriers	10.6
Yarn & label cores	5.4
Convertor cores	4.4
Metal foil & strapping cores	4.1
Other	14.9

Source: *Paperboard Packaging*, August 2003, p. 23, from CCTI.

★ 827 ★
Boxes
SIC: 2657; NAICS: 322212

Box Demand, 2000 and 2005

Demand is shown in billions of dollars. Corrugated and paperboard box sales will see modest growth through 2005. Growth will come largely from the food and beverage markets.

	2000	2005	Share
Corrugated boxes	$ 23.90	$ 26.20	72.4%
Folding cartons	8.89	9.99	27.6

Source: *Converting*, August 2003, p. 28, from Freedonia Group.

★ 828 ★
Coated Paper
SIC: 2671; NAICS: 322221

Leading Coated Freesheet Makers in North America

Market shares are shown based on 3.2 million short tons annually.

Sappi	28.0%
MeadWestvaco	23.0
International Paper	15.0
Stora Enso	14.0
Belgravia	7.0
Arjo Wiggins	6.0
Domstar	4.0
Cascades	2.0
Glatfelter	1.0
Smart Papers	1.0

Source: *Folio*, April 15, 2003, p. 32, from JP Management Consulting's JPSmart Terminal.

★ 829 ★
Tape
SIC: 2672; NAICS: 322222

Pressure Sensitive Tape Shipments

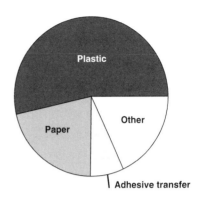

Total shipments are expected to hit $5.7 billion by 2006.

	2001	2006	Share
Plastic	$ 2,445	$ 3,025	53.49%
Paper	1,035	1,210	21.40
Adhesive transfer	295	395	6.98
Other	840	1,025	18.13

Source: *Adhesives & Sealants Industry*, July-August 2003, p. 20, from Freedonia Group.

★ 830 ★
Tape
SIC: 2672; NAICS: 322222

Tape Market Segments

Shares are shown by category of tape. Distribution is based on a total of 504 million dry pounds.

Industrial	37.0%
Packaging	32.0
Consumer	14.0
Surgical	7.0
Masking	5.0
Electrical	5.0

Source: *Adhesives Age*, April-May 2003, p. S13, from ChemQuest Group.

★ 831 ★

Tape

SIC: 2672; NAICS: 322222

Top Scotch Tape Brands, 2003

Market shares are shown based on sales at super-markets, drug stores and mass merchandisers (but not Wal-Mart) for the year ended May 18, 2003.

Scotch .	48.8%
Scotch Magic	24.1
Manco	8.6
Quickstik	1.7
Tartan .	1.5
3M .	1.1
Manco E-Z Start	0.8
Action .	0.5
3M Highland	0.5
Other	12.4

Source: *Grocery Headquarters*, August 2003, p. S6, from Information Resources Inc.

★ 832 ★

Tape

SIC: 2672; NAICS: 322222

Top Scotch Tape Makers, 2003

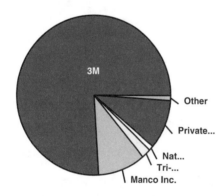

Market shares are shown based on sales at super-markets, drug stores and mass merchandisers (but not Wal-Mart) for the year ended May 18, 2003.

3M .	76.2%
Manco Inc.	9.7
Tri-Pak Inds.	1.8
Nat Tape Corp.	0.6
Private label	10.3
Other	1.4

Source: *Grocery Headquarters*, August 2003, p. S6, from Information Resources Inc.

★ 833 ★

Tape

SIC: 2672; NAICS: 322222

Transparent Tape Market

Market shares are estimated in percent.

3M .	90.0%
Other	10.0

Source: *Star Tribune*, November 10, 2003, p. 1D.

★ 834 ★

Food and Trash Bags

SIC: 2673; NAICS: 322223, 326111

Bag and Wrap Sales, 2002

Data show supermarket sales in millions of dollars.

Bags, tall kitchen .	$ 376.37
Aluminum foil .	364.70
Bags, food storage	238.92
Bags, trash/compactor	226.65
Bags, freezer	221.58
Bags, sandwich	194.69
Plastic wrap .	144.38
Bags, leaf & lawn	81.75
Bags, oven	36.88
Bags, waste	33.93

Source: *Progressive Grocer*, September 15, 2003, p. 19, from *Progressive Grocer's 56th Consumer Expenditures Study*.

★ 835 ★

Food and Trash Bags

SIC: 2673; NAICS: 322223

Top Food and Trash Brands, 2003

Brands are ranked by supermarket, drug store and discount store (excluding Wal-Mart) sales for the year ended December 28, 2003.

	($ mil.)	Share
Ziploc food bags	$ 225.8	13.68%
Glad trash bags	170.7	10.35
Hefty Cinch Sack trash bags	136.7	8.28
Hefty One Zip food bags	99.0	6.00
Glad Lock food bags	79.6	4.82

Continued on next page.

★ 835 ★

[Continued]
Food and Trash Bags
SIC: 2673; NAICS: 322223

Top Food and Trash Brands, 2003

Brands are ranked by supermarket, drug store and discount store (excluding Wal-Mart) sales for the year ended December 28, 2003.

	($ mil.)	Share
Glad Quick Tie trash bags	$33.0	2.00%
Private label	225.8	13.68
Other	679.4	41.18

Source: *MMR*, May 31, 2004, p. 33, from Information Resources Inc.

★ 836 ★

Diapers
SIC: 2676; NAICS: 322291

Private Label Diaper Market

Market shares are shown in percent.

Tyco	95.0%
Other	5.0

Source: *Nonwovens Industry*, May 2003, p. 29.

★ 837 ★

Diapers
SIC: 2676; NAICS: 322291

Top Adult Incontinence Brands

Market shares are shown based on drug store sales.

Depend	32.1%
Depend Poise	15.6
Serenity	8.6
Serenity Night and Day	1.5
Entrust Plus	1.1
Sure Care Slip-On	0.9
Attends	0.8
Private label	37.0
Other	2.4

Source: *Chain Drug Review*, January 5, 2004, p. 45.

★ 838 ★

Diapers
SIC: 2676; NAICS: 322291

Top Adult Incontinence Firms Worldwide, 2000

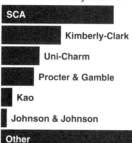

Market shares are shown in percent.

SCA	21.0%
Kimberly-Clark	11.0
Uni-Charm	7.0
Procter & Gamble	6.0
Kao	2.0
Johnson & Johnson	1.0
Other	52.0

Source: *Nonwovens Industry*, February 2002, p. 12, from International Research Associates.

★ 839 ★

Diapers
SIC: 2676; NAICS: 322291

Top Adult Incontinence Markets Worldwide, 2004 and 2007

The total market is expected to grow from $2.1 billion in 2002 to $2.7 billion in 2007. The industry's two major segments are retail and institutional. The retail sector is driven by comfort, discretion and ease of use. The typical buyer, according to the source, will find a product he or she likes and stick with it. The institutional sector is much more driven by price. Sales are shown in millions of dollars.

	2004	2007	Share
North America	$860	$951.0	34.36%
Asia-Pacific	645	713.0	25.76
Western Europe	605	728.0	26.30
Latin America	228	260.0	9.39
Africa/Middle East	31	34.0	1.23
Australasia	27	42.0	1.52
Eastern Europe	22	40.1	1.45

Source: *Nonwovens Industry*, March 2004, p. 44, from Euromonitor.

★ 840 ★

Diapers

SIC: 2676; NAICS: 322291

Top Diaper Makers in Brazil, 2001

Between 1995 and 2000 the consumption grew roughly by 19% a year. Sales in 2001 stood at $5 billion.

Kimberly-Clark	22.0%
MPC	18.0
Johnson & Johnson	12.0
Procter & Gamble	12.0
Pompom	8.0
Aloes	4.0
Others	24.0

Source: *Nonwoven Industry*, March 2003, p. 26.

★ 841 ★

Diapers

SIC: 2676; NAICS: 322291

Top Diaper Makers in the U.K.

Pampers launched the first paper diaper in 1972 and quickly became a market leader. Huggies entered the market in 1991 and proved to be a strong competititor. By 2000, the brand had a 30% share.

Procter & Gamble (Pampers)	48.0%
Kimberly Clark (Huggies)	41.9
Private label	10.0
Other	0.1

Source: *Marketing*, August 7, 2003, p. 13, from Euromonitor.

★ 842 ★

Diapers

SIC: 2676; NAICS: 322291

Top Disposable Diaper Brands, 2003

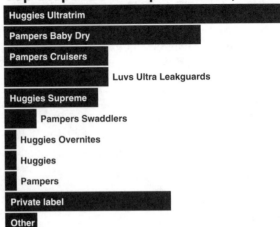

Market shares are shown based on sales at supermarkets, drug stores and mass merchandisers (but not Wal-Mart) for the year ended May 18, 2003.

Huggies Ultratrim	27.0%
Pampers Baby Dry	18.6
Pampers Cruisers	10.4
Luvs Ultra Leakguards	10.4
Huggies Supreme	8.5
Pampers Swaddlers	2.6
Huggies Overnites	1.4
Huggies	1.3
Pampers	0.8
Private label	16.0
Other	3.0

Source: *Grocery Headquarters*, August 2003, p. S6, from Information Resources Inc.

★ 843 ★
Diapers
SIC: 2676; NAICS: 322291
Top Disposable Diaper Makers, 2003

Market shares are shown based on sales at super-markets, drug stores and mass merchandisers (but not Wal-Mart) for the year ended May 18, 2003.

Procter & Gamble	44.3%
Kimberly-Clark	38.2
ASSC Hygienic Prods.	1.3
Private label	16.0
Other	0.2

Source: *Grocery Headquarters*, August 2003, p. S6, from Information Resources Inc.

★ 844 ★
Diapers
SIC: 2676; NAICS: 322291
Top Training Pants Brands, 2003

Market shares are shown based on sales at super-markets, drug stores and mass merchandisers (but not Wal-Mart) for the year ended May 18, 2003.

Huggies Pull-Ups	40.9%
Huggies Pull-Ups GoodNites	18.0
Pampers Easy-Ups	13.9
Huggies Little Swimmers	5.1
Drypers	0.7
Luvs Sleepdrys	0.6
Luvs Splashwear	0.3
Fitti	0.3
I M Bigg	0.2
Private label	19.6
Other	0.4

Source: *Grocery Headquarters*, August 2003, p. S6, from Information Resources Inc.

★ 845 ★
Feminine Hygiene Products
SIC: 2676; NAICS: 322291
Feminine Hygiene Products (Private-label)

Sales are shown for private label products, the total market and the private label share of the segment.

	Private Sales	Total Sales	Private Share
Sanitary napkins/ tampons	$128.70	$1,470.80	8.7%
Sanitary napkins/ liners	93.30	885.60	10.5
Tampons	35.40	585.10	6.0
Tampon holders	0.17	0.72	23.5

Source: *Private Label Buyer*, September 2003, p. 31, from Information Resources Inc.

★ 846 ★
Feminine Hygiene Products
SIC: 2676; NAICS: 322291
Leading Tampon Brands

Market shares are shown based on sales at drug stores.

Tampax	25.5%
Playtex Gentle Glide	19.0
Tampax Pearl	12.5
O.B.	10.8
Kotex Security	9.4
Tampax Compak	4.3
Playtex	3.3
Playtex Portables	2.0
Other	13.2

Source: *Chain Drug Review*, January 5, 2004, p. 63.

★ 847 ★
Feminine Hygiene Products
SIC: 2676; NAICS: 322291
Panty Liner Market in Israel

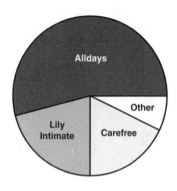

Market shares are shown in percent.

Alldays 54.0%
Lily Intimate 21.0
Carefree 18.0
Other 7.0

Source: *Haaretz*, January 28, 2004, p. NA, from
ACNielsen.

★ 848 ★
Feminine Hygiene Products
SIC: 2676; NAICS: 322291
Tampon Market in Israel

*Tampons have 20% of the overall feminine hygiene
market. Market shares are shown in percent.*

OB 50.0%
Procter & Gamble 36.0
Playtex (Hogla) 14.0

Source: *Haaretz*, January 28, 2004, p. NA, from
ACNielsen.

★ 849 ★
Feminine Hygiene Products
SIC: 2676; NAICS: 322291
Top Sanitary Napkin/Liner Brands, 2004

*Brands are ranked by sales at supermarkets,
drugstores and discount stores (but not Wal-Mart)
for the year ended January 25, 2004.*

	($ mil.)	Share
Always Sanitary	$ 290.5	33.44%
Kotex	153.7	17.70
Stayfree	129.9	14.96
Kotex Lightdays	63.7	7.33
Carefree	63.7	7.33
Always Alldays	33.0	3.80
Kotex Overnites	24.0	2.76
Stayfree Classic	5.0	0.58
Always Alldays Cleanweave . . .	3.8	0.44
Private label	89.1	10.26
Other	12.2	1.40

Source: *MMR*, April 19, 2004, p. 59, from Information Resources Inc.

★ 850 ★
Feminine Hygiene Products
SIC: 2676; NAICS: 322291
Top Sanitary Napkin Producers Worldwide, 2000

Market shares are shown in percent.

Procter & Gamble 27.0%
Kimberly-Clark 14.0
Johnson & Johnson 13.0
Uni-Charm 6.0
SCA 5.0
Kao 5.0
Other 30.0

Source: *Nonwovens Industry*, February 2002, p. 12, from
Intrnational Research Associates.

★ 851 ★
Sanitary Paper Products
SIC: 2676; NAICS: 322291

Disposable Hygiene Products Worldwide, 2002

Diapers and training pants generated $18.9 billion in sales. Top players in the global industry include Procter & Gamble, Kimberly-Clark, Johnson & Johnson, Kao, Oji Paper, and Pom-Pom Products.

Diaper/pants	46.0%
Sanitary protection	35.0
Wipes	11.0
Incontinence products	5.0
Cotton wool/buds	3.0

Source: *Medical Textiles*, December 2003, p. 2, from Euromonitor.

★ 852 ★
Sanitary Paper Products
SIC: 2676; NAICS: 322291

Disposable Paper Product Markets Worldwide

The market for away-from-home disposable paper products stood at $13 billion.

North America	37.6%
Western Europe	30.1
Asia Pacific	21.9
Eastern Europe	5.2
Latin America	5.2
Africa/Middle East	3.2

Source: *Brand Strategy*, September 2001, p. 20, from Euromonitor.

★ 853 ★
Sanitary Paper Products
SIC: 2676; NAICS: 322291

Disposable Wipes Markets, 2002

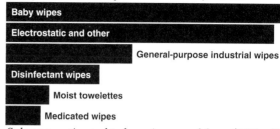

Sales are estimated to have increased from $820 million in 1997 to $1.29 billion in 2002.

	($ mil.)	Share
Baby wipes	$ 430	33.33%
Electrostatic and other	413	32.02
General-purpose industrial wipes	190	14.73
Disinfectant wipes	137	10.62
Moist towelettes	65	5.04
Medicated wipes	55	4.26

Source: *Research Alert*, June 3, 2003, p. 10, from Freedonia Group.

★ 854 ★
Sanitary Paper Products
SIC: 2676; NAICS: 322291

Paper Product Sales, 2002

Data show supermarket sales in millions of dollars.

	($ mil.)	Share
Toilet tissue	$ 2,756.80	17.28%
Paper towels, regular	972.60	6.10
Disposable dishes	790.87	4.96
Paper towels, jumbo	765.56	4.80
Paper napkins	440.50	2.76
Premoistened towelettes	383.67	2.41
Disposable cups	337.84	2.12
Coffee filters, disposable	117.21	0.73
Other	9,385.35	58.84

Source: *Progressive Grocer*, September 15, 2003, p. 19, from *Progressive Grocer's 56th Consumer Expenditures Study*.

★ 855 ★

Sanitary Paper Products

SIC: 2676; NAICS: 322291

Paper Towel Sales in New Zealand

*The company also holds 60% of the toilet paper and
46% of the facial tissue industry.*

Carter Holt Harvey	76.0%
Other	24.0

Source: *Dominion Post*, November 20, 2003, p. NA.

★ 856 ★

Sanitary Paper Products

SIC: 2676; NAICS: 322291

Top Baby Wipe Brands, 2004

*Brands are ranked by sales at supermarkets,
drugstores and discount stores (but not Wal-Mart)
for the year ended January 25, 2004.*

	($ mil.)	Share
Huggies Natural Care	$ 110.3	26.08%
Pampers Natural Aloe Touch	64.2	15.18
Huggies Supreme Care	30.4	7.19
Pampers Original Cotton Care	23.1	5.46
Huggies	18.1	4.28
Pampers Sensitive Touch	13.1	3.10
Luvs Natural	5.8	1.37
Luvs	5.8	1.37
Pampers Big Wipes	4.4	1.04
Huggies Original	4.1	0.97
Private label	115.8	27.38
Other	27.8	6.57

Source: *MMR*, April 19, 2004, p. 59, from Information Resources Inc.

★ 857 ★

Sanitary Paper Products

SIC: 2676; NAICS: 322291

Top Facial Tissue Makers, 2003

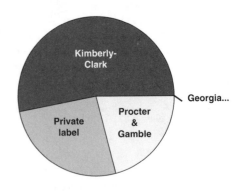

*Shares are shown based on dollar sales for the 52
weeks ended September 6, 2003. Figures exclude
Wal-Mart and club stores.*

Kimberly-Clark	53.0%
Private label and other	25.6
Procter & Gamble	21.0
Georgia Pacific	0.4

Source: *Advertising Age*, February 23, 2003, p. 24, from
ACNielsen.

★ 858 ★

Sanitary Paper Products

SIC: 2676; NAICS: 322291

Top Kitchen Towel Brands in the U.K., 2003

*Brands are ranked by sales in thousands of pounds
sterling for the year ended October 4, 2003.*

	(000)	Share
Bounty	£ 41,276	19.14%
Kittensoft	16,560	7.68
Wipe & Clean	5,076	2.35
Fiesta	2,704	1.25
Colourmani	941	0.44
Other	149,137	69.14

Source: *Grocer*, December 13, 2003, p. 66, from Information Resources Inc.

★ 859 ★
Sanitary Paper Products
SIC: 2676; NAICS: 322291

Top Moist Towelette Brands, 2004

Brands are ranked by sales at supermarkets, drugstores and discount stores (but not Wal-Mart) for the year ended January 25, 2004.

	($ mil.)	Share
Kleenex Cottonelle	$ 51.8	31.60%
Wet Ones	42.3	25.81
Pull-Ups Just for Kids	9.9	6.04
Quilted Northern	9.5	5.80
Charmin Fresh Mates	7.1	4.33
Pampers Tidy Tykes	5.9	3.60
Lever 2000	5.5	3.36
Nice'n Clean	3.7	2.26
Splash 'n Go	3.6	2.20
Comfort Bath	1.6	0.98
Private label	17.3	10.56
Other	5.7	3.48

Source: *MMR*, April 19, 2004, p. 59, from Information Resources Inc.

★ 860 ★
Sanitary Paper Products
SIC: 2676; NAICS: 322291

Top Moist Towelette Makers, 2003

Market shares are shown based on sales at supermarkets, drugstores and mass merchandisers for the year ended May 18, 2003. Figures exclude Wal-Mart.

Kimberly-Clark	42.2%
Playtex Products Inc.	26.6
Procter & Gamble	6.5
Georgia-Pacific	5.4
Private label	9.3
Other	10.0

Source: *Grocery Headquarters*, August 2003, p. S14, from Information Resources Inc.

★ 861 ★
Sanitary Paper Products
SIC: 2676; NAICS: 322291

Top Napkin Brands, 2003

Brands are ranked by supermarket, drug store and discount store (excluding Wal-Mart) sales for the year ended December 28, 2003.

	($ mil.)	Share
Mardi Gras	$ 51.2	10.79%
Vanity Fair	47.5	10.01
Bounty	35.2	7.42
Scott	30.2	6.36
Brawny	23.9	5.04
Private label	150.0	31.61
Other	136.6	28.78

Source: *MMR*, May 31, 2004, p. 33, from Information Resources Inc.

★ 862 ★
Sanitary Paper Products
SIC: 2676; NAICS: 322291

Top Paper Product Makers, 2003

Shares are shown based on $4.8 billion in sales of toilet paper, facial tissue and paper towels for the 52 weeks ended September 6, 2003. Figures exclude Wal-Mart and club stores.

Procter & Gamble	30.0%
Kimberly-Clark	29.0
Georgia-Pacific	22.0
Private label and other	19.0

Source: *Advertising Age*, February 23, 2003, p. 24, from ACNielsen.

★ 863 ★
Sanitary Paper Products
SIC: 2676; NAICS: 322291

Top Paper Towel Brands

Market shares are shown in percent.

Bounty	37.0%
Brawny	12.0
Scott	10.0
Kleenex Viva	9.0
Sparkle	8.0
Mardi Gras	2.0
Marcal	2.0
So Dri	1.0
Bounty Double Quilted	1.0
Private label	17.0

Source: *USA TODAY*, October 23, 2003, p. 3B, from Information Resources Inc.

★ 864 ★
Sanitary Paper Products
SIC: 2676; NAICS: 322291

Top Paper Towel Makers, 2004

Market shares are shown based on sales at supermarkets, drugstores and mass merchandisers (but not Wal-Mart) for the year ended January 25, 2004.

Procter & Gamble	38.20%
Georgia-Pacific	22.82
Kimberly Clark	19.77
Marcal Paper Mills	1.60
Private label	17.16
Other	0.45

Source: *Grocery Headquarters*, April 2004, p. 16, from Information Resources Inc.

★ 865 ★
Sanitary Paper Products
SIC: 2676; NAICS: 322291

Top Sanitary Paper Firms in Japan, 2002

Market shares are shown based on domestic output of 1.68 million tons.

Daio Paper	15.1%
Crecia	12.2
Oji Paper	9.8
Tokai Pulp & Paper	1.7
Mitsubishi Paper Mills	0.6
Other	60.6

Source: "Market Share Survey Report 2002." [online] from http://www.nni.nikkei.co.jp [accessed January 20, 2004], from Japan Paper Association.

★ 866 ★
Sanitary Paper Products
SIC: 2676; NAICS: 322291

Top Toilet Paper Brands

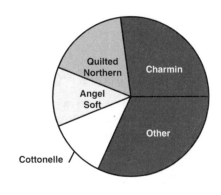

Market shares are shown in percent. Figures include Wal-Mart.

Charmin	27.1%
Quilted Northern	16.7
Angel Soft	12.4
Cottonelle	11.8
Other	32.0

Source: *Advertising Age*, January 12, 2004, p. 6, from A.C. Nielsen.

★ 867 ★
Sanitary Paper Products
SIC: 2676; NAICS: 322291

Top Toilet Paper Makers, 2003

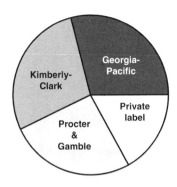

Shares are shown based on dollar sales for the 52 weeks ended September 6, 2003. Figures exclude Wal-Mart and club stores.

Georgia-Pacific	29.0%
Kimberly-Clark	28.0
Procter & Gamble	26.0
Private label and other	17.0

Source: *Advertising Age*, February 23, 2003, p. 24, from ACNielsen.

★ 868 ★
Sanitary Paper Products
SIC: 2676; NAICS: 322291

Top Toilet Tissue Brands in the U.K., 2003

Brands are ranked by sales in thousands of pounds sterling for the year ended October 4, 2003.

	(000)	Share
Andrex	£ 188,170	26.68%
Double Velvet	53,880	7.64
Charmin Ultra	41,863	5.94
Quilted Velvet	29,675	4.21
Nouvelle Quilted	25,682	3.64
Other	365,946	51.89

Source: *Grocer*, December 13, 2003, p. 66, from Information Resources Inc.

★ 869 ★
Stationery
SIC: 2678; NAICS: 322233

Top Office Stationery Makers in Germany

Sales of paper and stationery fell 5% to 2.1 billion euros in 2001. Market shares are shown in percent.

Lamy	9.7%
Pelikan	5.7
Brunnen	5.4
Faber-Castell	3.0
Leitz	2.7
Schwan-Stabilo	2.1
Staufen	2.0
Rotring	2.0
Other	67.4

Source: *Handelsbatt*, May 23, 2002, p. 15, from GfK.

★ 870 ★
Stationery
SIC: 2678; NAICS: 322233

Top Printing Paper Firms in Japan, 2002

Market shares are shown based on domestic output of 11.23 million tons.

Oji Paper	24.9%
Nippon Paper Industries	19.3
Daishowa Paper Mfg.	8.9
Daio Paper	8.5
Hokuetsu Paper Mills	7.9
Other	30.5

Source: "Market Share Survey Report 2002." [online] from http://www.nni.nikkei.co.jp [accessed January 20, 2004], from Nikkei estimate and Japan Paper Association.

★ 871 ★
Cigarette Paper
SIC: 2679; NAICS: 322299

Rolling Paper Market

Market shares are shown in percent.

Zig Zag 60.0%
Other 40.0

Source: *Forbes*, June 21, 2004, p. 177.

★ 872 ★
Coffee Filters
SIC: 2679; NAICS: 322299

Cone Paper Filter Market

Market shares are shown in percent. The company also has 36% of the basket filter market.

Merlitta 59.0%
Other 41.0

Source: *St. Petersburg Times*, April 5, 2004, p. NA.

★ 873 ★
Coffee Filters
SIC: 2679; NAICS: 322299

Top Coffee Filter Brands, 2003

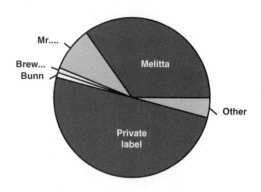

Brands are ranked by supermarket, drug store and discount store (excluding Wal-Mart) sales for the year ended December 28, 2003.

	($ mil.)	Share
Melitta	$ 45.9	34.90%
Mr. Coffee	12.0	9.13
Brew Rite	1.4	1.06
Bunn	1.1	0.84
Private label	66.4	50.49
Other	4.7	3.57

Source: *MMR*, May 31, 2004, p. 33, from Information Resources Inc.

SIC 27 - Printing and Publishing

★ 874 ★
Publishing
SIC: 2700; NAICS: 514191

Scientific/Technology Publishing Worldwide, 2002

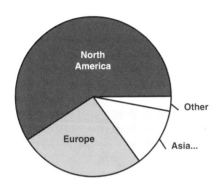

Europe is the market seeing the largest growth. Print takes the largest share of the industry but online services are very popular (and fueling much of the industry's growth).

North America	59.3%
Europe	26.0
Asia Pacific	12.0
Other	2.7

Source: *Electronic Information Report*, September 22, 2003, p. NA, from *Global STM Market Analysis & Forecast 2003 Report* by Simba Information.

★ 875 ★
Publishing
SIC: 2700; NAICS: 51111, 51112, 51113

Top Publishing Firms in Japan, 2002

Market shares are shown based on total sales of publications & ad revenue of 2.8 trillion yen.

Recruit	11.4%
Benesse	6.3
Kodansha	6.1
Shogakukan	5.4
Shueisha	5.2
Other	55.6

Source: "Market Share Survey Report 2002." [online] from http://www.nni.nikkei.co.jp [accessed January 20, 2004], from Research Institute for Publications and Dentsu.

★ 876 ★
Newspapers
SIC: 2711; NAICS: 51111

Largest Spanish Language Newspapers

Figures show circulation.

La Opinion	125,862
Hoy	91,156
El Nuervo Herald	90,264
El Mexicano	90,000
Diario Las Americas	69,032
Diario La Prensa	52,601
Tiempo de Laredo	28,300
El Dia	28,300
La Nacion USA	15,000

Source: *Wall Street Journal*, August 4, 2003, p. B1, from Audit Bureau of Circulations.

★ 877 ★

Newspapers

SIC: 2711; NAICS: 51111

Leading English-Language Newspapers Worldwide

Average circulation is for August 2001 to January 2002 for the U.K., from April to September 2001 for the U.S. and 2000 for India and Australia.

The Sun (U.K.)	3.47
The Daily Mail (U.K.)	2.48
USA TODAY	2.24
The Mirror (U.K.)	2.18
The Wall Street Journal	1.78
The Times of India	1.69
The New York Times	1.11
The Daily Telegraph (U.K.)	1.02
The Los Angeles Times	0.97
Daily Express (U.K.)	0.96

Source: *New York Times*, March 11, 2002, p. C13, from Audit Bureau of Circulations.

★ 878 ★

Newspapers

SIC: 2711; NAICS: 51111

Leading National Newspapers in the U.K., 2004

Table shows the leading national newpapers by circulation figures as of January 2004. According to the source, British newspapers are facing a shrinking number of readers and a tough marketplace as readers seem more interested in celebrity gossip than hard news. Shares are shown for the top 10 newspapers.

	(000)	% of Group
The Sun	3,400.00	27.7%
The Daily Mail	2,500.00	20.4
The Daily Mirror	1,900.00	15.5
The Daily Express	956.65	7.8
The Daily Telegraph	914.98	7.5
Daily Star	901.88	7.4
Times	660.71	5.4
Financial Times	422.54	3.5
Guardian	383.16	3.2
Independent	248.88	2.1

Source: *Wall Street Journal*, March 1, 2004, p. B4.

★ 879 ★

Newspapers

SIC: 2711; NAICS: 51111

Leading Newspaper Firms, 2002

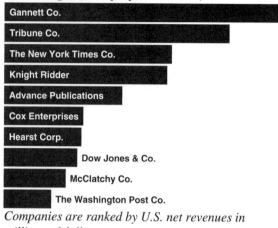

Companies are ranked by U.S. net revenues in millions of dollars.

Gannett Co.	$ 4,760
Tribune Co.	3,848
The New York Times Co.	2,864
Knight Ridder	2,786
Advance Publications	2,015
Cox Enterprises	1,350
Hearst Corp.	1,320
Dow Jones & Co.	1,250
McClatchy Co.	1,052
The Washington Post Co.	806

Source: *Advertising Age*, August 18, 2003, p. S-3, from BIA Financial Network, TNS Media Intelligence/Competitive Media Reporting, and Audit Bureau of Circulations.

★ 880 ★

Newspapers

SIC: 2711; NAICS: 51111

Leading Newspaper Markets

More than half (54.1%) of adults in the top 50 markets continue to read a newspaper every day and 62.5% of adults in the market read a newspaper each Sunday. Figures show markets with highest percentage of adult readership.

Hartford-New Haven, CT	65.7%
Providence, RI - New Bedford MA	64.5
Boston, MA	64.5
Cleveland, OH	63.4
Pittsburgh, PA	63.2
New York CIty, NY	62.6
Buffalo, NY	62.3
West Palm Beach, FL	61.8

Continued on next page.

★ 880 ★

[Continued]
Newspapers
SIC: 2711; NAICS: 51111

Leading Newspaper Markets

More than half (54.1%) of adults in the top 50 markets continue to read a newspaper every day and 62.5% of adults in the market read a newspaper each Sunday. Figures show markets with highest percentage of adult readership.

Harrisburg-Lancaster-Lebanon-York, PA	61.2%
Tampa-St.Petersburg-Sarasota, FL	61.0
Philadelphia, PA	60.5

Source: *Business Wire*, November 3, 2003, p. NA, from Newspaper Association of America.

★ 881 ★

Newspapers
SIC: 2711; NAICS: 51111

Leading Newspapers, 2003

Newspapers are ranked by average daily circulation.

USA Today	2,250,000
The Wall Street Journal	2,090,000
The New York Times	1,120,000
Los Angeles Times	955,211
The Washington Post	732,872
New York Daily News	729,124
New York Post	652,426
Chicago Tribune	613,509
Newsday of New York's Long Island	580,069
Houston Chronicle	553,018

Source: *Christian Science Monitor*, November 14, 2003, p. 24, from Audit Bureau of Circulations.

★ 882 ★

Newspapers
SIC: 2711; NAICS: 51111

Leading Newspapers in Spain

Data show circulation, in thousands.

El Pais	434
El Mundo	312
ABC	279
La Vanguardia	198
La Razon	149

Source: *The Economist*, April 5, 2003, p. 47, from Taylor Nelson Sofres and Officina de Justificacion de la Difusion.

★ 883 ★

Newspapers
SIC: 2711; NAICS: 51111

Tabloid Purchases by Age

Circulation is down significantly from the high point of the 1970s, affected by such things as tabloid television and the Internet. National Enquirer had circulation of 1.8 million and The Star had 1.53 million in 2002.

35-44	25.6
25-34	19.4
45-54	17.0
18-24	14.7
65+	13.3
55-64	10.1

Source: *American Demographics*, October 2003, p. 23, from Mediamark Research.

★ 884 ★
Comic Books
SIC: 2721; NAICS: 51112

Best-Selling Graphic Novels, 2003

Graphic novels have seen triple digit increases over the last three years. Much of this has come from the sales of Manga titles and other Japanese licensed characters. Manga titles, it should be noted, have been warmly received by girls, a group that traditionally has not been comic book readers. Data show unit sales at specialty stores for May 2003.

League of Extraordinary Gentlemen, Book 1	10,600
Marvel Encyclopedia: Hulk	5,500
Powers: Supergroup	4,900
Alan Moore: Portait of an Extraordinary Gentlemen	4,600
Love Hina, Vol. 10	4,100
Yu-Gi-Oh, Vol. 1	3,800
30 Days of Night	3,600

Source: *Daily Variety*, July 17, 2003, p. A1, from Diamond Comic Distributors.

★ 885 ★
Comic Books
SIC: 2721; NAICS: 51112

Manga Publishing in the United States

Viz claims to have half of the market for Japanese comics in the United States.

Viz	50.0%
Other	50.0

Source: *BP Report*, May 3, 2004, p. NA.

★ 886 ★
Comic Books
SIC: 2721; NAICS: 51112

Top Comic Book Publishers, 2003

Market shares are for comics, graphic novels, and magazines.

Marvel Comics	33.24%
DC Comics	29.89
Image Comics	7.24
Dark Horse Comics	5.53
Crossgen Entertainment	3.24
Dreamwave Entertainment	2.49
Wizard Entertainment	2.11
Tokyopop	2.09
Viz LLC	1.58
IDW Publishing	0.75
Fantagraphics Books/Eros Comix	0.66
Archie Comic Publications	0.48

Source: "2003 Year in Review." [online] from http://www.diamondcomics.com/market_share.html [accessed March 19, 2004], from Diamond Comics.

★ 887 ★
Comic Books
SIC: 2721; NAICS: 51112

Top Comic Book Publishers, 2004

Shares are shown based on sales of comics, magazines and graphic novels for January 2004.

Marvel Comics	38.36%
DC Comics	28.36
Dark Horse Comics	7.04
Image Comics	4.20

Continued on next page.

★ 887 ★
[Continued]
Comic Books
SIC: 2721; NAICS: 51112
Top Comic Book Publishers, 2004

Shares are shown based on sales of comics, magazines and graphic novels for January 2004.

Wizard Entertainment	2.11%
Viz	1.73
Dreamwave Productions	1.67
Tokyopop	1.63
Devils Due Publishing	1.39
Crossgen Entertainment	1.19
IDW Publishing	0.92
Fantagraphics Books/Eros Comix	0.80
Other	10.60

Source: *Dialogue*, March 2004, p. 41, from Diamond Comics.

★ 888 ★
Magazines
SIC: 2721; NAICS: 51112
Leading Bank/Finance Publications

Magazines are ranked by ad pages from January - August 2003.

American Banker	477.96
Financial Planning	449.00
Investment Advisor	409.75
Registered Representative	350.00
Traders	346.00
Research	304.67
On Wall Street	284.00
Wall Street & Technology	279.17
ABA Banking Journal	255.71

Source: *Min's B to B*, October 27, 2003, p. NA, from Competitive Media Reporting.

★ 889 ★
Magazines
SIC: 2721; NAICS: 51112
Leading General Interest Magazines Worldwide

Circulation is shown, in thousands.

Reader's Digest	12,558
National Geographic	7,739
People Weekly	3,714
Kampioen	3,684
Readers	2,850
Bosom Friend	2,600
Bild am Sonntag	2,335
Smithsonian	2,034
National Enquirer	1,935
Ba Xiao Shi Yi Wai	1,400

Source: *Financial Times*, September 17, 2002, p. 17, from *Zenith World Magazine Trends 2002-03*.

★ 890 ★
Magazines
SIC: 2721; NAICS: 51112
Leading Magazine Publishers in Australia

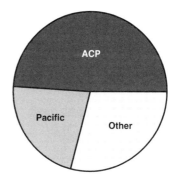

Market shares are shown in percent.

ACP	49.0%
Pacific	22.0
Other	29.0

Source: *Australasian Business Intelligence*, May 9, 2004, p. NA.

★ 891 ★
Magazines
SIC: 2721; NAICS: 51112

Leading Magazine Publishers in Australia

The total audited market stood at 111 million copies and was valued at $482 million. Market shares are estimated in percent.

ACP Publishing 48.2%
Pacific Publications 21.5
Time Inc. South Pacific 6.0
FBC Magazines 5.1
Murdoch Magazines 2.4
Readers Digest (Australia) 1.9
Horowitz Publications 1.9
John Fairfax Publications 1.8
EMAP Australia 1.8
Trader.com 1.6
Express Publications 1.6
Other 6.2

Source: *The Australian*, November 6, 2003, p. B10, from *Australian Magazine Industry Review 2003-04*.

★ 892 ★
Magazines
SIC: 2721; NAICS: 51112

Leading Magazine Publishers in Denmark, 2001

Market shares are shown in percent.

Allers 69.35%
Egmont 30.70

Source: *Boersen*, March 28, 2002, p. NA.

★ 893 ★
Magazines
SIC: 2721; NAICS: 51112

Leading Magazines Firms, 2002

Companies are ranked by U.S. net revenues in millions of dollars.

AOL Time Warner . . . . $ 4,850
Hearst Corp. 2,190
Advance Publications 1,950
Primedia 1,472
Reader's Digest Association 854
International Data Group 801
Gruner & Jahr USA (Bertelsmann) 772
Meredith Corp. 703
McGraw-Hill Cos. 698
Reed Elsevier 648

Source: *Advertising Age*, August 18, 2003, p. S-3, from BIA Financial Network, TNS Media Intelligence/Competitive Media Reporting, and Audit Bureau of Circulations.

★ 894 ★
Magazines
SIC: 2721; NAICS: 51112

Leading Magazines in Quebec

Data show readership.

7 Jours 1,194,000
Coup de Pouce 1,188,000
Selection Readers Digest 1,131,000
Chatelaine 1,024,000
L'actualite acute 986,000
Les Id'eacute es De Maison 847,000
Touring 847,000
Clin D'Oeil 836,000

Continued on next page.

★ 894 ★
[Continued]
Magazines
SIC: 2721; NAICS: 51112
Leading Magazines in Quebec

Data show readership.

Le Bel Age	798,000
Elle Quebec	793,000
Magazine Les Ailes	781,000

Source: *Strategy*, December 1, 2003, p. 17.

★ 895 ★
Magazines
SIC: 2721; NAICS: 51112
Leading Women's Magazines Worldwide

Top titles worldwide are ranked by circulation, in thousands.

Better Homes & Gardens	7,618
Family Circle	5,002
Good Housekeeping	4,558
Woman's Day	4,244
Ladies Home Journal	4,101
McCall's	4,006
Cosmopolitan	2,593
Martha Stewart Living	2,436
Redbook	2,269
Glamour	2,147
Bild der Frau	1,663

Source: *AdAgeGlobal*, October 2001, p. 45, from *FIPP/Zenith Media World Magazines Trends Report*.

★ 896 ★
Magazines
SIC: 2721; NAICS: 51112
Top Magazines by Ad Pages, 2003

Magazines are ranked by ad pages for the year. The magazines that saw the biggest increases in ad pages: Lucky (46%), Real Simple (40%) and Bridal Guide (35.1%). The titles with the biggest decreases: Martha Stewart Living (34.6%), Muscle & Fitness (20.2%) and Seventeen (20.1%).

People	3,705.31
The New York Times Magazine	3,363.20
Bridal Guide	3,128.05

Forbes	3,124.67
Fortune	3,054.14
In Style	3,045.65
BusinessWeek	3,034.65
Vogue	2,958.11
Bride's Magazine	2,956.50
Transworld Skateboarding	2,496.50

Source: *Advertising Age*, January 26, 2003, p. 36, from Publishers Information Bureau.

★ 897 ★
Magazines
SIC: 2721; NAICS: 51112
Top Magazines by Ad Revenue, 2003

Titles are ranked by ad revenues in millions of dollars.

People	$ 744.3
Better Homes and Gardens	654.3
Sports Illustrated	641.9
Parade	612.6
Time	604.9
Newsweek	430.9
Good Housekeeping	401.9
TV Guide	381.6
USA Weekend	377.7
BusinessWeek	336.1

Source: *Brandweek*, March 1, 2004, p. SR2, from Publishers Information Bureau and Competitive Media Reporting.

★ 898 ★
Magazines
SIC: 2721; NAICS: 51112
Top Magazines by Circulation, 2003

Magazines are ranked by paid circulation for the six months ended December 31, 2003. Game Informer Magazine saw the largest increase (45.2%) in circulation over the same period in 2002, followed by Bicycling (41.8%), and Official Xbox Magazine (37.5%). The biggest decreases were Soap Opera Digest (39.7%), Globe (15.7%) and Premier (15.3%).

AARP The Magazines	22,052,328
Reader's Digest	11,044,694
TV Guide	9,009,571
Better Homes & Gardens	7,606,820
National Geographic	6,602,650
Good Housekeeping	4,755,893
Family Circle	4,641,656
Woman's Day	4,279,375

Continued on next page.

★ 898 ★

[Continued]
Magazines
SIC: 2721; NAICS: 51112

Top Magazines by Circulation, 2003

Magazines are ranked by paid circulation for the six months ended December 31, 2003. Game Informer Magazine saw the largest increase (45.2%) in circulation over the same period in 2002, followed by Bicycling (41.8%), and Official Xbox Magazine (37.5%). The biggest decreases were Soap Opera Digest (39.7%), Globe (15.7%) and Premier (15.3%).

Time	4,112,311
Ladies' Home Journal	4,102,373
People	3,603,115
Westways	3,511,833

Source: *Advertising Age*, February 23, 2004, p. 39, from Audit Bureau of Circulations.

★ 899 ★

Magazines
SIC: 2721; NAICS: 51112

Top Magazines in the Restaurant Trade

Nation's Restaurant News enjoys its lead in this category in part because it is a weekly. Its competitors are monthly magazines. The industry also isn't seeing the ad pages that it did during its peak in the 1980s.

Nation's Restaurant News	26.0%
Restaurants & Institutions	16.0
Other	58.0

Source: *Folio*, September 1, 2003, p. NA.

★ 900 ★

Magazines
SIC: 2721; NAICS: 51112

Top Men's Lifestyle Magazines in the U.K., 2003

The top magazines in the men's category are shown by circulation as of December 2003. Front magazine fell 27.5% over December 2002 circulation levels. Men's Fitness gained 17.8% for the same period.

FHM	601,166
Loaded	263,107
Maxim	243,341
GQ	124,022
Wallpaper	107,814
Front	103,203
Bizarre	95,095
Esquire	70,164
Stuff	65,016
Men's Fitness	60,017

Source: *Marketing*, February 19, 2004, p. 6, from Audit Bureau of Circulation.

★ 901 ★

Magazines
SIC: 2721; NAICS: 51112

Top Music Magazines, 2003

Titles are ranked by circulation for January 1 - June 30, 2003.

Rolling Stone	1,300,000
Vibe	831,188
Spin	527,384
The Source	501,743
Blender	469,819

Source: *Billboard*, December 13, 2003, p. 73.

★ 902 ★

Magazines
SIC: 2721; NAICS: 51112

Top Spanish Language Magazines, 2003

Titles are ranked by ad revenue from April - November 2003.

Vanidades	$ 23.27
People en Espanol	22.26
Latina	12.98
Glamour en Espanol	8.34
Vogue en Espanol	7.42
Cosmopolitan en Espanol	7.22

Continued on next page.

★ 902 ★

[Continued]
Magazines
SIC: 2721; NAICS: 51112

Top Spanish Language Magazines, 2003

Titles are ranked by ad revenue from April - November 2003.

Hispanic Business	.$ 6.48
Eres	5.82
Vista	4.58
Newsweek En Espanol	4.49

Source: *Advertising Age*, January 5, 2004, p. 16, from TNS Media Intelligence and Competitive Media Reporting.

★ 903 ★

Magazines
SIC: 2721; NAICS: 51112

Top Teen Lifestyle Magazines in the U.K., 2003

Titles are ranked by circulation as of December 2003. The category is in decline with teenagers spending their money elsewhere and (according to the source) a lack of pop stars/idols. Figures for Cosmo Girl are up over 39% from December 2002.

Sugar	291,794
Bliss	241,664
Cosmo Girl	198,324
J-17	134,650
Mizz	100,298

Source: *Marketing*, February 19, 2004, p. 6, from Audit Bureau of Circulation.

★ 904 ★

Magazines
SIC: 2721; NAICS: 51112

Top Teen Magazines

In 1998, Seventeen, YM, and Teen Magazine had 6.3 million readers. In the interim a number of magazines aimed at young women have come in the market (Teen People, Teen Vogue, etc.) making the publications compete for readers. Titles are ranked by circulation in millions.

Seventeen	2.1
YM	1.5
Teen People	1.5
CosmoGirl!	1.2
Teen Vogue	0.5

Source: *Newsweek*, April 19, 2004, p. 59, from Magazine Publishers of America and Hearst.

★ 905 ★

Magazines
SIC: 2721; NAICS: 51112

Top Video Game Magazines, 2003

Data show paid circulation for the six months ending December 2003.

Game Informer	1,425,683
Electronic Gaming Monthly	570,309
GamePro	509,943
Official Xbox Magazine	403,222
PSM	401,890
PC Gamer	307,691
Computer Gaming World	270,014

Source: *Electronic Gaming Business*, March 24, 2004, p. NA, from Audit Bureau of Circulation.

★ 906 ★
Books
SIC: 2731; NAICS: 51113

Best-Selling Children Books in the U.K., 2003

J.K. Rowling was the top selling author by both value and volume even though there was no new Harry Potter title. Rowling claimed 5 of the top 15 paperbacks (data below show hardcover and paperback). Paragon was the top selling imprint. Unit sales are for the 26 weeks ended February 22, 2003.

The Beano	256,251
The Dandy	116,356
Bob the Builder Annual	89,714
Girls in Tears	89,517
Barbie Annual	83,616
The Match Annual	83,362
Tweenies Annual	77,689
The Bad Beginning	70,536
Rupert Annual	68,819
How to be a Fairy Princess	62,819

Source: *The Bookseller*, March 21, 2003, p. S10, from Nielsen's BookScan's Total Consumer Market.

★ 907 ★
Books
SIC: 2731; NAICS: 51113

Best-Selling Children's Books

Data show hardcover frontlist sales.

Harry Potter and the Order of the Phoenix	12,193,847
The Slippery Slope (A Series of Unfortunate Events #10)	892,046
Eragon	864,253
The English Roses	718,942
Artemis Fowl: The Eternity Code . . .	492,610
Good Night, Sweet Butterflies . . .	455,631
Mr. Peabody's Apples	442,538
The Cat in the Hat Movie: Storybook . .	422,140
The Second Summer of the Sisterhood .	351,463

Source: *Publishers Weekly*, March 22, 2004, p. 35.

★ 908 ★
Books
SIC: 2731; NAICS: 51113

Best-Selling Children's Paperbacks, 2002

Sales of previously released titles are for 2002. The Harry Potter titles were written by J.K. Rowling. The Outsiders was written S.E. Hinton and Tales of a Fourth Grade Nothing by Judy Blume.

Harry Potter and the Chamber of Secrets	1,872,000
Harry Potter and the Prisoner of Azkaban	1,275,000
Harry Potter and the Sorcerer's Stone .	990,000
The Outsiders	506,171
Tales of a Fourth Grade Nothing . . .	442,299

Source: *Current Events*, December 5, 2003, p. 4, from *Publishers Weekly*.

★ 909 ★
Books
SIC: 2731; NAICS: 51113

Best-Selling Fiction Books, 2003

Titles are ranked by millions of units scanned.

Harry Potter and the Order of the Phoenix . .	8.0
The Da Vinci Code	3.8
The Five People You Meet in Heaven	1.7
The King of Torts	1.1
The Lovely Bones	0.9

Source: *Variety*, January 12, 2004, p. A1.

Books
SIC: 2731; NAICS: 51113

Book Publishing in the U.K., 2002

The number of new titles increased 5% over the previous year despite flat sales. STM stands for science, technical & medical titles.

	New Titles	Share
Academic/professional	48,083	38.35%
Non-fiction	31,849	25.40
STM	18,678	14.90
Fiction	11,797	9.41
Children's books	10,519	8.39
School textbooks	4,464	3.56

Source: *The Bookseller*, June 13, 2003, p. 6, from Whitaker Information Services.

Books
SIC: 2731; NAICS: 51113, 51223

Book Sales by Category, 2002 and 2003

Total estimated sales increased from $22.39 million in 2002 to $23.42 billion in 2003.

	2002	2003	Share
El-Hi	$ 4,185.7	$ 4,290.4	18.32%
Professional	3,840.4	3,978.7	16.99
Higher education	3,273.1	3,390.9	14.48
Adult hardcover	2,512.1	2,451.8	10.47

	2002	2003	Share
Book clubs & mail order	$ 1,422.8	$ 1,308.9	5.59%
Mass market paperback	1,239.1	1,218.0	5.20
Religion	840.1	1,261.8	5.39
Children's hardcover	542.8	698.0	2.98
Standardized tests	526.6	591.9	2.53
Adult paperback	474.2	1,465.8	6.26
Children's paperback	473.2	448.6	1.92
Other	2,067.8	2,315.9	9.89

Source: *Publishers Weekly*, April 5, 2004, p. 5, from Association of American Publishers.

Books
SIC: 2731; NAICS: 51113

Book Sales by Category, 2003

Consumers purchased 1.176 billion trade books in 2003, down from 1.777 billion in 2002.

Romance	19.1%
General fiction	14.6
Mystery/detective	7.5
Espionage/thriller	4.7
Children's (incl. Harry Potter)	4.6
Biography/autobiography	2.9
History	2.5
Cooking/wine	2.5
Suspense/psychology	2.4
Diet/health/fitness	2.1
Other	37.1

Source: *USA TODAY*, May 18, 2004, p. 5B, from Ipsos BookTrends.

Books
SIC: 2731; NAICS: 51113

Children's Book Sales, 2003

Retailers are hoping Harry Potter and other franchised titles will translate into big sales for the last six months of 2003. Consumer spending on books for children under 14 increased 10% to roughly $840 million.

	2002	2003
Picture/storybooks	26.7%	27.0%
Non-fiction reading	14.4	8.6
Coloring & activity books	12.5	13.1

Continued on next page.

★ 913 ★
[Continued]
Books
SIC: 2731; NAICS: 51113

Children's Book Sales, 2003

Retailers are hoping Harry Potter and other franchised titles will translate into big sales for the last six months of 2003. Consumer spending on books for children under 14 increased 10% to roughly $840 million.

	2002	2003
Series/chapter books	10.0%	14.6%
Educational workbooks	8.1	7.5
Novelty books	8.0	9.0
Religious books	5.0	4.1
Misc storybooks	4.9	5.4
Sound books	2.4	3.7
Classic literature	2.3	2.4
Leveled readers	2.1	2.8
Reference books	1.4	1.7
Other	0.1	0.2

Source: "Can Potter Save Christmas?" [online] from http://www.ipsos-na.com/news/pressrelease.cfm?id+1909 [accessed April 12, 2004], from Ipsos Book Trends.

★ 914 ★
Books
SIC: 2731; NAICS: 51113

Children's Trade Book Publishing, 2002

Companies are ranked by sales in millions of dollars.

Random House	$ 299
Penguin	235
Scholastic	208
HarperCollins	200
Simon & Schuster	115
Disney	100
Little, Brown	45
Houghton Mifflin	32
Harcourt	30
Candlewick	25

Source: *Publishers Weekly*, September 22, 2003, p. 37.

★ 915 ★
Books
SIC: 2731; NAICS: 51113, 51223

Christian Living Industry

Christian living, according to the source, covers "the subgenres of practical life, relationships and spiritual growth (each of which gets further broken down into specialty categories)." The report tracks sales of books in eight main categories through Christian chain and independent stores.

	Revenue	Units
Zondervan	23.6%	18.2%
Thomas Nelson	18.6	14.9
Other	57.8	66.9

Source: *Publishers Weekly*, March 22, 2004, p. S10, from *2003 STATS Christian Retail Trends*.

★ 916 ★
Books
SIC: 2731; NAICS: 51113

Leading Romance Novel Publishers, 2002

59% of paperback sales in 2002 were romance novels, a figure down from 55.9% in 2000 and 54.5% in 2001. Companies are ranked by number of titles released during the year. Torstar's imprints include Harlequin, Mills & Boon, MIRA, Red Dress and Silhouette and Steeple Hill.

Torstar	1,113
Kensington	219
Pearson	153
Dorchester	113
Betelsmann	110
BET/Arabesque	62

Continued on next page.

★ 916 ★

[Continued]

Books

SIC: 2731; NAICS: 51113

Leading Romance Novel Publishers, 2002

59% of paperback sales in 2002 were romance novels, a figure down from 55.9% in 2000 and 54.5% in 2001. Companies are ranked by number of titles released during the year. Torstar's imprints include Harlequin, Mills & Boon, MIRA, Red Dress and Silhouette and Steeple Hill.

Barbour	51
St. Martin's	49
Pocket/Sonnet	46
Avalon	32

Source: "2003 Romance Novel Sales Statistics." [online] available from http://www.rwanational.org [accessed December 1, 2003], from Romance Writers Association.

★ 917 ★

Books

SIC: 2731; NAICS: 51113

Leading Travel Publishers

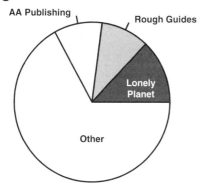

Lonely Planet is the world's most successful independent travel information company. It has printed over 54 million books since 1973. On Amazon.com the top selling Lonely Planet titles were Lonely Planet: Thailand, Lonely Planet: New Zealand, and Lonely Planet: Australia.

	Value	Volume
Lonely Planet	15.35%	12.84%
Rough Guides	10.28	9.66
AA Publishing	9.24	10.27
Other	65.13	67.23

Source: *Brand Strategy*, December 2003, p. 24.

★ 918 ★

Books

SIC: 2731; NAICS: 51113

Popular Politically-Themed Books, 2004

Data show the number of hardcover copies in print, in thousands, of some of the most popular books on politics sold in the first quarter of 2004.

Plan of Attack, Bob Woodward	750
Against All Enemies, Richard A. Clarke	750
The Price of Loyalty, Ron Suskind	400
Ten Minutes of Normal, Karen Hughes	320
Worse Than Watergate, John W. Dean	256

Source: *Wall Street Journal*, April 21, 2004, p. B1, from publishing companies.

★ 919 ★

Books

SIC: 2731; NAICS: 51113

Sports Book Publishing, 2003

Datas show share of sports book titles to be published in the last six months of the year. Popular titles already published include Seabiscuit on horse racing and cyclist Lance Armstrong's memoir It's Not About the Bike.

Baseball	130
Golf	53
Soccer	31
Hockey	28
Boxing	25
Other	306

Source: *BP Report*, September 29, 2003, p. NA, from R.R. Bowker's *Books in Print* and Simba.

★ 920 ★
Books
SIC: 2731; NAICS: 51113
STM Market Shares Worldwide, 2001

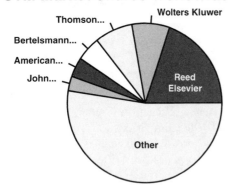

STM stands for science, technical and medical sector.

Reed Elsevier	19.6%
Wolters Kluwer	8.2
Thomson Corporation	7.6
Bertelsmann Springer	5.1
American Chemical Society	3.8
John Wiley	2.9
Other	52.8

Source: *Financial Times*, October 9, 2002, p. 16, from Merrill Lynch.

★ 921 ★
Books
SIC: 2731; NAICS: 51113
Top Book Publishers, 2001

Market shares are shown in percent.

Pearson	24.80%
McGraw Hill	18.32
Harcourt General	9.50
Verlagsgruppe Georg von Holzbrinck	8.70
Scholastic	7.70
Random House	6.90
Other	24.08

Source: "Publishing Industry Statistics." [online] from http://answers.google.com/answers/threadview?id14107 [accessed April 27, 2004], from Hoovers.

★ 922 ★
Books
SIC: 2731; NAICS: 51113
Top Book Publishers in Germany

Market shares are shown in percent. The industry is highly fragmented.

Random House	6.0%
Ullstein Heyne List	4.0
Other	90.0

Source: *Europe Intelligence Wire*, February 11, 2003, p. NA, from *Agence France Presse*.

★ 923 ★
Books
SIC: 2731; NAICS: 51113
Top Book Publishers in the U.K., 2003

Market shares are shown in percent.

Random House	13.0%
Penguin Group	10.8
Other	76.2

Source: *M2 Best Books*, January 30, 2004, p. NA, from *Book Sales Yearbook*.

★ 924 ★
Books
SIC: 2731; NAICS: 51113
Top Book Publishers (Trade) Worldwide, 2002

Companies are ranked by global sales in millions of dollars.

Random House	$ 2,102
Penguin Group	1,320
HarperCollins	1,149
Simon & Schuster	690
AOL TimeWarner Book Group	415

Source: *Publishers Weekly*, June 16, 2003, p. 9.

★ 925 ★
Books
SIC: 2731; NAICS: 51113

Top Hardcover Book Publishers, 2003

Data show the publisher's share of the 1,530 hardcover bestseller positions during 2003.

Random House	28.4%
Penguin USA	15.1
Time Warner	10.7
Simon & Schuster	10.7
HarperCollins	10.5
Von Holtzbrinck	7.1
Hyperion	6.1
Rodale	2.4
Thomas Nelson	1.5
Harcourt	0.7

Source: *Publishers Weekly*, January 12, 2004, p. 30.

★ 926 ★
Books
SIC: 2731; NAICS: 51113, 51223

Top Paperback Publishers, 2003

- Random House
- HarperCollins
- Penguin USA
- Simon & Schuster
- Time Warner
- Von Holtzbrinck
- Silhouette
- Harcourt
- Other

Data show the publisher's share of the 1,530 hardcover bestseller positions during 2003.

Random House	30.2%
HarperCollins	14.6
Penguin USA	14.1
Simon & Schuster	10.8
Time Warner	8.6
Von Holtzbrinck	6.2
Silhouette	3.3

Harcourt	3.3%
Other	8.9

Source: *Publishers Weekly*, January 12, 2004, p. 30.

★ 927 ★
Books
SIC: 2731; NAICS: 51113, 51223

Top Science Fiction Publishers in the U.K.

Companies are ranked by share of total imprints. HarperCollins benefited from sales of J.R.R. Tolkien backlist (which sold over 1 million copies).

NEL	22.2%
HarperCollins	17.2
Millennium	16.2
Orbit	13.0
Doubleday	6.6
Pocket Books	5.1
Corgi	3.2
Pan	3.0
Voyager	2.5
Gollancz	2.5
Other	8.5

Source: *The Bookseller*, April 19, 2002, p. S10.

★ 928 ★
Textbooks
SIC: 2731; NAICS: 51113

English Textbook Market in China

Market shares are shown in percent. PEP stands for People's Education Press.

PEP Primary English	60.0%
Other	40.0

Source: *Canadian Corporate News*, September 24, 2003, p. NA.

★ 929 ★
Textbooks
SIC: 2731; NAICS: 51113

Popular Pre-K-8 Textbooks, 2003

Market shares are shown in percent.

Scott Foresman Social Studies Horizons . . . 30.3%
Horizons 28.5
McGraw-Hill Science 6.6
Macmillan/McGraw-Hill Social Studies . . . 5.8
Early Childhood Program 5.6
Other 23.3

Source: *Educational Marketer*, May 10, 2004, p. NA, from Simba.

★ 930 ★
Textbooks
SIC: 2731; NAICS: 51113

Science Textbook Market in Tennessee

The state spent $38.5 million on new textbooks. Figures are for grades K-12.

Harcourt 45.8%
McGraw-Hill 33.6
Other 20.6

Source: *Educational Marketer*, October 13, 2003, p. NA.

★ 931 ★
Textbooks
SIC: 2731; NAICS: 51113

Textbook Market in Alabama

Market shares are shown for grades K-12.

McGraw-Hill 41.9%
Thomson Learning 34.5
Other 23.6

Source: *Educational Marketer*, October 6, 2003, p. NA.

★ 932 ★
Textbooks
SIC: 2731; NAICS: 51113

Textbook Market in North Carolina

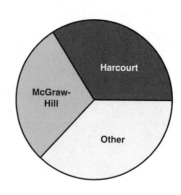

Market shares are shown for grades K-12. Harcourt had 79% of elementary sales.

Harcourt 33.7%
McGraw-Hill 29.3
Other 37.0

Source: *Educational Marketer*, October 6, 2003, p. NA.

★ 933 ★
Textbooks
SIC: 2731; NAICS: 51113

Top Textbook Publishers, 2003

The college market has a reputation for being stable with annual growth at 5-7%. Government statistics show increased college enrollments, which should translate into continued growth for the industry. Shares are shown based on $406.2 million in adoptions.

Pearson 27.8%
McGraw-Hill 25.8
Harcourt 24.9
Houghton Mifflin 16.7
Scholastic 1.9
Thomson Learning 1.4
Goodheart-Willcox 0.3
Sopris West 0.3
Clairmont Press 0.2
CPO Science 0.2
Other 0.5

Source: *Educational Marketer*, May 10, 2004, p. NA, from Simba.

★ 934 ★

Video Game Manuals

SIC: 2731; NAICS: 51113

Best-Selling Strategy Guides, 2002

Prima Games publishes about 130 to 140 titles a year (they control the PC game market) while BradyGames publishes about 60 titles. Brady published 6 of the top 7 titles shown in the table (Bethesda published Morrowind). Prima published Spiderman, Medal of Honor and Splinter Cell. Titles are ranked by unit sales.

Grand Theft Auto: Vice City	504,000
Final Fantasy X	284,000
Kingdom Hearts	195,000
Grand Theft Auto 3	181,000
Mortal Kombat: Deadly Alliance	105,000
Morrowind	103,000
Spiderman: the Movie	102,000
Medal of Honor Frontline	99,000
Madden NFL 2003	86,000
Splinter Cell	70,000

Source: *Electronic Gaming Business*, June 4, 2003, p. NA, from NPD Group/NPD Funworld/TRSTS.

★ 935 ★

Video Game Manuals

SIC: 2731; NAICS: 51113

Strategy Guide Industry

Figures are shown based on unit sales.

Prima Games	91.6%
Other	8.4

Source: *Business Wire*, October 2, 2003, p. NA, from NPD Group Inc. Gaming Guide Report.

★ 936 ★

Book Printing

SIC: 2732; NAICS: 323117

Leading Book Printers

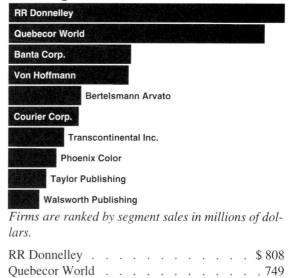

Firms are ranked by segment sales in millions of dollars.

RR Donnelley	$ 808
Quebecor World	749
Banta Corp.	355
Von Hoffmann	348
Bertelsmann Arvato	209
Courier Corp.	202
Transcontinental Inc.	159
Phoenix Color	137
Taylor Publishing	108
Walsworth Publishing	88

Source: *Printing Impressions*, December 2003, p. NA.

★ 937 ★

Directories

SIC: 2741; NAICS: 51114

Directories Market in the Twin Cities, MN

Market shares are shown in percent.

Dex	76.0%
Yellow Book	17.0
Other	7.0

Source: *Saint Paul Pioneer Press*, April 17, 2004, p. NA, from Yellow Pages Industry Association.

★ 938 ★

Directories

SIC: 2741; NAICS: 51114

Leading Independent Publishers

Companies are ranked by number of directories published.

Yellow Book USA	550
TransWestern Publishing	334
Phone Directories Co.	118
White Directory Publishers	57
Associated Publishing	10

Source: *Yellow Pages & Directory Report*, January 30, 2004, p. NA, from Simba Information.

★ 939 ★

Directories

SIC: 2741; NAICS: 51114

Leading Independent Publishers in California

Valley Yellow Pages	
United Yellow Pages	
TransWestern Publishing	
Yellow Book USA	
Clarke Directory Publishers	
West Coast Yellow Pages	

Companies are ranked by circulation, in thousands.

Valley Yellow Pages	5,200
United Yellow Pages	2,600
TransWestern Publishing	2,500
Yellow Book USA	2,100
Clarke Directory Publishers	900
West Coast Yellow Pages	130

Source: *Yellow Pages & Directory Report*, March 28, 2003, p. NA, from Simba Information.

★ 940 ★

Directories

SIC: 2741; NAICS: 51114

Leading Independent Publishers in Michigan

Companies are ranked by circulation, in thousands.

Yellow Books USA	5,300
TransWestern Publishing	2,500
Hometown Directories	1,400
Review Directories	190
Central Michigan Directories	98

Source: *Yellow Pages & Directory Report*, October 31, 2003, p. NA.

★ 941 ★

Directories

SIC: 2741; NAICS: 51114

Yellow Pages Industry, 2008

Revenues for the industry are shown by segment.

Printed directories	77.0%
Digital directories	23.0

Source: *Investor's Business Daily*, December 1, 2003, p. A9, from comScore Networks and Kelsey Group.

★ 942 ★

Trading Cards

SIC: 2741; NAICS: 511199

Trading Card Market

The typical customer of the $350 to $400 million market is between 25 to 40 years of age. Most are men. In the 1960s collectors were mostly preteen boys. The wholesale market reached about $1.1 billion in sales in 1991, the industry's high point.

Upper Deck	35.0%
Topps	35.0
Other	30.0

Source: *San Diego Tribune*, April 3, 2004, p. NA.

★ 943 ★
Printing
SIC: 2750; NAICS: 323110
Digital Color Printing

There were 700 large printing firms in 2000, a figure that is forecasted to fall to 600 in 2020. Medium firms will fall from 8,500 fto 5,000. Small firms will fall from 30,000 to 11,000.

Corporate and in-house departments	50.0%
Primedia and large printing companies	40.0
Small printing companies	5.0
Medium-size printing companies	5.0

Source: *Electronic Publishing*, December 2003, p. 24.

★ 944 ★
Printing
SIC: 2750; NAICS: 323110
Document Outsourcing Market in Canada

Figures are in millions of dollars.

	2002	2007	Share
Contract print services . .	$ 3,401	$ 4,192	74.13%
Facilities management . . .	869	1,077	19.05
Statement printing	365	386	6.83

Source: "Infotrends/CP Ventures Releases Canadian Document Outsourcing Forecast." [online] from http://www.capv.com [Press release May 19, 2004], from Cap Ventures and Infotrends.

★ 945 ★
Printing
SIC: 2750; NAICS: 323110
Leading Catalog Printers

Firms are ranked by segment sales in millions of dollars.

RR Donnelley	$ 998
Quebecor World	998
Quad Graphics	954
Banta Corp.	218
Arandell Corp.	208
Perry Judd's	90
The Dingley Press	76
Brown Printing	76

Trend Offset	.$ 75
Spencer Press	73

Source: *Printing Impressions*, December 2003, p. NA.

★ 946 ★
Printing
SIC: 2750; NAICS: 323110
Leading Direct Mail Printers

Firms are ranked by segment sales in millions of dollars.

Quebecor World	$ 624
Vertis Inc.	335
Banta Corp.	191
RR Donnelley	142
The Instant Web Cos.	93
Von Hoffman	85
Clondalkin Group	80
Japs-Olson Co.	76
Consolidated Graphics	71
Holden Communications	52

Source: *Printing Impressions*, December 2003, p. NA.

★ 947 ★
Printing
SIC: 2750; NAICS: 323110

Leading Financial Printers

Firms are ranked by segment sales in millions of dollars.

Bowne & Co.	$ 642
RR Donnelley	475
Merrill Corp.	232
Ennis Business Forms	50
St. Ives Burrups	25

Source: *Printing Impressions*, December 2003, p. NA.

★ 948 ★
Printing
SIC: 2750; NAICS: 323110

Leading In-House Printers

The leading plants are ranked by sales in millions of dollars. Shares are shown based on the top 50 in plants.

	($ mil.)	Share
U.S. Government Printing Office	$ 159.20	18.29%
Allstate Print Communications Center	100.00	11.49
California Office of State Publishing	69.22	7.95
Washington State Department of Printing	33.00	3.79
Wal-Mart	27.75	3.19
State of Oregon Publishing & Distribution	24.55	2.82
John Hancock Financial Services	19.50	2.24
University of California	19.11	2.20
Spartan Stores	19.02	2.19
ING Americas	19.00	2.18
Other	380.11	43.67

Source: *In-Plant Graphics*, December 2003, p. 1.

★ 949 ★
Printing
SIC: 2750; NAICS: 323110

Leading Printers in the U.K.

Companies are ranked by sales in millions of British pounds.

De la Rue	£ 583
Chesapeake	523
Clondalkin Group	500
Polestar	484
St. Ives	437
MY Holdings	400
British Polyethylene Industries	350
Communisis	262
Adare	180
Williams Lea	165

Source: *Print Week*, November 27, 2003, p. 16.

★ 950 ★
Printing
SIC: 2750; NAICS: 323110

Leading Printing Markets

Markets are ranked by value of potential market in billions of dollars.

Government (federal & state)	$ 3,829
Energy	3,489
Banking, insurance services	2,531
Health care	1,786
Automotive	1,721
Real estate	1,273
Telecommunications	937
Discount retail	790

Continued on next page.

★ 950 ★
[Continued]
Printing
SIC: 2750; NAICS: 323110
Leading Printing Markets

Markets are ranked by value of potential market in billions of dollars.

Consumer electronics	$ 692
Home improvements	662

Source: *Printing Impressions*, January 2004, p. 1.

★ 951 ★
Printing
SIC: 2750; NAICS: 323110
Leading Publication Printers

Firms are ranked by segment sales in millions of dollars.

Quebecor World	$ 1,622
RR Donnelley	1,046
Quad/Graphics	648
Cadmus Communications	321
Brown Printing	304
Perry Judd's	189
Banta Corp.	177
Vertis Inc.	167
Publishers Printing/Publishers Press	160
The Sheridan	146

Source: *Printing Impressions*, December 2003, p. NA.

★ 952 ★
Printing
SIC: 2750; NAICS: 323110
Top Printing Firms

Companies are ranked by most recent fiscal year sales in millions of dollars.

Quebecor World	$ 6,240.0
R.R. Donnelley & Sons	4,754.9
Moore Wallace Incorporated	3,583.6
Quad/Graphics	1,800.0
Mail-Well Inc.	1,728.0
Vertis	1,700.0

Banta Corporation	$ 1,457.9
Deluxe Corporation	1,284.0
Transcontinental Printing Inc.	1,141.0
Standard Register	1,028.0

Source: *Graphic Arts Monthly*, November 2003, p. 43, from *Graphic Arts Monthly 101, 21st Century*.

★ 953 ★
Labels
SIC: 2752; NAICS: 323110, 323114
Label Shipments, 2002 and 2007

Label shipments are expected to grow 8% annually through 2006 to 8 billion square meters ($14 billion). New labeling applications will come from reduced space, bar coding technologies and plateless digital printing. Shipments are shown in millions of dollars.

	2002	2007
Pressure sensitive	$ 7,218	$ 9,645
Glue-applied	2,232	2,640
Other	1,200	1,665

Source: *Adhesives & Sealants Industry*, November 2003, p. 20, from Freedonia Group.

★ 954 ★
Labels
SIC: 2752; NAICS: 323110, 323114
Label Stock Market in North America

The industry is valued at $2 billion.

UPM/Avery/Bemis	70.0%
Other	30.0

Source: *Saint Paul Pioneer Press*, July 26, 2003, p. NA.

★ 955 ★
Labels
SIC: 2761; NAICS: 323116

Global Label Market

Pressure-sensitive labeling has grown into the dominant labeling format. In Europe it took 43.6% of the market followed by glue-applied levels 41.5%.

Europe 36.0%
North America 28.0
Other 36.0

Source: *Paper, Film & Foil Converter*, September 1, 2003, p. NA.

★ 956 ★
Greeting Cards
SIC: 2771; NAICS: 511191

Greeting Card Market

The $7.5 billion industry is estimated in percent.

Hallmark 50.0%
American Greetings 35.0
Other 15.0

Source: *The Plain Dealer*, July 6, 2003, p. G1.

★ 957 ★
Platemaking
SIC: 2796; NAICS: 323122

Platesetter Market

The platesetter was introduced in 1995. It has been installed on more than 400 plants worldwide.

Esko Graphics' Cyrel Digital Imager (CDI) . . 75.0%
Other 25.0

Source: *Package Printing*, April 2004, p. 24.

SIC 28 - Chemicals and Allied Products

★ 958 ★
Chemicals
SIC: 2800; NAICS: 325132, 325192, 325181

Chemicals Industry in China, 2003

China's chemicals industry accounts for 10% of it's Gross Domestic Product.

Chemicals based on coal, metals, salt and organic compounds	48.0%
Petrochemicals and natural gas	20.0
Pharmaceuticals	17.0
Chemical fibers	9.0
Commodities	6.0

Source: *PROCESS Chemical and Pharmaceutical Engineering*, 3, p. NA, from ACHEM Worldwide News.

★ 959 ★
Chemicals
SIC: 2800; NAICS: 325181

Global Catalyst Market, 2001 and 2007

Sales are shown in millions of dollars.

	2001	2007	Share
Environmental	$ 2,502	$ 3,713	28.73%
Polymers	2,268	3,042	23.54
Refining	2,218	2,473	19.13
Petrochemicals	2,069	2,069	16.01
Fine chemicals/ intermediates/other	1,100	1,628	12.60

Source: *Chemical Market Reporter*, June 2, 2003, p. S6, from Catalyst Group Resources.

★ 960 ★
Chemicals
SIC: 2800; NAICS: 325132, 325181, 325131

Raw Materials Consumption in the U.S. and Europe, 2001

Consumption of raw materials for cosmetics and toiletries totaled $1.92 billion in 2001. Market segments are shown in millions of dollars.

	($ mil.)	Share
Conditioning polymers	$ 450	23.0%
Specialty surfactants	350	18.0
Antimicrobials	220	13.0
Emollients	200	10.0
Rheology control agent	190	10.0
Specialty actives	180	9.0
Hair fixatives	170	9.0
UV absorbers	160	8.0

Source: *Chemical Market Reporter*, November 11, 2002, p. FR 4, from Kline & Company.

★ 961 ★
Chemicals
SIC: 2800; NAICS: 325181

Rubber Chemical Market Worldwide, 2001

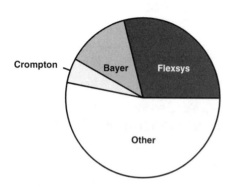

The market was valued at $2.18 billion.

	($ mil.)	Share
Flexsys	$ 600	28.90%
Bayer	280	13.49
Crompton	106	5.11
Other	1,090	52.50

Source: *Rubber & Plastics News*, November 18, 2002, p. 1.

★ 962 ★
Chemicals
SIC: 2800; NAICS: 325181

Rubber Processing Chemicals Demand Worldwide, 2001 and 2006

The world market for rubber processing chemicals is forecasted to increase from $685.5 million in 2001 to $1.84 billion in 2006.

	2001	2006	Share
North America	$ 152.0	$ 189	22.45%
Western Europe	140.0	154	18.29
China	104.0	140	16.63
Rest of world	98.5	125	14.85
Japan	74.5	81	9.62
Other Asia/Pacific	116.5	153	18.17

Source: *Rubber World*, October 22, 2002, p. 14, from Freedonia Group.

★ 963 ★
Chemicals
SIC: 2800; NAICS: 325181

Top Chemical Firms, 2003

The top chemical firms in the U.S. are ranked by sales in millions of dollars.

Dow Chemical	$ 32,632.0
DuPont	30,249.0
ExxonMobil	20,190.0
General Electric	8,371.0
Chevron Phillips	7,018.0
Huntsman Corp.	6,990.2
PPG Industries	6,606.0
Equistar Chemicals	6,545.0
Air Products	6,029.5
Eastman Chemical	5,800.0
Rohm and Haas	5,620.0
Praxair	5,613.0

Source: *C&EN*, May 17, 2004, p. 27.

★ 964 ★
Chemicals
SIC: 2800; NAICS: 325181

Top Chemical Firms in Europe, 2002

Firms are ranked by sales in millions of dollars.

BASF	$ 33,778
Bayer	31,061
Atofina	20,626
Akzo Nobel	14,681
BP Chemicals	12,507
Degussa	12,336
Shell Chemicals	11,490
ICI	9,858
Solvay	8,302
Air Liquide	8,284

Source: *European Chemical News*, December 1, 2003, p. 79.

★ 965 ★

Chemicals

SIC: 2800; NAICS: 325181

Top Chemical Firms Worldwide, 2002

Companies are ranked by chemical sales in billions of dollars. Shares are shown based on the top 50 firms.

	($ bil.)	Share
Dow Chemical	$ 27.60	6.85%
DuPont	26.70	6.63
BASF	25.27	6.27
Total	18.26	4.53
Bayer	17.75	4.40
ExxonMobil	16.40	4.07
Royal Dutch/Shell	15.20	3.77
BP	13.06	3.24
Degussa	11.12	2.76
Akzo Nobel	9.42	2.34
Other	222.18	55.14

Source: *C&EN*, July 28, 2003, p. 18.

★ 966 ★

Chemicals

SIC: 2800; NAICS: 325181

Top Chemical/Petrochemical Producers Worldwide, 2002

Companies are ranked by estimated annual sales in millions of dollars.

ExxonMobil Chemical Company	$ 19,312
ATOFINA	17,686
Mitsubishi Chemical	13,422
Shell Chemical Limited	13,260
BP Chemical	11,515
Asahi Kasei Corporation	9,012
Bayer Corporation	8,686
Solvay, S.A.	7,729
Saudi Basic Industries	7,672
Ashland Inc.	7,543

Source: *World Trade*, May 2003, p. 16.

★ 967 ★

Chemicals

SIC: 2800; NAICS: 325181

Water Treatment Chemicals, 2002

Sales reached $2.2 billion.

Corrosion and scale inhibitors	27.7%
Biocides and disinfecting chemicals	26.4
Coagulants and flocculants	16.4
Filter media and absorbent chemicals	15.7
Other	13.8

Source: *Chemical Week*, May 21, 2003, p. 19, from Business Communications Co.

★ 968 ★

Alkalies and Chlorine

SIC: 2812; NAICS: 325181

Caustic Soda Demand Worldwide, 2003

Total demand was 48.5 million dry metric tons.

Organics	18.0%
Pulp & paper	16.0
Inorganics	15.0
Soaps/detergents/textiles	13.0
Alumina	9.0
Water treatment	5.0
Other	24.0

Source: *Chemical Market Reporter*, November 10, 2003, p. 6, from Chemical Market Associates Inc.

★ 969 ★
Alkalies and Chlorine
SIC: 2812; NAICS: 325181
Global Chlorine Use, 2003

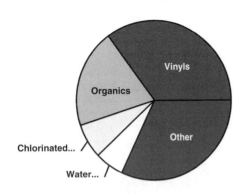

Total demand is 45.3 million metric tons.

Vinyls	35.0%
Organics	20.0
Chlorinated intermediates	7.0
Water treatment	6.0
Other	32.0

Source: *Chemical Market Reporter*, April 26, 2004, p. 16.

★ 970 ★
Surfactants
SIC: 2812; NAICS: 325181
Household Surfactant Demand

*Surfactants are soluble chemical compounds that re-
duce the surface tension between two liquids. They
are used in many detergents and soapy cleaning
compounds. Total consumption of surfactants in the
household product market was 15.9 billion pounds in
2002.*

Heavy-duty detergents	53.0%
Bleaches	15.0
Hard-surface cleaners	10.0
Fabric softeners	8.0
Light-duty liquids	7.0
Autodish products	6.0
Prewash products	1.0

Source: *C&EN*, January 26, 2004, p. 30, from Colin A.
Houston & Associates.

★ 971 ★
Surfactants
SIC: 2812; NAICS: 325181
Surfactant Demand in North America

Consumption reached 4.37 billion lbs. in 2002.

United States	70.0%
Mexico	17.0
Canada	7.0

Source: *Chemical Week*, August 20, 2003, p. 24, from
Colin A. Houston & Associates.

★ 972 ★
Surfactants
SIC: 2812; NAICS: 325181
Surfactant End Markets

*Surfactants in cosmetics and toiletries consumption
was 2.14 billion pounds.*

Anionics	88.0%
Nonionics	7.0
Amphoterics	3.0
Cationics	2.0

Source: *Chemical Market Reporter*, September 29, 2003,
p. 13, from Impact Marketing.

★ 973 ★
Industrial Gases
SIC: 2813; NAICS: 32512
Electronic Gases Market Worldwide

Market shares are shown in percent.

BOC Gases	23.0%
Air Liquide	21.0
Other	46.0

Source: *Electronic Materials Update*, December 2003,
p. NA.

★ 974 ★
Industrial Gases
SIC: 2813; NAICS: 32512

Global Home Health Care Gases, 2002

Home care markets cover a variety of sectors, such as home medical equipment and intravenous nutrition and medication. It has been estimated at $15 billion.

Air Liquide	14.0%
Apria	14.0
Lincare	11.0
Air Products	7.0
BOC	7.0
Linde	6.0
Praxair	6.0
Messer	2.0
Other	33.0

Source: *Chemical Week*, March 5, 2003, p. 23, from Merrill Lynch and J.R. Campbell & Associates.

★ 975 ★
Industrial Gases
SIC: 2813; NAICS: 32512

Industrial Gas Demand, 2006

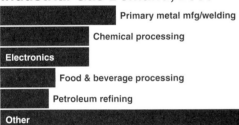

Primary metal mfg/welding
Chemical processing
Electronics
Food & beverage processing
Petroleum refining
Other

Demand is shown in millions of dollars. The strongest growth segments are in petroleum refining and electronics.

	2001	2006	Share
Primary metal mfg/welding	$ 935	$ 1,120	16.59%
Chemical processing	730	900	13.33
Electronics	580	880	13.04
Food & beverage processing	450	570	8.44
Petroleum refining	300	500	7.41
Other	1,885	2,780	41.19

Source: *Welding Design & Fabrication*, January 2003, p. 4, from Freedonia Group.

★ 976 ★
Industrial Gases
SIC: 2813; NAICS: 32512

Industrial Gas Demand Worldwide

Figures are in millions of dollars. The electronics sector is forecasted to see the strongest annual growth between 2003 and 2008 (11%). The growth that will come as the segment recovers from disappointing sales in the overall electronics and semiconductor industry.

	2003	2008	Share
Metal manufacturing and fabrication	$ 5,641	$ 7,234	13.94%
Chemicals and refining related processing	5,581	6,790	13.09
Electronics	3,365	5,670	10.93
Other	21,550	32,185	62.04

Source: *Chemical Market Reporter*, June 2, 2003, p. FR17, from Business Communications Co.

★ 977 ★
Industrial Gases
SIC: 2813; NAICS: 32512

Industrial Gas Industry in Latin America

Market shares are shown in percent.

Praxair	70.0%
Linde	20.0
Other	10.0

Source: *Chemical Week*, April 10, 2002, p. 37.

★ 978 ★
Industrial Gases
SIC: 2813; NAICS: 32512

Leading Gas Players in Europe

Market shares are shown in percent.

Owens-Illinois	35.0%
Saint Gobain	22.0
Other	33.0

Source: *America's Intelligence Wire*, February 18, 2004, p. NA.

★ 979 ★
Industrial Gases
SIC: 2813; NAICS: 32512

Leading Industrial Gas Makers Worldwide, 2002

Air Liquide's share is just under 16% of the $36 billion a year market in 2002.

Air Liquide	16.0%
Praxair	12.0
BOC	11.0
Other	61.0

Source: *Chemical Week*, January 28, 2004, p. 8.

★ 980 ★
Inorganic Pigments
SIC: 2816; NAICS: 325131

Worldwide Demand for Titanium Dioxide, 2004

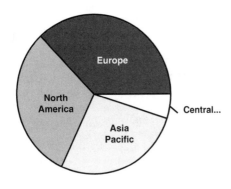

Total demand is forecasted to reach 4.26 million.

	(000)	Share
Europe	1,568	36.76%
North America	1,340	31.41
Asia Pacific	1,147	26.89
Central & South America	211	4.95

Source: *Chemical Market Reporter*, March 29, 2004, p. 6, from Millenium Chemicals, Inc.

★ 981 ★
Inorganic Chemicals
SIC: 2819; NAICS: 325188

Boric Acid Consumption, 2002

The United States is one of the world's largest boron producers. In 2002, the country produced 1.05 million metric tons.

Insulation-grade glass fibers	50.0%
Textile-grade fibers	19.0
Soaps and detergents	6.0
Borosilicate glasses	5.0
Enamels, frits and glazes	4.0
Other	8.0

Source: *Ceramic Industry*, January 2004, p. 12.

★ 982 ★
Inorganic Chemicals
SIC: 2819; NAICS: 325998

Hydrogen Peroxide Market

Companies are ranked by capacity in millions of pounds. Wood pulp bleaching takes 56% of the market. Total demand was 935 million pounds.

	(mil.)	Share
FMC	352	36.36%
Solvay Interox	290	29.96
Degussa	170	17.56
Atofina Chemicals	150	15.50
Georgia-Pacific	6	0.62

Source: *Chemical Market Reporter*, February 2, 2004, p. 23.

★ 983 ★
Inorganic Chemicals
SIC: 2819; NAICS: 325188

Leading Sodium Chlorate Makers Worldwide

Companies are ranked by capacity in thousands of metric tons per year.

	Tons	Share
Eka Chemicals	258	32.70%
Finnish Chemicals	191	24.21
Erco	126	15.97
Kerr-McGee	122	15.46

Continued on next page.

★ 983 ★

[Continued]
Inorganic Chemicals
SIC: 2819; NAICS: 325188

Leading Sodium Chlorate Makers Worldwide

Companies are ranked by capacity in thousands of metric tons per year.

	Tons	Share
Pioneer	24	3.04%
James River	17	2.15
Potlatch	15	1.90
Weyerhaeuser	15	1.90
St. Anne Chemical	11	1.39
Other	10	1.27

Source: *Chemical Week*, March 26, 2003, p. 34.

★ 984 ★

Inorganic Chemicals
SIC: 2819; NAICS: 325188

Sulfur Dioxide Market

The market is shown by application. Leading companies include Calabrain, Rhodia, and PVS Chemicals.

Chemicals	45.0%
Pulp & paper	15.0
Food and agriculture	15.0
Water and waste management	10.0
Metal and ore refining	6.0
Other	9.0

Source: *Chemical Market Reporter*, January 12, 2004, p. 31.

★ 985 ★

Inorganic Chemicals
SIC: 2819; NAICS: 325998

World Potash Consumption, 2003

In 2003, a total of 24.3 million tons of potash was consumed around the world. The market shares listed below are based on consumption by region.

Asia	32.0%
North America	23.0
Western Europe	18.0
Latin America	16.0
Former Soviet Union	5.0
Eastern Europe	3.0
Oceania	2.0
Africa	1.0

Source: *Fertilizer International*, March-April 2004, p. 33, from Lomikin and International Fertilizer Association.

★ 986 ★

Plastics
SIC: 2821; NAICS: 325211

Coating Resins Market

The total market was 6.67 billion pounds in 2002.

Acrylics	35.0%
Vinyl	23.0
Alkyl	13.0
Epoxy	9.0
Polyester	8.0
Urethane	5.0
Other	7.0

Source: *Chemical Week*, November 12, 2003, p. 27, from The ChemQuest Group.

★ 987 ★

Plastics

SIC: 2821; NAICS: 325211

Glass-Mat Thermoplastics Market in Europe

The company claims 85% of the glass-mat thermoplastics composites market in Europe and 50% of the global market.

Quadrant AG 85.0%
Other 15.0

Source: *Plastics News*, September 15, 2003, p. 4.

★ 988 ★

Plastics

SIC: 2821; NAICS: 325211

HDPE End Markets, 2002

The market for high-density polyethylene is expected to grow to 13,600 million pounds in 2002 to 16,220 million pounds in 2006.

Blow molding 40.0%
Film 20.0
Injection molding 20.0
Pipe & conduit 13.0
Sheet 6.0
Wire and cable 1.0

Source: *Chemical Market Reporter*, December 8, 2003, p. 31.

★ 989 ★

Plastics

SIC: 2821; NAICS: 325211

How Low-Density Polyethylene is Used, 2002

In 2002, total demand was 6,010 million pounds, forecasted to increase to 6,255 million pounds in 2006.

Film 48.0%
Extrusion coating 24.0
Injection molding 9.0
Wire and cable 5.0
Adhesives and sealants 3.0
Sheet 3.0
Other 8.0

Source: *Chemical Market Reporter*, December 1, 2003, p. 39.

★ 990 ★

Plastics

SIC: 2821; NAICS: 325181

How Polyethylene is Used

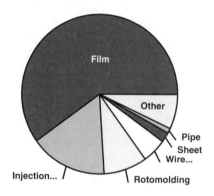

In 2002, total demand was 8,740 million pounds, forecasted to increase to 10,830 million pounds in 2006.

Film 60.0%
Injection molding 16.0
Rotomolding 9.0
Wire and cable 5.0
Sheet 2.0
Pipe 1.0
Other 7.0

Source: *Chemical Market Reporter*, December 1, 2003, p. 39.

★ 991 ★
Plastics
SIC: 2821; NAICS: 325211
PET End Markets

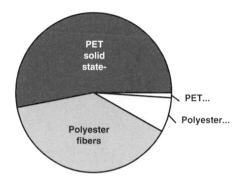

Total demand was 9,780 million pounds in 2002, up steadily from 8,590 million pounds in 1997. PET stands for polyethylene terephthalate.

PET solid state-resins	53.0%
Polyester fibers	39.0
Polyester films	7.0
PET engineering resins	1.0

Source: *Chemical Market Reporter*, January 26, 2004, p. 31.

★ 992 ★
Plastics
SIC: 2821; NAICS: 325211
Polyurethane Demand in North America

Current consumption is roughly double what it was in 1989, the first year for which data is available. Flexible slabstock was the top product. Demand is shown in millions of pounds.

	2000	2002	Share
Construction	1,469	1,459	22.82%
Transportation	1,328	1,326	20.74
Furniture	544	505	7.90
Carpet cushions	466	436	6.82
Appliances	283	278	4.35
Packaging	243	255	3.99
Bedding	239	230	3.60
Textiles and fibers	199	184	2.88

Source: *Rubber World*, November 2003, p. 12, from Alliance for the Polyurethane Industry.

★ 993 ★
Plastics
SIC: 2821; NAICS: 325211
PVC End Markets

Market shares are shown in percent. Top producers of polyvinyl chloride are OxyVinyls, PolyOne, Shintech and Georgia Gulf.

Construction	74.0%
Consumer goods	9.0
Packaging films and containers	6.0
Electrical fittings/wire/cable coatings	5.0
Transportation	2.0
Home furnishings	2.0
Other	2.0

Source: *Chemical Market Reporter*, November 3, 2003, p. 27.

★ 994 ★
Plastics
SIC: 2821; NAICS: 325211
Top 10 PVC Producers Worldwide, 2002

Companies are ranked by production capacity in thousand tons per year. PVC stands for polyvinyl chloride.

Shin-Etsu	3,320
Formosa	2,885
Oxyvinyls LP	2,070
Solvay	1,940
EVC (Ineos)	1,400
Georgia Gulf	1,305
LG Chem	1,000
Atofina	960
Vinnolit	650
Tayio Vinyls	590

Source: *European Chemical News*, December 8, 2003, p. 20, from Chemical Market Associates Inc. & Solvay.

★ 995 ★

Plastics

SIC: 2821; NAICS: 325211

Top ABS Resin Firms in Japan, 2002

Market shares are shown based on total shipments of 362,000 tons. ABS stands for acrylonitrile-butadiene-styrene.

Techno Polymer	26.0%
UMG ABS	23.0
Nippon A&L	13.0
Denki Kagaku Kogyu	10.5
Toray Industries	10.1
Other	17.4

Source: "Market Share Survey Report 2002." [online] from http://www.nni.nikkei.co.jp [accessed January 20, 2004], from Nikkei estimate and Japan ABS Resin Industry Association.

★ 996 ★

Plastics

SIC: 2821; NAICS: 325211

Top LDPE Makers in Japan

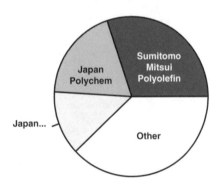

Market shares are shown in percent. LDPE stands for low-density polyethylene.

Sumitomo Mitsui Polyolefin	30.2%
Japan Polychem	18.7
Japan Polyolefins	12.9
Other	38.2

Source: *Nikkei Weekly*, July 21, 2003, p. 1, from Nihon Keizai Shimbun.

★ 997 ★

Plastics

SIC: 2821; NAICS: 325211

Top LLDPE Makers in North America, 2004

Market shares are shown based on total capacity. LLDPE stands for linear low-density polyethylene.

Dow Chemical	30.0%
ExxonMobil Chemical	17.7
Nova Chemicals Corp.	17.0
Equistar Chemicals	7.3
Other	28.0

Source: *Plastics News*, November 24, 2003, p. 3.

★ 998 ★

Plastics

SIC: 2821; NAICS: 325211

Top Markets for Nylon Resins in North America, 2003

The total market for North America was placed at 1.04 billion pounds through November.

Automotive	42.7%
Consumer products	10.5
Film & coating	9.7
Electrical/electronic	4.9
Wire & cable	4.6
Other	27.6

Source: *Plastics News*, January 26, 2004, p. 3, from American Plastics Council.

★ 999 ★

Plastics

SIC: 2821; NAICS: 325211

Top Polyethylene Makers Worldwide, 2007

Market shares are shown based on total forecasted capacity of 36.6 million tons. By end use, film & sheet have half of the market.

Dow Chemical	9.47%
ExxonMobil	8.46
Chevron Phillips	5.04

Continued on next page.

★ 999 ★
[Continued]
Plastics
SIC: 2821; NAICS: 325211

Top Polyethylene Makers Worldwide, 2007

Market shares are shown based on total forecasted capacity of 36.6 million tons. By end use, film & sheet have half of the market.

SABIC	4.49%
BP Solvay	4.19
Basell	3.52
Equistar	3.28
Borealis	2.76
Atofina	2.57
Polimeri Europa	2.14
Other	54.08

Source: *Hydrocarbon Processing*, May 2003, p. 23.

★ 1000 ★
Plastics
SIC: 2821; NAICS: 325211

Top Polypropylene Makers Worldwide, 2005

Market shares are shown based on total forecasted capacity of 20.08 million tons.

Basell	10.6%
BP/Solvay	6.1
ExxonMobil	4.6
Atofina	4.4
Sabic	4.3
Borealis	3.0
Dow	2.6
Formosa Plastics	2.6
Reliance Ind.	2.1
Sonoco	1.8
Other	57.9

Source: *Hydrocarbon Processing*, June 2003, p. 23.

★ 1001 ★
Plastics
SIC: 2821; NAICS: 325211

TPU End Markets

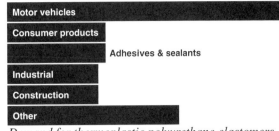

Demand for thermoplastic polyurethane elastomers is forecasted to increase to 70.3 kilotonnes in 2007.

Motor vehicles	37.0%
Consumer products	13.0
Adhesives & sealants	13.0
Industrial	12.0
Construction	12.0
Other	23.0

Source: *Urethanes Technology*, February-March 2004, p. 33, from Freedonia Group.

★ 1002 ★
Plastics
SIC: 2821; NAICS: 325211

World Demand for Thermoplastic Elastomers, 2002 and 2007

Thermoplastic elastomers are defined as a very flexible type of thermoplastic that has the properties of natural rubber and is often used for insulation and as a jacketing compound for portable cords. The world demand for this thermoplastic is presented by region for 2002 and forecast demand for 2007.

	2002	2007	Share
North America	561	752	33.42%
Western Europe	450	558	24.80
China	288	449	19.96
Japan	131	158	7.02
Other	220	333	14.80

Source: *Rubber World*, January 2004, p. 11, from Freedonia Group.

★ 1003 ★
Rubber
SIC: 2822; NAICS: 325212

Largest (Non-Tire) Rubber Makers Worldwide, 2002

Companies are ranked by sales in millions of dollars.

Hutchinson	$ 2,297.9
Bridgestone	2,145.4
Freudenberg Group	2,048.1
Parker-Hannifin Corp.	1,650.0
Cooper Tire & Rubber Co.	1,586.0
Trelleborg AB	1,500.0
Continental AG	1,350.0
HOK Inc.	1,256.6
Tomkins	1,189.5
Tokai Rubber Industries Ltd.	1,132.7

Source: *European Rubber Journal*, September 2003, p. 13.

★ 1004 ★
Rubber
SIC: 2822; NAICS: 325212

Largest Rubber Consuming Nations, 2002

Figures are estimated in thousands of metric tons. Global consumption increased slightly from 17.35 million metric tons to 17.96 million metric tons.

	(000)	Share
China	3,060	17.04%
United States	3,001	16.71
Japan	1,876	10.45
India	871	4.85
Germany	859	4.78
Korea	710	3.95%
France	700	3.90
Russia Fed.	571	3.18
Brazil	553	3.08
Spain	476	2.65
Other	5,283	29.42

Source: *Rubber World*, May 2003, p. 11, from International Rubber Study Group.

★ 1005 ★
Rubber
SIC: 2822; NAICS: 325212

Leading Rubber Markets Worldwide

Consumption is shown in thousands of metric tons. The growth rate is forecast to be the highest since the 1970s (North America 12% and Asia/Pacific 8.8%).

	2003	2004	Share
Asia/Pacific	9,191	9,675	47.55%
North America	3,789	3,962	19.47
European Union	3,503	3,645	17.92
Latin America	1,148	1,224	6.02
Africa	244	252	1.24
Other Europe	1,514	1,588	7.80

Source: *Rubber World*, September 2003, p. 11, from International Rubber Study Group.

★ 1006 ★
Rubber
SIC: 2822; NAICS: 325212

Leading SBR Producers Worldwide

Synthetic rubber takes 53% of the global rubber market (natural rubber has the balance). The styrene butadience rubber (SBR) industry is part of the synthetic category. The leaders of the 3.97 million ton industry are shown below.

Goodyear	10.0%
Chinese producers	8.0
Bayer	8.0
Russian producers	6.0
Michelin	5.0
Kumho	5.0
Dow Chemicals	5.0

Continued on next page.

★ 1006 ★
[Continued]
Rubber
SIC: 2822; NAICS: 325212

Leading SBR Producers Worldwide

*Synthetic rubber takes 53% of the global rubber mar-
ket (natural rubber has the balance). The styrene
butadiene rubber (SBR) industry is part of the synthetic category. The leaders of the 3.97 million ton
industry are shown below.*

Randflex	4.0%
Firestone	4.0
Enichem	4.0
Other	41.0

Source: *European Chemical News*, February 2, 2004, p. 19,
from Festel Capital.

★ 1007 ★
Rubber
SIC: 2822; NAICS: 325212

Polybutadiene Rubber End Markets

*Total demand was 531,000 metric tons in 2003. Ba-
yer and Goodyear Tire and Rubber were the top producers.*

Tires and treads for automobiles, trucks and buses	77.0%
High-impact resin modification	19.0
Industrial products and other applications	4.0

Source: *Chemical Market Reporter*, April 28, 2004, p. 27.

★ 1008 ★
Rubber
SIC: 2822; NAICS: 325212

Top Synthetic Rubber Firms in Japan, 2002

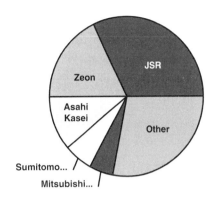

Market shares are shown based on total shipments.

JSR	31.5%
Zeon	18.1
Asahi Kasei	11.3
Sumitomo Chemical	5.6
Mitsubishi Chemical	5.1
Other	28.4

Source: "Market Share Survey Report 2002." [online]
from http://www.nni.nikkei.co.jp [accessed January 20,
2004], from Nikkei estimate and Japan Rubber Manufacturers Association.

★ 1009 ★
Rubber
SIC: 2822; NAICS: 325212

World Rubber Consumption, 2002 and 2003

*In the next two years industry consumption will in-
crease about 5% . Demand is higher for natural
rubber than synthetic rubber. Consumption is shown
in metric tons.*

	2002 (000)	2003 (000)	Share
China	2,885	3,450	18.40%
United States	3,006	3,070	16.38
Japan	1,826	1,879	10.02
Germany	859	936	4.99
India	871	919	4.90
France	700	779	4.16
South Korea	710	704	3.76
Brazil	584	596	3.18

Continued on next page.

★ 1009 ★

[Continued]
Rubber
SIC: 2822; NAICS: 325212

World Rubber Consumption, 2002 and 2003

In the next two years industry consumption will increase about 5%. Demand is higher for natural rubber than synthetic rubber. Consumption is shown in metric tons.

	2002 (000)	2003 (000)	Share
Russian Federation	516	549	2.93%
Spain	476	482	2.57
Malasia	438	465	2.48
Taiwan	395	406	2.17
Thailand	426	398	2.12
Italy	395	398	2.12
Canada	383	390	2.08
United Kingdom	246	258	1.38
Indonesia	241	251	1.34
Africa	237	245	1.31
Mexico	207	224	1.19
Belgium/Luxembourg . . .	162	170	0.91
Australia	69	71	0.38
Other European Countries . .	860	915	4.88
Other European Union Countries	462	465	2.48
Other Asia	424	421	2.25
Other Latin American Countries	301	305	1.63

Source: *Rubber World*, February 2004, p. 11, from International Rubber Study Group.

★ 1010 ★

Fibers
SIC: 2823; NAICS: 325221

Manmade Fiber Production Worldwide, 2003

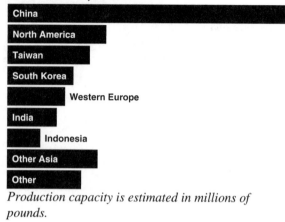

Production capacity is estimated in millions of pounds.

	(mil.)	Share
China	27,061	33.84%
North America	9,406	11.76
Taiwan	8,083	10.11
South Korea	6,563	8.21
Western Europe	5,576	6.97
India	4,491	5.62
Indonesia	3,296	4.12
Other Asia	8,542	10.68
Other	6,949	8.69

Source: *Textile World*, October 2003, p. 64, from Fiber Economics Bureau.

★ 1011 ★

Fibers
SIC: 2823; NAICS: 325221

Polyester Fiber Uses

Demand is forecasted to grow from 4.15 million pounds in 2002 to 4.3 million in 2008.

Apparel	27.0%
Industrial	24.0
Fiberfill	15.0
Home textiles	13.0
Carpets & rugs	11.0
Nonwoven fabrics	10.0

Source: *Chemical Market Reporter*, March 8, 2004, p. 41.

★ 1012 ★
Fibers
SIC: 2823; NAICS: 325221

South American Fiber Consumption, 2001

The data show fiber consumption by country in total pounds and in pounds consumed per capita. Shares are shown based on a total of 5.33 million pounds in South America.

	Lbs. (000)	Lbs. Per capita	Share
Brazil	3,542	20.0	26.63%
Colombia	476	11.9	15.85
Argentina	361	9.6	12.78
Peru	346	12.4	16.51
Chile	194	12.4	16.51
Other	415	8.8	11.72

Source: *Textile World*, September 2002, p. 72, from Fiber Economics Bureau and Author's Estimates.

★ 1013 ★
Fibers
SIC: 2823; NAICS: 325221

Top Synthetic Fiber Makers Worldwide

Companies are ranked by annual capacity in tons of acrylic, nylon, polyester and spandex. Olefin and Aramid are not included.

E.I. duPont de Nemours	1,210,000
Nan Ya Plastics Corp.	1,025,000
Reliance Industries	800,000
Hualon Corp.	790,000
Sinopec	710,000
Huvis Corporation	690,000
Far Eastern Textiles Ltd.	680,000
Teijin	650,000
Yizheng	640,000
koSa	630,000
Toray Industries Inc.	630,000

Source: *DNR*, September 23, 2002, p. NA.

★ 1014 ★
Fibers
SIC: 2824; NAICS: 325222

Fiber Consumption in South America, 2002

Total consumption of the region was 5 billion pounds. Fibers include man-made, cotton, and wool.

	(mil)	Share
Brazil	3,331	66.5%
Colombia	467	9.4
Argentina	349	7.0
Peru	344	6.9
Chile	183	3.7
Other	341	6.8

Source: *Fiber World*, March 2004, p. 44, from Fiber Economics Bureau.

★ 1015 ★
Fibers
SIC: 2824; NAICS: 325222

Top Synthetic Geotextile Manufacturers in Japan, 2001

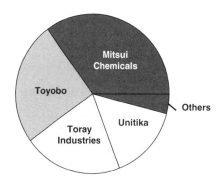

Demand for geotextiles grew in the late 1990s. Single sheets of membranes were once used as liners in waste disposal areas. Seepage issues now mean liners are doubled or tripled. The top four firms have 96% of the market.

Mitsui Chemicals	35.0%
Toyobo	25.0
Toray Industries	21.0
Unitika	15.0
Others	4.0

Source: *Nonwoven Industry*, November 2002, p. 26.

★ 1016 ★

Nylons

SIC: 2824; NAICS: 325222

Leading Nylon Makers in Western Europe

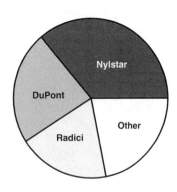

Market shares are shown in percent.

Nylstar	36.0%
DuPont	23.0
Radici	19.0
Other	22.0

Source: *Textile World*, August 2001, p. 62.

★ 1017 ★

Polyester

SIC: 2824; NAICS: 325222

Top Polyester Filament Firms in Japan, 2002

Market shares are shown based on domestic output of 323,057 tons.

Toray Industries	31.4%
Teijin	25.6
Toyobo	14.2
Unitika	11.2
Kanebo Gohsen	7.4
Other	10.2

Source: "Market Share Survey Report 2002." [online] from http://www.nni.nikkei.co.jp [accessed January 20, 2004], from Nikkei estimates.

★ 1018 ★

Herbal Medicines

SIC: 2833; NAICS: 325412

Traditional Herbal Medicines in Japan, 2003

Share is for the leader in the traditonal herbal medicines market in Japan as of the last quarter of 2003.

Tsumura and Company	75.0%
Others	25.0

Source: *Asia Africa Intelligence Wire*, October 31, 2003, p. NA.

★ 1019 ★

Vitamins

SIC: 2833; NAICS: 325411

Eye Vitamin Market

Bausch & Lomb manufactures Ocuvite PreserVision the number one eye vitamin recommended by vitreoretinal specialists.

Bausch & Lomb	70.0%
Other	30.0

Source: *Daily Record*, December 16, 2003, p. NA.

★ 1020 ★

Vitamins

SIC: 2833; NAICS: 325411

Top Vitamin Brands (Mineral Supplements)

Market shares are shown based on sales at drug stores.

Nature Made	5.8%
Nature's Bounty	5.0
Osteo-Bi-Flex	4.3
Nature's Resource	3.2
Sundown	2.9
Os-Cal	2.6
Natrol	2.4
Citracal	2.2
Flex-a-min	1.7
Other	69.9

Source: *Chain Drug Review*, January 5, 2004, p. 63.

★ 1021 ★
Vitamins
SIC: 2833; NAICS: 325411

Top Vitamin Makers

Market shares are shown in percent.

Roche/DSM	27.0%
BASF	21.0
Other	52.0

Source: *Prepared Foods*, September 2003, p. 31, from Business Communications Co.

★ 1022 ★
Vitamins
SIC: 2833; NAICS: 325411

Vitamin Market by Segment

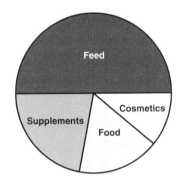

Market shares are shown in percent.

Feed	50.0%
Supplements	22.0
Food	17.0
Cosmetics	11.0

Source: *Food Ingredient News*, August 2003, p. NA, from Business Communications Co.

★ 1023 ★
Vitamins
SIC: 2833; NAICS: 325411

Vitamin Sales, 2003

Sales are shown for food, drug and mass merchandiser outlets (but not Wal-Mart) for the year ended March 23, 2003.

Nutritional supplements	$ 1,942.49
Vitamins, multiple	565.18
Complete nutritional products	493.23
Vitamins, remaining	470.53
Mineral supplements	434.15
Vitamins, children's flavored chewable	84.12
Vitamins -- B complex W/C	36.89
Protein supplements	34.36
Vitamins/tonics, liquid and powder	31.08

Source: *Retail Merchandiser*, June 2003, p. 32, from ACNielsen Strategic Planner.

★ 1024 ★
Analgesics
SIC: 2834; NAICS: 325412

Best-Selling Analgesics/Tablets (Internal), 2003

Market shares are shown based on drug store sales.

Tylenol	14.3%
Advil	12.9
Aleve	7.1
Bayer	5.4
Tylenol PM	5.2
Motrin IB	4.1
Excedrin	2.9
Tylenol Arthritis	2.7
Ecotrin	2.2
Excedrin Migraine	2.1
Private label	24.3
Other	16.8

Source: *Chain Drug Review*, January 5, 2004, p. 57, from Information Resources Inc.

★ 1025 ★
Analgesics
SIC: 2834; NAICS: 325412
Fiber Laxative Market

Market shares are shown in percent.

Procter & Gamble	40.0%
GlaxoSmithKline	20.0
Other	40.0

Source: *Pittsburgh Tribune-Review*, March 31, 2004, p. NA.

★ 1026 ★
Analgesics
SIC: 2834; NAICS: 325412
Gastrointestinal Remedies Market in Japan, 2003

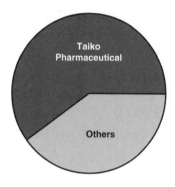

Shares shown are for the gastrointestinal medicines sector of the pharmaceuticals market in Japan.

Taiko Pharmaceutical of Osaka	60.0%
Others	40.0

Source: *Bangkok Post*, January 30, 2004, p. NA.

★ 1027 ★
Analgesics
SIC: 2834; NAICS: 325412
Pain Management Market

The industry is valued at $7.3 billion.

Prescription pain	63.0%
Over-the-counter products	36.0
Supplements	1.0

Source: *Nutraceuticals World*, April 2004, p. 40.

★ 1028 ★
Analgesics
SIC: 2834; NAICS: 325412
Top Acne Remedy Brands, 2003

Brands are ranked by sales in millions of dollars at drug stores, supermarkets and discount stores for the year ended December 28, 2003. Figures exclude Wal-Mart.

Neutrogena Acne Wash	$ 24.6
Clearasil	24.6
Johnson's Clean & Clear	23.1
Oxy	21.1
L'Oreal Pure Zone	15.6
Aveeno	12.4
Neutrogena Clear Pore	12.1
Stridex	11.8
Neutrogena On the Spot	9.8
Other	126.4

Source: *MMR*, February 9, 2004, p. 24, from Information Resources Inc.

★ 1029 ★
Analgesics
SIC: 2834; NAICS: 325412
Top Acne Treatment Brands, 2003

Market shares are shown based on drug store sales.

Clean & Clear	8.4%
Clearasil	7.7
Neutrogena acne wash	7.1
Oxy	6.7
L'Oreal Pure Zone	6.3

Continued on next page.

★ 1029 ★
[Continued]
Analgesics
SIC: 2834; NAICS: 325412

Top Acne Treatment Brands, 2003

Market shares are shown based on drug store sales.

Aveeno	4.8%
Neutrogena Clear Pore	4.3
Dermafina	3.5
Neutrogena On the Spot	3.5
Stri-Dex	3.0
Other	44.7

Source: *Chain Drug Review*, January 5, 2004, p. 45.

★ 1030 ★
Analgesics
SIC: 2834; NAICS: 325412

Top Analgesic (External) Brands, 2003

Market shares are shown based on drug store sales.

Icy Hot	11.3%
Bengay	11.3
Joint-Ritis	6.3
Salonpas	6.2
Aspercreme	4.1
Super Strength Blue Emu	3.7
Absorbine Jr.	3.6
Tiger Balm	2.8
Jointflex	2.8%
Mineral Ice	2.7
Private label	7.5
Other	37.7

Source: *Chain Drug Review*, January 5, 2004, p. 45.

★ 1031 ★
Analgesics
SIC: 2834; NAICS: 325412

Top Analgesic (Internal/Liquid) Brands, 2004

Brands are ranked by sales at supermarkets, drug stores and mass merchandisers (but not Wal-Mart) for the year ended January 25, 2004.

	($ mil.)	Share
Tylenol	$ 79.7	30.30%
Children's Motrin	64.1	24.37
Infants Motrin	23.4	8.90
Advil	3.8	1.44
Private label	44.7	17.00
Other	47.3	17.98

Source: *MMR*, April 19, 2004, p. 59, from Information Resources Inc.

★ 1032 ★
Analgesics
SIC: 2834; NAICS: 325412

Top Analgesic (Internal/Tablet) Firms, 2003

Market shares are shown based on sales at supermarkets, drug stores and mass merchandisers (but not Wal-Mart) for the year ended May 18, 2003.

McNeil Consumer Prods.	28.2%
Wyeth	14.3
Bayer Consumer Health	13.4
Bristol Myers-Squibb	7.5
Private label	20.4
Other	16.2

Source: *Grocery Headquarters*, August 2003, p. S14, from Information Resources Inc.

★ 1033 ★
Analgesics
SIC: 2834; NAICS: 325412
Top Antacid Tablet Brands, 2003

Market shares are shown based on drug store sales.

Zantac 75	11.4%
Pepcid AC	10.6
Tums Extra	6.8
Prilosec	5.9
Pepcid Complete	5.9
Gas X	5.4
Rolaids	3.4
Tums Ultra	2.6
Tums	2.5
Tagamet HB 200	2.5
Private label	21.3
Other	21.7

Source: *Chain Drug Review*, January 5, 2004, p. 45.

★ 1034 ★
Analgesics
SIC: 2834; NAICS: 325412
Top Antacid (Tablet) Makers, 2003

GlaxoSmithKline
Johnson & Johnson-Merck
Pfizer Inc.
Novartis Consumer Health
Private label
Other

Market shares are shown based on sales at supermarkets, drug stores and mass merchandisers for the year ended May 18, 2003. Figures exclude Wal-Mart.

GlaxoSmithKline	23.2%
Johnson & Johnson-Merck	19.9
Pfizer Inc.	16.8
Novartis Consumer Health	9.0
Private label	19.3
Other	11.8

Source: *Grocery Headquarters*, August 2003, p. S14, from Information Resources Inc.

★ 1035 ★
Analgesics
SIC: 2834; NAICS: 325412
Top Anti-Acne Treatments in Germany, 2001

Market shares are shown in percent.

Clearasil	32.2%
Aok	18.0
Jade	11.9
Other	37.9

Source: *Lebensmittel Zeitung*, April 12, 2002, p. 12, from ACNielsen.

★ 1036 ★
Analgesics
SIC: 2834; NAICS: 325412
Top Anti-Fungal Brands in Drug Stores, 2002

Brands are ranked by drug store sales in millions of dollars for the 52 weeks ended December 29, 2002. Total anti-fungal sales in drug stores were $292.4 million.

	($ mil.)	Share
Dr. Scholl (devices)	$ 37.1	12.69%
Lamasil AT	23.5	8.04
Lotrimin AF	18.2	6.22
Tinactin	14.3	4.89
Dr. Scholl Advantage	7.5	2.56
Pro Foot Triad	6.7	2.29
Dr. Scholl (medications)	6.4	2.19
Desenex	6.3	2.15
Airplus	5.7	1.95
Lotrimin Ultra	5.5	1.88
Other	161.2	55.13

Source: *Drug Store News*, May 19, 2003, p. 60, from Information Resources Inc.

★ 1037 ★

Analgesics

SIC: 2834; NAICS: 311111

Top Anti-Itch Treatments (with Calamine), 2004

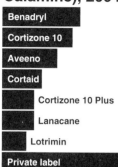

Benadryl
Cortizone 10
Aveeno
Cortaid
Cortizone 10 Plus
Lanacane
Lotrimin
Private label
Other

Brands are ranked by sales at supermarkets, drug stores and discount stores (but not Wal-Mart) for the year ended January 25, 2004.

	($ mil.)	Share
Benadryl	$ 30.4	10.37%
Cortizone 10	27.7	9.45
Aveeno	19.3	6.58
Cortaid	14.9	5.08
Cortizone 10 Plus	12.9	4.40
Lanacane	11.8	4.02
Lotrimin	9.9	3.38
Private label	60.5	20.63
Other	105.8	36.08

Source: *MMR*, April 19, 2004, p. 59, from Information Resources Inc.

★ 1038 ★

Analgesics

SIC: 2834; NAICS: 325412

Top Antidiarrhea Tablets, 2004

Brands are ranked by sales at supermarkets, drug stores and discount stores (but not Wal-Mart) for the year ended January 25, 2004.

	($ mil.)	Share
Imodium AD	$ 55.0	38.73%
Imodium Advanced	49.8	35.07
Kaopectate	3.2	2.25
Private label	33.7	23.73
Other	0.3	0.21

Source: *MMR*, April 19, 2004, p. 59, from Information Resources Inc.

★ 1039 ★

Analgesics

SIC: 2834; NAICS: 325412

Top Chest Rub Brands, 2004

Brands are ranked by sales at supermarkets, drug stores and discount stores (but not Wal-Mart) for the year ended January 25, 2004.

	($ mil.)	Share
Vicks VapoRub	$ 40.2	63.41%
Triaminic Vapor Patch	8.7	13.72
Mentholatum Ointment	5.1	8.04
Theraflu Vapor Stick	1.2	1.89
TheraPatch	0.9	1.42
Private label	6.4	10.09
Other	0.9	1.42

Source: *MMR*, April 19, 2004, p. 59, from Information Resources Inc.

★ 1040 ★

Analgesics

SIC: 2834; NAICS: 325412

Top Cold/Allergy/Sinus (Liquid/ Powder) Brands, 2003

Market shares are shown based on drug store sales.

Vicks Nyquil	14.4%
Dimetapp	5.8
Benadryl	5.7
Robitussin CF	5.0
Triaminic	4.7
Pediacare	4.6
Tylenol Plus	4.0
Robitussin	4.0
Motrin	3.9
Vicks Dayquil	3.3
Private label	20.1
Other	24.5

Source: *Chain Drug Review*, January 5, 2004, p. 45.

★ 1041 ★
Analgesics
SIC: 2834; NAICS: 325412

Top Cold/Allergy/Sinus Tablet Makers, 2003

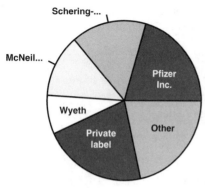

Market shares are shown based on sales at super-markets, drug stores and mass merchandisers (but not Wal-Mart) for the year ended May 18, 2003.

Pfizer Inc.	20.6%
Schering-Plough Corp.	15.7
McNeil Consumer Products	13.0
Wyeth	7.5
Private label	21.6
Other	21.6

Source: *Grocery Headquarters*, August 2003, p. S14, from Information Resources Inc.

★ 1042 ★
Analgesics
SIC: 2834; NAICS: 325412

Top Cold/Allergy/Sinus (Tablets/Powders) Brands, 2003

Market shares are shown based on drug store sales.

Claritin	10.2%
Benadryl	6.7
Claritin D	6.5
Alavert	3.4
Tylenol Cold	3.2
Alka-Seltzer Plus	3.2
Theraflu	3.0
Sudafed	2.9
Tylenol Sinus	2.7
Advil Cold & Sinus	2.5

Private label	23.7%
Other	32.0

Source: *Chain Drug Review*, January 5, 2004, p. 45.

★ 1043 ★
Analgesics
SIC: 2834; NAICS: 325412

Top Cold & Flu Brands in the U.K.

Market shares are estimated for 2002. Top manufac-turers in the market are Reckitt Benckiser, GlaxoSmithKline, Pfizer, Crookes and Boots.

Lemsip	36.0%
Night Nurse/Day Nurse	28.0
Beechams	13.0
Sudafed	5.0
Boots Cold & Flu treatments	4.0
Nurofen Cold & Flu	3.5
Benylin Day & Night	2.0
Other	8.5

Source: *Chemist & Druggist*, October 18, 2003, p. S12, from Information Resources Inc.

★ 1044 ★
Analgesics
SIC: 2834; NAICS: 325412

Top Cold Remedy Makers in Japan, 2002

Market shares are shown based on domestic ship-ments of 77 billion yen.

Taisho Pharmaceutical Co.	29.5%
Takeda Chemical Industries Ltd.	12.1
Sankyo Co.	10.4
SSP Co.	7.7
Nippon Zenyaku Kogyo Co.	7.6
Other	32.7

Source: "Market Share Survey Report 2002." [online] from http://www.nni.nikkei.co.jp [accessed January 20, 2004], from Nikkei estimate.

★ **1045** ★
Analgesics
SIC: 2834; NAICS: 325412

Top Cough/Cold Remedies in Drug Stores, 2002

Brands are ranked by drug store sales in millions of dollars for the 52 weeks ended December 29, 2002. Total sales of cough and cold remedies in drug stores was $1.47 billion.

	($ mil.)	Share
Benadryl	$ 57.3	3.88%
Vicks Nyquil	42.6	2.88
Halls	41.1	2.78
Robitussin DM	38.2	2.58
Alka Seltzer Plus	27.2	1.84
Tylenol Cold	24.5	1.66
Theraflu	24.2	1.64
Sudafed	24.2	1.64
Tylenol Sinus	22.2	1.50
Afrin	22.2	1.50
Other	1,154.7	78.10

Source: *Drug Store News*, May 19, 2003, p. 60, from Information Resources Inc.

★ **1046** ★
Analgesics
SIC: 2834; NAICS: 325412

Top Cough Syrup Brands, 2004

Brands are ranked by sales at supermarkets, drug stores and discount stores (but not Wal-Mart) for the year ended January 25, 2004.

	($ mil.)	Share
Robitussin DM	$ 74.4	28.75%
Robitussin	38.0	14.68
Delsym	34.2	13.21
Vicks Formula 44E	6.8	2.63
Vicks Formula 44	6.7	2.59
Diabetic Tussin	5.1	1.97
Simply Cough	4.3	1.66
Robitussin Pediatric	3.7	1.43
Robitussin Honey Cough	3.1	1.20
Vicks Pediatric Foruma 44E	2.0	0.77
Private label	69.2	26.74
Other	11.3	4.37

Source: *MMR*, April 19, 2004, p. 59, from Information Resources Inc.

★ **1047** ★
Analgesics
SIC: 2834; NAICS: 325412

Top Digestive Aids in Drug Stores, 2002

Brands are ranked by drug store sales in millions of dollars for the 52 weeks ended December 29, 2002. Total sales of digestive aids in drug stores were $954 million.

	($ mil.)	Share
Zantac 75	$ 39.8	4.17%
Pepcid AC	37.6	3.94
Metamucil	35.2	3.69
Imodium AD	27.3	2.86
Imodium Advanced	24.8	2.60
Tums EX	24.2	2.54
Dulcolax	23.4	2.45
Gas X	19.4	2.03
Mylanta	16.2	1.70
Pepcid Complete	11.8	1.24
Other	694.3	72.78

Source: *Drug Store News*, May 19, 2003, p. 60, from Information Resources Inc.

★ **1048** ★
Analgesics
SIC: 2834; NAICS: 32562

Top Douche Brands, 2004

Brands are ranked by sales at supermarkets, drug stores and discount stores (but not Wal-Mart) for the year ended January 25, 2004.

	($ mil.)	Share
Summer's Eve	$ 15.9	36.38%
Massengill	13.8	31.58
Summer's Eve Ultra	2.5	5.72
Vagi-Gard	1.2	2.75
Private label	9.7	22.20
Other	0.6	1.37

Source: *MMR*, April 19, 2004, p. 59, from Information Resources Inc.

★ 1049 ★
Analgesics
SIC: 2834; NAICS: 325412

Top Feminine Hygiene/Medicinal Treatment Brands, 2004

Brands are ranked by sales at supermarkets, drug stores and discount stores (but not Wal-Mart) for the year ended January 25, 2004.

	($ mil.)	Share
Summer's Eve	$ 20.7	28.91%
Vagisil	16.9	23.60
FDS	11.5	16.06
Playtex	6.7	9.36
Always	4.0	5.59
Norform	2.2	3.07
Azo Yeast	2.0	2.79
Gynecort	1.6	2.23
FDS Pursonals	1.3	1.82
Massengill	0.9	1.26
Other	3.8	5.31

Source: *MMR*, April 19, 2004, p. 59, from Information Resources Inc.

★ 1050 ★
Analgesics
SIC: 2834; NAICS: 325412

Top Feminine Pain Reliever Brands, 2004

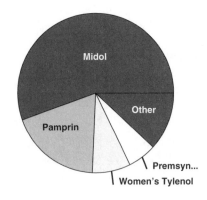

Brands are ranked by sales at supermarkets, drug stores and discount stores (but not Wal-Mart) for the year ended January 25, 2004.

	($ mil.)	Share
Midol	$ 28.9	55.58%
Pamprin	9.9	19.04
Women's Tylenol	4.0	7.69
Premsyn PMS	3.0	5.77
Other	6.2	11.92

Source: *MMR*, April 19, 2004, p. 59, from Information Resources Inc.

★ 1051 ★
Analgesics
SIC: 2834; NAICS: 325412

Top First Aid Ointments/Antiseptics Brands, 2003

Market shares are shown based on drug store sales.

Neosporin Plus	10.0%
Neosporin	8.1
Maderma	8.0
Aquaphor	3.6
Solarcaine	2.5
Polysporin	2.5
Bactine	2.4
Betadine	2.1
BD	2.0
Zims Crack Creme	1.6

Continued on next page.

★ **1051** ★

[Continued]
Analgesics
SIC: 2834; NAICS: 325412

Top First Aid Ointments/Antiseptics Brands, 2003

Market shares are shown based on drug store sales.

Private label	35.0%
Other	22.0

Source: *Chain Drug Review*, January 5, 2004, p. 45.

★ **1052** ★

Analgesics
SIC: 2834; NAICS: 325412

Top Hair Growth Brands, 2004

Brands are ranked by sales at supermarkets, drug stores and discount stores (but not Wal-Mart) for the year ended January 25, 2004.

	($ mil.)	Share
Rogaine	$ 39.4	57.69%
Nu Hair	1.0	1.46
Doo Gro	0.6	0.88
Barre	0.4	0.59
Private label	26.9	39.39

Source: *MMR*, April 19, 2004, p. 59, from Information Resources Inc.

★ **1053** ★

Analgesics
SIC: 2834; NAICS: 325412

Top Hemmorroidal Treatments, 2004

Brands are ranked by sales at supermarkets, drug stores and discount stores (but not Wal-Mart) for the year ended January 25, 2004.

	($ mil.)	Share
Preparation H	$ 42.7	61.71%
Anusol	3.8	5.49
Nupercainal	3.2	4.62
Anusol HC 1	2.7	3.90
Tronolane	1.8	2.60
Balneol	1.6	2.31
Hemorid	1.1	1.59

	($ mil.)	Share
Private label	$ 10.5	15.17%
Other	1.8	2.60

Source: *MMR*, April 19, 2004, p. 59, from Information Resources Inc.

★ **1054** ★

Analgesics
SIC: 2834; NAICS: 325412

Top Laxative Tablets, 2003

Market shares are shown based on drug store sales.

Dulcolax	9.6%
Ex-Lax	6.2
Metamucil	6.1
Colace	6.0
Fibercon	4.7
Senokot S	4.3
Senokot	3.9
Fleet	3.2
Correctol	3.1
Citrucel	3.0
Private label	36.6
Other	13.3

Source: *Chain Drug Review*, January 5, 2004, p. 57, from Information Resources Inc.

★ **1055** ★

Analgesics
SIC: 2834; NAICS: 325412

Top Lice Medications

Market shares are shown based on sales at drug stores.

Rid	29.1%
Nix	18.0
Pronto Plus	4.0
Lice Free	3.0
Acumed	2.5
Pronto	2.3
Lice Guard Robi Comb	2.2
Clear	1.9
Pin X	1.4

Continued on next page.

★ 1055 ★

[Continued]
Analgesics
SIC: 2834; NAICS: 325412

Top Lice Medications

Market shares are shown based on sales at drug stores.

A-200	1.0%
Other	34.6

Source: *Chain Drug Review*, January 5, 2004, p. 52.

★ 1056 ★

Analgesics
SIC: 2834; NAICS: 325412

Top Lip Balms, 2004

Chapstick
Abreva
Blistex
Carmex
Mentholatum Soft Lips
Campho Phenique
Herpecin L
Chapstick Flava Craze
Other

Brands are ranked by sales at supermarkets, drug stores and discount stores (but not Wal-Mart) for the year ended January 25, 2004.

	($ mil.)	Share
Chapstick	$ 71.3	24.27%
Abreva	51.4	17.49
Blistex	24.1	8.20
Carmex	16.6	5.65
Mentholatum Soft Lips	10.0	3.40
Campho Phenique	8.2	2.79
Herpecin L	5.9	2.01
Chapstick Flava Craze	5.6	1.91
Other	100.7	34.28

Source: *MMR*, April 19, 2004, p. 59, from Information Resources Inc.

★ 1057 ★

Analgesics
SIC: 2834; NAICS: 325412

Top Nasal Care Products, 2003

Market shares are shown based on drug store sales.

Zicam	11.1%
Primatene Mist	10.6
Breathe Right nasal strips	9.9
Afrin	9.6
Afrin No Drip	5.1
Vicks Sinex	4.6
Nasalcrom	3.7
Neo-Synephrine	3.0
Breathe Right nasal spray	2.7
4-Way	2.5
Private label	15.9
Other	21.3

Source: *Chain Drug Review*, January 5, 2004, p. 57, from Information Resources Inc.

★ 1058 ★

Analgesics
SIC: 2834; NAICS: 325412

Top Oral Pain Remedies, 2003

Market shares are shown based on drug store sales.

Anbesol	17.6%
Orajel	15.8
Baby Orajel	7.5
Colgate Peroxyl	7.1
Glyoxide	4.2
Dentemp	3.7
Zilactin	3.5
Dentek	3.5
Orabase B	2.4
Hyland's	2.3
Private label	5.8
Other	26.6

Source: *Chain Drug Review*, January 5, 2004, p. 57, from Information Resources Inc.

★ 1059 ★
Analgesics
SIC: 2834; NAICS: 325412

Top Pain Reliever Brands in Drug Stores, 2002

Brands are ranked by drug store sales in millions of dollars for the 52 weeks ended December 29, 2002. Total sales of pain relievers in drug stores were $1.17 billion.

	($ mil.)	Share
Tylenol	$ 141.1	11.96%
Advil	112.6	9.54
Aleve	60.7	5.15
Bayer	49.0	4.15
Tylenol PM	45.5	3.86
Motrin IB	35.2	2.98
Tylenol	33.7	2.86
Children's Motrin	31.7	2.69
Excedrin	30.5	2.59
ThermoCare	26.5	2.25
Other	613.2	51.98

Source: *Drug Store News*, May 19, 2003, p. 60, from Information Resources Inc.

★ 1060 ★
Drugs
SIC: 2834; NAICS: 325412

Animal Health Industry Leaders, 2002

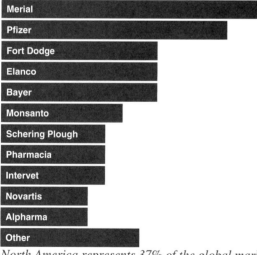

North America represents 37% of the global market for animal health products. Market shares are shown for the United States.

Merial	16.0%
Pfizer	13.0
Fort Dodge	9.0%
Elanco	9.0
Bayer	9.0
Monsanto	7.0
Schering Plough	6.0
Pharmacia	6.0
Intervet	6.0
Novartis	5.0
Alpharma	5.0
Other	8.0

Source: *Agri Marketing*, October 2003, p. S4, from Wood Mackenzie.

★ 1061 ★
Drugs
SIC: 2834; NAICS: 325412

Animal Health Market in New Zealand

Over 60% of thje country's export earnings come from agriculture.

Anthelmintics	49.2%
Inter mammary prep	8.4
Vaccines	6.5
Hormones	3.2
Anti bacterials parenteral	3.1
Minerals	2.9

Source: "Animal Remedies and Animal Health." [online] from http://www.usatrade.gov [accessed June 1, 2004].

★ 1062 ★
Drugs
SIC: 2834; NAICS: 325412

Anti-Aging Treatment Industry

According to the American Society for Asthetic Plastic Surgery nonsurgical procedures have increased more than 3 fold since 1997. Anti-aging cosmetic treatments of all kinds could hit $11 billion by 2007, according to FIND/SVP. The company Inamed is making a product to compete with Botox (which is made by Allergan).

Botox	89.0%
Other	11.0

Source: *BusinessWeek Online*, May 8, 2003, p. NA.

★ 1063 ★
Drugs
SIC: 2834; NAICS: 325412

Anti-Anxiety Market Worldwide

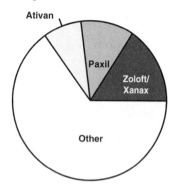

Market shares are shown in percent.

Zoloft/Xanax	16.0%
Paxil	11.0
Ativan	8.0
Other	65.0

Source: *Pharmaceutical Executive*, December 2002, p. 22, from Front Line Strategic Consulting.

★ 1064 ★
Drugs
SIC: 2834; NAICS: 325412

Anti-Depressant Drug Market

Market shares are shown in percent.

Par Pharmaceutical	45.0%
Apotex	40.0
Other	15.0

Source: *The Record (Bergen County, NJ)*, March 12, 2004, p. B8.

★ 1065 ★
Drugs
SIC: 2834; NAICS: 325412

Anti-Depressant Market Leaders Worldwide, 2004

Shares are shown based on estimated revenues.

Paxil	65.0%
Celexa	23.0
Effexor	17.0
Lexapro	9.0
Zoloft	6.0
Prozac	3.0
Wellbutrin	2.0

Source: *Financial Times*, June 4, 2004, p. 17, from SG Cowen.

★ 1066 ★
Drugs
SIC: 2834; NAICS: 325412

Anti-Obesity Drug Market, 2003

Total sales were $191.6 million.

	($ mil.)	Share
Meridia	$ 75,416	39.35%
Phentermine HCl	50,715	26.46
Adipex-P	26,876	14.02
Didnex	16,315	8.51
Ionamin	7,736	4.04
Other	14,590	7.61

Source: *Chemical Market Reporter*, March 1, 2004, p. 8, from IMS Health.

★ 1067 ★
Drugs
SIC: 2834; NAICS: 325412
Antipsychotic Market Shares, 2002

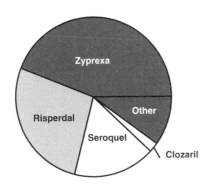

Total sales reached $5.2 billion.

Zyprexa	44.0%
Risperdal	27.0
Seroquel	17.0
Clozaril	2.0
Other	10.0

Source: *Wall Street Journal*, April 11, 2003, p. 1, from NDCHealth.

★ 1068 ★
Drugs
SIC: 2834; NAICS: 325412
Best-Selling Statins, 2003

Sales reached $10.27 billion. Statins are the best selling class of drugs in the United States. They are used to lower cholesterol and reduce the chances of heart attack.

Lipitor	49.1%
Zocor	31.6
Pravachol	14.8
Mevacor	0.3
Other	4.2

Source: *Wall Street Journal*, November 11, 2003, p. A1.

★ 1069 ★
Drugs
SIC: 2834; NAICS: 325412
Biologic Drug Market

Market shares are shown in percent.

Enbrel/Remicade/Humira	95.0%
Other	5.0

Source: *Investor's Business Daily*, November 10, 2003, p. A9.

★ 1070 ★
Drugs
SIC: 2834; NAICS: 325412
Crohn's Disease Market Worldwide, 2010

The market is forecasted to hit $2 billion 2010, up from $700 million in 2003. Crohn's Disease refers to an inflammation in the intestines which generally affects patients in their twenties and thirties.

Remicade	45.0%
Humira	26.0
CDP 870	16.0
Leukine	13.0

Source: *Investor's Business Daily*, April 26, 2004, p. A11, from Merrill Lynch and company data.

★ 1071 ★
Drugs
SIC: 2834; NAICS: 325412
DMARDS Market Shares, 2003

The disease-modifying anti-rheumatic drug market is shown for October 2002 - September 2003.

Etanercept (Enbrel)	59.0%
Leftunomide	15.0
Methotrexate	14.0
Hydroxychloroquine	9.0
Anakinra (Kineret)	4.0
Sulfasalazine	2.0
Infliximab (Remicade)	1.0

Source: *Managed Healthcare Executive*, January 2004, p. 40, from NDCHealth.

★ 1072 ★
Drugs
SIC: 2834; NAICS: 325412
ED Drug Market in Australia

The market for erectile dysfunction (ED) treatments is shown for June 2003. Viagra's share in other markets for this time period: 85% in the U.K., 74% in Brazil and 75% in Spain.

Viagra 63.0%
Cialis 33.0
Levitra 4.0

Source: *Medical Marketing & Media*, October 2003, p. 50, from IMS Health and IMS Midas.

★ 1073 ★
Drugs
SIC: 2834; NAICS: 325412
ED Drug Market in France

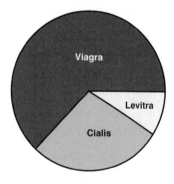

The market for erectile dysfunction (ED) treatments is shown for August 2003.

Viagra 63.0%
Cialis 28.0
Levitra 9.0

Source: *Seattle Times*, October 23, 2003, p. E2, from IMS Health.

★ 1074 ★
Drugs
SIC: 2834; NAICS: 325412
ED Drug Market in Germany

The market for erectile dysfunction (ED) treatments is shown for June 2003.

Viagra 56.0%
Cialis 30.0
Levitra 14.0

Source: *Puget Sound Business Journal*, August 19, 2003, p. NA.

★ 1075 ★
Drugs
SIC: 2834; NAICS: 325412
ED Drug Market Shares

The erectile dysfunction (ED) market is shown by brand.

Viagra 79.0%
Levitra 11.0
Cialis 10.0

Source: "Pfizer Inc. Supplemental Information." [online] from http://biz.yahoo.com/prnews/040420/ nytu091a_1.html [accessed April 20, 2004].

★ 1076 ★
Drugs
SIC: 2834; NAICS: 325412
Generic Drug Industry Worldwide, 2002

In 2002 the generic drug industry had a value of $35.1 billion.

North America 42.7%
Asia Pacific 27.1
Europe 26.2
Other 4.0

Source: *Datamonitor Industry Market Research*, October 1, 2003, p. NA, from Datamonitor.

★ 1077 ★
Drugs
SIC: 2834; NAICS: 325412
Generic Drug Market

The company has the leading share of the store-brand prescription drug market.

Perrigo Co. 65.0%
Other 35.0

Source: *Grand-Rapids Press*, October 29, 2003, p. A11.

★ 1078 ★
Drugs
SIC: 2834; NAICS: 325412
Generic Drug Market in France, 2003

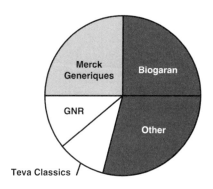

Generic drug sales in France represented 5.4% of the total domestic pharmaceuticals sector by value in 2003. Total sales totaled 855 million euros ($1.09 billion).

Biogaran 25.0%
Merck Generiques 25.0
GNR 11.0
Teva Classics 10.3
Other 28.7

Source: *Pharma Marketletter*, February 23, 2004, p. NA.

★ 1079 ★
Drugs
SIC: 2834; NAICS: 325412
Generic Drug Sales in Europe, 2001

Sales are shown in millions of dollars worth of sales by country.

Italy . . . . $ 1,495
France 1,470
Germany 1,404
United Kingdom 838
Spain 705

Source: *Chemical Market Reporter*, June 17, 2002, p. 6, from IMS Health.

★ 1080 ★
Drugs
SIC: 2834; NAICS: 325412
Hepatitis B Therapy Market

The market is forecasted to grow to $2.8 billion in 2012, up from $1.1 billion in 2002. Therapeutic vaccines have less than 1% of the market.

Antivirals 59.0%
Prophylactic vaccines 27.0
Pegylated interferons 12.0
Conventional interferons 1.0
Therapeutic vacccines 1.0

Source: *Chemical Market Reporter*, April 26, 2004, p. 8, from Decision Resources.

★ 1081 ★

Drugs

SIC: 2834; NAICS: 325412

Hypertension Drug Market Shares, 2003

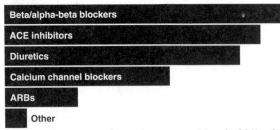

Market shares are shown in percent. Nearly 80% of prescriptions are written for new drugs such as ACE inhibitors and calcium channel blockers. Such drugs are more expensive and are generally more lucrative for drug companies than other medications.

Beta/alpha-beta blockers	27.0%
ACE inhibitors	25.0
Diuretics	23.0
Calcium channel blockers	16.0
ARBs	7.0
Other	2.0

Source: *Wall Street Journal*, February 17, 2004, p. D1, from NDCHealth, Eckerd.com, and Medlineplus.gov.

★ 1082 ★

Drugs

SIC: 2834; NAICS: 325412

Leading Over-the-Counter Drug Brands, 2003

Sales are shown for food stores, drug stores and mass merchandisers (but exclude Wal-Mart) for the year ended December 28, 2003.

Private-label internal analgesic tablets	$ 457.2
Private-label cold/allergy/sinus tablets/ packets	372.5
Private-label mineral supplements	358.0
Tylenol internal analgesic tablets	299.8
Advil internal analgesic tablets	285.5
Private-label 1&2 letter vitamins	193.3
Nicorette anti-smoking gum	189.3
Claritin cold/allergy/sinus tablets/packets	166.7
Private-label multi-vitamins	164.9
Aleve internal analgesic tablets	151.2

Source: *Supermarket News*, April 12, 2004, p. 25, from Information Resources Inc.

★ 1083 ★

Drugs

SIC: 2834; NAICS: 325412

Leading Therapy Classes Worldwide, 2003

Sales cover direct and indirect pharmaeutical channel purchases in U.S. dollars from pharmaceutical wholesalers and manufacturers. The figures below include prescription and certain over-the-counter data and represent manufacturer prices.

	($ bil.)	Share
Cholesterol & triglyceride reducers	$ 26.1	6.0%
Antiulcerants	24.3	5.0
Antidepressants	19.5	4.0
Antirheumatic nonsteroids	12.4	3.0
Antipsychotics	12.2	3.0
Calcium antagonists plain	10.8	2.0
Erythropoietin	10.1	2.0
Anti-epileptics	9.4	2.0
Oral antidiabetics	9.0	2.0
Cephalosporins & cominations	8.3	2.0

Source: "Leading Therapy Classes by Global Pharmaceutical Sales." [online] from http://www.imshealth.com [accessed April 15, 2004], from IMS Health.

★ 1084 ★

Drugs

SIC: 2834; NAICS: 325412

Leading Veterinary Health Suppliers Worldwide, 2002

Companies are ranked by sales in millions of dollars.

Merial	$ 1,505
Pfizer	1,119
Intervet	1,019
Bayer	802
Elanco	693
Schering-Plough	677
Fort Dodge	653
Novartis	624
Pharmacia	506
Virbac	333

Source: *Agri Marketing*, October 2003, p. S4, from Wood Mackenzie.

★ 1085 ★

Drugs

SIC: 2834; NAICS: 325412

Medical Skin Care Market in Thailand, 2003

The medical skin care market is also referred to as the active cosmetics market.

Beiersdorf 70.0%
Others 30.0

Source: *Bangkok Post*, April 7, 2004, p. NA.

★ 1086 ★

Drugs

SIC: 2834; NAICS: 325412

Neurology Drug Leaders

Market shares are shown in percent.

Pfizer 37.0%
Johnson & Johsnon 12.0
Novartis 11.0
Other 40.0

Source: *Pharma Marketletter*, March 29, 2004, p. NA, from Decision Resources.

★ 1087 ★

Drugs

SIC: 2834; NAICS: 325412

Pharmaceutical Outsourcing Market Worldwide, 2002

The industry was valued at $30 billion in 2002.

Active ingredients 30.0%
Dosage and packaging 26.0
Clinical 22.0
Process development 9.0
Discovery 7.0
Preclinical 6.0

Source: *C&EN*, April 21, 2003, p. 40, from PharmaSource.

★ 1088 ★

Drugs

SIC: 2834; NAICS: 325412

Prescription Drug Sales Worldwide, 2003

It is important to remember that drug prices are generally higher in the United States.

U.S. 49.0%
Europe 28.0
Japan 11.0
Asia 8.0
Latin America 4.0

Source: *Wall Street Journal*, April 30, 2004, p. B1, from IMS Health.

★ 1089 ★

Drugs

SIC: 2834; NAICS: 325412

Prescription Ophthalmic Drug Market

The market is seeing growth from an aging population that needs eye care and direct-to-consumer advertising. Sales are shown in millions of dollars.

	2002	2007	Share
Glaucoma treatment	$ 1,374.5	$ 2,041.2	45.05%
Ocular infection treatments	500.0	748.2	16.51
Ocular allergy treatments	397.1	638.4	14.09
Other	545.6	1,103.0	24.34

Source: *Industries in Transition*, July 2003, p. NA, from Business Communications Co.

★ 1090 ★

Drugs

SIC: 2834; NAICS: 325412

Top 10 Drugs Sold Worldwide, 2002

North America, Europe and Japan took 85% of the $400.6 billion audited world market for pharmaceuticals in 2002. The top 10 products had sales of $44 billion and 11% of the market.

	($ bil.)	Market Share
Lipitor (atorvastin)	$ 8.6	19.24%
Zocor (simvastatin)	6.2	13.87
Losec/Prilosec (omeprazole)	5.2	11.63
Zyprexa (olanzapine)	4.0	8.95
Norvasc (amlodipine)	4.0	8.95
Erypo (epoetin alfa)	3.8	8.50
Ogastro/Prevacid (lansoprazole)	3.6	8.05
Seroxat/Paxil (paroxetine)	3.3	7.38
Celebrex (celecoxib)	3.1	6.94
Zoloft (sertraline)	2.9	6.49

Source: *Chemical Market Reporter*, March 17, 2020, p. 6, from *IMS World Review 2003*.

★ 1091 ★

Drugs

SIC: 2834; NAICS: 325412

Top Anti-Infective Drugs Worldwide, 2002

According to Merrill Lynch & Company, the oral antibiotics market is worth $10 billion each year. Nearly half (12 of 29) of key products will see their patents expire before 2011.

	($ mil.)	Share
Augmetin	$ 1,787	17.87%
Zithromax	1,516	15.16
Cipro	1,334	13.34
Biaxin	1,102	11.02
Levaquin, Floxin	1,032	10.32
Rocephin	994	9.94
Cravit	592	5.92
Primaxin	585	5.85
Zosyn	406	4.06
Ceftin	365	3.65
Other	287	2.87

Source: *Med Ad News*, January 2004, p. 39, from Merrill Lynch & Company.

★ 1092 ★

Drugs

SIC: 2834; NAICS: 325412

Top Antihistimines, 2002

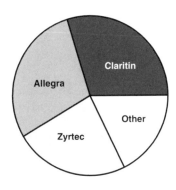

Market shares are for January - November 2002.

Claritin	30.1%
Allegra	28.7
Zyrtec	23.5
Other	17.7

Source: *USA TODAY*, April 23, 2003, p. A1, from IMS Health.

★ 1093 ★

Drugs

SIC: 2834; NAICS: 325412

Top Diabetes Drugs Worldwide, 2002

Because of an aging and increasingly overweight population the market for Type-2 diabetes drugs may climb to $20.2 billion by 2012.

Actos	$ 1,294
Avandia	1,214
Humulin	1,004
Humalog	834
Glucophage Line	778

Source: *Med Ad News*, January 2004, p. 4.

★ 1094 ★

Drugs

SIC: 2834; NAICS: 325412

Top Drug Firms, 2003

Market shares are shown based on sales from April 2002 through March 2003.

Pfizer	10.0%
GlaxoSmithKline	9.0
Johnson & Johnson	6.8
Merck & Co.	6.5
AstraZeneca	5.4
Bristol-Meyers Squibb Co.	4.5
Novartis	4.1
Pharmacia Corp.	3.8
Wyeth	3.7
Eli Lilly and Co.	3.5
Aventis	3.3
Other	47.5

Source: *Modern Healthcare*, August 18, 2003, p. 1, from IMS Health.

★ 1095 ★

Drugs

SIC: 2834; NAICS: 325412

Top Drug Firms by Prescriptions, 2003

Market shares are shown based on total prescriptions.

Pfizer	11.0%
Novartis	6.7
Teva	6.0
Mylan Labs	6.0
Watson	4.8
GlaxoSmithKline	4.6
Merck & Co.	3.7
Johnson & Johnson	3.0
Abbott	2.8
AstraZeneca	2.7
Bristol-Myers Squibb	2.6
Wyeth	2.4
Other	43.7

Source: "Leading 20 Corporations by Total U.S. Dispensed Prescriptions." [online] from http:// www.imshealth.com [accessed April 15, 2004], from IMS Health.

★ 1096 ★

Drugs

SIC: 2834; NAICS: 325412

Top Drug Firms by Promotional Spending

According to the source promotional spending ''represents the cost of detailing office and hospital-based physicians, the cost of advertising in medical journals and the retail value of samples. Data run by customer design to include completed mergers and acquisitions. Excludes co-marketing agreements. Joint-ventures assigned to product owner.''

	($ mil.)	Share
Pfizer	$ 3,714.2	18.3%
GlaxoSmithKline	1,950.1	9.6
Merck & Co.	1,790.0	8.8
AstraZeneca	1,370.4	6.7
Johnson & Johnson	1,231.3	6.1
Norvartis	894.5	4.4
Wyeth	891.7	4.4
Lilly	768.7	3.8

Source: ''Top 10 Corporations.'' [online] from http://www.imshealth.com [accessed April 15, 2004], from IMS Health.

★ 1097 ★

Drugs

SIC: 2834; NAICS: 325412

Top Drug Firms in Australia, 2001-2002

Market shares are shown based on processed PBS prescriptions.

Alphapharm	13.70%
Pfizer	7.79
GlaxoSmithKline	7.52
Merck Sharp & Dohme	7.49
Aventis Pharma	5.92
Pharmacia Australia	5.80
Sanofi Synthelabo	5.77
AstraZeneca	5.74
Bristol-Myers Squibb	4.51
Sigma	4.00
Other	31.76

Source: ''Pharmaceutical Products.'' [online] from http://www.usatrade.gov [accessed January 5, 2004], from U.S. Commercial Service and *Pharmaceutical Benefits Pricing Authority Annual Report.*

★ 1098 ★

Drugs

SIC: 2834; NAICS: 325412

Top Drug Firms in Croatia, 2003

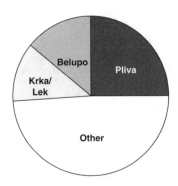

The current market has been growing 10-15% each year since 2000 with a total value of $620 million in 2003.

Pliva	25.0%
Belupo	14.0
Krka/Lek	12.0
Other	49.0

Source: ''Pharmaceuticals.'' [online] from http://www.export.gov [accessed May 4, 2004], from U.S. Commercial Service.

★ 1099 ★

Drugs

SIC: 2834; NAICS: 325412

Top Drug Firms in Greece, 2002

The market was worth $1.5 billion, most of which was imports.

Novartis	7.0%
Vianex	6.0
Janssen-Cilag	6.0
Glaxosmithkline	6.0
Roche	5.0
Pfizer	5.0
Astrazeneca	5.0
Squibb	4.0
Farmaserve Lily	4.0
Aventis	4.0
Other	48.0

Source: ''Greek Market for Drugs & Pharmaceuticals.'' [online] from http://www.export.gov [accessed May 4, 2004], from SFEE Data.

★ 1100 ★
Drugs
SIC: 2834; NAICS: 325412

Top Drug Firms in India

India's $5 billion a year drug industry is preparing for the introduction of patent protections this year. This is just one aspect of the industry which is, according to the article, seeing some substantial overhalls in the coming year.

Cipla	5.5%
GSK	5.5
Ranbaxy	4.7
Nicholas Piramal	4.3
Zydus	3.9
Sun	3.1
Other	73.0

Source: *Financial Times*, July 8, 2004, p. 18, from ORG MAT and Bloomberg.

★ 1101 ★
Drugs
SIC: 2834; NAICS: 325412

Top Drug Firms in Japan

Companies are ranked by sales in hundred million yen. Figures are after the merger of Yamanouchi and Fujisawa.

Takeda	¥ 10,461
Yamanouchi + Fujisawa	8,887
Sankyo	5,699
Eisai	4,666
Daiichi	3,220
Shionogi	2,852
Mitsubishi	2,808
Taisho	2,741
Chugai	2,374
Banyu	1,855

Source: *R&D Directions*, April 2004, p. 16.

★ 1102 ★
Drugs
SIC: 2834; NAICS: 325412

Top Drug Firms in Mexico, 2001

About 390 companies are in the market. Market shares are shown in percent.

Roche-Syntex	8.15%
Aventis Pharma	6.15
Glaxo-Wellcome	3.72
Novartis	3.27
Abbott	3.24
Wyeth	3.11
Pfizer	2.90
Boheringer Ingelheim Pharma	2.76
Bayer	2.76
Janssen	2.50
Other	61.44

Source: "Drugs and Pharmaceuticals." [online] from http://www.usatrade.gov [accessed January 5, 2004], from International Market Service.

★ 1103 ★
Drugs
SIC: 2834; NAICS: 325412

Top Drug Firms in Poland, 2002

Companies are ranked by drug sales in thousands of zlotys. The size of the Polish pharmaceutical market in 2002 was 11.7 billion zlotys.

GSK Pharmaceuticals	$ 1,120,916
Polpharm	791,824
Novartis	530,000
Sanofi-Synthelabo	322,135
Roche	300,635
Polfa Tarchomin	296,898
Novo Nordisk Pharma	287,885
Polfa Warsaw	286,517
Jelfa	247,728
Polfa Kutno	211,209

Source: *Warsaw Rzeczpospolita in Polish*, August 14, 2003, p. NA, from Rzceczpospolita questionnaire.

★ 1104 ★
Drugs
SIC: 2834; NAICS: 325412
Top Drug Firms in Portugal, 2002

▮ Merck Sharp & Dohme

▮ Novartis Farma

▮ Pfizer Laboratories

▮ Servier Portugal

▮ Pharmacia Corp.

▮ AstraZeneca

▮ Sanofi Synthelab

▮ Other

Shares are shown for the National Health System Market. The NHS paid for about 70% of the overall cost of drug products in 2002. Pain relievers, cough/ cold remedies, and digestive aids were the top selling classes by units. The total market value for the Portugese industry was 3.4 billion euros.

Merck Sharp & Dohme	8.07%
Novartis Farma	5.62
Pfizer Laboratories	4.56
Servier Portugal	4.35
Pharmacia Corp.	3.99
AstraZeneca	3.75
Sanofi Synthelab	2.82
Other	66.84

Source: "Market for Pharmaceuticals." [online] from http://www.export.gov [accessed May 4, 2004].

★ 1105 ★
Drugs
SIC: 2834; NAICS: 325412
Top Drug Firms in Vietnam, 2003

▮ Zuellig Pharma

▮ Diethelm

▮ Mega

▮ Other

The top firms and the top importers and distributors in the country.

Zuellig Pharma	17.0%
Diethelm	10.0
Mega	7.0
Other	66.0

Source: *Vietnam Economic Times*, March 26, 2020, p. 3.

★ 1106 ★
Drugs
SIC: 2834; NAICS: 325412
Top Drug Firms Worldwide, 2002

Market shares are shown as percent of worldwide industry sales.

Pfizer	7.3%
GlaxoSmithKline	7.1
Merck	5.1
AstrZeneca	4.6
Johnson & Johnson	4.6
Novartis	4.0
Bristol-Myers Squibb	3.7
Aventis	3.6
Roche	3.1
Pharacia	3.0
Other	53.9

Source: *C & EN*, March 17, 2003, p. 13, from IMS Health.

★ 1107 ★
Drugs
SIC: 2834; NAICS: 325412
Top Drug Firms Worldwide, 2003

Market shares are shown in percent.

Pfizer	9.2%
GlaxoSmithKline	7.0
Sanofi/Aventis	6.6
Merck	5.2
Johnson & Johnson	4.5
AstraZeneca	4.0
Novartis	3.7
Hoffmann-La Roche	3.5
Bristol-Myers Squibb	3.4
Wyeth	2.8
Other	50.1

Source: *Financial Times*, January 27, 2004, p. 18, from Wood Mackenzie and Thomson Datastream.

★ 1108 ★
Drugs
SIC: 2834; NAICS: 325412

Top Drug Sales Worldwide, 2003

*Sales cover direct and indirect pharmaeutical chan-
nel purchases in U.S. dollars from pharmaceutical
wholesalers and manufacturers. The figures above
include prescription and certain over-the-counter data and represent manufacturer prices.*

	($ bil.)	Share
Lipitor	$ 10.3	2.0%
Zocor	6.1	1.0
Zyprexa	4.8	1.0
Norvasc	4.5	1.0
Erypo	4.0	1.0
Ogastro/Prevacid	4.0	1.0
Nexium	3.8	1.0
Plavix	3.7	1.0
Seretide	3.7	1.0
Zoloft	3.4	1.0

Source: "Leading Therapy Classes by Global Pharmaceutical Sales." [online] from http://www.imshealth.com
[accessed April 15, 2004], from IMS *World Review 2004*.

★ 1109 ★
Drugs
SIC: 2834; NAICS: 325412

Top Generic Drug Firms, 2003

*Shares are shown based on generic prescriptions
dispensed. According to market research firm
Datamonitor "more than 30 of the nation's 37 largest drugs are up for patent expiration by 2008, representing total sales of more than $60 billion.*

Teva	13.9%
Mylan	13.0
Watson	9.6
Sandoz	8.8
Alpharma	4.8
Ivax	4.8
Mallinckrodt	4.3
Qualitest	4.0
Par	3.7
Other	32.1

Source: *Drug Store News*, February 16, 2004, p. 43, from
IMS Health.

★ 1110 ★
Drugs
SIC: 2834; NAICS: 325412

Top HIV Drug Producers

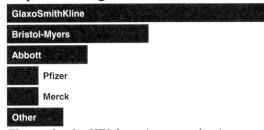

*The market for HIV drugs is expected to increase this
year by about 13% with year-to-year growth of 7%
over the rest of the decade. There are several reasons
for this. The HIV virus continues to mutate rapidly
and is becoming resistant to older drugs. Also, patents are set to expire on many of these drugs (AZT,
one of the biggest, expires in 2005) allowing for
cheap knockoffs.*

GlaxoSmithKline	45.0%
Bristol-Myers	23.0
Abbott	13.0
Pfizer	5.0
Merck	5.0
Other	9.0

Source: *Wall Street Journal*, September 22, 2003, p. B3,
from IMS Health, Evaluate Pharma, and Defined Health.

★ 1111 ★
Drugs
SIC: 2834; NAICS: 325412

Top Hospital Drugs, 2002

*Products are ranked by wholesale acquistion cost
dollars in millions of dollars.*

Procrit	$ 929.64
Lovenox	739.41
Epogen	733.00
Rocephin	574.07
Levaquin	516.10
Zofran	510.94
Neupogen	461.17
Zocor	452.11
Remicade	452.03
Rituxan	390.59

Source: *Drug Topics*, April 7, 2003, p. 29, from
NDCHealth.

★ 1112 ★
Drugs
SIC: 2834; NAICS: 325412

Top Prescription Drugs, 2003

The top classes are ranked by sales in billions of dollars. Sales include prescription products only at wholesale prices.

	($ bil.)	Share
Lipitor	$ 6.8	3.14%
Zocor	4.4	2.03
Prevacid	4.0	1.85
Procrit	3.3	1.52
Zyprexa	3.2	1.48
Nexium	3.1	1.43
Epogen	3.1	1.43
Zoloft	2.9	1.34
Celebrex	2.6	1.20
Neurontin	2.4	1.11
Other	180.7	83.46

Source: *Business Wire*, February 17, 2004, p. NA, from IMS National Sales Perspective.

★ 1113 ★
Drugs
SIC: 2834; NAICS: 325412

Top Therapeutic Classes, 2003

The top 10 classes had sales of $76.5 billion. Sales include prescription products only at wholesale prices.

	($ bil.)	Share
Cholesterol reducers	$ 13.9	6.42%
Proton pump inhibitors (anti-ulcerants)	12.9	5.96
SSRI/SNRI (antidepressants)	10.9	5.04
Antipsychotics	8.1	3.74
Erythropoietins (anemia)	7.4	3.42
Seizure disorders	6.9	3.19
COX-2 inhibitors (anti-arthritics)	5.3	2.45
Calcium blockers	4.4	2.03
Antihistamines	3.5	1.62
Codeine & combinations	3.2	1.48
Other	139.9	64.65

Source: *Business Wire*, February 17, 2004, p. NA, from IMS National Sales Perspective.

★ 1114 ★
Drugs
SIC: 2834; NAICS: 325412

World Sales of Over-The-Counter Healthcare Products, 2000 and 2005

Total sales are forecasted to increase from $82.3 billion in 2000 and $95.9 billion in 2005.

	2000	2005	Share
North America	$ 28.7	$ 30.8	32.12%
Asia-Pacific	26.1	32.1	33.47
Western Europe	17.2	19.8	20.65
Latin America	5.1	6.2	6.47
Eastern Europe	2.3	3.4	3.55
Other	2.9	3.6	3.75

Source: *Brand Strategy*, January 2002, p. 22, from Euromonitor.

★ 1115 ★
Smoking Cessation Products
SIC: 2834; NAICS: 325412

Top Smoking Cessation Products (Gum), 2004

Brands are ranked by sales at supermarkets, drug stores and discount stores (but not Wal-Mart) for the year ended January 25, 2004.

	($ mil.)	Share
Nicorette	$ 187.100	68.56%
Rugby	0.300	0.11
Cigarest	0.007	0.00
Private label	85.500	31.33

Source: *MMR*, April 19, 2004, p. 59, from Information Resources Inc.

★ 1116 ★
Smoking Cessation Products
SIC: 2834; NAICS: 325412

Top Smoking Cessation Products (Patch), 2004

Brands are ranked by sales at supermarkets, drug stores and discount stores (but not Wal-Mart) for the year ended January 25, 2004.

	($ mil.)	Share
Nicoderm CQ'	$ 87.64	62.88%
Nicotrol (Pharmacia)	6.70	4.81
Nicotrol (McNeil Consumer Products)	0.04	0.03
Private label	45.00	32.29

Source: *MMR*, April 19, 2004, p. 59, from Information Resources Inc.

★ 1117 ★
Smoking Cessation Products
SIC: 2834; NAICS: 325412

Top Smoking Cessation Products (Tablet), 2004

Brands are ranked by sales at supermarkets, drug stores and discount stores (but not Wal-Mart) for the year ended January 25, 2004.

	($ mil.)	Share
Commit	$ 42.80	81.00%
Smoke Away	10.00	18.93
Natra Bio Stop It Smoking	0.02	0.04
Natra Bio Smoking Withdrawal Relief	0.02	0.04

Source: *MMR*, April 19, 2004, p. 59, from Information Resources Inc.

★ 1118 ★
Weight Control Products
SIC: 2834; NAICS: 325411

Top Weight Control Candy/Tablet Brands, 2004

Market shares are shown based on sales at drug stores, supermarkets and discount stores (but not Wal-Mart) for the year ended February 22, 2004.

Metabolife 356	7.88%
Stacker 2	7.86
Hydroxycut	7.31%
Dexatrim Natural	6.70
Xenadrine EFX	4.91
TrimSpa	3.89
Mega-T	3.61
Metabolife Ultra	3.44
Metabolife	2.19
Zantrex 3	2.16
Other	50.05

Source: *Chain Drug Review*, April 12, 2004, p. 43, from Information Resources Inc.

★ 1119 ★
Biological Substances
SIC: 2835; NAICS: 325412, 325413

Botulinum Toxin type Market in Brazil

The market is valued at roughly R$100 million. The overall lifestyle and behavioral drug market has been very successful in the country.

Botox	85.0%
Other	15.0

Source: *America's Intelligence Wire*, March 15, 2004, p. NA.

★ 1120 ★
Blood Testing
SIC: 2835; NAICS: 325413

Blood Testing Market

Market shares are shown in percent.

Gen-Probe Inc.	75.0%
Roche	25.0

Source: *Investor's Business Daily*, September 15, 2003, p. A9.

★ 1121 ★
Diagnostics
SIC: 2835; NAICS: 325413
IVD Product Industry in Spain

The $522 invitro diagnostics industry is shown by segment. The market has developed because of an aging population, free access to analysts and medical practice requirements for a precise diagnosis.

Clinical chemistry systems	29.0%
Immuno-chemistry systems	25.0
Infectious-immunology systems	21.0
Hematology systems	13.5
Microbiology culture	11.5

Source: "In Vitro Clinical Diagnostic Reagents." [online] from http://www.usatrade.gov [accessed February 1, 2004].

★ 1122 ★
Diagnostics
SIC: 2835; NAICS: 325413
Largest IVD Markets Worldwide

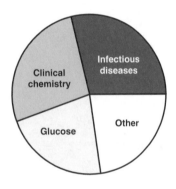

The global invitro diagnostics market was estimated at 19.5 billion euros.

	(mil.)	Share
Infectious diseases	5,627	28.86%
Clinical chemistry	5,271	27.03
Glucose	4,209	21.58
Other	4,393	22.53

Source: *Medical Device Technology*, November 2003, p. 10, from Research and Markets.

★ 1123 ★
Diagnostics
SIC: 2835; NAICS: 325413
Mad Cow Testing Worldwide

BSE testing (Bovine spongiform encephalopathy, also known as Mad Cow disease) is used to test cattle for the disease. The company has more than half of the market.

Prionics AG	50.0%
Others	50.0

Source: *Europe Intelligence Wre*, December 31, 2003, p. NA.

★ 1124 ★
Pregnancy Test Kits
SIC: 2835; NAICS: 325413
Leading Ovulation Prediction Kits, 2003

Brands are ranked by supermarket, drug store and discount store sales (not Wal-Mart) in millions of dollars for the year ended December 28, 2003.

	($ mil.)	Share
Clearplan Easy	$ 20.9	20.9%
First Response	4.1	4.1
Answer Quick & Simple	3.4	3.4
Inverness Medical	1.9	1.9
Private label	6.5	6.5
Other	63.2	63.2

Source: *MMR*, May 3, 2004, p. 32, from Information Resources Inc.

★ 1125 ★
Biotechnology
SIC: 2836; NAICS: 325414

Largest Biotech Firms Worldwide, 2002

Firms are ranked by revenues in millions of dollars.

Amgen	$ 5,500
Genentech	2,700
Biogen Idec	1,500
Genzyme	1,300
Chiron	1,300
MedImmune	850

Source: *Wall Street Journal*, June 24, 2003, p. A3, from companies.

★ 1126 ★
Blood
SIC: 2836; NAICS: 325414

Who Controls the Blood Market

America's Blood Centers

Red Cross

Other

In the summer of 2003 the American Red Cross began giving hospitals the option of buying blood that has not been filtered of white blood cells. The move saves money but, according to critics, may risk patients' lives.

America's Blood Centers	47.0%
Red Cross	45.0
Other	8.0

Source: *Rochester Democrat and Chronicle*, August 25, 2003, p. 1A.

★ 1127 ★
Detergents
SIC: 2841; NAICS: 325611

Global Laundry Detergent Sales, 2005 and 2007

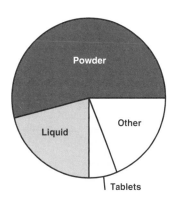

Segments of the world market are ranked by estimated retail sales. Figures are forecasted.

	2005	2007	Share
Powder	$ 17,427.9	$ 18,029.1	54.42%
Liquid	6,472.4	6,948.7	20.97
Tablets	1,874.2	2,019.0	6.09
Other	5,895.8	6,131.9	18.51

Source: *Household & Personal Products Industry*, January 2004, p. 78, from Euromonitor.

★ 1128 ★
Detergents
SIC: 2841; NAICS: 325611

Industrial Cleaning Products

Ecolab

Johnson Diversey

Other

Market shares are shown in percent.

Ecolab	17.0%
Johnson Diversey	14.0
Other	69.0

Source: *Knight Ridder/Tribune Business News*, April 13, 2003, p. NA.

★ 1129 ★
Detergents
SIC: 2841; NAICS: 325611

Leading Laundry Detergent Makers in China

Market shares are shown in percent.

Procter & Gamble 20.1%
Nice Group 17.4
Shanghai Whitecat Group 12.1
Hefei Unilever Detergent Co. 10.6
Xuzhou Henkel Detergent Co. 8.7
Other 11.1

Source: *Chinese Markets for Laundry Care Products*, January 2003, p. NA.

★ 1130 ★
Detergents
SIC: 2841; NAICS: 325611

Top Detergent Firms in Japan

Market shares are shown in percent.

Kao 32.4%
Procter & Gamble 31.9
Lion 26.4
Other 9.3

Source: *Cosmetics & Toiletries Household Products Marketing News in Japan*, November 25, 2003, p. NA, from Japan Soap and Detergent Association.

★ 1131 ★
Detergents
SIC: 2841; NAICS: 325611

Top Detergent Makers Worldwide, 2001

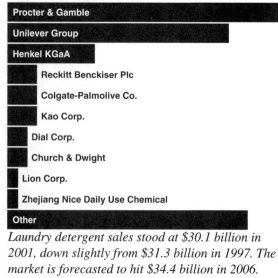

Procter & Gamble
Unilever Group
Henkel KGaA
Reckitt Benckiser Plc
Colgate-Palmolive Co.
Kao Corp.
Dial Corp.
Church & Dwight
Lion Corp.
Zhejiang Nice Daily Use Chemical
Other

Laundry detergent sales stood at $30.1 billion in 2001, down slightly from $31.3 billion in 1997. The market is forecasted to hit $34.4 billion in 2006.

Procter & Gamble 28.7%
Unilever Group 23.0
Henkel KGaA 8.8
Reckitt Benckiser Plc 3.2
Colgate-Palmolive Co. 3.1
Kao Corp. 2.7
Dial Corp. 1.7
Church & Dwight 1.5
Lion Corp. 1.3
Zhejiang Nice Daily Use Chemical 1.0
Other 25.0

Source: *Household & Personal Products Industry*, January 2003, p. 77, from Euromonitor.

★ 1132 ★
Detergents
SIC: 2841; NAICS: 325611

Top Laundry Detergent Brands in the U.K., 2001

Market shares are shown in percent.

Persil	28.0%
Ariel	19.0
Own-brand	15.0
Bold	14.0
Daz	9.0
Surf	7.0
Fairy	7.0

Source: *Marketing*, May 1, 2003, p. 15, from Mintel.

★ 1133 ★
Detergents
SIC: 2841; NAICS: 325611

Top Laundry Detergent Makers Worldwide, 2001

Market shares are shown in percent.

Procter & Gamble	28.7%
Unilever	23.0
Henkel	8.8
Reckitt Benckiser	3.2
Colgate-Palmolive	3.1
Kao Corp.	2.7
Dial Corp.	1.7
Church & Dwight	1.5
Lion Corp.	1.0
Other	26.3

Source: *Household and Personal Products Industry*, January 2003, p. 77, from Euromonitor.

★ 1134 ★
Detergents
SIC: 2841; NAICS: 325611

Top Liquid Laundry Detergent Brands, 2003

Brands are ranked by sales in millions of dollars for the year ended November 30, 2003.

	($ mil.)	Share
Tide	$ 974.22	37.3%
Purex	270.81	10.4
All	248.35	9.5
Wisk	151.62	5.8
Gain	145.65	5.6
XTRA	139.37	5.3
Arm & Hammer	133.52	5.1
Cheer Liquid	123.63	4.7
Era	100.17	3.8
All Surf	41.37	1.6
Dynamo	39.29	1.5
Dreft	35.85	1.4

Source: *Chemical Market Reporter*, January 26, 2004, p. 265, from Information Resources Inc.

★ 1135 ★
Detergents
SIC: 2841; NAICS: 325611

Top Powdered Laundry Detergent Brands, 2003

Brands are ranked by sales in millions of dollars for the year ended November 30, 2003. Consumers are moving from powder for liquid laundry detergents. Sales reflect this: powdered detergents had sales of $980 million compared to $2.6 billion in sales for liquid detergents.

	($ mil.)	Share
Tide	$ 456.0	46.53%
Gain	134.3	13.70
Cheer	68.8	7.02
Arm & Hammer	67.0	6.84
Surf	49.0	5.00
Purex	21.6	2.20
Sun	18.7	1.91
All	17.7	1.81
Ariel	17.5	1.79
Private label	28.1	2.87
Other	101.3	10.34

Source: *Household & Personal Products Industry*, January 2004, p. 68, from Information Resources Inc.

★ 1136 ★
Dishwashing Detergents
SIC: 2841; NAICS: 325611

Leading Dishwashing Detergent Brands in Spain

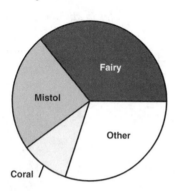

The washing-up liquid market was valued at 165 million euros in 2001. In terms of channel, 42% were sold at supermarkets and 26% were sold at hypermarkets.

Fairy	36.0%
Mistol	24.3
Coral	9.7
Other	30.0

Source: *Expansion*, July 9, 2002, p. 13, from AC Nielsen.

★ 1137 ★
Dishwashing Detergents
SIC: 2841; NAICS: 325611

Top Dishwashing Detergent Brands, 2003

Dawn

Palmolive

Joy

Other

Market shares are shown for the 52 weeks ended June 15, 2003.

Dawn	35.0%
Palmolive	28.0
Joy	11.2
Other	25.8

Source: *New York Times*, July 17, 2003, p. C7, from Information Resources Inc.

★ 1138 ★
Dishwashing Detergents
SIC: 2841; NAICS: 325611

Top Kitchen-Use Detergent Firms in Japan, 2002

Market shares are shown as percentages based on domestic sales of 47.52 billion yen. Total may not add to 100 due to rounding.

Kao	32.4%
P&G	31.9
Lion	26.4

Source: "Market Share Survey Report 2002." [online] from http://www.nni.nikkei.co.jp [accessed January 20, 2004], from Nikkei estimate and Japan Soap and Detergent Association.

★ 1139 ★
Laundry Aids
SIC: 2841; NAICS: 325611

Fabric Softener Market in France, 2001

The value of each sector of the market is shown in millions of euros.

	(mil.)	Share
Liquid softeners	76	36.36%
Pre-measured doses	59	28.23
Ultra	42	20.10
Eco-refill	14	6.70
Tumble-drier sheets	11	5.26
Easy iron products	7	3.35

Source: *LSA Libre Service Actualities*, June 19, 2002, p. 72, from Information Resources Inc. Secodop.

★ **1140** ★
Laundry Aids
SIC: 2841; NAICS: 325611

Leading Collar Cleaner Makers in China

Market shares are shown in percent.

Xi'an Kaimi Stock Co. Ltd.	20.8%
Beijing Goldfish Technology	19.1
Shanghai Zhengzhang Industrial Company	14.0
Shanghai Whitecat Group	12.8
Beijing Luowa Science and Technology Enterprise	12.1
Other	21.2

Source: *Chinese Markets for Laundry Care Products*, January 2003, p. NA.

★ **1141** ★
Laundry Aids
SIC: 2841; NAICS: 325611

Top Fabric Softener Sheet Brands, 2003

Brands are ranked by supermarket, drug store and discount store (excluding Wal-Mart) sales for the year ended December 28, 2003.

	($ mil.)	Share
Bounce	$ 144.0	39.97%
Snuggle	41.1	11.41
Downy	34.6	9.60
Bounce Free	22.6	6.27
Arm & Hammer Fresh & Soft	21.9	6.08
Private label	60.2	16.71
Other	35.9	9.96

Source: *MMR*, May 31, 2004, p. 33, from Information Resources Inc.

★ **1142** ★
Laundry Aids
SIC: 2841; NAICS: 325611

Top Pre-Laundry Treatment Brands, 2003

Brands are ranked by supermarket, drug store and discount store (excluding Wal-Mart) sales for the year ended December 28, 2003.

	($ mil.)	Share
Shout	$ 64.9	17.54%
Spray & Wash	50.2	13.57
Oxi Clean	46.1	12.46
Woolite	43.3	11.70
Other	165.5	44.73

Source: *MMR*, May 31, 2004, p. 33, from Information Resources Inc.

★ **1143** ★
Soap
SIC: 2841; NAICS: 325611

Bath and Shower Market, 2003

Sales are shown in millions of euros.

	(mil.)	Share
Bar soap	1,385.0	32.39%
Shower gel/body wash	1,097.4	25.66
Bath additives	1,054.6	24.66
Liquid soap	538.9	12.60
Other	200.6	4.69

Source: *Soap Perfumery & Cosmetics*, February 2004, p. 28, from Euromonitor.

★ 1144 ★
Soap
SIC: 2841; NAICS: 325611

Global Market for Bath and Shower Products, 2002

Shares are based on retail sales value during 2002.

Unilever Group	20.3%
Colgate-Palmolive	9.4
Procter & Gamble	7.3
Sara Lee	2.8
Henkel	2.7
Johnson & Johnson	2.6
Limited Brands	2.5
Dial	2.3
Kao	2.1
Other	48.0

Source: *Soap Perfumery & Cosmetics*, February 2004, p. 28, from Euromonitor.

★ 1145 ★
Soap
SIC: 2841; NAICS: 325611

Leading Liquid Soap Makers Worldwide, 2000

Market shares are shown in percent.

Colgate-Palmolive	15.1%
Unilever	6.9
Dial Corp.	6.6
Kao Corporation	4.8
Reckitt Benckiser	3.3
Procter & Gamble	3.2
Henkel	2.8
Gojo Industries	2.8
Sara Lee Corporation	2.5
Paterson Zochonis	2.3
Other	49.7

Source: *Chemical Market Reporter*, January 31, 2002, p. FR6, from Euromonitor.

★ 1146 ★
Soap
SIC: 2841; NAICS: 325611

Leading Soap Brands in Drug Stores

Brands are ranked by drug store sales in millions of dollars for the 52 weeks ended December 29, 2002.

	($ mil.)	Share
Dove (non-deodorant soap)	$ 30.4	7.95%
Dove (liquid soap)	11.5	3.01
Irish Spring (deodorant soap)	9.9	2.59
Olay Complete (liquid soap)	9.9	2.59
Lever 2000 (deodorant soap)	9.8	2.56
Clairol Herbal Essences (liquid soap)	9.6	2.51
Caress (liquid soap)	8.3	2.17
Dial (deodorant soap)	6.9	1.81
St. Ives Swiss Formula (liquid soap)	6.8	1.78
Caress (non-deodorant soap)	6.3	1.65
Other	272.8	71.38

Source: *Drug Store News*, May 19, 2003, p. 60, from Information Resources Inc.

★ 1147 ★
Soap
SIC: 2841; NAICS: 325611
Soap Market in Germany, 2003

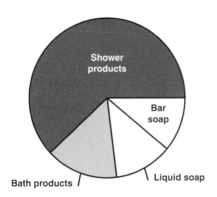

Sales are shown in millions of euros.

	(mil.)	Share
Shower products	416.0	62.37%
Bath products	99.1	14.86
Liquid soap	77.5	11.62
Bar soap	74.4	11.15

Source: *European Cosmetic Markets*, January 2003, p. 9, from industry estimates.

★ 1148 ★
Soap
SIC: 2841; NAICS: 325611
Top Baby Soap Makers

Market shares are shown in percent. They do not include Wal-Mart sales.

Johnson & Johnson	59.2%
Playtex	16.4
Gerber	15.2
Del Labs	0.7
Coty Baby	0.6
Avent America	0.3
Lander	0.2
Chattem	0.2
Yardley of London	0.1
Private label	6.7
Other	0.4

Source: *Household & Personal Products Indsutry*, August 2003, p. 49, from Information Resources Inc.

★ 1149 ★
Soap
SIC: 2841; NAICS: 325611
Top Bar Soap Brands (Deodorant)

Brands are ranked by sales in millions for the year ended September 7, 2003.

Lever 2000	$ 77.6
Irish Spring	55.6
Dial	55.1
Zest	35.5
Coast	26.0
Irish Spring Aloe	20.4
Safeguard	18.3
Dial Spring Water	15.4
Zest Whitewater Fresh	12.0
Dial Mountain Fresh	11.8

Source: *Household & Personal Products Industry*, November 2003, p. 80, from Information Resources Inc.

★ 1150 ★
Soap
SIC: 2841; NAICS: 325611
Top Bar Soaps (Nondeodorant), 2004

Brands are ranked by sales at supermarkets, drug stores and discount stores (but not Wal-Mart) for the year ended January 25, 2004.

	($ mil.)	Share
Dove	$ 219.4	45.27%
Caress	50.5	10.42
Ivory	40.4	8.34
Olay	33.7	6.95
Dial	17.3	3.57
Irish Spring	14.3	2.95
Dave Nutrium	12.1	2.50
Jergens	9.2	1.90
Tone Island Mist	7.9	1.63
Tone	7.1	1.46
Other	72.8	15.02

Source: *MMR*, March 22, 2004, p. 31, from Information Resources Inc.

★ 1151 ★

Soap

SIC: 2841; NAICS: 325611

Top Bath Fragrance/Bubble Bath Brands, 2004

Brands are ranked by sales at supermarkets, drug stores and discount stores (but not Wal-Mart) for the year ended January 25, 2004.

	($ mil.)	Share
Mr. Bubbles	$ 7.0	7.24%
Vaseline Intensive Care	6.9	7.14
Village Naturals	5.2	5.38
Calgon	3.9	4.03
Batherapy	3.8	3.93
Coty Healing Garden	3.2	3.31
Lander	2.9	3.00
Alpha Keri	2.2	2.28
Sesame Street	2.0	2.07
Village Naturals Spa	2.0	2.07
Private label	19.5	20.17
Other	38.1	39.40

Source: *MMR*, April 19, 2004, p. 59, from Information Resources Inc.

★ 1152 ★

Soap

SIC: 2841; NAICS: 325611

Top Bath Product Brands in Italy, 2003

Felce Azzurra
Neutro Roberts
Nivea Bagno
Dove Bagno
Venus Bagno
Malizia Bagno
Palmolive Bagno
Borotalco Bagno
Other

Market shares are shown for the 12 months ended September - October 2002. The country saw the lowest penetration in shower products among the top 5 European countries (54.2% compared to the big 5 average of 69.5%) and the highest weighted penetration of bath products (39.6% compared to the big 5 average of 22%).

Felce Azzurra	9.9%
Neutro Roberts	8.7
Nivea Bagno	6.0

Dove Bagno	5.4%
Venus Bagno	4.2
Malizia Bagno	4.1
Palmolive Bagno	4.0
Borotalco Bagno	3.6
Other	54.1

Source: *European Cosmetic Markets*, January 2003, p. 9, from industry estimates.

★ 1153 ★

Soap

SIC: 2841; NAICS: 325611

Top Bath Product Brands in Spain, 2002

Market shares are shown based on sales of 74.5 million units for the 12 months ended January - February 2002.

Sanex	12.5%
Dermo	6.6
Lactovit	5.9
Hidro Genesse	5.2
Natural Honey	4.2
Neutro Balance	4.0
Avena Kinesia	3.7
Fa	3.1
La Toja Hidrotermal	3.0
Other	51.8

Source: *European Cosmetic Markets*, January 2003, p. 9, from industry estimates.

★ 1154 ★

Soap

SIC: 2841; NAICS: 325611

Top Bath Product Brands in Western Europe, 2001

Market shares are shown in percent.

Dove	7.4%
Palmolive	5.7
Nivea Bath Care	5.2
Fa	3.6
Sanex	2.4
Imperial Leather	2.4
Radox	2.2

Continued on next page.

★ 1154 ★

[Continued]
Soap
SIC: 2841; NAICS: 325611

Top Bath Product Brands in Western Europe, 2001

Market shares are shown in percent.

Lux	2.2%
Badedas	1.8
Neutro Roberts	1.5
Private label	10.5
Other	55.1

Source: *Soap Perfumery & Cosmetics*, February 2003, p. 21, from Euromonitor.

★ 1155 ★

Soap
SIC: 2841; NAICS: 325611

Top Bath Product Makers in Asia, 2002

Market shares are shown in percent.

L'Oreal Groupe	9.3%
Unilever Group	8.5
Procter & Gamble Co.	8.1
Colgate-Palmolive	4.4
Gillette Co.	3.9
Estee Lauder Co.	3.7
Beiersdorf	2.9
Avon Products Inc.	2.8
Shiseido Co.	2.7
Johnson & Johnson	2.2
Other	51.5

Source: *Global Cosmetic Industry*, December 2003, p. 43, from Euromonitor.

★ 1156 ★

Soap
SIC: 2841; NAICS: 325611

Top Hand Sanitizers, 2004

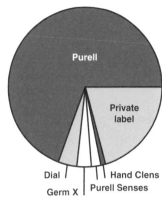

Brands are ranked by sales at supermarkets, drug stores and discount stores (but not Wal-Mart) for the year ended January 25, 2004.

	($ mil.)	Share
Purell	$ 24.9	69.55%
Dial	1.6	4.47
Germ X	0.9	2.51
Purell Senses	0.7	1.96
Hand Clens	0.3	0.84
Private label	7.4	20.67

Source: *MMR*, April 19, 2004, p. 59, from Information Resources Inc.

★ 1157 ★

Cleaning Products
SIC: 2842; NAICS: 325612

Cleaning Products Market in the U.K., 2002

Shares are for the 52 weeks ended July 21, 2002.

Flash	23.2%
Cif	14.6
Mr. Muscle	10.0
Detox	7.9
Other	44.3

Source: *Marketing Week*, September 26, 2002, p. 32, from Taylor Nelson Sofres Superpanel.

★ 1158 ★

Cleaning Products

SIC: 2842; NAICS: 325612

Household Cleaning Sales, 2003

Sales are shown in thousands of dollars. Data are from food, drug and mass merchandiser sales (excluding Wal-Mart) for the year ended October 4, 2003.

	($ 000)	Share
Liquid cleaners	$ 661,843.4	33.86%
Toilet bowl cleaners	275,581.7	14.10
Bathroom cleaners	223,280.6	11.42
Rug cleaners	157,853.9	8.08
Disinfectants	139,956.4	7.16
Window cleaners	119,480.6	6.11
Abrasives	115,882.3	5.93
Oven cleaners	43,043.3	2.20
Ammonia	18,749.0	0.96
Powdered cleaners	3,844.5	0.20
Other	195,241.3	9.99

Source: *Household & Personal Products Industry*, December 2003, p. 95, from ACNielsen Strategic Planner.

★ 1159 ★

Cleaning Products

SIC: 2842; NAICS: 325612

Leading Household Cleaner Makers Worldwide

Market shares are shown for 2000.

Procter & Gamble	18.1%
Unilever	14.3
Reckitt Benckiser	8.0
S.C. Johnson & Son	5.9
Henkel	5.0%
Colgate-Palmolive	4.3
Clorox	3.0
Kao	2.2
Sara Lee	1.8
Lion	1.6
Other	35.8

Source: *Household & Personal Products Industry*, February 2002, p. 82, from Euromonitor.

★ 1160 ★

Cleaning Products

SIC: 2842; NAICS: 325612

Top Cleaning Product Brands in the U.K., 2003

Brands are ranked by sales in thousands of pounds sterling for the year ended October 4, 2003.

	(000)	Share
Flash (all-purpose cleaners)	£ 37,509	7.23%
Domestos (bleach)	34,929	6.74
Cif (all purpose cleaner)	13,724	2.65
Cif Oxy Gel (all-purpose cleaner)	12,855	2.48
Cif (bathroom cleaner)	12,228	2.36
Flash (bathroom cleaner)	10,650	2.05
Bloo (cistern block)	10,235	1.97
Toilet Duck Active	9,760	1.88
Parozone (bleach)	9,337	1.80
Other	367,220	70.83

Source: *Grocer*, December 13, 2003, p. 66, from Information Resources Inc.

★ 1161 ★

Cleaning Products

SIC: 2842; NAICS: 325612

Top Floor Cleaner/Wax Remover Brands, 2003

Market shares are shown based on sales at supermarkets, drug stores and mass merchandisers (but not Wal-Mart) for the year ended May 18, 2003.

Swiffer WetJet	16.4%
Clorox ReadyMop	14.9
Mop & Glo Triple Action	12.7
Armstrong	11.9

Continued on next page.

★ **1161** ★

[Continued]
Cleaning Products
SIC: 2842; NAICS: 325612

Top Floor Cleaner/Wax Remover Brands, 2003

Market shares are shown based on sales at super-markets, drug stores and mass merchandisers (but not Wal-Mart) for the year ended May 18, 2003.

Future	9.1%
Pledge	6.4
Brite	5.1
Murphy's Oil Soap	5.0
Lysol	3.7
Pine-Sol Spray & Mop	2.5
Other	12.3

Source: *Grocery Headquarters*, August 2003, p. S6, from Information Resources Inc.

★ **1162** ★

Cleaning Products
SIC: 2842; NAICS: 325612

Top Floor Cleaner/Wax Remover Makers, 2003

Market shares are shown based on sales at super-markets, drug stores and mass merchandisers (but not Wal-Mart) for the year ended May 18, 2003.

SC Johnson & Son Inc.	35.6%
Reckitt Benckiser	18.7
Clorox Co.	17.3
Procter & Gamble	16.4
The Murphy-Phoenix Co.	5.0
Other	7.0

Source: *Grocery Headquarters*, August 2003, p. S6, from Information Resources Inc.

★ **1163** ★

Cleaning Products
SIC: 2842; NAICS: 325612

Top Floor Cleaner/Wax Removers, 2003

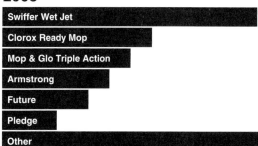

Brands are ranked by supermarket, drug store and discount store (but not Wal-Mart) sales for the year ended December 28, 2003.

	($ mil.)	Share
Swiffer Wet Jet	$ 20.9	23.91%
Clorox Ready Mop	12.4	14.19
Mop & Glo Triple Action	10.2	11.67
Armstrong	9.1	10.41
Future	7.4	8.47
Pledge	4.8	5.49
Other	22.6	25.86

Source: *MMR*, May 31, 2004, p. 33, from Information Resources Inc.

★ **1164** ★

Cleaning Products
SIC: 2842; NAICS: 325612

Top Floor Polish Brands, 2001

Market shares are shown in percent.

Mop & Glo	22.8%
Future	19.8
Step Saver	5.4
Brite	2.8
Private label	5.5
Other	43.7

Source: *Soap & Cosmetics*, January 2003, p. 20, from Euromonitor.

★ 1165 ★
Cleaning Products
SIC: 2842; NAICS: 325612
Top Furniture Polish Brands, 2001

Market shares are shown in percent.

Pledge/Pronto	50.6%
Old English	13.4
Endust	11.4
Scott's Liquid Gold	5.2
Behold	3.4
Private label	2.5
Other	13.5

Source: *Soap & Cosmetics*, January 2003, p. 20, from Euromonitor.

★ 1166 ★
Cleaning Products
SIC: 2842; NAICS: 325612
Top Metal Polish Brands, 2001

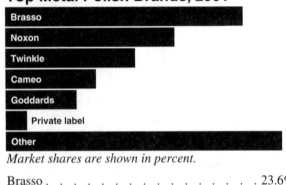

Market shares are shown in percent.

Brasso	23.6%
Noxon	17.1
Twinkle	13.2
Cameo	9.3
Goddards	6.9
Private label	2.0
Other	27.9

Source: *Soap & Cosmetics*, January 2003, p. 20, from Euromonitor.

★ 1167 ★
Cleaning Products
SIC: 2842; NAICS: 325612
Top Shoe Polish/Accessory Brands, 2003

Brands are ranked by supermarket, drug store and discount store (but not Wal-Mart) sales for the year ended December 28, 2003.

	($ mil.)	Share
Kiwi polish	$ 34.9	34.42%
Kiwi laces/accessories	8.5	8.38
Griffin laces/accessories	5.9	5.82
Lynk laces/accessories	4.4	4.34
Kiwi scuff polish	3.8	3.75
Private label	9.0	8.88
Other	34.9	34.42

Source: *MMR*, May 31, 2004, p. 33, from Information Resources Inc.

★ 1168 ★
Starches
SIC: 2842; NAICS: 325612
Leading Starch Makers

Market shares are shown in percent.

Cargill	13.0%
ADM	9.0
CPI	8.0
Cerestar	8.0
Roquette	6.0
Avebe	2.0
Other	54.0

Source: *Chemical Market Reporter*, November 5, 2001, p. 2, from Cerestar.

★ **1169** ★

Baby Care

SIC: 2844; NAICS: 325611, 32562

Baby Care Market, 2003

Market shares are shown in percent.

	($ mil.)	Share
Baby care	$ 641.5	50.00%
Baby skin care	199.3	15.53
Baby toiletries	185.4	14.45
Baby hair care	154.8	12.07
Baby sun care	102.0	7.95

Source: *Soap Perfumery & Cosmetics*, March 2004, p. 18, from Euromonitor.

★ **1170** ★

Baby Care

SIC: 2844; NAICS: 325611, 32562

Baby Care Market in the U.K., 2003

Shares are shown based on sales for the year ended October 12, 2003.

Nappies	36.6%
Toiletries	30.0
Baby food, drinks, and milks	22.8
Baby access	6.0
Healthcare	3.8
Breast/nursing pads	0.5
Sterilants	0.4

Source: *Grocer*, January 17, 2004, p. 41, from TNS Superpanel.

★ **1171** ★

Baby Care

SIC: 2844; NAICS: 325611, 32562

Top Baby Care Brands Worldwide, 2003

Johnson's Baby
Penaten
Nivea Baby
L'Oreal Kids
Nivea Sun
Bubchen
Baby Magic
Pigeon
Nenuco
Other

Market shares are shown for the global market.

Johnson's Baby	31.2%
Penaten	2.1
Nivea Baby	2.0
L'Oreal Kids	1.9
Nivea Sun	1.6
Bubchen	1.6
Baby Magic	1.6
Pigeon	1.2
Nenuco	1.2
Other	56.8

Source: *Soap Perfumery & Cosmetics*, March 2004, p. 18, from Euromonitor.

★ **1172** ★

Baby Care

SIC: 2844; NAICS: 325611, 32562

Top Baby Lotion Brands, 2003

Brands are ranked by sales at supermarkets, drug stores and discount store (but not Wal-Mart) for the year ended November 30, 2003.

	($ mil.)	Share
Johnson's	$ 16.8	37.25%
Playtex Baby Magic	8.0	17.74
Aveeno	6.0	13.30
Johnson & Bedtime Lotion	5.3	11.75
Gerber	2.4	5.32
Gerber Skin Nutrients	1.7	3.77

Continued on next page.

★ 1172 ★
[Continued]
Baby Care
SIC: 2844; NAICS: 325611, 32562

Top Baby Lotion Brands, 2003

Brands are ranked by sales at supermarkets, drug stores and discount store (but not Wal-Mart) for the year ended November 30, 2003.

	($ mil.)	Share
Johnson's Soft Lotion	$ 0.6	1.33%
Gerber Teeny Faces	0.6	1.33
Lander	0.5	1.11
Burt's Bees	0.3	0.67
Other	2.9	6.43

Source: *MMR*, January 26, 2004, p. 19, from Information Resources Inc.

★ 1173 ★
Baby Care
SIC: 2844; NAICS: 325611, 32562

Top Baby Needs (Petroleum Jelly), 2004

Brands are ranked by sales at supermarkets, drug stores and discount stores (but not Wal-Mart) for the year ended January 25, 2004.

	($ mil.)	Share
Vaseline	$ 26.9	60.18%
Lander	0.3	0.67
Personal Cue	0.3	0.67
Eboline	0.2	0.45
White Rose	0.1	0.22
Private label	16.6	37.14
Other	0.3	0.67

Source: *MMR*, April 19, 2004, p. 59, from Information Resources Inc.

★ 1174 ★
Baby Care
SIC: 2844; NAICS: 325611, 32562

Top Baby Oil Brands, 2004

Brands are ranked by sales at supermarkets, drug stores and discount stores (but not Wal-Mart) for the year ended January 25, 2004.

	($ mil.)	Share
Johnson's	$ 25.7	66.24%
Playtex Baby Magic	0.9	2.32

	($ mil.)	Share
Lander	$ 0.8	2.06%
Personal Care	0.3	0.77
Burt's Bees	0.1	0.26
Johnson & Johnson	0.1	0.26
Private label	10.6	27.32
Other	0.3	0.77

Source: *MMR*, April 19, 2004, p. 59, from Information Resources Inc.

★ 1175 ★
Baby Care
SIC: 2844; NAICS: 325611, 32562

Top Baby Ointment Brands, 2004

Brands are ranked by sales at supermarkets, drug stores and discount stores (but not Wal-Mart) for the year ended January 25, 2004.

	($ mil.)	Share
Desitin	$ 29.2	38.57%
A and D	19.9	26.29
Balmex	9.4	12.42
Aveeno	2.8	3.70
Johnson's No More Rash	2.3	3.04
Dr. Smiths	2.2	2.91
Aquaphor Baby	1.7	2.25
Johnson's Baby	1.2	1.59
Triple Paste	1.1	1.45
Boudreax's Butt Paste	0.6	0.79
Private label	2.9	3.83
Other	2.4	3.17

Source: *MMR*, April 19, 2004, p. 59, from Information Resources Inc.

★ 1176 ★
Cosmaceuticals
SIC: 2844; NAICS: 32562

Cosmaceutical Demand, 2002

Cosmaceuticals are cosmetics with active ingredients. It is one of the fastest growing segments in the department store skin care business because these products are more inexpensive and more available than other skin improvement products like Botox.

Skin care	59.4%
Hair care	15.3
Professional	7.2
Other	18.1

Source: *Financial Times*, February 21, 2004, p. 8, from Freedonia Group.

★ 1177 ★
Cosmetics
SIC: 2844; NAICS: 32562

Cosmetics Industry in Canada

The market is valued at $1.1 billion and should grow 3-4% each year to reach $1.7 billion in 2006.

Facial treatments	13.6%
Shampoos/conditioners	12.4
Women's fragrances	8.5
Personal cleaning products	6.9
Hand/body creams, lotions, treatments . . .	5.9
Hair coloring	5.3
Toothpastes	4.8
Hair styling products & sprays	4.8
Deodorants	4.8
Face makeup	4.7
Other	28.3

Source: "Cosmetics and Toiletries." [online] available from http://www.export.gov [accessed December 8, 2003], from Kline & Co.

★ 1178 ★
Cosmetics
SIC: 2844; NAICS: 32562

Cosmetics Market in the U.K.

Sales are shown in millions of British pounds. The average British shopper spent 4.42 British pounds on face make-up in 2002. They are second in spending only to Norway.

	(mil.)	Share
Face	£ 264	32.51%
Eye	240	29.56
Lip	237	29.19
Other	71	8.74

Source: *M2 Presswire*, October 9, 2003, p. NA, from Datamonitor.

★ 1179 ★
Cosmetics
SIC: 2844; NAICS: 32562

Global Makeup Market, 2003 and 2007

Sales are shown in millions of dollars. Face makeup was the leading segment with forecasted sales of $9.5 billion in 2007, followed by lip products at $7.9 billion, eye makeup at $6.7 billion and nail products at $2.5 billion. In that year, North/South America will have 37.5% of the market.

	2003	2005	2007
North/South America . . .	$ 9,483.32	$ 9,768.64	$ 10,024.91
Europe	7,801.52	8,350.97	8,969.72
Asia Pacfic . . .	5,990.43	6,474.11	7,006.52
Other	526.69	603.74	690.35

Source: *Chemical Market Reporter*, December 1, 2003, p. FR3, from Datamonitor.

★ 1180 ★
Cosmetics
SIC: 2844; NAICS: 32562

Largest Cosmetics Firms Worldwide

Companies are ranked by sales in billions of dollars. Unilever, Johnson & Johnson and Wella's figures are estimates.

L'Oreal Group	$ 13.20
Procter & Gamble	9.98
Unilever	6.68

Continued on next page.

★ 1180 ★

[Continued]
Cosmetics
SIC: 2844; NAICS: 32562

Largest Cosmetics Firms Worldwide

Companies are ranked by sales in billions of dollars.
Unilever, Johnson & Johnson and Wella's figures
are estimates.

Shiseido Co.	$ 4.83
Estee Lauder Cos. Inc.	4.70
Avon Products Inc.	3.89
Johnson & Johnson	3.56
Beiersdorf	3.20
Wella	3.11
Alberto-Culver Co.	3.11

Source: *WWD*, December 8, 2003, p. 34S.

★ 1181 ★

Cosmetics
SIC: 2844; NAICS: 32562

Leading Cosmetic Brands in Drug Stores, 2002

Brands are ranked by drug store sales in millions of
dollars for the 52 weeks ended December 29, 2002.
Total sales in drug stores were $894.6 million.

	($ mil.)	Share
Revlon Super Lustrous	$ 30.5	3.52%
Cove Girl Outlast	30.0	3.46
Cover Girl Clean (face)	27.3	3.15
Maybelline Expert Eyes	27.2	3.14
Maybelline Great Lash	22.3	2.57
Maybelline Wet Shine (lip)	20.2	2.33
Max Factor Lipfinity (lip)	19.5	2.25
L'Oreal Endless (lip)	18.7	2.16
Revlon Colorstay (face)	17.2	1.98
L'Oreal Colour Riche (lip)	16.8	1.94
Other	637.7	73.52

Source: *Drug Store News*, May 19, 2003, p. 60, from Information Resources Inc.

★ 1182 ★

Cosmetics
SIC: 2844; NAICS: 32562

Makeup Market Segments

Sales are shown in millions of dollars. In 2007, face
makeup is projected to take 36% of the market.

	2003	2005	2007
Facial makeup	$ 2,751.4	$ 2,796.8	$ 2,825.8
Lip products	2,086.5	2,161.5	2,223.5
Eye makeup	2,085.9	2,151.9	2,209.1
Nail products	666.7	643.0	625.1

Source: *Chemical Market Reporter*, December 1, 2003,
p. FR3, from Datamonitor.

★ 1183 ★

Cosmetics
SIC: 2844; NAICS: 32562

Top Cosmetics Firms in Japan, 2002

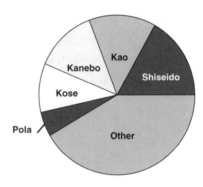

Market shares are shown in percent.

Shiseido	16.7%
Kao	13.7
Kanebo	12.6
Kose	10.1
Pola	4.6
Other	42.3

Source: *Cosmetics & Toiletries Household Products Marketing News in Japan*, November 25, 2003, p. NA, from Ministry of Economy, Trade and Industry.

★ 1184 ★
Cosmetics
SIC: 2844; NAICS: 32562
Top Eye Makeup Brands, 2003

Market shares are shown based on sales at drug stores for the year ended November 2, 2003.

Expert Eyes	6.2%
Great Lash	5.8
Voluminous	3.5
Wear Infinite	3.5
Almay One Coat	3.3
Cover Girl Eye Enhancers	3.1
ColorStay	2.8
Double Extend	2.7
Lash Expansion	2.2
Prestige	2.2
Other	64.7

Source: *Chain Drug Review*, January 19, 2004, p. 14, from Information Resources Inc.

★ 1185 ★
Cosmetics
SIC: 2844; NAICS: 32562
Top Face Makeup Brands, 2003

Market shares are shown based on sales at drug stores for the year ended November 2, 2003.

Cover Girl Clean	5.6%
ColorStay	3.4
Age Defying	3.3
New Complexion	3.2
Visible Lift	2.9
Cover Girl Smoothers	2.9
Neutrogena	2.4
Feel Naturale	2.2
Skinlights	2.1
Healthy Skin	1.9
Other	70.1

Source: *Chain Drug Review*, January 19, 2004, p. 14, from Information Resources Inc.

★ 1186 ★
Cosmetics
SIC: 2844; NAICS: 32562
Top Face Makeup Firms, 2003

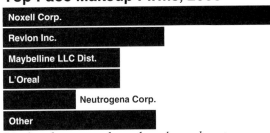

Market shares are shown based on sales at super-markets, drug stores and mass merchandisers for the year ended May 18, 2003. Figures exclude Wal-Mart.

Noxell Corp.	31.3%
Revlon Inc.	18.3
Maybelline LLC Dist.	12.6
L'Oreal	12.5
Neutrogena Corp.	7.7
Other	17.3

Source: *Grocery Headquarters*, August 2003, p. S14, from Information Resources Inc.

★ 1187 ★
Cosmetics
SIC: 2844; NAICS: 32562
Top Lip Makeup Brands, 2003

Market shares are shown based on sales at drug stores for the year ended November 2, 2003.

Cover Girl Outlast	6.8%
Super Lustrous	6.1
Endless	5.0
Max Factor Lipfinity	4.7
Colour Riche	3.7
Lipglide	3.6
ColorStay	3.5
ColorStay Overtime	3.4
Wet Shine	3.1
Moisture Whip	3.1
Other	57.0

Source: *Chain Drug Review*, January 19, 2004, p. 14, from Information Resources Inc.

★ 1188 ★
Cosmetics
SIC: 2844; NAICS: 32562

Top Makeup Removal (Implement) Brands, 2004

Brands are ranked by sales at supermarkets, drug stores and discount stores (but not Wal-Mart) for the year ended January 25, 2004.

	($ mil.)	Share
Almay	$ 10.1	47.42%
Andrea EyeQ's	2.1	9.86
Buf Puf	1.6	7.51
Private label	5.5	25.82
Other	2.0	9.39

Source: *MMR*, April 19, 2004, p. 59, from Information Resources Inc.

★ 1189 ★
Denture Care
SIC: 2844; NAICS: 32562

Top Denture Adhesives

Market shares are shown based on sales at drug stores.

Fixodent	42.9%
Super Poligrip	10.5
Sea-Bond	9.6
Fixodent Free	8.1
Poligrip Free	6.7
Poligrip Ultra Fresh	4.2
Super Wernets	3.6
Cushion Grip	3.4
Fixodent Fresh	2.9
Rigident	1.8
Other	6.3

Source: *Chain Drug Review*, January 5, 2004, p. 52.

★ 1190 ★
Denture Care
SIC: 2844; NAICS: 32562

Top Denture Cleaners (Tablets)

Market shares are shown based on sales at drug stores.

Efferdent	24.9%
Polident	24.4
Efferdent Plus	14.8
Polident Overnight	10.0
Smoker's Polident	4.3
Polident for Partials	1.6
Fixodent	0.7
Other	19.3

Source: *Chain Drug Review*, January 5, 2004, p. 52.

★ 1191 ★
Deodorants
SIC: 2844; NAICS: 32562

Deodorant Market in Germany

The market fell slightly from 537 million euros in 2001 to 523.8 million euros in 2002. Sure/Rexona is the leading brand.

	2001	2002
Spray aerosol	41.7%	44.8%
Spray vaporiser	20.8	20.6
Roll-on	19.2	20.2
Stick	12.7	10.4
Stick cream/gel	2.5	1.5
Tube	2.4	2.0
Wipes	0.4	0.3
Other	0.3	0.3

Source: *European Cosmetic Markets*, July 2003, p. 249, from Information Resources GfK GmbH.

★ 1192 ★
Deodorants
SIC: 2844; NAICS: 32562

Top Deodorant Brands, 2003

Market shares are shown based on sales at drug stores for the year ended November 2, 2003.

Mennen Speed Stick	7.7%
Degree	5.8
Dove	5.5
Right Guard Sport	5.3
Old Spice High Endurance	5.3
Mitchum	4.6
Secret Platinum	4.4
Ban	3.9
Secret	3.8
Secret Sheer Dry	3.4
Other	55.6

Source: *Chain Drug Review*, January 19, 2004, p. 14, from Information Resources Inc.

★ 1193 ★
Deodorants
SIC: 2844; NAICS: 32562

Top Deodorant Brands in Colombia

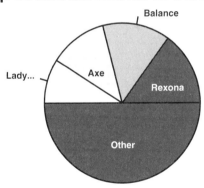

Market shares are shown in percent. By company, Unilever had a 27% share, Gillette 21%, Colgate Palmolive 17% and Prebel 12%.

Rexona	15.0%
Balance	14.0
Axe	12.0
Lady Speed Stick	9.0
Other	50.0

Source: *South American Business Information*, January 27, 2004, p. NA.

★ 1194 ★
Deodorants
SIC: 2844; NAICS: 32562

Top Deodorant Brands in Russia, 2002

Roll-ons are the most popular format in the Russian market. Antiperspirants are also now nearly as popular as deodorants. Market shares are shown in percent.

Fa	17.5%
Rexona	16.4
Nivea Deo	10.5
Lady Speed Stick	10.4
Gillette Series	8.8
Secret	5.9
Other	30.5

Source: *European Cosmetic Markets*, July 2003, p. 249, from ACNielsen.

★ 1195 ★
Deodorants
SIC: 2844; NAICS: 32562

Top Deodorant Brands in Spain, 2002

Market shares are shown in percent. Aerosols have 58%, roll ons 20% and sticks 10.4% of sales.

Axe	11.6%
Sanex	11.5
Rexona	8.0
Nivea	5.8
Dove	5.7
Fa	4.4
Byly	3.5
Williams	3.2
Mum	3.0
Neutro Balance	2.4
Other	40.1

Source: *European Cosmetic Markets*, July 2003, p. 249, from Fragrancias y Cosmetica from ACNielsen data.

★ 1196 ★
Deodorants
SIC: 2844; NAICS: 32562

Top Deodorant Brands in the U.K., 2002

Market shares are shown in percent. Aerosols have 61% of the 252.62 million pounds sterling (based on turnover).

Sure	29.3%
Right Guard	9.2
Dove	9.1
Soft & Gentle	8.7
Own label	5.3
Gillette Series	4.2
Nivea	3.5
Other	30.7

Source: *European Cosmetic Markets*, July 2003, p. 249, from industry estimates.

★ 1197 ★
Deodorants
SIC: 2844; NAICS: 32562

Top Deodorant Makers, 2003

Market shares are shown based on sales at supermarkets, drug stores and mass merchandisers (but not Wal-Mart) for the year ended May 18, 2003.

Procter & Gamble	27.3%
The Gillette Co.	20.0
Mennen Co.	14.6
Helene Curtis Inds. Inc.	9.8
Church & Dwight Co. Inc.	7.9
Other	20.4

Source: *Grocery Headquarters*, August 2003, p. S14, from Information Resources Inc.

★ 1198 ★
Depilatories
SIC: 2844; NAICS: 32562

Top Depilatory Brands, 2004

Brands are ranked by sales at supermarkets, drug stores and discount stores (but not Wal-Mart) for the year ended January 25, 2004.

	($ mil.)	Share
Nair	$ 27.8	24.09%
Sally Hansen	26.0	22.53

	($ mil.)	Share
Nad's	$ 10.7	9.27%
Veet Neat	7.2	6.24
Epil Stop	5.6	4.85
Magic	5.3	4.59
Bikini Zone	4.0	3.47
Nair 3 in 1	3.6	3.12
Hair Off	3.1	2.69
Nair for Men	2.8	2.43
Other	19.3	16.72

Source: *MMR*, April 19, 2004, p. 59, from Information Resources Inc.

★ 1199 ★
Depilatories
SIC: 2844; NAICS: 32562

Women's Hair Removal Market in Spain

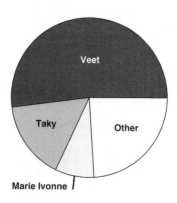

Market shares are shown for waxes. Gillette for Women was the top shaving product with 85.1% of the market.

Veet	51.5%
Taky	16.3
Marie Ivonne	8.0
Other	24.2

Source: *Distribucion Actualidad*, May 2002, p. 60.

★ 1200 ★
Ear Care
SIC: 2844; NAICS: 32562

Top Ear Drop/Treatment Brands, 2004

Brands are ranked by sales at supermarkets, drug stores and discount stores (but not Wal-Mart) for the year ended January 25, 2004.

	($ mil.)	Share
Similasan	$ 8.5	20.63%
Murine Ear	7.7	18.69
Debrox	7.6	18.45
Auro Dri	2.5	6.07
Swim Ear	1.9	4.61
Physicians' Choice	1.5	3.64
Private label	7.1	17.23
Other	4.4	10.68

Source: *MMR*, April 19, 2004, p. 59, from Information Resources Inc.

★ 1201 ★
Eye Care
SIC: 2844; NAICS: 32562

Top Eye Care/Lens Solution Makers, 2003

Market shares are shown based on sales at supermarkets, drug stores and mass merchandisers (but not Wal-Mart) for the year ended May 18, 2003.

Bausch & Lomb Inc.	22.4%
Alcon/Nestle	20.5
Allergan Pharm.	12.9
Pfizer Inc.	9.8
Private label	10.5
Other	23.9

Source: *Grocery Headquarters*, August 2003, p. S14, from Information Resources Inc.

★ 1202 ★
Eye Care
SIC: 2844; NAICS: 32562

Top Eye/Lens Care Brands, 2003

Market shares are shown based on drug store sales.

Renu Multiplus	7.1%
Opti-Free Express	7.0
Renu	3.6
Refresh Tears	3.5
Refresh Plus	2.9
Genteal	2.9
Visine	2.3
Opti-Free	2.1
Clear Eyes	2.1
Visine Advanced Relief	1.9
Private label	11.6
Other	53.0

Source: *Chain Drug Review*, January 5, 2004, p. 45.

★ 1203 ★
Eye Care
SIC: 2844; NAICS: 32562

Top Eye/Lens Care (Tablet/Accessories) Brands, 2003

Market shares are shown based on drug store sales.

Optic Shop	7.1%
Magnivision	5.7
Aosept	4.8
Ultraxyme	4.7
Flents	4.7
Renu	4.5
Ocusoft	4.5
Coverlet	3.9
Ultra Care	3.8
Lami	3.7
Private label	19.4
Other	33.2

Source: *Chain Drug Review*, January 5, 2004, p. 45.

★ 1204 ★

Foot Care

SIC: 2844; NAICS: 32562

Foot Care Market in the U.K., 2003

Sectors are ranked by value in thousands of pounds for the year ended April 2003.

	(000)	Share
Antifungals	£ 423,254	46.60%
Wart/corn/verruca removers	290,893	32.03
Corn plasters	91,901	10.12
Foot shoe deodorants	63,252	6.96
Preventative footcare	35,840	3.95
Foot bath products	1,720	0.19
Foot powder	1,436	0.16

Source: *Community Pharmacy*, July 21, 2003, p. 28, from IMS Health.

★ 1205 ★

Foot Care

SIC: 2844; NAICS: 32562

Foot Care Product Sales

Sales are shown in millions of dollars for the year ended July 12, 2003. Data are for food, drug stores and mass outlets and exclude Wal-Mart (which had foot care product sales of $194.25 million).

	($ mil.)	Share
Foot preparations, athlete's foot	$ 193.19	35.18%
Foot preparations, remaining	173.12	31.53
Insoles	109.71	19.98
Foot comfort products	73.10	13.31

Source: *Retail Merchandiser*, September 2003, p. 28, from ACNielsen Strategic Planner.

★ 1206 ★

Foot Care

SIC: 2844; NAICS: 32562

Top Foot Care Device Brands, 2004

Brands are ranked by sales at supermarkets, drug stores and discount stores (but not Wal-Mart) for the year ended January 25, 2004.

	($ mil.)	Share
Dr. Scholl's	$ 76.9	29.60%
Dr. Scholl's Advantage	17.8	6.85
Dr. Scholl's Tri Comfort	15.1	5.81
Airplus	7.7	2.96

	($ mil.)	Share
Dr. Scholl's Air Pillo	$ 7.1	2.73%
Dr. Scholl's Double Air Pillo	6.5	2.50
Pro Foot Triad	6.2	2.39
Johnson's Odor Eaters	5.9	2.27
Private label	23.8	9.16
Other	92.8	35.72

Source: *MMR*, April 19, 2004, p. 59, from Information Resources Inc.

★ 1207 ★

Foot Care

SIC: 2844; NAICS: 32562

Top Foot Care Medication Brands, 2004

Brands are ranked by sales at supermarkets, drug stores and discount stores (but not Wal-Mart) for the year ended January 25, 2004.

	($ mil.)	Share
Lamisil AT	$ 39.4	15.14%
Lotrimin AF	32.3	12.41
Tinactin	29.6	11.38
Dr. Scholl's	12.4	4.77
Desenex	11.7	4.50
Lotrimin Ultra	11.7	4.50
Gold Bond	8.8	3.38
Other	114.3	43.93

Source: *MMR*, April 19, 2004, p. 59, from Information Resources Inc.

★ 1208 ★

Fragrances

SIC: 2844; NAICS: 32562

Global Fragrance Market, 2003

Latin America was the fastest growing market from 2002 to 2003 (+14%). Eastern Europe was the second fastest growing (+1.6%).

	($ mil.)	Share
Latin America	$ 2,126.4	27.58%
Western Europe	2,033.3	26.37
North America	1,469.0	19.05
Eastern Europe	701.5	9.10
Africa and Middle East	684.3	8.87
Asia Pacific	581.2	7.54
Australasia	115.2	1.49

Source: *Global Cosmetic Industry*, May 2004, p. 40.

★ 1209 ★

Fragrances

SIC: 2844; NAICS: 32562

Prestige Fragrance Market in Canada

Market shares are shown in percent.

	Men	Women
Prestige	59.7%	19.6%
Direct sales	7.5	21.5
Mass	6.3	37.0
Other	26.5	21.9

Source: *Cosmetics Magazine Newsletter*, April 11, 2003, p. NA, from Trendex North America.

★ 1210 ★

Fragrances

SIC: 2844; NAICS: 32562

Top Fragrance Brands in Drug Stores

Brands are ranked by drug store sales in millions of dollars for the 52 weeks ended December 29, 2002. Total sales of fragrances in drug stores was $490.7 million.

	($ mil.)	Share
Elizabeth Taylor's White Diamonds	$ 9.6	1.96%
Old Spice	9.2	1.87
Calgon	8.1	1.65
Drakkar Noir	$ 7.9	1.61%
Coty's Healing Garden	7.8	1.59
Gold Bond	7.3	1.49
Coty Stetson	7.2	1.47
Jean Nate	6.7	1.37
Body Fantasy	6.1	1.24
Davidoff Cool Water	5.6	1.14
Other	415.2	84.61

Source: *Drug Store News*, May 19, 2003, p. 60, from Information Resources Inc.

★ 1211 ★

Fragrances

SIC: 2844; NAICS: 32562

Top Fragrance Brands Worldwide, 2003

Shares are shown for mass market fragrances.

Avon	14.7%
Adidas	2.1
Bath & Body Works	1.6
Ekos	1.3
Axe/Lynx/Ego	1.3
Old Spice	1.2
Yves Rocher	1.0
Charlie	1.0
Brut	1.0
Jafra	0.9
Other	73.9

Source: *Global Cosmetic Industry*, May 2004, p. 40.

★ 1212 ★
Fragrances
SIC: 2844; NAICS: 32562

Top Fragrance Makers in France, 2002

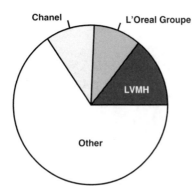

Retail sales were valued at 969.5 million euros.

LVMH	14.2%
L'Oreal Groupe	10.4
Chanel	10.0
Other	65.4

Source: *Soap Perfumery & Cosmetics*, October 2003, p. 22, from Euromonitor.

★ 1213 ★
Fragrances
SIC: 2844; NAICS: 32562

Top Fragrance Makers in Italy, 2002

Retail sales were valued at 393.1 million euros.

Unilever	11.6%
L'Oreal Groupe	11.2
LVMH	6.3
Chanel	6.1
Weruska & Joel	3.8
Other	61.0

Source: *Soap Perfumery & Cosmetics*, October 2003, p. 22, from Euromonitor.

★ 1214 ★
Fragrances
SIC: 2844; NAICS: 32562

Top Fragrance Makers in Spain, 2002

Retail sales were valued at 494.4 million euros.

Antonio Puig	24.9%
L'Oreal Groupe	9.8
Coty Inc.	7.7
LVMH	6.0
Unilever	4.6
Other	47.0

Source: *Soap Perfumery & Cosmetics*, October 2003, p. 22, from Euromonitor.

★ 1215 ★
Fragrances
SIC: 2844; NAICS: 32562

Top Fragrance Makers in Western Europe, 2001

Market shares are shown based on retail value.

LVMH Moet Hennessy Louis	14.8%
L'Oreal Groupe	8.9
Unilever Group	7.9
Coty Inc.	6.3
Estee Lauder Cos. Inc.	5.4
Chanel SA	5.2
Procter & Gamble Co.	4.8
Antonio Puig SA	3.4
Gucci Group	2.7
Other	38.1

Source: *Soap Perfumery & Cosmetics*, October 2002, p. 30, from Euromonitor.

★ 1216 ★

Fragrances

SIC: 2844; NAICS: 32562

Top Fragrances (Men's), 2004

	($ mil.)	Share
Axe		
Old Spice		
Gillette Series		
Coty Stetson		
Brut		
Nivea for Men		
Drakkar Noir		
Davidoff Cool Water		
Old Spice High Endurance		
Coty Adidas Moves		
Other		

Brands are ranked by sales at supermarkets, drug stores and discount stores (but not Wal-Mart) for the year ended January 25, 2004.

	($ mil.)	Share
Axe	$ 50.1	13.28%
Old Spice	18.6	4.93
Gillette Series	12.3	3.26
Coty Stetson	10.8	2.86
Brut	10.6	2.81
Nivea for Men	9.8	2.60
Drakkar Noir	8.8	2.33
Davidoff Cool Water	7.7	2.04
Old Spice High Endurance	7.7	2.04
Coty Adidas Moves	7.3	1.93
Other	233.6	61.91

Source: *MMR*, April 19, 2004, p. 59, from Information Resources Inc.

★ 1217 ★

Fragrances

SIC: 2844; NAICS: 32562

Top Fragrances (Women's), 2004

Brands are ranked by sales at supermarkets, drug stores and discount stores (but not Wal-Mart) for the year ended January 25, 2004.

	($ mil.)	Share
Calgon	$ 15.2	4.42%
Gold Bond	13.7	3.98
Shower to Shower	11.9	3.46

	($ mil.)	Share
Elizabeth Taylor White Diamonds	$ 11.0	3.20%
Body Fantasy	9.1	2.65
Celine Dion	8.8	2.56
Jean Nate	7.1	2.07
Coty Javon Musk for Women	6.3	1.83
Coty Healing Garden	5.9	1.72
Davidoff Cool Water	5.9	1.72
Private label	15.3	4.45
Other	233.6	67.95

Source: *MMR*, April 19, 2004, p. 59, from Information Resources Inc.

★ 1218 ★

Hair Care

SIC: 2844; NAICS: 32562

Global Hair Care Market

In 2002, North America and South America took 45% of the worldwide industry.

	2000	2002	Share
Shampoos & conditioners	$ 16,255.5	$ 17,508.9	40.01%
Colorants	8,419.4	9,501.5	21.71
Styling agents/ hairspray	7,114.6	7,755.0	17.72
Salon	4,514.0	4,860.1	11.11
Perms & relaxants	574.4	696.3	1.59

Source: *Soap Perfumery & Cosmetics*, November 2003, p. 22, from Datamonitor.

★ 1219 ★

Hair Care

SIC: 2844; NAICS: 32562

Leading Ethnic Hair Care Product Makers, 2003

Market shares are shown based on 5.19 million units sold at drug stores, supermarkets and discount stores (but not Wal-Mart) for the year ended March 2, 2003.

J.M. Products	19.3%
Ampro Industries	12.7
Carson Products	11.3
Advanced Research Laboratories	7.0
Bonner Bros.	6.8

Continued on next page.

★ 1219 ★

[Continued]
Hair Care
SIC: 2844; NAICS: 32562

Leading Ethnic Hair Care Product Makers, 2003

Market shares are shown based on 5.19 million units sold at drug stores, supermarkets and discount stores (but not Wal-Mart) for the year ended March 2, 2003.

Luster Products	5.7%
Golden Sun	4.7
Andrew Jergens (John Frieda)	3.7
Alberto-Culver (Pro-Line)	3.4
Other	25.4

Source: *Chain Drug Review*, April 7, 2003, p. 44, from Information Resources Inc.

★ 1220 ★

Hair Care
SIC: 2844; NAICS: 32562

Top African-American Hair Care Categories

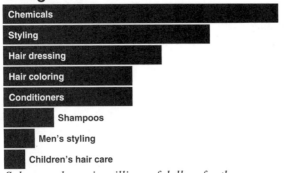

Sales are shown in millions of dollars for the year ended December 28, 2003.

	($ mil.)	Share
Chemicals	$ 44.03	27.61%
Styling	33.58	21.05
Hair dressing	26.15	16.39
Hair coloring	20.45	12.82
Conditioners	19.96	12.51
Shampoos	7.80	4.89
Men's styling	5.10	3.20
Children's hair care	2.43	1.52

Source: *Household & Personal Products Industry*, April 2004, p. 86.

★ 1221 ★

Hair Care
SIC: 2844; NAICS: 32562

Top Conditioner Brands in Spain, 2002

Market shares are shown in percent.

Pantene	20.6%
Elvive	15.5
Flex	11.2
Fructis	9.4
Wella	3.5
Timotei	3.3
Lanofil	3.1
Starpack	3.1
Dove	3.0
Other	30.4

Source: *European Cosmetic Markets*, September 2003, p. 335, from Distribucion Actualidad based on ACNielsen data.

★ 1222 ★

Hair Care
SIC: 2844; NAICS: 32562

Top Conditioner/Cream Rinse Firms, 2003

Market shares are shown based on sales at supermarkets, drug stores and mass merchandisers for the year ended May 18, 2003. Figures exclude Wal-Mart.

Procter & Gamble	20.7%
Helene Curtis Inds. Inc.	17.6
Clairol Inc.	16.1
Alberto Culver Co.	10.5
L'Oreal	5.6
Other	29.5

Source: *Grocery Headquarters*, August 2003, p. S14, from Information Resources Inc.

★ 1223 ★
Hair Care
SIC: 2844; NAICS: 32562

Top Hair Care Brands in Western Europe, 2002

Market shares are shown in percent.

Pantene Pro-V	7.5%
Elseve/Elvive	5.7
Fructis	4.6
Studio Line	3.7
Poly	2.9
Excellence	2.8
Taft/Drei Wetter Taft	2.6
Organics	2.4
Nivea Hair Care	2.2
Belle Color	2.0
Private label	3.6
Other	60.0

Source: *Soap Perfumery & Cosmetics*, November 2003, p. 22, from Euromonitor.

★ 1224 ★
Hair Care
SIC: 2844; NAICS: 32562

Top Hair Care Markets in Asia/ Pacific, 2002

The markets include shampoo, conditioner, hair styling and hair coloring. The hair care market grew 2.8% from 2001 to 2002. Shampoo and conditioners enjoyed good sales through the region with the exception of China, where some companies saw losses due to heavy promotional spending in the competitive market.

Korea	$ 380.0
China	244.5
Philippines	180.3
Taiwan	167.9
Urban Thailand	92.0
Peninsular Malaysia	60.8

Source: *Soap, Perfumery & Cosmetics Asia*, May 2003, p. 9, from Taylor Nelson Sofres.

★ 1225 ★
Hair Care
SIC: 2844; NAICS: 32562

Top Hair Coloring Brands, 2003

Market shares are shown based on sales at drug stores for the year ended November 2, 2003. Figures exclude Wal-Mart.

Preference	11.2%
Excellence	8.7
Feria	7.8
Nice 'n Easy	7.3
Just For Men	6.7
Natural Instincts	5.6
Couleur Experts	4.6
Garnier Nutrisse	4.4
Hydrience	3.4
Colorsilk	3.2
Other	37.1

Source: *Chain Drug Review*, January 19, 2004, p. 19, from Information Resources Inc.

★ 1226 ★

Hair Care

SIC: 2844; NAICS: 32562

Top Hair Coloring Firms, 2003

Market shares are shown based on sales at super-markets, drug stores and mass merchandisers for the year ended May 18, 2003. Figures exclude Wal-Mart.

L'Oreal	$42.9
Clairol Inc.	33.7
Combe Inc.	8.7
Revlon Inc.	7.0
Garnier Inc.	5.5
Other	2.2

Source: *Grocery Headquarters*, August 2003, p. S14, from Information Resources Inc.

★ 1227 ★

Hair Care

SIC: 2844; NAICS: 32562

Top Hair Sprays/Spritzes, 2003

Brands are ranked by supermarket, drug store and discount store sales for the 52 weeks ended September 7, 2003. Figures exclude Wal-Mart.

	($ mil.)	Share
Rave	$30.2	7.70%
Suave	24.1	6.14
Pantene Pro V	19.4	4.95
Clairol Herbal Essences	19.0	4.84
Sebastian Shaper	16.2	4.13
Aquanet	15.9	4.05
Tresemme Tres Two	13.6	3.47
White Rain Classic Care	13.5	3.44
Pantene Classic Care	13.4	3.42
Salon Selectives	12.8	3.26
Other	214.2	54.60

Source: *MMR*, November 3, 2003, p. 32, from Information Resources Inc.

★ 1228 ★

Hair Care

SIC: 2844; NAICS: 32562

Top Hair Styling Brands in France, 2003

The styling market had sales of 392 million euros. Brand shares are shown in percent.

Studio Line	27.0%
Elnett	16.0
Vivelle	15.5
Fructis Style	8.0
Taft	6.0
Jean-Louis David	4.5
Grafic	4.5
Jacques Dessange	4.4
Cadonett	4.4
Timotei	3.5
Other	6.2

Source: *European Cosmetic Markets*, October 2003, p. 368, from Information Resources Inc. - Secodip Infoscan.

★ 1229 ★

Hair Care

SIC: 2844; NAICS: 32562

Top Shampoo Brands (Dandruff) in the UK, 2002

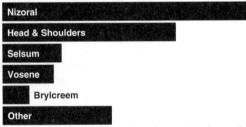

Brands are ranked by sales through independent pharmacies.

	(mil.)	Share
Nizoral	£22,872	39.95%
Head & Shoulders	14,240	24.87
Selsum	4,831	8.44
Vosene	4,179	7.30
Brylcreem	2,173	3.80
Other	8,952	15.64

Source: *Community Pharmacy*, July 21, 2003, p. 36, from IMS Health Pharmatrend.

★ 1230 ★
Hair Care
SIC: 2844; NAICS: 32562

Top Shampoo Brands in France, 2002

The shampoo industry had sales of 760.3 million euros, a rise of 6.7% over the previous year. Indeed, the entire hair care market enjoyed strong growth and sales, up 6.5% to 1.82 billion euros.

Elseve	18.0%
Fructis	11.5
Ultra Doux	8.0
Jacques Dessange	7.5
Head & Shoulders	6.5
Dop	5.0
Timotei	4.0
Dove	4.0
Organics	3.5
Jean-Louis David	3.5
Other	28.5

Source: *European Cosmetic Markets*, September 2003, p. 326, from industry estimates.

★ 1231 ★
Hair Care
SIC: 2844; NAICS: 32562

Top Shampoo Brands in the U.K., 2002

Market shares are shown in percent.

Head & Shoulders	12.3%
Pantene	12.2
Herbal Essences	6.8
Elvive	6.6
Neutrogena	6.1

Dove	4.2%
Fructis	3.6
Organics	3.3
VO5	3.2
Supersoft	0.9
Other	40.8

Source: *European Cosmetic Markets*, September 2003, p. 335, from industry estimates.

★ 1232 ★
Hair Care
SIC: 2844; NAICS: 32562

Top Shampoo Makers in Russia, 2002

The total hair care market was worth $796.7 million. Top shampoo and conditioners and market shares: Schauma with 15.8%, Timotei with 14.4% and Pantene Pro-V with 13.5%. Pantene Pro-V is the leading hair care brand overall.

Procter & Gamble	12.9%
Henkel	11.5
Wella AG	9.1
L'Oreal	9.0
Unilever	7.8
Kalina OAO	4.6
Beiersdorf	3.3
Linda	2.8
Svoboda	2.7
Green Mama	1.1
Other	35.2

Source: *European Cosmetic Markets*, September 2003, p. 343, from Euromonitor.

★ 1233 ★

Hair Care

SIC: 2844; NAICS: 32562

Top Shampoo Makers in the U.K., 2002

Shampoo has 41% of the overall hair care market followed by conditioners with 23.8% of the total. Shares are shown for the year ended August 2002.

P&G	21.3%
L'Oreal/Lab. Garnier	16.0
Wella	9.2
Own label	9.2
Lever Faberge	8.6
Alberto Culver	8.4
Other	27.3

Source: *Marketing Week*, October 17, 2002, p. 32, from Information Resources Inc.

★ 1234 ★

Lip Care

SIC: 2844; NAICS: 32562

Top Lip Balm/Cold Sore Medication Makers, 2003

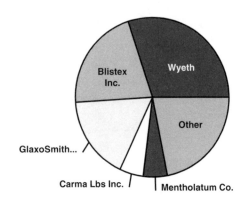

Market shares are shown based on sales at supermarkets, drug stores and mass merchandisers (but not Wal-Mart) for the year ended May 18, 2003.

Wyeth	29.9%
Blistex Inc.	21.3
GlaxoSmithKline	16.7
Carma Lbs Inc.	5.3
Mentholatum Co.	5.2
Other	21.6

Source: *Grocery Headquarters*, August 2003, p. S14, from Information Resources Inc.

★ 1235 ★

Lip Care

SIC: 2844; NAICS: 32562

Top Lip Care Brands

Market shares are shown based on sales at drug stores.

Abreva	22.1%
Chapstick	20.9
Blistex	8.0
Carmex	5.8
Mentholatum Soft Lips	3.0
Herpecin L	2.4
Campho-Phenique	2.4
Blistex OCT	1.8
Blistex Lip Medex	1.8
Kanka	1.5
Other	27.9

Source: *Chain Drug Review*, January 5, 2004, p. 52.

★ 1236 ★

Nail Care

SIC: 2844; NAICS: 32562

Leading Nail Care Brands in Drug Stores

Brands are ranked by drug store sales in millions of dollars for the 52 weeks ended December 29, 2002. Total sales of nail care products were $406.8 million.

	($ mil.)	Share
Kiss (nails)	$ 23.6	5.80%
Revlon (accessories)	19.9	4.89
Nailene (nails)	17.7	4.35
LaCross (accessories)	16.5	4.06
Sally Hansen Hard as Nails (polish/treatments)	14.4	3.54
Revlon (polish/treatment)	12.6	3.10
Broadway nails (nails)	11.7	2.88
Sally Hansen Maximum Growth (polish/treatment)	10.6	2.61
Maybelline Express Finish (polish/treatment)	10.4	2.56
L'Oreal Jet Set (polish/treatment) .	9.0	2.21
Other	260.4	64.01

Source: *Drug Store News*, May 19, 2003, p. 60, from Information Resources Inc.

★ 1237 ★

Nail Care

SIC: 2844; NAICS: 32562

Top Artificial Nail Brands, 2004

Broadway Nails		
Kiss		
Fing'rs		
Nailene		
	Fing'rs California Girl	
	Kiss Custom Ft	
	Kiss 1 Easy Step	
	Nailene Color Express	
	IBD 5 Second	
Other		

Brands are ranked by sales at supermarkets, drug stores and discount stores for the year ended January 28, 2004.

Broadway Nails	19.10%
Kiss	15.67
Fing'rs	7.97
Nailene	6.07
Fing'rs California Girl	5.57
Kiss Custom Ft	3.61
Kiss 1 Easy Step	3.43
Nailene Color Express	3.18
IBD 5 Second	2.84
Other	32.56

Source: *Chain Drug Review*, March 15, 2004, p. 35, from Information Resources Inc.

★ 1238 ★

Nail Care

SIC: 2844; NAICS: 32562

Top Nail Polish Remover Brands, 2004

Brands are ranked by sales at supermarkets, drug stores and discount stores (but not Wal-Mart) for the year ended January 25, 2004.

	($ mil.)	Share
Cutex Quick & Gentle	$ 10.1	18.67%
Cutex Essential Care	4.2	7.76
Pretty Nails	3.1	5.73
Sally Hansen	2.2	4.07
Cutex	1.4	2.59
Revlon	1.3	2.40

	($ mil.)	Share
Onyx Professional	$ 1.2	2.22%
Sally Hansen Kwik Off	1.2	2.22
Calico	0.8	1.48
Sally Hansen Pro Vitamin	0.3	0.55
Other	28.3	52.31

Source: *MMR*, April 19, 2004, p. 59, from Information Resources Inc.

★ 1239 ★

Nail Care

SIC: 2844; NAICS: 32562

Top Nail Polish/Treatment Brands

Brands are ranked by sales at supermarkets, drug stores and discount stores for the year ended January 28, 2004.

Sally Hansen Hard as Nails	7.50%
Revlon	6.40
Sally Hansen Maximum Growth	5.20
Maybelline Express Finish	4.06
Sally Hansen Teflon Tuff	3.16
Maybelline Wet Shine	2.73
Cover Girl Nail Slicks	2.70
Sally Hansen	2.68
L'Oreal Jet Set Shine	2.67
Wet 'n' Wild	2.61
Other	60.29

Source: *Chain Drug Review*, March 15, 2004, p. 35, from Information Resources Inc.

★ 1240 ★
Nasal Care
SIC: 2844; NAICS: 32562

Top Nasal Aspirator Brands, 2004

Brands are ranked by sales at supermarkets, drug stores and discount stores (but not Wal-Mart) for the year ended January 25, 2004.

	($ mil.)	Share
First Years	$ 1.2	37.50%
Safety 1st	0.7	21.88
Gerber	0.5	15.63
Little Noses	0.2	6.25
Ross	0.1	3.13
Private label	0.3	9.38
Other	0.2	6.25

Source: *MMR*, April 19, 2004, p. 59, from Information Resources Inc.

★ 1241 ★
Nasal Care
SIC: 2844; NAICS: 32562

Top Nasal Sprays/Drops/Inhaler Brands, 2004

Brands are ranked by sales at supermarkets, drug stores and discount stores (but not Wal-Mart) for the year ended January 25, 2004.

	($ mil.)	Share
Zicam	$ 44.1	12.94%
Primatene Mist	41.8	12.26
Afrin	39.7	11.65
Afrin No Drip	20.4	5.98
Vicks Sinex	20.4	5.98
4 Way	15.8	4.63
Nasalcrom	13.3	3.90
Vicks	11.1	3.26

	($ mil.)	Share
Breath Right	$ 10.5	3.08%
Neo Synephrine	10.3	3.02
Private label	56.9	16.69
Other	56.6	16.60

Source: *MMR*, April 19, 2004, p. 59, from Information Resources Inc.

★ 1242 ★
Nasal Care
SIC: 2844; NAICS: 32562

Top Nasal Strip Brands, 2004

Brands are ranked by sales at supermarkets, drug stores and discount stores (but not Wal-Mart) for the year ended January 25, 2004.

	($ mil.)	Share
Breathe Right	$ 44.00	92.83%
Clear Passage	0.10	0.21
Snore Fix	0.03	0.06
Breathe Right Near Clear	0.01	0.02
Maxair	0.01	0.02
Private label	3.20	6.75
Other	0.05	0.11

Source: *MMR*, April 19, 2004, p. 59, from Information Resources Inc.

★ 1243 ★
Oral Care
SIC: 2844; NAICS: 32562

Leading Oral Care Makers in Western Europe

Market shares are shown in percent.

Colgate-Palmolive	23.0%
GlaxoSmithKline	21.0
Unilever	15.0
Henkel	8.0
Procter & Gamble	7.0
Private label	4.0
Other	22.0

Source: *Chemical Market Reporter*, May 10, 2004, p. FR10, from JPMorgan.

★ 1244 ★
Oral Care
SIC: 2844; NAICS: 32562

Leading Oral Care Makers Worldwide

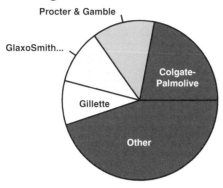

Market shares are shown in percent.

Colgate-Palmolive 22.0%
Procter & Gamble 13.0
GlaxoSmithKline 11.0
Gillette 9.0
Other 45.0

Source: *Chemical Market Reporter*, May 10, 2004,
p. FR10, from JPMorgan.

★ 1245 ★
Oral Care
SIC: 2844; NAICS: 32562

Leading Whitening Product Makers

| Procter & Gamble |
| Colgate |
| Other |

Market shares are shown in percent.

Procter & Gamble 59.0%
Colgate 29.0
Other 12.0

Source: *Chemical Market Reporter*, May 10, 2004,
p. FR10, from JPMorgan.

★ 1246 ★
Oral Care
SIC: 2844; NAICS: 32562

Top Bleaching/Whitening Brands, 2003

*Shares are shown based on drug store sales only for
the year ended March 2003.*

Crest Whitestrips 21.2%
Colgate Simply White 8.0
Rembrandt Dazzling White 2.9
Rembrandt Plus 1.6
Plus White Ultra 1.3
Plus White 1.3
Natural White Pro 1.2
Mentadent 1.1
Dr. Georges Dental White 1.0
Biodent Oral Care Optiwhite 1.0
Other 59.4

Source: *Chemical Market Reporter*, May 12, 2003, p. 14,
from Information Resources Inc.

★ 1247 ★
Oral Care
SIC: 2844; NAICS: 32562

Top Dental Floss Brands, 2004

*Brands are ranked by sales at supermarkets, drug
stores and discount stores (but not Wal-Mart) for the
year ended January 25, 2004.*

	($ mil.)	Share
Reach	$ 24.8	20.08%
Glide	24.5	19.84
Reach Easy Slide	8.0	6.48
Reach Dentotape	6.4	5.18
Reach Gentle Gum Care	5.5	4.45
Oral B Satinfloss	5.4	4.37
Glide Comfort Plus	4.2	3.40
J&J Reach Whitening	4.1	3.32
Oral B Essential Floss	3.5	2.83
Oral B Satintape	3.4	2.75
Private label	23.4	18.95
Other	10.3	8.34

Source: *MMR*, April 19, 2004, p. 59, from Information Resources Inc.

★ 1248 ★
Oral Care
SIC: 2844; NAICS: 32562
Top Dental Rinse Makers, 2003

Market shares are shown based on sales at super-markets, drug stores and mass merchandisers for the year ended May 18, 2003.

Pfizer Inc. 52.2%
Procter & Gamble 15.1
Johnson & Johnson 5.2
Laclede Prof. Prods. 1.6

Source: *Grocery Headquarters*, August 2003, p. S14, from Information Resources Inc.

★ 1249 ★
Oral Care
SIC: 2844; NAICS: 32562
Top Oral Care Products

Market shares are shown in percent.

Listerine Pocketpaks 39.4%
Trident White Chewing Gum 22.8
Wrigley's Eclipse Flash Strips 11.1
Orbit White Chewing Gum 5.5
Altoids Strips 4.6
Arm & Hammer Dental Care Chewing Gum . . 3.6
Arm & Hammer Advance Whitening Gum . . 1.7
Wrigley's Winterfresh Thin Ice Breath 1.3
Other 10.0

Source: *Candy Industry*, October 2003, p. 42, from Information Resources Inc.

★ 1250 ★
Oral Care
SIC: 2844; NAICS: 32562
Top Portable Oral Care Products, 2003

Market shares are shown based on food store sales for the year ended August 10, 2003.

Trident White 29.6%
Listerine Pocketpaks 28.5
Wrigley's Eclipse Flash Strips 14.0
Altoids 6.7

Orbit White 6.1%
Arm & Hammer Dental Care 4.3
Wrigley's Winterfresh Thin Ice 2.7
Arm & Hammer Advance White 2.4
Other 5.7

Source: *Progressive Grocer*, October 1, 2003, p. 74, from Information Resources Inc.

★ 1251 ★
Oral Care
SIC: 2844; NAICS: 32562
Top Toothpaste Firms in Japan, 2002

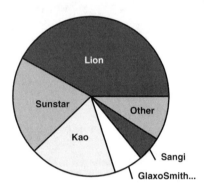

Market shares are shown based on domestic sales of 64.5 billion yen.

Lion 42.3%
Sunstar 20.1
Kao 18.0
GlaxoSmithKline 6.2
Sangi 4.8
Other 8.6

Source: "Market Share Survey Report 2002." [online] from http://www.nni.nikkei.co.jp [accessed January 20, 2004], from Nikkei estimate.

★ 1252 ★
Oral Care
SIC: 2844; NAICS: 32562

Top Toothpaste Makers, 2003

Market shares are shown based on sales at supermarkets, drug stores and mass merchandisers for the year ended May 18, 2003.

Colgate Oral Pharm.	34.6%
Procter & Gamble	29.5
GlaxoSmithKline	9.5
Chesebrough Pond's USA	6.5
Church & Dwight	5.7

Source: *Grocery Headquarters*, August 2003, p. S14, from Information Resources Inc.

★ 1253 ★
Oral Care
SIC: 2844; NAICS: 32562

Top Toothpaste Makers in Europe, 2002

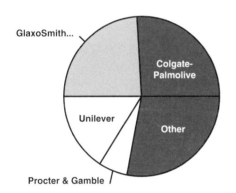

GlaxoSmith...
Colgate-Palmolive
Unilever
Other
Procter & Gamble

Market shares are shown in percent.

Colgate-Palmolive	26.0%
GlaxoSmithKline	24.0
Unilever	16.0
Procter & Gamble	6.0
Other	28.0

Source: *Advertising Age*, February 23, 2004, p. 29, from Credit Suisse First Boston.

★ 1254 ★
Oral Care
SIC: 2844; NAICS: 32562

Top Toothpaste Makers in New Zealand, 2002

In October 2002 Colgate launched At Home Whitening, which created a whole new category for oral care - the teeth whitening industry. GSK makes Macleans and Sensodyne. Lever Rexona makes Close Up and Aim.

Colgate	56.9%
GSK	35.0
Lever Rexona	9.0

Source: *Grocer's Review*, June 2003, p. NA.

★ 1255 ★
Personal Care Products
SIC: 2844; NAICS: 325611, 32562

Cosmetics & Toiletries Market in Argentina, 2003 and 2005

Sales are shown in millions of dollars.

	2003	2005
Hair care	$ 752.0	$ 803.6
Cosmetic coloring	355.2	423.1
Deodorants	344.1	372.1
Fragrances	333.1	344.7
Skin care	327.2	357.1
Bath and shower products	236.0	247.4
Men's hygiene	218.8	240.6
Oral hygiene	208.9	233.8
Baby care	28.6	29.4
Solar care	27.5	29.5

Source: "Cosmetics and Toiletries." [online] from http://www.usatrade.gov [accessed January 5, 2004], from U.S. Commercial Service and Euromonitor.

★ 1256 ★
Personal Care Products
SIC: 2844; NAICS: 325611, 32562

Cosmetics & Toiletries Market in China

Procter & Gamble controls 13.5% of the market, Unilever 6.2% and Colgate 3.5% of the market.

Pantene	2.9%
Rejoice	2.8
Colgate	2.8
Lux	2.6
Safeguard	2.4
Olay	2.3
Hazeline	2.1
Zhong Hua	2.0
Slek	1.7
Liangmiamzhen	1.6
Other	76.8

Source: *Soap Perfumery & Cosmetics Asia*, March 2004, p. 25, from Euromonitor.

★ 1257 ★
Personal Care Products
SIC: 2844; NAICS: 325611, 32562

Cosmetics & Toiletries Market in Germany, 2002

L'Oreal Groupe	
Beiersdorf AG	
Henkel KGaA	
Procter & Gamble	
Unilever Group	
Coty Inc.	
Wella AG	
Colgate-Palmolive	
GlaxoSmithKline	
Gillette	
Other	

Sales in the personal care sector dropped slightly to 11.1 billion euros in 2002, according to market research firm IKW. Soap, cosmetics and oral care all saw drops. Skin care was stable and body care increased slightly.

L'Oreal Groupe	13.0%
Beiersdorf AG	12.4
Henkel KGaA	9.3
Procter & Gamble	6.3

Unilever Group	4.8%
Coty Inc.	4.1
Wella AG	3.7
Colgate-Palmolive	3.3
GlaxoSmithKline	3.3
Gillette	3.0
Other	32.4

Source: *Soap Perfumery & Cosmetics*, November 2003, p. 22, from Euromonitor.

★ 1258 ★
Personal Care Products
SIC: 2844; NAICS: 325611, 32562

Cosmetics & Toiletries Market in South Africa

Revlon was the top brand with 4% of the market, followed by Charlie with 3.4%.

Unilever	16.6%
Revlon Inc.	11.9
Procter & Gamble	7.1
L'Oreal Groupe	6.8
Gillette Co.	6.3
National Brands Ltd.	5.1
Colgate-Palmolive	5.1
Estee Lauder Cos. Inc.	4.4
Coty Inc.	3.0
GlaxoSmithKline	2.4
Other	31.4

Source: *Soap Perfumery & Cosmetics*, April 2004, p. 25, from Euromonitor.

★ 1259 ★
Personal Care Products
SIC: 2844; NAICS: 325611, 32562

Cosmetics & Toiletries Market in South Korea, 2002

The market is considered unusual because local firms dominate while multinationals have 35% of the market. The top two firms are Amore Pacific Group and LG Group.

Amore	7.7%
Isa Knox	5.1
LacVert	4.5
Hera	4.1
Sulwhasoo	3.8

Continued on next page.

★ 1259 ★

[Continued]
Personal Care Products
SIC: 2844; NAICS: 325611, 32562

Cosmetics & Toiletries Market in South Korea, 2002

The market is considered unusual because local firms dominate while multinationals have 35% of the market. The top two firms are Amore Pacific Group and LG Group.

Amway	3.3%
Hercyna	1.5
Calli	1.5
Entia	1.2
Enprani	1.2
Other	66.1

Source: *Soap Perfumery & Cosmetics*, August - September 2003, p. 9.

★ 1260 ★

Personal Care Products
SIC: 2844; NAICS: 325611, 32562

Cosmetics & Toiletries Market in the Philippines, 2001

Skin care had the largest share of cosmetics & toiletries sales (20.2% share).

Unilever Group	17.0%
Colgate-Palmolive	12.9
Procter & Gamble	10.6
Johnson & Johnson	7.9
Avon Products	7.1
Gillette Co.	6.4
Sara Lee Corp.	3.8
Splash Manufacturing Corp.	3.7
Other	30.6

Source: *Soap Perfumery & Cosmetics Asia*, March 2003, p. 1, from Euromonitor.

★ 1261 ★

Personal Care Products
SIC: 2844; NAICS: 325611, 32562

Cosmetics & Toiletries Market in the U.K., 2002

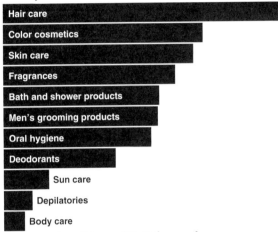

Sales are in millions of British pounds.

	(mil.)	Share
Hair care	£ 1,132.8	18.49%
Color cosmetics	818.3	13.36
Skin care	779.1	12.72
Fragrances	703.3	11.48
Bath and shower products	635.8	10.38
Men's grooming products	629.9	10.28
Oral hygiene	601.5	9.82
Deodorants	455.3	7.43
Sun care	178.8	2.92
Depilatories	110.7	1.81
Body care	79.7	1.30

Source: *Soap Perfumery & Cosmetics*, July 2003, p. 22, from Euromonitor.

★ 1262 ★

Personal Care Products
SIC: 2844; NAICS: 325611, 32562

Leading Health/Beauty Aid Categories

Products are ranked by sales in millions of dollars.

Analgesics, internal/tablets	$ 2,020.0
Cold/allergy/sinus (tablets)	1,290.0
Toothpaste	1,250.0

Continued on next page.

★ 1262 ★

[Continued]
Personal Care Products
SIC: 2844; NAICS: 325611, 32562

Leading Health/Beauty Aid Categories

Products are ranked by sales in millions of dollars.

Deodorants	$ 1,170.0
Hair coloring	1,100.0
Shampoo	1,040.0
Diet aids (liquid/powder)	1,010.0
Sanitary napkins/liners	897.4
Hand and body lotion	799.5
Hair conditioners	797.4

Source: *MMR*, April 21, 2003, p. 60, from Information Resources Inc.

★ 1263 ★

Personal Care Products
SIC: 2844; NAICS: 325611, 32562

Leading Personal Care Brands in Drug Stores, 2002

Brands are ranked by drug store sales in millions of dollars for the 52 weeks ended December 29, 2002. Total sales of razors, deodorants, shaving cream and similar personal care products in drug stores was $850 million.

	($ mil.)	Share
Gillette Mach 3	$ 75.8	8.92%
Gillette Mach 3 Turbo	25.8	3.04
Mennen Speed Stick	23.8	2.80
Gillette Venus	23.8	2.80
Gilette Sensor Excel	22.0	2.59
Right Guard Sport	19.6	2.31
Degree	19.4	2.28
Gillette Sensor	18.9	2.22
Skintimate	16.2	1.91
Dove	16.0	1.88
Other	588.7	69.26

Source: *Drug Store News*, May 19, 2003, p. 60, from Information Resources Inc.

★ 1264 ★

Personal Care Products
SIC: 2844; NAICS: 325611, 32562

Leading Personal Care Product Makers

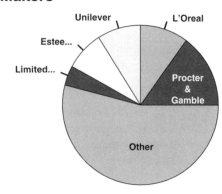

Cosmetics is the top segment of the industry with $15.2 billion. Skin care is close behind at $15 billion. The top 5 firms have almost half of the market. Men's products is a newer market that is becoming competitive as many men spend more money on grooming products.

Procter & Gamble	14.8%
L'Oreal	10.2
Unilever	9.1
Estee Lauder	7.6
Limited Brands	4.2
Other	54.1

Source: *Investor's Business Daily*, April 5, 2004, p. A12, from Datamonitor, Kline & Co., Mintel, and comseticindustry.com.

★ 1265 ★

Personal Care Products
SIC: 2844; NAICS: 325611, 32562

Men's Cosmetics Market in Italy, 2002

The market for male cosmetics in Italy reached a value of 639.5 million euros in 2002. The industry is shown by segment.

Fragrances	52.4%
Aftershaves	26.2
Shaving creams	12.8
Treatment creams	4.3
Gift sets	4.3

Source: *European Cosmetic Markets*, March 2004, p. 100, from Unipro.

★ 1266 ★
Personal Care Products
SIC: 2844; NAICS: 325611, 32562

Men's Grooming Brands Worldwide, 2001

Market shares are shown in percent.

Gillette	8.1%
Gillette Mach 3	6.6
Schick	4.1
Axe/Lynx/Ego	4.1
Gillette Sensor Excel	3.7
Wilkinson Sword	2.7
Nivea for Men	2.7
Gillette Series	2.4
Gillette Sensor	2.3
Other	63.3

Source: *Soap Perfumery & Cosmetics*, December 2002, p. 16, from Euromonitor.

★ 1267 ★
Personal Care Products
SIC: 2844; NAICS: 325611, 32562

Men's Grooming Market in the U.K., 2003

Market shares are shown in percent.

Gillette UK	35.0%
Lever Faberge	24.1
Wilkinson Sword	5.8
Sara Lee Household & Body Care	5.3
Beiersdorf	3.7
Coty	3.0
Biro BIC	1.7
KMI International	1.7
Private label	9.3
Other	10.4

Source: *Marketing*, April 1, 2004, p. 15, from Euromonitor.

★ 1268 ★
Personal Care Products
SIC: 2844; NAICS: 325611, 32562

Men's Grooming Market Worldwide, 2002

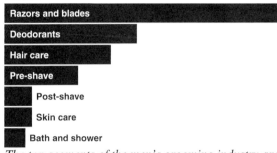

The top segments of the men's grooming industry are shown by retail value shown in millions of dollars. The market is expected to grow 11% between 2004 and 2006 according to Kline & Co. in part because of the rise of the "metrosexual" (heterosexual men concerned with fashion and grooming).

	($ mil.)	Share
Razors and blades	$ 5,792.1	41.54%
Deodorants	2,840.4	20.37
Hair care	2,229.0	15.99
Pre-shave	1,523.3	10.93
Post-shave	617.1	4.43
Skin care	536.5	3.85
Bath and shower	404.8	2.90

Source: *Soap Perfumery & Cosmetics*, December 2003, p. 16, from Euromonitor.

★ 1269 ★
Personal Care Products
SIC: 2844; NAICS: 325611, 32562

Men's Grooming Products in the U.K., 2003

The sector is worth 954 million pounds but is declining year over year. Market shares are shown for the year ended May 25, 2003.

Deodorants	32.8%
Razor blades	25.7
Fragrances	13.8
Shaving soaps	9.2
Shower products	7.1
Skin care	5.8
Hair care	4.6
Hair sprays	0.5
Shampoo	0.2

Source: *Grocer*, August 9, 2003, p. 31, from TNS Superpanel.

★ 1270 ★
Personal Care Products
SIC: 2844; NAICS: 325611, 32562

Personal Care Industry in Latin America, 2003 and 2005

Sales are shown in millions of dollars. Argentina , Brazil, and Mexico account for two-thirds of the market. The strongest growth in the region is coming from Mexico.

	2003	2005	Share
Hair care	$ 3,973.3	$ 4,252.5	21.77%
Fragrances	2,784.9	3,264.6	16.71
Oral hygiene	2,167.1	2,295.8	11.75
Skin care	1,942.1	2,087.5	10.69
Bath and shower . . .	1,881.1	1,915.6	9.81
Color cosmetics . . .	1,875.0	2,001.5	10.25
Men's grooming . . .	1,411.0	1,494.1	7.65
Deodorants	1,303.9	1,399.7	7.17
Baby care	355.7	395.5	2.02
Sun care	277.1	327.7	1.68
Depilatories	97.5	100.3	0.51

Source: *Household & Personal Products Industry*, February 2004, p. 46, from UBS Warburg.

★ 1271 ★
Personal Care Products
SIC: 2844; NAICS: 325611, 32562

Top Personal Care Product Makers Worldwide, 2001

Skin care had 25.1% of the market in 2002, followed by hair care 24.1%, make-up 20%, personal hygiene 17.6%. Europe had 33.4 of the industry for the year, then Asia-Pacific with 27.1%. The top 8 firms had just over 60% of the market in 2001.

L'Oreal	15.1%
Unilever	14.1
Procter & Gamble	9.2
Gillette	7.0
Colgate-Palmolive	6.8
Avon Products	4.7
Kao Corporation	2.6
Henkel	2.4
Other	38.1

Source: *Datamonitor Industry Market Research*, October 1, 2003, p. NA, from Datamonitor.

★ 1272 ★
Shaving Cream
SIC: 2844; NAICS: 32562

Top Shaving Cream Brands, 2004

Brands are ranked by sales at supermarkets, drug stores and discount stores (but not Wal-Mart) for the year ended January 25, 2004.

	($ mil.)	Share
Skintimate	$ 59.9	22.47%
Edge	50.2	18.83
Gillette Series	29.3	10.99
Gillette Satin Care	22.1	8.29
Gillette Foamy	20.0	7.50
Colgate	14.0	5.25
Edge Active Care	13.2	4.95
Barbasol	12.8	4.80
Aveeno	7.2	2.70
Noxzema	5.6	2.10
Private label	13.0	4.88
Other	19.3	7.24

Source: *MMR*, April 19, 2004, p. 59, from Information Resources Inc.

★ 1273 ★
Shaving Cream
SIC: 2844; NAICS: 32562

Top Shaving Foam Brands in Italy, 2002

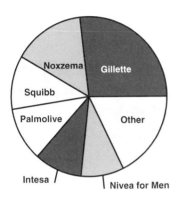

Shares are for the 12 months to April 2002.

Gillette	26.5%
Noxzema	15.0
Squibb	11.0
Palmolive	11.0
Intesa	10.0
Nivea for Men	9.0
Other	17.5

Source: *European Cosmetic Markets*, March 2003, p. 87, from industry estimates.

★ 1274 ★
Skin Care
SIC: 2844; NAICS: 32562

Global Skin Care Market

Sales are shown in millions of dollars. In 2007, face care is projected to have sales of $21 billion and 48% of the market. Hand care was second with sales of $15.2 billion and body care with $2.8 billion. According to the figures, Asia-Pacific will have about 39% of the industry in 2007.

	2003	2005	2007
Asia Pacific	$ 14,142.5	$ 15,475.0	$ 16,790.8
Europe	11,296.8	13,163.6	14,305.9
North/South America	10,184.4	10,797.5	11,488.2
Other	379.5	421.9	470.1

Source: *Chemical Market Reporter*, December 1, 2003, p. FR3, from Datamonitor.

★ 1275 ★
Skin Care
SIC: 2844; NAICS: 32562

Leading Ethnic Skin Care Products, 2003

Market shares are shown based on 7.79 million units sold at drug stores, supermarkets and discount stores (but not Wal-Mart) for the year ended March 2, 2003.

E.T. Browne Drug	53.3%
J. Strickland	14.0
Kiwi Brands	10.8
General Therapeutics	4.6
Hollywood Beauty	4.0
BioCosmetic Labs	3.5
Summit Labs	2.9
Wolstra	2.0
Keystone Labs	1.8
Other	3.1

Source: *Chain Drug Review*, April 7, 2003, p. 44, from Information Resources Inc.

★ 1276 ★
Skin Care
SIC: 2844; NAICS: 325611

Leading Skin Care Brands in Drug Stores, 2002

Brands are ranked by drug store sales in millions of dollars for the 52 weeks ended December 29, 2002. Total sales of skin care products at drug stores were $1.16 billion.

	($ mil.)	Share
Vaseline Intensive Care	$ 26.4	2.28%
Nivea	24.0	2.07
Ponds	22.8	1.97
Olay Total Effects	21.9	1.89
Olay	19.4	1.67
Sally Hansen	18.8	1.62
Lubriderm	18.3	1.58
Eucerin	17.1	1.47
Roc Actif Pur	16.2	1.40
Cetophil	15.8	1.36
Other	959.3	82.70

Source: *Drug Store News*, May 19, 2003, p. 60, from Information Resources Inc.

★ 1277 ★
Skin Care
SIC: 2844; NAICS: 32562

Men's Skin Care Market in Germany, 2003

Shares are for the leading mass market brands for male skin care products sold in Germany in 2003.

Nivea (Beiersdorf)	24.8%
Gillette	8.9
Own label	6.5
Tabac (Maurer + Wirtz)	6.1
Palmolive	6.0
Adidas (Coty/Reckitt Benckiser)	5.2
Axe (Lynx/Lever Faberge)	3.9
Wilkinson (Wilkinson Sword/Schick)	2.9
Other	35.7

Source: *European Cosmetic Markets*, March 2004, p. 96.

★ 1278 ★
Skin Care
SIC: 2844; NAICS: 32562

Men's Skin Care Products in the U.K., 2003

The market for male skin care products in the United Kingdom reached a value of 518.9 million pounds sterling for the 52 weeks endind December 27, 2003. The market includes shaving products and face care items.

Gillette	42.9%
Nivea (Beiersdorf)	22.7
King of Shaves	7.5
Colgate Palmolive	4.6
Simple for Men (Accantia)	2.6
Wilkinson Sword (Schick/Energizer)	1.7
Lynx (Lever Faberge)	1.1
Imperial Leather (PZ Cussons)	0.1
Others	16.7

Source: *European Cosmetic Markets*, March 2004, p. 104, from Information Resources Inc. InfoScan.

★ 1279 ★
Skin Care
SIC: 2844; NAICS: 32562

Top Aftershave Brands in Italy, 2002

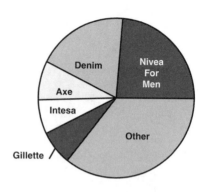

The market declined 6% during the year. This is part of a downward trend of the last several years.

Nivea For Men	23.9%
Denim	18.5
Axe	7.8
Intesa	7.2
Gillette	6.6
Other	36.0

Source: *European Cosmetic Markets*, March 2003, p. 87, from ACNielsen.

★ 1280 ★
Skin Care
SIC: 2844; NAICS: 32562

Top Face Care Brands Worldwide, 2002

The market was worth $26 billion. The U.S. market size was $4.6 billion and Japan's was $5.7 billion.

Nivea Visage/Vital	4.6%
Olay	3.7
L'Oreal Plenitude	3.3
Avon	3.1
Lancome	2.8
Clinique	2.8
Pond's	2.7
Estee Lauder	2.7
Pond's	2.0
Sofina	1.4

Continued on next page.

★ 1280 ★

[Continued]
Skin Care
SIC: 2844; NAICS: 32562

Top Face Care Brands Worldwide, 2002

The market was worth $26 billion. The U.S. market size was $4.6 billion and Japan's was $5.7 billion.

Private label	1.7%
Other	69.2

Source: *Soap Perfumery & Cosmetics*, June 2003, p. 22, from Euromonitor.

★ 1281 ★

Skin Care
SIC: 2844; NAICS: 32562

Top Face Care Markets Worldwide, 2002

Figures are in millions of dollars.

	($ mil.)	Share
Asia Pacific	$ 11,888.8	45.68%
Western Europe	6,622.2	25.45
North America	4,993.5	19.19
Latin America	1,128.1	4.33
Eastern Europe	727.1	2.79
Africa and Middle East	454.3	1.75
Australasia	209.5	0.81

Source: *Soap Perfumery & Cosmetics*, June 2003, p. 22, from Euromonitor.

★ 1282 ★

Skin Care
SIC: 2844; NAICS: 32562

Top Face Moisturizer Brands, 2004

Brands are ranked by sales at supermarkets, drug stores and discount stores (but not Wal-Mart) for the year ended January 25, 2004.

	($ mil.)	Share
Olay	$ 45.8	17.83%
Olay Complete	35.1	13.66
Pond's	21.5	8.37
Neutrogena Moisture	16.0	6.23
Aveeno	13.4	5.22

	($ mil.)	Share
Neutrogena Healthy Skin	$ 11.8	4.59%
Neutrogena Healthy Defense	8.9	3.46
Olay ProVital	8.4	3.27
L'Oreal Plenitude Future	6.2	2.41
Cetaphil	6.1	2.37
Other	83.7	32.58

Source: *MMR*, April 19, 2004, p. 59, from Information Resources Inc.

★ 1283 ★

Skin Care
SIC: 2844; NAICS: 32562

Top Facial Cleanser Brands, 2003

Market shares are shown based on sales at drug stores for the year ended November 2, 2003.

Pond's	9.2%
Cetaphil	6.6
Olay Daily Facials	6.2
Clean & Clear	4.8
Neutrogena Deep Clean	4.6
Olay	3.9
St. Ives Swiss Formula	3.6
Neutrogena	3.2
Dove	3.1
Biore	2.9
Other	55.0

Source: *Chain Drug Review*, January 19, 2004, p. 14, from Information Resources Inc.

★ 1284 ★
Skin Care
SIC: 2844; NAICS: 32562
Top Hand/Body Lotion Brands, 2004

Brands are ranked by sales at supermarkets, drug stores and discount stores (but not Wal-Mart) for the year ended January 25, 2004.

	($ mil.)	Share
Vaseline Intensive Care	$ 65.6	8.42%
Nivea	54.0	6.93
Aveeno	46.0	5.90
Lubriderm	43.5	5.58
Jergens	40.1	5.14
Curel	35.9	4.61
St. Ives Swiss Formula	30.6	3.93
Eucerin	29.2	3.75
Cetaphil	26.6	3.41
Other	408.0	52.34

Source: *MMR*, April 19, 2004, p. 59, from Information Resources Inc.

★ 1285 ★
Skin Care
SIC: 2844; NAICS: 32562
Top Hand/Body Lotion Firms, 2003

Market shares are shown based on sales at supermarkets, drugstores and mass merchandisers for the year ended May 18, 2003. Figures exclude Wal-Mart.

Andrew Jergens Co.	14.9%
Beiersdorf Inc.	12.9
Chesebrough-Pond's	11.7
Pfizer Inc.	8.6
Private label	6.0
Other	44.9

Source: *Grocery Headquarters*, August 2003, p. S14, from Information Resources Inc.

★ 1286 ★
Skin Care
SIC: 2844; NAICS: 32562
Top Skin Care Brands in China, 2002

Total skin care sales reached 12,447.7 million rembini. Facial care took 11,314.2 million rembini in sales, body care 826.2 million, hand care 307.3 million and sun protection 95.6 million.

Olay	7.9%
Dabao	5.0
Pond's	4.4
Avon	3.7
Aupres	2.8
Artistry	2.8
Maxam	2.1
Yue-Sai	1.7
Mininurse	1.5
Vaseline	1.4
Other	68.2

Source: *Soap & Cosmetics Asia*, November 2003, p. 11, from Euromonitor.

★ 1287 ★
Skin Care
SIC: 2844; NAICS: 32562
Top Skin Fade/Age/Bleach Creams, 2004

Brands are ranked by sales at supermarkets, drug stores and discount stores (but not Wal-Mart) for the year ended January 25, 2004.

	($ mil.)	Share
Olay Total Effects	$ 46.7	12.31%
Olay Regenerist	35.2	9.28
Neutrogena Healthy Skin	23.2	6.12
Neutrogena Visibly Firm	19.3	5.09
Nivea Visage Q10	18.5	4.88
ROC Actif Pur Skin	14.5	3.82
L'Oreal Plenitude Revitalift . . .	12.0	3.16
L'Oreal Plenitude Age Perfect . .	11.9	3.14
Vita K Solutions	11.3	2.98
L'Oreal Derm Expertis Wrinkle		
Decrs	9.6	2.53
Other	177.1	46.69

Source: *MMR*, April 19, 2004, p. 59, from Information Resources Inc.

★ 1288 ★
Sun Care
SIC: 2844; NAICS: 32562

Global Sun Care Products Market by Country, 2003

Figures are in millions of euros for France, Germany, Italy, and Spain. For the United States and World figures, the measure is millions of dollars. The figure for the United Kingdom is millions of pounds sterling.

United States	1,052.5
Italy	308.3
France	251.6
Spain	249.2
United Kingdom	219.5
Germany	166.6

Source: *Soap Perfumery & Cosmetics*, April 2004, p. 64, from *Euromonitor*.

★ 1289 ★
Sun Care
SIC: 2844; NAICS: 32562

Leading Sun Tan Lotion Makers, 2003

Companies are ranked by sales in millions of dollars for the year ended December 28, 2003. Figures exclude Wal-Mart.

	($ mil.)	Share
Schering-Plough	$ 138.80	33.29%
Playtex Products	89.00	21.34
Neutrogena Corp.	64.77	15.53
Tanning Research Lab	40.88	9.80
Solar Cosmetic Lab	9.52	2.28
Chattem Inc.	7.38	1.77

	($ mil.)	Share
European Tanning System	$ 5.20	1.25%
Sun & Skin Care Research	4.35	1.04
Sea & Ski Corp.	3.58	0.86
Other	53.52	12.83

Source: *Household & Personal Products Industry*, March 2004, p. 78, from Information Resources Inc.

★ 1290 ★
Sun Care
SIC: 2844; NAICS: 32562

Top Global Sun Care Brands, 2003

The global market was worth $4.3 billion.

Nivea Sun	11.7%
Ambre Solaire	7.2
Coppertone	6.1
Banana Boat	4.0
Neutrogena	3.1
Delial	2.3
Hawaiian Tropic	2.1
Piz Buin	1.8
Soltan	1.6
Clarins	1.5
Private Label	5.3
Others	53.4

Source: *Soap Perfumery & Cosmetics*, April 2004, p. 64, from Euromonitor.

★ 1291 ★
Sun Care
SIC: 2844; NAICS: 32562

Top Sun Care Brands in Spain, 2002

Market shares are shown based on mass merchandiser sales. Lotions and milks took 50.4% of sales while creams took 11.5% of the industry.

Nivea	19.9%
Delial	18.7
Ambre Solaire	7.5
Nenuco	7.2
Juper	4.1
Babaria	4.0
Piz Buin	2.6
Anne Molle	2.0

Continued on next page.

★ 1291 ★
[Continued]
Sun Care
SIC: 2844; NAICS: 32562
Top Sun Care Brands in Spain, 2002

Market shares are shown based on mass merchandiser sales. Lotions and milks took 50.4% of sales while creams took 11.5% of the industry.

Johnson's	0.8%
Astor-Natural Act	0.1
Private label	7.8
Other	25.3

Source: *European Cosmetic Markets*, April 2003, p. 125, from ACNielsen.

★ 1292 ★
Paints and Coatings
SIC: 2851; NAICS: 32551
Coatings Market in North America, 2002

The market was valued at nearly $19 billion in 2002.

Waterborne coatings	41.0%
Low-solids solvent-based coatings	32.0
Solvent-based with high solids content	14.0
Other	13.0

Source: *Polymers Paint Colour Journal*, January 2004, p. 42, from Kusumgar, Nerlfi and Growney Inc.

★ 1293 ★
Paints and Coatings
SIC: 2851; NAICS: 32551
Industrial Coatings Market in Western Europe

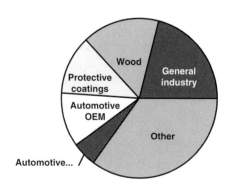

Global players like Akzo and Becker have 65% of the automotive coatings market. Seven suppliers have 70% of the furniture foil coatings industry (a segment of the wood coatings market).

General industry	21.0%
Wood	16.0
Protective coatings	12.0
Automotive OEM	11.0
Automotive repair	5.0
Other	35.0

Source: *Industrial Paint & Powder*, May 2003, p. 12, from Wifar Chemical Consultants.

★ 1294 ★
Paints and Coatings
SIC: 2851; NAICS: 32551
Paint Industry

The U.S. paint market is about 20% of the global industry. 2003 is expected to be a less successful year for the industry as it endures such things as the weak economic recovery and bad weather (which affects architectural painting). Figures are in millions of gallons.

	1998	2002	Share
Architectural	719	632	51.26%
Product coatings	412	428	34.71
Special-purpose coatings	183	173	14.03

Source: *C&EN*, November 3, 2003, p. 24, from U.S. Bureau of the Census.

★ 1295 ★
Paints and Coatings
SIC: 2851; NAICS: 32551

Paint Industry in China

Production is shown by segment.

Interior decorative	21.0%
Exterior decorative	14.0
Heavy duty	12.0
Automotive	12.0
Functional coatings	8.0
Other	33.0

Source: *Chemical Market Reporter*, November 10, 2003, p. FR13, from IRL and CNCIA.

★ 1296 ★
Paints and Coatings
SIC: 2851; NAICS: 32551

Paint Market by Region, 2007

Demand is forecasted to grow 3.5% a year through 2007 to 28.8 million metric tons.

North America	28.0%
Western Europe	21.0
Asia Pacific	14.0
China	10.0
Japan	7.0
Other	20.0

Source: *Chemical Week*, April 21, 2004, p. 30, from Freedonia Group.

★ 1297 ★
Paints and Coatings
SIC: 2851; NAICS: 32551

Paints and Coatings Market in South East Asia, 2002

Market shares are by application.

Construction	62.4%
Manufacturing	9.6
Marine Industry	9.5
Automotive	6.9
Heavy Industry	6.6
Furniture	0.5
Other	4.4

Source: *Asian Pacific Coatings Journal*, October 2003, p. 46.

★ 1298 ★
Paints and Coatings
SIC: 2851; NAICS: 32551

Pigment Demand, 2002 and 2007

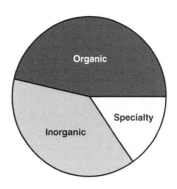

Demand for pigment is projected to increase 5% annually to $3.6 billion in 2007.

	2002	2007	Share
Organic	$ 1,280	$ 1,680	46.41%
Inorganic	1,155	1,380	38.12
Specialty	405	560	15.47

Source: *Industrial Paint & Powder*, November 2003, p. 6, from Freedonia Group.

★ 1299 ★
Paints and Coatings
SIC: 2851; NAICS: 32551
Popular Car Colors in Europe, 2001

Figures show the leading colors for consumers based on a survey. Silver was the leader in North America with 21% and silver/gray was the leader in Japan with silver/gray 43%.

Silver/gray	26.0%
Blue met.	18.0
Black	13.0
Other	43.0

Source: *Auto Interiors*, January - February 2002, p. 7.

★ 1300 ★
Paints and Coatings
SIC: 2851; NAICS: 32551
Popular Colors for Luxury Cars in North America, 2003

Figures show percentage of full/intermediate sized vehicles manufactured by color.

Medium/dark gray	23.3%
Silver	18.8
White metalic	17.8
White	12.6
Black	10.9
Other	16.6

Source: *Coatings World*, January 2004, p. 12, from *DuPont Automotive 2003 Color Popularity Survey*.

★ 1301 ★
Paints and Coatings
SIC: 2851; NAICS: 32551
Popular Colors for Sports/Compact Cars in North America, 2003

Figures show percentage of vehicles manufactured by color.

Silver	20.1%
Black	13.6
Medium/dark gray	11.9
Medium/dark blue	11.1
Medium red	9.2
Other	34.1

Source: *Coatings World*, January 2004, p. 12, from *DuPont Automotive 2003 Color Popularity Survey*.

★ 1302 ★
Paints and Coatings
SIC: 2851; NAICS: 32551
Top Coatings Makers in North America

Firms are ranked by estimated coatings sales in millions of dollars.

Sherwin-Williams	$ 3.800
PPG Industries	3.137
Valspar Corp.	1.550
DuPont Coatings & Color Technologies Group	1.500
ICI Paints North America	1.500
RPM Inc.	1.130
Akzo Nobel Coatings	1.100
Benjamin Moore & Co.	0.900
Behr Process Corp.	0.800
BASF Coatings	0.780
Professional Paint Inc.	0.400

Source: *Industrial Paint & Powder*, October 2003, p. 16.

★ 1303 ★
Paints and Coatings
SIC: 2851; NAICS: 32551

Top Coatings Makers Worldwide, 2002

Firms are ranked by sales in billions of dollars. Data include paint, coatings, adhesives and sealants.

Akzo Nobel	$ 5.33
PPG Industries	4.48
ICI Group	4.39
Sherwin-Williams	4.25
Henkel	3.85
DuPont Performance Coatings	2.60
Valspar	2.13
BASF	1.98
RPM Inc.	1.98
SigmaKalon	1.60

Source: *Coatings World*, July 2003, p. 26.

★ 1304 ★
Paints and Coatings
SIC: 2851; NAICS: 32551

Top Paint Firms in North America

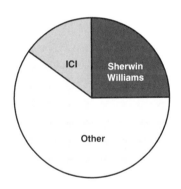

Sherwin Williams has 20-25% of the market and ICI has 10-15% of the market.

Sherwin Williams	25.0%
ICI	15.0
Other	60.0

Source: *Plain Dealer Reporter*, May 15, 2004, p. C1, from Orr & Boss Inc.

★ 1305 ★
Paints and Coatings
SIC: 2851; NAICS: 32551

Top Paint Firms in the U.K.

Market shares are shown in percent. Decorative paints have 59% of the industry followed by automotive OEM with 5% of the industry.

Akzo Nobel	23.0%
ICI	20.0
SigmaKalon	17.0
DuPont	4.0
PPG Industries	3.0
Other	33.0

Source: *Urethanes Technology*, February/March 2002, p. 37, from Industrial Research.

★ 1306 ★
Paints and Coatings
SIC: 2851; NAICS: 32551

Top Paint Firms in Western Europe, 2001

Market shares are shown in percent.

Akzo Nobel	16.0%
BASF	9.0
DuPont	8.0
TotalFinaElf Group	7.0
ICI	5.0
PPG Industries	5.0
Other	50.0

Source: *Coatings World*, June 2002, p. 14, from Information Research Ltd.

★ 1307 ★
Organic Chemicals
SIC: 2865; NAICS: 32511
Ethylene Capacity Worldwide by Region, 1991 and 2007

The petrochemical market has begun to strengthen after nearly a decade of decline.

	1991	2007
North America	33.0%	27.0%
Europe	25.0	20.0
Asia	20.0	27.0
Eastern Europe/Russia	10.0	6.0
Middle East/Africa	7.0	15.0
Latin America	6.0	5.0

Source: *Chemical Week*, March 31, 2004, p. 21.

★ 1308 ★
Organic Chemicals
SIC: 2865; NAICS: 32511
Largest Cumene Producers

Companies are ranked by production in thousands of metric tons annually.

Shell Chemicals	725
Georgia Gulf	680
Flint Hills Resources	676
Sunoco Chemicals	544
Citgo Petroleum	500
Marathon Ashland Petroleum	364
JLM Chemicals	66

Source: *Chemical Week*, April 14, 2004, p. 41.

★ 1309 ★
Organic Chemicals
SIC: 2865; NAICS: 32511
Leading Toluene Makers

Companies are ranked by production in metric tons annually.

	(000)	Share
ExxonMobil Chemical	1,100	15.68%
BP	1,030	14.68
Sunoco Chemical	604	8.61
Chevron Philllips Chemical	600	8.55
Hovensa	490	6.98
Atofina	480	6.84
Flint Hill Resources	475	6.77
Tosco Phillips	448	6.38
Equistar Chemicals	325	4.63
Citgo	315	4.49
Other	1,150	16.39

Source: *Chemical Week*, March 17, 2004, p. 25.

★ 1310 ★
Organic Chemicals
SIC: 2869; NAICS: 325199
Acetic Acid Market in China

Company shares are shown for the 1.4 million metric ton market.

Celanese	16.0%
Yaraco	14.0
Jilin	14.0
BP	12.0
Wujing	11.0
Sopo	10.0
Yangzi Petrochemical	7.0
Daqing	7.0
Other	9.0

Source: *C&EN*, July 21, 2003, p. 13, from BP Chemicals.

★ 1311 ★
Organic Chemicals
SIC: 2869; NAICS: 325199
Acrylic Acid Market

The global market is valued at 3.1 million metric tons.

BASF 25.0%
Rohm and Haas 18.0
Nippon Shokubai 13.0
Other 44.0

Source: *Chemical Week*, January 28, 2004, p. 15.

★ 1312 ★
Organic Chemicals
SIC: 2869; NAICS: 325188
Cement & Concrete Additives Demand in China, 2007

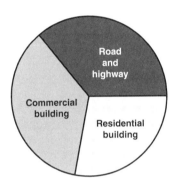

The total consumption is forecasted to reach 1.8 million metric tons in 2007.

Road and highway construction 36.0%
Commercial building 36.0
Residential building 28.0

Source: *Chinese Markets for Cement Additives*, December 2003, p. NA.

★ 1313 ★
Organic Chemicals
SIC: 2869; NAICS: 325199
Citric Acid Consumption Worldwide

The market has been troubled by weak pricing and overabundance of capacity, according to the source.

Beverages 44.0%
Food 24.0
Detergents 20.0
Pharma & cosmetics 8.0
Industrial 4.0

Source: *Chemical Market Reporter*, May 7, 2001, p. 4.

★ 1314 ★
Organic Chemicals
SIC: 2869; NAICS: 325199
Ethylene End Markets

Total demand reached 58.9 billion pounds in 2002 and is forecasted to hit 63.7 million in 2006. Top producers include Dow Chemical, Shell Chemicals, Westlake Petrochemicals, Equistar Chemicals and ExxonMobil Chemical.

Polyethylene 53.7%
Ethylene dichloride 17.7
Ethylene oxide 12.4
Alpha-olefins 8.5
Ethylebenzene 5.6
Other 2.6

Source: *Chemical Market Reporter*, September 29, 2003, p. 27.

★ 1315 ★
Organic Chemicals
SIC: 2869; NAICS: 325199
Leading Ethylene Dichloride Makers

Companies are ranked by production in thousands of metric tons.

	(000)	Share
Dow Chemical	2,900	16.88%
OxyVinyls	2,600	15.13
Georgia Gulf	2,300	13.38
Formosa Plastics	2,220	12.92
OxyMar	1,530	8.90
Westlake	1,300	7.57

Continued on next page.

★ 1315 ★

[Continued]
Organic Chemicals
SIC: 2869; NAICS: 325199

Leading Ethylene Dichloride Makers

Companies are ranked by production in thousands of metric tons.

	(000)	Share
OxyChem	1,300	7.57%
PHH Monomer	835	4.86
Vulcan Chemicals	460	2.68
Other	1,739	10.12

Source: *Chemical Week*, September 10, 2003, p. 44.

★ 1316 ★

Organic Chemicals
SIC: 2869; NAICS: 325199

Leading Ethylene Makers in Asia

Companies are ranked by capacity in thousands of metric tons.

Formosa Petrochemical	1,600
Yeochon NCC	1,440
Honam Petrochemical	1,300
Mitsubishi Chemical	1,270
LG Petrochemical	1,210
Petrochemical Corp. of Singapore	1,140
Chinese Petroleum Corp.	1,070
Indian Petrochemicals	850
Reliance Industries	800
Rayong Olefins	800

Source: *Chemical Week*, February 4, 2004, p. 20, from company reports.

★ 1317 ★

Organic Chemicals
SIC: 2869; NAICS: 325199

Solvents Demand, 2002 and 2007

Demand is expected to incrase 1.2% annually to 11.2 billion pounds in 2007. Figures are in millions of pounds.

	2002	2007	Share
Conventional	9,450	9,850	88.06%
Green	1,010	1,335	11.94

Source: *Industrial Paint & Powder*, July 2003, p. 6, from Freedonia Group.

★ 1318 ★

Organic Chemicals
SIC: 2869; NAICS: 325199

World Consumption of Fine Chemicals, 2001

Fine chemicals are those used primarily in the production of pharmaceuticals and agricultural applications. Market shares are shown by percent of consumption worldwide.

United States	55.0%
Europe	30.0
Asia	15.0

Source: *C&EN*, February 17, 2020, p. 58, from Degussa.

★ 1319 ★

Organic Chemicals
SIC: 2869; NAICS: 325199

World Production of Fine Chemicals, 2002

Fine chemicals are those used primarily in the production of pharmaceuticals and agricultural applications. Market shares are shown by percent of production worldwide.

Europe	50.0%
United States	25.0
Japan	10.0
Rest of Asia	10.0
Rest of the world	5.0

Source: *C&EN*, February 17, 2003, p. 58, from Degussa.

★ 1320 ★
Agrichemicals
SIC: 2879; NAICS: 32532

Global Agrichemical Sales by Active Ingredient, 2002

Industry sales are shown for active ingredients in both volume and dollars.

	Tons	($ mil.)
Glyphosate	178,600	$ 4,705
Atrazine	45,600	280
Malathion	35,100	412
Trifluralin	22,400	294
Acephate	17,800	330
Acetochlor	16,000	304
Pendimethalin	15,220	350
2, 4-D	10,850	325
Paraquat-dichloride	10,630	405
Chlorpyriphos	9,850	295
Carbofuran	8,750	283
S-metolachlor	8,200	244
Diquat dibromide	3,570	301
Azoxystrogin	3,310	472
Kresoxin-methyl	3,050	408
Glufosinate-ammonium	2,720	310
Imidacloprid	1,840	920
Permethrin	1,800	270
Fipronil	805	366
Deltamethrin	510	238
Lambda-cyhalothrin	480	275
Imazethapyr	380	282

Source: *Specialty Chemicals*, October 2003, p. 32.

★ 1321 ★
Agrichemicals
SIC: 2879; NAICS: 32532

Global Agrichemicals Market, 2002

Shares are shown based on an industry valued at $27.8 billion.

Bayer CropScience	20.0%
Syngenta	19.0
BASF	11.0
Monsanto	10.0
Dow AgroSciences	9.0
DuPont	8.0
Other	23.0

Source: *Chemical Week*, March 5, 2003, p. 23, from Allan Woodburn Associates.

★ 1322 ★
Herbicides
SIC: 2879; NAICS: 32532

Global Herbicide Market, 2001

Agricultural herbicides represented $14 billion of the $17 billion total. Corn, soybeans, cotton and small grains represent 65% of the herbicide industry.

Monsanto	29.0%
Syngenta	23.0
BASF	14.0
Aventis/Bayer	13.0
DuPont	10.0
Dow AgroSciences	9.0
Other	2.0

Source: *Chemical Market Reporter*, September 9, 2002, p. 10, from SRI Consulting.

★ 1323 ★
Insecticides
SIC: 2879; NAICS: 32532

Household Insecticide Market

Market shares are shown in percent. S.C. Johnson markets the Raid and Off brands.

S.C. Johnson & Son 15.0%
Bayer 12.0
Other 73.0

Source: *Milwaukee Journal Sentinel*, October 17, 2002, p. NA.

★ 1324 ★
Insecticides
SIC: 2879; NAICS: 32532

Top Insecticide Brands in India

Good Knight

Jet

Other

The insect repellant market was worth 835.65 crore. Market shares are for the coil segment, which had 52% of market value. In the refills segment, the second largest market portion, All Out had 63.3% and Good Knight 29.6%.

Good Knight 20.2%
Jet 14.1
Other 65.7

Source: *Business Standard*, March 4, 2004, p. 1.

★ 1325 ★
Insecticides
SIC: 2879; NAICS: 32532

Top Sunscreen/Insect Repellants, 2004

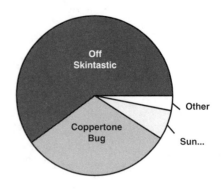

Brands are ranked by sales at supermarkets, drug stores and discount stores (but not Wal-Mart) for the year ended January 25, 2004.

	($ mil.)	Share
Off Skintastic	$ 2.1	60.00%
Coppertone Bug & Sun	1.1	31.43
Sun & Bug Stuff	0.2	5.71
Other	0.1	2.86

Source: *MMR*, April 19, 2004, p. 59, from Information Resources Inc.

★ 1326 ★
Adhesives
SIC: 2891; NAICS: 32552

Adhesives Industry in Developing Countries, 2003

The use of adhesives in the developing world totalled $6,200 million in 2003.

	($ mil.)	Share
Forest products	$ 1,450	23.4%
Packaging	850	13.7
Woodworking	600	9.7
Footwear	550	8.9
Consumer	550	8.9
Pressure sensitive	500	8.1
Other	1,700	27.5

Source: *Adhesives & Sealants Industry*, April 2004, p. 34, from *Adhesives in Developing Regions*.

★ 1327 ★
Adhesives
SIC: 2891; NAICS: 32552

Adhesives Market in Europe

Market shares are shown by application. Germany is at the top of the adhesives market in Europe with about 31% of the market, followed by France with about 16% of the industry.

Building and construction	45.7%
Transport	38.3
Glazing	16.0

Source: *Urethanes Technology*, August-September 2003, p. 28, from IAL Consultants Ltd.

★ 1328 ★
Adhesives
SIC: 2891; NAICS: 32552

Global Adhesives Market by Region, 2002

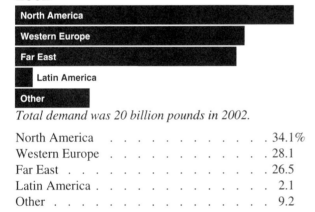

Total demand was 20 billion pounds in 2002.

North America	34.1%
Western Europe	28.1
Far East	26.5
Latin America	2.1
Other	9.2

Source: *Adhesives & Sealants Industry*, February 2004, p. 18, from CHEM Research GmbH and DPNA International.

★ 1329 ★
Adhesives
SIC: 2891; NAICS: 32552

Liner Release Market

Self-adhesive types make up 90% of the North American market. The industry is shown by usage.

Polyethylene	53.0%
Polyester	30.0
Polypropylene	15.0
Other	2.0

Source: *Paper, Film & Foil Converter*, October 1, 2003, p. NA, from AWA Alexander Watson Associates.

★ 1330 ★
Adhesives
SIC: 2891; NAICS: 32552

Medical Adhesives Demand, 2002 and 2007

Total medical adhesives demand is forecasted to grow from $900 million in 2002 to $1.3 billion in 2007. The best opportunities are for cyanoacrylate, polyethyleneglycol, and plasma/protein types. Figures for 2007 are forecasted.

	2002	2007
Dental	$ 524	$ 660
Medical, internal	354	579
Medical, external	31	66

Source: *Adhesives & Sealants Industry*, October 2003, p. 16, from Freedonia Group.

★ 1331 ★
Adhesives
SIC: 2891; NAICS: 32552

Specialty Adhesive Demand

Demand is shown in millions of dollars.

	2002	2007	Share
Manufacturing and assembly	$ 1,725	$ 2,450	81.67%
Consumer and household . .	320	380	12.67
On-line construction	120	170	5.67

Source: *Adhesives & Sealants Industry*, September 2003, p. 22, from Freedonia Group.

★ 1332 ★
Laminates
SIC: 2891; NAICS: 32552

Decorative Overlay Laminate Shipments

Paper overlays include low-basis weight papers and decoration foils. Figures are in billions of square feet.

	(bil.)	Share
Paper overlays	6.2	56.36%
Vinyl films	2.4	21.82
High pressure laminates	2.2	20.00
Edgebanding	0.2	1.82

Source: *Wood & Wood Products*, May 2003, p. 76, from Laminating Materials Association.

★ 1333 ★
Ink
SIC: 2893; NAICS: 32552

Leading Ink Makers in North America

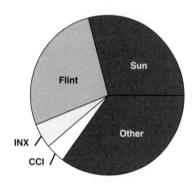

Market shares are shown based on sales of $4 billion.

Sun	29.0%
Flint	27.0
INX	5.0
CCI	4.0
Other	35.0

Source: *Chemical Week*, September 17, 2003, p. 19.

★ 1334 ★
Ink
SIC: 2893; NAICS: 32591

Leading Printing Ink Makers in Europe, 2002

The market had sales of $4.2 billion.

Sun	37.0%
Flint	10.0
Slegwerk	10.0
BASF	9.0
Other	34.0

Source: *Chemical Week*, September 17, 2003, p. 19, from Sun Chemical and *Chemical Week* estimates.

★ 1335 ★
Ink
SIC: 2893; NAICS: 32591

Printing Ink Market in North America

The growth of flexible films has translated into growth for flexible printing as well. Demand for labels and tags has also helped because of the reliance on flexo printing methods.

	($ mil.)	Share
Flexo	$ 950	67.0%
Water-based flexo	570	26.0

Source: *Ink World*, October 2003, p. 32, from National Association of Printing Ink Manufacturers.

★ 1336 ★
Ink
SIC: 2893; NAICS: 32591

Top Ink and Graphic Arts Companies Worldwide, 2002

Companies are ranked by sales volume in dollars.

Dainippon Ink & Chemicals	$ 4,400.0
Flint Ink	1,400.0
Toyo Ink	1,000.0
BASF Drucksysteme GmbH	762.5
Sakata Inx	742.1
SICPA	725.0
Tokyo Printing Ink	454.3
Huber Group	380.0

Continued on next page.

★ 1336 ★

[Continued]
Ink
SIC: 2893; NAICS: 32591

Top Ink and Graphic Arts Companies Worldwide, 2002

Companies are ranked by sales volume in dollars.

Siegwerk Druckfarben AG	$ 380.0
Inctec Inc.	360.0
Akzo Nobel Inks	275.0
T&K Toka	240.0
Dainichiseika Color & Chemicals	230.0
Sericol International	200.0
Royal Dutch Printing Ink Van Son	150.0

Source: *Ink World*, November 2003, p. 21.

★ 1337 ★

Carbon Black
SIC: 2895; NAICS: 325182

Carbon Black Demand, 2001 and 2006

Demand is thought to hit $8.6 billion. Carbon black is generally used as a reinforcement of vulcanized rubber goods. Figures are in thousands of metric tons.

	2001	2006	Share
Tires and tire components	4,940	5,670	65.78%
Non-tire rubber products	1,850	2,380	27.61
Special blacks	480	570	6.61

Source: *Rubber World*, April 2003, p. 16, from Freedonia Group.

★ 1338 ★

Carbon Black
SIC: 2895; NAICS: 325182

Carbon Black Production, 2003

Total production is expected to reach 7.8 million metric tons, up 3.1% in 2002 and up 6% from its level in 2001.

NAFTA	25.0%
China	12.0
Central/Eastern Europe	11.0
Other	52.0

Source: *Rubber World*, December 2003, p. 12, from Notch Consulting Group.

★ 1339 ★

Carbon Black
SIC: 2895; NAICS: 325182

Leading Carbon Black Makers Worldwide

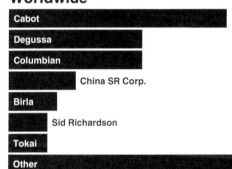

Companies are ranked by capacity in thousands of kilotons.

	Capacity	Share
Cabot	1,797	22.78%
Degussa	1,137	14.42
Columbian	1,135	14.39
China SR Corp.	570	7.23
Birla	371	4.70
Sid Richardson	345	4.37
Tokai	282	3.58
Other	2,250	28.53

Source: *European Rubber Journal*, December 2003, p. 26.

★ 1340 ★

Air Fresheners

SIC: 2899; NAICS: 325998

Top Air Freshener Brands, 2003

*Brands are ranked by supermarket sales for the year
ended December 28, 2003.*

	($ mil.)	Share
Glade Plug In	$ 119.8	26.04%
Wizard	85.7	18.63
Glade	44.1	9.58
Renuzit Longlast Adjustable . . .	39.2	8.52
Private label	9.1	1.98
Other	162.2	35.25

Source: *MMR*, May 31, 2004, p. 33, from Information Resources Inc.

★ 1341 ★

Firestarters

SIC: 2899; NAICS: 325998

Top Firestarter Brands, 2003

*Market shares are shown based on sales at super-
markets, drug stores and mass merchandisers (but
not Wal-Mart) for the year ended May 18, 2003.*

Starter Logg	2.4%
Quick Start	2.2
Diamond SuperMatch	0.7
Duraflame Firestart	0.7
Firemaster	0.3
Fatwood	0.2
Pine Mountain	0.2
Coleman	0.1
Pine Mountain Snap N Start	0.1
Other	93.1

Source: *Grocery Headquarters*, August 2003, p. S6, from
Information Resources Inc.

SIC 29 - Petroleum and Coal Products

★ 1342 ★
Biodiesel Fuels
SIC: 2911; NAICS: 32411

Major Biodiesel Producers in Europe, 2002

Shares are for the major producers of biodiesel fuel in Europe during 2002. The table shows production capacity by company in tons per year. Total European capacity totals 2,115,000 tons annually.

	Tons	Share
Oelmuhl Hbg/ADM	150,000	7.06%
Dico-Saipol/Diester	150,000	7.06
Connemann/ADM	115,000	5.41
Novaol	110,000	5.18
Rheinische BioEster	100,000	4.71
Maschinenringe SH	100,000	4.71
Jenamethyl AG	100,000	4.71
ICI Novaol	100,000	4.71
Bioenergie West	100,000	4.71
Biodiesel GmbH	100,000	4.71
Other	999,000	47.03

Source: *Oil & Fats International*, July 2002, p. 22.

★ 1343 ★
Gasoline
SIC: 2911; NAICS: 32411

FBO Fuel Market at Memphis International Airport, TN

FBO (fixed base operators) provide gas and maintenance to commerical airlines.Wilson Air started in 1996. Within a year it took 22% of the market.

Wilson Air	60.0%
Other	40.0

Source: *Commercial Appeal*, April 15, 2004, p. NA.

★ 1344 ★
Gasoline
SIC: 2911; NAICS: 32411

Gasoline Market Shares

Market shares are shown based on gross sales of 136.5 billion gallons.

Shell	14.04%
ExxonMobil	13.72
ConocoPhillips	13.00
BP	12.69
Citgo	11.11
Valero	9.94
MarathonAshland Petroleum	8.77
ChevronTexaco	8.31
Sunoco	4.70
Amerada Hess	3.73
Other	6.26

Source: *National Petroleum News*, July 15, 2003, p. 123.

★ 1345 ★
Gasoline
SIC: 2911; NAICS: 32411
Top Gasoline Firms in Japan, 2002

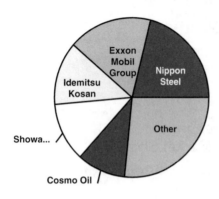

Market shares are shown based on domestic sales of 60.35 million kiloliters.

Nippon Steel	23.0%
Exxon Mobil Group	19.3
Idemitsu Kosan	14.0
Showa Shell Sekiyu	13.4
Cosmo Oil	11.2
Other	29.1

Source: "Market Share Survey Report 2002." [online] from http://www.nni.nikkei.co.jp [accessed January 20, 2004], from Nikkei estimate and Petroleum Association of Japan.

★ 1346 ★
Petroleum Refining
SIC: 2911; NAICS: 32411
Leading Petroleum Firms in Europe

Market shares are shown in percent.

Independents	43.0%
Shell	15.0
BP	14.0
TotalFinaElf	13.0
ExxonMobil	10.0
ChevronTexaco	3.0
ConocoPhillips	2.0

Source: *Weekly Petroleum Argus*, April 7, 2003, p. 9, from Wood Mackenzie.

★ 1347 ★
Petroleum Refining
SIC: 2911; NAICS: 32411
Leading Petroleum Refiners in Argentina

Market shares are shown in percent.

Petrobras	35.4%
Shell	16.4
Esso	12.6
Other	35.6

Source: *America's Intelligence Wire*, May 28, 2003, p. NA.

★ 1348 ★
Petroleum Refining
SIC: 2911; NAICS: 32411
Who Leads the Global Refining Catalysts Market

The industry was valued at $2 billion.

Grace	29.0%
Akzo Nobel	29.0
Engelhard	12.0
Criterion	12.0
Other	18.0

Source: *Global Refining & Fuels Report*, April 28, 2004, p. NA, from Albemarle.

★ 1349 ★
Motor Oil
SIC: 2992; NAICS: 324191
Top Motor Oil Brands, 2003

Shares are for the first four months of the year. Figures are for the "do-it-for-me" market.

Pennzoil	27.4%
Valvoline	16.2
Castrol	13.8
Other	42.6

Source: *New York Times*, July 2, 2003, p. C8, from *Car Care Trac Report* and NPD Group.

★ 1350 ★
Motor Oil
SIC: 2992; NAICS: 324191

Top Motor Oil Brands (DIY), 2003

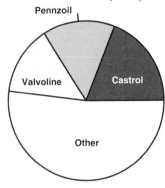

Shares are for the first four months of the year.
Figures are for the "do-it-yourself" market.

Castrol	18.6%
Pennzoil	15.3
Valvoline	14.2
Other	51.9

Source: *New York Times*, July 2, 2003, p. C8, from *Car Care Trac Report* and NPD Group.

SIC 30 - Rubber and Misc. Plastics Products

★ 1351 ★

Tires

SIC: 3011; NAICS: 326211

Agricultural Tire Market in the U.S./Canada

Market shares are shown in percent.

Firestone	. 50.0%
Other	. 50.0

Source: *Business Record (Des Moines)*, May 3, 2004, p. 3.

★ 1352 ★

Tires

SIC: 3011; NAICS: 326211

Aircraft Tire Market Worldwide

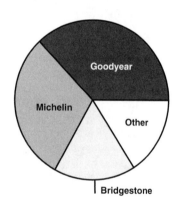

Total sales hit $343 million.

Goodyear	. 37.0%
Michelin	. 30.0
Bridgestone	. 17.0
Other	. 16.0

Source: *European Rubber Journal*, July-August 2003, p. 12, from Michelin.

★ 1353 ★

Tires

SIC: 3011; NAICS: 326211

Global Tire Market

Market shares are shown by segment.

Passenger car/light truck	. 51.0%
Trucks	. 33.0
Earthmovers	. 6.0
Agricultural	. 3.0
Other	. 7.0

Source: "Driving the Turnaround." [online] at http://www.goodyear.com/investor/pdf/Detroit.Press.1.7.04.pdf [accessed March 1, 2004], p. NA.

★ 1354 ★

Tires

SIC: 3011; NAICS: 326211

Leading HP/UHP Tire Brands

Market shares are shown for the replacement market. HP stands for ultra high performance. UHP stands for ultra high performance.

Goodyear	. 17.5%
Michelin	. 13.0
Bridgestone	. 8.0
Yokohama	. 6.5
BFGoodrich	. 6.5
Toyo	. 6.0
Dunlop	. 6.0
Kumho	. 5.0
Firestone	. 4.5
Falken	. 4.5
Sumitomo	. 3.0
Pirelli	. 3.0
Other	. 22.5

Source: *Modern Tire Dealer*, Annual Fact Book 2004, p. NA, from *Modern Tire Dealer* estimates.

★ 1355 ★
Tires
SIC: 3011; NAICS: 326211
Motorcycle Tire Market in Europe, 2001

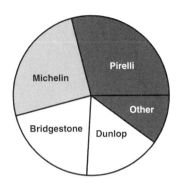

Market shares are shown in percent.

Pirelli 29.0%
Michelin 25.0
Bridgestone 20.0
Dunlop 16.0
Other 10.0

Source: *Michelin Fact Book 2001* [online] retrieved from http://www.michelin.com [accessed January 1, 2003], p. NA, from Michelin.

★ 1356 ★
Tires
SIC: 3011; NAICS: 326211
OTR Tire Market, 2001 and 2003

Data show replacement shipments for civilian vehicles.

	2001	2003
Bias	69,196	59,567
Radial	66,064	70,863

Source: *Tire Business*, March 29, 2004, p. 12, from Continental Tire North America.

★ 1357 ★
Tires
SIC: 3011; NAICS: 326211
Top Highway Truck Tire Makers, 2003

Market shares are shown in percent.

Goodyear 19.0%
Michelin 18.0
Bridgestone 16.0
Yokohama 5.0
General 5.0
Toyo 4.0
Dunlop 3.0
Continental 3.0
Sumitomo 3.0
Kumho 2.0
Kelly-Springfield 2.0
Hankook 2.0
Cooper 2.0
BFGoodrich 2.0
Other 8.0

Source: *Tire Business*, February 2, 2004, p. 9.

★ 1358 ★
Tires
SIC: 3011; NAICS: 326211
Top Light Truck Replacement Brands, 2003

Market shares are shown based on the shipment of 34.5 million replacement tires.

Goodyear 12.0%
BFGoodrich 9.0
Bridgestone 7.0
Cooper 6.5
Michelin 6.5
Firestone 5.5
General 5.5
Multi-Mile 5.0
Kelly 3.5
Cordovan 3.0

Continued on next page.

★ 1358 ★
[Continued]
Tires
SIC: 3011; NAICS: 326211

Top Light Truck Replacement Brands, 2003

Market shares are shown based on the shipment of 34.5 million replacement tires.

Sears	3.0%
Toyo	3.0
Uniroyal	3.0
Other	27.5

Source: *Modern Tire Dealer*, Annual Fact Book 2004, p. 8, from *Modern Tire Dealer* estimates.

★ 1359 ★
Tires
SIC: 3011; NAICS: 326211

Top Tire Brands in Canada, 2003

Market shares are shown based on the shipment of 15.3 million replacement tires.

Motomaster	18.5%
Goodyear	14.5
Michelin	9.5
Bridgestone	6.5
Hankook	4.0
Uniroyal	3.5
Dayton	3.5
Cooper	3.5
Toyo	3.0
President	3.0
Firestone	3.0
Other	27.5

Source: *Modern Tire Dealer*, Annual Fact Book 2004, p. 8, from *Modern Tire Dealer* estimates.

★ 1360 ★
Tires
SIC: 3011; NAICS: 326211

Top Tire Firms in Japan, 2002

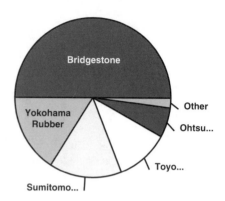

Market shares are shown based on domestic output of 1.19 million tons.

Bridgestone	49.9%
Yokohama Rubber	15.9
Sumitomo Rubber Industries	15.4
Toyo Tire & Rubber	11.3
Ohtsu Tire & Rubber	5.8
Other	1.7

Source: "Market Share Survey Report 2002." [online] from http://www.nni.nikkei.co.jp [accessed January 20, 2004], from Nikkei estimate.

★ 1361 ★
Tires
SIC: 3011; NAICS: 326211

Top Tire Makers, 2003

Shares of the consumer market are shown for both the United States and Canada. Figures exclude imports.

Goodyear	34.4%
General	14.1
Michelin	13.5
Bridgestone	11.2
Firestone	10.0
BFGoodrich	5.2
Continental	3.9
Dunlop	3.8
Uniroyal	1.9

Source: *Modern Tire Dealer*, Annual Fact Book 2004, p. 8, from *Modern Tire Dealer* estimates.

★ 1362 ★

Tires

SIC: 3011; NAICS: 326211

Top Tire Makers in North America, 2003

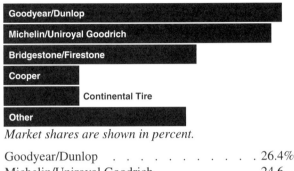

Market shares are shown in percent.

Goodyear/Dunlop 26.4%
Michelin/Uniroyal Goodrich 24.6
Bridgestone/Firestone 17.9
Cooper 7.2
Continental Tire 6.8
Other 17.1

Source: *Tire Business*, February 2, 2004, p. 9.

★ 1363 ★

Tires

SIC: 3011; NAICS: 326211

Top Tire Makers Worldwide, 2002

Market shares are shown in percent.

Michelin 19.5%
Bridgestone 19.1
Goodyear 17.4
Continental 6.8
Sumitomo 3.8
Pirelli 3.8
Yokohama 3.3
Cooper 2.4
Kumho 2.0
Toyo 1.8
Hankook 1.8
Other 18.3

Source: *Tire Business*, February 2, 2004, p. 12, from *Tire Business*.

★ 1364 ★

Tires

SIC: 3011; NAICS: 326211

Top Tire Marketers, 2003

Market shares are shown based on the shipment of 194 million replacement tires.

TBC Corp. 8.5%
Treadways 3.5
Kumho 2.5
Hercules 2.5
Del-Nat 2.5
Hankook 2.0
American Tire Distributors 1.5
SURE Tire 1.0
Other 76.0

Source: *Modern Tire Dealer*, Annual Fact Book 2004, p. 8, from *Modern Tire Dealer* estimates.

★ 1365 ★

Tires

SIC: 3011; NAICS: 326211

Top Tire Replacement Brands, 2003

Market shares are shown based on the shipment of 194 million replacement passenger tires.

Goodyear 14.5%
Michelin 8.0
Firestone 7.5
Bridgestone 6.0
Cooper 5.5
BFGoodrich 5.0
Sears 4.0
General 4.0
Uniroyal 3.0
Multi-Mile 3.0
Other 39.5

Source: *Modern Tire Dealer*, Annual Fact Book 2004, p. 8, from *Modern Tire Dealer* estimates.

★ 1366 ★
Footwear
SIC: 3021; NAICS: 316219
Non-Slip Footwear Sales

Market shares are shown in percent.

Albahealth 50.0%
Other 50.0

Source: *Hospital Materials Management*, January 2004, p. 8.

★ 1367 ★
Condoms
SIC: 3069; NAICS: 326299
Top Condom Brands, 2004

Brands are ranked by sales at supermarkets, drug stores and discount stores (but not Wal-Mart) for the year ended January 25, 2004.

	($ mil.)	Share
Trojan	$ 63.9	27.55%
Trojan Enz	39.4	16.99
Lifestyles	22.1	9.53
Durex Extra Sensitive	15.6	6.73
Trojan Magnum	13.9	5.99
Trojan Ultra Pleasure	10.1	4.36
Trojan Her Pleasure	8.4	3.62
Other	58.5	25.23

Source: *MMR*, April 19, 2004, p. 59, from Information Resources Inc.

★ 1368 ★
Condoms
SIC: 3069; NAICS: 326299
Top Condom Makers, 2003

Market shares are shown based on sales at supermarkets, drug stores and mass merchandisers for the year ended May 18, 2003. Figures exclude Wal-Mart.

Church & Dwight Co. Inc. 64.0%
Durex Consumer Products Inc. 13.2
Ansell Personal Prods. 12.7
Personal Prods. Co. 4.1
Apothecus Inc. 1.3
Other 4.7

Source: *Grocery Headquarters*, August 2003, p. S14, from Information Resources Inc.

★ 1369 ★
Plastic Film
SIC: 3081; NAICS: 326113
Largest Plastic Film/Sheet Producers in North America

Companies are ranked by film & sheet sales in millions of dollars.

Bemis Co. Inc. . . . . $ 1,870.1
DuPont Co. 1,261.0
Tyco Plastics 1,100.0
Cryovac Inc. 1,020.0
Printpack Inc. 950.0
Sigma Plastics Group 880.0
Pliant Corp. 742.6
Pechiney Plastic Packaging 700.0
Pactiv Corp. 664.0
Glad Products Co. 635.0

Source: *Plastics News*, December 29, 2003, p. 45.

★ 1370 ★
Sun Blocking Films
SIC: 3081; NAICS: 326113

Sun Control Film Market in India

The company manufactures films for vehicle and residential uses.

Garware Polyester 75.0%
Other 25.0

Source: *Asia Africa Intelligence Wire*, December 22, 2003, p. NA.

★ 1371 ★
Plastic Sheet
SIC: 3083; NAICS: 32613

Heavy Gauge Sheet Market

The global heavy gauge steel market is a substantial industry with demand placed at 200,000 tons in Europe alone.

Acrylics 76.0%
Polycarbonates 16.0
Other 8.0

Source: *Modern Plastics*, August 2003, p. 32, from Eastman Chemical.

★ 1372 ★
Plastic Pipe
SIC: 3084; NAICS: 326122

Plastic Pipe Demand Worldwide, 2002 and 2007

Demand is forecasted to increase over 4% annually through 2007. Growth will outpace growth for the overall pipe market, in which plastic takes about 47% off the total. Figures are in millions of meters.

	2002	2007	Share
North America	1,835	2,145	34.27%
Western Europe	1,249	1,440	23.00
Asia/Pacific	1,210	1,535	24.52
Other	879	1,140	18.21

Source: *Underground Construction*, January 2004, p. 8, from Freedonia Group.

★ 1373 ★
Thermoses
SIC: 3085; NAICS: 32616

Vacuum Flask Container Market

Market shares are shown in percent.

Thermos 53.0%
Other 47.0

Source: *Daily Herald*, March 26, 2004, p. NA.

★ 1374 ★

Cosmetics Storage

SIC: 3089; NAICS: 326199

Top Cosmetics Storage Brands, 2004

*Brands are ranked by sales at supermarkets, drug
stores and discount stores (but not Wal-Mart) for the
year ended January 25, 2004.*

	($ mil.)	Share
Living Things	$ 14.1	23.94%
Caboodles	8.2	13.92
Modella	5.1	8.66
Studio	4.3	7.30
Stuff	2.5	4.24
Studio Basics	2.2	3.74
Basics	1.9	3.23
Goody	1.5	2.55
Revlon	1.2	2.04
Private label	10.9	18.51
Other	7.0	11.88

Source: *MMR*, April 19, 2004, p. 59, from Information Resources Inc.

★ 1375 ★

Household Plastic Containers

SIC: 3089; NAICS: 326121

Top Household Container Brands, 2003

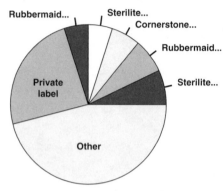

*Brands are ranked by supermarket, drug store and
discount store (excluding Wal-Mart) sales for the
year ended December 28, 2003.*

	($ mil.)	Share
Sterilite supply containers	$ 12.6	7.31%
Rubbermaid trash receptacle . . .	12.6	7.31
Cornerstone trash receptacle . . .	10.5	6.09
Sterilite trash receptable	8.5	4.93
Rubbermaid supply container . . .	8.3	4.81
Private label	41.1	23.84
Other	78.8	45.71

Source: *MMR*, May 31, 2004, p. 33, from Information Resources Inc.

★ 1376 ★

Plastic Bags

SIC: 3089; NAICS: 314911

Leading T-Shirt and Merchandise Bag Makers in North America

*The top producers in the North America are shown
by share of market.*

Formosa Plastics Corp./Superbag Corp.	15.7%
Consumer Products Division (Sonoco Products)	15.5
Vanguard Plastics	15.0
API	14.0
Other	39.8

Source: *Plastics Technology*, July 2003, p. 68, from Mastio
& Company.

★ 1377 ★
Plastic Cards
SIC: 3089; NAICS: 326199

Plastic Card Industry Worldwide, 2002

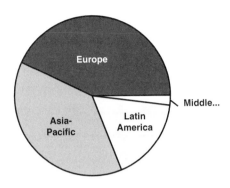

The world market grew 10% in unit shipments but only slightly in revenues. Traditional cards made up 84% of units shipped but this represented only a quarter of revenues. Chip cards repsented only 16.4% of unit shipments but 75% of card industry revenues.

	($ mil.)	Share
Europe	$ 1,840	42.82%
Asia-Pacific	1,620	37.70
Latin America	742	17.27
Middle East-Africa	95	2.21

Source: *Cardline*, October 10, 2003, p. 1, from International Card Manufacturers Association.

★ 1378 ★
Plastic Lumber
SIC: 3089; NAICS: 326199

Composite and Plastic Lumber Demand, 2001

Demand is shown by application.

Decking	38.3%
Molding and trim	30.8
Fencing	15.0
Windows and doors	6.1
Other	9.8

Source: *Builder*, January 2004, p. 356, from Freedonia Group, Industry Study No. 1551.

SIC 31 - Leather and Leather Products

★ 1379 ★

Footwear

SIC: 3140; NAICS: 316213, 316214

Leading Casual Footwear Makers, 2003

Firms are ranked by sales in millions of dollars.

Skechers	$ 563.0
Vans	411.4
Clarks	325.0
Rockport	319.0
GBM	260.0

Source: *Sporting Goods Business*, May 1, 2004, p. NA.

★ 1380 ★

Footwear

SIC: 3140; NAICS: 316213, 316214

Leading Outdoor/Rugged Footwear Makers, 2003

Firms are ranked by sales in millions of dollars.

Timberland	$ 676
Wolverine	300
Merrell	$ 160
Columbia	78
Genfoot/Kamik	60
Teva	54
Rocky	48
LaCrosse	40
Danner	29

Source: *Sporting Goods Business*, May 1, 2004, p. NA.

★ 1381 ★

Footwear

SIC: 3143; NAICS: 316213

Hunting Boot Market

Market shares are shown in percent.

Rocky	45.0%
Other	55.0

Source: *Investor's Business Daily*, January 5, 2004, p. B2.

★ 1382 ★

Footwear

SIC: 3143; NAICS: 316213

Men's Casual Footwear Sales, 2003

Sales in billions of dollars are for December 2002 - November 2003.

Active casual	$ 2.7
Dress casual	2.0
Casual	2.0
Dress	1.5

Source: *Footwear News*, January 26, 2004, p. 31, from NPD Fashionworld.

★ 1383 ★

Footwear

SIC: 3144; NAICS: 316214

Women's Casual Boot Market, 2003

The top casual boot brands are Clarks England, Sporto, Steve Madden, Easy Spirit and Timberland.

Under $50.00	38.4%
$50-74.99	30.4
$75-99.99	15.5
$100-124.99	8.2
$125-$149.99	2.5
$150	1.3

Source: *Footwear News*, April 12, 2004, p. 30, from NPD Group/NPD Fashion World Consumer.

★ 1384 ★

Footwear

SIC: 3144; NAICS: 316214

Women's Casual Footwear Sales, 2003

Sales in billions of dollars are for December 2002 - November 2003.

Dress casual	$ 7.2
Casual	3.0
Dress	2.7
Active casual	2.2

Source: *Footwear News*, January 26, 2004, p. 31, from NPD Fashionworld.

★ 1385 ★

Athletic Footwear

SIC: 3149; NAICS: 316211

Athletic Footwear Sales

Unit sales are shown, in thousands, for October 2000 - September 2001, October 2001- September 2002 and October 2002 - September 2003. Men's footwear takes about 44% of sales.

	Sep. 2001	Sep. 2002	Sep. 2003
Men	176,908	198,835	194,204
Women	119,610	122,268	126,347
Children	105,463	113,727	121,547

Source: *Footwear News*, December 15, 2003, p. C1, from NPD Group/NPD Fashionworld/consumer data estimates.

★ 1386 ★

Athletic Footwear

SIC: 3149; NAICS: 316211

Athletic Shoe Market, 2002

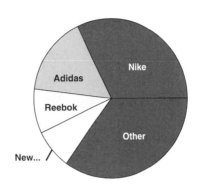

The U.S. has about 43% of the global market. Market shares are shown in percent.

Nike	32.2%
Adidas	15.5
Reebok	9.1
New Balance	8.1
Other	35.1

Source: *The Oregonian*, July 6, 2003, p. NA, from Sporting Goods Intelligence.

★ 1387 ★

Athletic Footwear

SIC: 3149; NAICS: 316211

Athletic Shoe Production Worldwide

Data are estimates. Nike leads the global industry.

China	46.0%
Indonesia	28.0
Vietnam	11.0
Thailand	9.0
Other	6.0

Source: *Wall Street Journal*, December 19, 2002, p. A1, from Sporting Goods Intelligence and WSJ research.

★ 1388 ★
Athletic Footwear
SIC: 3149; NAICS: 316211
Athletic Shoe Sales, 2002

Market shares are shown in percent.

	($ bil.)	Share
Running	$ 4.49	29.0%
Basketball	3.30	21.0
Cross training	2.00	12.8
Walking	1.10	7.0
Low performance	0.86	5.5
Hiking	0.66	4.2
Tennis	0.66	4.2
Sport sandals	0.31	2.0
Other	2.35	14.0

Source: *St. Petersburg Times*, September 6, 2003, p. 1E, from NPD Group Inc.

★ 1389 ★
Athletic Footwear
SIC: 3149; NAICS: 316211
Basketball Shoe Market

Market shares are shown in percent.

Nike	65.0%
Other	35.0

Source: *Boston Globe*, October 12, 2003, p. NA.

★ 1390 ★
Athletic Footwear
SIC: 3149; NAICS: 316211
Footwear Sales by Gender, 2002

Women's footwear sales fell 11% over the previous year to $19.2 billion. Men's sales were essentially flat. Boys' footwear sales grew 8% to $2 billion and girls' footwear sales were flat at $1.8 billion. Infants' shoe sales grew 20% over the year.

	($ bil.)	Share
Women's	$ 19.200	47.51%
Men's	16.500	40.83
Boys' 4-12	2.000	4.95
Girls' 4-12	1.800	4.45
Infants'	0.911	2.25

Source: *Children's Business*, August 2003, p. 19, from NPD Data.

★ 1391 ★
Athletic Footwear
SIC: 3149; NAICS: 316211
Global Athletic Shoe Market, 2002

Market shares are shown in percent.

Nike	34.1%
Adidas	16.5
Other	49.4

Source: *New York Times*, May 23, 2004, p. 8.

★ 1392 ★
Athletic Footwear
SIC: 3149; NAICS: 316211
Soccer Shoe Market

Market shares are shown in percent.

Adidas 50.0%
Other 50.0

Source: *The Business Journal (Portland)*, September 8, 2003, p. NA.

★ 1393 ★
Athletic Footwear
SIC: 3149; NAICS: 316219
Sports Shoe Market in Israel, 2003

Shares of the 1.3 billion Israeli shekel sports footwear market.

Nike 22.0%
New Balance 18.0
Diadora 17.0
Puma 7.0
Other 36.0

Source: *Haaretz*, March 25, 2020, p. NA, from Life Sport.

★ 1394 ★
Athletic Footwear
SIC: 3149; NAICS: 316211
Top Sneaker Makers, 2002

According to the article, competition has heated up in the $15 billion market. Manufacturers are putting out more styles and at prices to benefit the consumer. Basketball shoes, the priciest and most profitable segment, took 16% of the market in 2002. Shares are shown based on wholesale shipments.

Nike 39.1%
Reebok 12.0
New Balance 11.6
Adidas 9.6
Other 27.7

Source: *USA TODAY*, April 3, 2003, p. B1, from Sporting Goods Intelligence.

★ 1395 ★
Athletic Footwear
SIC: 3149; NAICS: 316211
Top Tennis Shoe Makers

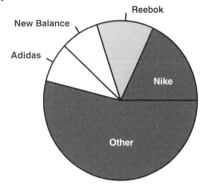

Market shares are shown in percent.

Nike 17.8%
Reebok 12.3
New Balance 7.9
Adidas 7.7
Other 54.3

Source: "Puma back in Serena endorsement derby." [online] available from http://sports.espn.go.com/espn/print?id1585126&typestory, from National Sporting Goods Association.

★ 1396 ★
Luggage
SIC: 3161; NAICS: 316991
Luggage and Leather Goods Market in the U.K.

The market includes hand luggage, business cases, handbags and small leather goods. It was was estimated at 1.03 billion British pounds in 2002.

	1998	2002
Small leather goods	58.4%	34.6%
Hand luggage	24.0	37.2
Other	17.6	28.2

Source: "Hand Luggage and Leather Goods Market Report 2003." [online] from http://www.researchandmarkets.com [accessed June 1, 2004], from researchandmarkets.com.

★ 1397 ★
Luggage
SIC: 3161; NAICS: 316991

Premium Luggage Market in India, 2003

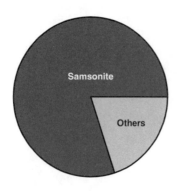

Shares are for the Rs 90 crore market.

Samsonite	80.0%
Others	20.0

Source: *The Financial Express*, April 6, 2004, p. NA.

SIC 32 - Stone, Clay, and Glass Products

★ 1398 ★
Glass
SIC: 3211; NAICS: 327211
Glass Reinforcement Market, 2001

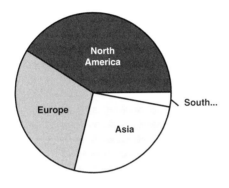

The market represents 2.5 million tons and excludes glass mats and AR glass.

North America	41.0%
Europe	30.0
Asia	26.0
South America	3.0

Source: *Reinforced Plastics*, January 2003, p. 44, from Saint-Gobain Vetrotex.

★ 1399 ★
Glass
SIC: 3211; NAICS: 327211
Top Sheet Glass Firms in Japan, 2002

Market shares are shown based on total shipments of 308.4 million square miles.

Asahi Glass	40.4%
Nippon Sheet Glass	29.9
Central Glass	16.1
PPG-CI	1.9
Guardian Japan	1.8
Other	9.9

Source: "Market Share Survey Report 2002." [online] from http://www.nni.nikkei.co.jp [accessed January 20, 2004], from Nikkei estimates.

★ 1400 ★
Glassware
SIC: 3220; NAICS: 327213
Glassware Sales, 2002

Shipments are shown in millions of dollars. In the consumer glassware segment, stemware sales were $148.5 million and glass tableware were $264.2 million.

	($ mil.)	Share
Consumer glassware	$ 1,600	35.56%
Lighting and electronic glassware	1,100	24.44
Other	1,800	40.00

Source: *Ceramic Industry*, October 2003, p. 33, from Freedonia Group.

★ 1401 ★
Canning Jars
SIC: 3221; NAICS: 327213

Home Canning Jars, 2001

Market shares are shown in percent.

Ball Corp. 80.0%
Other 20.0

Source: *Forbes*, October 27, 2003, p. 159.

★ 1402 ★
Crystal
SIC: 3229; NAICS: 327212

Retail Crystal Sales, 2002

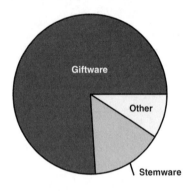

*Crystal sales declined from 2001. Crystal Clear In-
dustries claims that the decline came from shrinking
consumer confidence, direct imports and the strength
of the euro. Department stores have 50% of the market.*

Giftware 76.0%
Stemware 15.0
Other 9.0

Source: *HFN*, September 8, 2003, p. 12S.

★ 1403 ★
Automotive Mirrors
SIC: 3231; NAICS: 327215

Automotive Electrochromic Mirror Market

Market shares are shown in percent.

Gentex 78.0%
Magna Doneelley 19.0
Other 13.0

Source: *The Star-Ledger*, August 1, 2003, p. 33.

★ 1404 ★
Automotive Mirrors
SIC: 3231; NAICS: 327215

Rearview Mirror Market

*Shares are for the automatic dimming market only,
which makes up only 13% of the overall market.*

Gentex 80.0%
Other 20.0

Source: *Investor's Business Daily*, September 24, 2003,
p. A10.

★ 1405 ★
Cement
SIC: 3241; NAICS: 32731

Cement Consumption, 2003 and 2005

*Figures are in thousands of metric tons. Data for
2005 are forecasted.*

	2003	2005	Share
Portland	104,355	108,034	79.98%
Cement and clinker			
imports	22,400	22,524	16.67
Masonry cement . . .	4,569	4,523	3.35

Source: *Rock Products*, January/February 2004, p. 14, from
McGraw-Hill Construction.

★ 1406 ★
Cement
SIC: 3241; NAICS: 32731

Leading Cement Producing Nations, 2003

Cement production is shown measured in thousand metric tons.

	(000)	Share
China	750,000	40.4%
India	110,000	6.0
United States and Puerto Rico	92,600	5.0
Japan	72,000	4.1
South Korea	56,000	3.1
Brazil	40,000	2.2
Italy	40,000	2.2
Russia	40,000	2.2
Spain	40,000	2.2
Indonesia	34,000	1.9
Thailand	35,000	1.9
Iran	31,000	1.7
Mexico	31,500	1.7
Germany	28,000	1.5
Egypt	26,000	1.4
Saudi Arabia	23,000	1.3
France	20,000	1.1
Other countries	360,000	19.4

Source: *Mineral Commodity Summaries — Cement*, January 2004, p. 43, from U.S. Geological Survey.

★ 1407 ★
Cement
SIC: 3241; NAICS: 32731

Leading End Markets for Cement, 2002

Roughly 85 million tons of portland cement and 4 million tons of masonry cement were produced during the year. Sales are shown by market.

Ready-mixed concrete producers	75.0%
Concrete product makers	13.0
Contractors (mainly road paving)	6.0
Building materials dealers	3.0
Other	3.0

Source: "Cement." [online] from http://www.ers.usgs.gov [accessed March 22, 2004], from U.S. Geological Survey.

★ 1408 ★
Cement
SIC: 3241; NAICS: 32731

Top Cement Makers in Chile, 2003

Market shares are shown in percent.

Cementos Melon/Lafarge	36.4%
Cementos Polpaico/Holcim	35.2
Cementos Bio Bio/Briones	28.4

Source: *America's Intelligence Wire*, January 14, 2004, p. NA, from Business News Americas.

★ 1409 ★
Cement
SIC: 3241; NAICS: 32731

Top Cement Makers in Ghana

GHACEM has had a monopoly in the market since 1967. In March 2000, this monopoly was broken by Diamond Cement Limited. Market shares are shown in percent.

	2000	2001	2002
GHACEM	81.0%	69.0%	70.0%
Other	19.0	21.0	30.0

Source: *Africa News*, August 18, 2003, p. NA.

★ 1410 ★
Cement
SIC: 3241; NAICS: 32731

Top Cement Makers in Japan, 2002

Market shares are shown based on total domestic shipments.

Taiheiyo Cement	36.9%
Ube-Mitsubishi Cement	24.3
Sumitomo Osaka Cement	19.0
Tokuyama	6.8
Aso Cement	3.3
Other	9.7

Source: "Market Share Survey Report 2002." [online] from http://www.nni.nikkei.co.jp [accessed January 20, 2004], from Japan Cement Association.

★ 1411 ★
Concrete
SIC: 3241; NAICS: 32731

Top Cement Makers in the U.K.

The ready mixed concrete market is shown by company.

RMC	26.4%
Hanson	22.2
Tarmac	20.1
Lafarge	8.8
Aggregate Industries	5.3
Other	17.2

Source: *Contract Journal*, February 5, 2003, p. 14, from BDS Marketing Research.

★ 1412 ★
Advanced Ceramics
SIC: 3250; NAICS: 327121, 327331, 327122

Advanced Ceramics Market, 2003 and 2008

Figures are in millions of dollars. Data for 2008 are forecasted.

	2003	2008	Share
Electronic ceramics	$ 5,720	$ 8,520	66.15%
Chemical processing and environmental-related	1,550	2,170	16.85
Ceramic coatings	860	1,290	10.02
Structural ceramics	515	900	6.99

Source: *Industries in Transition*, February 2004, p. NA, from Business Communications Co.

★ 1413 ★
Advanced Ceramics
SIC: 3250; NAICS: 327121, 327331, 327122

Engineering Ceramics Market

Figures are in millions of dollars. The top six manufacturing companies supply 55% of the engineering ceramics market.

	($ mil.)	Share
Catalyst supports and membranes	$ 547	40.58%
Mechanical and wear parts	539	39.99
High temperature process parts	262	19.44

Source: *Advanced Ceramics Report*, February 2004, p. 9, from Materials Technology Publications.

★ 1414 ★
Bricks
SIC: 3251; NAICS: 327121, 327331

Brick Industry by Region, 2002

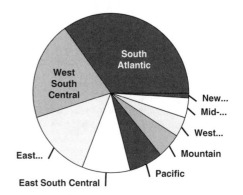

The entire masonry construction market (brick, concrete and natural stone) added 93 million square feet from 1997 to 2002.

South Atlantic	35.0%
West South Central	20.0
East North Central	14.0
East South Central	10.0
Pacific	7.0
Mountain	5.0
West North Central	4.0
Mid-Atlantic	4.0
New England	1.0

Source: *Masonry Construction*, November-December 2003, p. 44, from Ducker Worldwide.

★ 1415 ★
Bricks
SIC: 3251; NAICS: 327121, 327331
Leading Light-Mass Brick Producer in Thailand, 2003

Quality Construction Products Plc 71.0%
Others 29.0

Source: *Asia Africa Intelligence Wire*, March 18, 2004, p. NA.

★ 1416 ★
Tiles
SIC: 3251; NAICS: 327121
Clay Tile Market in France, 2002

Market shares are shown in percent.

Poliet/Coverland 50.0%
Imetal 40.0
Other 10.0

Source: ''Building Products.'' [online] from http:// www.usatrade.gov [accessed January 5, 2004], from U.S. Commercial Service.

★ 1417 ★
Tiles
SIC: 3253; NAICS: 327122
Ceramic Tile Market, 2002

Total factory shipments and imports of ceramic tiles in 2002 totaled 2.63 billion square feet. Shares are for sales in the United States by country of manufacture.

Italy 26.9%
U.S. 22.7
Spain 14.9
Mexico 11.0
Brazil 9.1
Other 15.4

Source: *Ceramic Industry*, October 2003, p. 21, from U.S. Bureau of the Census and U.S. Customs Department.

★ 1418 ★
Tiles
SIC: 3253; NAICS: 327122
Ceramic Tile Sales

Figures are shown based on a survey of floor covering retailers.

12x12 . . . . 56.0%
13x13 . . . . 22.0
18x18 . . . . 9.0
16x16 . . . . 5.0
Other 8.0

Source: *National Floor Trends*, November 2003, p. 10, from study by the source and Business News Publishing Co.

★ 1419 ★
Refractories
SIC: 3255; NAICS: 327124
Refractories Demand, 2002 and 2007

According to the source the improved outlook is based on ''improved fundamentals for many of the major end use market, particularly iron and steel after the industry's collapse starting in late 1997''. Demand is shown in millions of dollars.

	2002	2007	Share
Bricks & shapes	$ 1,210	$ 1,345	55.35%
Monolithics	575	635	26.13
Other	395	450	18.52

Source: *Research Studies Freedonia Group*, September 3, 2003, p. 1, from Freedonia Group.

★ 1420 ★
Plumbing Fixtures
SIC: 3261; NAICS: 327111

Sink Sales by Type

Figures show manufacturer dollar sales of sinks. By 2005, kitchen sink sales are forecasted to reach $474.3 million, wash sinks $66.4 million and bar sinks $24.1 million.

	2000	2002	Share
Kitchen	416.9	474.3	85.52%
Wash	63.1	59.6	10.75
Bar	21.3	20.7	3.73

Source: *Supply House Times*, February 2004, p. 46, from U.S. Department of Commerce.

★ 1421 ★
Plumbing Fixtures
SIC: 3261; NAICS: 327111

Toilet Tank Market, 2003-2005

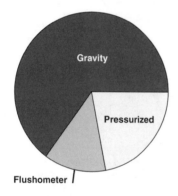

Gravity

Pressurized

Flushometer

Manufacturer sales of flush tanks totaled 315.6 million in 2001 and are forecasted to hit 350.4 million units in 2005. For the same period sales of water closets grew from 425.1 million to 448.1 million.

	2003	2004	2005
Gravity	73.0%	70.0%	65.0%
Flushometer	14.0	13.0	13.0
Pressurized	13.0	17.0	22.0

Source: *Supply House Times*, September 2003, p. 76, from Chicago Faucets and Geberit.

★ 1422 ★
Sanitaryware
SIC: 3261; NAICS: 327111

Sanitaryware Industry in Thailand

Market shares are shown in percent. UMI-Laudfen's share is between 10-12%.

Cotto	40.0%
American Standard	30.0
UMI-Laufen	12.0
Other	18.0

Source: *Asia Africa Intelligence Wire*, September 27, 2002, p. NA, from *The Nation*.

★ 1423 ★
Sanitaryware
SIC: 3261; NAICS: 327111

Top Faucets/Sanitaryware Market in South Korea, 2003

The table shows the top three companies in the faucet and sanitary ware market in South Korea.

Daelim Trading	27.0%
Royal Toto Metal	19.0
Data Corp.	11.0
Other	43.0

Source: ''Korea's Faucet and Sanitaryware Market'' [online] http://www.export.gov/comm_svc/index.html [accessed March 30, 2004], March 10, 2020, p. NA.

★ 1424 ★
Sanitaryware
SIC: 3261; NAICS: 327111

Top Sanitary Ceramics Makers in Japan, 2002

Market shares are shown based on domestic shipments of 8.4 million units.

Toto	62.0%
INAX	28.8
Asahi Eito	4.0
Janis	3.9
Other	1.3

Source: ''Market Share Survey Report 2002.'' [online] from http://www.nni.nikkei.co.jp [accessed January 20, 2004], from Nikkei estimates.

★ 1425 ★

Gypsum

SIC: 3275; NAICS: 32742

Gypsum Demand in North America

Demand is in millions of dollars. Gypsum board is the prominent gypsum product taking three quarters of demand.

2007	$ 46,800
2002	42,080
1997	35,890

Source: *Concrete Products*, October 1, 2003, p. 10.

★ 1426 ★

Gypsum

SIC: 3275; NAICS: 32742

World Gypsum Production, 2003

Demand for gypsum turns largely on the health of the construction industry. In the United States, 95% of gypsum is used in wallboard, cement, and plaster manufacturing.

	(000)	Share
United States	16,000	15.70%
Iran	11,500	11.30
Canada	9,000	8.90
Spain	7,500	7.40
China	6,900	6.80
Mexico	6,800	6.70
Thailand	6,500	6.40
Japan	5,700	5.60
Australia	4,000	4.00
France	3,500	3.50
India	2,300	2.30
Egypt	2,000	2.00
Brazil	1,650	1.70
United Kingdom	1,500	1.50
Italy	1,200	1.20
Poland	1,100	1.10
Uruguay	1,100	1.08
Austria	1,000	1.00
Other countries	12,500	12.30

Source: *Mineral Commodity Summaries — Gypsum*, January 2004, p. 77, from U.S. Geological Survey.

★ 1427 ★

Interior Finishing

SIC: 3275; NAICS: 32742

Interior Finishing Industry

Drywall has been gradually replacing plaster.

Conventional drywall	90.0%
Other	10.0

Source: *Walls & Ceiling*, March 2004, p. 34.

★ 1428 ★

Wallboard

SIC: 3275; NAICS: 32742

Wallboard Market Leaders

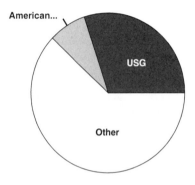

Market shares are shown in percent.

USG	30.0%
American Gypsum	8.0
Other	62.0

Source: *Crain's Chicago Business*, March 8, 2004, p. 4.

★ 1429 ★
Abrasives
SIC: 3291; NAICS: 32791

Abrasives Demand, 2002 and 2007

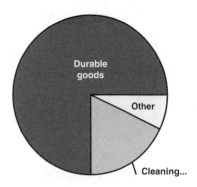

Demand for abrasives is expected to grow about
3.7% a year until becoming a $5.4 billion market in
2007.

	2002	2007	Share
Durable goods	$ 3,325	$ 4,070	75.23%
Cleaning & maintenance . .	870	960	17.74
Other	325	380	7.02

Source: *American Ceramic Society Bulletin*, February
2004, p. 8, from Freedonia Group.

SIC 33 - Primary Metal Industries

★ 1430 ★
Steel
SIC: 3312; NAICS: 331111

Specialty Steel Consumption

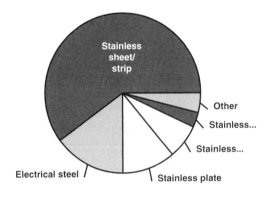

Figures are for year-to-date July 2003. The specialty steel industry is struggling with declining domestic demand. Stainless steel rods saw a decline of 18% over the previous year-to-date July 2002. Other declines: bars 6%, plates 7%, sheets and strips 8%.

	Tons	Share
Stainless sheet/strip	915,864	60.42%
Electrical steel	229,833	15.16
Stainless plate	161,354	10.64
Stainless bar	109,817	7.24
Stainless rod	42,352	2.79
Other	56,590	3.73

Source: *PR Newswire*, October 6, 2003, p. NA, from Specialty Steel Industry of North America.

★ 1431 ★
Steel
SIC: 3312; NAICS: 331111

Top Crude Steel Firms in Japan, 2002

Market shares are shown based on domestic output of 109.8 million tons.

Nippon Steel	27.2%
JFE Holdings	24.1
Sumitomo Metal Industries	9.8
Kobe Steel	6.2
Tokyo Steel Manufacturing	3.6
Other	29.1

Source: ''Market Share Survey Report 2002.'' [online] from http://www.nni.nikkei.co.jp [accessed January 20, 2004], from Nikkei estimate and Japan Iron and Steel Federation.

★ 1432 ★
Steel
SIC: 3312; NAICS: 331111

Top Crude Steel Makers Worldwide, 2002

Market shares are shown based on total output of 902.79 million tons.

Arcelor	4.9%
Nippon Steel Corp.	3.4
Posco	3.2
LNM Group	3.0
Shanghai Boasteel Group	2.2
Other	83.3

Source: ''Market Share Survey Report 2002.'' [online] from http://www.nni.nikkei.co.jp [accessed January 20, 2004], from Metal Bulletin Plc of the U.K.

★ 1433 ★

Steel

SIC: 3312; NAICS: 331111

Top Stainless Steel Firms in Japan, 2002

Market shares are shown based on domestic output of 3.09 million tons.

Nippon Steel	25.2%
Nisshin Steel	19.3
JFE Holdings	16.8
Nippon Yakin Kogyo	10.6
Nippon Metal Industry	9.5
Other	18.6

Source: "Market Share Survey Report 2002." [online] from http://www.nni.nikkei.co.jp [accessed January 20, 2004], from Nikkei estimates.

★ 1434 ★

Steel

SIC: 3312; NAICS: 331111

Top Steel Firms Worldwide, 2002

Firms are ranked by production in millions of tons.

Arcelor	44.0
Nippon Steel	30.9
Posco	28.9
LNM	27.5
Shanghai Baosteel	19.5
ThyssenKrupp Steel	17.0
Corus	16.8
NKK	16.5
Riva	15.2
US Steel	14.5

Source: *Financial Times*, August 28, 2003, p. 17, from Thomson Datastream and Metal Bulletin.

★ 1435 ★

Steel

SIC: 3312; NAICS: 331111

Top Steel Producers in Poland, 2004

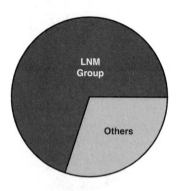

The steel market in Poland is dominated by one player since the acquisition of Ispat Polaska Stal (PHS) by LNM in the first quarter of 2004.

LNM Group	70.0%
Others	30.0

Source: *European Intelligence Wire*, March 8, 2004, p. NA.

★ 1436 ★

Steel

SIC: 3312; NAICS: 331111

Top Steel Producing Countries, 2003

Countries are ranked by production in millions of metric tons. China has 30% of global production. With its booming economy, China saw production increase 21% over 2002. It is also the world's largest steel consumer.

China	220.1
Japan	110.5
United States	90.4
Russia	62.7
South Korea	46.3
Germany	44.8
Ukraine	36.9
India	31.8
Brazil	31.1
Italy	26.7

Source: *Wall Street Journal*, March 31, 2004, p. A6, from International Iron and Steel Institute.

★ 1437 ★
Steel Strapping
SIC: 3315; NAICS: 331222

Steel Strapping Market

Market shares are estimated in percent.

ITW 35.0%
Acme Packaging 35.0
Other 30.0

Source: *Knight Ridder/Tribune Business News*, August 19, 2003, p. NA.

★ 1438 ★
Steel Beams
SIC: 3316; NAICS: 331221

Top H-Beam Firms in Japan, 2002

Market shares are shown based on domestic output of 4.35 million tons.

Tokyo Steel Manufacturing 36.3%
Nippon Steel 16.1
Sumikin Steel & Shapes 11.2
NKK Bars & Shapes 9.3
JFE Holdings 7.4
Other 19.7

Source: "Market Share Survey Report 2002." [online] from http://www.nni.nikkei.co.jp [accessed January 20, 2004], from Nikkei estimate.

★ 1439 ★
Steel Pipe
SIC: 3317; NAICS: 33121

Steel Pipe Demand, 2002 and 2007

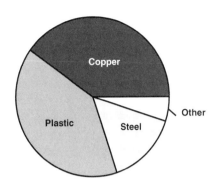

There is forecasted to be a 2.5% annual increase in the industry coming from efforts to improve old sewer systems and driveway water systems. Demand is in millions of feet.

	2002	2007	Share
Copper	5,519	6,281	40.47%
Plastic	5,330	6,140	39.56
Steel	2,226	2,387	15.38
Other	665	712	4.59

Source: *Welding Design & Fabrication*, October 2003, p. 6, from Freedonia Group.

★ 1440 ★
Castings
SIC: 3321; NAICS: 331511

Largest Ferrous Castings Producers Worldwide

Market shares are shown in percent.

China 24.0%
United States 16.0
Russia 10.0
Japan 8.0
Germany 7.0
India 5.0
Other 30.0

Source: *Advanced Manufacturing Technology*, September 15, 2003, p. 10.

★ 1441 ★
Foundries
SIC: 3321; NAICS: 331511

Top Foundries Worldwide, 2002

Market shares are shown based on sales.

	($ bil.)	Share
TSMC	$4.66	40.0%
UMC	1.94	16.7
IBM Micro	0.73	6.3
Chartered	0.44	3.9
TI	0.32	2.7
NEC	0.31	2.7
Hitachi	0.24	2.1
Anam	0.22	1.9
Hynix	0.15	1.3

Source: *Electronic Business*, August 1, 2003, p. 38, from
SEMICO Research.

★ 1442 ★
Foundries
SIC: 3321; NAICS: 331511

Top Nations for Foundries, 2001

Shipments are in millions of tons.

China	14.8
United States	11.8
Japan	5.8
Germany	4.6
India	3.1
France	2.5
Italy	2.3
Mexico	1.8
Brazil	1.7

Source: *Modern Casting*, December 2002, p. 22, from
*Modern Casting's 36th Annual Census of World Casting
Production.*

★ 1443 ★
Aluminum
SIC: 3334; NAICS: 331312

Aluminum End Markets, 2002

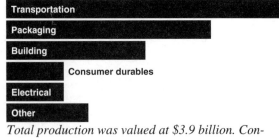

*Total production was valued at $3.9 billion. Con-
sumption is shown by segment.*

Transportation	34.0%
Packaging	25.0
Building	17.0
Consumer durables	7.0
Electrical	7.0
Other	10.0

Source: "Aluminum." [online] from http://
www.ers.usgs.gov [accessed March 22, 2004], from U.S.
Geological Survey.

★ 1444 ★
Aluminum
SIC: 3334; NAICS: 331312

Aluminum Market in Russia

*The company is one of the top three worldwide and
has 10% of the world market.*

RusAl	70.0%
Other	30.0

Source: *Metals & Mining Report*, April 15, 2004, p. NA.

★ 1445 ★

Aluminum

SIC: 3334; NAICS: 331312

Largest Aluminum Producers

Companies are ranked by production of refined aluminum in millions of metric tons.

Alcoa	3.5
Alcan	2.2
Norsk Hydro	1.3
BHP Billiton	1.0
Rio Tinto	0.8

Source: *New York Times*, July 8, 2003, p. C1, from Bloomberg Financial Markets and Merrill Lynch.

★ 1446 ★

Aluminum

SIC: 3334; NAICS: 331312

World Aluminum Production, 2003

Countries are ranked by aluminum production for the year 2003, measured in thousand metric tons.

	(000)	Share
China	5,200	19.1%
Russia	3,400	12.5
Canada	2,800	10.3
United States	2,700	9.9
Australia	1,850	6.8
Brazil	1,390	5.1
Norway	1,150	4.3
South Africa	690	2.6
Venezuela	580	2.2
France	430	1.6
Other countries	7,150	26.2

Source: *Mineral Commodity Summaries — Aluminum*, January 2004, p. 21, from U.S. Geological Survey.

★ 1447 ★

Nickel

SIC: 3339; NAICS: 331419

World Nickel Production, 2003

Stainless steel accounts for two-thirds of the primary market for nickel. World mine production was at an all time high in 2003. Production is in metric tons of nickel content.

	Tons	Share
Russia	330,000	23.6%
Australia	220,000	15.8
Canada	180,000	12.9
Indonesia	120,000	8.6
New Caledonia	120,000	8.6
Cuba	75,000	5.4
Colombia	65,000	4.7
China	56,000	4.0
Brazil	46,000	3.3
South Africa	40,000	2.9
Dominican Republic	39,000	2.8
Philippines	27,000	2.0
Greece	23,000	1.7
Venezuela	21,000	1.5
Botswana	18,000	1.3
Zimbabwe	8,000	0.6
Other countries	12,000	0.9

Source: *Mineral Commodity Summaries — Nickel*, January 2004, p. 115, from U.S. Geological Survey.

★ 1448 ★
Tin
SIC: 3339; NAICS: 331419

Leading Tin Product Makers

Market shares are shown in percent.

U.S. Steel	45.0%
Weirton Steel	25.0
Other	30.0

Source: *The Times (Munster, Indiana)*, February 19, 2004, p. NA.

★ 1449 ★
Zinc
SIC: 3341; NAICS: 331492

World Zinc Production, 2003

Countries are ranked by zinc production for the year 2003, measured in thousand metric tons.

	(000)	Share
China	1,700	20.0%
Australia	1,600	18.9
Other countries	1,300	15.3
Peru	1,250	14.7
Canada	1,000	11.8
United States	770	9.1
Mexico	500	5.9
Kazakhstan	350	4.2

Source: *Mineral Commodity Summaries — Zinc*, January 2004, p. 189, from U.S. Geological Survey.

★ 1450 ★
Aluminum Foil
SIC: 3353; NAICS: 331315

Top Aluminum Foil Brands, 2003

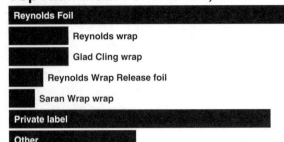

Brands are ranked by supermarket, drug store and discount store (excluding Wal-Mart) sales for the year ended December 28, 2003.

	($ mil.)	Share
Reynolds Foil	$ 201.7	33.36%
Reynolds wrap	43.5	7.19
Glad Cling wrap	39.7	6.57
Reynolds Wrap Release foil	21.9	3.62
Saran Wrap wrap	20.9	3.46
Private label	185.3	30.65
Other	91.6	15.15

Source: *MMR*, May 31, 2004, p. 33, from Information Resources Inc.

★ 1451 ★
Aluminum Rolling
SIC: 3353; NAICS: 331315

Top Rolled Aluminum Firms in Japan, 2002

Market shares are shown based on domestic output of 2.29 million tons.

Sumitomo Light Metal Industries	16.2%
Kobe Steel	15.3
Furukawa Electric	11.4
Mitsubishi Aluminum	7.4
Sky Aluminum	6.3
Other	43.3

Source: "Market Share Survey Report 2002." [online] from http://www.nni.nikkei.co.jp [accessed January 20, 2004], from Nikkei estimate.

★ 1452 ★
Fiber Optics
SIC: 3357; NAICS: 335921
Gyro Fiber Market

The company has 100% of the European market. Its domestic share exceeds 60%.

Fibercore Limited 60.0%
Other 40.0

Source: *Military & Aerospace Electronics*, March 2004, p. 6.

★ 1453 ★
Fiber Optics
SIC: 3357; NAICS: 335921
Top Fiber Optic Firms in Japan, 2002

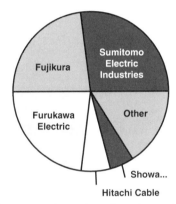

Market shares are shown based on domestic output of 16.5 million km core.

Sumitomo Electric Industries 27.0%
Fujikura 23.0
Furukawa Electric 23.0
Hitachi Cable 6.0
Showa Electric Wire & Cable 5.0
Other 16.0

Source: "Market Share Survey Report 2002." [online] from http://www.nni.nikkei.co.jp [accessed January 20, 2004], from Nikkei estimates.

★ 1454 ★
Fiber Optics
SIC: 3357; NAICS: 335921
Undersea Cable Systems Worldwide, 1999-2003

Market shares are shown in percent.

Alcatel 29.3%
TyCom 25.5
TBA 15.0
KDD-SCS 14.2
NEC 7.1
Fujitsu 6.4
Other 22.5

Source: *Telephony*, March 4, 2002, p. 22, from Pionner Consulting.

★ 1455 ★
Fiber Optics
SIC: 3357; NAICS: 335921
Worldwide Fiber Optic Demand, 2003

Total demand was 55 million kilometers.

Japan 30.0%
North America 25.0
China 25.0
Western Europe 10.0
Latin America/rest of world 5.0
Other Asian Countries 5.0

Source: *Fiber Optics Weekly Update*, March 19, 2004, p. 1, from Corning OFC 2004 Presentation.

★ 1456 ★
Castings
SIC: 3360; NAICS: 331521, 331522
Casting Capacity, 2004

Metal castings are ranked by capacity in tons.

Iron 11,930,000
Aluminum 2,915,000
Steel 1,510,000
Zinc/lead 410,000

Continued on next page.

★ 1456 ★
[Continued]
Castings
SIC: 3360; NAICS: 331521, 331522

Casting Capacity, 2004

Metal castings are ranked by capacity in tons.

Copper-base 400,000
Investment 200,000
Magnesium 140,000
Other nonferrous 70,000

Source: *Modern Casting*, January 2004, p. 27.

★ 1457 ★
Castings
SIC: 3360; NAICS: 331521, 331525

Largest Nonferrous Castings Producers

Market shares are shown in percent.

United States 24.0%
Japan 12.0
China 11.0
Italy 9.0
Mexico 8.0
Germany 8.0
Russia 6.0
Other 22.0

Source: *Advanced Manufacturing Technology*, September 15, 2003, p. 10.

★ 1458 ★
Castings
SIC: 3360; NAICS: 331524, 331525, 331513

Metal Casting Industry

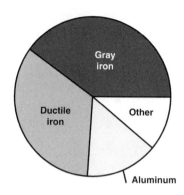

Total metal casting shipments were valued at $16.9 billion in 2001, according to the U.S. Department of Commerce. Automotive and light trucks are the biggest end use markets with a 35% share.

Gray iron 40.0%
Ductile iron 34.0
Aluminum 15.0
Other 11.0

Source: *Advanced Manufacturing Technology*, September 15, 2003, p. 10, from *DOE's Metal Casting Industry of the Future 2002 Annual Report*.

SIC 34 - Fabricated Metal Products

★ 1459 ★
Aerosol Cans
SIC: 3411; NAICS: 332431

Aerosol Can Industry in Europe, 2002

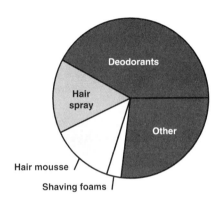

A total of 1.75 billion aluminum cans were produced in 2002.

Deodorants	42.0%
Hair spray	15.0
Hair mousse	13.0
Shaving foams	3.0
Other	27.0

Source: *Global Cosmetic Industry*, September 2003, p. 30, from European Association of Aluminum Aerosol Container Manufacturers.

★ 1460 ★
Razor Blades
SIC: 3421; NAICS: 332211

Razor Blade Market

Market shares are shown for the 52 weeks ended September 7, 2003.

Gillette	70.0%
Schick	25.0
Other	5.0

Source: *USA TODAY*, October 14, 2003, p. 6B, from Information Resources Inc.

★ 1461 ★
Razor Blades
SIC: 3421; NAICS: 332211

Razor Blade Market in Oman

Market shares are shown in percent for May - June 2003.

SuperMax	39.0%
Gillette	37.0
Other	24.0

Source: *Cosmetics International*, September 26, 2003, p. 4, from ACNielsen.

★ 1462 ★
Razor Blades
SIC: 3421; NAICS: 332211
Razor Market in Canada

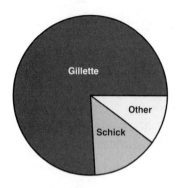

The industry was valued at $270 million.

Gillette 76.0%
Schick 14.0
Other 10.0

Source: *Strategy*, May 3, 2004, p. 2, from ACNielsen.

★ 1463 ★
Razor Blades
SIC: 3421; NAICS: 332211
Razor Market in Mexico

Market shares are shown in percent.

Gillette de Mexico 75.0%
Other 25.0

Source: *Internet Securities*, October 1, 2003, p. NA.

★ 1464 ★
Razor Blades
SIC: 3421; NAICS: 332211
Top Razor Blade (Refill) Makers, 2003

Market shares are shown based on sales at super-markets, drugstores and mass merchandisers for the year ended May 18, 2003.

The Gillette Co. 88.2%
Pfizer Inc. 7.4
American Safety Razor Co. 0.6
Noxell Corp. 0.1

Source: *Grocery Headquarters*, August 2003, p. S14, from Information Resources Inc.

★ 1465 ★
Razor Blades
SIC: 3421; NAICS: 332211
Top Razor Brands, 2004

Market shares are shown based on sales at super-markets, drug stores, mass merchandisers (but not Wal-Mart) for the year ended February 12, 2004. According to consumer research and Gillette, 68 million men and 94 million women shave with a blade and a razor.

Schick Quattro 19.59%
Gillette Mach3 Turbo 18.88
Gillette Venus 16.72
Schick Intuition 9.03
Gillette Mach3 . . . . 8.22
Gillette Mach3 Turbo G Force 5.17
Gillette Sensor Excel 3.61
Gillette Venus Passion 3.25
Gillette Sensor Excel Women 3.10
Other 12.43

Source: *DSN Retailing Today*, March 8, 2004, p. 23, from Information Resources Inc.

★ 1466 ★
Razor Blades
SIC: 3421; NAICS: 332211
Top Razors (Disposable)

Market shares are shown based on sales at drug stores.

Shick Xtreme3 . . . . 14.7%
Schick Slim Twin 12.6
Custom Plus 9.4
Good News 6.8

Continued on next page.

★ 1466 ★

[Continued]
Razor Blades
SIC: 3421; NAICS: 332211

Top Razors (Disposable)

Market shares are shown based on sales at drug stores.

Daisy Plus 6.2%
Good News Plus 6.0
Sensor 3 . . . . 4.1
Bic Softwin 4.1
Other 36.1

Source: *Chain Drug Review*, January 5, 2004, p. 63, from Information Resources Inc.

★ 1467 ★

Razor Blades
SIC: 3421; NAICS: 332211

Top Razors (Refill)

Market shares are shown based on sales at drug stores.

Mach3 . . . . 29.4%
Mach3 Turbo 18.9
Venus 11.3
Sensor Excel 9.1
Sensor 7.2
Atra Plus 3.1
Trac II Plus 2.9
Shick Extreme3 . . . . 1.9
Sensor Excel for Women 1.9
Other 14.3

Source: *Chain Drug Review*, January 5, 2004, p. 63, from Information Resources Inc.

★ 1468 ★

Razor Blades
SIC: 3421; NAICS: 332211

Wet Shaving Industry Worldwide

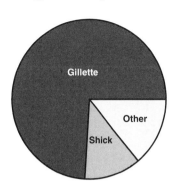

The global industry is valued at $7 billion.

Gillette 74.0%
Shick 12.0
Other 14.0

Source: *BusinessWeek*, January 26, 2004, p. 46, from industry research.

★ 1469 ★

Steel Files
SIC: 3423; NAICS: 332212

Steel File Market Worldwide

The company has over 90% of the market.

Yamond Ltd. 90.0%
Other 10.0

Source: *Asia Africa Intelligence Wire*, April 30, 2004, p. NA.

★ 1470 ★

Locks

SIC: 3429; NAICS: 33251

Door Lock Market

The company has an estimated 55-65% of the market.

Black & Decker 65.0%
Other 35.0

Source: *Baltimore Sun*, July 2, 2003, p. NA.

★ 1471 ★

Locks

SIC: 3429; NAICS: 332722

Global Lock Market, 2002

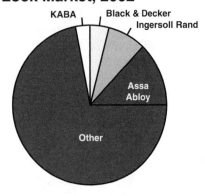

Market shares are shown based on total sales.

Assa Abloy 13.0%
Ingersoll Rand 8.0
Black & Decker 4.0
KABA 3.0
Other 72.0

Source: *Financial Times*, January 2, 2003, p. 12, from company reports and C.S. First Boston.

★ 1472 ★

Luggage Boxes

SIC: 3429; NAICS: 332439

Rooftop Luggage Boxes

Thule makes luggage rack and boxes for vehicles to help drivers carry everything from luggage to golf clubs. It makes 80% of the luggage boxes.

Thule Holding 80.0%
Other 20.0

Source: *Waterbury Republican-American*, January 21, 2004, p. NA.

★ 1473 ★

Luggage Racks

SIC: 3429; NAICS: 332439

Roof Rack Market in North America

The company also has 50% of the market worldwide.

Franklin Aluminum Company 66.0%
Other 34.0

Source: *Modern Machine Shop*, April 2003, p. 104.

★ 1474 ★

Solar Equipment

SIC: 3433; NAICS: 333414

Solar Panel Production Worldwide, 2003

Global solar cell production rose 40% in 2003 to 742 Megawatts.

Japan 49.0%
U.S. 12.0
Other 39.0

Source: *PR Newswire*, March 10, 2004, p. NA, from Solarbuzz Inc.

★ 1475 ★
Solar Equipment
SIC: 3433; NAICS: 333414

Solar Power Equipment Manufacturers Worldwide, 2003

Shares are for the top manufacturers of solar power equipment based on capacity measured in megawatts sold in 2003. Companies are ranked by solar power equipment sales by capacity in megawatts. Shares are shown based on worldwide capacity was about 750 megawatts (MW) in 2003.

	MW	Share
Sharp	198.0	26.40%
Shell Solar	77.0	10.27
Kyocera	72.0	9.60
BP Solar	70.2	9.36
RWE	42.0	5.60
Mitsubishi	40.0	5.33
Isofoton	35.2	4.69
Sanyo	35.0	4.67
Q-Cells	28.0	3.73
Photowatt	20.0	2.67
Other	132.6	17.68

Source: *New York Times*, March 13, 2004, p. B2, from PV Energy Systems.

★ 1476 ★
Solar Equipment
SIC: 3433; NAICS: 333414

Top Solar Batteries Producers Worldwide, 2002

Market shares are shown based on total worldwide production of 520.15 MW (megawatts).

Sharp Corp.	23.6%
BP Solar	13.5
Kyocera Corp.	11.5
Shell Solar	9.1
Sanyo Electric Co.	6.7
Other	35.6

Source: "Market Share Survey Report 2002." [online] from http://www.nni.nikkei.co.jp, from Japan Electronics and Information Technology Industries Assocation.

★ 1477 ★
Solar Equipment
SIC: 3433; NAICS: 333414

Top Solar Battery Makers in Japan, 2002

Market shares are shown based on domestic production of 250 megawatts.

Sharp	49.2%
Kyocera	24.0
Sanyo Electric	14.0
Mitsubishi Electric	9.6
Kaneka	3.0
Other	0.2

Source: "Market Share Survey Report 2002." [online] from http://www.nni.nikkei.co.jp [accessed January 20, 2004], from Nikkei estimate and Japan Refrigeration and Air Condtioning Association.

★ 1478 ★
Swimming Pool Heaters
SIC: 3433; NAICS: 333414

Swimming Pool Heater Market

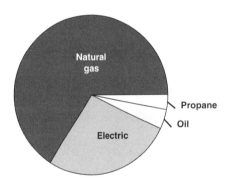

Data are for in-ground existing sales. In-ground pool sales increased from 150,000 in 1996 to 170,700 in 2000. Total pool sales were 315,000 and 366,700 for the same period.

Natural gas	66.0%
Electric	27.0
Oil	4.0
Propane	3.0

Source: *LP/Gas*, January 2004, p. 26, from *Thermodrive Heat Pump Pool Heater Market Research Report*.

★ 1479 ★
Metal Sashes and Doors
SIC: 3442; NAICS: 332321

Power Sliding Door Market in Europe

Market shares are shown in percent.

Delphi 75.0%
Other 25.0

Source: *PR Newswire*, March 4, 2003, p. NA.

★ 1480 ★
Metal Sashes and Doors
SIC: 3442; NAICS: 332321

Top Aluminum Sash/Door Makers in Japan, 2002

Market shares are shown based on domestic shipments.

Tostem 35.5%
YKK 28.4
Sankyo Aluminum 15.7
Shin Nikkei 12.8
Tateyama Aluminum 5.4
Other 2.2

Source: "Market Share Survey Report 2002." [online] from http://www.nni.nikkei.co.jp [accessed January 20, 2004], from Nikkei estimate.

★ 1481 ★
Radiators
SIC: 3443; NAICS: 332313, 33241, 33242

Global Radiator Market

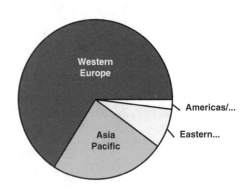

China controls 20% of the world market by volume and will increase by $76 million between 2000 and 2004 as the Asia/Pacific region becomes the dominant region in this market.

	($ mil.)	Share
Western Europe	$ 2,211.1	65.87%
Asia Pacific	804.9	23.98
Eastern Europe	269.5	8.03
Americas/Other	71.3	2.12

Source: *Supply House Times*, July 2002, p. 21, from BSRIA.

★ 1482 ★
Duct
SIC: 3444; NAICS: 332322

Duct Market Shares, 2002

Rectangular
Spiral
Oval
Other

In five years, spiral is forecasted to take 34% of the market at the expense of rectangular, which will see its share fall to 58% of the market.

Rectangular 65.0%
Spiral 29.0
Oval 3.0
Other 3.0

Source: *Snips*, June 2003, p. 6, from Sheet Metal and Air Conditioning Contractors National Association and *2002 Duct Fabrication Market Survey*.

★ **1483** ★
Push Poles
SIC: 3462; NAICS: 332111
Push Pole Market

Push poles are increasingly becoming staples for boaters. They can be made of any substance (PVC, wood) but perhaps the most common form is a one piece pole made of fiberglass, graphite or some composite of the two. They have a number of uses, such as propelling boats and canoes through marshes. Roughly 4,500 push poles are sold each year by eight firms.

Stiffy	50.0%
Other	50.0

Source: *Post and Courier*, January 25, 2004, p. C13.

★ **1484** ★
Automotive Trim
SIC: 3465; NAICS: 33637
Automotive Interior Trim Industry Worldwide

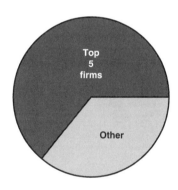

The worldwide market stood at $17 billion in 2003. The top five firms (Faurecia, Visteon, Johnson Controls, Collins & Aikman and Lear) have nearly $11 billion. There are about 87 firms in the industry.

Top 5 firms	64.0%
Other	36.0

Source: *PR Newswire*, May 13, 2003, p. NA, from CSM Worldwide.

★ **1485** ★
Hubcaps
SIC: 3465; NAICS: 33637
Small-Vehicle Hubcap Market Worldwide

The company has 90% of the OEM (original equipment market) for hubcaps for golf carts and other small wheeled vehicles.

Cycle Country	90.0%
Other	10.0

Source: "Cycle Country Accessories" [online] from http://www.topstock.com/Featured_Issues/Cycle%20Country%20Accessories.htm [accessed June 1, 2004].

★ **1486** ★
Cookware
SIC: 3469; NAICS: 332214
Pressure Cooker Market in China, 2004

Zhejiang's share is over 50%. ASD's share is between 20% and 30% of the market.

Zhejiang Supor Cookware Co. Ltd.	50.0%
ASD Co. Ltd.	30.0
Other	20.0

Source: *Asia Africa Intelligence Wire*, February 11, 2004, p. NA.

★ **1487** ★
Powder Coatings
SIC: 3479; NAICS: 332812
Powder Coatings Market

Market shares are shown in percent.

Europe	43.0%
Asia	26.0
North America	23.0
Other	8.0

Source: *Coatings World*, September 2002, p. 36, from Irfab Chemical Consultants.

★ 1488 ★
Firearms
SIC: 3484; NAICS: 332994

Leading Firearm Manufacturers, 2001

Companies are ranked by production of pistols, revolvers, rifles and shotguns. In 2002, the industry produced 943,213 handguns, 1,284,554 rifles and 679,813 shotguns. Totals have been declining since 1996.

	Units	Share
Remington Arms	565,586	19.45%
Sturm, Ruger & Co.	515,031	17.71
Marlin Firearms	258,383	8.89
H&R 1871	192,541	6.62
O.F. Mossberg & Sons	169,096	5.82
U.S. Repeating Arms	158,371	5.45
Smith & Wesson	155,560	5.35
Savage Arms	72,295	2.49
Bryco Arms	66,874	2.30
Beemiller Inc.	64,328	2.21
Argus Publications	63,037	2.17
Beretta U.S.A.	58,536	2.01
Other	567,942	19.53

Source: *Shooting Industry*, July 2003, p. 28, from Bureau of Alcohol, Tobacco and Firearms.

★ 1489 ★
Firearms
SIC: 3484; NAICS: 332994

Leading Handgun Manufacturers, 2001

Companies are ranked by production.

	Units	Share
Sturm, Ruger & Co.	263,691	27.96%
Smith & Wesson	155,560	16.49
Bryco Arms	66,874	7.09
Beretta	58,151	6.17
Beemiller	50,878	5.39
Kel-Tec	45,658	4.84
Arms Technology	38,145	4.04
Heritage Mfg. Inc.	34,100	3.62
Kimber Mfg.	32,746	3.47
Colt's Mfg.	31,648	3.36
Other	165,762	17.57

Source: *Shooting Industry*, July 2003, p. 28, from Bureau of Alcohol, Tobacco and Firearms.

★ 1490 ★
Firearms
SIC: 3484; NAICS: 332994

Leading Long-Gun Manufacturers, 2001

Companies are ranked by production.

	Units	Share
Remington Arms	565,586	28.79%
Marlin Firearms	258,383	13.15
Sturm, Ruger & Co.	251,340	12.79
H&R 1871	192,541	9.80
O.F. Mossberg & Sons	169,096	8.61
U.S. Repeating Arms	158,371	8.06
Savage Arms	72,295	3.68
Argus Publications	63,037	3.21
Bushmaster Firearms	31,346	1.60
Other	202,372	10.30

Source: *Shooting Industry*, July 2003, p. 28, from Bureau of Alcohol, Tobacco and Firearms.

★ 1491 ★
Firearms
SIC: 3484; NAICS: 332994

Leading Pistol Manufacturers, 2001

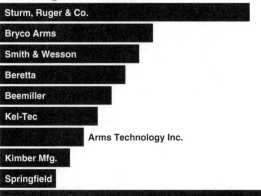

Companies are ranked by production.

	Units	Share
Sturm, Ruger & Co.	112,847	18.11%
Bryco Arms	66,874	10.73
Smith & Wesson	63,235	10.15
Beretta	58,151	9.33
Beemiller	50,878	8.17

Continued on next page.

★ 1491 ★
[Continued]
Firearms
SIC: 3484; NAICS: 332994

Leading Pistol Manufacturers, 2001

Companies are ranked by production.

	Units	Share
Kel-Tec	45,658	7.33%
Arms Technology Inc.	38,145	6.12
Kimber Mfg.	32,746	5.26
Springfield	27,186	4.36
Other	127,350	20.44

Source: *Shooting Industry*, July 2003, p. 28, from Bureau of Alcohol, Tobacco and Firearms.

★ 1492 ★
Valves
SIC: 3491; NAICS: 332911

Global Valve Market

The global market is thought to be about $10 billion. Market shares are shown in percent.

Tyco	6.0%
Flowserve	4.0
Emerson	3.0
SPX	1.0
Metso	1.0
KSB	1.0
Kitz	1.0
Dresser	1.0
Circor	1.0
Other	81.0

Source: *Supply House Times*, January 2003, p. 30, from McIlvane Co.

★ 1493 ★
Valves
SIC: 3491; NAICS: 332911

Valve Market Worldwide, 2002 and 2007

Demand is forecasted to increase 5.5% annually through 2007, representing a $60 billion market. The industry will benefit from increased energy consumption, particularly in Latin America, Asia and Eastern Europe.

	2002	2007	Share
Western Europe . . .	$ 15,320	$ 19,180	31.55%
North America	12,500	15,610	25.67
Asia/Pacific	11,830	16,890	27.78
Other	6,850	9,120	15.00

Source: *Process Heating*, April 2004, p. 12, from Freedonia Group.

SIC 35 - Industry Machinery and Equipment

★ 1494 ★

Turbines

SIC: 3511; NAICS: 333611

Leading Wind Generator Manufacturers Worldwide, 2003

Vestas and NEG Micon are planning to merge and create the world's largest wind turbine company. The share assigned to Enercon is an estimate based on the source.

Vestas/NEG Micon	35.0%
Enercon	18.0
Gamesa Eoilica	11.8
GE Wind	8.8
Nordex	7.0
Bonus Energy	7.0
Other	12.4

Source: *Modern Power Systems*, January 2004, p. 3.

★ 1495 ★

Turbines

SIC: 3511; NAICS: 333611

Leading Wind Turbine Makers, 2003

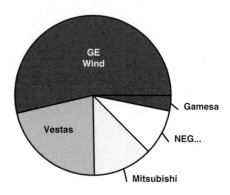

Market shares are shown based on sales. California and Texas had the most megawatts of wind energy installed. Worldwide investment on new wind farms in 2003 was $9 billion.

GE Wind	51.8%
Vestas	21.3
Mitsubishi	11.9
NEG Micron	9.4
Gamesa	3.3

Source: *Manufacturing & Technology News*, May 4, 2004, p. 8, from American Wind Energy Association.

★ 1496 ★
Turbofans
SIC: 3511; NAICS: 333611

Leading Turbofan Makers Worldwide, 2004-2013

Accoring to the source a total of 40,989 turbofan engines will be manufactured from 2004-2013. Production is estimated at $160 billion.

General Electric 36.0%
Rolls-Royce 24.0
Pratt & Whitney 20.0
Snecma 12.0
Honeywell 2.0

Source: *PR Newswire*, April 23, 2004, p. NA, from Teal Group.

★ 1497 ★
Engines
SIC: 3519; NAICS: 333618, 336399

Diesel Engine Production, 2004

NAFTA's production of diesel engines is shown by application.

On-highway 78.0%
Off-highway 10.4
Agricultural 6.1
Gen-set 2.4
Industrial 2.2
Mar/loc 0.9

Source: *Diesel Progress North American Edition*, December 2003, p. 26, from *Future of Diesel Engines, 7th Edition*.

★ 1498 ★
Outboard Motors
SIC: 3519; NAICS: 333618

Top Outboard Motor Brands in Panama

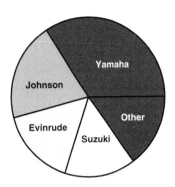

Market shares are shown in percent.

Yamaha 34.0%
Johnson 20.0
Evinrude 16.0
Suzuki 15.0
Other 15.0

Source: "Recreational and Pleasure Boats Industry." [online] from http://www.usatrade.gov [accessed January 5, 2004], from U.S. Commercial Service and company reports.

★ 1499 ★
Farm Equipment
SIC: 3523; NAICS: 333111

Leading Power Tillers/Cultivator Makers in Japan, 2000

Market shares are estimated in percent.

Kubota 22.2%
Iseki 10.9
Honda Motor 10.4
Seirei Industry 8.0
Mitsubishi Agricultural Machinery 4.4
Ishikawajima Shibaura Kikai 3.0
Other 40.1

Source: "Farm Equipment." [online] from http://www.usatrade.gov [accessed January 5, 2004], from U.S. Commercial Service and Yano Research Institute.

★ 1500 ★
Farm Equipment
SIC: 3523; NAICS: 333111

Leading Tractor Makers in Japan, 2000

Market shares are estimated in percent.

Kubota 41.3%
Yanmar Diesel Engine 14.4
Iseki 9.9
Ishikawajima Shibaura Kikai 8.1
Mitsubishi Agricultural Machinery 5.4
Other 20.9

Source: ''Farm Equipment.'' [online] from http://www.usatrade.gov [accessed January 5, 2004], from U.S. Commercial Service and Yano Research Institute.

★ 1501 ★
Farm Equipment
SIC: 3523; NAICS: 333111

Top Tractor Makers in the U.K., 2002

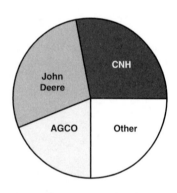

Market shares are shown in percent.

CNH (Case and New Holland) 28.3%
John Deere 27.8
AGCO (MF and Fendt) 19.0
Other 24.9

Source: *Arable Farming*, February 16, 2004, p. 3.

★ 1502 ★
Farm Equipment
SIC: 3523; NAICS: 333111

Tractor and Combine Sales, 2003

Sales are shown for year to date December 2003.

	Units	Share
2 WD 0-40 HP	125,333	60.45%
2 WD 40-100 HP	60,304	29.08
2 WD 100+ HP	14,223	6.86
Self-propelled	4,644	2.24
4 WD	2,837	1.37

Source: *Implement & Tractor*, January/February 2004, p. 25.

★ 1503 ★
Farm Equipment
SIC: 3523; NAICS: 333111

Tractor Sales in France, 2002

New tractor sales hit 38,192 units.

	Sales	Share
John Deere	6,875	18.00%
Renault	6,271	16.42
New Holland	6,206	16.25
MF	3,773	9.88
Case/Steyr	2,578	6.75
Fendt	1,848	4.84
SLH	1,806	4.73
Valtra	1,796	4.70
Deutz-Fahr	1,447	3.79
Landini	1,050	2.75
Other	4,542	11.89

Source: *Implement & Tractor*, July-August 2003, p. 10.

★ 1504 ★
Farm Equipment
SIC: 3523; NAICS: 333111

Tractor Sales in Italy, 2002

	Sales	Share
New Holland		
SLH		
Landini		
John Deere		
MF		
Fendt		
Deutz-Fahr		
Case/Steyr		
Renault		
Valtra		
Other		

New tractor sales hit 30,102 units.

	Sales	Share
New Holland	8,030	26.68%
SLH	7,474	24.83
Landini	3,733	12.40
John Deere	2,328	7.73
MF	798	2.65
Fendt	716	2.38
Deutz-Fahr	450	1.49
Case/Steyr	385	1.28
Renault	145	0.48
Valtra	117	0.39
Other	5,926	19.69

Source: *Implement & Tractor*, July-August 2003, p. 10.

★ 1505 ★
Farm Equipment
SIC: 3523; NAICS: 333111

Tractor Sales in Switzerland, 2002

New tractor sales hit 2,383 units.

	Sales	Share
New Holland	422	16.81%
John Deere	412	16.41
SLH	347	13.82
Case/Steyr	282	11.23

	Sales	Share
Fendt	213	8.48%
Deutz-Fahr	195	7.77
Renault	138	5.50
MF	128	5.10
Landini	89	3.54
Valtra	55	2.19
Other	230	9.16

Source: *Implement & Tractor*, July-August 2003, p. 10.

★ 1506 ★
Farm Equipment
SIC: 3523; NAICS: 333111

Tractor Sales in Western Europe, 2002

New tractor sales hit 169,541 units. France was the largest market (38,192) and Italy was number two (30,192).

	Units	Share
New Holland	27,909	16.46%
John Deere	25,723	15.17
SLH	14,386	8.49
MF	10,981	6.48
Case/Steyr	10,754	6.34
Fendt	9,128	5.38
Renault	7,806	4.60
Valtra	7,649	4.51
Landini	7,135	4.21
Deutz-Fahr	6,603	3.89
Other	41,467	24.46

Source: *Implement & Tractor*, July-August 2003, p. 10.

★ 1507 ★
Lawn & Garden Equipment
SIC: 3524; NAICS: 332212, 333112

Commerical Mower Production

Total sales by year: 157 million units in 1998, 184.7 million in 2000 and 185.9 million in 2002.

	1998	2002	Share
Zero-turn mowers	68,906	98,224	52.82%
Commercial walk- behind mowers	51,267	44,187	23.76
Riding rotary turf mowers	19,862	24,646	13.25
Riding reel mowers . . .	16,982	18,912	10.17

Source: *Diesel Progress North American Edition*, July 2003, p. 17, from Power Systems Research.

★ 1508 ★
Construction Equipment
SIC: 3531; NAICS: 33312

Concrete Mixer Sales

The company makes 85% of all concrete mixers sold in the country. It also makes 27% of all garbage trucks sold and 29% of all fire trucks.

Oshkosk Truck	85.0%
Other	15.0

Source: *Fortune*, December 22, 2003, p. 71, from Oshkosh Truck.

★ 1509 ★
Construction Equipment
SIC: 3531; NAICS: 33312

Construction Equipment Population

Since 1999, the hydraulic excavator population grew 41%, all directional boring grew 36% and off-highway haulers grew 24%.

Skid-steer loaders	281,728
Backhoe loaders	254,712
Wheel loaders	176,748
Hydraulic excavators, crawler	156,535
Trenchers, rubber-tired	63,896
Motor graders, articulated	48,276
Rough-terrain forklifts, telescopic	31,096
Asphalt pavers	15,971
Directional-boring equipment	11,648

Off-highway haulers, articulated	7,254
Concrete pavers, slab	4,665

Source: *Construction Equipment*, August 2003, p. 20, from MacKay & Co.

★ 1510 ★
Construction Equipment
SIC: 3531; NAICS: 33312

Hydraulic Excavator Market in China, 2003

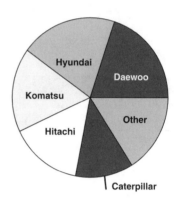

Market shares are shown in percent.

Daewoo	20.3%
Hyundai	20.0
Komatsu	16.7
Hitachi	15.0
Caterpillar	12.2
Other	15.8

Source: *ENR*, April 12, 2004, p. 16.

★ 1511 ★
Construction Equipment
SIC: 3531; NAICS: 33312
Largest Construction Machinery Markets, 2001

Total revenues for the year were 438 billion euros.

United States	18.9%
Germany	18.1
Japan	16.3
Italy	9.8
U.K.	5.7
France	5.6
Other	35.4

Source: *Handelsblatt*, April 16, 2002, p. 14, from VDMA.

★ 1512 ★
Construction Equipment
SIC: 3531; NAICS: 333923
Leading All-Terrain Crane Makers in Germany, 2002

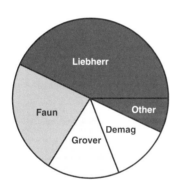

Market shares are shown for the first six months of the year.

Liebherr	43.0%
Faun	23.0
Grover	15.0
Demag	12.0
Other	7.0

Source: *Cranes Today*, September 2002, p. 18.

★ 1513 ★
Construction Equipment
SIC: 3531; NAICS: 33312
Leading Grader Manufacturers in North America

The market for graders is cyclical. It has been mostly stable for the past 20 years. During the last five, however, sales have dropped from 4,500 in 1998 to 3,250 in 2002. Shares are estimates. Other includes Case, Shannon Chastain and B.R. Lee Industries.

Caterpillar	40.0%
Volvo	20.0
Deere	20.0
Komatsu	10.0
Other	10.0

Source: *Diesel Progress North American Edition*, June 2003, p. 4.

★ 1514 ★
Construction Equipment
SIC: 3531; NAICS: 33312
Leading Hydraulic Excavator Makers in Japan, 2002

Market shares are shown based on domestic shipments of 18,308 units.

Komatsu	28.5%
Shin Caterpillar Mitsubishi	25.4
Hitachi Construction Machinery	20.9
Kobelco Construction Machinery	13.8
Sumitomo Construction Machinery	7.0
Other	4.4

Source: "Market Share Survey Report 2002." [online] from http://www.nni.nikkei.co.jp [accessed January 20, 2004], from Nikkei estimate and Japan Construction Equipment Manufacturers Association.

★ 1515 ★
Construction Equipment
SIC: 3531; NAICS: 33312
Top Construction Equipment Producers Worldwide, 2003

The top 50 firms worldwide sold $65.84 billion in construction equipment.

Caterpillar	20.8%
Komatsu	9.9
Terex	5.9

Continued on next page.

★ 1515 ★

[Continued]
Construction Equipment
SIC: 3531; NAICS: 33312

Top Construction Equipment Producers Worldwide, 2003

The top 50 firms worldwide sold $65.84 billion in construction equipment.

Volvo Construction Equipment	4.9%
Liebherr	4.7
CNH	4.5
Ingersoll-Rand	4.4
Hitachi	4.2
Deere	4.1
Metso Minerals	3.1
Sandvik Mining and Construction	3.0
JCB	2.3
Other	28.2

Source: *International Construction*, April 2004, p. 15.

★ 1516 ★

Oil & Gas Equipment
SIC: 3533; NAICS: 333132

Leading Oil and Gas Equipment Makers, 2002

Selected firms are ranked by revenues in billions of dollars.

Schlumberger	$ 13.5
Halliburton	12.5
Ingersoll-Rand Company	8.0
Baker Hughes	5.0
Cooper Cameron Corporation	1.5

Source: "Oil and Gas Field Machinery in USA." [online] from http://www.euromonitor.com [accessed June 9, 2004], from *Euromonitor*.

★ 1517 ★

Oil & Gas Equipment
SIC: 3533; NAICS: 333132

Oil and Gas Equipment Market Worldwide

The global industry is shown by region.

Africa	20.0%
North America	19.0
Western Europe	16.0
Middle East	15.0
Asia	12.0
Other	18.0

Source: "French and Oil and Gas Equipment Market in France." [online] from http://www.export.gov [accessed May 4, 2004].

★ 1518 ★

Elevators and Escalators
SIC: 3534; NAICS: 333921

Escalators and Escalator Sales

Figures are in millions of dollars.

	2002	2007	Share
Associated products	$ 1,040	$ 1,450	22.83%
Passenger & freight elevators	980	1,325	20.87
Escalators & moving walkways	345	500	7.87
Other elevating/lifting equipment	2,265	3,075	48.43

Source: *Research Studies - Freedonia Group*, August 26, 2003, p. NA, from Freedonia Group.

★ 1519 ★
Elevators and Escalators
SIC: 3534; NAICS: 333921

Top Elevator Firms Worldwide

The top eight firms control 75% of the market: Schindler, Kone, Thyssen, Mitsubishi, Hitachi, Toshiba and Fujitech.

Top 8 firms 75.0%
Other 25.0

Source: *The Australian*, May 18, 2004, p. 28.

★ 1520 ★
Cranes
SIC: 3536; NAICS: 333923

Crane Market Shares

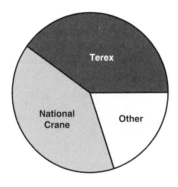

Over the previous decade Terex has brought National's share down from the mid 50s to the point where they are now roughly equal. Market shares are estimated in percent.

Terex 40.0%
National Crane 40.0
Other 20.0

Source: *Cranes Today*, June 2003, p. 11.

★ 1521 ★
Industrial Vehicles
SIC: 3537; NAICS: 333924

Top Industrial Vehicle Makers Worldwide, 2002

Market shares are shown based on global sales of 550,121 units.

Toyota Industries Corp. 24.0%
Linde 19.9
NACCO Material Handling Group Inc. . . . 11.7
Jungheinrich AG 9.9
Mitsubishi Heavy Industries 7.2
Other 27.3

Source: "Market Share Survey Report 2002." [online] from http://www.nni.nikkei.co.jp [accessed January 20, 2004], from Nikkei estimates.

★ 1522 ★
Lift Trucks
SIC: 3537; NAICS: 333924

Leading Lift Truck Makers Worldwide

Firms are ranked by worldwide revenues in millions of dollars.

Toyota . . . . $ 3,100
Linde 3,000
NACCO Industries 1,600
Jungheinrich 1,500
Crown 984
Komatsu 769
Mitsubishi/Caterpillar 704
Manitou 700
Nissan 700
TCM 600

Source: *Modern Materials Handling*, August 2003, p. 43.

★ 1523 ★
Lift Trucks
SIC: 3537; NAICS: 333924

Lift Truck Market in Western Europe

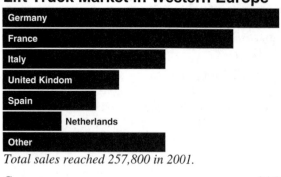

Total sales reached 257,800 in 2001.

Germany	24.0%
France	20.0
Italy	14.0
United Kindom	10.0
Spain	8.0
Netherlands	5.0
Other	14.0

Source: *Handelsblatt*, July 20, 2002, p. 14.

★ 1524 ★
Machine Tools
SIC: 3540; NAICS: 333512

Leading Molding Producers in North America, 2001

Companies are ranked by sales in millions of dollars.

Husky Injection Moulding Systems . . .	$ 100.0
Wentworth Technologies Co. Ltd.	67.0
Stack Teck Systems Inc.	47.7
Reko International Group Inc.	40.0
Hallmark Technologies Inc.	40.0
Active Burgess Mould & Design	40.0
Windsor Mould Inc.	30.0
Build-A-Mould Ltd.	25.0

Source: *Canadian Machinery and Metalworking*, June-July 2003, p. 15, from Global Market Intelligence Report *Tool Die, and Mould Industries* and K&H Global Business Planning Consultants.

★ 1525 ★
Machine Tools
SIC: 3541; NAICS: 333512

CNC Machine Tool Market

The company has two thirds of the market for computer numerically controlled machines costing $10,000 or less.

ShopBot Tools	66.0%
Other	34.0

Source: *PR Newswire*, April 7, 2004, p. NA.

★ 1526 ★
Machine Tools
SIC: 3541; NAICS: 333512

Leading Lathe/Turning Centers in Canada

Market shares are shown in percent. Ontario is the home of two-thirds of all machine tool installations.

Okuma	19.3%
Mazak	18.3
Haas	15.3
Daewoo	12.5
Hyundai	7.5
Other	27.1

Source: *Canadian Machinery and Metalworking*, March 2003, p. 14, from Candian Machine Tool Distributors Association.

★ 1527 ★
Machine Tools
SIC: 3541; NAICS: 333512

Leading Machine Tool Consumers Worldwide, 2002

Countries are ranked by estimated value of tools delivered in millions of dollars. Estimated output of the surveyed countries was $31 billion.

	($ mil.)	Share
China	$ 5,696.0	18.61%
Germany	4,815.2	15.74
Japan	3,441.0	11.25
United States	3,324.8	10.87
Italy	2,931.5	9.58
South Korea	1,223.3	4.00
France	1,164.7	3.81

Continued on next page.

★ 1527 ★

[Continued]
Machine Tools
SIC: 3541; NAICS: 333512

Leading Machine Tool Consumers Worldwide, 2002

Countries are ranked by estimated value of tools delivered in millions of dollars. Estimated output of the surveyed countries was $31 billion.

	($ mil.)	Share
Taiwan	$ 976.9	3.19%
Canada	875.0	2.86
Spain	818.9	2.68
Other	5,332.7	17.43

Source: *Modern Machine Shop*, May 2003, p. 97, from *World Machine Tool Output & Consumption Survey*.

★ 1528 ★

Machine Tools
SIC: 3541; NAICS: 333512

Leading Machine Tool Producers Worldwide, 2002

Countries are ranked by estimated value of tools produced in millions of dollars.

	($ mil.)	Share
Germany	$ 6,737.5	21.72%
Japan	6,379.0	20.57
Italy	3,775.8	12.17
China, Peoples Rep.	3,025.0	9.75
United States	1,913.3	6.17
Taiwan	1,753.8	5.65
Switzerland	1,715.9	5.53
Spain	862.2	2.78
Korea, Rep. Of	833.3	2.69
France	812.3	2.62
Other	3,207.7	10.34

Source: *Metalworking Insiders Report*, February 15, 2003, p. 1, from Gardner Publications.

★ 1529 ★

Machine Tools
SIC: 3541; NAICS: 333512

Leading Milling Center Makers in Canada

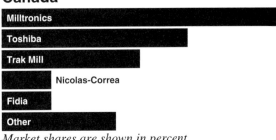

Market shares are shown in percent.

Milltronics	34.2%
Toshiba	22.9
Trak Mill	17.1
Nicolas-Correa	5.7
Fidia	5.7
Other	14.3

Source: *Canadian Machinery and Metalworking*, March 2003, p. 14, from Candian Machine Tool Distributors Association.

★ 1530 ★

Machine Tools
SIC: 3541; NAICS: 333512

Machine Tool Installations in Canada

Market shares are shown in percent.

Ontario	66.8%
Quebec	23.1
West	8.9
East	1.2

Source: *Canadian Machinery and Metalworking*, March 2003, p. 14, from Candian Machine Tool Distributors Association.

★ 1531 ★
Machine Tools
SIC: 3541; NAICS: 333512

Top Carbide Machine Tool Firms in Japan, 2002

Market shares are shown based on domestic sales of 189.7 billion yen.

Mitsubishi Materials	14.3%
Toshiba Tungaloy	14.0
Sumitomo Electric Industries	12.7
Hitachi Tool Engineering	6.0
OSG	5.2
Other	47.8

Source: "Market Share Survey Report 2002." [online] from http://www.nni.nikkei.co.jp [accessed January 20, 2004], from Nikkei estimate.

★ 1532 ★
Machine Tools
SIC: 3541; NAICS: 333512

Top Machining Center Makers in Japan

Shares are shown based on production.

Yamazaki Mazak	24.5%
Makino Milling Machine Co.	20.5
Mori Seiki	19.7
Okuma	16.6

Source: *Metalworking Insiders Report*, August 8, 2003, p. 2, from *Nikkei Business Daily*.

★ 1533 ★
Machine Tools
SIC: 3541; NAICS: 333512

Top NC Lathe Makers in Japan

Data refer to numerically controlled lathes.

Yamazaki Mazak Corp.	30.7%
Mori Seiki Co.	23.7
Okuma Corp.	20.1
Other	25.5

Source: *Metalworking Insiders Report*, August 8, 2003, p. 2, from *Nikkei Business Daily*.

★ 1534 ★
Dies and Molds
SIC: 3544; NAICS: 333511, 333514

Top Producers of Dies and Molds Worldwide

Market shares are shown in percent for 1999.

Japan	41.0%
U.S.	18.0
Germany	10.0
Italy	5.7
France	5.1
Taiwan	4.6
U.K.	4.4
Canada	3.0
Spain	2.8
South Korea	2.1
Other	2.9

Source: *Nikkei Weekly*, December 17, 2001, p. 1, from International Special Tooling & Machining Association and Ministry of Economy, Trade and Industry.

★ 1535 ★
Printing Equipment
SIC: 3555; NAICS: 333293
Digital Printer Sales

Color printers have 15% of large printing companies, 25% of medium sized firms, 30% of corporate and in-house departments.

Corporate and in-house departments 50.0%
Primedia and large printing companies 40.0
Small printing companies 5.0
Medium-size printing companies 5.0

Source: *Electronic Publishing*, December 2003, p. 24.

★ 1536 ★
Food Processing Equipment
SIC: 3556; NAICS: 333294
Leading Food Processing Equipment Makers, 2002

Selected firms are ranked by revenues in millions of dollars.

Invensys . . . . $ 9,900.0
FMC Corporation 1,852.9
Key Tecchnology Inc. 73.0

Source: "Industrial Food Processing Machinery in USA." [online] from http://www.euromonitor.com [accessed June 9, 2004], from Euromonitor.

★ 1537 ★
Automatic Ball Bonders
SIC: 3559; NAICS: 333298
Ball Bonder Market Worldwide

The world ball bonder market increased from $334.5 million in 2001 to $356.2 million in 2002.

Kulicke & Soffa 36.0%
Shinkawa 22.0
ASM Pacific 19.0
Other 23.0

Source: *Business Wire*, April 21, 2003, p. NA, from VLSI Research.

★ 1538 ★
Cigarette Making Machines
SIC: 3559; NAICS: 333319
Leading Cigarette Making Machine Producers Worldwide

Market shares are shown in percent.

Hauni 90.0%
Other 10.0

Source: "Is it the Name?" [online] available from http://www.the managementor.com/kuniverse/kmailers_universe/mktg_kmailers [accessed February 26, 2003].

★ 1539 ★
Plastics Machinery
SIC: 3559; NAICS: 33322
High-Volume PET Machinery

Since creating its first mold for a coffee cup in 1958 the company has been a significant presence in the market for producing customized machines used to create preformed PET (polyethylene terephthalate) molds.

Husky 76.0%
Other 24.0

Source: *Canadian Business*, March 17, 2003, p. 5.

★ 1540 ★
Plastics Machinery
SIC: 3559; NAICS: 33322
Leading Injection Molding Machine Makers in Japan, 2002

Market shares are shown based on domestic production.

Nissei Plastic Industrial 20.0%
Sumitomo Heavy Industries 18.8
Fanuc 17.0
Japan Steel Works 15.1
Toshiba Machine 12.5
Other 16.6

Source: "Market Share Survey Report 2002." [online] from http://www.nni.nikkei.co.jp [accessed January 20, 2004], from Nikkei estimate.

★ 1541 ★
Rubber Machinery
SIC: 3559; NAICS: 33322
Rubber Machinery Sales Worldwide, 2002

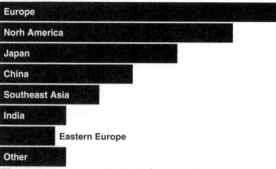

The sector was worth about $1.7 billion in 2002. Many consolidations took place. European companies have seen some success in the United States and China. Figures are from an annual survey by the source.

Europe 25.0%
Norh America 21.0
Japan 16.0
China 12.0
Southeast Asia 9.0
India 6.0
Eastern Europe 5.0
Other 6.0

Source: *European Rubber Journal*, March 2003, p. 20.

★ 1542 ★
Semiconductor Equipment
SIC: 3559; NAICS: 333295
CMP Industry Shares Worldwide

Chemical mechanical planarization or polishing (CMP) is a process involving a chemical reaction that enhances the mechanical removal rate of a material. CMP removes films and similar imperfections on the film or wafer and then flattens it (planarization). The industry is valued at $1.7 billion and is forecasted to reach $3.3 billion in 2008. CMP equipment has 55% of the market and slurries take 24%.

Asia 50.0%
North America 36.0
Europe 12.0
Other 2.0

Source: *Electronic News*, December 22, 2003, p. NA, from Business Communications Co.

★ 1543 ★
Semiconductor Equipment
SIC: 3559; NAICS: 333295

Global Deposition Industry

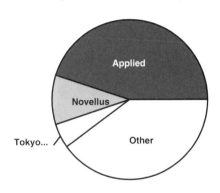

The market was valued at $5.3 billion.

Applied	45.0%
Novellus	10.0
Tokyo Electron	5.0
Other	40.0

Source: *Electronic News*, April 28, 2003, p. NA, from VLSI Research.

★ 1544 ★
Semiconductor Equipment
SIC: 3559; NAICS: 333295

High-Speed Amplifier Market Worldwide, 2002

Analog Devices

Intersil

Other

Market shares are shown in percent.

Analog Devices	41.0%
Intersil	11.0
Other	38.0

Source: *Electronic Buyer's News*, May 19, 2003, p. 8.

★ 1545 ★
Semiconductor Equipment
SIC: 3559; NAICS: 333295

Leading Lithography Tool Providers Worldwide

The global industry was valued at $3.5 billion.

ASML	45.0%
Nikon Corp.	25.0
Canon Inc.	20.0
Other	10.0

Source: *Electronic News*, April 28, 2003, p. NA, from VLSI Research.

★ 1546 ★
Semiconductor Equipment
SIC: 3559; NAICS: 333295

Leading Wafer Fab Equipment Makers Worldwide, 2002

Market revenues declined from $24.1 billion in 2001 to $16.5 billion in 2002, a nearly 32% fall. Companies are ranked by revenues in millions of dollars.

	($ mil.)	Share
Applied Materials	$ 3,672	22.2%
Tokyo Electron	1,671	10.1
ASML	1,596	9.7
KLA-Tencor	1,209	7.3
Nikon	801	4.8
Novellus Systems	797	4.8
Lam Research	589	3.6
Hitachi	529	3.2
Canon	516	3.1
Dainippon Screen	398	2.4
Other	4,750	28.7

Source: "Gartner Says Worldwide Wafer Equipment Declined 32%." [online] from http://www.gartner.com [press release April 7, 2003], from Gartner.

★ 1547 ★
Semiconductor Equipment
SIC: 3559; NAICS: 333295

Process Diagnostic Equipment Market Worldwide

The global industry was valued at $2.8 billion.

KLA-Tencor Corp.	40.0%
Applied Materials	10.0
Hitachi High Technologies Corp.	5.0
Other	45.0

Source: *Electronic News*, April 28, 2003, p. NA, from VLSI Research.

★ 1548 ★
Semiconductor Equipment
SIC: 3559; NAICS: 333295

Wafer Fab Materials Market Worldwide

The industry was valued at $12.98 billion in 2002.

Silicon wafers	43.0%
Photomasks	16.0
Electronic gases	14.0
Photoresists & ancillaries	10.0
Wet chemicals	5.0
Other	12.0

Source: *Chemical Week*, July 23, 2003, p. 10, from Semiconductor Equipment Manufacturers Institute.

★ 1549 ★
Fire Pumps
SIC: 3561; NAICS: 333911

Truck-Mounted Fire Pumps Market

The company has 50% share of the U.S. market.

Hale Products	50.0%
Other	50.0

Source: "Market Leadership." [online] from http://www.idexcorp.com/about/leadership.asp [accessed May 25, 2004].

★ 1550 ★
Pumps
SIC: 3561; NAICS: 333911

Sewage Pump Sales Worldwide

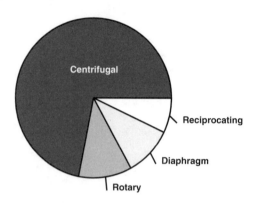

Figures show sales for new and replacement sewer pipe in millions of dollars. The U.S. remains the home of some of the world's largest pump firms, but the industry is splintered and contains more than 1,000 companies. Shares are for the replacement market.

	New	Replacement	Share
Centrifugal	$ 121	$ 729	72.32%
Rotary	19	114	11.31
Diaphragm	16	97	9.62
Reciprocating	11	68	6.75

Source: *Water and Waste Water International*, February 2003, p. 45, from McIlvaine Company's *2002 World Pump Report*.

★ 1551 ★
Compressors
SIC: 3563; NAICS: 333912

Compressors Market in Mindanao, Philippines

Total market was valued at $2.6 million, up steadily from $1.12 million in 1998.

Danfoss	50.0%
Grasso	21.7
York	16.5
Mycom	11.8

Source: "Refrigeration and Cold Storage Equipment in Mindanao." [online] from http://www.usatrade.gov [accessed june 1, 2004], from Philippine Business Profiles and Perspectives.

★ 1552 ★
Packaging Machinery
SIC: 3565; NAICS: 333993

Packaging Machinery Industry

The company has a 65% of the global market as well.

Better Packages 75.0%
Other 25.0

Source: *Knight Ridder/Tribune Business News*, May 30, 2003, p. NA.

★ 1553 ★
Packaging Machinery
SIC: 3565; NAICS: 333993

Packaging Machinery Market Worldwide

The company also holds 75% of the U.S. market.

Better Packages 65.0%
Other 35.0

Source: *Knight Ridder/Tribune Business News*, May 30, 2003, p. NA, from company reports.

★ 1554 ★
Packaging Machinery
SIC: 3565; NAICS: 333993

Packaging Machinery Sales Worldwide, 2002

Total sales worldwide were $601 million.

United States 27.6%
Germany 17.7
Japan 14.9
Italy 12.6
China 11.0
Spain 4.0
U.K. 3.3

France 3.1%
Switzerland 2.6
Netherlands 1.0
Other 2.2

Source: *Food Engineering*, October 2003, p. 18, from Confederation of Packaging Machinery Associations.

★ 1555 ★
Packaging Machinery
SIC: 3565; NAICS: 333993

Packaging Machinery Spending, 2003

Data show estimated spending by market segment.

	($ mil.)	Share
Food products	$ 2,062	42.90%
Beverage products	921	19.16
Pharmaceutical/medical/ consumer/industrial	370	7.70
Durable hard goods	370	7.70
Personal care products	321	6.68
Chemicals & cleaning	312	6.49
Paper products/textiles/all other	294	6.12
Converters/printers/other	156	3.25

Source: *Packaging Digest*, May 2003, p. 60, from Packaging Machinery Manufacturers Institute.

★ 1556 ★
Incinerators
SIC: 3567; NAICS: 333994

Leading Incinerator Makers in Japan, 2002

Market shares are shown based on domestic orders of 3,659 metric tons.

Mitsubishi Heavy Industries 30.3%
NKK 23.6
Hitachi Zosen 16.3
Kawasaki Heavy Idnustries 14.5
Kawasaki Steel 11.4
Other 3.9

Source: "Market Share Survey Report 2002." [online] from http://www.nni.nikkei.co.jp [accessed January 20, 2004], from Nikkei estimate.

★ 1557 ★

Bearings

SIC: 3568; NAICS: 333613

Top Bearings Makers in Japan, 2002

Market shares are shown based on domestic sales of 389.2 billion yen.

NSK	35.2%
Koyo Seiko	28.4
NTN	25.3
Nachi-Fujikoshi	5.9
Minebea	4.2
Other	1.0

Source: "Market Share Survey Report 2002." [online] from http://www.nni.nikkei.co.jp [accessed January 20, 2004], from Nikkei estimate.

★ 1558 ★

Firefighting Equipment

SIC: 3569; NAICS: 333999

Fire Rescue Tool Market

The company has 50% share of the U.S. market.

Hale Products	50.0%
Other	50.0

Source: "Market Leadership." [online] from http://www.idexcorp.com/about/leadership.asp [accessed May 25, 2004].

★ 1559 ★

Robots

SIC: 3569; NAICS: 333999

Largest Robot Stocks Worldwide

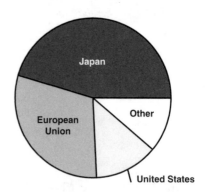

Total operational stock increased to 769,888 units in 2002, up slightly from 756,377 in 2001. Robots are most commonly used in the automotive field, taking a 53% of the market in Germany, 63% in France, 60% in the U.K. and 50% in the United States.

	Units	Share
Japan	350,169	45.48%
European Union	233,139	30.28
United States	103,515	13.45
Other	83,065	10.79

Source: *Advanced Manufacturing & Technology*, December 15, 2003, p. 11, from United Nations Economic Commission for Europe and International Federation of Robotics.

★ 1560 ★

Robots

SIC: 3569; NAICS: 333999

New Orders for Robots in North America, 2003

Material handling > 10 lbs.	29.0%
Spot welding	27.0
Arc welding	18.0
Material handling, 10 lbs	8.0
Dispensing/coating	8.0
Other	10.0

Source: *Advanced Manufacturing Technology*, March 15, 2004, p. 2, from Robotic Industries Association.

★ 1561 ★
Robots
SIC: 3569; NAICS: 333999
Robot Sales in North America

Sales are shown by application.

Material handling	34.0%
Spot welding	31.0
Arc welding	18.0
Dispensing & coating	8.0
Assembly	6.0
Material removal	3.0

Source: *Assembly*, May 2004, p. 41, from Robotics Industry Association.

★ 1562 ★
Robots
SIC: 3569; NAICS: 333999
Top Multi-Joint Robot Makers Worldwide, 2002

Market shares are shown based on total shipments of 493 billion yen.

ABB	17.0%
Fanuc Ltd.	16.9
Yaskawa Electric Corp.	16.5
KUKA Roboter GmbH	9.1
Kawasaki Heavy Industries	6.8
Other	33.7

Source: "Market Share Survey Report 2002." [online] from http://www.nni.nikkei.co.jp [accessed January 20, 2004], from Nikkei estimates.

★ 1563 ★
Computers
SIC: 3571; NAICS: 334111
Government PC Market, 2003

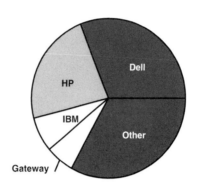

Shares are for the first quarter.

Dell	31.4%
HP	23.2
IBM	7.1
Gateway	5.6
Other	32.7

Source: *Investor's Business Daily*, July 31, 2003, p. A4, from Gartner Inc. and Dataquest Inc.

★ 1564 ★
Computers
SIC: 3571; NAICS: 334111
Leading Contract Computer Manufacturers Worldwide

Market shares are among the top 15 contractors. Computers include PCs, desktop and notebooks.

Solectron	23.0%
Quanta	20.0
Asustek	13.0
Sanmina-SCI	12.0
Compal	10.0
Other	22.0

Source: *Investor's Business Daily*, February 5, 2003, p. A6, from Deutsche Banc. and Alexander Brown.

★ 1565 ★
Computers
SIC: 3571; NAICS: 334111

Leading Electronic Dictionary Producers in China

Market shares are shown in percent.

Wenquxin	26.5%
Noahark	15.7
Besta	13.7
Instant-Dict	12.2

Source: *Asia Africa Intelligence Wire*, August 19, 2003, p. NA, from Sino-Market Research.

★ 1566 ★
Computers
SIC: 3571; NAICS: 334411

Leading Thin Client Suppliers Worldwide, 2003

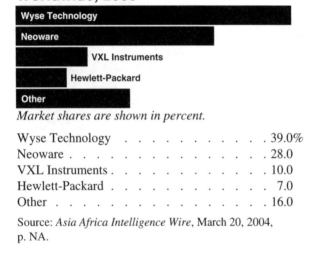

Wyse Technology
Neoware
VXL Instruments
Hewlett-Packard
Other

Market shares are shown in percent.

Wyse Technology	39.0%
Neoware	28.0
VXL Instruments	10.0
Hewlett-Packard	7.0
Other	16.0

Source: *Asia Africa Intelligence Wire*, March 20, 2004, p. NA.

★ 1567 ★
Computers
SIC: 3571; NAICS: 334111

Tablet PC Sales

Sales are forecasted in thousands of units.

2007	6,200
2006	4,400
2005	2,300
2004	760
2003	260

Source: *Computer Reseller News*, November 17, 2003, p. 35, from International Data Corp.

★ 1568 ★
Computers
SIC: 3571; NAICS: 334111

Thin-Client Industry Worldwide

The source defines thin clients as "terminals on desktops that connect directly to a server rather than operate with their own hard drives." Thin client systems are cheaper than standard client/server PC setups.

Wyse Technology	41.0%
Neoware	30.0
Compaq	6.0
Sun Microsystems	3.9
MXT/Visara	2.7
TeleVideo	2.2
Igel	2.2
Other	12.0

Source: *Investor's Business Daily*, August 12, 2002, p. A8, from Commerce Capital Markets Inc. and First Call.

★ 1569 ★
Computers
SIC: 3571; NAICS: 334111

Top Computer Makers in Altai Region, Russia

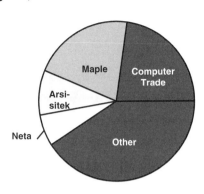

The Altai Region was known primarily for its agricultural output. The region now has a strong telecommunications infrastructure, according to the source. In 1990, the first three computer firms came to the region. By August 1998, there were 50 such firms. The monthly turnover in the computer market for the region was about $2 - 5 million.

Computer Trade	25.0%
Maple	23.0
Arsi-sitek	10.0
Neta	7.0
Other	45.0

Source: "Information Technology and Telecommunications." [online] from http://www.bisnis.doc.gov [accessed May 10, 2004].

★ 1570 ★
Computers
SIC: 3571; NAICS: 334111

Top Notebook Makers Worldwide

Market shares are shown for the second quarter of the year.

Hewlett-Packard	17.4%
Dell	16.1
Toshiba	11.7
IBM	11.6
Acer	5.4

Source: *New York Times*, October 6, 2003, p. C9, from Gartner Dataquest.

★ 1571 ★
Computers
SIC: 3571; NAICS: 334111

Top Notebook Makers in Germany, 2003

Notebook computers rose 44% to 2.5 million units, according to estimates by International Data Corp.

	Units	Share
Acer	368,139	14.5%
Fujitsu Siemens	332,589	13.1
Toshiba	254,779	10.0
Hewlett-Packard	240,542	9.4
Gericom	234,280	9.2
Dell	166,391	6.5
IBM	164,804	6.5
Medion	154,920	6.1
Vobis	112,241	4.4

Source: *Europe Intelligence Wire*, January 27, 2004, p. NA, from RSDL Europe and International Data Corp.

★ 1572 ★
Computers
SIC: 3571; NAICS: 334111

Top Notebook Makers in Russia

Market shares are shown in percent.

Rover Computers	29.5%
Toshiba	11.8
Hewlett-Packard	11.4
Other	47.3

Source: *Kommersant*, February 25, 2003, p. 16.

★ 1573 ★

Computers

SIC: 3571; NAICS: 334111

Top Notebook Makers in Taiwan, 2003

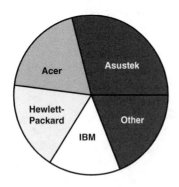

Market shares are determined by shipment volume.

Asustek	28.90%
Acer	18.70
Hewlett-Packard	18.40
IBM	15.04
Other	18.96

Source: *Taiwan Economic News*, March 12, 2020, p. NA, from Frost & Sullivan.

★ 1574 ★

Computers

SIC: 3571; NAICS: 334111

Top Notebook Makers in the Ukraine, 2002

PC demand is estimated to reach 780,000 units in 2003 and 930,000 units in 2004.

Toshiba	26.0%
HP/Compaq	24.0
IBM	10.0
Other	40.0

Source: "Computer Equipment Manufacturing." [online] from http://www.usatrade.gov [accessed February 1, 2004], from Halystky Kontraky.

★ 1575 ★

Computers

SIC: 3571; NAICS: 334111

Top PC Firms, 2002-2003

Total shipments fell from 57.7 million in 2002 to 51.3 million in 2003. Data include PCs, mobile PCs and IA-32 servers.

	2002	2003
Dell	25.3%	27.6%
Hewlett-Packard	17.9	18.6
Gateway	5.3	3.5
IBM	4.9	4.7
Apple	3.3	2.9
Other	43.2	42.7

Source: "Gartner Says PC Vendors Experiences a Happy Holiday Season." [online] from http://www.gartner.com [press release January 14, 2004], from Gartner Dataquest.

★ 1576 ★

Computers

SIC: 3571; NAICS: 334111

Top PC Firms in Asia/Pacific, 2033

Market shares are shown based on 28.39 million units. Figures exclude Japan.

Lenovo	12.7%
Hewlett-Packard	9.7
IBM	7.0
Dell	6.3
Founder	5.0
Other	59.3

Source: "Asia/Pacific PC Market Successfully Sailed Past Market." [online] from http://www.idc.com [Press release dated January 1, 2004], from International Data Corp.

★ 1577 ★
Computers
SIC: 3571; NAICS: 334111
Top PC Firms in Australia, 2003

Computer firms shipped 618,827 notebooks and personal computers during the fourth quarter. Notebooks grew 35% between 2002 and 2003.

Hewlett-Packard	17.7%
Dell	12.7
IBM	8.5
Acer	7.7
Toshiba	5.7
Apple	3.9
Other	43.8

Source: ''What a Year for the Australian PC Market.'' [online] from http://www.idc.com [Press release dated January 30, 2004], from International Data Corp.

★ 1578 ★
Computers
SIC: 3571; NAICS: 334111
Top PC Firms in Brazil

Market shares are shown in percent.

Metron	6.0%
Itautec	5.0
Hewlett-Packard	5.0
Other	84.0

Source: *Latin Trade*, May 2003, p. 28, from Gartner Dataquest.

★ 1579 ★
Computers
SIC: 3571; NAICS: 334111
Top PC Firms in Canada, 2003

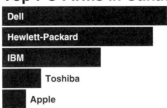

A total of 3,303,644 computers are thought to have been shipped for the year. Figures are preliminary.

	Units	Share
Dell	722,199	21.9%
Hewlett-Packard	669,823	20.3
IBM	426,300	12.9
Toshiba	162,492	4.9
Apple	104,918	3.2
Others	1,217,912	36.9

Source: ''Canadian PC Market Closes the Year on a High Note.'' [online] from http://www.idc.com [press release January 30, 2004], from International Data Corp. Canada.

★ 1580 ★
Computers
SIC: 3571; NAICS: 334111
Top PC Firms in China, 2003

The top three PC firms control only 17.6% of the market showing China's PC market to be very diversified.

Dell	6.8%
Founder	6.2
IBM	4.6
Other	82.4

Source: ''China's Laptop PC Market Remains Attractive'' [Online] http://www.chinadaily.com.cn/english/ [accessed March 19, 2004], March 8, 2004, p. NA.

★ 1581 ★

Computers

SIC: 3571; NAICS: 334111

Top PC Firms in EMEA, 2003

Total shipments in Europe, the Middle East and Africa (EMEA) increased from 46.67 million units in 2002 to 52.67 million units in 2003.

	2002	2003
Hewlett-Packard	15.6%	15.7%
Dell	8.0	8.9
Fujitsu Siemens	6.2	6.3
IBM	4.2	4.4
Acer	4.0	5.4
Other	62.1	59.3

Source: "Gartner Says EMEA PC Market Recovered from Downturn." [online] from http://www.gartner.com [Press release February 24, 2004], from Gartner Dataquest.

★ 1582 ★

Computers

SIC: 3571; NAICS: 334111

Top PC Firms in France

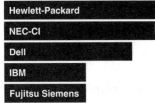

The market had shipments of 5.57 million.

	Units	Share
Hewlett-Packard	1,350,000	24.2%
NEC-CI	712,492	12.8
Dell	626,877	11.2
IBM	383,417	6.9
Fujitsu Siemens	368,349	6.6

Source: *Europe Intelligence Wire*, January 30, 2004, p. NA, from Gartner Dataquest.

★ 1583 ★

Computers

SIC: 3571; NAICS: 334111

Top PC Firms in Germany

Market shares are for the second quarter of 2003. Total units are estimated at 7.2 million for 2003, up from 6.8 million.

Fujitsu Siemens	16.9%
HP	12.6
Medion AG	11.6
Dell	7.5
Acer	4.9
Other	46.5

Source: "Personal Computers." [online] from http://www.usatrade.gov [accessed January 5, 2004], from U.S. Commercial Service and International Data Corp.

★ 1584 ★

Computers

SIC: 3571; NAICS: 334111

Top PC Firms in India, 2003

Market shares are shown for the second quarter of 2003.

HCL	9.6%
Hewlett-Packard	8.3
IBM	8.1
Other	74.0

Source: *AsiaPulse News*, August 22, 2003, p. NA, from International Data Corp. India.

★ 1585 ★

Computers

SIC: 3571; NAICS: 334111

Top PC Firms in Indonesia

Demand for PCs has grown at an average rate of 20% over the last three years, according to the source. The increase is a result of more expensive, higher quality PCs and a population with improving income and advanced education.

Hewlett-Packard	14.0%
IBM	5.0
Dell	3.5
Acer	3.0
Zyrex	3.0
Other	71.5

Source: "Indonesian Personal Computer and Peripheral Market." [online] from http://www.usatrade.gov [accessed June 1, 2004], from APW/Komitel.

★ 1586 ★

Computers

SIC: 3571; NAICS: 334111

Top PC Firms in Japan

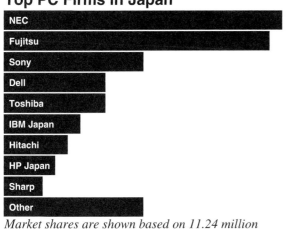

Market shares are shown based on 11.24 million units.

NEC	22.2%
Fujitsu	21.2
Sony	11.1
Dell	8.1
Toshiba	8.0
IBM Japan	6.3
Hitachi	5.0
HP Japan	3.8
Sharp	3.0
Other	11.3

Source: *Nikkei Weekly*, May 12, 2003, p. 1, from Multimedia Research Institute.

★ 1587 ★

Computers

SIC: 3571; NAICS: 334111

Top PC Firms in Latin America, 2003

Total shipments increaed from 8.40 million units in 2002 to 9.05 million units in 2003.

	2002	2003
Hewlett-Packard	13.7%	11.2%
Dell	5.6	6.6
IBM	5.5	4.0
Alaska	2.6	2.2
Toshiba	1.5	1.6
Other	70.8	74.4

Source: "Gartner Says Strong Notebook Sales Helped Drive Latin America PC Market." [online] from http://www.gartner.com [Press release February 24, 2004], from Gartner Dataquest.

★ 1588 ★

Computers

SIC: 3571; NAICS: 334111

Top PC Firms in the Czech Republic, 2003

Market shares are shown abased on sales of 413,000 units.

Hewlett-Packard	16.0%
Acer	11.0
Dell	10.0
Brave	8.0
Autocont	6.0
Other	49.0

Source: *Europe Intelligence Wire*, March 24, 2020, p. NA, from International Data Corp.

★ 1589 ★

Computers

SIC: 3571; NAICS: 334111

Top PC Firms in the U.K.

Market shares are shown for the fourth quarter of 2002 and 2003.

	4Q 2002	4Q 2003
Hewlett-Packard	16.9%	19.2%
Dell	16.4	17.6
NEC	9.2	6.8
Time Group	6.4	5.6
eMachines	5.6	5.5
Other	45.5	45.3

Source: "4Q03 Seasonal Demand Helps Fuel Another Quarter." [online] available from http://www.idc.com [accessed February 9, 2004], from International Data Corp.

★ 1590 ★

Computers

SIC: 3571; NAICS: 334111

Top PC Firms Worldwide, 2002-2003

Market shares for 2003 are preliminary. Total shipments are estimated to have increased from 152.29 million in 2002 to 168.85 million units in 2003.

	2002	2003
Hewlett-Packard	14.2%	14.3%
Dell	13.2	15.0
IBM	5.2	5.1
Fujitsu/Fujitsu Siemens	3.8	3.8
Toshiba	2.8	2.9
Other	60.9	58.9

Source: "Gartner Says PC Vendors Experiences a Happy Holiday Season." [online] from http://www.gartner.com [press release January 14, 2004], from Gartner Dataquest Inc.

★ 1591 ★

Computers

SIC: 3571; NAICS: 334111

Top Supercomputer Makers

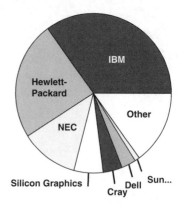

Shares are for processing power at 500 largest installations.

IBM	35.0%
Hewlett-Packard	24.0
NEC	12.0
Silicon Graphics	6.0
Cray	4.0
Dell	3.0
Sun Microsystems	1.0
Other	15.0

Source: *Wall Street Journal*, June 23, 2003, p. B5, from *Top500List*.

★ 1592 ★

Personal Digital Assistants

SIC: 3571; NAICS: 334111

Global PDA Shipments by Operating System

Market shares are shown in percent.

	2002	2004
Palm	57.0%	46.0%
Microsoft	25.0	45.0
Other	18.0	9.0

Source: *Business 2.0*, June 2004, p. 97, from International Data Corp.

★ 1593 ★
Personal Digital Assistants
SIC: 3571; NAICS: 334111
Handheld Device Shipments

Shipments are shown in millions of units.

2006 . . . . 6.8
2005 . . . . 6.7
2004 . . . . 6.6
2003 . . . . 6.3
2002 . . . . 6.0

Source: *CFO*, Winter 2003, p. 45, from International Data
Corp.

★ 1594 ★
Personal Digital Assistants
SIC: 3571; NAICS: 334111
School PDA Market

*Shares are for grades K-12. An estimated 62.5% of
schools use handheld devices.*

PalmOne 82.0%
Other 18.0

Source: *Electronic Education Report*, October 10, 2003,
p. NA, from Quality Education Data.

★ 1595 ★
Personal Digital Assistants
SIC: 3571; NAICS: 334111
Smart Hand-Held Device Market in Australia, 2003

Fourth quarter saw 93.4% year-on-year growth .

Palm 29.9%
Hewlett-Packard 26.3
Nokia 13.1
RIM 7.3
Sony Ericsson 4.0
Other 19.4

Source: "New Leader in the Growing SHD Market."
[online] from http://www.idc.com [Press release dated
March 11, 2004], from International Data Corp.

★ 1596 ★
Personal Digital Assistants
SIC: 3571; NAICS: 334111
Top PDA Makers, 2003

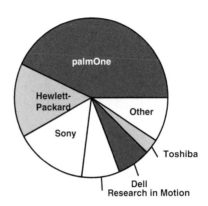

*PDA stands for personal digital assistant. Total ship-
ments were 5.84 million in 2003, down from 5.96
million in 2002.*

	Units	Share
palmOne	12,537,300	43.4%
Hewlett-Packard	887,500	15.2
Sony	866,500	14.8
Research in Motion	435,500	7.5
Dell	433,000	7.4
Toshiba	178,361	3.1
Other	504,530	8.6

Source: "Gartner Says Worldwide PDA Industry Suffers
5% Shipment Decline." [online] from http://
www.gartner.com [Press release March 16, 2004], from
Gartner.

★ 1597 ★
Personal Digital Assistants
SIC: 3571; NAICS: 334111
Top PDA Makers in China, 2002

Market shares are shown in percent.

Hi-Tech Wealth 24.0%
Meijin Computer Technology Ltd. 20.0
Legend Group 18.0
Group Sense PDA Ltd. 16.0
Inventec Besta Co. Ltd. 9.0
Other 13.0

Source: *Electronic Business*, May 15, 2003, p. 52, from
Gartner Dataquest.

★ 1598 ★
Personal Digital Assistants
SIC: 3571; NAICS: 334111
Top PDA Makers in Spain

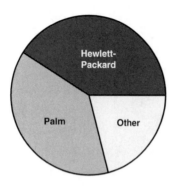

Market shares are shown in percent.

Hewlett-Packard	40.8%
Palm	38.0
Other	21.2

Source: *Europe Intelligence Wire*, February 20, 2004, p. NA, from Canalys.

★ 1599 ★
Personal Digital Assistants
SIC: 3571; NAICS: 334111
Top PDA Makers Worldwide, 2002

Shipments fell from 13.2 million in 2001 to 12 million in 2002. Market shares are shown in percent.

Palm	36.8%
Hewlett-Packard	13.5
Sony	11.0
Handspring	5.8
Toshiba	3.7
Casio	3.3
RIM	2.3
Nokia	2.2
Hi-Tech Wealth	2.1
Sharp	1.9
Other	17.4

Source: *Econtent*, August/September 2003, p. 17, from Gartner Dataquest.

★ 1600 ★
Personal Digital Assistants
SIC: 3571; NAICS: 334111
Top PDA Makers Worldwide, 2003

Shares are based on shipments of handheld computers during 2003.

PalmOne	38.1%
Hewlett-Packard	22.0
Lunn Poly	18.2
Sony	13.4
Dell	5.9
Toshiba	3.0
Other	17.6

Source: "Slight Quarterly Growth in Worldwide Handheld Devices Market." [online] http://www.idc.com [Press release January 27, 2004], p. NA.

★ 1601 ★
Computer Data Storage
SIC: 3572; NAICS: 334112
Archival Storage Market

Market shares are shown in percent.

Plasmon	49.0%
Hewlett-Packard	45.0
Other	6.0

Source: *The Gazette (Colorado Springs, CO)*, December 5, 2003, p. NA, from International Data Corp.

★ 1602 ★
Computer Data Storage
SIC: 3572; NAICS: 334112
CD-Rewritable Disc Drive Market

Unit shares are shown for August 2003.

EPO Technology	14.4%
I/O Magic	9.8
Memorex	9.6
Sony	8.9
Samsung	7.3

Source: *New York Times*, October 13, 2003, p. C6, from NPD Group and NPD Techworld.

★ 1603 ★
Computer Data Storage
SIC: 3572; NAICS: 334112
Computer Storage Area Network Market Worldwide

Market shares are shown based on revenue for the third quarter of 2003.

Hewlett-Packard 31.2%
EMC 27.1
IBM 14.5
Network Applications 7.8
Other 19.4

Source: *InfoStor*, February 2004, p. 2, from International Data Corp.

★ 1604 ★
Computer Data Storage
SIC: 3572; NAICS: 334112
Disk Storage Market in Asia/Pacific, 2003

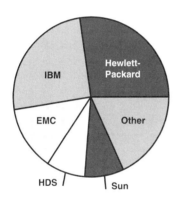

Revenues increased from $544.5 million in the third quarter to $602.3 million in the fourth quarter.

	3Q	4Q
Hewlett-Packard	27.2%	27.4%
IBM	26.9	24.9
EMC	11.6	13.2
HDS	10.3	7.9
Sun	6.7	8.2
Other	17.3	18.3

Source: "Asia/Pacific Disk Storage Systems Market." [online] from http://www.idc.com [Press release dated March 24, 2004], from International Data Corp.

★ 1605 ★
Computer Data Storage
SIC: 3572; NAICS: 334112
Flash Drive Market

Market shares are shown in percent.

Lexar's JumpDrive 60.0%
Other 40.0

Source: *East Bay Business Times*, August 18, 2003, p. NA, from WR Hambrecht.

★ 1606 ★
Computer Data Storage
SIC: 3572; NAICS: 334112
Sales of Hard Disk Drives Worldwide, 2004

Shares are based on sales in the first quarter of 2004.

Maxtor 23.0%
Toshiba 21.0
Seagate 16.0
Hitachi 16.0
Western Digital 8.0
Others 16.0

Source: *Investor's Business Daily*, May 17, 2004, p. A5, from International Data Corp.

★ 1607 ★
Computer Data Storage
SIC: 3572; NAICS: 334112
Top External Disk Storage Market Worldwide, 2003

The $12.9 billion external, controller-based disk storage systems market is shown by company.

EMC 20.6%
HP 18.6
IBM 13.1
Hitachi 8.3
Sun Microsystems 6.8
Dell 4.9

Source: *CNET Asia*, March 8, 2020, p. NA, from Gartner.

★ 1608 ★
Computer Peripherals
SIC: 3572; NAICS: 334112

Top FPD Makers in Germany, 2002

Market shares are shown in percent. FPD stands for flat panel displays.

Ingram	15.8%
Fujitsu Siemens	7.9
Medion	7.3
Acer	7.2
Samsung	6.2
Dell	6.0
LG	5.8
Hewlett-Packard	5.6
Vobis	4.3
Philips	4.0
Other	29.9

Source: "Personal Computers." [online] from http://www.usatrade.gov [accessed January 5, 2004], from U.S. Commercial Service and International Data Corp.

★ 1609 ★
Computer Peripherals
SIC: 3577; NAICS: 334119

Color Toner Market Worldwide, 2003, 2005, and 2007

Figures show revenues in billions of dollars. Figures for 2005 and 2007 are projections.

	2003	2005	2007
Monochrome toner	$ 17.8	$ 17.5	$ 17.0
Color toner	1.7	3.0	4.5

Source: "Worldwide Revenue from Color Toner Expected to Reach $4.5B in 2007." [online] from http://lyra.com [accessed May 25, 2004], from Lyra Research.

★ 1610 ★
Computer Peripherals
SIC: 3577; NAICS: 334111

Computer Equipment Market

Data are in units. Mainframes actually have less than 0.1% of the market. Market shares forecasted for 2008: Desktops 60%, mobiles 35.9%, Servers 2.9%, industrial PCs 0.9% and motherboards/misc. 7.9%.

	2004	2005	2008
Desktop	119.4	125.9	142.2
Mobiles	59.6	66.5	96.3
Motherboards and other	17.9	18.9	21.3
Servers	3.9	4.6	7.7
Industrial PCs	0.7	0.8	0.9
Mainframes	0.1	0.1	0.1

Source: "Computer Equipment - Markets & Connectors Use." [online] from http://www.bishop-associates.com [accessed January 7, 2004], from Bishop & Associates.

★ 1611 ★
Computer Peripherals
SIC: 3577; NAICS: 334111

Computer Product Industry

Overall sales for the first nine months of the year reached $21.7 billion. Consumables had $5 billion in sales, notebooks and desktops $2.7 billion. Market shares are for the first nine months of each year.

	2002	2003
Consumables	23.1%	23.4%
Desktops	15.0	12.2
Notebooks	11.6	12.4
Printers	10.1	10.7
Digital cameras	7.7	8.8
Displays	6.9	6.6
Storage media	4.5	5.7

Source: *Business Wire*, November 17, 2003, p. 5076, from NPD Group and NPD Techworld.

★ 1612 ★
Computer Peripherals
SIC: 3577; NAICS: 334119
Ink Cartridge Market Worldwide, 2003

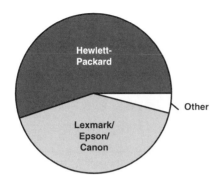

The retail market for ink cartridges was $4.15 billion in 2003.

Hewlett-Packard 55.0%
Lexmark/Epson/Canon 41.0
Other 4.0

Source: *International Herald Tribune*, April 20, 2004, p. 15, from NPD Group.

★ 1613 ★
Computer Peripherals
SIC: 3577; NAICS: 334119
Leading VSAT Makers in Canada

VSAT stands for very small aperture terminals.

Telesat 95.0%
Other 5.0

Source: "Space News." [online] available from http:// www.spacenews/spacenews/archive03/ telesatarch_52003.html.

★ 1614 ★
Computer Peripherals
SIC: 3577; NAICS: 334119
PC Camera and Video Products

The total market was valued at $700 million.

Logitech 42.0%
Other 58.0

Source: *Chief Executive*, July 2003, p. 42.

★ 1615 ★
Computer Printers
SIC: 3577; NAICS: 334119
Computer Printer Market in Europe, 2001

Market shares are shown in percent.

Hewlett-Packard 46.5%
Brother 12.3
Lexmark 11.1
Kyocera 8.1
Canon 6.9
Other 15.1

Source: *Computerwoche*, April 19, 2002, p. 24, from International Data Corp.

★ 1616 ★
Computer Printers
SIC: 3577; NAICS: 334119
Computer Printer Market in Japan, 2007

Total demand for computer printers is forecasted to increase from $2.21 billion in 2002 to $6.58 billion in 2007 to $31 billion in 2012. The overall PC industry is seeing stable growth.

	($ mil.)	Share
Individual consumers	$ 2,292.5	34.76%
Government	1,073.7	16.28
Financial	816.1	12.37
Education	730.2	11.07
Communications	524.0	7.94
Manufacturing	429.5	6.51

Continued on next page.

★ 1616 ★

[Continued]
Computer Printers
SIC: 3577; NAICS: 334119

Computer Printer Market in Japan, 2007

Total demand for computer printers is forecasted to increase from $2.21 billion in 2002 to $6.58 billion in 2007 to $31 billion in 2012. The overall PC industry is seeing stable growth.

	($ mil.)	Share
Health Care	$ 257.7	3.91%
Other	472.4	7.16

Source: *Chinese Markets for Printers*, December 2003, p. NA.

★ 1617 ★

Computer Printers
SIC: 3577; NAICS: 334119

Computer Printer Market in Spain, 2003

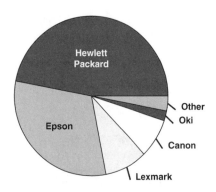

Printer sales in Spain during 2003 totaled 328.6 million euros. Shares of this market are shown in percent by company and cover all printer types; color and monochrome; laser jet and ink jet.

Hewlett Packard	47.0%
Epson	31.0
Lexmark	9.0
Canon	8.0
Oki	2.0
Other	3.0

Source: *European Intelligence Wire*, March 15, 2004, p. NA.

★ 1618 ★

Computer Printers
SIC: 3577; NAICS: 334119

Inkjet and Color Electrophotographic Printer Demand Worldwide

Global revenues for inkjet and color electrophotographic printers (digital presses, connected color copiers and desktop laser printers) and their related consumables are forecasted to increase from $55 billion in 2002 to nearly $92 billion in 2007. Ink and toner revenues are expected to take 54% of the market in 2007.

	2002	2007
Inkjet printers, media and ink	$ 33	$ 50
Color EP printers, media toner	22	42

Source: *Photo Maketing Newsline*, January 14, 2004, p. 3, from IP Strategies.

★ 1619 ★

Computer Printers
SIC: 3577; NAICS: 334119

Inkjet Printer Market in India, 2003

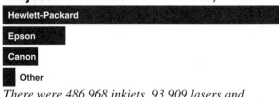

There were 486,968 inkjets, 93,909 lasers and 316,554 dot matrix printers sold in 2003. The inkjet printer market overall was characterized as being of high volume and low value, according to the source. Sales by the top three firms was $59 million.

	Units	Share
Hewlett-Packard	493,896	71.93%
Epson	112,733	16.42
Canon	60,000	8.74
Other	20,000	2.91

Source: "Computer Peripherals." [online] from http://www.export.gov [accessed February 1, 2004], from Dataquest and Manufacturers Association of Information Technology (MAIT).

★ 1620 ★
Computer Printers
SIC: 3577; NAICS: 334119

Inkjet Printer Market in Western Europe, 2002 and 2007

Market shares are by product type based on sales in millions of dollars. Turkey and Greece show strong growth potential. Home working is forecasted to take 70% of the industry in 2007.

	2002	2007	Share
Inkjet cartridges	$ 7,659.15	$ 9,740.03	79.29%
Coated paper	1,288.38	1,700.80	13.85
Uncoated paper	804.48	827.80	6.74
Film	99.68	15.14	0.12

Source: *Office Products International*, February 2004, p. 72, from CAP Ventures.

★ 1621 ★
Computer Printers
SIC: 3577; NAICS: 334119

Top Computer Printer Makers, 2003

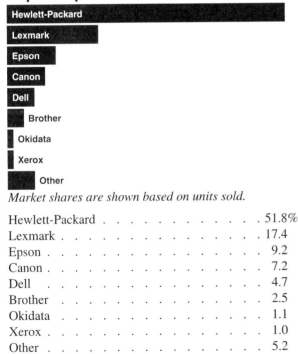

Market shares are shown based on units sold.

Hewlett-Packard	51.8%
Lexmark	17.4
Epson	9.2
Canon	7.2
Dell	4.7
Brother	2.5
Okidata	1.1
Xerox	1.0
Other	5.2

Source: *Atlanta Journal-Constitution*, June 5, 2004, p. F1, from International Data Corp.

★ 1622 ★
Computer Printers
SIC: 3577; NAICS: 334119

Top Computer Printer Makers in Germany, 2002

Market shares are shown based on 5.5 million units.

Hewlett-Packard	43.4%
Lexmark	17.1
Canon	14.9
Epson	14.7
Kyocera	3.6
Oki	1.2
Samsung	0.9
Minolta/QMS	0.7
Other	1.2

Source: "Personal Computers." [online] from http://www.usatrade.gov [accessed January 5, 2004], from U.S. Commercial Service and International Data Corp.

★ 1623 ★
Computer Printers
SIC: 3577; NAICS: 334119

Top Computer Printer Makers Worldwide, 2002

Market shares are shown based on total worldwide shipments of 58.9 million units.

Hewlett-Packard	39.7%
Seiko Epson Corp.	26.0
Canon Inc.	17.2
Lexmark International	13.5
Legend Holdings	1.2
Other	2.4

Source: "Market Share Survey Report 2002." [online] from http://www.nni.nikkei.co.jp [accessed January 20, 2004], from Nikkei estimates.

★ 1624 ★
Computer Printers
SIC: 3577; NAICS: 334119

Top Inkjet Printer Makers in Japan, 2002

Market shares are shown based on domestic shipments of 5.7 million units.

Seiko Epson	50.8%
Canon	41.7
Hewlett-Packard Japan	3.5
NEC	1.6
Lexmark International	1.3
Other	1.1

Source: ''Market Share Survey Report 2002.'' [online] from http://www.nni.nikkei.co.jp [accessed January 20, 2004], from Gartner Japan.

★ 1625 ★
Computer Printers
SIC: 3577; NAICS: 334119

Top Inkjet Printer Makers Worldwide, 2003

Market shares are shown based on units sold.

Hewlett-Packard	44.1%
Epson	20.1
Lexmark	15.6
Canon	14.9
Other	5.3

Source: *New York Times*, May 24, 2004, p. C4, from International Data Corp.

★ 1626 ★
Computer Printers
SIC: 3577; NAICS: 334119

Top Laser Printer Makers Worldwide, 2003

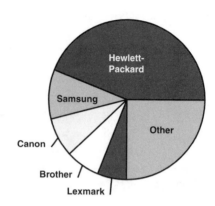

Market shares are shown based on unit sales of black and white laser printers.

Hewlett-Packard	44.1%
Samsung	9.8
Canon	7.7
Brother	7.4
Lexmark	5.8
Other	25.1

Source: *New York Times*, May 24, 2004, p. C4, from International Data Corp.

★ 1627 ★
Computer Printers
SIC: 3577; NAICS: 334119

Top Laser Printer Market in India, 2003

| Hewlett-Packard |
| Samsung |
| Other |

Market shares are shown in percent.

Hewlett-Packard	75.0%
Samsung	20.0
Other	5.0

Source: *Asia Africa Intelligence Wire*, January 26, 2004, p. NA, from International Data Corp.

★ 1628 ★
Computer Printers
SIC: 3577; NAICS: 334119

Top Printer/Copier/MFP Makers in Europe, 2003

*Companies are ranked by shipments of copiers, prin-
ters and multi-functional peripherals for the year.
The industry saw healthy growth in the fourth quarter with Eastern Europe performing particularly
well.*

	Units	Share
Hewlett-Packard	14,795	42.9%
Epson	6,331	18.3
Lexmark	4,865	14.1
Canon	4,363	12.6
Samsung Electronics	905	2.6
Other	3,255	9.4

Source: "Gartner Says European Printer, Copier and Multi
Functional Product Market." [online] from http://
www.gartner.com [Press release March 16, 2004], from
Gartner.

★ 1629 ★
Computer Printers
SIC: 3577; NAICS: 334119

Top Printer Server Makers in Australia, 2003

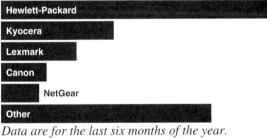

Data are for the last six months of the year.

Hewlett-Packard	37.1%
Kyocera	14.7
Lexmark	9.8
Canon	5.5
NetGear	5.3
Other	27.6

Source: "Printer Market Posts Lowest Results in Over 2
Years." [online] from http://www.idc.com [Press release
dated March 26, 2004], from International Data Corp.

★ 1630 ★
Automated Teller Machines
SIC: 3578; NAICS: 334119

ATMs in Western Europe, 2002

*The table shows the three Western European coun-
tries with the largest number of ATMs as of the end
of 2002. There are 283,590 ATMs in the region. The
U.K. saw the highest growth. Switzerland saw the
highest average withdrawl.*

	ATMs	Share
Germany	50,487	18.0%
Spain	49,925	18.0
United Kingdom	40,795	14.0
Others	142,383	50.0

Source: *European Banker*, February 2004, p. 9, from Retail
Banking Research.

★ 1631 ★
Automated Teller Machines
SIC: 3578; NAICS: 334119

Casino ATM Market

*The company has at least 70% of casino ATM opera-
tions and transaction processing.*

Global Cash	70.0%
Other	30.0

Source: *ATM & Debit News*, March 4, 2004, p. 1.

★ 1632 ★
Automated Teller Machines
SIC: 3578; NAICS: 333313

Leading ATM Shippers, 2003

Companies are ranked by unit shipments.

	(mil.)	Share
Diebold	15,590	27.78%
Triton	11,190	19.94
NCR	9,400	16.75
Tranax	9,000	16.04
NexTran	3,000	5.35
Tidel	2,868	5.11

Continued on next page.

★ 1632 ★
[Continued]
Automated Teller Machines
SIC: 3578; NAICS: 333313

Leading ATM Shippers, 2003

Companies are ranked by unit shipments.

	(mil.)	Share
Wincor	2,488	4.43%
Lipman	1,000	1.78
Greenlink	798	1.42
Fujitsu	778	1.39

Source: *ATM & Debit News*, February 26, 2004, p. 3, from
ATM & Debit News research.

★ 1633 ★
Automated Teller Machines
SIC: 3578; NAICS: 334119

Top ATM Makers in Western Europe, 2002

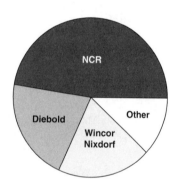

*In 2002 there were 283,590 ATMs in operation in
Western Europe.*

NCR	47.5%
Diebold	20.6
Wincor Nixdorf	20.2
Other	11.6

Source: *Electronic Payment International*, January 2004,
p. 12, from Retail Banking Research.

★ 1634 ★
Currency Equipment
SIC: 3578; NAICS: 333311

Currency-Acceptancy Equipment in South Africa

*The company has the lion's share of the market for
currency acceptancy devices for slot and vending
machines.*

Global Payment	80.0%
Other	20.0

Source: *Long Island Business News*, January 23, 2004,
p. NA.

★ 1635 ★
POS Terminals
SIC: 3578; NAICS: 333313

Leading POS Terminal Makers, 2003

*Market shares are shown in percent. POS stands for
point-of-sale.*

	Units	Share
VeriFone Inc.	656,428	29.17%
Hypercom	625,800	27.81
Ingenico	443,600	19.72
Thales e-Transactions	52,500	2.33
Other	471,672	20.96

Source: *ATM & Debit News*, March 4, 2004, p. 1.

★ 1636 ★
POS Terminals
SIC: 3578; NAICS: 333313

POS Network Market Shares

*Shares are shown based on March 2003 PIN-based
debit transaction activity.*

Star	56.1%
Interlink	15.5
NYCE	10.0
Pulse	9.6
Other	8.8

Source: *ATM & Debit News*, September 25, 2003, p. 4,
from *ATM & Debit News EFT Data Book, 2004*.

★ 1637 ★
Postage Meters
SIC: 3578; NAICS: 333313
Global Postage Meter Market

The company has 62% of the global market and 80%
of the domestic one.

Pitney Bowes 62.0%
Other 38.0

Source: *Chief Executive*, October 2003, p. 38.

★ 1638 ★
Postage Meters
SIC: 3578; NAICS: 333313
Postage Meter Market

Market shares are estimated in percent.

Pitney Bowes 80.0%
Hasler 8.0
Neopost 8.0
FP 4.0

Source: *Chicago Tribune*, January 12, 2004.

★ 1639 ★
Postage Meters
SIC: 3578; NAICS: 333313
Postage Meter Market in Spokane, WA

| Pitney Bowes |
| Northwest Mailing |
| Other |

Market shares are shown in percent.

Pitney Bowes 60.0%
Northwest Mailing 28.0
Other 12.0

Source: *Spokesman-Review*, May 7, 2004, p. NA, from
companies.

★ 1640 ★
Self-Checkout Industry
SIC: 3578; NAICS: 334119
Self-Checkout Market

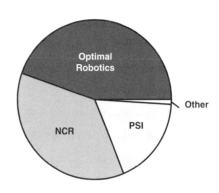

Market shares are shown based on installed lanes.

	2001	2002
Optimal Robotics	47.5%	44.5%
NCR	36.4	36.7
PSI	15.4	18.0
Other	0.7	0.8

Source: *Computer Reseller News*, January 5, 2004, p. 55,
from IHL Consulting Group.

★ 1641 ★
Automated Beverage-Container Systems
SIC: 3581; NAICS: 333311
Automated Bottle Collection Machines Worldwide

Automated beverage-container collection systems are
sometimes called "reverse vending machines".
These are devices that collect empty beverage cans
and bottles at supermarkets and then return a deposit
refund to the user. The company has more than
50,000 devices in 40 nations.

Asker 90.0%
Other 10.0

Source: *BusinessWeek*, January 12, 2004, p. 60.

★ 1642 ★
Heating and Cooling
SIC: 3585; NAICS: 333415

Electric Heating Element Shipments in North America, 2002

Tubular	
Flexible	
Open coil	
Glass top range	
Cartridge	

The overall market is mature with sales of 23 types of electric heating elements exceeding $1 billion in sales for the year. The highest growth rates are forecast for flexible heating elements. Data are in millions of dollars.

	($ mil.)	Share
Tubular	$ 300.5	30.05%
Flexible	131.6	13.16
Open coil	110.2	11.02
Glass top range	102.6	10.26
Cartridge	75.2	7.52

Source: "$1 Billion North American Electric Heating Element Industry." [online] available from http://www.vdc-corp.com [accessed December 17, 2003], from Venture Development Corp.

★ 1643 ★
Heating and Cooling
SIC: 3585; NAICS: 333415

Largest Room Air Conditioner Makers, 2002

Market shares are shown based on shipments.

GE/GE Profile	17.0%
Fedders/Maytag	15.0
Kenmore	14.1
Whirlpool	8.8
LG/Goldstar	8.0
Frigidaire	7.1
Hampton Bay	4.1
Sharp	3.5
Friedrich	3.3
Haier	2.4
Other	16.7

Source: *HFN*, December 22, 2003, p. 29.

★ 1644 ★
Heating and Cooling
SIC: 3585; NAICS: 333415

Top Home Air Conditioner Makers in Japan, 2002

Market shares are shown based on domestic shipments of 6.9 million units.

Matsushita Electric Industrial	15.4%
Mitsubishi Electric	15.3
Toshiba Carrier	14.2
Daikin Industries	13.0
Hitachi	11.0
Other	31.1

Source: "Market Share Survey Report 2002." [online] from http://www.nni.nikkei.co.jp [accessed January 20, 2004], from Nikkei estimate and Japan Refrigeration and Air Conditioning Association.

★ 1645 ★
Pumps and Mixing Equipment
SIC: 3586; NAICS: 333913

High Pressure Sample Injection

The company has 50% share of the U.S. market for "high-pressure sample injection, fluid switching and fluid management systems."

Idex	50.0%
Other	50.0

Source: "Market Leadership." [online] from http://www.idexcorp.com/about/leadership.asp [accessed May 25, 2004].

★ 1646 ★
Pumps and Mixing Equipment
SIC: 3586; NAICS: 333913

Paint Dispensing/Mixing Equipment Market Worldwide

The company has 50% share of the world market for "automatic and manually operated dispensing, metering and mixing equipment for paints and coatings market, paint mixers and shakers and car refinish products."

Idex	50.0%
Other	50.0

Source: "Market Leadership." [online] from http://www.idexcorp.com/about/leadership.asp [accessed May 25, 2004].

★ 1647 ★
Carwashing Equipment
SIC: 3589; NAICS: 333319

Carwashing Equipment Industry in Europe

Market shares are shown in percent.

WashTec 50.0%
Other 50.0

Source: *Professional Carwashing & Detailing Online*, February 18, 2003, p. NA.

★ 1648 ★
Filters
SIC: 3599; NAICS: 336399

Filter Market, 2006

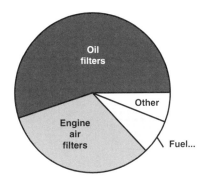

The category is projected to see sales of $2.9 billion by 2006.

	($ mil.)	Share
Oil filters	$ 1,600	55.17%
Engine air filters	930	32.07
Fuel filters	200	6.90
Other	170	5.86

Source: *Aftermarket Business*, January 2004, p. 30, from Freedonia Group.

SIC 36 - Electronic and Other Electric Equipment

★ 1649 ★

Contract Manufacturing

SIC: 3600; NAICS: 334111, 33422

Electronic Manufacturing Services Industry Worldwide, 2001 and 2006

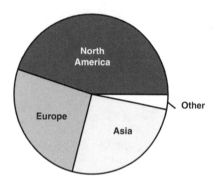

Fueled by the growth of the OEM (original equipment manufacturing) industry, the EMS market is expected to grow from $98 billion in 2001 to $202 billion in 2006.

	2001	2006
North America	51.0%	45.0%
Europe	26.0	26.0
Asia	20.0	26.0
Other	3.0	3.0

Source: *Electronic Packaging & Production*, November 2002, p. 18, from Electronic Trend Publications.

★ 1650 ★

Contract Manufacturing

SIC: 3600; NAICS: 334111, 33422

Leading Wireless Infrastructure Manufacturers Worldwide

Market shares are among the top 15 contractors.

Flextronics	23.0%
Celestina	23.0
Solectron	20.0
Sanmina-SCI	14.0
Other	20.0

Source: *Investor's Business Daily*, February 5, 2003, p. A6, from Deutsche Banc. and Alexander Brown.

★ 1651 ★

Atomic Power Plant Equipment

SIC: 3621; NAICS: 335312

Atomic Power Plant Technology Worldwide

Siemens/Framatome

BNF/LIABB/Westinghouse

General Electric

Other

Global shares are shown in percent.

Siemens/Framatome	40.0%
BNF/LIABB/Westinghouse	20.0
General Electric	11.0
Other	19.0

Source: "Market Shares of Atomic Power Plant Manufacturers." [online] available from http://www.siemens-boykott.de [accessed September 29. 2003].

★ 1652 ★
Motors and Generators
SIC: 3621; NAICS: 335312

Leading Motor and Generator Makers, 2002

Selected firms are ranked by revenues in millions of dollars.

General Electric	$ 130.80
Emerson Electric Co.	13.80
A O Smith Corporation	1.50
Baldor Electric Company	0.54

Source: "Motors and Generators in USA." [online] from http://www.euromonitor.com [accessed June 9, 2004], from Euromonitor.

★ 1653 ★
Appliances
SIC: 3630; NAICS: 335221, 335222, 335224

Appliance Industry in Europe

Washing machines and refrigerators were the industry's top sectors with each taking 25% of production. Dishwashers took 11% of the category, coming in third.

Italy	36.0%
Germany	18.0
France	12.0
Spain	10.0
U.K.	7.0
Turkey	6.0
Poland	3.0
Slovenia	3.0%
Hungary	2.0
Russia	2.0
Sweden	1.0

Source: *Appliance*, November 2002, p. S15, from European Trade Federation.

★ 1654 ★
Appliances
SIC: 3630; NAICS: 335221, 335222, 335224

Appliance Industry in Mexico

Figures show the size of selected markets in millions of dollars.

Washing machines	$ 232.0
Refrigerators	180.0
Microwave ovens	124.8
Food grinders	94.0
Vacuum cleaners	28.0
Dryers	24.0
Household electrical appliances	11.3
Dishwashers	5.0

Source: "Household Consumer Goods." [online] available from http://www.export.gov [accessed December 8, 2003].

★ 1655 ★
Appliances
SIC: 3630; NAICS: 335221, 335222, 335224

Appliance Market in Europe, 2001

Market shares are shown based on volume.

BSH	16.5%
Electrolux	16.2
Merloni	10.7
Brandt	5.5
Candy	4.4
GDA	3.3
Other	43.8

Source: *Financial Times*, February 5, 2002, p. 22, from industry estimates.

★ 1656 ★
Appliances
SIC: 3630; NAICS: 335221, 335222, 335224

Appliance Production in Europe

Production is shown by country.

Italy	36.0%
Germany	18.0
France	12.0
Spain	10.0
U.K.	7.0
Turkey	6.0
Slovenia	3.0
Poland	3.0
Russia	2.0
Hungary	2.0
Sweden	1.0

Source: *Appliance*, November 2002, p. S15, from European Trade Federation.

★ 1657 ★
Appliances
SIC: 3630; NAICS: 335221, 335222, 335224

Top Appliance Makers

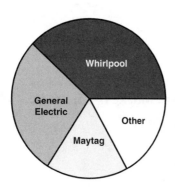

Market shares are shown in percent.

Whirlpool	38.0%
General Electric	28.0
Maytag	17.0
Other	17.0

Source: *Brandweek*, August 18, 2003, p. 20.

★ 1658 ★
Cooking Equipment
SIC: 3631; NAICS: 335221

Grill Sales

Gas grills have nearly doubled in sales in the last 10 years from $5.8 million in 1995 to $9.6 million in 2002. Total grill sales increased from $11.4 million to $15.2 million for the same period.

	1995	2000	2002
Gas	$ 5,800,878	$ 9,320,000	$ 9,583,500
Charcoal	5,321,924	5,898,000	5,363,500
Electric	261,267	211,000	238,200

Source: *Retail Merchandiser*, August 2003, p. 35, from Hearth Patio & Barbecue Association.

★ 1659 ★
Cooking Equipment
SIC: 3631; NAICS: 335221

Largest Gas Range Makers, 2002

Market shares are shown based on shipments.

GE/GE Profile	22.9%
Kenmore	11.8
Maytag	7.8
Whirlpool	7.4
Hotpoint	7.4
Magic Chef	3.6
Amana	3.2
KitchenAid	1.8
Roper	1.4
Other	8.6

Source: *HFN*, December 22, 2003, p. 29.

★ 1660 ★
Refrigerators
SIC: 3632; NAICS: 335222

Built-in Refrigerator Market

Market shares are estimated in percent.

Sub-Zero Freezer Co.	70.0%
Other	30.0

Source: *The Capital Times*, June 12, 2003, p. 1E.

Refrigerators
SIC: 3632; NAICS: 335222

Frost-Free Refrigerator Market in India, 2003

Market shares in the frost-free segment are shown. In the overall market LG has a 24% share, Whirlpool has 23% and Godrej has 21%.

LG	38.0%
Whirlpool	22.0
Godrej	17.0
Samsung	16.0
Other	7.0

Source: *Asia Africa Intellegence Wire*, March 25, 2020, p. NA, from Francis Kanoi Marketing Research.

Refrigerators
SIC: 3632; NAICS: 335222

Largest Refrigerator Makers, 2002

Market shares are shown based on shipments.

Kenmore	25.5%
GE/GE Profile	18.6
Whirlpool	13.9
Frigidaire	12.9
Maytag	8.6
Amana	5.6
KitchenAid	2.7

Hotpoint	2.6%
Roper	2.1
Magic Chef	0.8
Other	6.7

Source: *HFN*, December 22, 2003, p. 29.

Refrigerators
SIC: 3632; NAICS: 335222

Minifridge Market

Market shares are shown in percent.

Haier	50.0%
Other	50.0

Source: *Forbes*, May 10, 2004, p. 48.

Refrigerators
SIC: 3632; NAICS: 335222

Top Refrigerator Makers in Europe, 2000

Market shares are shown based on production.

Electrolux	14.62%
Bosch-Siemens	11.78
Whirlpool	8.20
Arcelik	5.74
Merloni	5.47
Fagor	4.92
Gorenje	4.55
Liebherr	3.14
Other	41.58

Source: *Appliance*, December 2001, p. S21, from *Appliance Magazine* research.

★ 1665 ★
Refrigerators
SIC: 3632; NAICS: 335222

Top Refrigerator Makers in India

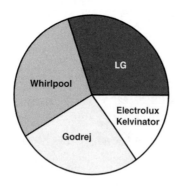

Market shares are shown in percent.

LG 24.0%
Whirlpool 23.0
Godrej 21.0
Electrolux Kelvinator 12.0

Source: *Hindu Business Line*, March 25, 2004, p. NA, from industry sources.

★ 1666 ★
Refrigerators
SIC: 3632; NAICS: 335222

Top Refrigerator Makers in Japan, 2002

Market shares are shown based on domestic shipments of 4.4 million units.

Matsushita Electric Industrial 19.5%
Toshiba 15.9
Sanyo Electric 15.5
Hitachi 15.2
Sharp 15.0
Other 18.9

Source: "Market Share Survey Report 2002." [online] from http://www.nni.nikkei.co.jp [accessed January 20, 2004], from Nikkei estimate and Japan Electrical Manufacturers Association.

★ 1667 ★
Wine Cellars
SIC: 3632; NAICS: 335222

Wine Cellar Market, 2003

Wine cellars are small refrigerators with racks used to chill wine.

Haier America 50.0%
Other 50.0

Source: *Business 2.0*, October 2003, p. 66, from Haier America and industry analysts.

★ 1668 ★
Wine Chillers
SIC: 3632; NAICS: 335222

Wine Chiller Market

Market shares are shown in percent.

Haier 50.0%
Other 50.0

Source: *Forbes*, May 10, 2004, p. 48.

★ 1669 ★
Laundry Equipment
SIC: 3633; NAICS: 335224

Largest Washer Makers, 2002

Market shares are shown based on shipments.

Kenmore 30.7%
Maytag 21.5
Whirlpool 20.2
GE/GE Profile 12.3
Frigidaire 4.8
Roper 2.6
Amana 2.3
Hotpoint 1.2
Crosley 0.8

Source: *HFN*, December 22, 2003, p. 29.

★ 1670 ★
Laundry Equipment
SIC: 3633; NAICS: 335224

Leading Dryer Makers, 2002

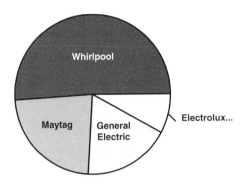

Market shares are shown in percent.

Whirlpool	51.0%
Maytag	23.0
General Electric	18.0
Electrolux (Frigidaire)	8.0

Source: "Markets, Metrics and Madness: Counting Beans or Changing Markets." [online] from http://www.acee.org [accessed June 1, 2004], from *Appliance Magazine*.

★ 1671 ★
Laundry Equipment
SIC: 3633; NAICS: 335224

Top Dryer Makers in Europe, 2000

Market shares are shown based on production.

Crosslee	17.10%
Electrolux	16.27
Whirlpool	15.47
GDA	14.90
Bosch-Siemens	11.33
Miele	6.72
Ardo Merloni	3.73
Groupe Brandt	3.46
Other	11.02

Source: *Appliance*, December 2001, p. S21, from *Appliance* research.

★ 1672 ★
Laundry Equipment
SIC: 3633; NAICS: 335224

Top Washing Machine Makers in Europe, 2000

Market shares are shown based on production.

Ardo Merloni	20.06%
Electrolux	17.78
Bosch-Siemens	12.73
Whirlpool	7.58
Candy	7.12
Groupe Brandt	6.05
Arcelik	4.92
GDA	4.60
Miele	3.37
Other	15.79

Source: *Appliance*, December 2001, p. S21, from *Appliance* research.

★ 1673 ★
Laundry Equipment
SIC: 3633; NAICS: 335224

Top Washing Machine Makers in Germany, 2000

Market shares are shown based on production.

Bosch-Siemens	44.0%
Miele	26.0
Electrolux	20.0
Whirlpool	8.0
Group Brandt	2.0

Source: *Appliance*, December 2001, p. S21, from *Appliance* research.

★ 1674 ★
Laundry Equipment
SIC: 3633; NAICS: 335224

Top Washing Machine Makers in Japan, 2002

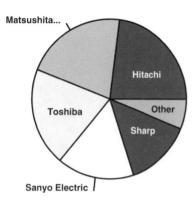

Market shares are shown based on domestic shipments of 4.14 million units.

Hitachi	22.5%
Matsushita Electric Industrial	21.2
Toshiba	20.0
Sanyo Electric	16.2
Sharp	13.9
Other	6.2

Source: "Market Share Survey Report 2002." [online] from http://www.nni.nikkei.co.jp [accessed January 20, 2004], from Nikkei estimate and Japan Electrical Manufacturers Association.

★ 1675 ★
Laundry Equipment
SIC: 3633; NAICS: 335224

Top Washing Machine Makers in Turkey, 2000

Market shares are shown based on production.

Arcelik	72.0%
BSH	28.0

Source: *Appliance*, December 2001, p. S21, from *Appliance* research.

★ 1676 ★
Laundry Equipment
SIC: 3633; NAICS: 335224

Top Washing Machine Producers in Thailand

Market shares are shown in percent.

LG Electronics	20.5%
Samsung Electronics	16.4
Hitachi	14.8
Matsushita Electric Industrial	11.4
Sharp	10.0
Other	26.9

Source: *Nikkei Weekly*, August 12, 2002, p. 20.

★ 1677 ★
Personal Care Appliances
SIC: 3634; NAICS: 335211

Beard and Mustache Trimmer Market

Shares are estimated.

Wahl Clipper	26.0%
Remington	26.0
Other	48.0

Source: *Chicago Tribune*, June 18, 2003, p. NA.

★ 1678 ★
Personal Care Appliances
SIC: 3634; NAICS: 335211

Electric Toothbrush Market in Australia

Market shares are shown in percent.

Oral-B	70.0%
Other	30.0

Source: *Australasian Business Intelligence*, November 20, 2003, p. NA.

★ 1679 ★
Personal Care Appliances
SIC: 3634; NAICS: 335211

Electronic Grooming Market in the U.K., 2002

Market shares are shown based on retail volume.

	Hair Care	Body Shavers
Gillette	23.2%	19.5%
Conair	17.7	0.0
Remington	11.1	17.1
Philips	0.0	25.2
Private label	17.5	14.1
Other	30.5	24.1

Source: *Marketing*, July 24, 2003, p. 11, from Euromonitor.

★ 1680 ★
Personal Care Appliances
SIC: 3634; NAICS: 335211

Men's Shaver Market in the U.K.

Market shares are shown in percent.

Gillette	50.0%
King of Shaves	13.0
Palmolive	4.0
Wilkinson Sword	0.6
Other	32.4

Source: *Marketing*, April 28, 2004, p. 22.

★ 1681 ★
Personal Care Appliances
SIC: 3634; NAICS: 335211

Shaving Device Sales in Argentina, 2003

The company's share is based on rechargeable and disposable shavers in Argentina. By volume, the company has a 75% share. The total market size for this segment in 2003 was 220 million Argentine Pesos.

Gillette	85.0%
Others	15.0

Source: *South American Business Information*, April 16, 2004, p. NA.

★ 1682 ★
Personal Care Appliances
SIC: 3634; NAICS: 335211

Top Dental Equipment Brands, 2004

Brands are ranked by sales at supermarkets, drug stores and discount stores (but not Wal-Mart) for the year ended January 25, 2004.

	($ mil.)	Share
Dentek	$ 14.5	11.16%
Teledyne Water Pik	9.6	7.39
Oral B	7.4	5.70
Glide	7.3	5.62
Private lebal	6.9	5.31
Doctor's NightGuard	6.6	5.08
Reach Access	5.5	4.23
Butler GUM	5.2	4.00
Oral B Super Floss	4.4	3.39
Butler Proxabrush	4.1	3.16
Stim-u-dent	4.1	3.16
Other	54.3	41.80

Source: *MMR*, April 19, 2004, p. 59, from Information Resources Inc.

★ 1683 ★
Personal Care Appliances
SIC: 3634; NAICS: 335211

Top Groomer/Shaving Implement Brands, 2004

Brands are ranked by sales at supermarkets, drug stores and discount stores (but not Wal-Mart) for the year ended January 25, 2004.

	($ mil.)	Share
Lacross	$ 20.0	15.69%
Conair	15.3	12.00
Revlon	15.0	11.76
Wahl Clip 'n Trim	8.3	6.51
Trim	7.7	6.04
Micro Touch	6.5	5.10
Tweezerman	5.9	4.63
Vidal Sassoon	5.9	4.63
Norelco	4.2	3.29
Wahl	4.0	3.14
Other	34.7	27.22

Source: *MMR*, April 19, 2004, p. 59, from Information Resources Inc.

★ 1684 ★
Personal Care Appliances
SIC: 3634; NAICS: 335211

Top Power Toothbrush Brands, 2003

Brands are ranked by sales in millions of dollars at drug stores, supermarkets and discount for the year ended December 28, 2003. Figures exclude Wal-Mart.

	($ mil.)	Share
Sonicare Advance	$ 43.5	13.22%
Crest Spinbrush Pro	42.4	12.89
Braun Oral B	41.6	12.64
Braun Oral B Flexisoft	30.9	9.39
Braun Oral B Crossaction	21.2	6.44
Crest Spinbrush Classic	18.2	5.53
Sonicare Elite	17.7	5.38
Other	113.5	34.50

Source: *MMR*, February 9, 2004, p. 24, from Information Resources Inc.

★ 1685 ★
Small Appliances
SIC: 3634; NAICS: 333414, 335211, 339999

Leading Electrical Appliance Makers in Germany

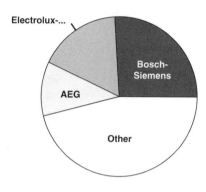

The market for large appliances (washers, dishwashers, refrigerators etc.) was worth $4.6 billion. The small domestics market was worth $1.7 billion. Germany was the largest market in Europe with 38 million households.

Bosch-Siemens	26.0%
Electrolux-Group	16.8
AEG	11.0
Other	46.2

Source: ''Household Appliances.'' [online] from http://www.usatrade.gov [accessed January 5, 2004], from U.S. Commercial Service.

★ 1686 ★
Small Appliances
SIC: 3634; NAICS: 335211

Slow Cooker Market

Market shares are shown in percent.

Rival	85.0%
Other	15.0

Source: *Daily News*, February 4, 2004, p. U10.

★ 1687 ★
Vacuum Cleaners
SIC: 3635; NAICS: 335212
Vacuum Cleaner Market

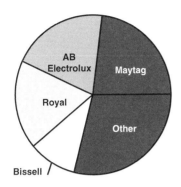

Shares are shown based on a $3.4 billion market.

Maytag	23.3%
AB Electrolux	20.1
Royal	17.7
Bissell	10.1
Other	28.8

Source: *Advertising Age*, October 13, 2003, p. 3, from Mintel.

★ 1688 ★
Vacuum Cleaners
SIC: 3635; NAICS: 335212
Vacuum Cleaner Shipments, 2002 and 2003

Figures are in millions of units sold. Sales of upright vacuums are doing well but other segments are trending downwards.

	2002	2003
Upright	15.9	18.0
Hand	6.2	5.8
Steam carpet extractor	5.2	4.8
Stick	4.1	3.3
Canister	3.1	2.4
Wet/dry	2.0	1.4

Source: *Home Channel News*, April 26, 2004, p. 13, from NPD Group/NPD Houseworld-Consumer.

★ 1689 ★
Dishwashers
SIC: 3639; NAICS: 335228
Largest Dishwasher Makers, 2002

Market shares are shown based on shipments.

Kenmore	24.1%
GE/GE Profile	17.9
Maytag	16.8
Whirlpool	16.6
Frigidaire	8.5
KitchenAid	6.0
Bosch	3.5
Amana	0.8
Other	4.3

Source: *HFN*, December 22, 2003, p. 29.

★ 1690 ★
Dishwashers
SIC: 3639; NAICS: 335228
Top Dishwasher Makers in Europe, 2000

Market shares are shown in percent.

Bosch-Siemens	29.71%
Electrolux	19.66
Merloni	11.01
Whirlpool	8.60
Miele	6.65
Bonferraro	6.05
Groupe Brandt	5.48
Arcelik	4.31
Candy	3.41
Fagor	3.23
Other	1.89

Source: *Appliance*, December 2001, p. S21, from *Appliance* research.

★ 1691 ★
Dishwashers
SIC: 3639; NAICS: 335228

Top Dishwasher Makers in Japan, 2002

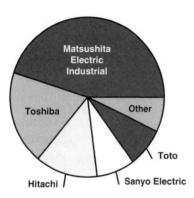

Market shares are shown based on domestic shipments of 719,000 units.

Matsushita Electric Industrial	45.0%
Toshiba	18.5
Hitachi	13.1
Sanyo Electric	8.4
Toto	7.9
Other	7.1

Source: "Market Share Survey Report 2002." [online] from http://www.nni.nikkei.co.jp [accessed January 20, 2004], from Nikkei estimate and Japan Electrical Manufacturers Association.

★ 1692 ★
Light Bulbs
SIC: 3643; NAICS: 335931

Top Light Bulb Brands, 2003

Brands are ranked by supermarket, drug store and discount store (excluding Wal-Mart) sales for the year ended December 28, 2003.

	($ mil.)	Share
GE	$ 352.9	52.70%
Sylvania	45.0	6.72
Reveal	42.7	6.38
GE Miser	26.5	3.96
GE Long Life	24.1	3.60
Other	178.4	26.64

Source: *MMR*, May 31, 2004, p. 33, from Information Resources Inc.

★ 1693 ★
Light Bulbs
SIC: 3643; NAICS: 335931

Top Light Bulb Makers, 2003

Market shares are shown based on sales at supermarkets, drug stores and mass merchandisers (but not Wal-Mart) for the year ended May 18, 2003.

General Electric Co.	70.6%
Osram Sylvania	7.3
Philips Lighting	4.0
Feit Electric Co.	0.6
Private label	14.6
Other	2.9

Source: *Grocery Headquarters*, August 2003, p. S6, from Information Resources Inc.

★ 1694 ★
Automotive Lighting
SIC: 3647; NAICS: 336321

Lens Coating Market

The world market is about the same: 80% in uv-curable and 20% in thermal cured.

UV-curable	81.0%
Thermal cured	19.0

Source: *Products Finishing*, April 2004, p. 22.

★ 1695 ★
Automotive Lighting
SIC: 3647; NAICS: 336321

Rear Light Market in Europe

Market shares are shown in percent.

Valeo Lighting Systems	35.0%
Automotive Lighting	32.0
Schefenacker	13.0
Hella	10.0
Other	10.0

Source: *Automotive News Europe*, March 24, 2003, p. 14.

★ 1696 ★
Consumer Electronics
SIC: 3651; NAICS: 33431
Flat Panel TV Market

Consumers are expected to spend $10 billion on flat panel TVs for the first time in 2003. The entire market is worth about $41 billion. Sales are in millions of units. Liquid crystal displays (LCD) have 61% of unit sales. Data are for Japan, Europe and the United States.

	2002	2004	2006
LCD	1.65	5.65	11.16
Plasma	0.50	2.18	6.11
Other	0.00	0.00	0.80

Source: *Business Wire*, March 18, 2003, p. NA, from Strategy Analytics.

★ 1697 ★
Consumer Electronics
SIC: 3651; NAICS: 33431
Global Television Market

Market shares are shown in percent.

LG Electronics	7.3%
Philips	6.3
Sony	6.2
Funai	6.1
Samsung	5.9
TCL	5.0
Thomson	4.9
Konka	4.6
Other	53.7

Source: *Financial Times*, November 4, 2003, p. 17, from Bloomberg.

★ 1698 ★
Consumer Electronics
SIC: 3651; NAICS: 33431
Jukebox Market

The company has recently filed for bankruptcy protection.

Rowe International	60.0%
Other	40.0

Source: *The Grand Rapids Press*, September 4, 2003, p. A12.

★ 1699 ★
Consumer Electronics
SIC: 3651; NAICS: 33431
Leading Digital Music Players, 2004

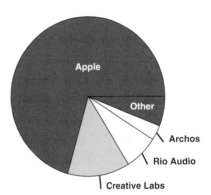

Market shares for hard drive based players are shown for January 2004.

Apple	70.4%
Creative Labs	13.1
Rio Audio	7.1
Archos	3.1
Other	6.3

Source: *USA TODAY*, March 5, 2004, p. B1, from NPD Group.

★ 1700 ★
Consumer Electronics
SIC: 3651; NAICS: 33431
Leading MP-3 Players

Data are for flash memory. Apple has no presence in this sector but has 76.2% of hard drive MP-3 player sales.

iRiver	21.5%
Digitalway	18.5
RCA	11.8
Rio	10.1
Creative Labs	3.9
Other	34.2

Source: *Business Week*, January 26, 2004, p. 22, from NPD Group.

★ 1701 ★
Consumer Electronics
SIC: 3651; NAICS: 33431

Technology and U.S. Households

Figures show the penetration of technology in U.S. households. The article discusses the appeal of multitasking - how technology allows to be involved in several means of communications at once. Some theorize that users may even get a rush of dopamine at the use of all these devices — that is, a chemical release in the brain to enhance pleasure and stimulation.

	2000	2002
VCRs	90.0%	61.0%
Desktop PCs	51.0	54.0
Cellphones	39.0	48.0
DVD players	10.0	31.0
Laptop PCs	9.0	14.0
Digital cameras	8.0	21.0
Personal digital devices	3.0	8.0
MP3 players	2.0	4.0
Personal video recorders	0.0	7.0

Source: *New York Times*, July 6, 2003, p. 8, from Yankee Group.

★ 1702 ★
Consumer Electronics
SIC: 3651; NAICS: 33431

Top 8-mm/Hi8 Camcorder Brands, 2002

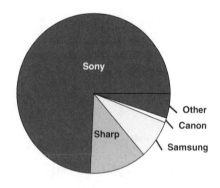

Market shares are estimated.

Sony	75.0%
Sharp	12.0
Samsung	7.5
Canon	1.0
Other	4.5

Source: *Dealerscope*, August 2003, p. 32, from *Dealerscope 81st Annual Statistical Survey and Report.*

★ 1703 ★
Consumer Electronics
SIC: 3651; NAICS: 33431

Top Camcorder Makers

Market shares are shown based on unit sales for March 2004.

Sony	47.7%
Samsung	13.6
Canon	13.3
J.V.C.	12.3
Panasonic	11.0
Other	2.1

Source: *New York Times*, May 31, 2004, p. C5, from NPD Group/NPD Techworld.

★ 1704 ★
Consumer Electronics
SIC: 3651; NAICS: 33431

Top Camcorder Makers in Japan, 2002

Market shares are shown based on domestic shipments of 1.44 million units.

Sony	41.0%
Matsushita Electric Industrial	28.0
Victor Co. of Japan	18.1
Canon	7.3
Sharp	4.9
Other	0.7

Source: ''Market Share Survey Report 2002.'' [online] from http://www.nni.nikkei.co.jp [accessed January 20, 2004], from Nikkei estimate and Japan Electronics and Information Technology.

★ **1705** ★
Consumer Electronics
SIC: 3651; NAICS: 33431

Top Camcorder Makers Worldwide, 2002

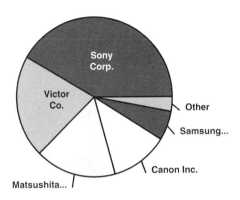

Market shares are shown based on 45.04 million units.

Sony Corp.	42.0%
Victor Co. of Japan	20.7
Matsushita Electric Industrial Co.	16.9
Canon Inc.	11.5
Samsung Electronics Co.	6.2
Other	2.7

Source: "Market Share Survey Report 2002." [online] from http://www.nni.nikkei.co.jp, from Japan Electronics and Information Technology Industries Assocation.

★ **1706** ★
Consumer Electronics
SIC: 3651; NAICS: 33431

Top Camcorder (VHS) Brands, 2002

Market shares are estimated.

JVC	62.0%
Panasonic	37.0
Other	1.0

Source: *Dealerscope*, August 2003, p. 32, from *Dealerscope 81st Annual Statistical Survey and Report.*

★ **1707** ★
Consumer Electronics
SIC: 3651; NAICS: 33431

Top CD Player Brands, 2002

Market shares are estimated.

Sony	47.8%
RCA	12.4
Technics	11.5
Yamaha	6.1
Philips	5.2
Kenwood	3.3
JVC	3.2
Other	10.5

Source: *Dealerscope*, August 2003, p. 32, from *Dealerscope 81st Annual Statistical Survey and Report.*

★ **1708** ★
Consumer Electronics
SIC: 3651; NAICS: 33431

Top DVD Player Brands, 2002

Market shares are estimated.

Apex Digital	15.2%
Sony	13.2
Panasonic	9.5
Toshiba	6.8
Samsung	6.3
Philips/Magnavox	4.5
Emerson	4.4
Other	40.1

Source: *Dealerscope*, August 2003, p. 32, from *Dealerscope 81st Annual Statistical Survey and Report.*

★ 1709 ★
Consumer Electronics
SIC: 3651; NAICS: 33431

Top DVD Player Makers in Japan, 2002

Market shares are shown based on domestic shipments of 623,000 units.

Matsushita Electric Industrial	40.3%
Toshiba	26.8
Pioneer	25.6
Sharp	3.6
Sony	1.6
Other	2.1

Source: "Market Share Survey Report 2002." [online] from http://www.nni.nikkei.co.jp [accessed January 20, 2004], from Nikkei estimate and Japan Electronics and Information Technology.

★ 1710 ★
Consumer Electronics
SIC: 3651; NAICS: 33431

Top DVD Player Producers Worldwide, 2002

Market shares are shown based on 45.04 million units.

Sony Corp.	15.5%
Matsushita Electric Industrial Co.	11.7
Samsung Electronics Co.	11.2
Toshiba Corp.	11.0
Pioneer Corp.	7.4
Other	43.2

Source: "Market Share Survey Report 2002." [online] from http://www.nni.nikkei.co.jp, from Japan Electronics and Information Technology Industries Assocation.

★ 1711 ★
Consumer Electronics
SIC: 3651; NAICS: 33431

Top Large Screen TV Brands, 2002

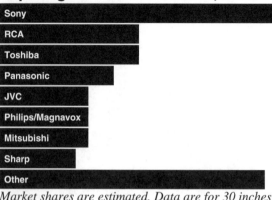

Market shares are estimated. Data are for 30 inches and above.

Sony	21.7%
RCA	11.0
Toshiba	10.9
Panasonic	8.7
JVC	7.1
Philips/Magnavox	7.0
Mitsubishi	6.5
Sharp	5.7
Other	21.4

Source: *Dealerscope*, August 2003, p. 32, from *Dealerscope 81st Annual Statistical Survey and Report.*

★ 1712 ★
Consumer Electronics
SIC: 3651; NAICS: 33431

Top LCD TV Makers in Spain, 2004

A total of 500,000 liquid crystal display televisions are expected to be sold during 2004.

Samsung	18.0%
Sony	16.0
Philips	16.0
Other	50.0

Source: *Europe Intelligence Wire*, April 22, 2004, p. NA, from RDSL Europe.

★ 1713 ★
Consumer Electronics
SIC: 3651; NAICS: 33431

Top LCD TV Producers Worldwide

Market shares are for second quarter 2003.

Sharp	31.00%
Sony	12.00
Samsung	11.00
Other	46.51

Source: ''DisplaySearch Reports Global LCD TV Shipments Jump 162%.'' [online] from http://www.displaysearch.com [accessed February 20, 2004], p. 19, from DisplaySearch.

★ 1714 ★
Consumer Electronics
SIC: 3651; NAICS: 33431

Top Minidisc Makers in Japan, 2002

Market shares are shown based on domestic shipments of 3.17 million units.

Sony	35.6%
Matsushita Electric Industrial	26.0
Sharp	21.5
Kenwood	9.1
Victor Co. of Japan	6.1
Other	1.7

Source: ''Market Share Survey Report 2002.'' [online] from http://www.nni.nikkei.co.jp [accessed January 20, 2004], from Nikkei estimate.

★ 1715 ★
Consumer Electronics
SIC: 3651; NAICS: 33431

Top Plasma TV Makers in Japan, 2002

Market shares are shown based on domestic shipments of 191,000 units.

Hitachi	32.6%
Pioneer	24.6
Matsushita Electric Industrial	23.0
Sony	8.5
Toshiba	7.0
Other	4.3

Source: ''Market Share Survey Report 2002.'' [online] from http://www.nni.nikkei.co.jp [accessed January 20, 2004], from Nikkei estimate and Japan Electronics and Information Technology.

★ 1716 ★
Consumer Electronics
SIC: 3651; NAICS: 33431

Top Projection TV Brands, 2002

Market shares are estimated.

Sony	20.7%
Mitsubishi	18.0
Toshiba	12.5
Hitachi	12.2
RCA	9.5
Panasonic	7.2
Other	19.9

Source: *Dealerscope*, August 2003, p. 32, from *Dealerscope 81st Annual Statistical Survey and Report.*

★ 1717 ★
Consumer Electronics
SIC: 3651; NAICS: 33431
Top Receiver (A/V and Stereo) Brands, 2002

Market shares are estimated.

Sony	28.5%
Yamaha	15.0
Onkyo	9.0
Pioneer	7.8
Denon	6.7
RCA	5.9
Kenwood	5.7
Other	21.4

Source: *Dealerscope*, August 2003, p. 32, from *Dealerscope 81st Annual Statistical Survey and Report.*

★ 1718 ★
Consumer Electronics
SIC: 3651; NAICS: 33431
Top TV Makers in Japan, 2002

Market shares are shown based on domestic shipments of 9.06 million units. Data refer to cathode-ray tubes and liquid crystal display.

Matsushita Electric Industrial	18.8%
Sony	17.2
Sharp	14.9
Toshiba	14.1
Mitsubishi Electric	8.3
Other	26.7

Source: "Market Share Survey Report 2002." [online] from http://www.nni.nikkei.co.jp [accessed January 20, 2004], from Nikkei estimate and Japan Electronics and Information Technology.

★ 1719 ★
Consumer Electronics
SIC: 3651; NAICS: 33431
Top VCR Makers in Japan, 2002

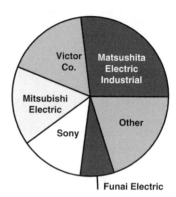

Market shares are shown based on domestic shipments of 4.72 million units

Matsushita Electric Industrial	27.0%
Victor Co. of Japan	17.2
Mitsubishi Electric	15.6
Sony	13.2
Funai Electric	6.8
Other	20.2

Source: "Market Share Survey Report 2002." [online] from http://www.nni.nikkei.co.jp [accessed January 20, 2004], from Nikkei estimate and Japan Electronics and Information Technology.

★ 1720 ★
Consumer Electronics
SIC: 3651; NAICS: 33431
U.S. Calculator Market

TI
HP
Other

The market is valued at $503 million.

TI	66.0%
HP	2.0
Other	32.0

Source: *Business 2.0*, March 2004, p. 36.

★ 1721 ★
Digital Video Recorders
SIC: 3651; NAICS: 33431

Digital Video Recorder Households

Digital video recorders store programs on hard drive rather than video tape. Figures show number of households with each brand.

Dish Network 740,000
TiVo 624,000
UltimateTV 145,000
ReplayTV 105,000

Source: *New York Times*, July 21, 2003, p. C3, from In-Stat/MDR.

★ 1722 ★
Digital Video Recorders
SIC: 3651; NAICS: 33431

Leading Digital Video Recorder Makers, 2003

Market shares are shown in percent.

TiVo 39.0%
EchoStar 36.0
Scientific-Atlanta 14.0
Other 11.0

Source: *New York Times*, April 26, 2004, p. C4, from International Data Corp.

★ 1723 ★
Digital Video Recorders
SIC: 3651; NAICS: 33431

Top Digital Video Recorder Makers Worldwide, 2003

Total sales were 2.69 million units in 2003. The market is forecasted to 9.16 million in 2005 and 21.21 million in 2007.

Scientific Atlanta 25.0%
Echostar 25.0
Pace 10.0
Hughes Network Systems 10.0
Motorola 7.0
Other 23.0

Source: *Business Wire*, March 17, 2004, p. NA, from Strategy Analytics.

★ 1724 ★
Personal Video Recorders
SIC: 3651; NAICS: 33431

PVR Homes by Region

PVR stands for personal video recorders. By 2010, Asia/Pacific will represent 40.4% of all personal video recorder homes. However PVRs will only be present in 13% of Asia-Pacific homes compared to 43% of U.S. TV homes.

	2006	2008	2010
North America	15,026	28,210	54,012
Asia Pacific	13,326	34,022	69,591
Europe	10,108	21,033	38,035
Latin America	2,345	5,370	10,404

Source: *Broadcasting & Cable's TV International*, January 8, 2003, p. 5, from Informa Media Group.

★ 1725 ★
Personal Video Recorders
SIC: 3651; NAICS: 33431

PVR Market Shares in North America

Shares are shown for North American households. According to the source, the market for digital television households stood at 20.3 million subscribers in 2002.

EchoStar 45.0%
TiVo 38.0
Other 17.0

Source: "Trace Strategies Announces New Research." [online] from http://www.tracestrategies.com/pr/02132003PR.html [accessed May 27, 2003], from Trace Strategies.

★ 1726 ★
Music
SIC: 3652; NAICS: 334612, 51222

Album Sales by Genre, 2003

Titles may appear in more than one genre.

	Units (000)	Share
R&B	150,789	26.13%
Alternative	128,375	22.25
Metal	73,816	12.79
Country	69,311	12.01
Christian/Gospel	47,083	8.16
Soundtrack	32,623	5.65
Latin	27,401	4.75

Continued on next page.

★ 1726 ★
[Continued]
Music
SIC: 3652; NAICS: 334612, 51222

Album Sales by Genre, 2003

Titles may appear in more than one genre.

	Units (000)	Share
Jazz	23,060	4.00%
Classical	18,853	3.27
New age	5,662	0.98

Source: *Business Wire*, December 31, 2003, p. NA, from Nielsen SoundScan.

★ 1727 ★
Music
SIC: 3652; NAICS: 334612, 51222

Background Music Industry

Muzak serves 350,000 business locations. While background music was once the subject of some disdain the company now sells customized packages to some of its customers and also offers a basic service with music culled from a variety of performances of original artists.

Muzak	60.0%
Other	40.0

Source: *International Herald Tribune*, February 17, 2004, p. 15.

★ 1728 ★
Music
SIC: 3652; NAICS: 334612, 51222

Best-Selling Albums, 2003

Data show unit sales from January 1, 2003 - December 28, 2003. Artists are in parentheses.

Get Rich or Die Tryin' (50 Cent)	6,535,809
Come Way With Me (Norah Jones)	5,137,468
Meteora (Linkin Park)	3,478,361
Fallen (Evanescence)	3,364,738
Speakerxx-Love (Outkast)	3,089,849
Dangerously in Love (Beyonce)	2,527,485

Chocolate Factory (R. Kelly)	2,439,536
Metamorphosis (Hilary Duff)	2,405,544
Shock N Y'All (Toby Keith)	2,324,437
Rush of Blood to the Head (Coldplay)	2,183,997

Source: *Business Wire*, December 31, 2003, p. NA, from Nielsen SoundScan.

★ 1729 ★
Music
SIC: 3652; NAICS: 334612, 51222

Best-Selling Box Sets

Figures show estimated grosses since 1991. The source calculated estimated grosses by multiplying the unit sales by the average retail price. Sales for Jimmy Buffet's release was 780,000 units, for Bob Marley's release 645,000 units and Metallica's release 548,000 units.

Boots, Beaches, Bars and Ballads, Jimmy Buffet	$ 42.1
Songs of Freedom, Bob Marley	34.8
Live S---, Metallica	29.6
Complete Studio Recordings, Led Zepplin	25.9
1972-99 Selected Works, Eagles	15.9
Pandora's Box, Aerosmith	15.3
Tracks, Bruce Springsteen	12.6
Ken Burns' Jazz	10.5
Jimi Hendrix Experience	10.3
Collection, Patsy Cline	10.0

Source: *USA TODAY*, December 19, 2003, p. 2E, from Soundscan.

★ 1730 ★
Music
SIC: 3652; NAICS: 334612, 51222

Country Music Listeners

Listeners are shown by marketing area. According to the source, those 35-44 years of age composed 24% of all listeners, the largest segment. 52% of listeners are women, 95% are white and 62% are married.

Southeast	24.0%
West Central	19.0
East Central	17.0
Southwest	14.0
Pacific	14.0
New England	13.0
Mid Atlantic	9.0

Source: *American Demographics*, November 2003, p. 21, from Mediamark Research.

★ 1731 ★

Music

SIC: 3652; NAICS: 334612, 51222

Largest Music Markets Worldwide, 2002

The market fell from $33 billion in 2001 to $30 billion in 2002. Sales are on the decline as downloading music from online becomes more popular. From 2001 to 2002 sales of CDs dropped 6%, singles declined 16% and casettes 36%. Data show the top markets ranked by retail sales in millions of dollars.

	($ mil.)	Share
United States	$ 12,325	39.78%
Japan	4,593	14.83
United Kingdom	2,859	9.23
France	1,990	6.42
Germany	1,988	6.42
Canada	588	1.90
Italy	555	1.79
Spain	542	1.75
Australia	500	1.61
Mexico	445	1.44
Other	4,596	14.83

Source: *Billboard*, April 19, 2003, p. 1, from International Federation of the Phonographic Industry.

★ 1732 ★

Music

SIC: 3652; NAICS: 334612, 51222

Latin Music Shipments by Category

Shipments are for the first six months of each year.

	2002	2003	Share
Regional			
Mexican . . .	11,148,727	12,220,419	67.87%
Pop	5,897,975	4,352,036	24.17
Tropical	1,831,812	1,433,609	7.96

Source: *Billboard*, September 13, 2003, p. 28, from Recording Industry Association of America.

★ 1733 ★

Music

SIC: 3652; NAICS: 334612, 51222

Leading Music Firms in Europe, 2003

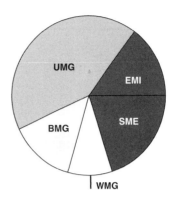

Market share leaders in both the album and singles categories are shown for the first six months of 2003.

	Albums	Singles
EMI	29.1%	14.4%
UMG	24.8	40.0
BMG	16.3	12.5
WMG	13.2	8.8
SME	11.4	18.6

Source: *Music & Copyright*, September 3, 2003, p. 5, from Music & Media.

★ 1734 ★

Music

SIC: 3652; NAICS: 334612, 51222

Music Market in the Middle East

The table compares sales in selected countries. In the eight countries for which there is data — Bahrain, Egypt, Kuwait, Lebanon, Oman, Qatar, Saudi Arabia and the United Arab Emirates — fell 19% to $112 million in 2002. The fall in sales (expected again this year) is the result of economic problems, conservative attitudes in these countries and piracy.

	2000	2001	2002
Saudia Arabia	$ 209.3	$ 191.1	$ 116.2
Egypt	50.9	24.5	25.7
UAE	35.1	31.3	29.5

Source: *Music & Copyright*, September 17, 2003, p. 8, from International Federation of the Phonographic Industry and *Music & Copyright* research.

★ 1735 ★

Music

SIC: 3652; NAICS: 334612, 51222

Music Sales by Format, 2002

In 1993, CDs accounted for 51% of music purchases while cassettes had 38% of sales. Vinyl LPs share increased from 0.5% in 2000.

CDs	91.0%
Prerecorded cassettes	2.4
Vinyl LPs	0.7
Other	5.9

Source: *Seattle Post-Intelligencer*, November 18, 2003, p. C1, from Recording Industry Association of America.

★ 1736 ★

Music

SIC: 3652; NAICS: 334612, 51222

Top Latin Music Firms, 2003

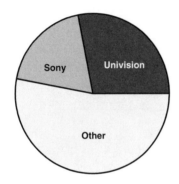

Market shares are shown in percent.

Univision	28.18%
Sony	18.58
Other	53.24

Source: *Billboard*, January 31, 2004, p. 5.

★ 1737 ★

Music

SIC: 3652; NAICS: 334612, 51222

Top Music Firms, 2003

Sales have dropped in recent years. Several companies have started cutting prices in an effort to stimulate sales.

Universal	28.0%
Warner . . . . — . .	16.0
BMG	15.0
Sony	14.0
EMI	10.0
Other	17.0

Source: *Forbes*, April 26, 2004, p. 60, from Nielsen SoundScan.

★ 1738 ★

Music

SIC: 3652; NAICS: 334612, 51222

Top Music Firms, 2004

Shares are shown based on units sold from January 1 - April 25, 2004.

Universal	26.3%
BMG	16.7
Warner Music	15.1
Sony Music	13.7
EMI Music	11.2

Source: *New York Times*, May 3, 2004, p. C1.

★ 1739 ★

Music

SIC: 3652; NAICS: 334612, 51222

Top Music Firms in Argentina, 2003

The industry has begun to emerge from a recession. For the first nine months of 2002, 4 million units were sold. In 2003, 10 million are forecasted to be sold.

Universal	25.0%
Warner	16.0
Sony	16.0
EMI	16.0
BMG	16.0

Source: *Billboard*, January 10, 2004, p. 26.

★ 1740 ★
Music
SIC: 3652; NAICS: 334612, 51222
Top Music Firms in Asia, 2002

Market shares are shown in percent. Figures exclude Japan.

UMG	16.2%
SME	12.5
WMG	10.5
EMI	7.7
BMG	7.0

Source: *Music & Copyright*, June 11, 2003, p. 8.

★ 1741 ★
Music
SIC: 3652; NAICS: 334612, 51222
Top Music Firms in Europe, 2003

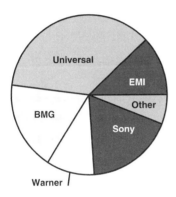

Market shares are shown in percent. Europe's top selling albums were "Come Away with Me" by Norah Jones and "Escapology" by Robbie Williams. "Lose Yourself" by Eminem and "Where is the Love" by Black Eyed Peas were the top selling singles.

	Albums	Singles
EMI	25.9%	12.1%
Universal	23.1	36.2
BMG	17.7	18.3
Warner	14.5	9.9
Sony	13.6	17.8
Other	5.2	5.7

Source: *Billboard*, December 27, 2003, p. 63, from Billboard Information Group.

★ 1742 ★
Music
SIC: 3652; NAICS: 334612, 51222
Top Music Firms in France, 2003

Total sales reached $1.4 billion and 116.3 million units. CDs made up 85.6 million units and 30.7 million units were singles.

	2002	2003
Universal Music	35.5%	33.6%
Sony Music	22.5	20.5
EMI	19.1	18.1
Warner Music	11.2	14.2
BMG	9.4	9.4

Source: *Billboard*, February 7, 2004, p. 49.

★ 1743 ★
Music
SIC: 3652; NAICS: 334612, 51222
Top Music Firms in Japan, 2002

Market shares are shown in percent.

Sony	14.2%
Universal	11.3
Alex	11.0
Toshiba-EMI	10.9
Victor	8.6
Warner	6.7
BMG Funhouse	6.3
Toy's Factory	3.5
Pony Canyon	3.5
JDISC	3.4
Other	20.6

Source: *Billboard*, May 8, 2003, p. 55, from SoundScan Japan.

★ 1744 ★
Music
SIC: 3652; NAICS: 334612, 51222

Top Music Firms in Latin America, 2002

Market shares are shown in percent.

SME 22.2%
UMG 21.4
WMG 15.9
BMG 15.0
EMI 11.3
Other 14.1

Source: *Music & Copyright*, April 2, 2003, p. 6, from *Music & Copyright* research.

★ 1745 ★
Music
SIC: 3652; NAICS: 334612, 51222

Top Music Firms in Sweden

The industry declined 5.7% to $189 million. Market shares are shown in percent.

EMI Recorded Music Sweden 23.7%
Universal Music 20.2
Sony Music 16.7
Warner Music 13.2
BMG 11.4
Other 14.8

Source: *Billboard*, March 15, 2003, p. 55, from GLF, an affiliate of the International Federation of the Phonographic Industry.

★ 1746 ★
Music
SIC: 3652; NAICS: 334612, 51222

Top Music Firms in Switzerland

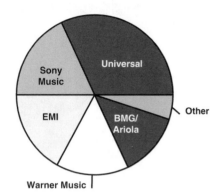

Market shares are shown in percent.

Universal 32.0%
Sony Music 18.0
EMI 17.0
Warner Music 15.0
BMG/Ariola 13.0
Other 5.0

Source: *HandelsZeitung*, July 30, 2003, p. NA.

★ 1747 ★
Music
SIC: 3652; NAICS: 334612, 51222

Top Music Firms Worldwide

Market shares are shown in percent.

Universal 25.9%
Independents 25.0
Sony 14.1
EMI 12.0
Warner 11.9
BMG 11.1

Source: *USA TODAY*, September 23, 2003, p. 2B, from International Federation of the Phonographic Industry.

★ 1748 ★
Music
SIC: 3652; NAICS: 334612, 51222
Top R&B Distributors

Market shares are shown in percent.

Universal	.40.7%
BMG	.18.4
Sony	.14.7
WEA	.10.5
Indies	.8.4
EMM	.7.3

Source: *Billboard*, January 17, 2004, p. 18, from Nielsen Soundscan.

★ 1749 ★
Music
SIC: 3652; NAICS: 334612, 51222
Top Rap Distributors

Market shares are shown in percent.

Universal	.50.6%
Indies	.13.1
BMG	.11.8
WEA	.10.3
EMM	.7.4
Sony	.6.9

Source: *Billboard*, January 17, 2004, p. 18, from Nielsen Soundscan.

★ 1750 ★
Online Music Downloading
SIC: 3652; NAICS: 45122
Market for Legally Downloaded Music

iTunes Music Stores for Macs and Windows is thought to have more than 80% of the market.

iTunes Music Stores	.80.0%
Other	.20.0

Source: *Seattle Post-Intelligencer*, November 10, 2003, p. C1.

★ 1751 ★
Online Music Downloading
SIC: 3652; NAICS: 334612, 51222
Music Downloading Services, 2003 and 2004

Data show millions of individual users.

	Dec. 2003	March 2004
Kazaa	7.3	5.3
iMesh	0.8	1.0
Morpheus	0.7	0.6
iTunes	0.7	1.9
BearShare	0.6	0.5

Source: *USA TODAY*, April 20, 2004, p. 3B, from Nielsen/ NetRatings.

★ 1752 ★
Online Music Downloading
SIC: 3652; NAICS: 334612, 51222
Online Music Sales Worldwide

World retail music sales have been declining in recent years. Online sales have been growing, however, with retail sales growing from $1.2 billion in 2004 to $2.09 billion in 2007.

	2004	2007	Share
Europe	$ 455.4	$ 687.6	32.82%
North America	451.1	922.7	44.04
Asia Pacific	288.4	435.1	20.77
Latin America	22.7	44.6	2.13
Other	1.3	5.0	0.24

Source: *Music & Copyright*, December 11, 2002, p. 1, from Informa Media Group.

★ 1753 ★

Online Music Downloading

SIC: 3652; NAICS: 334612, 51222

Who Uses File-Sharing Web Sites, 2002

Over 600 million files are thought to de downloaded or copied from March - June 2003.

13-17 years	26.0%
30-39	21.0
18-22	21.0
40-49	13.0
23-29	13.0
50 and over	6.0

Source: *New York Times*, September 8, 2003, p. C11, from NPD Group.

★ 1754 ★

Cable Modems

SIC: 3661; NAICS: 33421

Worldwide Cable Modem Market, 2002

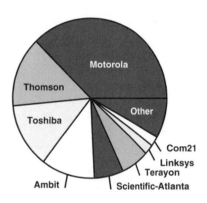

Shares are shown based on shipments of DOCSIS cable modems during the fourth quarter of 2002. DOCSIS stands for Data Over Cable Service Interface Specification.

	Units	Shares
Motorola	1,085,000	36.81%
Thomson	405,000	13.74
Toshiba	385,000	13.06
Ambit	329,536	11.18
Scientific-Atlanta	189,000	6.41

	Units	Shares
Terayon	175,000	5.94%
Linksys	65,849	2.23
Com21	63,000	2.14
Other	250,000	8.48

Source: *CED*, March 2003, p. 12, from Kinetic Strategies and company reports.

★ 1755 ★

Fax Machines

SIC: 3661; NAICS: 33421

Top Fax Machine Makers, 2003

Market shares are shown based on shipments of 4.54 million units.

Hewlett-Packard	21.6%
Brother	21.5
Matsushita	19.7
Sharp	15.3
Lexmark	12.1
Other	9.8

Source: *Wall Street Journal*, June 24, 2004, p. B6, from Gartner Dataquest.

★ 1756 ★

Smartphones

SIC: 3661; NAICS: 33421

Top Operating Systems for Smartphones, 2003 and 2007

Market shares are shown as percentage of market by operating system. The market in 2003 totalled 13 million handsets and is forecast to reach 87 million handsets in 2007.

	2003	2007
Symbian	71.0%	66.0%
Microsoft	15.0	23.0
Palm	14.0	12.0

Source: *2.5G-3G*, January 2004, p. 1, from International Data Corp.

★ 1757 ★
Speakerphones
SIC: 3661; NAICS: 33421

Global Speakerphone Market, 2003

Share is for the leader in this market as of early 2003.

Polycom 94.0%
Other 6.0

Source: *Across the Board*, July 24, 2003, p. NA.

★ 1758 ★
Telephone Equipment
SIC: 3661; NAICS: 33421

Leading SS7 Phone Switch Manufacturers Worldwide, 2003

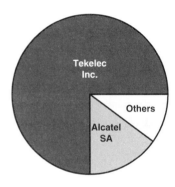

SS7 stands for signaling system number 7. This is a worldwide standard that defines the procedures and protocol by which network elements in the public switched telephone network exchange information over a digital signaling network to effect wireless (cellular) and wireline call setup, routing and control.

Tekelec Inc. 75.0%
Alcatel SA 15.0
Others 10.0

Source: *Los Angeles Business Journal*, January 26, 2004, p. 31, from Robert W. Baird.

★ 1759 ★
Telephone Recording Equipment
SIC: 3661; NAICS: 33421

Phone Recording and Monitoring Market Worldwide, 2003

The phone recording and monitoring market covers systems used primarily in commercial settings to monitor incoming calls for quality and training purposes. Figures are for the second quarter of 2003.

NICE Systems 22.0%
Witness Systems 14.0
Other 64.0

Source: *The Denver Post*, January 2, 2004, pp. C-1, from Datamonitor.

★ 1760 ★
Teletypes
SIC: 3661; NAICS: 33421, 334418

Leading Teletype/Fax Equipment Vendors to the Federal Government, 2002

Market shares are shown based on total purchases of $65 million.

Ricoh Corp. 24.25%
Oce-Van der Grinten 10.80
Xerox Corp. 6.79
ITC 5.29
Sindo Systems Co. 4.78
Minolta Corp. 4.39
Northrop Grumman Corp. 4.12
Atlantic Duncans Inc. 3.93
Other 35.65

Source: *Government Executive*, September 4, 2003, p. NA.

★ 1761 ★
Antennas
SIC: 3663; NAICS: 33422

High-Gain Satcom Antenna Market

Global shares are shown in percent. More than 1,300 systems have been installed on commercial and business aircraft.

CMC 75.0%
Other 25.0

Source: *Interavia*, September 2002, p. 14.

★ 1762 ★
Broadcasting Equipment
SIC: 3663; NAICS: 33422

Conditional Access Market Worldwide, 2001

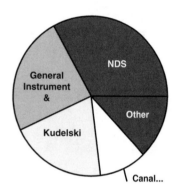

Market shares are shown in percent.

NDS 33.0%
General Instrument & Scientific Atlanta . . . 24.0
Kudelski 20.0
Canal Plus Technologies 10.0
Other 13.0

Source: *Financial Times*, March 6, 2003, p. 17, from CS First Boston and Thomson Datastream.

★ 1763 ★
Broadcasting Equipment
SIC: 3663; NAICS: 33422

Digital Set-Top Box Market

Figures are in millions of units. DVR stands for digital video recorder. HD stands for high definition.

	2003	2005	2007
Basic boxes	30.8	32.1	29.6
Total High end boxes	2.1	11.9	24.3
Total DVR equipped	1.4	8.9	18.4
Boxes with DVRs	1.3	6.7	12.5
Boxes with HD capability . .	1.1	7.6	18.7
Home networking boxes . . .	0.7	3.0	5.9
Home media servers	0.2	2.2	5.9

Source: *Cable World*, May 12, 2003, p. NA.

★ 1764 ★
Broadcasting Equipment
SIC: 3663; NAICS: 33422

Low Noise Block Down-Convertors

Low noise block down-convertors (known by the acronym LNB) are part of a satellite's tuner. As the receiver takes in high-frequencey signals the LNB filters out background noise.

Rogers Corp. 70.0%
Other 30.0

Source: *Hartford Courant*, January 25, 2004, p. NA.

★ 1765 ★
Broadcasting Equipment
SIC: 3663; NAICS: 33422

Pay TV Access Systems

Market shares are shown based on Kudelski Group's purchase of MediaGuard from Thomson, the French technology group. There are 100 million subscribers.

Kudelski 40.0%
NDS 30.0
Other 30.0

Source: *Financial Times*, August 5, 2003, p. 14, from company reports.

★ 1766 ★
Broadcasting Equipment
SIC: 3663; NAICS: 33422

Set-Top Box Shipments in Western Europe

Shipments of digital set-top TV boxes are shown by platform.

	2002	2008	Share
DTH and SMATV	5,600	8,600	53.09%
Cable and MMDS	820	2,600	16.05
DTT	600	4,800	29.63
DSL	10	200	1.23

Source: *TV International*, March 12, 2004, p. 10, from IMS Research.

★ 1767 ★
Broadcasting Equipment
SIC: 3663; NAICS: 33422

Top Cable TV Set-Top Box Suppliers, 2003

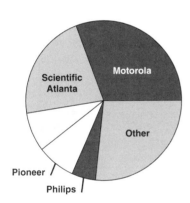

Market shares are estimated in percent.

Motorola	30.5%
Scientific Atlanta	22.2
Pace Micro Technology PLC	8.0
Pioneer	8.0
Philips	4.8
Other	26.5

Source: *The Palm Beach Post*, July 14, 2003, p. 1D, from Digital Tech Consulting.

★ 1768 ★
Broadcasting Equipment
SIC: 3663; NAICS: 33422

Top CMTS Producers Worldwide, 2002

CMTS stands for cable modem termination systems. Market shares are shown based on $396 million in revenues in 2002, which may reach $692 million in 2007.

	($ mil.)	Share
Cisco	$ 213	53.92%
ADC	73	18.48
Motorola Broadband	43	10.89
Terayon	24	6.08
Arris	17	4.30
Juniper Networks	8	2.03
Com21	7	1.77
Other	10	2.53

Source: *CED*, August 2003, p. 42, from Gartner Dataquest Inc.

★ 1769 ★
Broadcasting Equipment
SIC: 3663; NAICS: 33422

Top Converged Device Makers Worldwide, 2003

Market shares are shown based on shipments.

Nokia	56.9%
Sony Ericsson	8.5
Motorola	8.1
RIM	5.1
Samsung	3.0
Other	18.4

Source: "2003 Worldwide Mobile Phone Shipments up 29.7% in Fourth Quarter." [online] available from http://www.idc.com [accessed February 3, 2004], from International Data Corp.

★ 1770 ★
Broadcasting Equipment
SIC: 3663; NAICS: 33422
Top Digital Set-Top Box Suppliers Worldwide, 2002

Market shares are shown based on a total of 27.2 million subscribers.

STMicroelectronics NV 32.8%
Broadcom Corp. 27.0
Koninklijke Philips Electronics 24.7
IBM Corp. 6.8
LSI LogicCorp. 2.4
Intel Corp. 0.2

Source: *Electronic Business*, September 1, 2003, p. 52, from Acacia Research.

★ 1771 ★
Broadcasting Equipment
SIC: 3663; NAICS: 33422
Top Satellite Set-Top Box Suppliers Worldwide, 2003

Market shares are estimated in percent.

Echostar 20.5%
Thomson 20.0
Hughes Network Systems 11.0
Pace Micro Technology 9.0
Sony 5.5
Other 34.0

Source: *The Palm Beach Post*, July 14, 2003, p. 1D, from Digital Tech Consulting.

★ 1772 ★
Camera Phones
SIC: 3663; NAICS: 33422
Camera Phone Sales, 2003-2006

Sales are projected in millions of dollars by year. According to the source, 11 million Americans are expected to purchase a camera phone this year.

2006 . . . . $ 77.3
2005 . . . . 68.9
2004 . . . . 37.6
2003 . . . . 11.3

Source: *Investor's Business Daily*, October 29, 2003, p. A6, from Gartner Inc.

★ 1773 ★
Camera Phones
SIC: 3663; NAICS: 33422
Leading Camera Phone Makers Worldwide, 2003

A total of 65 million camera phones will be sold worldwide with Japan and South Korea being major growth markets. 25 million camera phones were shipped during the first six months of 2003 compared to 20 million digital still cameras. Shares are for the first six months of the year.

NEC 15.0%
Panasonic 15.0
Nokia 14.0
Other 56.0

Source: *M2 Presswire*, September 25, 2003, p. NA, from Strategy Analytics.

★ 1774 ★
Cellular Phones
SIC: 3663; NAICS: 33422
Cellular Industry in Canada

Figures are for June 2003. CDMA stands for code division multiple access. TDMA stands for time division multiple access. GSM stands for global systems for mobile communications.

CDMA 48.0%
US TDMA 29.0
GSM 15.0
Analogue 8.0

Source: *North American Mobile Communications Report*, August 2003, p. 43.

★ 1775 ★

Cellular Phones

SIC: 3663; NAICS: 33422

Mobile Phone Shipments

Shipments are shown in millions of units.

2007	114
2006	99
2005	87
2004	75
2003	72
2002	69

Source: *CFO*, Winter 2003, p. 45, from International Data Corp.

★ 1776 ★

Cellular Phones

SIC: 3663; NAICS: 33422

Top CDMA Phone Makers Worldwide, 2003

Market shares are shown based on shipments.
CDMA stands for code division multiple access.

	Q2	Q3
Samsung	21.0%	20.0%
LG	20.0	23.0
Motorola	16.0	20.0
Kyocera	12.0	10.0
Nokia	11.0	13.0
Other	20.0	14.0

Source: *Investor's Business Daily*, December 26, 2003, p. A4, from Strategy Analytics and J.D. Power & Associates.

★ 1777 ★

Cellular Phones

SIC: 3663; NAICS: 33422

Top Cell Phone Makers in Europe

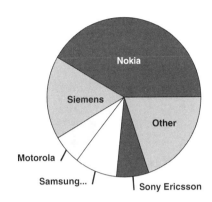

Share are for July - September in 2002 and 2003.

	July-Sept. 2002	July-Sept. 2003
Nokia	51.2%	42.1%
Siemens	9.5	17.0
Motorola	7.8	6.3
Samsung Electronics	7.6	8.6
Sony Ericsson	4.0	6.5
Other	19.9	19.5

Source: *Nordic Business Report*, December 5, 2003, p. NA, from Strategy Analytics.

★ 1778 ★

Cellular Phones

SIC: 3663; NAICS: 33422

Top Cellular Phone Makers in Australia, 2003

Market shares are shown in percent.

Nokia	65.0%
Motorola	11.0
Siemens	5.0
Samsung	5.0
Panasonic	5.0
Other	9.0

Source: *East Africa Intelligence Wire*, January 8, 2004, p. NA, from Australian Mobile Telecommunications Association.

★ 1779 ★
Cellular Phones
SIC: 3663; NAICS: 33422

Top Cellular Phone Makers in China, 2003

Market shares are shown for the first six months of the year.

Ningo Bird	15.1%
Motorola	14.2
TCL	11.6
Nokia	9.7
Other	49.4

Source: *China Economic Review*, October 7, 2003, p. 9, from Ministry of Information Industry.

★ 1780 ★
Cellular Phones
SIC: 3663; NAICS: 33422

Top Cellular Phone Makers in India

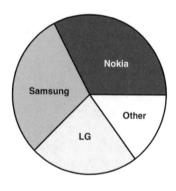

Market shares are shown in percent.

Nokia	32.6%
Samsung	29.6
LG	22.8
Other	15.0

Source: *IPR Strategic Business Information Database*, December 21, 2003, p. NA, from Gartner.

★ 1781 ★
Cellular Phones
SIC: 3663; NAICS: 33422

Top Cellular Phone Makers Worldwide, 2003

Market shares are shown based on shipments. Figures are preliminary.

	(mil.)	Share
Nokia	179.33	33.6%
Motorola	75.43	14.1
Samsung	53.00	9.9
Siemens	45.34	8.5
LG Electronics	27.49	5.2
Other	152.73	28.6

Source: "2003 Worldwide Mobile Phone Shipments up 29.7% in Fourth Quarter." [online] available from http://www.idc.com [accessed February 3, 2004], from International Data Corp.

★ 1782 ★
Cellular Phones
SIC: 3663; NAICS: 33422

Top Wireless Services in Taiwan, 2003

Shares are for the top two mobile phone manufacturers selling in Taiwan based on market position for the month of October, 2003.

Nokia	17.0%
Inventec Company	12.8
Other	80.2

Source: *Taipei Times*, November 27, 2003, p. NA.

★ 1783 ★
Cellular Phones
SIC: 3663; NAICS: 33422
Wireless Phone Market in Western Europe, 2003

Share are percent of sales in Western Europe.

Nokia 44.4%
Siemens 15.7
Samsung 8.1
Motorola 7.6
Sony Ericsson 5.9
Others 18.3

Source: *Business Wire*, March 16, 2004, p. 5833.

★ 1784 ★
Global Positioning Satellites
SIC: 3663; NAICS: 33422
GPS Market Shares Worldwide

The global positioning satellite market is forecasted to hit $1.2 billion in revenues by 2008. It is the fastest growing segment of the marine and aviation sectors. Figures are estimates. Garmin has less than 50% of the market, Magellan less than 40%, Lowrance less than 10% and Cobra less than 2%.

Garmin 50.0%
Magellan 40.0
Lowrance 10.0
Cobra 2.0

Source: *Business 2.0*, December 2003, p. 66, from companies.

★ 1785 ★
Mobile Content
SIC: 3663; NAICS: 33422
Global Ringtone Industry

Global mobile content is forecasted to grow to 10 billion euros in 2006. About half of the market is thought to be for entertainment. Some 50-75% of the entertainment market is thought to be for ringtones. The market is shown by region in billions of euros.

	2002	2004	2006
Asia-Pacific	1.30	3.1	4.5
Europe	0.90	1.5	2.0
North America	0.08	0.4	1.0

Source: *Mobile Messaging Analyst*, August 2003, p. 10, from W2Forum.

★ 1786 ★
Satellites
SIC: 3663; NAICS: 33422
Commercial Launch Market Worldwide

Commercial launches vary from year to year. In 1998, there were 40 launches, down to 16 in 2001. In 2004, 26 commercial launches are forecasted. Non-commercial launches numbered between 40 and 56 from 1998 - 2004. Market shares are shown in percent.

	2003	2004
United States	31.0%	23.0%
Russia	30.0	34.0
Europe	26.0	27.0
Multinational	13.0	12.0
Japan	0.0	4.0

Source: *Interavia Business & Technology*, July-September 2003, p. 46, from Futron.

★ 1787 ★
Satellites
SIC: 3663; NAICS: 33422
Commercial Satellite Market Worldwide, 2002

Shares are shown for total orders of commercial GEO communications satellites.

CAST/Alcatel 29.0%
Israel Aircraft Industries 29.0
Alcatel 14.0
Boeing 14.0
Orbital 14.0

Source: *Financial Times*, August 5, 2003, p. 16, from Futron.

★ 1788 ★
Satellites
SIC: 3663; NAICS: 33422
Largest Fixed Satellite Operators Worldwide

Firms are ranked by revenues in millions of dollars.

SES Global . . . . $ 1,410.0
Intelsat ltd. 992.0
PanAmSat Corp. 812.3

Continued on next page.

★ 1788 ★
[Continued]
Satellites
SIC: 3663; NAICS: 33422

Largest Fixed Satellite Operators Worldwide

Firms are ranked by revenues in millions of dollars.

Eutelsat S.A.	$ 690.8
Loral Skynet	391.2
JSAT Corp.	380.8
Space Communications Corp.	218.7
Telesat Canada	207.4
New Skies Satellites	200.5
Arabsat	147.0
AsiaSat	122.0

Source: "Top 20 Fixed Satellite Operators, 2002." [online] from http://www.space.com/spacenews/top20_satellite_2002.html.

★ 1789 ★
Satellites
SIC: 3663; NAICS: 33422

Leading Satellite Operators in Europe, 2001

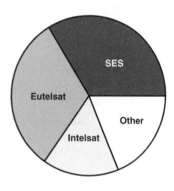

Market shares are shown in percent.

SES	33.9%
Eutelsat	31.5
Intelsat	15.7
Other	18.9

Source: *Financial Times*, December 10, 2002, p. 20, from Euroconsult.

★ 1790 ★
Door Entry Devices
SIC: 3669; NAICS: 33429

Garage Door/Commercial Door Operator Business

The company has over half of the market for garage door openers and commercial door operators. It has a growing presence in the gate operator and telephone entry system industry.

Chamberlain	50.0%
Other	50.0

Source: "Management." [online] from http://www.brivo.com/about/management.jsp [accessed May 25, 2004].

★ 1791 ★
Networking Equipment
SIC: 3669; NAICS: 33429

ATM/MPLS Multiservice WAN Switch Market Worldwide, 2001

Market shares are shown based on $3.9 billion in revenues worldwide for 2001. MPLS stands for multiprotocol label switching.

Nortel	28.8%
Lucent	27.5
Alcatel	18.9
Cisco	14.2
Marconi	4.5
Other	6.1

Source: *Network World*, May 20, 2002, p. 14, from Del'Oro Group.

★ 1792 ★
Networking Equipment
SIC: 3669; NAICS: 33429

Broadband Access Technology Market Worldwide

The top two technologies have 95% of the dollar market and 93% of the unit market. CATV stands for community access television. DSL stands for digital subscriber line.

CATV/DSL	95.0%
Other	5.0

Source: *EDN*, March 4, 2004, p. 9.

★ 1793 ★
Networking Equipment
SIC: 3669; NAICS: 33429

Content Addressable Memory Market Worldwide, 2002

The global market for memory for network search applications is valued at $78.8 million.

Integrated Device Technology	53.3%
Cypress Semiconductor	20.3
NetLogic/SiberCore	18.0
Other	8.4

Source: *Electronic Buyer's News*, October 13, 2003, p. 17, from Semico Research Group.

★ 1794 ★
Networking Equipment
SIC: 3669; NAICS: 33429

Enterprise Hardware Market Worldwide

Market shares are shown in percent.

Cisco	55.1%
3Com	4.7
Nortel	4.2
Hewlett-Packard	4.1
Avaya	1.3
Other	30.6

Source: *Computerworld*, January 19, 2004, p. 43, from International Data Corp.

★ 1795 ★
Networking Equipment
SIC: 3669; NAICS: 33429

Enterprise VoIP Equipment Worldwide

Market shares are shown in percent.

Cisco	54.3%
Avaya	8.1
Nortel	6.5
3Com	5.1
Mitel	4.6
Other	21.4

Source: *Computer Reseller News*, April 28, 2003, p. 100, from Synergy Research Group.

★ 1796 ★
Networking Equipment
SIC: 3669; NAICS: 33429

Ethernet LAN Switching Market, 2003

The 10-gigabit ethernet LAN switching global market is shown for the first three quarters of the year.

Cisco	40.9%
Foundry	35.4
Extreme	10.5
Force10	5.5
Nortel	4.1
Other	3.6

Source: *Computer Reseller News*, January 12, 2004, p. 25, from Synergy Research Group.

★ 1797 ★

Networking Equipment
SIC: 3669; NAICS: 33429

Ethernet Switch Market Worldwide

Market shares for the third quarter are estimated based on revenues.

Cisco	73.6%
Nortel	3.8
3Com	3.7
Foundry	3.1
Hewlett-Packard	3.0
Other	12.7

Source: "Gartner Says Worldwide Ethernet Switch Shipments Increased 10%" [online] from http://www.4gartner.com [Press release November 13, 2003], from Gartner Dataquest.

★ 1798 ★

Networking Equipment
SIC: 3669; NAICS: 33429

High-End IAD Market Shares Worldwide

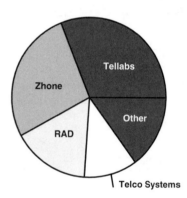

IAD stands for integrated access devices.

Tellabs	31.0%
Zhone	27.0
RAD	16.0
Telco Systems	11.0
Other	15.0

Source: *Telephony*, December 2, 2002, p. 24, from Yankee Group.

★ 1799 ★

Networking Equipment
SIC: 3669; NAICS: 33429

High-End Router Market

The market refers to the sale of high-end equipment to Internet service providers and telecommunications companies that serve as gatekeepers for Internet traffic.

Cisco	71.0%
Juniper	21.0
Other	8.0

Source: *New York Times*, February 10, 2004, p. C4, from Del'Oro Group.

★ 1800 ★

Networking Equipment
SIC: 3669; NAICS: 33422

Leading Broadband Equipment Makers, 2003

Market shares are shown for the fourth quarter of 2003.

Alcatel	26.8%
Cisco	9.1
Siemens	7.2
Thomson	6.2
Motorola	5.4
Other	45.3

Source: "Broadband Equipment Market Posts 32% Annual Growth." [online] from http://www.srgresearch.com [Press release February 19, 2004], August 20, 2002, p. NA, from Synergy Research Group.

★ 1801 ★

Networking Equipment
SIC: 3669; NAICS: 33429

Leading Broadband Equipment Makers in China, 2003

In the third quarter of 2003, the broadband equipment market grew 90% sequentially. The market is primarily being driven by file downloading, Voice over IP and gaming applications. Shares are shown for third quarter 2003.

Alcatel	35.9%
Huawei	30.7
UTStarcom	11.4
Other	22.0

Source: *Internet Wire*, December 3, 2003, p. NA, from Synergy Research Group.

★ 1802 ★
Networking Equipment
SIC: 3669; NAICS: 33429

Leading Enterprise Telephony Market

The market shares for enterprise IP (Internet proto-col) telephony line shipments are shown for the third quarter of the year.

Cisco	27.4%
Avaya	20.2
Nortel	13.3
Mitel	7.5
3Com	6.4

Source: "U.S. Enterprise IP Telephony Market Posts Record Growth." [online] from http://www.srgresearch.com [Press release November 18, 2003], from Synergy Research.

★ 1803 ★
Networking Equipment
SIC: 3669; NAICS: 33429

Leading Global Mobile Network Makers, 2002

Market shares are shown in percent.

Ericsson	29.5%
Nokia	12.9
Siemens	11.7
Lucent	11.0
Motorola	10.0
Nortel	9.4
Alcatel	6.5
Other	9.0

Source: *Wall Street Journal*, July 21, 2003, p. B4, from Gartner Dataquest and Thomson Financial Datastream.

★ 1804 ★
Networking Equipment
SIC: 3669; NAICS: 33429

Leading Metro SONET/SDH Makers Worldwide, 2003

Metro SONET/SDH makes up 56% of total optical equipment sales, representing sales of $1.1 billion. Figures are for the third quarter of 2003.

Alcatel	16.0%
Fujitsu	14.0
Other	70.0

Source: *Fiber Optics Weekly Update*, December 5, 2003, p. 7, from Infonetics Research.

★ 1805 ★
Networking Equipment
SIC: 3669; NAICS: 33429

Leading Mobile Terminal Vendors Worldwide

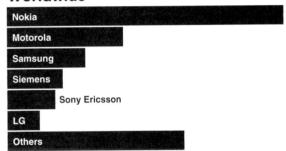

Market shares for the third quarter are estimated based on unit shipments.

Nokia	35.9%
Motorola	14.6
Samsung	9.9
Siemens	7.0
Sony Ericsson	5.5
LG	3.8
Others	23.3

Source: "Gartner Says Worldwide Mobile Terminal Market Increased" [online] from http://www.4gartner.com [Press release November 13, 2003], from Gartner Dataquest.

★ 1806 ★
Networking Equipment
SIC: 3669; NAICS: 33429

Leading Optical Hardware Makers Worldwide, 2003

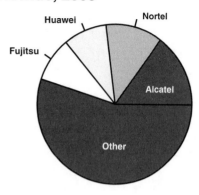

Market shares are shown in percent for the second quarter of 2003. Total revenues worldwide were $2.1 billion for the period.

Alcatel	15.0%
Nortel	12.0
Huawei	9.0
Fujitsu	9.0
Other	55.0

Source: *PR Newswire*, August 21, 2003, p. NA, from Infonetics Research.

★ 1807 ★
Networking Equipment
SIC: 3669; NAICS: 33422

Leading Router Makers Worldwide, 2003

Market shares are shown for the fourth quarter of 2003.

Cisco	71.1%
Juniper	25.8
Avici	2.7
Other	0.4

Source: "Strong Growth in Core Routers Driven by Carriers." [online] from http://www.srgresearch.com [Press release February 12, 2004], p. NA, from Synergy Research Group.

★ 1808 ★
Networking Equipment
SIC: 3669; NAICS: 33429

Leading Service Provider Router Vendors Worldwide

Market shares for the third quarter are estimated based on revenues.

Cisco	55.2%
Juniper	26.4
Nortel	5.3
Redback	4.0
Other	9.1

Source: "Gartner Says Worldwide Service Provider Router Revenue Increased" [online] from http://www.4gartner.com [Press release November 13, 2003], from Gartner Dataquest.

★ 1809 ★
Networking Equipment
SIC: 3669; NAICS: 33429

Leading Switch Makers Worldwide, 2003

Market shares are shown for the third quarter of 2003.

Cisco	32.0%
Nortel	27.0
F5	13.0
Other	28.0

Source: *Investor's Business Daily*, February 5, 2004, p. A8, from Del'Oro Group and Synergy Research Group.

★ 1810 ★
Networking Equipment
SIC: 3669; NAICS: 33422

Leading Wi-Fi Gear Makers, 2003

Figures are for the fourth quarter of 2003. Wi-Fi stands for wireless fidelity. Products certified as Wi-Fi are interoperable with each other even if they are from different manufacturers. A user with a Wi-Fi product can use any brand of Access Point with any other brand of client hardware that is built to the Wi-Fi standard.

Linksys	22.3%
D-Link Systems	17.9
Other	59.8

Source: *Globe and Mail*, February 11, 2004, p. NA, from Synergy Research Group.

★ 1811 ★
Networking Equipment
SIC: 3669; NAICS: 33429

Leading xDSL CO Vendors Worldwide

Market shares for the third quarter are estimated based on unit shipments.

Alcatel	34.4%
Huawei	17.7
NEC	8.8
Sumitomo	6.6
Siemens	5.4
Lucent Technologies	5.4
Other	21.6

Source: "Gartner Says Worldwide DSL Equipment Market Posted Record Growth" [online] from http:// www.4gartner.com [Press release November 13, 2003], from Gartner Dataquest.

★ 1812 ★
Networking Equipment
SIC: 3669; NAICS: 33429

Managed IP-VPN Providers

IP-VPN stands for Internet Protocol-Virtual Private Network. DIY stands for Do-it-yourself.

DIY	63.5%
AT&T	7.7
WorldCom	6.7
Savvis	5.9
Sprint	4.9
Genuity	4.5
Qwest	2.8
Equant	1.9
XO	1.0
InfoNet	0.7
SBC	0.5

Source: *Telephony*, April 21, 2003, p. 25, from International Data Corp.

★ 1813 ★
Networking Equipment
SIC: 3669; NAICS: 33429

Metro WDM Market

The total market was valued at $350 million. WDM stands for wave division multiplex.

Nortel	30.0%
ADVA	22.0
Ciena	14.0
Cisco	7.0
Alcatel	4.0
Lucent	3.0
Other	19.0

Source: *Fiber Optics Weekly Update*, September 19, 2003, p. 1, from ADVA Optical Networking.

★ 1814 ★
Networking Equipment
SIC: 3669; NAICS: 33429

Network Security Market Worldwide

The market exceeded $3 billion in 2003. Shares are for fourth quarter.

Hybrid Solutions	69.8%
VPN Gateways	18.1
IDS/IPS	12.1

Source: "Network Security Market Eclipses $3B in 2003." [online] from http://wwww.srgresearch.com [Press release February 27, 2003], from SRG Research.

★ 1815 ★
Networking Equipment
SIC: 3669; NAICS: 33429

Security Appliance Market Worldwide, 2003

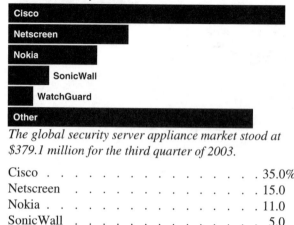

The global security server appliance market stood at $379.1 million for the third quarter of 2003.

Cisco	35.0%
Netscreen	15.0
Nokia	11.0
SonicWall	5.0
WatchGuard	3.0
Other	31.0

Source: *Investor's Business Daily*, December 23, 2003, p. A4, from International Data Corp.

★ 1816 ★
Networking Equipment
SIC: 3669; NAICS: 33429

SOHO/Home WLAN Market Worldwide, 2002

The SOHO/Home WLAN market was 55% of the worldwide WLAN market and up 80% over the previous year. SOHO - small office home office. WLAN - Wireless local area network.

Linksys	20.7%
Buffalo	18.1
D-Link	16.0
Netgear	13.0
Other	32.2

Source: *Internet Wire*, February 12, 2003, p. NA, from Synergy Research Group.

★ 1817 ★
Networking Equipment
SIC: 3669; NAICS: 33422

Wi-Fi Equipment Makers Worldwide, 2002

Market shares are shown in percent.

	3Q	4Q
Cisco	14.6%	13.7%
Linksys	11.4	12.9
Buffalo	9.2	9.6
Netgear	9.1	8.3
D-Link	9.1	12.7
Symbol	6.4	6.3
Proxim	5.7	4.8
Avaya	4.4	2.7
3Com	2.9	2.8
Other	27.2	26.2

Source: *Wireless Data News*, February 26, 2003, p. NA, from Synergy Research Group.

★ 1818 ★
Networking Equipment
SIC: 3669; NAICS: 33429

WLAN Hardware Market Worldwide

The market for wireless local area networks is shown by region.

North America	52.0%
Europe/Middle East/Africa	25.0
Asia Pacific	19.0
Other	4.0

Source: *EBN*, December 1, 2003, p. 8, from Infonetics Research.

★ 1819 ★
Networking Equipment
SIC: 3669; NAICS: 33429
WLAN Market in North America

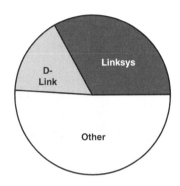

Market shares are shown for the second quarter of 2003. WLAN stands for Wireless Local Area Network.

Linksys	33.0%
D-Link	16.0
Other	51.0

Source: *Taiwan Economic News*, December 18, 2003, p. NA, from Dell'Oro Group.

★ 1820 ★
Networking Equipment
SIC: 3669; NAICS: 33429
Worldwide Switching and Routing Market, 2003

Shares are based on worldwide sales in the 4th quarter of 2002 through the 3rd quarter of 2003. The estimated size of this market in 2003 was between $5.3 and $5.5 billion.

Cisco	45.0%
Nortel	19.0
Juniper	10.0
Lucent	8.0
Alcatel	6.0
Ericcson	3.0
Redback	2.0
Marconi	2.0
Others	5.0

Source: *Lightwave*, January 2004, p. 46, from RHK.

★ 1821 ★
Radio Frequency Identification Hardware
SIC: 3669; NAICS: 33429
RFID Hardware Shipments Worldwide

Shipments are shown in millions of dollars. Figures for 2005 are projected.

	2003	2005	Share
Security/access control . .	$ 196.9	$ 240.4	24.84%
Supply chain management . .	123.8	235.0	24.28
Automobile immobilization	109.5	125.7	12.99
Transportation	106.2	153.5	15.86
Toll collection	93.6	115.1	11.88
Asset management	65.1	98.2	10.15

Source: *New York Times*, September 29, 2003, p. C4, from Venture Development Corporation.

★ 1822 ★
Security Equipment
SIC: 3669; NAICS: 33429
Security Equipment Market in the U.K., 2001 and 2004

Market sectors are shown in billions of dollars. 2004 figures are projected.

	2001	2004	Share
Manned security	$ 3.43	$ 4.43	43.86%
Electronic security	2.22	2.28	22.57
Fire protection equipment . .	1.54	1.98	19.60
Physical security	0.95	0.96	9.50
Vehicle security	0.46	0.45	4.46

Source: "Security and Safety Equipment." [online] from http://www.usatrade.gov [accessed January 5, 2004], from U.S. Commercial Service.

★ 1823 ★
Security Equipment
SIC: 3669; NAICS: 33429

Security Equipment Sales in Germany

The total market grew from 10.16 billion to $10.97 billion.

	1999	2000	Share
Security surveillance systems	$ 3,119	$ 3,323	30.28%
Security lock fittings for buildings	1,171	1,115	10.16
Fire alarms and systems . .	1,047	1,098	10.01
Holdup and burglary equipment	994	1,021	9.30
Security doors	867	892	8.13
Video surveillance equipment	324	356	3.24
Security windows	274	284	2.59
Access control equipment . .	207	222	2.02
Money safes and containers	151	156	1.42
Other security technology . .	2,016	2,506	22.84

Source: "Admission Control and Video Surveillance." [online] from http://www.usatrade.gov [accessed January 5, 2004], from U.S. Commercial Service and BBE.

★ 1824 ★
Optoelectronics
SIC: 3670; NAICS: 334419

Global Optoelectronics Market

The industry has seen a decline in demand because of economic troubles. Markets such as computers and telecommunications are seeing overcapacity. In the next four years, however, the industry is expected to benefit from growth in the semiconductor market. Global revenues by year: $4.63 billion in 1999, $4.23 billion in 2002, $7.23 billion in 2009.

Laser diodes	32.7%
LEDs	25.3
Photodetectors	20.3

Source: *Lightwave*, January 2004, p. 37.

★ 1825 ★
Optoelectronics
SIC: 3670; NAICS: 334419

Optoelectronics Market in Japan, 2002

Production is expected to increase 4% to $53 billion. The segments with the largest growth are plasma panel displays (87.6%), solid-state lasers (34.9%) and excimer-laser devices (21.7%).

I/O devices	34.4%
Optoelectronic communications tools and devices	7.8
Production devices using lasers	7.7
Optoelectronic sensing devices	3.5
Other	46.6

Source: *Optoelectronics Report*, May 15, 2003, p. 1, from Optoelectronic Industry and Technology Development Association.

★ 1826 ★
Circuit Boards
SIC: 3672; NAICS: 334412

Worldwide PCB Market, 2001-2005

The printed circuit board (PCB) market is shown by number of units produced in each category. Figures for 2003 and 2005 are estimated.

	2001 (mil.)	2003 (mil.)	2005 (mil.)
Multilayer	1,648	2,800	4,449
Single-sided	1,687	1,957	2,295
Flexible	190	490	1,101
Double-sided	676	818	901

Source: *Printed Circuit Design & Manufacture*, March 2004, p. 48, from Chinese Printed Circuit Association.

★ 1827 ★
Flash Memory
SIC: 3674; NAICS: 334413

Flash Memory Card Sales

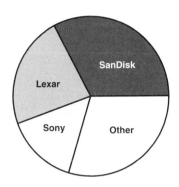

Market shares are shown based on sales of $950 million.

SanDisk	33.0%
Lexar	22.5
Sony	14.8
Other	29.7

Source: *San Francisco Chronicle*, March 1, 2004, p. NA, from NPD.

★ 1828 ★
Flash Memory
SIC: 3674; NAICS: 334413

Flash Memory Market

Market shares are for November 2003.

SD Memory Card	41.8%
Compact Flash Card	26.5
Other	31.7

Source: *PR Newswire*, January 8, 2004, p. NA, from Gartner.

★ 1829 ★
Flash Memory
SIC: 3674; NAICS: 334413

Top Flash Memory Suppliers Worldwide, 2002

Market shares are shown based on total worldwide sales of $7.8 billion.

Intel Corp.	26.1%
Samsung Electronics Corp.	15.4
Toshiba Corp.	10.7
Advanced Micro Devices	9.2
Fujitsu	8.3
Other	30.3

Source: "Market Share Survey Report 2002." [online] from http://www.nni.nikkei.co.jp [accessed January 20, 2004], from iSuppli Corp.

★ 1830 ★
Flash Memory
SIC: 3674; NAICS: 334413

Top Flash Memory Suppliers Worldwide, 2003

Market shares are shown based on $7.8 billion in sales. The market saw significant growth from 2001 (36% increase in sales and a 21% increase in units). Continued growth will depend on the health of the wireless communications industry.

Intel	27.0%
Samsung	14.0
Toshiba	11.0
AMD	10.0
Fujitsu	9.0
STMicroelectronics	8.0
Sharp	5.0
Mitsubishi	5.0
Atmel	5.0
Other	6.0

Source: "Intel Remains Leading Flash Memory Supplier." [online] from http://www.icinsights.com [Press release accessed Janaury 1, 2004], from IC Insights.

★ 1831 ★
Graphics Chips
SIC: 3674; NAICS: 334413

Leading Graphics Chips, 2003

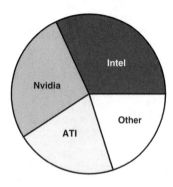

Data are for second quarter and include stand-alone and integrated chip sets. Total for the year was 207 million units.

Intel	32.0%
Nvidia	27.0
ATI	21.0
Other	20.0

Source: *Electronic Business*, October 2003, p. 34, from Mercury Research.

★ 1832 ★
Graphics Chips
SIC: 3674; NAICS: 334413

Leading Graphics Chips Makers Worldwide

Market shares are shown in percent. In 2003, discrete chips had 45% of the market with the balance held by integrated chip sets.

	2Q 2003	3Q 2003
Intel	32.0%	34.0%
Nvidia	28.0	25.0
ATI	22.0	21.0
Via/S3	8.0	9.0
SiS	8.0	9.0
Other	2.0	2.0

Source: *Investor's Business Daily*, February 4, 2004, p. A4, from Mercury Research and Jon Peddie Research.

★ 1833 ★
Graphics Chips
SIC: 3674; NAICS: 334413

Mobile Graphics Market Worldwide, 2002

Market shares are shown for the fourth quarter.

ATI Technolgies	49.0%
VIA Technologies	17.0
Nvidia	17.0
Intel	9.0
Trident Microsystems	5.0
Silicon Motion	3.0

Source: *Electronic Business*, April 15, 2003, p. 24, from Jon Peddie Research.

★ 1834 ★
Lasers
SIC: 3674; NAICS: 334413

Blue-Violet Laser Diodes

Nichia is the first company in the world to succeed in the development of blue-violet laser diodes.

Nichia	99.0%
Other	1.0

Source: *Knight Ridder/Tribune Business News*, April 22, 2004, p. NA.

★ 1835 ★
Lasers
SIC: 3674; NAICS: 334413

Diode Laser Sales Worldwide

The market declined 16% to $2.4 billion largely because of depression in the telecom industry.

	2002 ($ 000)	2003 ($ 000)	Share
Optical storage	$ 1,396,992	$ 1,556,800	55.39%
Telecom-munications	665,310	883,913	31.45
Solid-state laser pumping	118,550	135,060	4.81
Medical therapeutics	44,040	53,020	1.89

Continued on next page.

★ 1835 ★
[Continued]
Lasers
SIC: 3674; NAICS: 334413
Diode Laser Sales Worldwide

The market declined 16% to $2.4 billion largely because of depression in the telecom industry.

	2002 ($ 000)	2003 ($ 000)	Share
Image recording . .	$ 41,006	$ 44,428	1.58%
Entertainment . . .	25,280	22,880	0.81
Barcode scanning . .	14,664	14,872	0.53
Inspection, measurement & control	7,988	7,988	0.28
Sensing	5,600	6,500	0.23
Materials processing . . .	3,720	4,395	0.16
Other	80,616	80,816	2.88

Source: *Laser Focus World*, February 2003, p. 63, from Strategies Unlimited and *Laser Focus World 2003 Annual Review.*

★ 1836 ★
Lasers
SIC: 3674; NAICS: 334413
High-Brightness LED Market Worldwide

The high-brightness light emitting diode market has been valued at $1.8 billion.

Mobile appliances	40.0%
Signs	23.0
Automotive	18.0
Illumination	5.0
Signals	2.0
Other	12.0

Source: *Laser Focus World*, May 2003, p. S3.

★ 1837 ★
Lasers
SIC: 3674; NAICS: 334413
Industrial Laser Shipments in North America

Shipments are shown in thousands of dollars.

	($ 000)	Share
CO2	$ 243,390	58.02%
Nd:YAG	175,766	41.90
Other	348	0.08

Source: *Assembly*, May 2004, p. 28, from Association for Manufacturing Technology's Laser Systems Product Group.

★ 1838 ★
Lasers
SIC: 3674; NAICS: 334413
Industrial Laser Systems Worldwide

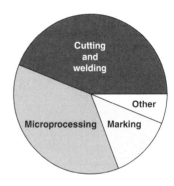

Sales of laser systems for materials processing is expected to grow from $3.6 billion to $9.8 billion worldwide.

	2002	2010	Share
Cutting and welding	$ 1.9	$ 4.3	43.88%
Microprocessing	1.0	3.6	36.73
Marking	0.5	1.3	13.27
Other	0.2	0.6	6.12

Source: *Optoelectronics Report*, October 1, 2003, p. 4, from Optech Consulting.

★ 1839 ★
Lasers
SIC: 3674; NAICS: 334413
Nondiode Laser Sales Worldwide

Nondiode lasers represented 44% of the overall $4.3 billion market in 2002 and 41% of the $4.8 billion market in 2003.

	2002 ($ mil.)	2003 ($ mil.)	Share
Materials processing	$ 1,258,870	$ 1,316,900	66.85%
Medical therapeutics	347,327	382,612	19.42
Basic research	141,884	146,994	7.46
Instrumentation	46,840	51,884	2.63
Image recording	16,760	16,060	0.82
Sensing	14,280	15,430	0.78
Inspection, measurement & control	11,432	10,315	0.52
Entertainment	10,320	12,955	0.66
Barcode scanning	1,215	1,005	0.05
Optical storage	625	625	0.03
Other	13,600	15,260	0.77

Source: *Laser Focus World*, February 2003, p. 63, from Strategies Unlimited and *Laser Focus World 2003 Annual Review*.

★ 1840 ★
Microprocessors
SIC: 3674; NAICS: 334413
8-bit Microcontroller Industry

Market shares are shown based on a 3 billion ($5 billion) market.

Microchip Technology	16.0%
Motorola	12.0
Other	72.0

Source: *Arizona Republic*, July 7, 2003, p. D1, from Gartner Dataquest.

★ 1841 ★
Microprocessors
SIC: 3674; NAICS: 334413
DRAM Module Market Worldwide

The DRAM module market is forecasted to grow 27% in 2004.

Kingston Technology	20.9%
Smart Modular Technologies	8.1
TwinMOS Technologies	6.0
Other	65.0

Source: *Computer Reseller News*, April 19, 2004, p. NA, from iSuppli.

★ 1842 ★
Microprocessors
SIC: 3674; NAICS: 334413
FPGA Synthesis Market Worldwide

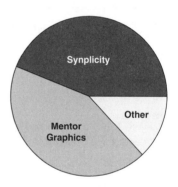

Market shares are shown in percent.

Synplicity	44.0%
Mentor Graphics	43.0
Other	13.0

Source: *Electronic Engineering Times*, March 15, 2004, p. 39, from Dataquest.

★ 1843 ★
Microprocessors
SIC: 3674; NAICS: 334413
Global Standard Logic, 2002

Market shares are shown in percent.

Texas Instruments	25.2%
Toshiba	18.6
Fairchild	14.3
Philips Semiconductor	12.3
On Semiconductor	11.8
Other	17.8

Source: *EBN*, August 25, 2003, p. 24, from iSupply.

★ 1844 ★
Microprocessors
SIC: 3674; NAICS: 334413
Integrated Circuit Market in China

The market is estimated to grow at 17% annually, driven by telecommunications manufacturing and increased capacity in the consumer and computer markets. Demand is shown in millions of dollars.

	2003	2006	Share
Computers	$ 9,247	$ 15,221	37.78%
Communications	6,936	13,889	34.47
Consumer	5,864	9,962	24.73
Industrial	539	818	2.03
Automotive	346	399	0.99

Source: *Electronic Design*, April 26, 2004, p. S4, from Databeans.

★ 1845 ★
Microprocessors
SIC: 3674; NAICS: 334413
Leading DSP Makers Worldwide, 2003

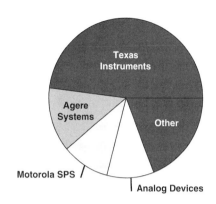

Market shares are shown based on $6.13 billion in revenues. DSP stands for digital signal processor.

Texas Instruments	47.7%
Agere Systems	13.1
Motorola SPS	10.3
Analog Devices	9.5
Other	19.4

Source: *RCR Wireless News*, April 12, 2004, p. 6, from Forward Concepts.

★ 1846 ★
Microprocessors
SIC: 3674; NAICS: 334413
Leading Fabless IC Suppliers Worldwide, 2003

Sales are forecasted to reach $20.6 billion.

	($ mil.)	Share
Qualcomm	$ 2,510	12.16%
Nvidia	1,835	8.89
Broadcom	1,595	7.73
Xilinx	1,265	6.13
MediaTek	1,170	5.67
ATI	1,135	5.50
SanDisk	930	4.51
Marvell	830	4.02
Altera	780	3.78

Continued on next page.

★ 1846 ★
[Continued]
Microprocessors
SIC: 3674; NAICS: 334413

Leading Fabless IC Suppliers Worldwide, 2003

Sales are forecasted to reach $20.6 billion.

	($ mil.)	Share
Conexant	$ 650	3.15%
Other	7,940	38.47

Source: "IC Insights Mclean Report 2004 Forecasts."
[online] from http://www.icinsights.com [Press release accessed January 1, 2004], from IC Insights.

★ 1847 ★
Microprocessors
SIC: 3674; NAICS: 334413

Leading Photoresist Suppliers Worldwide

Revenues fell from $859.4 million in 2000 to $662.9 million in 2001.

	($ mil.)	Share
TOK	$ 150.1	22.6%
Shipley	139.2	21.0
JSR Corp.	117.6	17.7
Shin-Etsu	70.1	10.6
Arch	63.7	9.6
Other	122.2	18.5

Source: *C&EN*, July 15, 2002, p. 24, from Gartner Dataquest.

★ 1848 ★
Microprocessors
SIC: 3674; NAICS: 334413

Leading PLD Makers Worldwide

The market for programmable logic devices (PLD) is expected to grow from $1.9 billion in 2002 to $2.5 billion in 2007.

Xilinx	49.0%
Altera	31.0
Lattice	10.0
Actel	6.0
Cypress	2.0
Atmel	1.0
Quicklogic	1.0

Source: *Purchasing*, October 23, 2003, p. 20, from IC Insights.

★ 1849 ★
Microprocessors
SIC: 3674; NAICS: 334413

Leading Silicon/Epitaxial Wafer Makers Worldwide, 2002

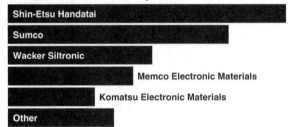

Market shares are shown based on total worldwide revenues of $5.66 billion.

	($ mil.)	Share
Shin-Etsu Handatai	$ 1,635.9	28.8%
Sumco	1,319.3	23.3
Wacker Siltronic	874.7	15.4
Memco Electronic Materials . . .	723.9	12.8
Komatsu Electronic Materials . . .	485.6	8.6
Other	629.0	11.1

Source: *American Ceramic Society Bulletin*, August 2003, p. 9, from Gartner Dataquest.

★ 1850 ★

Microprocessors

SIC: 3674; NAICS: 334413

Leading Wi-Fi Chip Makers Worldwide, 2003

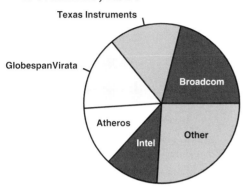

Texas Instruments

GlobespanVirata

Broadcom

Atheros

Other

Intel

Market shares are shown based on unit sales.

Broadcom	21.0%
Texas Instruments	15.0
GlobespanVirata	15.0
Atheros	12.0
Intel	11.0
Other	26.0

Source: *Investor's Business Daily*, February 10, 2004, p. A4, from International Data Corp., Piper Jaffray & Co., and iSuppli Corp.

★ 1851 ★

Microprocessors

SIC: 3674; NAICS: 334413

Leading Wireless Communications IC Suppliers, 2003

Sales are forecasted to reach $22.8 billion.

	($ mil.)	Share
TI	$ 2,575	11.29%
Qualcomm	2,510	11.01
STMicroelectronics	1,760	7.72
Motorola	1,690	7.41
Intel	1,550	6.80
Philips	1,420	6.23
Infineon	1,260	5.53
NEC	750	3.29
Toshiba	690	3.03

	($ mil.)	Share
RF Micro Devices	$ 585	2.57%
Other	8,015	35.15

Source: "IC Insights New Energing IC Markets." [online] from http://www.icinsights.com [Press release accessed January 1, 2004], from IC Insights.

★ 1852 ★

Microprocessors

SIC: 3674; NAICS: 334413

Microprocessor Industry Sales Worldwide, 2002

In June 2003, the Semiconductor Industry Association lowered its estimated industry growth to 10% from 19.8% in February. Slow PC sales continue to affect growth.

PCs	78.3%
Printers, copier and other data processing	15.7
Communications electronics	2.3
Consumer electronics	2.2
Automotive electronics	1.0
Industrial electronics	0.3
Military/civil aerospace	0.2

Source: *Investor's Business Daily*, June 25, 2003, p. 1, from Gartner Inc.

★ 1853 ★

Microprocessors

SIC: 3674; NAICS: 334413

MPU Sales for Telematic Equipment Sales Worldwide

Motorola

Hitachi

Other

Global shipments increased from 1.74 million units to 2.31 million units.

Motorola	89.2%
Hitachi	5.3
Other	5.6

Source: *EBN*, October 21, 2002, p. 3, from Telematics Research Group.

★ 1854 ★
Microprocessors
SIC: 3674; NAICS: 334413

Nor Chip Market Leaders Worldwide, 2002

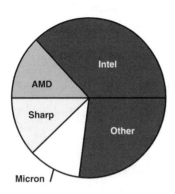

Market shares are shown in percent.

Intel	. . . . 37.0%
AMD	. . . . 13.0
Sharp	. . . . 12.0
Micron	. . . . 11.0
Other	. . . . 27.0

Source: *Investor's Business Daily*, March 10, 2003, p. A4, from Semico Research Group.

★ 1855 ★
Microprocessors
SIC: 3674; NAICS: 334413

Photomask Market Shares Worldwide, 2001

Market shares are shown in percent.

DNP	. . . . 26.8%
DPI	. . . . 22.5
Toppan	. . . . 17.4
Other	. . . . 13.2

Source: *Solid State Technology*, August 2002, p. 48.

★ 1856 ★
Microprocessors
SIC: 3674; NAICS: 334413

Smart Card Security Chip Market Worldwide

Market shares are shown in percent.

Infineon Technologies	. . . . 48.1%
STMicroelectronics	. . . . 30.7
Hitachi Ltd.	. . . . 6.6
Philips Electronics	. . . . 5.3
Atmel Corp.	. . . . 3.9
Other	. . . . 5.4

Source: *Investor's Business Daily*, March 12, 2002, p. A6, from Frost & Sullivan and International Biometric Group.

★ 1857 ★
Microprocessors
SIC: 3674; NAICS: 334413

Top CPLD Makers Worldwide

Shares are estimated in the complex programmable logic display market.

Altera	. . . . 42.0%
Lattice	. . . . 32.0
Xilinx	. . . . 22.0
Other	. . . . 4.0

Source: *EBN*, August 4, 2003, p. 1, from Xilinx.

★ 1858 ★
Microprocessors
SIC: 3674; NAICS: 334413

Top Logic IC Makers in Japan, 2002

*Market shares are shown based on domestic ship-
ments of 1.79 trillion yen.*

NEC Electronics 13.7%
Toshiba 12.0
Intel 8.5
Hitachi 8.3
Fujitsu 7.2
Other 50.3

Source: "Market Share Survey Report 2002." [online]
from http://www.nni.nikkei.co.jp [accessed January 20,
2004], from Nikkei estimate.

★ 1859 ★
Microprocessors
SIC: 3674; NAICS: 334413

World LDI Market Leaders, 2003

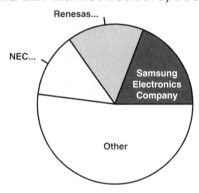

*LDI stands for liquid crystal display driver internal
controller. LDIs are non-memory semiconductors
used to drive liquid crystal display panels.*

Samsung Electronics Company 18.8%
Renesas Technology Corporation 16.0
NEC Electronics 13.0
Other 52.2

Source: *Yonhap News Agency of Lorea*, March 31, 2004,
p. NA, from Gartner Dataquest.

★ 1860 ★
Microprocessors
SIC: 3674; NAICS: 334413

x86 Microprocessor Market, 2003

Market shares are shown in percent.

	Q3	Q4
Intel	82.60%	83.50%
AMD	16.50	15.50
Via Technology	0.81	0.90
Transmeta	0.10	0.06

Source: *Investor's Business Daily*, February 18, 2004,
p. A4, from Intrenational Data Corp.

★ 1861 ★
Semiconductors
SIC: 3674; NAICS: 334413

Baseband Semiconductor Industry Worldwide

Market shares aer shown in percent.

Texas Instruments 25.0%
Qualcomm 19.0
STMicroelectronics 10.0
Intel 1.0
Other 46.0

Source: *New York Times*, July 19, 2004, p. C4, from
Gartner Dataquest.

★ 1862 ★
Semiconductors
SIC: 3674; NAICS: 334413

Leading Consumer Electronics Semiconductor Makers Worldwide

*Consumer chips are expected to be a key driver to
the industry. Numerous products are making the
switch from analog to digital: VCRs, cameras, DVD
players and game consoles. Market shares are shown
based on total revenues of $24.1 billion.*

Toshiba 9.4%
Hitachi 6.4
Sony 5.5
Philips Semiconductors 5.2
STMicroelectronics 5.1
NEC 4.6

Continued on next page.

★ 1862 ★
[Continued]
Semiconductors
SIC: 3674; NAICS: 334413

Leading Consumer Electronics Semiconductor Makers Worldwide

Consumer chips are expected to be a key driver to the industry. Numerous products are making the switch from analog to digital: VCRs, cameras, DVD players and game consoles. Market shares are shown based on total revenues of $24.1 billion.

Sanyo	4.6%
Matsushita	4.5
Rohm	4.4
Mitsubishi	3.7
Sharp	3.6
Other	43.0

Source: *Electronic Business*, May 15, 2003, p. 20, from Gartner Dataquest and IC Insights.

★ 1863 ★
Semiconductors
SIC: 3674; NAICS: 334413

Leading Semiconductor IP Vendors Worldwide, 2002

The total semiconductor intellectual property (IP) market worldwide was worth $933.8 million.

ARM	19.8%
Rambus	10.4
Synopsys	7.8
TTPCom	6.2
Parthus Ceva	5.5
Virage Logic	5.1
Artisan	4.7
MIPS Technologies	4.6
Mentor Graphics	2.8
MonolithicSystem Technology	2.7
Other	30.4

Source: *Electronics Weekly*, June 25, 2003, p. 11, from Gartner Dataquest Inc.

★ 1864 ★
Semiconductors
SIC: 3674; NAICS: 334413

Leading Semiconductor Suppliers Worldwide, 2003

The total global market was valued at $175 billion for the year.

	($ mil.)	Share
Intel	$ 28,050	16.0%
Samsung	10,320	5.9
Renesas	7,516	4.3
Toshiba	7,422	4.2
Texas Instruments	7,400	4.2
STM	7,100	4.1
Infineon	6,979	4.0
NEC	6,413	3.7
Motorola	4,700	2.7
Philips	4,440	2.5
Other	84,674	48.4

Source: *Air Cargo World*, January 2004, p. 55, from Gartner Dataquest.

★ 1865 ★
Semiconductors
SIC: 3674; NAICS: 334413

Semiconductor Laser Market

Market share is estimated.

Excimer	90.0%
Other	10.0

Source: *Buyside*, May 2003, p. 31.

★ 1866 ★

Semiconductors

SIC: 3674; NAICS: 334413

Semiconductor Market by Region, 2004 and 2006

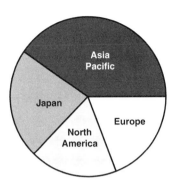

Total sales are forecasted to reach $194.6 billion in 2004, $206.1 billion in 2005 and $219.7 billion in 2006.

	2004 ($ bil.)	2006 ($ bil.)	Share
Asia Pacific	$ 75.0	$ 88.2	40.15%
Japan	44.7	48.9	22.26
North America	37.5	40.6	18.48
Europe	37.4	42.0	19.12

Source: *CircuiTree*, December 2003, p. 60, from Semiconductor Industry Association and Custer Consulting Group.

★ 1867 ★

Capacitors

SIC: 3675; NAICS: 334414

Global Aluminum Electrolytic Capacitor Market, 2001

Shares are for the largest producers of aluminum capacitors in 2001.

Nichicon	22.0%
Nippon Chemi-Con	22.0
Rubycon Corporation	18.0
Matsushita Electric Industrial	9.0
Bccomponents	3.0
Elna Capacitor	3.0
Others	23.0

Source: *Passive Component Industry*, Nov./Dec. 2002, p. 29, from Polmonole Publications Inc.

★ 1868 ★

Connectors

SIC: 3678; NAICS: 334417

Global Connector Market, 2003

Demand fell in 2001 and 2002, although the market is forecasted to rebound in 2003. Global sales are forecasted at $25.4 billion in 2003, up from $23.12 billion in 2002. Printed circuit boards was the leading product market with sales of $7.3 billion in 2002.

	2002	2003	Share
North America	$ 7.62	$ 7.68	30.16%
Europe	5.53	6.46	25.37
Asia Pacific	4.84	3.00	11.78
Japan	3.86	4.38	17.20
China	2.14	2.59	10.17
Other	1.24	1.35	5.30

Source: "World Markets." [online] from http://www.bishop-associates.com [accessed January 7, 2004], from Bishop & Associates.

★ 1869 ★

Connectors

SIC: 3679; NAICS: 334419

Connectors Market in North America

The industry is shown by segment.

Computers & peripherals	31.2%
Telecom datacom	19.0
Automotive	13.7
Industrial equipment	9.5
Military & aerospace	8.2
Other	18.5

Source: "North American Electronic Connector Market." [online] from http://www.bishopassociates.com [accessed January 12, 2004, *from Bishop & Associates.*

★ 1870 ★
EMI/RFI Shielding
SIC: 3679; NAICS: 334419
EMI/RFI Shielding Industry

Demand for electromagnetic interface/radio frequen-cy interference is shown in millions of dollars.

	2002	2008
Conductive coatings	$ 235	$ 267
Metal cabinets	100	134
Laminates/tapes	15	19
Conductive plastics/elastomers	11	11
Other	162	198

Source: *Circuits Assembly*, July 2003, p. 10, from Business Communications Co.

★ 1871 ★
Flat Panels
SIC: 3679; NAICS: 334419
Flat Panel Market Worldwide, 2005

The market for computer and TV flat panels is forecasted for 2005.

Samsung	33.0%
LG Philips	18.0
Chin Mei	11.0
QDI	10.0
Sharp	8.0
Other	13.0

Source: *Financial Times*, March 8, 2004, p. 15, from Philips, Lehman Brothers, and Banc of America Securities.

★ 1872 ★
LED Equipment
SIC: 3679; NAICS: 334419
High-brightness LED Market Worldwide, 2002

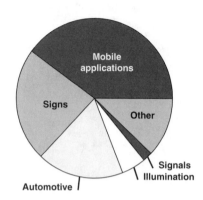

LED stands for light emitting diodes. The industry grew 50% in 2002 to $1.8 billion. The top market segments are shown in the table.

Mobile applications	40.0%
Signs	23.0
Automotive	18.0
Illumination	5.0
Signals	2.0
Other	12.0

Source: "Mobile Applications Prompt Strong Growth in LED Market." [online] http://compoundsemiconductor.net/ [accessed April 5, 2004], from Strategies Unlimited.

★ 1873 ★
Liquid Crystal Displays
SIC: 3679; NAICS: 334419
Liquid Crystal Market Worldwide

Liquid crystals are used in the manufacturing of elec-tronic displays in mobile phones and notebooks.

Merck	64.0%
Chisso	26.0
Other	10.0

Source: *Wall Street Journal*, October 22, 2003, p. B2.

★ 1874 ★
Liquid Crystal Displays
SIC: 3679; NAICS: 333313

Top LCD Makers

Market shares are shown in percent.

LG Philips LCD 21.5%
Samsung 20.0
AU Optronics 11.8
CMO 10.0
CPT 7.6
Other 29.1

Source: *Investor's Business Daily*, December 11, 2003,
p. A6, from DisplaySearch.

★ 1875 ★
Liquid Crystal Displays
SIC: 3679; NAICS: 334419

Top LCD Makers in Japan, 2002

Market shares are shown based on domestic production of 1.26 trillion yen.

Sharp 33.7%
Toshiba Matsushita Display Technology . . . 18.6
Hitachi 11.6
Seiko Epson 7.8
Sanyo Electric 7.0
Other 21.3

Source: "Market Share Survey Report 2002." [online]
from http://www.nni.nikkei.co.jp [accessed January 20,
2004], from Nikkei estimate and Ministry of Economy,
Trade and Industry.

★ 1876 ★
Liquid Crystal Displays
SIC: 3679; NAICS: 333313

Top OLED Display Makers, 2003

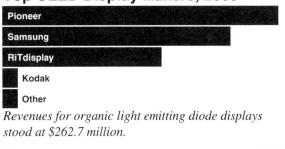

Revenues for organic light emitting diode displays stood at $262.7 million.

Pioneer 40.0%
Samsung 33.0
RiTdisplay 23.1
Kodak 2.2
Other 1.7

Source: *Investor's Business Daily*, January 21, 2004, p. A5,
from DisplaySearch.

★ 1877 ★
Liquid Crystal Displays
SIC: 3679; NAICS: 334419

Top TFT-LCD Makers Worldwide, 2003

Market shares are shown for the third quarter of 2003. TFT stands for thin film transistor.

LG Philips LCD 21.2%
Samsung 18.9
AUO 11.9
Other 31.7

Source: *Taiwan Economic News*, December 11, 2003,
p. NA, from International Display Technology of Japan.

★ 1878 ★
Liquid Crystal Displays
SIC: 3679; NAICS: 334419

Worldwide LCD Market by Application, 2003

LCD stands for liquid crystal display and these devices are used in monitors used on PCs and TVs. Shares shown here are for the 4th quarter of 2003.

LCD Monitors	51.0%
Notebook PCs	40.0
LCD TVs	7.0
Other	2.0

Source: *Investor's Business Daily*, March 30, 2004, p. A4, from DisplaySearch.

★ 1879 ★
Liquid Crystal Displays
SIC: 3679; NAICS: 334419

Worldwide Market for TFT LCD Devices, 2003

TFT stands for thin film transistor and LCD stands for liquid crystal display. The TFT LCD market includes all thin film liquid crystal display devices. The share data is for the 4th quarter of 2003.

LG Phillips LCD	23.0%
Samsung	20.3
AUO	12.2
CMO	10.4
CPT	7.4
Other	27.2

Source: "DisplaySearch Press Release." [online] http://www.displaysearch.com/press/2004/031704.htm [accessed April 8, 2004].

★ 1880 ★
Batteries
SIC: 3691; NAICS: 335911

Auto Battery Market in Western Europe

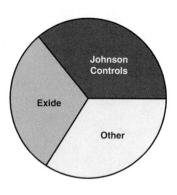

The $1.7 billion market is shown by company. Data are based on Johnson Control's recent purchase of Vanta AG's battery automotive business.

Johnson Controls	36.0%
Exide	30.0
Other	34.0

Source: *Milwaukee Journal-Sentinel*, August 7, 2002, p. NA.

★ 1881 ★
Batteries
SIC: 3691; NAICS: 335911

Automobile Battery Market in Thailand, 2002

Shares are by company and based on sales of automobile batteries sold for replacement.

GS Battery	35.0%
Thai Storage	26.0
FB	18.0
Yuasa	10.0
Other	11.0

Source: *Bangkok Post*, November 19, 2003, p. NA.

★ 1882 ★
Batteries
SIC: 3691; NAICS: 335911

Automotive OE Market in India

The company also has half of the industrial battery market.

Exide 85.0%
Other 15.0

Source: *Battery & EV Technology*, April 2004, p. NA.

★ 1883 ★
Batteries
SIC: 3691; NAICS: 335911

Battery Market in South America

The industry is shown by country.

Brazil 66.0%
Argentina 9.8
Venezuela 6.6
Colombia 6.3
Other 11.3

Source: *Batteries International*, July 2003, p. 61.

★ 1884 ★
Batteries
SIC: 3691; NAICS: 335911

Industrial Battery Sales in North America, 2002

North American industrial battery sales amounted to $864 million.

Industrial trucks 96.0%
Mining vehicles 2.0
Railroad/locomotives 2.0

Source: *Batteries International*, July 2003, p. 61, from Hollingsworth & Vose.

★ 1885 ★
Batteries
SIC: 3691; NAICS: 335911

Military Battery Market, 2003

The figure provided is for the company that sells most batteries to the U.S. Government for use in military applications.

Saft America Inc. 90.0%
Others 10.0

Source: *The Oakland Press*, May 27, 2004, p. B2.

★ 1886 ★
Batteries
SIC: 3691; NAICS: 335911

Small Rechargable Battery Market Worldwide

The rechargable business is valued at $9 billion, with lithium representing $3.5 billion, nickel rechargable $5 billion, small lead and rechargable alkaline representing $500 million in sales. Rayovac has 60% of the U.S. rechargable market due to quick charger technologies. Sanyo is the world market leader in the small rechargable market. Japan's control of the rechargable market is falling (79.8% in 2001 to a forecasted 54.5% in 2003).

	2001	2003	Share
NiCd	1,940	2,010	34.30%
NiMH	1,720	1,950	33.28
Li-Ion	700	1,300	22.18
Rechargable alkaline . . .	280	400	6.83
Li-polymer	20	200	3.41

Source: *Battery & EV Technology*, January 2003, p. NA, from BCC Inc.

★ 1887 ★
Batteries
SIC: 3691; NAICS: 335911

Top Battery Brands, 2003

Market shares are shown for the year ended November 30, 2003. Figures exclude Wal-Mart.

Duracell 31.5%
Energizer 21.9
Duracell Ultra 6.0
Duracell (other) 4.2
Energizer (other) 4.1
Rayovac Maximum 3.5

Continued on next page.

[Continued]
Batteries
SIC: 3691; NAICS: 335911

Top Battery Brands, 2003

Market shares are shown for the year ended November 30, 2003. Figures exclude Wal-Mart.

Duracell Ultra (other) 2.4%
Energizer e2 Titanium 2.2
Energizer e2 Lithium 2.1
Private label 6.0
Other 16.1

Source: *Grocery Headquarters*, February 2004, p. 52, from Information Resources Inc.

★ 1888 ★
Batteries
SIC: 3691; NAICS: 335911

Top Battery Makers, 2003

Market shares are shown based on sales at supermarkets, drug stores and mass merchandisers (but not Wal-Mart) for the year ended May 18, 2003.

Duracell 48.2%
Energizer 32.4
Rayovac 7.1
Panasonic Battery Co. 0.6
Private label 11.3
Other 0.4

Source: *Grocery Headquarters*, August 2003, p. S6.

★ 1889 ★
Batteries
SIC: 3691; NAICS: 335911

Top Battery Producers Worldwide, 2002

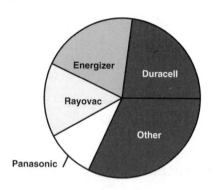

The world alkaline battery market was placed at $5.9 billion in 2002.

Duracell 23.3%
Energizer 20.3
Rayovac 14.7
Panasonic 10.0
Other 31.7

Source: *Office Products International*, January 2004, p. 28, from Frost & Sullivan.

★ 1890 ★
Batteries
SIC: 3691; NAICS: 335911

Top Lithium-Ion Battery Makers in Japan, 2002

Market shares are shown based on domestic sales of 180.2 million units.

Sanyo Electric 41.1%
Sony 24.5
Matsushita Battery Industrial 12.2
Toshiba 7.2
NEC Tokin 4.4
Other 10.6

Source: ''Market Share Survey Report 2002.'' [online] from http://www.nni.nikkei.co.jp [accessed January 20, 2004], from Nikkei estimate and Battery Association of Japan.

★ 1891 ★

Batteries

SIC: 3691; NAICS: 335911

UMI Battery Market in India, 2004

Market shares are shown in percent.

Indo National	34.0%
Novino	18.0
GEEP	3.0
Other	45.0

Source: *Battery & EV Technology*, April 2004, p. NA.

★ 1892 ★

Vehicle Stability Systems

SIC: 3694; NAICS: 336322

Electronic Stability Systems in Europe

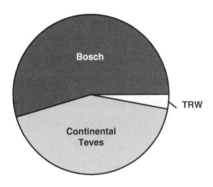

The market for such devices has been valued at 2.5 billion euros. Shares are estimated, with TRW's share placed at just under 3%.

Bosch	55.0%
Continental Teves	43.0
TRW	3.0

Source: *Automotive News Europe*, November 17, 2003, p. 3.

★ 1893 ★

Recording Media

SIC: 3695; NAICS: 334613

Consumer Recorder Market, 2003

The market is shown for the first three months of the year by format.

DVD-RAM/R-format	70.2%
Other	29.8

Source: *PR Newswire*, July 14, 2003, p. NA.

★ 1894 ★

Recording Media

SIC: 3695; NAICS: 334613

Recordable DVD Media Formats

Market shares are shown by format.

	July 2001	July 2003
DVD-R/RW	71.0%	44.0%
DVD-RAM	27.0	1.0
DVD + R/RW	2.0	55.0

Source: *DVD Report*, October 27, 2003, p. NA, from NPD Group Inc. and DVD + RW Alliance.

★ 1895 ★

Recording Media

SIC: 3695; NAICS: 334613

Top Blank CD-R Media Brands, 2003

Market shares are shown based on sales at supermarkets, drug stores and discount stores (but not Wal-Mart) for the year ended November 2, 2003.

	($ mil.)	Share
Memorex	$ 38.8	21.08%
TDK	24.5	13.31
Maxell	11.7	6.36
Fuji	11.6	6.30
Sony	5.7	3.10
Imation	4.9	2.66
Verbatim	4.7	2.55
Imix	1.5	0.81
Emtex	0.3	0.16

Continued on next page.

★ 1895 ★
[Continued]
Recording Media
SIC: 3695; NAICS: 334613
Top Blank CD-R Media Brands, 2003

Market shares are shown based on sales at super-markets, drug stores and discount stores (but not Wal-Mart) for the year ended November 2, 2003.

	($ mil.)	Share
JVC	$ 0.1	0.05%
Other	80.3	43.62

Source: *Chain Drug Review*, January 19, 2004, p. 19, from Information Resources Inc.

★ 1896 ★
Video Tape
SIC: 3695; NAICS: 334613
Leading Blank Video Cassette Brands, 2003

Brands are ranked by supermarket, discount and drug store sales in millions of dollars for the year ended November 30, 2003. Figures exclude Wal-Mart.

	($ mil.)	Share
Sony	$ 31.1	14.06%
Sony V	23.3	10.53
Fuji HQ	18.5	8.36
TDK Revue	17.3	7.82
Fuji	14.7	6.65
Maxell GX Silver	14.2	6.42
TDK	11.9	5.38

	($ mil.)	Share
Panasonic	$ 8.8	3.98%
Maxell HGX Gold	7.9	3.57
RCA	7.6	3.44
Other	65.9	29.79

Source: *MMR*, January 12, 2004, p. 73, from Information Resources Inc.

★ 1897 ★
Video Tape
SIC: 3695; NAICS: 334613
Top Blank Video Tape Makers, 2003

Market shares are shown based on sales at super-markets, drug stores and mass merchandisers (but not Wal-Mart) for the year ended May 18, 2003.

Sony Corp.	28.2%
TDK Electronics Corp.	22.2
Maxell Corp. of America	20.5
Fuji Photo Film U.S.A.	18.6
Thomson	3.7
Other	6.8

Source: *Grocery Headquarters*, August 2003, p. S6, from Information Resources Inc.

★ 1898 ★
Kiosks
SIC: 3699; NAICS: 335999
Airport Kiosk Market

Kinetics is the largest supplier of airport self-service kiosks and has about 3,000 units spread across North America.

Kinetics	70.0%
Other	30.0

Source: *Aviation Daily*, June 24, 2003, p. 8.

SIC 37 - Transportation Equipment

★ 1899 ★
Auto Auctioning

SIC: 3711; NAICS: 336111

Auto Auctioning Industry

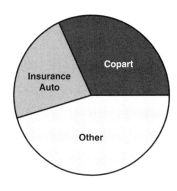

Market shares are shown in percent. Copart's share is estimated and Insurance Auto has 20-25% of the market.

Copart	35.0%
Insurance Auto	25.0
Other	50.0

Source: *Crain's Chicago Business*, November 24, 2003, p. 4.

★ 1900 ★
Autos

SIC: 3711; NAICS: 336111, 336112, 336211

Auto Segment Market Shares, 2002

Market shares are shown in percent.

Midsize car	21.7%
Compact car	14.4
Full-size pickups	13.5
Midsize SUV	10.2
Entry SUV	6.7
Compact van	6.7

Compact pickup	5.2%
Full-size SUV	4.6
Entry luxury car	4.4
Luxury car	3.3
Sports car	3.1
Luxuty SUV	2.2
Full-size car	2.2
Full-size van	2.0

Source: *Motor Trend*, April 2003, p. 42, from J.D. Power & Associates.

★ 1901 ★
Autos

SIC: 3711; NAICS: 336111

Automobile Sales in Europe, 2002-2003

The major auto segments of the European market are shown for 2002 and 2003. Sales figures are in thousands. The top sellers for 2003 in selected segments: minicars (Renault Twingo 114,812), upper medium (Volkswagen Passat 259,362), compact minivans (Renault Scenic 250,317).

	2002	2003	% Change
Small Minivan	243	412	69.6%
Large Minivan	308	351	14.2
Compact SUV	323	350	8.5
Compact Minivan . . .	877	933	6.4
Small	3,478	3,658	5.2
Entry Premium	577	567	-1.7
Medium Premium . . .	552	551	-1.7
Lower Premium	1,115	1,022	-8.3
Lower Medium	3,446	3,132	-9.1
Upper Medium	1,570	1,415	-9.9
Minicar	1,024	795	-22.3

Source: *Automotive News Europe*, February 9, 2020, p. 18, from JATO Dynamics.

★ 1902 ★

Autos

SIC: 3711; NAICS: 336111

Best-Selling Autos in China, 2002

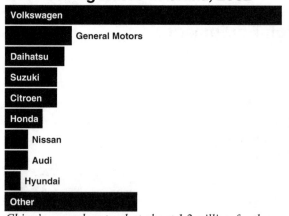

China's car sales stood at about 1.2 million for the year. The rapidly growing middle class (about 100 million people) is the industry's major market.

Volkswagen	38.0%
General Motors	9.0
Daihatsu	8.0
Suzuki	7.0
Citroen	7.0
Honda	5.0
Nissan	3.0
Audi	3.0
Hyundai	2.0
Other	18.0

Source: *Financial Times*, August 25, 2003, p. 13, from Deutsche Bank.

★ 1903 ★

Autos

SIC: 3711; NAICS: 336111

Best-Selling Autos in China by Price, 2003

Passenger car sales rose 61% over 2002 to reach 1,879,271 vehicles.

$15,000-$22,000	26.0%
$12,000-$15,000	21.0
$4,200-$8,500	18.8
$22,000-$32,000	17.2
$8,500-$12,000	13.5
Above $32,000	3.5

Source: *Automotive News*, March 15, 2004, p. 32, from Automotive Resources Asia.

★ 1904 ★

Autos

SIC: 3711; NAICS: 336111

Best-Selling Autos in Hungary, 2003

Market shares are shown in percent.

	Units	Shares
Suzuki	39,747	19.1%
Opel	27,043	13.0
Renault	19,830	9.5
Skoda	15,204	7.3
Volkswagen	14,805	7.1
Peugeot	14,579	7.0
Daewoo	11,579	5.6
Ford	10,498	5.0

Source: *Europe Intelligence Wire*, January 20, 2004, p. NA, from Hungarian News Agency and Hungarian Car Importers Association.

★ 1905 ★

Autos

SIC: 3711; NAICS: 336111

Best-Selling Autos in the U.K., 2003

The table shows leading auto brands by registrations during 2003.

Focus (Ford)	131,684
Corsa (GM)	108,387

Continued on next page.

★ 1905 ★

[Continued]

Autos

SIC: 3711; NAICS: 336111

Best-Selling Autos in the U.K., 2003

The table shows leading auto brands by registrations during 2003.

Astra (GM)	96,929
Fiesta (Ford)	95,887
Clio (Renault)	83,972
206 (Peugeot)	82,667
Megane (Renault)	71,660
Golf (VW)	67,226
3 Series (BMW)	65,489
Mondeo (Ford)	60,046

Source: *European Rubber Journal*, April 1, 2004, p. 30, from SMMT.

★ 1906 ★

Autos

SIC: 3711; NAICS: 336111

Best-Selling Cars, 2003

Data show sales for model year 2003.

Toyota Camry	416,948
Honda Accord	409,242
Ford Taurus	327,447
Honda Civic	309,857
Toyota Corolla	265,688
Chevrolet Impala	244,543
Chevrolet Cavalier	239,421
Ford Focus	230,827
Nissan Altima	200,749

Source: *Automotive News*, October 6, 2003, p. NA.

★ 1907 ★

Autos

SIC: 3711; NAICS: 336111

Best-Selling Cars in Australia, 2003

The top selling marquees are shown for the first ten months of the year.

	Units	Share
Toyota	153,709	20.3%
Holden	146,923	19.4
Ford	106,196	14.0
Mitsubishi	60,998	8.1
Nissan	48,563	6.4
Mazda	44,876	5.9
Hyundai	25,627	3.4
Honda	25,007	3.3
Subaru	24,299	3.2
Mercedes-Benz	15,936	2.1

Source: *AsiaPulse News*, November 25, 2003, p. NA, from VFACTS.

★ 1908 ★

Autos

SIC: 3711; NAICS: 336111

Best-Selling Cars in Japan, 2002

Data show unit sales.

Honda Fit	250,790
Toyota Corolla	226,222
Nissan March	139,332
Toyota Ist	103,579
Toyota Vitz	100,801
Toyota Noah	97,080
Toyota Estima	95,765

Continued on next page.

★ 1908 ★
[Continued]
Autos
SIC: 3711; NAICS: 336111
Best-Selling Cars in Japan, 2002

Data show unit sales.

Toyota Voxy	77,958
Nissan Cube	75,215
Honda Mobilio	72,242

Source: *America's Intelligence Wire*, January 9, 2003, p. NA, from Japan Automobile Manufacturers Association.

★ 1909 ★
Autos
SIC: 3711; NAICS: 336111
Best-Selling Cars in Northeast Ohio, 2003

A total of 245,880 vehicles were sold in 2003. The source covers 234 dealers and 19 counties in Ohio.

	Units	Share
Chevrolet	44,544	18.12%
Ford	42,535	17.30
Honda	20,824	8.47
Toyota	17,350	7.06
Dodge	15,401	6.26
Other	105,226	42.80

Source: *The Plain Dealer*, January 10, 2004, p. C1, from Greater Cleveland Automobile Dealers AE Association.

★ 1910 ★
Autos
SIC: 3711; NAICS: 336111
Best-Selling Cars in Vietnam, 2002

Data show unit sales. Total sales of locally produced vehicles reached 26,872 vehicles. Company market shares: Toyota Vietnam 27%, Vietnam Daewoo Motors (GM) 14% and Ford Vietnam 14%.

Toyota Zace	1,906
Mercedes-Benz 140	1,794
Toyota Altis	1,603
Vinastar Jolie	1,434
Daewoo Lanos 1.5	1,423
Suzuki Carry Truck	1,304
Ford LAa	1,246

Daewoo Nubira 1.6	1,092
Hiace Commuter	1,032

Source: "Automotive Market." [online] from http://www.usatrade.gov [accessed January 5, 2004], from U.S. Commercial Service.

★ 1911 ★
Autos
SIC: 3711; NAICS: 336111
Best-Selling Small Cars, 2003

Data show unit sales.

Toyota Corolla/Matrix	325,477
Honda Civic	299,672
Chevy Cavalier	256,550
Ford Focus	229,353
VW Golf/Jetta	147,209
Dodge Neon	120,101
Saturn Ion	117,230
Nissan Sentra	94,500
Mazda 3/Protege	70,869
Pontiac Vibe	56,922

Source: *Detroit News*, February 19, 2004, p. B1, from Autodata.

★ 1912 ★
Autos
SIC: 3711; NAICS: 336111
Hybrid Electric Vehicle Market

Total registrations were 43,435 in 2003. California and Virginia topped the list of registrations. Women accounted for 43% of HEV registrations.

Honda Civic HEV	50.0%
Toyota Prius	47.0
Honda Insight	3.0

Source: *Electric and Hybrid Vehicles Today*, April 26, 2004, p. NA, from R.L. Polk & Company.

★ 1913 ★
Autos
SIC: 3711; NAICS: 336111
Hybrid Vehicle Market

Analysts expect optional hybrid systems on 28 car and truck models by 2008. 4 million hybrid vehicles could be on the road in 10 years.

GM	33.0%
Dodge	16.0
Toyota Motor	10.0
Honda Motor	10.0
Ford	6.0
Other	25.0

Source: *The Marion Star*, November 23, 2003, p. NA, from J.D. Power & Associates.

★ 1914 ★
Autos
SIC: 3711; NAICS: 336111
Hybrid Vehicle Registrations, 2003

Total hybrid vehicles registration were 43,435 in 2003, up 26% from 2002. Since 2000 hybrid sales grew at an average annual rate of nearly 89%.

	Units	Share
California	11,425	26.30%
Virginia	3,376	7.77
Florida	1,996	4.60
Washington	1,972	4.54
Maryland	1,851	4.26
New York	1,653	3.81
Texas	1,651	3.80
Illinois	1,502	3.46
Massachusetts	1,335	3.07
Pennsylvania	1,217	2.80%
Other	15,457	35.59

Source: *Wall Street Journal*, April 22, 2004, p. D4, from R.L. Polk & Co.

★ 1915 ★
Autos
SIC: 3711; NAICS: 336112
Light Truck Sales (Domestic and Foreign)

The data for 2003 are for the period January through October.

	Asian/European Trucks	Domestic Trucks
2003	26.6%	73.4%
2002	23.9	76.1
2001	23.1	76.9
2000	21.2	78.8
1999	18.4	81.6
1998	16.2	83.8
1997	15.4	84.6

Source: *Detroit Free Press*, November 10, 2003, p. A1, from Autodata Corp.

★ 1916 ★
Autos
SIC: 3711; NAICS: 336112
Light-Truck Sales Leaders, 2003

Data show sales for model year 2003.

Ford F-series	820,868
Chevrolet Silverado	689,404
Dodge Ram pickup	427,764
Ford Explorer	388,627
Chevrolet TrailBlazer	268,686
Dodge Caravan/Grd Caravan	237,326
Ford Ranger	215,002
Jeep Grand Cherokee	207,808
GMC Sierra	198,970

Source: *Automotive News*, October 6, 2003, p. NA, from Automotive News Data Center.

★ 1917 ★
Autos
SIC: 3711; NAICS: 336112

Light Vehicle Sales, 2003

Sales stood 16.6 million in 2003, down from 16.8 million in 2002 and more than 17 million in previous years. The source points out industry sales have been buttressed by 0% interest loans and large rebates.

	2002	2003
Middle sedans	19.2%	18.2%
Sports utility	17.7	17.2
Small sedans	13.9	13.4
Vans	8.7	8.4
Cross/utilities	7.4	10.0
Luxury sedans	7.3	6.9

Source: *WARD's Dealer Business*, March 1, 2004, p. 3.

★ 1918 ★
Autos
SIC: 3711; NAICS: 336111

Luxury Car Market in Spain, 2003

Data show unit sales.

Audi	41,526
BMW	40,641
Mercedes-Benz	36,650
Volvo	13,192
Jaguar	2,621
Lexus	1,400

Source: *Automotive News Europe*, January 26, 2004, p. 9, from Precisa Urban Science Spain.

★ 1919 ★
Autos
SIC: 3711; NAICS: 336111

Luxury Car Market Worldwide, 2000

Market shares are shown in percent.

Mercedes-Benz E-Class	35.0%
BMW 5 Series	29.0
Audi AG	23.0
Jaguar S-Type	8.0
Lexus GS	5.0
Other	10.0

Source: *BusinessWeek*, March 18, 2002, p. 92A, from JATO Dynamics.

★ 1920 ★
Autos
SIC: 3711; NAICS: 336111

Market for Vans in the U.K., 2003

Shares are by manufacturer for van sales in the United Kingdom in 2003.

Ford	28.3%
Vauxhall	16.8
Citroen	8.4
Mercedes Benz	7.7
Renault	6.5
Peugeot	5.4
Volkswagen	5.4
Fiat	3.6
LDV	3.0
Nissan	2.9
Toyota	2.2
Iveco	1.8

Source: *Commercial Motor*, January 15, 2004, p. NA.

★ 1921 ★
Autos
SIC: 3711; NAICS: 336111
Motor Vehicles Sales in the Philippines, 2004

Shares are shown for the leading motor vehicle manufacturers selling in the Philippines based on sales during the month of January 2004.

Toyota 37.56%
Mitsubishi 16.12
Honda 15.63
Other 30.69

Source: *Asia Africa Intelligence Wire*, February 12, 2004, p. NA.

★ 1922 ★
Autos
SIC: 3711; NAICS: 336111
New Car Registrations in Europe

Data refer to European Union and EFTA countries (Iceland, Liechtenstein, Norway, Switzerland). Total registrations were 14.2 million.

	2002	2003	Share
Germany	3,252,898	3,235,960	22.76%
United Kingdom	2,563,631	2,579,050	18.14
Italy	2,279,612	2,251,307	15.83
France	2,145,071	2,009,254	14.13
Spain	1,331,877	1,383,017	9.73
Netherlands	510,702	488,944	3.44
Belgium	467,569	458,796	3.23
Austria	279,493	300,714	2.12
Greece	268,489	257,293	1.81
Sweden	254,589	261,206	1.84

Source: "New Passenger Car Registrations by Market." [online] from http://www.acea.be [Press release February 12, 2004], from Association des Constructeurs Europeens d'Automobiles.

★ 1923 ★
Autos
SIC: 3711; NAICS: 336111
New Car Sales in Europe, 2003

Companies are shown based on share of new car registrations in Europe and the EFTA countires (Iceland, Lichtenstein, Norway, and Switzerland).

	2002	2003
VW Group	18.4%	18.2%
PSA Group	15.0	14.8
Ford Group	11.4	11.0
GM Group	9.9	9.8
Fiat Group	8.2	7.4
DaimlerChrysler	6.6	6.5
BMW Group	4.3	4.4
Other	26.2	27.9

Source: "New Passenger Car Registrations by Manufacturer." [online] http://www.acea.be [Press Release: January 1, 2004], from Association des Constructeurs Europeens d'Automobiles.

★ 1924 ★
Autos
SIC: 3711; NAICS: 336111, 336112
New Car Sales in Illinois

Between 1998 and 2003 the big three automakers (Ford, Chrysler, GM) saw it share fall from 44% to 21.7% in the domestic car market. Japanese brands saw their share increase from 17.9% to 22.2%. Share of total sales is shown by county.

Cook 48.5%
DuPage 14.7
Lake 11.0
Other 25.8

Source: *Chicago Tribune*, February 8, 2004, p. NA, from *Chicago Auto Outlook* and Auto Outlook Inc.

★ 1925 ★
Autos

SIC: 3711; NAICS: 336112

Passenger Van Market, 2003

Ford dominates the market for large 15-passenger vans.

	Units	Share
Ford Club Wagon	29,319	53.0%
Chevrolet Express	16,023	29.0
Dodge/Freightliner Sprinter	7,155	12.0
GMC Savana	3,089	6.0

Source: *Detroit News*, March 14, 2003, p. C1, from Ward's.

★ 1926 ★
Autos

SIC: 3711; NAICS: 336111, 336112

Sedan Sales and the Big Three

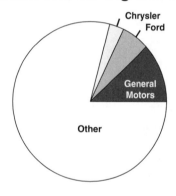

After concentrating on SUV sales in recent years automakers are focusing on the car industry again (cars represent 50% of the new vehicle market, according to CNW Market Research). Market shares are shown in percent.

	1995	2000	2003
General Motors	19.9%	14.4%	11.6%
Ford	12.2	8.8	6.2
Chrysler	5.3	3.7	2.8
Other	62.6	73.1	79.4

Source: *Brandweek*, January 5, 2004, p. 20, from Global Insight.

★ 1927 ★
Autos

SIC: 3711; NAICS: 336111, 336112

Top Auto and Truck Firms in Canada, 2002-2003

Data show unit sales.

	2002	2003	Share
General Motors	519,195	453,881	28.48%
Ford Motor	272,647	256,889	16.12
DaimlerChrysler . . .	261,297	226,811	14.23
Honda	165,331	154,630	9.70
Toyota	152,766	165,024	10.36
Hyundai	95,931	95,901	6.02
Mazda	71,140	65,550	4.11
Nissan	64,661	69,534	4.36
Volkswagen	50,211	46,708	2.93
Subaru	17,236	15,762	0.99
BMW	16,622	17,868	1.12
Suzuki	11,558	9,361	0.59
Mitsubishi	3,223	14,122	0.89
Porsche	1,193	1,612	0.10

Source: *Automotive News*, January 19, 2004, p. NA, from Automotive News Data Center and Association of International Automobile Manufacturers of Canda.

★ 1928 ★
Autos

SIC: 3711; NAICS: 336111, 336112

Top Auto and Truck Firms in Mexico, 2002-2003

Data show unit sales for the first 11 months of each year.

	2002	2003	Share
General Motors	206,241	187,746	21.87%
Nissan	189,696	188,297	21.94
Volkswagen	169,514	171,570	19.99
Ford	144,359	145,284	16.93
DaimlerChrysler . . .	106,010	92,121	10.73
Honda	26,952	25,636	2.99
Renault	13,511	16,487	1.92
Toyota	3,354	10,030	1.17
Other	14,875	21,114	2.46

Source: *Automotive News*, December 29, 2003, p. NA, from Automotive News Data Center and Mexican Automobile Industry Association.

★ 1929 ★
Autos
SIC: 3711; NAICS: 336111, 336112
Top Auto Makers in Canada

Market shares are shown in percent.

	2002	2003
General Motors	30.3%	28.4%
Ford	15.2	15.2
DaimlerChrysler	14.5	13.4
Other	40.0	43.0

Source: *Toronto Star*, December 11, 2004, p. A1.

★ 1930 ★
Autos
SIC: 3711; NAICS: 336111
Top Auto Makers in China, 2003

Companies are ranked by unit sales.

	Units	Share
Volkswagen	694,000	34.02%
General Motors	387,710	19.01
Honda Motors	123,000	6.03
PSA Peugeot Citroen	103,000	5.05
Suzuki Motor Corp.	100,000	4.90
Toyota Motor Corp.	98,000	4.80
SAIC-Chery	90,000	4.41
Mazda Motor Corp.	80,000	3.92
Geely Group	80,000	3.92
Nissan Motor Company	73,000	3.58
Other	211,290	10.36

Source: "Car Makers' Sales, Market Share China, 2003" [online] http://www.forbes.com [accessed March 29, 2004], p. NA.

★ 1931 ★
Autos
SIC: 3711; NAICS: 336111
Top Auto Makers in Europe, 2003

Shares are for January - April 2003.

VW Group	16.62%
Peugeot Group	15.76
Ford Group	11.17
Renault Group	11.14
GM Group	9.97
Fiat Group	8.56
DaimlerChrysler	6.37
Other	20.41

Source: *Automotive Industries*, June 2003, p. 6.

★ 1932 ★
Autos
SIC: 3711; NAICS: 336111
Top Auto Makers in Iran

The two companies control 90% of the market.

Iran Khodro/SAIPA Khodro	90.0%
Other	10.0

Source: "Malaysia's Proton to set up Plants in Iran, China." [online] from http://www.iranmania.com/news/200504b.asp.

★ 1933 ★
Autos
SIC: 3711; NAICS: 336111
Top Auto Makers in Poland, 2003

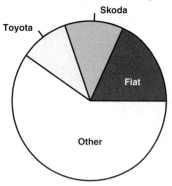

New car sales jumped 16.3% to 358,432 units. Market shares are shown in percent.

Fiat	18.40%
Skoda	12.11
Toyota	10.30
Other	59.19

Source: *Poland Business News*, January 23, 2004, p. NA.

★ 1934 ★
Autos
SIC: 3711; NAICS: 336111
Top Auto Makers in Russia, 2002

Market shares are shown in percent. The top brand for each company is shown in parentheses.

AvtoVAZ (Lada)	70.0%
AvtoGAZ (Volga)	20.0
Kamaz (Oka)	5.0
Ford (Focus)	3.0
Other	2.0

Source: *Automotive News Europe*, December 1, 2003, p. 21, from Emerging Markets.

★ 1935 ★
Autos
SIC: 3711; NAICS: 336111
Top Auto Makers in South Korea

Market shares are shown in percent.

Hyundai Motors	47.8%
Kia Motors	23.8
Ssangyong	9.8
GM Daewoo	9.7
Renault Samsung	8.4

Source: *Korea Times*, January 11, 2004, p. NA.

★ 1936 ★
Autos
SIC: 3711; NAICS: 336111
Top Auto Makers Worldwide, 2003

Firms are ranked by global unit sales. Shares are shown based on sales by the top 39 companies.

	Units	Share
General Motors	8,594,605	14.42%
Toyota Motor Corp.	6,783,463	11.38
Ford Motor Co.	6,541,562	10.98
Volkswagen AG	5,015,911	8.42
DaimlerChrysler	4,355,800	7.31
PSA/Peugeot-Citroen	3,286,100	5.51
Hyundai Automotive Group .	3,046,333	5.11
Nissan Motor Co.	2,968,357	4.98
Honda Motor Co.	2,910,000	4.88
Renault SA	2,388,958	4.01
Fiat S.p.A.	1,989,921	3.34
Suzuki Motor Co.	1,824,977	3.06
Other	9,896,407	16.60

Source: *Automotive News*, May 17, 2004, p. 8, from *Automotive News* research.

★ 1937 ★
Autos
SIC: 3711; NAICS: 336111

Top Auto Registrations, 2003

*Data show the top registrations for October 2002 -
September 2003. Total vehicle registrations (cars &
trucks) were 16.43 million.*

Toyota Camry	413,628
Honda Accord	403,463
Ford Taurus	328,401
Toyota Corolla	322,174
Honda Civic	308,007
Chevrolet Impala	264,996
Chevrolet Cavalier	237,066
Ford Focus	233,575
Nissan Altima	196,778
Chevrolet Malibu	158,794

Source: *PR Newswire*, December 8, 2003, p. NA.

★ 1938 ★
Autos
SIC: 3711; NAICS: 336111

Top Auto Sellers in California, 2003

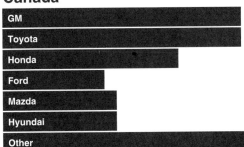

*Total vehicle sales were 1,953,243 units, nearly 12%
of all vehicle sales in the country.*

Toyota Motor Sales	20.8%
General Motors	17.1
Other	62.1

Source: *Automotive News*, March 1, 2004, p. 4, from R.L.
Polk & Co.

★ 1939 ★
Autos
SIC: 3711; NAICS: 336111

Top Compact/Subcompact Makers in Canada

*Smaller cars dominate the Canadian market because
of higher gas taxes and lower disposable incomes. In
the United States, mid-sized cars and full-sized
pickups have about a third of the market.*

	1999	2003
GM	28.4%	19.2%
Toyota	16.9	19.3
Honda	14.4	13.8
Ford	6.7	7.6
Mazda	6.2	8.8
Hyundai	5.6	8.9
Other	21.8	22.4

Source: *Globe and Mail*, February 21, 2004, p. NA, from
Desrosiers Automotive Consultants Inc. Annual Reports.

★ 1940 ★
Autos
SIC: 3711; NAICS: 336111

Top Convertibles, 2002

*Convertibles made up 3.8% of all passenger car
registrations for the year. Data show number of
registrations. Los Angeles is the top market for
convertibles with 30,418 registrations.*

	Units	Share
Chrysler Sebring	43,809	14.48%
Ford Mustang	42,418	14.02
Ford Thunderbird	19,536	6.46
Mitsubishi Eclipse	15,887	5.25
Lexus SC 430	14,925	4.93
Mazda Miata	14,089	4.66
Mercedes SL	12,415	4.10

Continued on next page.

★ 1940 ★

[Continued]
Autos
SIC: 3711; NAICS: 336111

Top Convertibles, 2002

Convertibles made up 3.8% of all passenger car registrations for the year. Data show number of registrations. Los Angeles is the top market for convertibles with 30,418 registrations.

	Units	Share
Chevrolet Corvette	11,959	3.95%
Porsche Boxster	10,300	3.40
Honda S2000	9,728	3.22
Other	107,434	35.52

Source: *Research Alert*, October 3, 2003, p. 2, from R.L. Polk & Co.

★ 1941 ★

Autos
SIC: 3711; NAICS: 336111

Top Convertibles, 2003

Total convertible registrations increased 2.3% over 2002 to reach 296,433 units for the calendar year 2003.

	Units	Share
Chrysler Sebring	42,476	14.33%
Ford Mustang	41,289	13.93
Volkswagen New Beetle	23,316	7.87
BMW Z4	18,852	6.36
Ford Thunderbird	18,056	6.09
Mercedes-Benz SL	13,009	4.39
Mitsubishi Eclipse	12,382	4.18
Mazda Miata	11,308	3.81
Chevrolet Corvette	10,928	3.69
Lexus SC430	10,548	3.56
Other	94,269	31.80

Source: *Just-Auto.com*, March 23, 2004, p. NA, from R.L. Polk & Co.

★ 1942 ★

Autos
SIC: 3711; NAICS: 336112

Top Light Vehicle Makers, 2003

Shares of the consumer market are shown for United States and Canada.

General Motors	35.0%
Ford	24.1
DaimlerChrysler	15.0
Toyota	8.7
Honda	8.5
Nissan	3.8
Mazda	1.2
BMW	1.2
Mitsubishi	1.0
Other	1.5

Source: *Modern Tire Dealer*, Annual Fact Book 2004, p. 8, from *Modern Tire Dealer* estimates.

★ 1943 ★

Autos
SIC: 3711; NAICS: 336112

Top Light Vehicle Makers, 2004

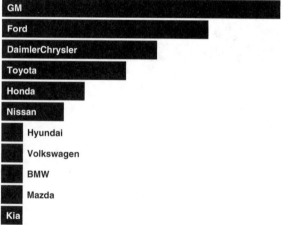

Companies are ranked by sales for the first five months of the year.

	Units	Share
GM	1,896,956	27.2%
Ford	1,400,397	20.1
DaimlerChrysler	1,012,505	14.5
Toyota	834,270	12.0
Honda	569,923	8.2
Nissan	394,677	5.7

Continued on next page.

★ **1943** ★

[Continued]

Autos

SIC: 3711; NAICS: 336112

Top Light Vehicle Makers, 2004

Companies are ranked by sales for the first five months of the year.

	Units	Share
Hyundai	163,675	2.4%
Volkswagen	134,758	1.9
BMW	115,912	1.7
Mazda	113,574	1.6
Kia	108,265	1.6

Source: *Detroit Free Press*, June 3, 2004, p. 3A, from Autodata Corp.

★ **1944** ★

Autos

SIC: 3711; NAICS: 336112

Top Light Vehicle Makers Worldwide

Companies are shown ranked by millions of vehicles produced.

General Motors	8.79
Ford	7.60
Toyota	6.91
DaimlerChrysler	6.05
Renault/Nissan	5.42
Volkswagen	5.06
PSA	3.23
Honda	3.00
Suzuki	2.35
Hyundai	2.25

Source: *Wall Street Journal*, December 8, 2003, p. 1, from CSM Worldwide.

★ **1945** ★

Autos

SIC: 3711; NAICS: 336112

Top Light Vehicle Sellers, 2003

Sales are shown by nameplate.

Ford Motor	3,477,444
Chevrolet	2,642,583

DaimlerChrysler	2,346,168
Toyota Motor	1,866,314
Dodge	1,223,302
Nissan North America	794,417
General Motors	563,479
Pontiac	475,536
BMW Group	276,957
Mercedes-Benz	218,551
Subaru	186,819
Volvo	134,586
Lexus	126,820
Oldsmobile	125,897
Suzuki	58,438
Hummer	35,259
Porsche	28,416
Scion	10,898

Source: *Automotive News*, January 12, 2004, p. NA, from Automotive News Data Center.

★ **1946** ★

Autos

SIC: 3711; NAICS: 336111

Top Minivehicle Makers in Japan, 2002

Market shares are shown based on domestic sales of 1.83 million units.

Suzuki Motor	31.3%
Daihatsu Motor	26.8
Honda Motor	15.8
Mitsubishi Motors	13.1
Fuji Heavy Industries	8.2
Other	4.8

Source: "Market Share Survey Report 2002." [online] from http://www.nni.nikkei.co.jp [accessed January 20, 2004], from Japan Mini Vehicle Association.

★ 1947 ★
Autos
SIC: 3711; NAICS: 336112

Top Pickup Brands, 2003

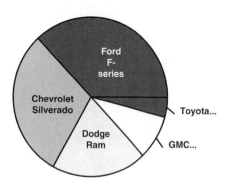

Shares are shown based on sales of 1.88 million vehicles for January - October 2003.

Ford F-series 36.9%
Chevrolet Silverado 30.2
Dodge Ram 19.9
GMC Sierra 8.6
Toyota Tundra 4.4

Source: *Advertising Age,* December 1, 2003, p. 11, from
Automotive News Data Center.

★ 1948 ★
Autos
SIC: 3711; NAICS: 336112

Top SUVs in Austria

*As of December 2002 there were nearly 3.9 million
registered cars on the road. Data show the best-selling
models.*

	2002	Jan-Jun 2003
Toyota	3,309	1,894
Suzuki Grand Vitara	1,124	624
Hyundai Santa Fe	934	677
BMW X5	850	450
Toyota Landcruiser	727	651
Nissan Terrano II	676	391

	2002	Jan-Jun 2003
Mitsubishi Pajero Sport	674	413
Nissan X-Trail	527	416
KIA Sorento	349	454
Volvo XC90	6	359

Source: "SUV Vehicles and Accessories." [online] from
http://www.usatrade.gov [accessed January 5, 2004], from
U.S. Commercial Service.

★ 1949 ★
Autos
SIC: 3711; NAICS: 336112

Top Truck Registrations, 2003

*Data show the top registrations for October 2002 -
September 2003. Total registrations for the model
year fell 4.1%.*

Ford F-series 782,376
Chevrolet Silverado 677,107
Dodge Ram 423,086
Ford Explorer 397,218
Chevrolet TrailBlazer 264,151
Dodge Caravan 233,947
Ford Ranger 215,470
Jeep Grand Cherokee 205,427
GMC Sierra 199,912
Chevrolet Tahoe 191,209

Source: *PR Newswire,* December 8, 2003, p. NA, from
R.L. Polk & Co.

★ 1950 ★
Autos
SIC: 3711; NAICS: 336112

Top Van (2.8-6.5 tonnes) Makers in the U.K., 2003

Market shares are shown in percent.

Ford 30.6%
Mercedes 14.7
VW 8.3
Vauxhall 7.0
LDV 6.9
Renault 6.7
Iveco 6.0
Citroen 4.8

Continued on next page.

[Continued]
Autos
SIC: 3711; NAICS: 336112
Top Van (2.8-6.5 tonnes) Makers in the U.K., 2003

Market shares are shown in percent.

Peugeot	3.7%
Fiat	3.7
Other	7.6

Source: *Company Van*, March - April 2004, p. 14, from Iveco.

★ 1951 ★
Autos
SIC: 3711; NAICS: 336111
Types of Cars Driven, 2002-2004

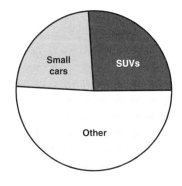

Market shares are shown in percent.

	2002	2003	2004
SUVs	25.9%	27.2%	26.1%
Small cars	23.6	22.8	22.9
Other	50.5	50.0	51.0

Source: *Washington Post*, June 13, 2004, p. F1, from National Transportation Research Service.

★ 1952 ★
Autos
SIC: 3711; NAICS: 336111, 336112
Vehicle Drive Production in North America, 2003 and 2008

Four-wheel drives are forecasted to have a 37% market penetration by 2008.

	2003	2008
Rear-wheel drive	87.0%	68.0%
Front-wheel drive	13.0	32.0

Source: *just-auto.com*, March 8, 2004, p. NA.

★ 1953 ★
Autos
SIC: 3711; NAICS: 336111, 336112
Vehicle Market Shares

The $400 billion auto industry is shown by segment.

Passenger cars	48.0%
SUVs	26.0
Pickup trucks	20.0
Minivans	6.0

Source: *Atlanta Journal-Constitution*, October 24, 2003, p. F1, from AutoPacific Group.

★ 1954 ★
Garbage Trucks
SIC: 3711; NAICS: 336112
Garbage Truck Market in North America

Market share is estimated.

Mack	70.0%
Other	30.0

Source: *Fleet Equipment*, March 2004, p. 12.

★ 1955 ★
Police Cars
SIC: 3711; NAICS: 336111

Police Car Market

Market shares are shown in percent.

Crown Victoria	85.0%
Other	15.0

Source: *Detroit Free Press*, July 31, 2003, p. 3C.

★ 1956 ★
Buses
SIC: 3713; NAICS: 336211

Pakistan's Bus Market, 2003

Total production was 1,296 vehicles in 2002-2003.

Hino	58.3%
Mazda	37.1
Nissan	4.6

Source: "U.S. Commercial Service" [online] http://www.export.gov/comm_svc/index.html [accessed March 30, 2004], March 13, 2020, p. NA.

★ 1957 ★
Buses
SIC: 3713; NAICS: 336211

Top Bus Companies in Africa, 2002

Market shares are shown in percent.

Changzhou Iveco Bus Co.	40.0%
Yutong	16.0
Other	44.0

Source: *Asia Africa Intelligence Wire*, November 10, 2003, p. NA, from *Business Daily Update*.

★ 1958 ★
Trucks
SIC: 3713; NAICS: 336211

Class 4 Truck Leaders, 2003

Ford
Isuzu
Chevrolet
GMC
Freightliner
Mitsubishi Fuso
Nissan Diesel
Hino
Other

Market shares are shown based on sales.

	Units	Share
Ford	16,195	17.84%
Isuzu	9,979	10.99
Chevrolet	7,365	8.11
GMC	5,119	5.64
Freightliner	2,996	3.30
Mitsubishi Fuso	2,544	2.80
Nissan Diesel	840	0.93
Hino	326	0.36
Other	45,429	50.04

Source: *Automotive News*, January 26, 2004, p. NA, from Automotive News Data Center.

★ 1959 ★
Trucks
SIC: 3713; NAICS: 336211

Class 5 Truck Leaders, 2003

Market shares are shown based on sales.

	Units	Share
Ford	17,854	30.80%
GMC	3,588	6.19
Isuzu	2,441	4.21
Chevrolet	2,398	4.14
Mitsubishi Faso	1,130	1.95
Nissan Diesel	681	1.17
Freightliner	482	0.83
Hino	377	0.65

Continued on next page.

★ 1959 ★

[Continued]
Trucks
SIC: 3713; NAICS: 336211

Class 5 Truck Leaders, 2003

Market shares are shown based on sales.

	Units	Share
Sterling	29	0.05%
Other	28,980	50.00

Source: *Automotive News*, January 26, 2004, p. NA, from Automotive News Data Center.

★ 1960 ★

Trucks
SIC: 3713; NAICS: 336211

Class 5 Truck Market in Canada, 2003

Ford

General Motors

Hino Canada

Freightliner

Market shares are shown in percent.

Ford	56.4%
General Motors	22.9
Hino Canada	19.4
Freightliner	1.3

Source: "Canadian Retail Truck Sales." [online] available from http://www.todaystrucking.com [accessed March 30, 2004], p. NA, from Canadian Vehicle Manufacturers Association.

★ 1961 ★

Trucks
SIC: 3713; NAICS: 336211

Class 6 Truck Market, 2003

Market shares are shown in percent.

International	37.8%
Freightliner	30.7
Ford	19.2
General Motors	3.2
Chevrolet	2.3
Sterling	2.1

Hino USA	2.0%
Nissan	1.1
Mitsubishi Fuso	1.1
Other	0.5

Source: "U.S. Retail Truck Sales." [online] available from http://www.todaystrucking.com [accessed March 30, 2004], p. NA.

★ 1962 ★

Trucks
SIC: 3713; NAICS: 336211

Class 6 Truck Market in Canada, 2003

Market shares are shown in percent.

International	47.2%
General Motors	17.2
Freightliner	13.9
Hino Canada	11.0
Other	10.7

Source: "Canadian Retail Truck Sales." [online] available from http://www.todaystrucking.com [accessed March 30, 2004], p. NA, from Canadian Vehicle Manufacturers Association.

★ 1963 ★

Trucks
SIC: 3713; NAICS: 336211

Class 7 Truck Market, 2003

Market shares are shown in percent.

International	42.6%
Freightliner	27.7
General Motors	6.1
Sterling	5.5
Kenworth	5.0
Peterbilt	4.8
Chevrolet	3.2
Ford	3.1
Mack	0.4
Hino USA	0.4
Other	1.2

Source: "U.S. Retail Truck Sales." [online] available from http://www.todaystrucking.com [accessed March 30, 2004], p. NA.

★ 1964 ★
Trucks
SIC: 3713; NAICS: 336211
Class 7 Truck Market in Canada, 2003

Market shares are shown in percent.

International	36.2%
General Motors	16.8
Freightliner	12.9
Peterbilt	9.3
Sterling	9.1
Kenworth	9.0
Hino Canada	3.5
Mack	2.3
Other	0.9

Source: "Canadian Retail Truck Sales." [online] available from http://www.todaystrucking.com [accessed March 30, 2004], p. NA, from Canadian Vehicle Manufacturers Association.

★ 1965 ★
Trucks
SIC: 3713; NAICS: 336211
Class 8 Truck Market, 2003

Market shares are shown in percent.

Freightliner	32.3%
International	15.9
Peterbilt	12.4
Mack	10.8
Kenworth	10.7
Volvo	9.7
Sterling	6.6
Other	1.6

Source: "U.S. Retail Truck Sales." [online] available from http://www.todaystrucking.com [accessed March 30, 2004], p. NA.

★ 1966 ★
Trucks
SIC: 3713; NAICS: 336211
Class 8 Truck Market in Canada, 2003

Market shares are shown in percent.

Freightliner	23.1%
International	19.0
Kenworth	14.9
Peterbilt	11.4
Volvo	9.9
Mack	7.5
Other	25.6

Source: "Canadian Retail Truck Sales." [online] available from http://www.todaystrucking.com [accessed March 30, 2004], p. NA, from Canadian Vehicle Manufacturers Association.

★ 1967 ★
Trucks
SIC: 3713; NAICS: 336211
Half-ton Pickup Market in Texas

Market shares are shown in percent.

General Motors	38.0%
Ford	36.0
Dodge	22.0
Other	4.0

Source: *San Antonio Express-News*, May 6, 2004, p. NA.

★ 1968 ★

Trucks

SIC: 3713; NAICS: 336211

Top Truck Importers in the U.K., 2003

There were 55,590 commercial vehicles over 3.5 tons registered in 2003, up 7.1% (3,670 units) from 2002.

	2002	2003
Paccar	23.5%	22.8%
DaimlerChrysler	17.9	18.3
Iveco Group	17.3	15.1
Volvo/Renault	14.7	15.0
MAN/ERF	11.7	10.8
Scania/VW	10.6	12.5
Other	4.4	5.5

Source: *Commercial Motor*, January 15, 2004, p. 22, from Society of Motor Manufacturers and Trading.

★ 1969 ★

Trucks

SIC: 3713; NAICS: 336211

Top Truck Makers, 2000-2002

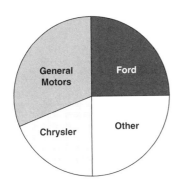

Market shares are shown in percent.

	2000	2001	2002
Ford	28.1%	27.3%	25.4%
General Motors	27.0	29.0	30.9
Chrysler	20.9	18.8	18.6
Other	24.0	24.9	25.1

Source: *Canadian Business*, October 26, 2003, p. NA, from Burnham Investment Research.

★ 1970 ★

Trucks

SIC: 3713; NAICS: 336211

Top Truck Makers in Denmark, 2002

Market shares are shown in percent.

Scania	29.0%
Volvo	22.1
MAN	15.0
Other	33.9

Source: *Boersen*, April 23, 2002, p. NA.

★ 1971 ★

Trucks

SIC: 3713; NAICS: 336211

Top Truck Producers

Market shares are shown in percent.

DaimlerChrysler	38.0%
Paccar	24.0
Volvo	21.0
Navistar	17.0

Source: *Forbes*, August 11, 2003, p. 67.

★ 1972 ★

Trucks

SIC: 3713; NAICS: 336211

Truck Market Segments

The compact pickup category has lost 36% of its market share in the last 10 years. Japan has recently moved into the market for full-sized pickups. Figures for 1993 are full year. For 2003 the figures are for the first six months only.

	1993	2003
Full-size pickup	9.7%	13.7%
Minivans	7.7	6.7
Compact pickup	7.7	4.9
Midsize SUV	7.5	10.1
Full-size SUV	1.3	4.1
Entry SUV	1.0	7.3
Luxury SUV	0.2	3.0

Source: *Motor Trend*, November 2003, p. 36, from J.D. Power & Associates.

★ 1973 ★
Trucks
SIC: 3713; NAICS: 336211

Used Truck Market in France, 2003

Shares are for truck sales in France during October 2003. These shares are for trucks of five tons or more.

	Units	Share
Renault	19,039	38.94%
Mercedes Benz	8,454	17.29
Volvo	5,274	10.79
Iveco	4,146	8.48
DAF	3,478	7.11
Scania	3,149	6.44
MAN	2,236	4.57
Other	3,111	6.36

Source: *Commercial Motor*, January 15, 2004, p. NA.

★ 1974 ★
Auto Parts
SIC: 3714; NAICS: 336312, 33633, 33634

Auto Electronics Market, 2008

Figures are in billions of dollars for North America.

	($ bil.)	Share
Engines and drivetrains	$ 12.9	38.17%
Security and safety electronics	11.6	34.32
Auto comfort, convenience and entertainment	5.8	17.16
Auto navigation and instrumentation	3.5	10.36

Source: *America's Intelligence Wire*, April 28, 2004, p. NA, from Freedonia Group.

★ 1975 ★
Auto Parts
SIC: 3714; NAICS: 33633, 33635

Automotive Cockpit Market (Outsourced) in Europe

Faurecia and joint venture partner Siemens VDO have more than 75% of the market. The industry is expected to see a 6% growth between 2003 and 2010. Four million cockpits are outsourced each year.

Faurecia/Siemens	75.0%
Other	25.0

Source: *Automotive News Europe*, November 3, 2003, p. 16.

★ 1976 ★
Auto Parts
SIC: 3714; NAICS: 336312, 33633, 33634

Automotive Cockpit Market Worldwide, 2003

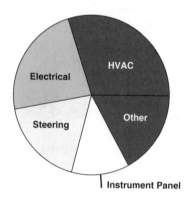

The $16.7 billion industry is shown by component. HVAC stands for heating, ventillating and air conditioning.

HVAC	30.0%
Electrical	23.0
Steering	18.0
Instrument Panel	12.0
Other	17.0

Source: *Plastic News*, March 22, 2004, p. 3, from ITB Group Ltd.

★ 1977 ★

Auto Parts

SIC: 3714; NAICS: 336312, 336322, 33633

Automotive Electronics Industry in Canada

Demand in the original equipment market is shown by segment. Total demand is expected to increase from $3.6 billion in 2002 to $5.4 billion.

	2002	2007	Share
Engines & drivetrain . . .	$ 1,650	$ 430	8.27%
Safety & security	1,120	2,130	40.96
Comfort/convenience/ entertainment	570	1,650	31.73
Navigation & instrumentation	300	990	19.04

Source: *Canadian Electronics*, November-December 2003, p. S3, from Freedonia Group.

★ 1978 ★

Auto Parts

SIC: 3714; NAICS: 33635

Automotive Throttle Market

Market shares are shown in percent. The company listed has more than 70% of the market.

Williams Controls	70.0%
Other	30.0

Source: *Crain's Detroit Business*, October 20, 2003, p. 28.

★ 1979 ★

Auto Parts

SIC: 3714; NAICS: 33634

Brake Pad Market

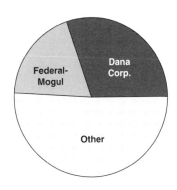

Market shares are shown in percent.

Dana Corp.	30.0%
Federal-Mogul	19.0
Other	51.0

Source: *Aftermarket Business*, February 2004, p. 6, from Frost & Sullivan.

★ 1980 ★

Auto Parts

SIC: 3714; NAICS: 33633

Commercial Vehicle Airspring Sales in Korea

The company makes 80% of all OEM (original e-quipment manufacturer) parts for commercial ve-hicles.

Dae Won Kang Up	80.0%
Other	20.0

Source: *European Rubber Journal*, March 2003, p. 3.

★ 1981 ★
Auto Parts
SIC: 3714; NAICS: 336312
Diesel Injection System Market

Shares are shown based on the global market.

Bosch 85.0%
Other 15.0

Source: *Handelsblatt*, May 25, 2002, p. 13, from Schroder
Smith Barney.

★ 1982 ★
Auto Parts
SIC: 3714; NAICS: 336399
Fifthwheel Market in the U.K., 2003

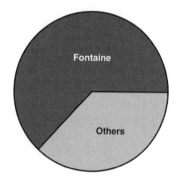

*A fifthwheel is a coupling device attached to a
tractor or dolly which supports the front of a
semitrailer and locks it to the tractor or dolly.*

Fontaine 63.0%
Others 37.0

Source: *Trailer/Body Builders*, February 1, 2004, p. NA.

★ 1983 ★
Auto Parts
SIC: 3714; NAICS: 33633
Leading Airbag Makers in Japan, 2000

Market shares are shown in percent.

Toyoda Gosei 35.0%
Takata 30.0
Autoliv (inc. NSK) 15.0
Tokai-Rika 6.0
Other 14.0

Source: "Market Consolidation Occupies Airbag Manufacturers." [online] from http://www.just-auto.com [accessed
January 6, 2003], from just-auto.com and industry estimates.

★ 1984 ★
Auto Parts
SIC: 3714; NAICS: 336399
Leading Airbag Makers in North America

*Market shares are shown based on production of
front and side airbags.*

Autoliv 35.0%
TRW Automotive 25.0
Takata 20.0
Delphi 13.0
Other 7.0

Source: *Automotive News*, May 17, 2004, p. 8, from *Automotive News* research.

★ 1985 ★

Auto Parts

SIC: 3714; NAICS: 33633

Leading Airbag Makers Worldwide, 2000

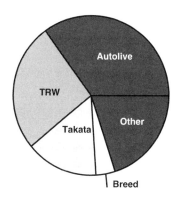

Market shares are shown in percent.

Autolive (inc. NSK)	35.0%
TRW	26.0
Takata (inc. Petri)	15.0
Breed	4.0
Other	20.0

Source: "Market Consolidation Occupies Airbag Manufacturers." [online] from http://www.just-auto.com [accessed January 6, 2003], from just-auto.com and industry estimates.

★ 1986 ★

Auto Parts

SIC: 3714; NAICS: 33634, 33635, 336399

OEM Sales in Germany

For the fifth year domestic auto sales fell (4.7%) while foreign sales increased (1.6%) particularly among Japanese automakers (8.8%). The total auto parts market was valued at $32 billion in 2002. OEM stands for original equipment manufacturers.

	1994	2000
Wheel/tire	24.0%	28.0%
Aerodynamics	17.0	16.0
Chassis	10.0	13.0
Mufflers	9.0	11.0
Audio	9.0	2.0
Motors	7.0	10.0

	1994	2000
Steering wheels	6.0%	4.0%
Seats	5.0	2.0
Interiors	5.0	6.0
Other	8.0	8.0

Source: "OEM Equipment." [online] from http://www.usatrade.gov [accessed January 5, 2004], from U.S. Commercial Service.

★ 1987 ★

Auto Parts

SIC: 3714; NAICS: 336312, 336322, 33635

Specialty Parts Sales, 2002-2003

Retail sales in the automotive aftermarket/equipment market rose 7.7% to $28.9 billion in 2003.

	2002	2003
Appearance accessories	51.1%	57.7%
Wheels, tires, suspension	24.9	25.1
Performance parts	24.1	17.3

Source: *Tire Business*, April 26, 2004, p. 6, from Specialty Equipment Market Association.

★ 1988 ★

Auto Parts

SIC: 3714; NAICS: 336312

Starters and Alternators Market

Market shares are shown in percent. American Generator & Armature Co. has less than 5% of the market.

Unit Parts Co./Worldwide Automotive	30.0%
AGA	5.0
Other	65.0

Source: *Chicago Tribune*, November 24, 2003, p. 1.

★ 1989 ★
Auto Parts
SIC: 3714; NAICS: 336312, 33634, 33635

Top Auto Parts Suppliers in North America, 2002

Companies are ranked by original equipment manufacturer sales in millions of dollars.

Delphi Corp.	$ 19,665
Visteon Corp.	12,168
Lear Corp.	9,504
Johson Controls Inc.	7,687
Magna International	7,650
Dana Corp.	5,340
TRW Automotive	4,950
Robert Bosch Corp.	4,390
Denso International America	3,769
American Axle & Manufacturing Holdings	3,341

Source: *Automotive News Fact Book*, Annual 2003, p. NA.

★ 1990 ★
Auto Parts
SIC: 3714; NAICS: 336312, 33634, 33635

Top Auto Parts Suppliers Worldwide, 2003

Companies are ranked by OEM (original equipment manufacturer) sales in millions of dollars.

Delphi Corp.	$ 26,200
Robert Bosch GmbH	23,200
Dense Corp.	16,856
Visleon Corp.	16,513
Lear Corp.	15,747
Magna International	15,345
Johnson Controls Inc.	15,192
Aisin Seiki Co. Ltd.	13,534
Faurecia	12,700
TRW Automotive	11,300

Source: *Automotive News*, June 28, 2004, p. 16.

★ 1991 ★
Auto Parts
SIC: 3714; NAICS: 336399

Top Bumper Makers in Europe

Market shares are shown in percent.

Venture Holdings	28.0%
Plastic Omnium	15.0
Dynamit Nobel	13.0
Decoma	10.0
Faurecia	8.0
Collins & Aikman	5.0
Compla	4.0
Other	17.0

Source: *Automotive News Europe*, December 1, 2003, p. 20, from Decoma.

★ 1992 ★
Turbochargers
SIC: 3714; NAICS: 336312

Leading Turbocharger Makers in Europe, 2001

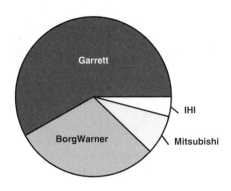

Market shares are shown in percent.

Garrett	58.0%
BorgWarner	30.0
Mitsubishi	8.0
IHI	4.0

Source: *Business Wire*, May 10, 2004, p. NA, from researchandmarkets.com.

★ 1993 ★
Truck Trailers
SIC: 3715; NAICS: 336212

Leading Truck Trailer Makers, 2003

*The top 30 manufacturers produced 174,991 trailers
in 2003. Shares are shown based on this top 30 total.*

	Units	Share
Great Dane Limited Partnership . .	41,000	23.43%
Wabash National Corporation . . .	36,320	20.76
Utility Trailer Manufacturing . . .	23,688	13.54
Stoughton Trailers	9,900	5.66
MANAC	6,300	3.60
Strick Corporation	6,000	3.43
Trailmobile Canada Ltd.	5,479	3.13
Fontaine Trailer Company	3,900	2.23
Transcraft	3,629	2.07
Dorsey Trailer Company/Fruehauf de Mexico	2,537	1.45
Other	36,238	20.71

Source: *Trailer/Body Business*, February 1, 2004, p. NA,
from *Trailer/Body Business* survey.

★ 1994 ★
Motor Homes
SIC: 3716; NAICS: 336213

Largest Class C Makers, 2003

Market shares are shown in percent.

Winnebago	23.4%
Thor	14.8
Coachmen	12.7
Gulfstream Coach Inc.	10.9
Other	38.2

Source: *RV Business*, April 2004, p. 23, from Statistical
Surveys Inc.

★ 1995 ★
Recreational Vehicles
SIC: 3716; NAICS: 336213

Motorized RV Market, 2003

Market shares are through November 2003.

Winnebago	19.0%
Fleetwood	18.0
Monaco	13.0
Thor	10.0
Coachmen	8.0
Other	32.0

Source: *Forbes*, March 29, 2004, p. 69, from Statistical
Surveys.

★ 1996 ★
Recreational Vehicles
SIC: 3716; NAICS: 336213

Towable RV Market, 2003

Market shares are through November 2003.

Thor	26.0%
Fleetwood	16.0
Forest River	15.0
Jayco	7.0
Coachmen	5.0
Other	31.0

Source: *Forbes*, March 29, 2004, p. 69, from Statistical
Surveys.

★ 1997 ★
Aircraft
SIC: 3721; NAICS: 336411

Business Jet Market Worldwide

Market shares are shown in percent.

	2003	2006
Cessna Aircraft	37.0%	40.0%
Raytheon Aircraft	18.0	16.0
Bombardier/Learjet	18.0	16.0
Gulfstream Aerospace	16.0	18.0
Dassault	10.0	10.0

Source: *Interavia Business & Technology*, July-September 2003, p. 19.

★ 1998 ★
Aircraft
SIC: 3721; NAICS: 336411

Fractional Jet Industry

There were 6,217 fractional jet owners in 2002, up from 89 in 1993. One can buy as little as one-sixteenth of a jet for 50 hours. Market shares are shown based on revenues.

	2001	2002
NetJets	55.0%	72.0%
Other	45.0	28.0

Source: *Columbus Dispatch*, October 17, 2003, p. NA.

★ 1999 ★
Aircraft
SIC: 3721; NAICS: 336411

General Aircraft Shipments

Total shipments fell 3.2% for the period from 2,207 in 2002 to 2,137 in 2003. Billings fell 16.7%, from $7.72 billion to $6.43 billion. Worldwide shipments were about the same (2,687 and 2,686) but the value of billings fell 15.5% from $11.2 billion to $9.9 billion.

	2002	2003	Share
Pistons	1,496	1,590	74.40%
Business jets	524	384	17.97
Turboprops	187	163	7.63

Source: *Business & Commercial Aviation*, March 2004, p. 11, from Aviation Research Group.

★ 2000 ★
Aircraft
SIC: 3721; NAICS: 336411

Global Aircraft Shipments, 2002 and 2003

Shipments were flat between 2002 and 2003. Business jets fell 23.4% in the period. Billings fell 15.5% to $9.99 billion, its worst showing in five years.

	2002	2003	Share
Pistons	1,731	1,896	70.59%
Business jets	676	518	19.29
Turboprops	280	272	10.13

Source: *Flight International*, February 17, 2020, p. 34, from General Aviation Manufacturers Association.

★ 2001 ★
Aircraft
SIC: 3721; NAICS: 336411

Largest Jet Makers Worldwide, 2003

By 2012, the top two firms are projected to switch places, with Gulfstream taking 27.9% of the market with Bombardier taking 22.4%.

Bombardier	25.5%
Gulfstream	25.1
Textron (Cessna unit)	19.4
Dassault Systems	16.5
Raytheon Corp.	12.0
Other	1.5

Source: *America's Intelligence Wire*, May 16, 2003, p. NA, from Teal Group and *Financial Post*.

★ 2002 ★
Aircraft
SIC: 3721; NAICS: 336411

Leading Aircraft Makers for the DoD, 2002

Market shares are shown based on total purchases of $32 billion. DoD stands for Department of Defense.

Boeing Co.	29.67%
Lockheed Martin Corp.	25.11
United Technologies Corp.	11.87
General Electric Co.	4.52
Northrop Grumman Corp.	2.90
Honeywell Inc.	1.92

Continued on next page.

★ 2002 ★

[Continued]
Aircraft
SIC: 3721; NAICS: 336411

Leading Aircraft Makers for the DoD, 2002

Market shares are shown based on total purchases of $32 billion. DoD stands for Department of Defense.

Textron Inc.	1.78%
Raytheon Co.	1.62
Veritas Capital Inc	0.98
Computer Sciences Corp.	0.84
Other	20.71

Source: *Government Executive*, September 4, 2003, p. NA.

★ 2003 ★

Aircraft
SIC: 3721; NAICS: 336411

Regional Jet Market Worldwide, 2003

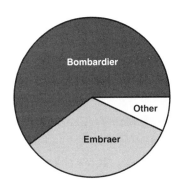

The total market is projected to reach $5.86 billion.

	($ bil.)	Share
Bombardier	$ 3.5	60.0%
Embraer	1.9	33.0
Other	0.4	7.0

Source: *Wall Street Journal*, August 7, 2003, p. A9, from Teal Group.

★ 2004 ★

Aircraft
SIC: 3721; NAICS: 336411

Types of U.S. Aircraft

Distribution of the 217,600 general aviation aircraft is shown. Figures are for 2000.

	No.	Share
Piston driven propeller	170,500	78.35%
Amateur-built/experimental craft	20,400	9.38
Helicopters and other rotocraft	7,200	3.31
Turbo-jet	7,000	3.22
Turbo-prop	5,800	2.67
Lighter-than-air craft	4,700	2.16
Gliders	2,000	0.92

Source: *New York Times*, December 9, 2003, p. C8, from General Aviation Manufacturers Association and Federal Aviation Adminsitration.

★ 2005 ★

Aircraft
SIC: 3721; NAICS: 336411

World Aircraft Fleet

The number of aircraft is forecasted to 16,858 in 2003 to 33,392 in 2023. Figures are as of December 31, 2003.

	2003	2023
Narrowbody	49.0%	52.0%
Turboprops	23.0	1.0
Widebody	16.0	20.0
Regional jets	12.0	27.0

Source: *Aviation Week & Space Technology*, April 26, 2004, p. 46, from BACK Aviation Solutions Fleet iNet and World Fleet Forecast.

★ 2006 ★
Helicopters
SIC: 3721; NAICS: 336411

Civilian Helicopter Market, 2003

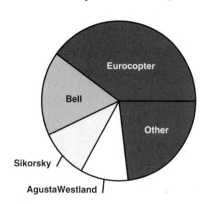

Shares are shown based on value of production.

Eurocopter 40.0%
Bell 17.0
Sikorsky 10.0
AgustaWestland 10.0
Other 23.0

Source: *Wall Street Journal*, January 2, 2004, p. A7, from Forecast International.

★ 2007 ★
Rotocraft
SIC: 3721; NAICS: 336411

Commercial Rotocraft Market, 2003

Shares are shown based on total value for fiscal year 2003.

Eurocopter 35.56%
Textron Canada 14.52
Sikorsky 11.65
Bell/Agusta 10.95
Agustawestland 8.05
MD Helicopters 5.04
Robinson 4.78
Other 9.45

Source: *Aerospace Daily*, January 15, 2004, p. 7, from Forecast International.

★ 2008 ★
Aircraft Engines
SIC: 3724; NAICS: 336412

Jet Engine Market

Market shares are shown based on engines in service and ordered.

CFM International 32.6%
General Electric 24.3
Rolls-Royce 19.0
Pratt & Whitney 11.5
IAE 9.6
Other 2.9

Source: *Airline Business*, April 2004, p. 52, from Airclaims CASE database.

★ 2009 ★
Aircraft Engines
SIC: 3724; NAICS: 336412

Jet Engine Market - Airbus A320 family

Market shares are shown based on engines in service and ordered.

CFM International 52.7%
IAE 39.2
Pratt & Whitney 0.5
Other 7.6

Source: *Airline Business*, April 2004, p. 52, from Airclaims CASE database.

★ 2010 ★
Aircraft Engines
SIC: 3724; NAICS: 336412

Jet Engine Market - Boeing 777

Market shares are shown based on engines in service and ordered.

General Electric 37.5%
Rolls-Royce 34.9
Pratt & Whitney 27.4

Source: *Airline Business*, April 2004, p. 52, from Airclaims CASE database.

★ 2011 ★

Aircraft Engines

SIC: 3724; NAICS: 336412

Regional Jet Engine Market

Market shares are shown based on engines in service and ordered.

General Electric 62.0%
Rolls-Royce 38.0

Source: *Airline Business*, April 2004, p. 52, from Airclaims CASE database.

★ 2012 ★

Aircraft Services

SIC: 3724; NAICS: 336412

Global MRO Market, 2002

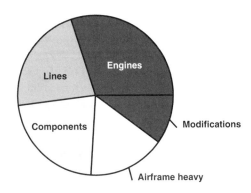

The aircraft maintenance & repair market is expected to grow at an annual rate of 5.3% through 2012. Market shares are shown in percent.

Engines 30.0%
Lines 22.0
Components 22.0
Airframe heavy 16.0
Modifications 10.0

Source: *Interavia*, September 2002, p. 24, from Aerostrategy.

★ 2013 ★

Aircraft Services

SIC: 3724; NAICS: 336412

Independent PMA Market

The company has over two thirds of the industry for U.S. Federal Aviation Administration parts manufacturing approval (PMA). The commercial aerospace spare parts market has been placed at $6 billion.

Heico Aerospace 66.0%
Other 34.0

Source: *Flight International*, December 9, 2003, p. 29.

★ 2014 ★

Full-Flight Simulators

SIC: 3728; NAICS: 336413

Full-Flight Simulator Industry, 2002

Market shares are shown in percent. CAE also has 67% of visual systems orders.

CAE 60.0%
TTS 40.0

Source: *Flight International*, March 4, 2003, p. 29.

★ 2015 ★

Deep-Sea Submersibles

SIC: 3731; NAICS: 48839

Deep-Sea Robotics Market

The company's deep-sea robotics manipulators are the industry standard, with 75-80% of the market. Most of the company's business comes from oil firms interested in drilling and exploring.

Schilling Robotics 80.0%
Other 20.0

Source: *Sacramento Bee*, November 7, 2003, p. NA.

★ 2016 ★
Ship Building
SIC: 3731; NAICS: 336611

Global Shipbuilding Market, 2003

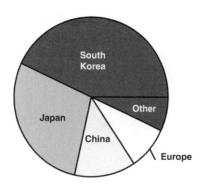

South Korea was in the lead for the first time since 2000.

South Korea	43.5%
Japan	28.6
China	12.6
Europe	8.7
Other	6.6

Source: *YON - Yonhap News Agency of Korea*, April 20, 2004, p. NA, from Ministry of Commerce, Industry and Energy.

★ 2017 ★
Ship Building
SIC: 3731; NAICS: 336611

Leading LNG Carrier Makers

LNG stands for liquified natural gas. The top 3 firms have 65% of the market for the construction of liquified natural gas tankers.

Samsung Heavy Industries/Daewoo Heavy Industries	48.0%
HHI	17.0
Other	35.0

Source: *MEED - Middle East Economic Digest*, April 2, 2004, p. NA.

★ 2018 ★
Ship Building
SIC: 3731; NAICS: 336611

Top Ship Builders in Japan

Market shares are shown in percent.

Universal Shipbuilding	19.6%
Imabari Shipbuilding	11.0
IHI Marine United	8.2
Other	61.2

Source: *Nikkei Weekly*, July 21, 2003, p. 1, from Nihon Keizai Shimbun.

★ 2019 ★
Boats
SIC: 3732; NAICS: 336612

Largest Yacht Builders Worldwide

The luxury yacht industry order book grew 5.2% in the last year, based on units of total construction. In terms of linear feet of yachts over 80 feet in length, the global industry grew 6% to 62,056 feet. Yard names are ranked by number of projects.

Azimut/Benetti	56
Ferretti	38
Rodiguez Group	27
Sunseeker	24
Royal Denship	15
Hatteras	14
Malora	14
Horizon	12
Feadship	9
Hargrave/Monte Fino	9

Source: "The Economic Stature of the Yachting Sector in 2004." [online] from http://www.monacoyachtshow.com [Press release 2004].

★ 2020 ★

Boats

SIC: 3732; NAICS: 336612

Pleasure Boat Industry in Italy, 2001

The Italian pleasure boat industry is the second largest in the world and valued at 1,388 million euros.

Outboard motor boats	62.8%
Inboard motorboats	15.8
Sailboats	11.8
Inflatable boats	10.1

Source: ''Recreational and Pleasure Boats Industry.'' [online] from http://www.usatrade.gov [accessed January 5, 2004], from U.S. Commercial Service.

★ 2021 ★

Boats

SIC: 3732; NAICS: 336612

Top Fiberglass Boat Builders

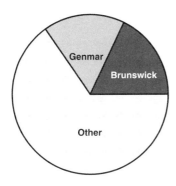

Market shares are shown in percent.

Brunswick	17.5%
Genmar	16.9
Other	65.5

Source: *Star Tribune*, March 9, 2004, p. 1D.

★ 2022 ★

Boats

SIC: 3732; NAICS: 336612

Yacht Industry Worldwide, 2004

Data show the types of yachts built.

Cruising yachts	77.0%
Sailing	12.0
Open	5.0
Expedition	4.0
Sportfinishing	2.0

Source: ''The Economic Stature of the Yachting Sector in 2004.'' [online] from http://www.monacoyachtshow.com [Press release 2004], from *ShowBoats International*.

★ 2023 ★

Railroad Equipment

SIC: 3743; NAICS: 33651

Expenditures on High Speed Trains Worldwide, 2003

Shares are shown for annual expenditures on high speed train engines by region. Expenditures are measured in millions of euros.

	(mil.)	Share
Western Europe	850	62.0%
Asia	500	36.4
Canada and the United States	10	0.8
Eastern Europe	10	0.8

Source: *Railway Age*, January 2004, p. NA, from SCI Verkehr for Vossloh.

★ 2024 ★
Railroad Equipment
SIC: 3743; NAICS: 33651

Global Railway Equipment Market, 2001-2002

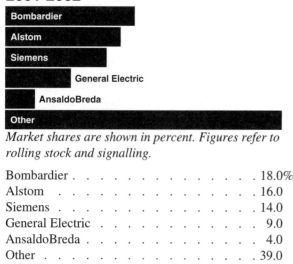

Market shares are shown in percent. Figures refer to rolling stock and signalling.

Bombardier	18.0%
Alstom	16.0
Siemens	14.0
General Electric	9.0
AnsaldoBreda	4.0
Other	39.0

Source: *International Railway Journal*, April 2003, p. S8.

★ 2025 ★
Railroad Equipment
SIC: 3743; NAICS: 33651

Passenger Car Purchases in North America, 2003

Purchasers are ranked by number of rail cars delivered to them during the year.

Oceanside, CA (NCTD)	280
New York City (NYC Transit)	160
New York City (LIRR)	110
Chicago (Metro)	88
Washington D.C. (WMATA)	86
San Jose (Santa Clara Velley TA)	74
VIA Rail Canada	50
Amtrak	46
San Francisco (MUNI)	45
Toronto (GO Transit)	32

Source: *Railway Age*, January 2004, p. 59.

★ 2026 ★
Railroad Equipment
SIC: 3743; NAICS: 33651

Railway Market Shares Worldwide, 2003 and 2008

The total market was valued at 56.78 million euros in 2003 and forecasted to reach 69.92 million euros in 2008. Top suppliers to the industry are Bombardier, Alstom, Siemens and General Electric.

	2003	2008
Western Europe	21.47	25.91
Asia	13.73	18.66
Canada/USA	9.42	10.77
Eastern Europe	4.51	5.61
Africa/Middle East	1.38	1.60
Latin America	1.29	1.51
Australia/New Zealand	0.82	1.00
Other	4.16	4.86

Source: *International Railway Journal*, December 2003, p. 14.

★ 2027 ★
Railroad Equipment
SIC: 3743; NAICS: 33651

Wagon Fleet in Europe

Data are for railway-owned cars, which made up 60% of all wagons in 2000 (down from 80.5% in 1990). The remaining 40% are privately owned.

Flat & combined transport wagons	38.0%
Covered wagons	29.0
Open wagons	20.0
Other	13.0

Source: *International Railway Journal*, June 2003, p. 22.

★ 2028 ★
Bicycles
SIC: 3751; NAICS: 336991

Bicycle Production in Europe, 2002

Total production stood at 10.15 million units for the year. Consumption was 15.6 million units, up from 2001 but down from 16.07 million and 16.68 million in 1999 and 2000.

	(000)	Share
Germany	3,050	30.03%
Italy	2,350	23.14
France	1,424	14.02

Continued on next page.

★ 2028 ★

[Continued]
Bicycles
SIC: 3751; NAICS: 336991

Bicycle Production in Europe, 2002

Total production stood at 10.15 million units for the year. Consumption was 15.6 million units, up from 2001 but down from 16.07 million and 16.68 million in 1999 and 2000.

	(000)	Share
Holland	1,159	11.41%
Spain	504	4.96
Portugal	387	3.81
United Kingdom	350	3.45
Greece	300	2.95
Belgium/Luxembourg	229	2.26
Denmark	124	1.22
Austria	92	0.91
Finland	79	0.78
Sweden	70	0.69
Ireland	37	0.36

Source: *Bicycle Retailer and Industry News*, January 2004, p. 24, from *Bike Europe*, National Cycle, Motorcycle and Accessories Association, and Comite de Liaison des Fabricators de Bicyclettes.

★ 2029 ★

Bicycles
SIC: 3751; NAICS: 336991

Specialty Bike Sales

19.5 million bikes were sold during 2002, the second level highest since 1992. A road bike was the most expensive type at an average price of $1,194.65.

	2000	2002
Mountain	41.00%	33.80%
Youth	28.50	28.30
Comfort	13.60	20.60
Hybrid	10.20	9.40
Road	3.60	5.30
Cruiser	2.80	2.20
Tandem	0.12	0.15

Source: *The Record*, October 31, 2003, p. B1, from National Bicycle Dealers Association.

★ 2030 ★

Bicycles
SIC: 3751; NAICS: 336991

Top Bicycle Producers in Switzerland, 2003

Companies are ranked by estimated unit sales. In 2002, a total of 263,000 bikes were sold (using this figure for 2003 would give Rek about 10% of the market). New bike sales had 47% of the entire $403 million bike market, followed by clothing/shoes and services with 10% shares each.

Rek	27,000
Intercycle	23,000
Scott	20,000
Komenda	20,000
Tour-de-Suisse Rad	14,000
BMC	13,000
Canyon	10,000
Belimport	9,000
Specialized Holland	8,000
Baltensperger	7,000

Source: "Bicycle Market." [online] available from http://www.export.gov [accessed December 1, 2003], from Swiss Bicycle Manufacturers, Wholesalers and Importers Association.

★ 2031 ★

Bicycles
SIC: 3751; NAICS: 336991

U.S. Bicycle Imports

Importers bought in 19.3 million bicycles in 2002, down from 20.2 million in 2000 (an all time record). Sales were down, however, leading analysts to suspect retailers have large inventories than usual.

	2000	2002	Share
10, 12, 16 kids imports	6,940,951	5,907,346	30.58%
26" imports	6,200,499	5,070,304	26.24
20" imports	4,966,398	5,978,308	30.94
24" imports	1,833,320	1,828,348	9.46
700c imports	337,923	535,961	2.77

Source: *Bicycle Retailer and Industry News*, April 1, 2003, p. 1, from Bicycle Product Supplier Association.

★ 2032 ★
Dirtbikes
SIC: 3751; NAICS: 336991
Top Dirtbike Brands, 2003

Date are forecasts for 2003.

Honda	46.18%
Yamaha	27.56
Suzuki	10.80
Kawasaki	10.08
KTM	5.36
Other	0.03

Source: *Dealernews*, March 2004, p. 88, from *Motorcycle Industry Council Retail Report*, SEC filings, and annual reports.

★ 2033 ★
Motorcycles
SIC: 3751; NAICS: 336991
ATV/Dirtbike Sales by State

Data show retail sales data through June.

	(000)	Share
California	154,724	14.25%
Texas	61,680	5.68
Pennsylvania	43,871	4.04
Ohio	38,774	3.57
Florida	38,225	3.52
New York	37,245	3.43
Michigan	36,574	3.37
Minnesota	35,829	3.30
Arizona	33,025	3.04
Wisconsin	31,422	2.89
Georgia	27,337	2.52
Other	546,784	50.37

Source: *Dealernews*, August 2003, p. 76, from *Motorcycle Industry Council Retail Report*, SEC filings, and companies.

★ 2034 ★
Motorcycles
SIC: 3751; NAICS: 336991
Motorcycle Sales by State

Data show retail sales data through June. Figures include sports bikes, touring, standard and cruisers.

	(000)	Share
California	63,050	11.20%
Florida	43,190	7.67
Texas	36,810	6.54
Ohio	25,460	4.52
Pennsylvania	25,352	4.50
New York	23,515	4.18
Illinois	22,022	3.91
Michigan	18,847	3.35
Georgia	16,353	2.91
Virginia	14,852	2.64
Indiana	14,116	2.51
Other	259,316	46.07

Source: *Dealernews*, August 2003, p. 76, from *Motorcycle Industry Council Retail Report*, SEC filings, and companies.

★ 2035 ★
Motorcycles
SIC: 3751; NAICS: 336991

New Streetbike Sales

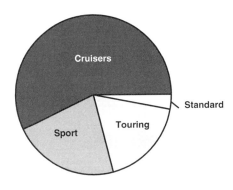

Data are based on sales by participants in the Motorcycle Industry Council Retail Sales Report. 2003 figures are unavailable although the estimate is for 1.96 million units which would be another record breaking year.

	2000	2003
Cruisers	52.96%	56.59%
Sport	22.58	21.89
Touring	19.09	18.10
Standard	5.37	3.33

Source: *Dealernews*, January 2004, p. 28, from *Motorycycle Industry Council Retail Sales Report* and DJB Composite Index.

★ 2036 ★
Motorcycles
SIC: 3751; NAICS: 336991

Top Motorcycle Firms in Japan, 2002

Market shares are shown based on domestic sales of 771,082 units.

Honda Motor	54.1%
Yamaha Motor	27.2
Suzuki Motor	15.4
Kawasaki Heavy Industries	3.3

Source: "Market Share Survey Report 2002." [online] from http://www.nni.nikkei.co.jp [accessed January 20, 2004], from Nikkei estimate and Japan Automobile Manufacturers Association.

★ 2037 ★
Motorcycles
SIC: 3751; NAICS: 336991

Top Motorcycle Makers, 2004

Data show two-wheel sales forecasts for calendar year 2004.

	Units	Share
Honda	262,922	28.37%
Harley-Davidson	241,710	26.08
Yamaha	162,455	17.53
Suzuki	111,126	11.99
Kawasaki	93,561	10.09
BMW	17,765	1.92
KTM	17,419	1.88
Buell	6,106	0.66
Triumph	5,886	0.64
Ducati	4,540	0.49
Victory	3,316	0.36

Source: *Dealernews*, March 2004, p. 88, from *Motorcycle Industry Council Retail Report*, SEC filings, and annual reports.

★ 2038 ★
Motorcycles
SIC: 3751; NAICS: 336991

Top Motorcycle Makers in Europe, 2000

Market shares are shown in percent.

Honda	21.8%
Yamaha	17.3
Suzuki	14.3
BMW	13.0
Kawasaki	9.4
Harley	7.4
Other	16.8

Source: *Investor's Business Daily*, July 24, 2001, p. 1, from company reports.

★ 2039 ★

Motorcycles

SIC: 3751; NAICS: 336991

Top Motorcycle Makers in Thailand

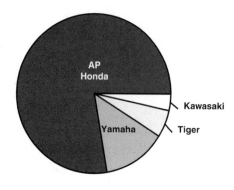

The *$1.4 billion market is shown by company. Tiger had a 3% share in 2002 and its share may hit 5% in 2003. Figures are as of July 2003.*

AP Honda	70.0%
Yamaha	12.0
Tiger	5.0
Kawasaki	3.0

Source: *Far Eastern Economic Review*, October 9, 2003, p. NA, from Kasikorn Research Centre.

★ 2040 ★

Powered Two Wheelers

SIC: 3751; NAICS: 336991

Powered Two Wheeler Market in Taiwan

Sales of domestic powered two-wheeled market grew 16% over 2002 to 764,700 units.

Kwang Yang	37.3
Sanyang	29.8
Yamaha Taiwan	25.5
Tailing	4.9
Motive Power	1.5
Other	1.0

Source: *Taiwan Economic News*, February 9, 2004, p. NA, from Ministry of Transportation and Communications (Taiwan).

★ 2041 ★

Scooters

SIC: 3751; NAICS: 336991

Largest Scooter Markets, 2003

Data show units sold. According to the "DJB Composite Index" roughly 42,000 scooters were sold in 2003. If one includes gray-market imports and non-MIC reporting OEMs the figure is closer to 60,000.

Los Angeles	2,039
Chicago	1,762
New York City	1,668
Minneapolis/St. Paul	1,401
Miami/Ft. Lauderdale	1,201
Denver	1,174
Seattle/Tacoma	1,031
Salt Lake City	1,022
Washington D.C./Maryland	1,014

Source: *Dealernews*, March 2004, p. 42, from Motorcycle Industry Council and OBM.

★ 2042 ★

Aerospace

SIC: 3761; NAICS: 336414, 54171

Largest Defense Contractors, 2002

Companies are ranked by value of military contracts, in billions, for fiscal year.

Lockheed Martin	$ 17.0
Boeing	16.6
Northop Grumman	8.7
Raytheon	7.0
General Dynamics	7.0
United Technologies	3.6
Science Applications	2.1
TRW	2.0
L-3 Communications	1.7
Health Net	1.7

Source: *Orbis*, Fall 2003, p. 693, from U.S. Department of Defense.

★ 2043 ★
Aerospace
SIC: 3761; NAICS: 336414, 54171
Largest Space Firms Worldwide, 2002

Companies are ranked by space sales in millions of dollars. Shares are shown based on the top 50 firms worldwide.

	($ mil.)	Share
Boeing Co.	$ 11,000	26.01%
Lockheed Martin Corp.	7,500	17.73
Raytheon Co.	3,122	7.38
Northop Grumman	2,672	6.32
EAADS Space	2,323	5.49
Arianespace	1,530	3.62
Alcatel Space	1,363	3.22
Alliant Techsystems Inc.	1,181	2.79
Hughes Electronics Corp.	1,170	2.77
Loral Space & Communications	853	2.02
Other	9,585	22.66

Source: "Space News Top 50." [online] from http://www.space.com/spacenews/top50_2003.html [accessed October 20, 2003], from *Space News* research and company reports.

★ 2044 ★
Aerospace
SIC: 3761; NAICS: 336414, 54171
Leading Civilian Contractors, 2002

- Lockheed Martin
- University of California
- Boeing Co.
- Bechtel Group Inc.
- Northrop Grumman
- Computer Sciences Corp.
- BNFL Inc.
- SAIC
- AmerisourceBergen Corp.
- California Institute of Technology
- **Other**

Companies are ranked by value of contracts in billions of dollars. Total contract awards for fiscal year 2002 was $80.52 billion.

	($ bil.)	Share
Lockheed Martin	$ 5.88	7.30%
University of California	4.10	5.09
Boeing Co.	2.80	3.48
Bechtel Group Inc.	$ 2.58	3.20%
Northrop Grumman	1.73	2.15
Computer Sciences Corp.	1.72	2.14
BNFL Inc.	1.61	2.00
SAIC	1.54	1.91
AmerisourceBergen Corp.	1.51	1.88
California Institute of Technology	1.41	1.75
Other	55.64	69.10

Source: *Government Executive*, September 4, 2003, p. NA.

★ 2045 ★
Aerospace
SIC: 3761; NAICS: 336414, 54171
Leading Missile Makers, 2002

Market shares are shown based on total purchases of $3.7 billion.

Lockheed Martin	42.58%
Raytheon Co.	40.25
Boeing Co.	3.80
RAM Systems GmbH	3.46
Northrop Grumman Corp.	2.92
Washington Group International	1.11
Carlyle Group	0.81
Sequa Corp.	0.61
Science & Applied Technology	0.50
Harris Corp.	0.40
Other	3.56

Source: *Government Executive*, September 4, 2003, p. NA.

★ 2046 ★
Travel Trailers
SIC: 3792; NAICS: 336214

Largest Travel Trailers and Fifth Wheel Makers, 2003

Market shares are shown in percent.

Thor	30.0%
Forest River	15.0
Fleetwood	13.0
Jayco	7.0
Coachmen	5.0
Other	30.0

Source: *RV Business*, April 2004, p. 23, from Statistical Surveys Inc.

★ 2047 ★
Trailer Hitches
SIC: 3799; NAICS: 336999

Air Suspension Hitches

The company has 75-80% of the market for air suspension hitches for medium sized trucks.

TrailerSaver	80.0%
Other	20.0

Source: *Capital Times*, April 28, 2004, p. 8C.